WORLDS TOGETHER,
WORLDS APART

Volume B

NORTH
AMERICA

ARCTIC
OCEAN

ASIA

North Magnetic Pole
North Pole

New Siberian Islands

Laptev Sea

Victoria Island

Baffin Bay

Franz Josef Land

Svalbard

Novaya Zemlya

GREENLAND

Iceland

ARCTIC CIRCLE

A R C T I C

Longitude West of Greenwich

QUEEN ELIZABETH ISLANDS

GREENLAND

Baffin Bay

Iceland

ARCTIC CIRCLE

N O R T H

A M E R I C A

Great Slave Lake

Hudson Bay

Lake Winnipeg

Lake Superior

Lake Michigan

Lake Huron

Lake Erie

Lake Ontario

Island of Newfoundland

Gulf of St. Lawrence

British

N O R T H

P A C I F I C

O C E A N

N O R T H

A T L A N T I C

O C E A N

TROPIC OF CANCER

Hawaii

Gulf of Mexico

CARIBBEAN SEA

CENTRAL AMERICA

M I D   A T L A N T I C   R I D G E

P O L Y N E S I A

Samoa Islands

Tahiti

EQUATOR

Amazon Basin

S O U T H

A M E R I C A

A N D E S

PERU-CHILE TRENCH

S O U T H

A T L A N T I C

O C E A N

S O U T H

P A C I F I C

O C E A N

TROPIC OF CAPRICORN

Falkland Islands

Cape Horn

Drake Passage

ANTARCTIC PENINSULA

ANTARCTIC CIRCLE

Alexander Island

WEDDELL SEA

ELLSWORTH LAND

Marie Byrd Land

Vinson Massif 16067 ft

A N T A

GLOBAL SATELLITE MOSAIC

The beauty and complexity of Earth's landscapes above and below the oceans is revealed with the Global Satellite Mosaic. The mosaic was prepared for the National Geographic Society by NASA's Jet Propulsion Laboratory, using more than 500 satellite images from the National Oceanic and Atmospheric Administration. The cloud-free images show Earth in its natural colors as it would be seen from space. One can easily identify the world's major glaciers, deserts, mountain ranges, and rain forests. For example, follow the green ribbon of lush vegetation along the Nile into the stark, dry Sahara. The mountain ranges seem to rise off the map thanks to digital elevation databases from the Department of Defense. The deepest areas of the ocean realm are colored dark blue in contrast to the light blue areas highlighting continental shelves, submarine ridges, and underwater mountains.

BIOSPHERE

Thousands of satellite images were combined to show a picture of biological productivity. In the oceans, red, yellow, and green indicate waters rich in phytoplankton. On the green areas show high-potential plant productivity; tan suffer from productivity limitations due to aridity and temperature.

THE W

SATEL

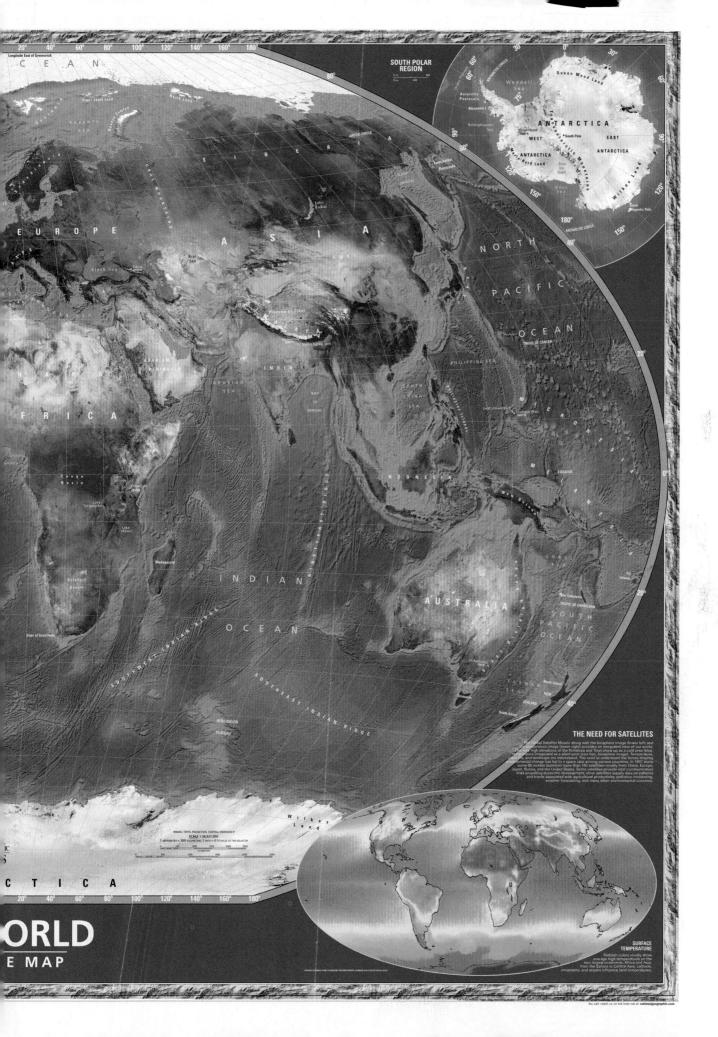

OCEAN

EUROPE

ASIA

SIBERIA

ASIA

Aral
Sea

Black Sea

Plateau of Tibet

HIMALAYA

Kamchatka
Peninsula

ARABIAN
PENINSULA

ARABIAN
SEA

INDIA

BAY
OF
BENGAL

AFRICA

Congo
Basin

Lake
Tanganyika

Lake
Nyasa

Madagascar

Kalahari
Desert

Cape of Good Hope

INDIAN

OCEAN

SOUTH
CHINA
SEA

PHILIPPINE SEA

TROPIC OF CANCER

NORTH

PACIFIC

OCEAN

MICRONESIA

MELANESIA

EQUATOR

INDONESIA

NEW GUINEA

AUSTRALIA

CORAL
SEA

TROPIC OF CAPRICORN

SOUTH
PACIFIC
OCEAN

TASMAN
SEA

NEW
ZEALAND

North Island

South Island

SOUTHWEST INDIAN RIDGE

SOUTHEAST INDIAN RIDGE

MID-INDIAN RIDGE

KERGUELEN
PLATEAU

Wilkes
Land

SOUTH POLAR
REGION

ANTARCTICA

Queen Maud Land

Weddell
Sea

Antarctic
Peninsula

Alexander I.

Bellingshausen
Sea

Marie Byrd Land

Ross
Ice
Shelf

Ross
Sea

WEST
ANTARCTICA

EAST
ANTARCTICA

South Pole

Transantarctic Mountains

Wilkes Land

South
Magnetic Pole

ANTARCTIC CIRCLE

ARCTIC CIRCLE

THE NEED FOR SATELLITES

This Optical Satellite Mosaic along with the biosphere image (lower left) and the temperature image (lower right) provides an integrated view of our world. The very high elevations of the Himalaya and Tibet show up as a cold area (blue in the temperature image and as a plant-poor area (tan, biosphere image). Temperature, biomass, and landscape are interrelated. The need to understand the forces shaping environmental change has led to a space race among various countries. In 1957 alone some 85 rockets launched more than 140 satellites—mostly from China, Europe, Japan, Russia, and the United States. Some satellites provide vital communication links propelling economic development; other satellites supply data on patterns and trends associated with agricultural productivity, pollution monitoring, weather forecasting, and many other environmental concerns.

WORLD
E MAP

SURFACE
TEMPERATURE

Reddish colors vividly show average high temperatures on the two largest continents, Africa and Asia, from the Sahara to Central Asia. Latitude, mountains, and oceans influence land temperatures.

You can reach us on the Internet at nationalgeographic.com

Political World

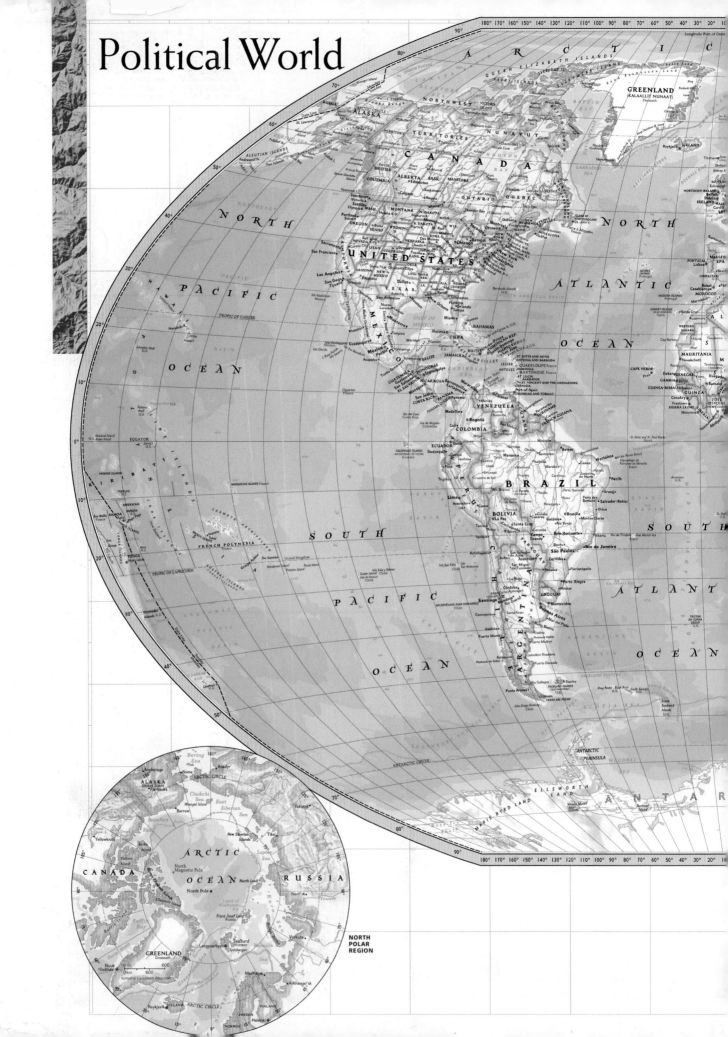

NORTH POLAR REGION

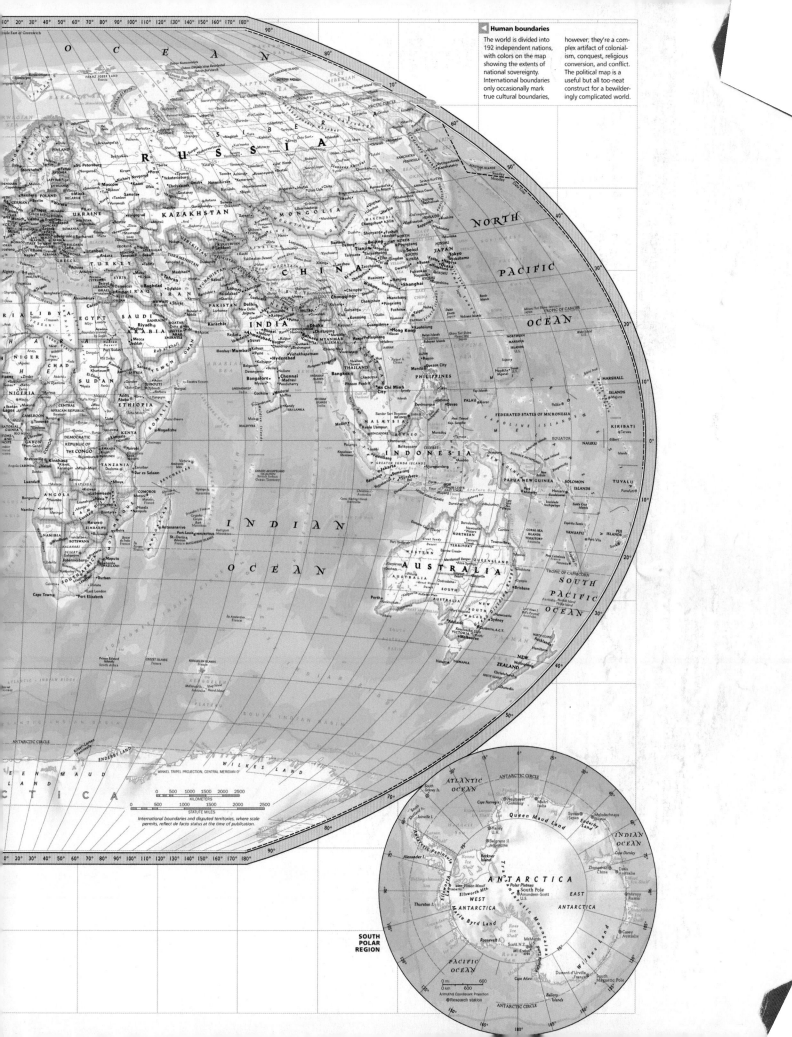

WINKEL TRIPEL PROJECTION, CENTRAL MERIDIAN 0°

0   500   1000   1500   2000   2500
KILOMETERS
0   500   1000   1500   2000   2500
STATUTE MILES

International boundaries and disputed territories, where scale permits, reflect de facto status at the time of publication.

SOUTH POLAR REGION

Armithal Equidistant Projection
⊛ Research station

0 km   600
0 mi   600

FIFTH EDITION

WORLDS TOGETHER,
WORLDS APART

Volume B: 600 to 1850

Robert **Tignor** · Jeremy **Adelman** · Stephen **Aron** · Peter **Brown**

Benjamin **Elman** · Stephen **Kotkin** · Xinru **Liu** · Suzanne **Marchand**

Holly **Pittman** · Gyan **Prakash** · Brent **Shaw** · Michael **Tsin**

W. W. Norton & Company, Inc.

New York · London

W. W. Norton & Company has been independent since its founding in 1923, when William Warder Norton and Mary D. Herter Norton first published lectures delivered at the People's Institute, the adult education division of New York City's Cooper Union. The firm soon expanded its program beyond the Institute, publishing books by celebrated academics from America and abroad. By midcentury, the two major pillars of Norton's publishing program—trade books and college texts—were firmly established. In the 1950s, the Norton family transferred control of the company to its employees, and today—with a staff of four hundred and a comparable number of trade, college, and professional titles published each year—W. W. Norton & Company stands as the largest and oldest publishing house owned wholly by its employees.

Editor: Jon Durbin
Associate Editor: Scott Sugarmann
Project Editor: Jennifer Barnhardt
Editorial Assistant: Kelly Rafey
Managing Editor, College: Marian Johnson
Managing Editor, College Digital Media: Kim Yi
Production Manager: Andy Ensor
Media Editor: Laura Wilk
Associate Media Editor: Michelle Smith
Media Project Editor: Rachel Mayer
Assistant Media Editor: Chris Hillyer
Marketing Manager, History: Sarah England Bartley
Design Director: Rubina Yeh
Book Design: Jillian Burr
Photo Editor: Travis Carr
Permissions Manager: Megan Schindel
Permissions Associate: Elizabeth Trammell
Composition: Cenveo® Publisher Services
Illustrations: Mapping Specialists, Ltd.
Manufacturing: Quad Graphics—Versailles

Permission to use copyrighted material is included on page C-1.

The Library of Congress has cataloged the one-volume edition as follows:

Names: Tignor, Robert L., author.
Title: Worlds together, worlds apart : a history of the world from the
    beginnings of humankind to the present / Robert Tignor ... [and eleven
    others].
Description: Fifth edition. | New York : W. W. Norton & Company, [2018] |
    Includes bibliographical references and index.
Identifiers: LCCN 2017032085 | **ISBN 9780393624786 (hardcover)**
Subject: LCSH: World history—Textbooks. | World
    history—Examinations—Study guides. | Advanced placement programs
    (Education)—Examinations—Study guides
Classification: LCC D21 .T53 2018 | DDC 909—dc23 LC record available at https://lccn.loc.gov/2017032085

ISBN this edition: 978-0-393-62487-8 (pbk.)

W. W. Norton & Company, Inc., 500 Fifth Avenue, New York, NY 10110-0017
wwnorton.com

W. W. Norton & Company Ltd., 15 Carlisle Street, London W1D 3BS
1 2 3 4 5 6 7 8 9 0

Chapter 9

NEW EMPIRES AND COMMON CULTURES, 600–1000 CE   **316**

Chapter 10

BECOMING "THE WORLD," 1000–1300 CE   **356**

Chapter 11

CRISES AND RECOVERY IN AFRO-EURASIA, 1300–1500   402

Chapter 12

CONTACT, COMMERCE, AND COLONIZATION, 1450–1600   **438**

Chapter 13
WORLDS ENTANGLED, 1600–1750   **476**

Chapter 14
CULTURES OF SPLENDOR
AND POWER, 1500–1780 **518**

Chapter 15

REORDERING THE WORLD, 1750–1850   **554**

Revolutionary Transformations and New Languages of Freedom   556

Worlds Together, Worlds Apart has set the standard for four editions for those who want to teach a globally integrated world history survey course. Just as the dynamic field of world history evolves, so, too, has Worlds Together, Worlds Apart. Building on the success of the first four editions, the Fifth Edition continues to offer a highly coherent, cutting-edge survey of the field built around world history stories of significance that make it possible for students to readily make connections and comparisons across time and place and make the teaching of the course more manageable for instructors (for example, the building of the Silk Road, the spread of the Black Death across Afro-Eurasia, the impact of New World silver on global trade, and alternative ways to organize societies during the rise of nineteenth-century capitalism). The Fifth Edition is the most accessible to date. Many of the chapters were substantially reorganized and streamlined to place greater emphasis on the main chapter ideas and amplify comparisons and connections—the book's greatest strength. The new edition will be the most relevant yet for students. They will find increased coverage on numerous topics, but in particular a topic students care a lot about: the environment's role in world history. The Fifth Edition pays considerable attention to the role of climate in producing radical changes in the lives of humans. For example, a long-term warming of the globe facilitated the domestication of plants and animals and led to an agricultural revolution and the emergence of settled societies. In the seventeenth century, the dramatic drop in global temperatures, now known as the Little Ice Age, produced political and social havoc and led to civil wars, population decline, and regime change all around the globe. These are the new focuses of Chapters 1 and 13. Indeed, all chapters have been substantially revised, not because they were inadequate when originally written, but because the recent studies of comparative and global historians have transformed our understanding of the history of the world.

The Fifth Edition is also the most interactive to date. Lead media author Alan Karras (University of California, Berkeley) has brought together an outstanding media team to develop the comprehensive ancillary package for the Fifth Edition, substantially increasing the learning and teaching support available to students and instructors.

- New **InQuizitive**, Norton's adaptive quizzing platform, uses interactive questions and guided feedback to support students' understanding of each chapter's focus questions.
- New **History Skills Tutorials** combine video and interactive activities to provide students with a framework for analyzing a variety of sources.
- New **Primary Source Exercises** in the Coursepack provide ready-made quizzes to assess students' ability to analyze images and documents tied to each chapter.
- New **Story Maps** break complex maps into a sequence of five annotated screens that focus on the story behind the geography.

Since work began on Worlds Together, Worlds Apart, world history has gained even more prominence in college classrooms and historical studies. Courses in the history of the world now abound, often replacing the standard surveys of European history and western civilization overviews. Graduate history students receive training in world history, and journals routinely publish studies in this field. A new generation of textbooks was needed to help students and instructors make sense of this vast, complex, and rapidly evolving field. We believe that Worlds Together, Worlds Apart remains the most current, cutting-edge, engaging, readable, interactive, and useful text available for all students of world history. We also believe that this text, one that has advanced the teaching of this field, could only have grown out of the highly collaborative effort of a team of scholars and teachers rather than the more typical single- or two-author efforts. Indeed, the idea to build each chapter around stories of world history significance and the execution of this model grew out of our monthly team meetings and our joint writing efforts during the development stage. As a team-driven text, *Worlds Together, Worlds Apart* also has the advantage of area experts to make sure the material is presented accurately, which is always a challenge for the single- or two-author texts, especially in world history. Finally, our book reads with a single voice, due to the extraordinary efforts of our general editor and leader, Robert Tignor, who with every edition makes the final major sweep through the text to make sure that the voice, style, and level of detail are consistent throughout. Building on these distinctive strengths, we have worked hard and thoughtfully to make the Fifth Edition of *Worlds Together, Worlds Apart* the best edition so far. While there are many exciting additions to the main text and support package, we have made every effort to remain true to our original vision.

OUR GUIDING PRINCIPLES

Five principles inform this book, guiding its framework and the organization of its individual chapters. The first is that **world history is global history**. There are many fine histories of the individual regions of the world, which we have endeavored to make good use of. But unlike the authors of many other so-called world histories, we have chosen not to deal with the great regions and cultures of the world as separate units, reserving individual chapters to East Asia, South Asia, Southwest Asia, Europe, Africa, and the Americas. Our goal is to place each of these regions in its largest geographical context. Accordingly, we have written chapters that are truly global in that most major regions of the world are discussed in each one. We achieved these globally integrated chapters by building each around a significant world history story or theme. There are a number of wonderful examples throughout the book: the peopling of the earth (Chapter 1), the building of the Silk Road (Chapter 6), the rise of universal religions (Chapters 8 and 9), the Black Death (Chapter 11), the Little Ice Age and its far-reaching impact on political systems globally as well as the effects of New World silver on the economies of the world (Chapter 13), alternative visions to nineteenth-century capitalism (Chapter 15), the rise of nation-states and empires (Chapter 16), and so on. It would be misleading, of course, to say that the context is the world, because none of these regions, even the most highly developed commercially, enjoyed commercial or cultural contact with peoples all over the globe before Columbus's voyage to the Americas and later expeditions of the sixteenth century. But the peoples living in the Afro-Eurasian landmass, probably the single most important building block for our study, were deeply influenced by one another, as were the more scattered peoples living in the Americas and in Africa below the Sahara. Products, ideas, and persons traveled widely across the large land units of Eurasia, Africa, and the Americas. Indeed, Afro-Eurasia was not divided or thought of as divided into separate landmasses until recent times. It is in this sense that our world history is global.

The second principle informing this work is **the importance of chronology in framing world history**. Rather than telling the story of world history by analyzing separate geographical areas, we have elected to frame the chapters around significant world history themes and periods that transcended regional and cultural boundaries—moments or periods of meaningful change in the way that human beings organized their lives. Some of these changes were dramatic and affected many people. Environments changed; the earth became drier and warmer; humans learned to domesticate plants and animals; technological innovations in warfare, political organization, and commercial activities occurred; diseases crossed political and cultural borders, as did dramatic changes in the world's climate; and new religious and cultural beliefs spread far and wide. These changes swept across large landmasses, paying scant heed to preexisting cultural and geographical unity. They affected peoples living in widely dispersed societies, and they often led to radically varied cultural responses in different regions of the world. In other cases, changes occurred in only one locality while other places retained their traditions or took alternative routes. Chronology helps us understand the ways in which the world has, and has not, shared a common history.

The third principle is **historical and geographical balance**. Ours is not a history focused on the rise of the west. We seek to pay attention to the global histories of all peoples and not to privilege those developments that led directly into European history as if the rest of the history of the world was but a prelude to the rise of the West. We deal with peoples living outside Europe on their own terms and try to see world history from their perspective. Even more significantly, while we describe societies that obviously influenced Europe's historical development, we do so in a context very different from that which western historians have stressed. Rather than simply viewing these cultures in terms of their role in western development, we seek to understand them in their own right and to illuminate the ways they influenced other parts of the world. From our perspective, it is historically inaccurate to annex Mesopotamia and Egypt to the West because these territories lay well outside Europe and had a large influence on Africa, South Asia, and East Asia as well as on Europe. Indeed, our presentation of Europe in the period leading up to and including the founding of the Roman Empire is different from many of the standard treatments. The Europeans we describe are rather rough, wild-living, warring peoples living on the fringes of the settled parts of the world and looked down on by more politically stable communities. They hardly seem to be made of the stuff that will catapult Europeans to world leadership a millennium later—indeed, they were very different people from those who, as the result of myriad intervening and contingent events, founded the nineteenth- and twentieth-century empires whose ruins are still all around us.

Our fourth principle is **an emphasis on connections and what we call disconnections across societal and cultural boundaries**. World history is not the history of separate regions of the world at different periods of time. It is the history of the connections among peoples living often at great distances from one another, and it is also the history of the resistance of peoples living within and outside societies to connections that threatened to put them in subordinate positions or to rob them of their independence.

A stress on connections inevitably foregrounds those elements within societies that promoted long-distance ties. Merchants are important, as are military men and political potentates seeking to expand their polities. So are scholars and religious leaders, particularly those who believed that they had universalistic messages with which to convert others to their visions. Perhaps most important of all in premodern world history, certainly the most understudied, are the nomadic pastoral peoples, who were often the agents for the transmission of products, peoples, and ideas across long and harsh distances. They exploded onto the scene of settled societies at critical junctures, erasing old cultural and geographical barriers and producing new unities, as the Arabs did in the seventh century CE and the Mongols did in the thirteenth century. *Worlds Together, Worlds Apart* is not intended to convey the message that the history of the world is a story of increasing integration. What for one ruling group brought benefits in the form of increased workforces, material prosperity, and political stability often meant enslavement, political subordination, and loss of territory for other groups. The historian's task, then, is not only to represent the different experiences of increased connectedness, describing worlds that came together, but also to be attentive to the opposite trends, describing peoples and communities that remained apart.

The fifth and final principle is that **world history is a narrative of big themes and high-level comparisons**. *Worlds Together, Worlds Apart* is not a book of record. Indeed, in a work that tells the story of humankind from the beginnings of history to the present, the notion that no event or individual worthy of attention would be excluded is the height of folly. We have sought to offer clear themes and interpretations in order to synthesize the vast body of data that often overwhelms histories of the world. Our aspiration is to identify the main historical forces that have moved history, to highlight those monumental innovations that have changed the way humans lived, and to describe the creation and evolution of those bedrock institutions, many of which, of course, endure. In this regard, self-conscious cross-cultural comparisons of developments, institutions, and even founding figures receive attention to make students aware that some common institutions, such as slavery, did not have the same features in every society. But conversely, the seemingly diverse terms that were used, say, to describe learned and religious men in different parts of the world—monks in Europe, *ulama* in Islam, Brahmans in India, and scholar-gentries in China—often meant much the same thing in very different settings. We have constructed *Worlds Together, Worlds Apart* around big ideas, stories, and themes rather than filling the book with names and dates that encourage students only to memorize rather than understand world history concepts.

OUR MAJOR THEMES

The primary organizing framework of *Worlds Together, Worlds Apart*—one that runs through the chapters and connects the different parts of the narrative—is the theme of **interconnection and divergence**. While describing movements that facilitated global connectedness, this book also shows how different regions developed their own ways of handling or resisting connections and change. Throughout history, different regions and different population groups often stood apart from the rest of the world until touched by traders or explorers or missionaries or soldiers. Some of these regions welcomed global connections; others sought to change the nature of their connections with the outside world; and yet others resisted efforts to bring them into the larger world. All, however, were somehow affected by their experience of connection. Thus, the history of the world is not simply one of increasing globalization, in which all societies eventually join a common path to the present. Rather, it is a history of the ways in which, as people became linked, their experience of these global connections diverged.

Besides the central theme of interconnection and divergence, other themes also stand out in *Worlds Together, Worlds Apart*. First, the book discusses **how the recurring efforts of people to cross religious, political, and cultural borders brought the world together.** Merchants and educated men and women traded goods and ideas. Whole communities, in addition to select groups, moved to safer or more promising environments. **The transregional crossings of ideas, goods, and peoples produced transformations and conflicts**—a second important theme. Finally, the movement of ideas, peoples, products, climates, and germs over long distances upset the balance of power across the world and within individual societies. Such movements changed the relationship of different population groups with other peoples and areas of the world and led over time to dramatic shifts in the ascendancy of regions. **Changes in power arrangements within and between regions explain which parts of the world and regional groups benefited from integration and which resisted it.** These three themes (exchange and migration, conflict and resistance, and alterations in the balance of power) weave themselves through every chapter of this work. While we highlight major themes throughout, we tell the stories of the people caught in these currents of exchange, conflict, and changing power relations, paying particular attention to the role that gender and the environment play in shaping the evolution of societies. The history of the world is not a single, sweeping narrative. On the contrary, the last 5,000 years have produced multiple histories, moving along many paths and trajectories. Sometimes these histories merge, intertwining themselves in substantial ways. Sometimes they disentangle themselves and simply stand apart. Much of the time, however, they are simultaneously together and apart. In place of a single narrative, the usual one being the rise of the west, this book maps the many forks in the road that confronted the world's societies at different times and the surprising turns and unintended consequences that marked the choices that peoples and societies made, including the unanticipated and dramatic rise of the west in the nineteenth century. Formulated in this way, world history is the unfolding of many possible histories, and readers of this book should come away with a reinforced sense of the unpredictability of the past, the instability of the present, and the uncertainty of the future.

OVERVIEW OF VOLUME ONE

Volume One of *Worlds Together, Worlds Apart* deals with the period from the beginnings of human history through the Mongol invasions of the thirteenth century and the spread of the Black Death across Afro-Eurasia. It is divided into eleven chapters, each of which marks a distinct historical period. Hence, each chapter has an overarching theme or small set of themes that holds otherwise highly diverse material together.

Chapter 1, "Becoming Human," presents biological and cultural perspectives on the way that early hominins became truly human. This chapter incorporates much new research, largely the result of new techniques and methods employed by climatologists, biologists specializing in DNA analysis, linguists, and paleoanthropologists in the tradition of Mary and Louis Leakey. These scientists have transformed our understanding of the evolution of human beings. So much of this work is now being incorporated into the history profession and history courses that it has acquired its own name, big history. We believe that this chapter is important in establishing the global context of world history. We believe, too, that our chapter is unique in its focus on how hominins became humans—how early hominins became bipedal and how they developed complex cognitive processes such as language and artistic abilities. We have incorporated a new understanding of evolution, which now appears to have taken place not in a steady and gradual way as was once thought, but in punctuated bursts, often in response to major climate and environmental challenges. In addition, our findings about the evolution of hominins from *Austrolopithecus* to *Homo sapiens* are based on more precise information than was available in earlier editions. Research indicates that *Homo sapiens* originated in Africa, probably no more than 200,000 years ago. These early men and women walked out of the African landmass sometime between 100,000 and 50,000 years ago, gradually populating all regions of the world. What is significant in this story is that the different population groups around the world, the so-called races of humankind, have only recently broken off from one another. Also in this chapter, we emphasize the role of climate in human evolution; indeed, the first group of *Homo sapiens* nearly went extinct because of severe freezing temperatures, produced by an eruption of vast quantities of lava into the atmosphere. This critical phase in human evolution was followed almost immediately by a strong warming trend that occurred 10,000 years ago and that has remained with us ever since, despite some significant drops in global temperatures. This warming trend led humans to domesticate plants and animals and to found the first village settlements, beginning in Southwest Asia.

Chapter 2, "Rivers, Cities, and First States, 3500–2000 BCE," covers the period during which five of the great river basins experienced extraordinary breakthroughs in human activity. On the floodplains of the Tigris and Euphrates in Mesopotamia, the Nile in Egypt, the Indus Valley in modern-day northern India and Pakistan, and the Yellow and Yangzi Rivers in China, men and women mastered annual floods and became expert in seeding and cultivating foodstuffs. In these areas, populations became dense. River-basin cultures had much in common. They had highly developed hierarchical political, social, and cultural systems, priestly and bureaucratic classes, and organized religious and cultural systems. But they also differed greatly, and these differences were passed from generation to generation. The development of these major complex societies certainly is a turning point in world history. We include in this chapter an expanded discussion on the rise of city-states and provide a greater emphasis on the political aspects leading to the emergence of city-states.

Extensive climatic and technological changes serve as major turning points for **Chapter 3, "Nomads, Chariots, Territorial States, and Microsocieties, 2000–1200 BCE."** Drought, environmental degradation, and political instability brought the first river-basin societies to a crashing end around 2000 BCE. When aridity forced tribal and nomadic peoples living on the fringes of the settled populations to move closer to settled areas, they brought with them an insurmountable military advantage. They had become adept at yoking horses to war chariots and hence were in a position to subjugate and later intermarry with the peoples in the settled polities in the river basins. Around 2000 BCE, these peoples established new territorial kingdoms in Mesopotamia, Egypt, the Indus Valley, and China, which gave way a millennium later (1000 BCE) to even larger and more militarily and politically powerful states. The section on China features a major rewriting and reorganization of the Shang territorial states in East Asia with a new section on Shang writing. In the Americas, the Mediterranean, sub-Saharan Africa, and the Pacific worlds, microsocieties arose as an alternative form of a political system in which peoples lived in much smaller-scale societies that showcased their own unique and compelling features.

Chapter 4, "First Empires and Common Cultures in Afro-Eurasia, 1250–325 BCE," describes the different ways in which larger-scale societies grew and became unified. In the case of the world's first empires, the neo-Assyrian and Persian, political power was the main unifying element. Both states established different models that future empires would emulate. The Assyrians used brute force to intimidate and subjugate different groups within their societies and neighboring states. The Persians followed a pattern that relied less on coercion and more on tributary relationships, while reveling in cultural diversity.

The Zhou state in China offered yet a third way of political unity, basing its rule on the doctrine of the mandate of heaven, which legitimated its rulers' succession as long as they were able to maintain stability and order. Vedic society in South Asia offers a dramatically different model in which religion and culture rather than centralizing monarchies were the main unifying forces. Religion moves to the forefront of the narrative in other ways in this chapter. The birth of monotheism occurred in the Zoroastrian and Hebrew faiths and the beginnings of Buddhism. All three religions endure today.

The last millennium before the Common Era witnessed some of the most monumental developments in human history. In the six and a half centuries discussed in **Chapter 5, "Worlds Turned Inside Out, 1000–350 BCE,"** teachers and thinkers, rather than kings, priests, and warriors, came to the fore. Men like Confucius, the Buddha, Plato, and Aristotle, to name only the best known of this brilliant group, offered new insights into the natural world and provided new guidelines for how to govern justly and live ethically. Drawing on the work of sociologist Karl Jaspars, we call this era the Axial Age, during which Greek, Chinese, and South Asian thinkers elaborated political, religious, and philosophical ideas that informed the societies in which they lived and that have been central to the lives of these societies ever since. In this era, small-scale societies, benefiting from more intimate relationships, took the place of the first great empires, now in decline. These highly individualistic cultures developed new strategies for political organization, even experimenting with a democratic polity. In Africa, the Bantu peoples spread across sub-Saharan Africa, and the Sudanic peoples of Meroe created a society that blended Egyptian and sub-Saharan influences. These were all dynamic hybrid societies building on existing knowledge. Equally dramatic transformations occurred in the Americas, where the Olmec and Chavin peoples were creating hierarchical societies of the like never before seen in their part of the world.

Chapter 6, "Shrinking the Afro-Eurasian World, 350 BCE–250 CE," describes three major forces that simultaneously integrated large segments of the Afro-Eurasian landmass culturally and economically. First, Alexander and his armies changed the political and cultural landscape of North Africa and Southwest and South Asia. Culturally, Alexander spread Hellenism through North Africa and Southwest and central Asia, making it the first cultural system to achieve a transregional scope. Second, it was in the post-Alexander world that long-distance trade was intensified and stabilized. For the first time, a trading network, known as the Silk Road, stretching from Palmyra in the west to central Asia in the east, came into being. This chapter incorporates new research on the origins of the Silk Road and its Afro-Eurasian political, commercial, and cultural importance. Despite the fact that the Silk Road was actually made up of many different roads and was not always accessible, and despite the fact that trade took place mainly over short distances, its reputation was well known to merchants, military adventurers, travelers, religious leaders, and political elites. Buddhism was the first religion to seize on the Silk Road's more formal existence as its followers moved quickly with the support of the Mauryan Empire to spread their ideas into central Asia. Finally, we witness the growth of a "silk road of the seas" as new technologies and bigger ships allowed for a dramatic expansion in maritime trade from South Asia all the way to Egypt and East Africa.

Chapter 7, "Han Dynasty China and Imperial Rome, 300 BCE–300 CE," builds on our comparison of the Neo-Assyrian and Persian Empires in Chapter 4 by comparing in great detail the Han dynasty and Roman Empire, the two political, economic, and cultural powerhouses that dominated much of the Afro-Eurasian landmass from 200 BCE to 200 CE. Both the Han dynasty and the Roman Empire ruled effectively in their own way, providing an instructive comparative case study. Both left their imprint on Afro-Eurasia; rulers for centuries afterward tried to revive these glorious imperial systems and use them as models of greatness. Only the Chinese were successful in restoring imperial rule and did so for more than two millennia. European efforts to re-create the Roman Empire, at least in western Europe, failed. This chapter also discusses the effect of state sponsorship on religion, as Christianity came into existence in the context of the late Roman Empire and Buddhism was introduced to China during the decline of the Han.

Out of the crumbling Roman Empire new political systems and a new religion emerged, the major topic of **Chapter 8, "The Rise of Universal Religions, 300–600 CE."** The Byzantine Empire, claiming to be the successor state to the Roman Empire, embraced Christianity as its state religion. The Tang rulers patronized Buddhism to such a degree that Confucian statesmen feared it had become the state religion. This chapter has new information on the Sogdians, a pastoral peoples who inhabited central Asia and were vital in spreading Buddhism and supporting Silk Road trade. Both Buddhism and Christianity enjoyed spectacular success in the politically fragmented post-Han era in China and in the feudal world of western Europe. These dynamic religions represent a decisive transformation in world history. Christianity enjoyed its eventual successes through

state sponsorship via the Roman and Byzantine Empires and by providing spiritual comfort and hope during the chaotic years of Rome's decline. Buddhism grew through imperial sponsorship and significant changes to its fundamental beliefs, when adherents to the faith deified Buddha and created notions of an afterlife. In Africa, a wide range of significant developments and myriad cultural practices existed; yet large common cultures also arose. The Bantu peoples spread throughout the southern half of the landmass, spoke closely related languages, and developed similar political institutions based on the prestige of individuals of high achievement. In the Americas, the Olmecs established their own form of the city-state, while the Maya owed their success to a decentralized common culture built around a strong religious belief system and a series of spiritual centers.

In **Chapter 9, "New Empires and Common Cultures, 600–1000 CE,"** we see another world religion, Islam, explode with world-changing consequences in a relatively remote corner of the Arabian Peninsula. The rise of Islam provides a contrast to the way universalizing religions and political empires interacted. Islam and empire arose in a fashion quite different from Christianity and the Roman Empire. Christianity took over an already existing empire—the Roman—after suffering persecution at its hands for several centuries. In contrast, Islam created an empire almost at the moment of its emergence. There is much new scholarship on early Islam, the life of Muhammad, and the creation of the Quran, based mainly on the writings of non-Muslim observers and scholars. Although these texts are often critical of Muhammad and early Islam, they must be used (albeit very carefully) because of the dearth of information on the beginnings of Islam found in the few Muslim and Arabic sources that remain to us. We have added this important perspective to our discussion of the birth of Islam. By the time the Abbasid Empire came into being in the middle of the eighth century, Islamic armies, political leaders, and clerics exercised power over much of the Afro-Eurasian landmass from southern Spain, across North Africa, all the way to central Asia. The Tang Empire in China, however, served as a counterweight to Islam's power both politically and intellectually. Confucianism enjoyed a spectacular recovery in this period. With the Tang rulers, Confucianism slowed the spread of Buddhism and further reinforced China's development along different, more secular pathways. Japan and Korea also enter world history at this time as tributary states to Tang China and as hybrid cultures that mixed Chinese customs and practices with their own. The Christian world split in this period between the western Latin church and the eastern Byzantine church. Both branches of Christianity played a role in unifying societies, especially in western Europe, which lacked strong political rule at a time when all of Europe experienced a profound and disabling drop in temperature.

In the three centuries from 1000 to 1300 (**Chapter 10, "Becoming 'The World,' 1000–1300 CE"**), Afro-Eurasia experienced an unprecedented rise in prosperity and population that even spread into West and East Africa. Just as importantly, the world in this period divided into regional zones that are recognizable today. And trade grew rapidly.

A view of the major trading cities of this time demonstrates how commerce transformed cultures. Sub-Saharan Africa also underwent intense regional integration via the spread of the Mande-speaking peoples and the Mali Empire. The Americas witnessed their first empire in the form of the Chimu peoples in the Andes. This chapter ends with the Mongol conquests of the twelfth and thirteenth centuries, which brought massive destruction. The Mongol Empire, however, once in place, promoted long-distance commerce, scholarly exchange, and travel on an unprecedented scale. The Mongols brought Eurasia, North Africa, and many parts of sub-Saharan Africa into a new connectedness. The Mongol story also underscores the important role that nomads played throughout the history of the early world. Just as much of Europe had suffered through a drop in temperature in the ninth and tenth centuries, as described in Chapter 9, now a radical fall in temperature in combination with drought troubled the eastern Mediterreanean and the Islamic world. Here the result was a steep decline in standards of living, leading to riots and political fragmentation. Even so, Islamic science flourished, and China became the most urbanized part of the world.

The Black Death brought Afro-Eurasia's prosperity and population growth to a catastrophic end, as discussed in **Chapter 11, "Crises and Recovery in Afro-Eurasia, 1300–1500."** The death and destruction of the fourteenth century saw traditional institutions give way, forcing peoples to rebuild their cultures. The political systems that came into being at this time and the intense religious experimentation that took place effected a sharp break with the past. The bubonic plague wiped out as much as two-thirds of the population in many of the densely settled locations of Afro-Eurasia. Societies once brought to their knees by the Mongols' depredations now suffered grievously from biological pathogens. In the face of one of humanity's grimmest periods, peoples and societies demonstrated tremendous resilience as they looked for new ways to rebuild their communities, some turning inward and others seeking inspiration, conquests, and riches elsewhere.

New dynasties emerged all across Afro-Eurasia. The Ming replaced the Mongol Yuan dynasty in China. A small band of Muslim warriors in Anatolia became sophisticated military tacticians and administrators and created an empire that would last as the Ottoman Empire until the end of World War I. New Muslim dynasts also took over South Asia (the Mughals) and the Iranian plateau (Safavids). Nor was Europe left behind, for here, too, new dynamic rulers came to the thrones in England, France, Spain, and Portugal, ready to project their power overseas. Volume One concludes on the eve of the Columbian Exchange, the moment when "old" worlds discovered "new" ones and a vast series of global interconnections and divergences commenced.

OVERVIEW OF VOLUME TWO

The organizational structure for Volume Two reaffirms the commitment to write a decentered, global history of the world. Christopher Columbus is not the starting point, as he is in so many modern world histories. Rather, we begin in the eleventh and twelfth centuries with two major developments in world history: the Mongols and the Black Death. The first, set forth in **Chapter 10, "Becoming 'The World,' 1000–1300 CE,"** describes a world that was divided for the first time into regions that are recognizable today. This world experienced rapid population growth, as is shown by a simple look at the major trading cities from Asia in the east to the Mediterranean in the west. Yet nomadic peoples remained a force, as revealed in the Mongol invasions of Afro-Eurasia.

Chapter 11, "Crises and Recovery in Afro-Eurasia, 1300–1500," describes how the Mongol warriors, through their conquests and the integration of the Afro-Eurasian world, unwittingly spread the bubonic plague, which brought death and depopulation to much of Afro-Eurasia. Both these stories set the stage for the modern world and are clear-cut turning points in world history. The primary agents of world connection described in this chapter were dynasts, soldiers, clerics, merchants, and adventurers who rebuilt the societies that disease and political collapse had destroyed.

The Mongols joined the two hemispheres, as we describe in **Chapter 12, "Contact, Commerce, and Colonization, 1450–1600,"** bringing the peoples and products of the Western Hemisphere into contact and conflict with Eurasia and Africa. It is the collision between the Eastern and Western Hemispheres that sets in motion modern world history and marks a distinct divide or turning point between the premodern and the modern. Here, too, disease and increasing trade linkages were vital. Unprepared for the advanced military technology and the disease pool of European and African peoples, the Amerindian population experienced a population decline even more devastating than that caused by the Black Death.

Europeans sailed across the Atlantic Ocean to find a more direct, less encumbered route to Asia and came upon lands, peoples, and products that they had not expected. One item, however, that they had sought in every part of the world and that they found in abundance in the Americas was precious metal. Although historians rightly emphasize the European intrusion into the Indian Ocean and their discovery of the Americas, we remind readers that the Europeans were not alone in expanding their influence through the oceans. The Ottomans made gains in the Red Sea and ventured into the Indian Ocean as rivals to the Portuguese.

In **Chapter 13, "Worlds Entangled, 1600–1750,"** we discuss how New World silver from Mexico and Peru became the major currency of global commerce, oiling the long-distance trading networks that had been revived after the Black Death. The effect of New World silver on the world economy was so great that it, even more than the Iberian explorations of the New World, brought the hemispheres together and marks the true genesis of modern world history. Sugar also linked the economies and political systems of western Europe, Africa, and the Americas and was a powerful force in a triangular trade centered on the Atlantic Ocean. This trade involved the shipment of vast numbers of African captives to the Americas, where they toiled as slaves on sugar, tobacco, cotton, and rice plantations.

For Europe and the rest of the world, the sudden dip in temperature in the seventeenth century, which historians now call the Little Ice Age, brought immense suffering not seen around the world since the Black Death. Wars broke out, and regimes were overthrown in China and Iran. Much of the new research into the Little Ice Age is based on a better understanding of the climate through the studies of climatologists, research that has transformed the way historians now look at the seventeenth century.

Chapter 14, "Cultures of Splendor and Power, 1500–1780," discusses the Ottoman scientists, Safavid and Mughal artists, Chinese literati, and European thinkers, whose notable achievements were rooted in their own cultures but tempered by awareness of the intellectual activities of others. In this chapter, we look closely at how culture is created as a historical process and describe how the massive increase in wealth during this period, growing out of global trade, led to one of the great periods of cultural flourishing in world history. In our discussion of Europe's scientific revolution, which got under way at the end of the sixteenth century and came to full fruition in the seventeenth century through the studies of Isaac Newton, we tackle the vexed question of why the scientific breakthrough occurred in Europe and not in China, India, and the Muslim world, which had been in the lead up to then. It was a turn to quantification that catapulted Europe ahead of the rest of the world, coupled with the fact that the Chinese had their exposure to European science through the Jesuits.

Around 1800, transformations reverberated outward from the Atlantic world and altered economic and political relationships in the rest of the world. In **Chapter 15, "Reordering the World, 1750–1850,"** we discuss how political revolutions in the Americas and Europe, new ideas about how to trade and organize labor, and a powerful rhetoric of freedom and universal rights underlay the beginning of "a great divide" between peoples of European descent and those who were not. These forces of laissez-faire capitalism, industrialization, the nation-state, and republicanism not only attracted diverse groups around the world; they also threatened groups that put forth alternative visions. Ideas of freedom, as manifested in trading relations, labor, and political activities, clashed with a traditional world based on inherited rights and statuses and further challenged the way men and women had lived in earlier times. These political, intellectual, and economic reorderings changed the way people around the world saw themselves and thus represent something quite novel in world history.

Much new comparative work has been done on the industrial revolution in the same way that historians have placed Europe's scientific revolution within a global context.

These new ways of envisioning the world did not go unchallenged, as **Chapter 16, "Alternative Visions of the Nineteenth Century,"** makes clear. Here, intense resistance to evolving modernity reflected the diversity of peoples and their hopes for the future. Wahabbism in Islam, the strongman movement in Africa, Indian resistance in America and Mexico, socialism and communism in Europe, the Taiping Rebellion in China, and the Indian mutiny in South Asia catapulted to historical prominence prophets and leaders whose visions often drew on earlier traditions and led these individuals to resist rapid change.

Chapter 17, "Nations and Empires, 1850–1914," discusses the political, economic, military, and ideological power that thrust Europe and North America to the fore of global events and led to an era of nationalism and modern imperialism, new forces in world history. Yet this period of seeming European supremacy was to prove short-lived. This chapter has new material on the Irish potato famine and an in-depth analysis of European colonialism.

As **Chapter 18, "An Unsettled World, 1890–1914,"** demonstrates, even before World War I shattered Europe's moral certitude, many groups at home (feminists, Marxists, and unfulfilled nationalists) and abroad (anticolonial nationalists) had raised a chorus of complaints about European and North American dominance. As in Chapter 14, we look at the processes by which specific cultural movements rose and reflected the concerns of individual societies. Yet here, too, syncretistic movements emerged in many cultures and reflected the sway of global imperialism, which by then had become a dominant force.

In keeping with our stress on the environment, this chapter discusses Teddy Roosevelt's promotion of the conservation of nature and other efforts by Europeans to be stewards of the earth. There is also a new environmentally oriented Current Trends in World History about the felt need for sustainable agricultural methods on the Russian steppe lands.

Chapter 19, "Of Masses and Visions of the Modern, 1910–1939," briefly covers World War I and then discusses how, from the end of World War I until World War II, different visions of being modern competed around the world. It is the development of modernism and its effects on multiple cultures that integrate the diverse developments discussed in this chapter. In the decades between the world wars, proponents of liberal democracy struggled to defend their views and often to impose their will on authoritarian rulers and anticolonial nationalists.

The chapter presents a number of revisionist views on the origins of World War I, the Armenian genocide, the Sykes-Picot agreement that was reached by Britain and France during World War I to partition the Ottoman Middle Eastern lands once the war was over, and the secularizing and modernizing ideas that animated Mustafa Kemal, later known as Ataturk, to create a new nation in Turkey.

Chapter 20, "The Three-World Order, 1940–1975," covers World War II and describes how new adversaries arose after the war. A three-world order came into being— the First World, led by the United States and extolling capitalism, the nation-state, and democratic government; the Second World, led by the Soviet Union and favoring authoritarian polities and economies; and the Third World, made up of former colonies seeking an independent status for themselves in world affairs. The rise of this three-world order dominated the second half of the twentieth century and constitutes another major theme of world history.

In **Chapter 21, "Globalization, 1970–2000,"** we explain that at the end of the cold war, the modern world, while clearly more unified than before, still had profound cultural differences and political divisions. At the beginning of the twenty-first century, capital, commodities, peoples, and ideas moved rapidly over long distances. But cultural tensions and political impasses continued to exist. The rise of this form of globalism represented a vital new element as humankind headed into a new century and millennium. This chapter contains an expanded discussion of the role of international and supranational financial organizations; the environmental crisis, brought on by the release of carbon emissions into the atmosphere and the resulting global warming; and the end of white rule in South Africa.

We close with the **Epilogue, "2001–The Present,"** which tracks developments since the turn of the millennium. These last few years have brought profound changes to the world order, yet we hope readers of *Worlds Together, Worlds Apart* will see more clearly how this most recent history is, in fact, entwined with trends of much longer duration that are the chief focus of this book.

We see the last half decade as pointing the peoples and countries of the world in more populist, ethnic nationalist, and violent directions. Britain's vote to withdraw from the European Union, known as Brexit; the election of Donald Trump to the American presidency; the rise of ethnic and religious consciousness in Turkey and India most notably and throughout the world in general; and the emergence of militant Islam in al-Qaeda and then in ISIS (the Islamic State in Iraq and Syria) all seem to us to be the consequence of various groups believing themselves to be disenfranchised and demanding to be heard.

MEDIA & PRINT ANCILLARIES

The Fifth Edition of *Worlds Together, Worlds Apart* is supported by an array of digital resources to help faculty meet their course goals—in the classroom and online—and activities for students to develop core skills in reading comprehension, historical analysis, and writing.

FOR STUDENTS

- **InQuizitive** (Shane Carter, Siobhan McGurk) is an adaptive quizzing tool that improves students' understanding of the themes and objectives of each chapter while honing their critical analysis skills with primary source, image, and map analysis questions. Students receive personalized quiz questions with detailed, guiding feedback on the topics in which they need the most help, while the engaging, gamelike elements motivate them as they learn.

- The **History Skills Tutorials** feature three modules—Images, Documents, and Maps—to support students' development of the key skills needed for the history course. These tutorials feature author videos modeling the analysis process, followed by interactive questions that will challenge students to apply what they have learned.

- The free and easy-to-use **Student Site** offers additional resources for students to use outside of class. Resources include interactive iMaps, author videos, and a comprehensive Online Reader featuring 100 additional sources.

- Free and included with new copies of the text, the **Norton Ebook Reader** provides an enhanced reading experience that works on all computers and mobile devices. Features include intuitive highlighting, note-taking, and book-marking, as well as pop-up definitions and enlargeable maps and images. Author videos are embedded throughout to create an engaging reading environment.

FOR INSTRUCTORS

- **Norton Coursepacks** allow instructors to bring strong assessment and lecture tools directly into their Learning Management System (LMS). Available at no cost to professors or students, Norton Coursepacks include chapter-based assignments, including Guided Reading Exercises, Primary Source Exercises, Chapter Review Quizzes, author videos, interactive iMaps, forum prompts, and more.

- **Story Maps** (Ruth Mostern) break complex maps into a sequence of five annotated screens that focus on the story behind the geography. Twelve maps, including two new maps, cover such topics as "The Silk Road," "The Spread of the Black Death," and "Population Growth and the Economy."

- The **Instructor's Manual** (Sharon Cohen) has everything instructors need to prepare lectures and classroom activities: lecture outlines, lecture ideas, classroom activities, and lists of recommended books, films, and Web sites.

- The **Test Bank** (Ryba Epstein, Derek O'Leary) contains approximately 1,400 multiple-choice, true/false, and essay questions. All test questions are now aligned with Bloom's Taxonomy for greater ease of assessment (available in print, PDF, Word, and Examview formats).

- **Lecture PowerPoints and Art PowerPoints** feature lecture outlines, key talking points, and the photographs and maps from the book to support in-class presentations.

ACKNOWLEDGMENTS

Worlds Together, Worlds Apart would never have happened without the full support of Princeton University. In a highly unusual move, and one for which we are truly grateful, the university helped underwrite this project with financial support from its 250th Anniversary Fund for undergraduate teaching and by allowing released time for the authors from campus commitments.

The history department's support of the effort over many years has been exceptional. Four chairs made funds and departmental support available, including the department's incomparable administrative talents. We would be remiss if we did not single out the department manager, Judith Hanson, who provided us with assistance whenever we needed it. We also thank Eileen Kane, who tracked down references and illustrations and merged changes into the manuscript. We also would like to thank Pamela Long, who made all of the complicated arrangements for ensuring that we were able to discuss matters in a leisurely and attractive setting. Sometimes that meant arranging for long-distance conference calls. She went even further and proofread the entire manuscript, finding errors that we had all overlooked.

We drew shamelessly on the expertise of the departmental faculty, and although it might be wise simply to include a roster of the Princeton history department, that would do an injustice to those of whom we took most advantage. So here they are: Mariana Candido, Robert Darnton, Sheldon Garon, Anthony Grafton, Molly Greene, David Howell, Harold James, William Jordan, Emmanuel Kreike, Michael Mahoney, Arno Mayer, Kenneth Mills, John Murrin, Susan Naquin, Willard Peterson, Theodore Rabb, Bhavani Raman, Stanley Stein, and Richard Turits. When necessary, we went outside the history department, getting help from Michael L. Bender, L. Carl Brown, Michael Cook, Norman Itzkowitz, Martin Kern, Thomas Leisten, Heath Lowry, and Peter Schaefer. Two departmental colleagues—Natalie Z. Davis and Elizabeth Lunbeck—were part of the original team but had to withdraw because of other commitments. Their contributions were vital, and we want to express our thanks to them. David Gordon, now at Bowdoin College, used portions of the text while teaching an undergraduate course at the University of Durban in South Africa and shared comments with us. Shamil Jeppie, like David Gordon a graduate of the Princeton history department, now teaching at the University of Cape Town in South Africa, read and commented on various chapters.

Beyond Princeton, we have also benefited from exceptionally gifted and giving colleagues who have assisted this book in many ways. Colleagues at Louisiana State

University, the University of North Carolina, the University of Pennsylvania, and the University of California at Los Angeles, where Suzanne Marchand, Michael Tsin, Holly Pittman, and Stephen Aron, respectively, are now teaching, pitched in whenever we turned to them. Especially helpful have been the contributions of Joyce Appleby, James Gelvin, Naomi Lamoreaux, and Gary Nash at UCLA; Michael Bernstein at Tulane University; and Maribel Dietz, John Henderson, Christine Kooi, David Lindenfeld, Reza Pirbhai, and Victor Stater at Louisiana State University. It goes without saying that none of these individuals bears any responsibility for factual or interpretive errors that the text may contain. Xinru Liu would like to thank her Indian mentor, Romila Thapar, who changed the way we think about Indian history.

The quality and range of reviews on this project were truly exceptional. The final version of the manuscript was greatly influenced by the thoughts and ideas of numerous instructors. We wish to particularly thank our consulting reviewers, who read multiple versions of the manuscript from start to finish.

First Edition Consultants

Hugh Clark, Ursinus College
Jonathan Lee, San Antonio College
Pamela McVay, Ursuline College
Tom Sanders, United States Naval Academy

Second Edition Consultants

Jonathan Lee, San Antonio College
Pamela McVay, Ursuline College
Steve Rapp, Georgia State University
Cliff Rosenberg, City University of New York

First Edition Reviewers

Lauren Benton, New Jersey Institute of Technology
Ida Blom, University of Bergen, Norway
Ricardo Duchesne, University of New Brunswick
Major Bradley T. Gericke, United States Military Academy
John Gillis, Rutgers University
David Kenley, Marshall University
John Kicza, Washington State University
Matthew Levinger, Lewis and Clark College
James Long, Colorado State University
Adam McKeown, Columbia University
Mark McLeod, University of Delaware
John Mears, Southern Methodist University
Michael Murdock, Brigham Young University
David Newberry, University of North Carolina, Chapel Hill

Tom Pearcy, Slippery Rock State University
Oliver B. Pollak, University of Nebraska, Omaha
Ken Pomeranz, University of California, Irvine
Major David L. Ruffley, United States Air Force Academy
William Schell, Murray State University
Major Deborah Schmitt, United States Air Force Academy
Sarah Shields, University of North Carolina, Chapel Hill
Mary Watrous-Schlesinger, Washington State University

Second Edition Reviewers

William Atwell, Hobart and William Smith Colleges
Susan Besse, City University of New York
Tithi Bhattacharya, Purdue University
Mauricio Borrerero, St. John's University
Charlie Briggs, Georgia Southern University
Antoinne Burton, University of Illinois, Urbana-Champaign
Jim Cameron, St. Francis Xavier University
Kathleen Comerford, Georgia Southern University
Duane Corpis, Georgia State University
Denise Davidson, Georgia State University
Ross Doughty, Ursinus College
Alison Fletcher, Kent State University
Phillip Gavitt, Saint Louis University
Brent Geary, Ohio University
Henda Gilli-Elewy, California State Polytechnic University, Pomona
Fritz Gumbach, John Jay College
William Hagen, University of California, Davis
Laura Hilton, Muskingum College
Jeff Johnson, Villanova University
David Kammerling-Smith, Eastern Illinois University
Jonathan Lee, San Antonio College
Dorothea Martin, Appalachian State University
Don McGuire, State University of New York, Buffalo
Pamela McVay, Ursuline College
Joel Migdal, University of Washington
Anthony Parent, Wake Forest University
Sandra Peacock, Georgia Southern University
David Pietz, Washington State University
Jared Poley, Georgia State University
John Quist, Shippensburg State University
Steve Rapp, Georgia State University
Paul Rodell, Georgia Southern University
Ariel Salzman, Queen's University
Bill Schell, Murray State University
Claire Schen, University at Buffalo
Jonathan Skaff, Shippensburg State University
David Smith, California State Polytechnic University, Pomona

Neva Specht, Appalachian State University

Ramya Sreeniva, State University of New York, Buffalo

Charles Stewart, University of Illinois, Urbana-Champaign

Rachel Stocking, Southern Illinois University, Carbondale

Heather Streets, Washington State University

Tim Teeter, Georgia Southern University

Charlie Wheeler, University of California, Irvine

Owen White, University of Delaware

James Wilson, Wake Forest University

Third Edition Reviewers

Henry Antkiewicz, Eastern Tennessee State University

Anthony Barbieri-Low, University of California, Santa Barbara

Andrea Becksvoort, University of Tennessee, Chattanooga

Hayden Bellonoit, United States Naval Academy

John Bloom, Shippensburg University

Kathryn Braund, Auburn University

Catherine Candy, University of New Orleans

Karen Carter, Brigham Young University

Stephen Chappell, James Madison University

Jessey Choo, University of Missouri, Kansas City

Timothy Coates, College of Charleston

Gregory Crider, Wingate University

Denise Davidson, Georgia State University

Jessica Davidson, James Madison University

Sal Diaz, Santa Rosa Junior College

Todd Dozier, Baton Rouge Community College

Richard Eaton, University of Arizona

Lee Farrow, Auburn University, Montgomery

Bei Gao, College of Charleston

Behrooz Ghamari-Tabrizi, University of Illinois, Urbana-Champaign

Steven Gish, Auburn University, Montgomery

Jeffrey Hamilton, Baylor University

Barry Hankins, Baylor University

Brian Harding, Mott Community College

Tim Henderson, Auburn University, Montgomery

Marjorie Hilton, University of Redlands

Richard Hines, Washington State University

Lisa Holliday, Appalachian State University

Jonathan Lee, San Antonio College

David Kalivas, University of Massachusetts, Lowell

Christopher Kelley, Miami University, Ohio

Kenneth Koons, Virginia Military Institute

Michael Kulikowski, Pennsylvania State University

Benjamin Lawrence, University of California, Davis

Lu Liu, University of Tennessee, Knoxville

David Longfellow, Baylor University

Harold Marcuse, University of California, Santa Barbara

Dorothea Martin, Appalachian State University

David Mayes, Sam Houston State University

James Mokhiber, University of New Orleans

Mark Munzinger, Radford College

David Murphree, Virginia Tech University

Joshua Nadel, North Carolina Central University

Wing Chung Ng, University of Texas, San Antonio

Robert Norrell, University of Tennessee, Knoxville

Chandrika Paul, Shippensburg University

Beth Pollard, San Diego State University

Timothy Pytell, California State University, San Bernardino

Stephen Rapp, professional historian

Alice Roberti, Santa Rosa Junior College

Aviel Roshwald, Georgetown University

James Sanders, Utah State University

Lynn Sargeant, California State University, Fullerton

William Schell, Murray State University

Michael Seth, James Madison University

Barry Stentiford, Grambling State University

Gabrielle Sutherland, Baylor University

Lisa Tran, California State University, Fullerton

Michael Vann, California State University, Sacramento

Peter Von Sivers, University of Utah

Andrew Wackerfuss, Georgetown University

Ted Weeks, Southern Illinois University, Carbondale

Angela White, Indiana University of Pennsylvania

Jennifer Williams, Nichols State University

Andrew Wise, State University of New York, Buffalo

Eloy Zarate, Pasadena City College

William Zogby, Mohawk Valley Community College

Fourth Edition Reviewers

Andrea Becksvoort, University of Tennessee, Chattanooga

Hayden Bellenoit, United States Naval Academy

Volker Benkert, Arizona State University

Gayle Brunelle, California State University, Fullerton

Jessica Clark, California State University, Chico

Brian Harding, Mott Community College

Emily Hill, Queen's University at Kingston

Laura Hilton, Muskingum University

Dennis Laumann, University of Memphis

Elaine MacKinnon, University of West Georgia

Ronald Mellor, University of California, Los Angeles

Carol Miller, Tallahassee Community College

Greg O'Malley, University of California, Santa Cruz

David Ortiz Jr., University of Arizona

Charles Parker, Saint Louis University

Juanjuan Peng, Georgia Southern University

Dana Rabin, University of Illinois, Urbana-Champaign

Matthew Rothwell, University of Southern Indiana

Teo Ruiz, University of California, Los Angeles

Jeffrey Shumway, Brigham Young University

Lisa Tran, California State University, Fullerton

Lela Urquhart, Georgia State University

Fifth Edition Reviewers

Andreas Agocs, University of the Pacific

Anthony Barbieri-Low, University of California, Santa Barbara

Michelle Benson-Saxton, University at Buffalo

Brett Berliner, Morgan State University

Carolyn Noelle Biltoft, Georgia State University

Edward Bond, Alabama A&M University

Gayle Brunelle, California State University, Fullerton

Grace Chee, West Los Angeles College

Stephen Colston, San Diego State University

Paula Devos, San Diego State University

Paul Hudson, Georgia Perimeter College

Alan Karras, University of California, Berkeley

Elaine MacKinnon, University of West Georgia

Harold Marcuse, University of California, Santa Barbara

Jeff McEwen, Chattanooga State Community College

Thomas McKenna, Concord University

Eva Moe, Modesto Junior College

Alice Pate, Kennesaw State University

Chandrika Paul, Shippensburg University

Jared Poley, Georgia State University

Dana Rabin, University of Illinois, Urbana-Champaign

Masako Racel, Kennesaw State University

Charles Reed, Elizabeth City State University

Alice Roberti, Santa Rosa Junior College

Steven Rowe, Chicago State University

Ariel Salzmann, Queen's University

Lynn Sargeant, California State University, Fullerton

Robert Saunders, Farmingdale State College

Sharlene Sayegh-Canada, California State University, Long Beach

Claire Schen, University at Buffalo

Jeffrey Shumway, Brigham Young University

Greg Smay, University of California, Berkeley

Margaret Stevens, Essex County College

Lisa Tran, California State University, Fullerton

Michael Vann, California State University, Sacramento

Theodore Weeks, Southern Illinois University

Krzysztof Ziarek, University of Buffalo

For the Fifth Edition, we also had a mix of new and returning authors who helped create the best support materials to accompany *Worlds Together, Worlds Apart*. Alan Karras served as the lead media author, directing the development of our ancillary author team. For their tremendous efforts, we would like to thank Sharon Cohen for authoring the Instructor's Manual, Ryba Epstein and Derek O'Leary for creating the test bank, and Shane Carter and Siobhan McGurk for developing InQuizitive.

For the Fifth Edition, we have some familiar and new friends at Norton to thank. Chief among them is Jon Durbin, who once again played a major role in bringing this edition to publication. Laura Wilk, our new media editor, has put together a fabulous package of support materials for students and instructors. Sarah England has put together a creative marketing plan for the book. Jillian Burr is responsible for the book's beautiful and effective design. Jennifer Barnhardt has done an amazingly efficient job as our project editor. Andy Ensor has shepherded the project through production beautifully. Kelly Rafey has done a masterful job compiling the manuscript with a special focus on photos, primary sources, and permissions. Michelle Smith and Chris Hillyer have done a fine job lending their support in strengthening the media support materials to meet the ever more complex classroom and assessment needs of instructors. Alice Vigliani did a spectacular job working on the manuscript, paying particular attention to our efforts to reorganize and streamline many of the chapters in both volumes. Janet Greenblatt did a superb job with the copyediting, turning the chapters around quickly to meet our schedule. A special shout-out goes to Debra Morton-Hoyt and her team of cover designers. *Worlds Together, Worlds Apart* has always been incredibly creative and distinctive looking, and the Fifth Edition covers are even more eye-catching and memorable than the first four editions. Bravo!

Finally, we must recognize that while this project often kept us apart from family members, their support held our personal worlds together.

ROBERT TIGNOR (*Ph.D. Yale University*) is professor emeritus and the Rosengarten Professor of Modern and Contemporary History at Princeton University and the three-time chair of the history department. With Gyan Prakash, he introduced Princeton's first course in world history nearly thirty years ago. Professor Tignor has taught graduate and undergraduate courses in African history and world history and written extensively on the history of twentieth-century Egypt, Nigeria, and Kenya. Besides his many research trips to Africa, Professor Tignor has taught at the University of Ibadan in Nigeria and the University of Nairobi in Kenya.

JEREMY ADELMAN (*D.Phil. Oxford University*) has lived and worked in seven countries and four continents. A graduate of the University of Toronto, he earned a master's degree in economic history at the London School of Economics (1985) and a doctorate in modern history at Oxford University (1989). He is the author or editor of ten books, including *Sovereignty and Revolution in the Iberian Atlantic* (2006) and *Worldly Philosopher: The Odyssey of Albert O. Hirschman* (2013), a chronicle of one of the twentieth century's most original thinkers. He has been awarded fellowships by the British Council, the Social Science and Humanities Research Council of Canada, the Guggenheim Memorial Foundation, and the American Council Learned Societies (the Frederick Burkhardt Fellowship). He is currently the Henry Charles Lea Professor of History and the director of the Global History Lab at Princeton University. His next book is called *Earth Hunger: Markets, Resources and the Need for Strangers*.

STEPHEN ARON (*Ph.D. University of California, Berkeley*) is professor of history and Robert N. Burr Chair at the University of California, Los Angeles and president of the Western History Association (2016–2017). Professor Aron is the author of *How the West Was Lost: The Transformation of Kentucky from Daniel Boone to Henry Clay*; *American Confluence: The Missouri Frontier from Borderland to Border State*; and *The American West: A Very Short Introduction*. He is currently writing a book with the tentative title *Can We All Get Along: An Alternative History of the American West*.

PETER BROWN (*B.A. Oxford University*) is the Rollins Professor of History emeritus at Princeton University. He previously taught at London University and the University of California, Berkeley. He has written on the rise of Christianity and the end of the Roman Empire. His works include *Augustine of Hippo*; *The World of Late Antiquity*; *The Cult of the Saints*; *Body and Society*; *The Rise of Western Christendom*; and *Poverty and Leadership in the Later Roman Empire*. His most recent book is *Treasure in Heaven*.

BENJAMIN ELMAN (*Ph.D. University of Pennsylvania*) is professor of East Asian studies and history at Princeton University. He has served as the chair of the Princeton East Asian Studies Department and as director of the East Asian Studies Program. He taught at the University of California, Los Angeles for over fifteen years, 1986–2002. His teaching and research fields include Chinese intellectual and cultural history, 1000–1900; the history of science in China, 1600–1930; the history of education in late imperial China; and Sino-Japanese cultural history, 1600–1850. He is the author of seven books, four of them translated into Chinese, Korean, or Japanese: *From Philosophy to Philology: Intellectual and Social Aspects of Change in Late Imperial China*; *Classicism, Politics, and Kinship: The Ch'angchou School of New Text Confucianism in Late Imperial China*; *A Cultural History of Civil Examinations in Late Imperial China*; *On Their Own Terms: Science in China, 1550–1900*; *A Cultural History of Modern Science in China*; *Civil Examinations and Meritocracy in Late Imperial China, 1400–1900*; and *Science in China, 1600–1900: Essays by Benjamin A. Elman*. He is the creator of Classical Historiography for Chinese History at http://libguides .princeton.edu/chinese-historiography, a bibliography and teaching Web site published since 1996.

ALAN KARRAS (*Ph.D. University of Pennsylvania*) is the Associate Director of International & Area Studies at the University of California, Berkeley, and has served as chair of the College Board's test development committee for world history and as co-chair of the College Board's commission on AP history course revisions. He studies the eighteenth-century Atlantic world and global interactions more broadly concerning illegal activities like smuggling and corruption.

STEPHEN KOTKIN (*Ph.D. University of California, Berkeley*) is Birkelund Professor of History and International Affairs at Princeton University and director of the Princeton Institute for International and Regional Studies. His books include *Stalin: Waiting for Hitler, 1929-1941*; *Stalin: Paradoxes of Power, 1878-1928*; *Magnetic Mountain: Stalinism as a Civilization*; *Uncivil Society: 1989 and the Implosion of the Communist Establishment*; and *Armageddon Averted: The Soviet Collapse, 1970-2000*. He has coedited many works, including *Mongolia in the Twentieth Century: Landlocked Cosmopolitan*.

XINRU LIU (*Ph.D. University of Pennsylvania*) is professor of early Indian history and world history at the College of New Jersey. She is associated with the Institute of World History and the Chinese Academy of Social Sciences. She is the author of *Ancient India and Ancient China, Trade and Religious Exchanges*, AD 1-600; *Silk and Religion, an Exploration of Material Life and the Thought of People*, AD 600-1200; *Connections across Eurasia: Transportation, Communication, and Cultural Exchange on the Silk Roads*, coauthored with Lynda Norene Shaffer; *A Social History of Ancient India* (in Chinese); and *The Silk Road in World History*. Professor Liu promotes South Asian studies and world history studies in both the United States and the People's Republic of China.

SUZANNE MARCHAND (*Ph.D. University of Chicago*) is Boyd Professor of European and Intellectual History at Louisiana State University, Baton Rouge. Professor Marchand also spent a number of years teaching at Princeton University. She is the author of *Down from Olympus: Archaeology and Philhellenism in Germany, 1750-1970* and *German Orientalism in the Age of Empire: Religion, Race and Scholarship*.

HOLLY PITTMAN (*Ph.D. Columbia University*) is professor of art history at the University of Pennsylvania, where she teaches art and archaeology of Mesopotamia and the Iranian Plateau. She also serves as curator in the Near East Section of the University of Pennsylvania Museum of Archaeology and Anthropology. Previously she served as a curator in the Ancient Near Eastern Art Department of the Metropolitan Museum of Art. She has written extensively on the art and culture of the Bronze Age in Southwest Asia and has participated in excavations in Cyprus, Turkey, Syria, Iraq, and Iran, where she currently works. Her research investigates works of art as media through which patterns of thought, cultural development, and historical interactions of ancient cultures of the Near East are reconstructed.

GYAN PRAKASH (*Ph.D. University of Pennsylvania*) is the Dayton-Stockton Professor of History at Princeton University, specializing in South Asian history. A member of the Subaltern Studies Collective until its dissolution in 2006, he directed the Shelby Cullom Davis Center for Historical Studies (2003-2008) and was awarded fellowships by the National Science Foundation, the Guggenheim Foundation, and the National Endowment of Humanities. He is the author of *Bonded Histories* (1990) and *Another Reason* (1999) and has edited several volumes of essays, including *After Colonialism* (1994), *The Spaces of the Modern City* (2009), *Utopia/Dystopia* (2010), and *Noir Urbanisms* (2010). His latest book is *Mumbai Fables*, and he wrote the script for the film *Bombay Velvet* (2015). He is currently writing a book on the history of Indira Gandhi's Emergency rule in India. With Robert Tignor, he introduced the modern world history course at Princeton University.

BRENT SHAW (*Ph.D. Cambridge University*) is the Andrew Fleming West Professor of Classics at Princeton University, where he has directed the Program in the Ancient World. He was previously at the University of Pennsylvania, where he chaired the Graduate Group in Ancient History. His principal areas of specialization as a Roman historian are Roman family history and demography, sectarian violence and conflict in Late Antiquity, and the regional history of Africa as part of the Roman Empire. His works include *Sacred Violence: African Christians and Sectarian Hatred in the Age of Augustine*; *Bringing in the Sheaves: Economy and Metaphor in the Roman World*; and *Spartacus and the Slave Wars*. He has also edited the papers of Sir Moses Finley, *Economy and Society in Ancient Greece*, and published in a variety of books and journals, including the *Journal of Roman Studies*, the *American Historical Review*, the *Journal of Early Christian Studies*, and *Past & Present*.

MICHAEL TSIN (*Ph.D. Princeton*) is associate professor of history and global studies at the University of North Carolina at Chapel Hill. He previously taught at the University of Illinois at Chicago, Princeton University, Columbia University, and the University of Florida. Professor Tsin's primary interests include the histories of modern China and colonialism. He is the author of *Nation, Governance, and Modernity in China: Canton, 1900-1927*. He is currently writing a cultural history of the reconfiguration of Chinese identity in the twentieth century.

THE GEOGRAPHY OF THE ANCIENT AND MODERN WORLDS

Today, we believe the world to be divided into continents, and most of us think that it was always so. Geographers usually identify six inhabited continents: Africa, North America, South America, Europe, Asia, and Australia. Inside these continents they locate a vast number of subcontinental units, such as East Asia, South Asia, Southeast Asia, the Middle East, North Africa, and sub-Saharan Africa. Yet this geographical understanding would have been completely alien to premodern men and women, who did not think that they inhabited continents bounded by large bodies of water. Lacking a firm command of the seas, they

saw themselves living on contiguous landmasses, and they thought these territorial bodies were the main geographical units of their lives. Hence, in this volume we have chosen to use a set of geographical terms, the main one being Afro-Eurasia, that more accurately reflect the world that the premoderns believed that they inhabited.

The most interconnected and populous landmass of premodern times was Afro-Eurasia. The term Eurasia is widely used in general histories, but we think it is in its own ways inadequate. The preferred term from our perspective must be Afro-Eurasia, for the interconnected

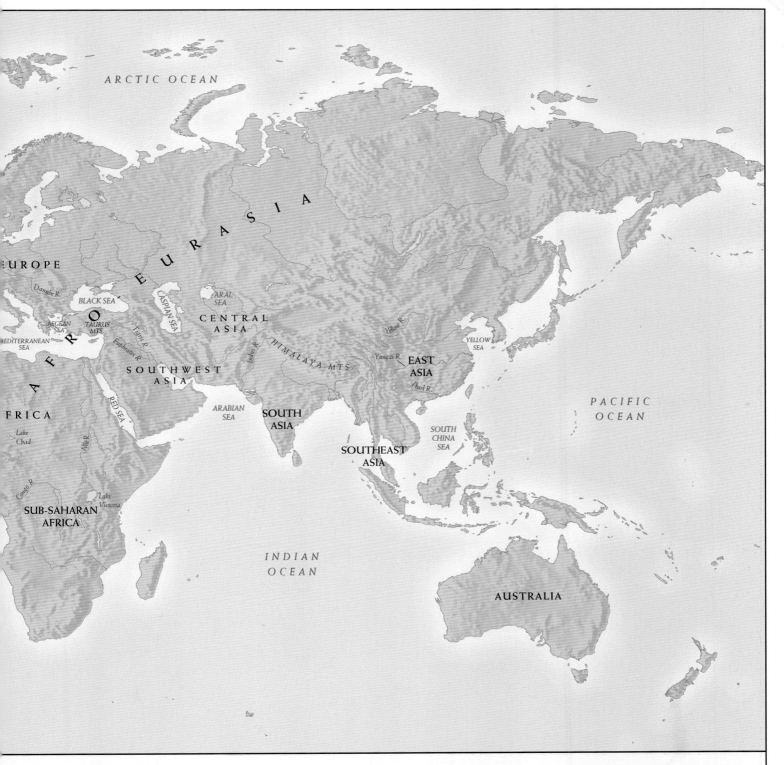

landmass of premodern and indeed much of modern times included large parts of Europe and Asia and significant regions in Africa. The major African territories that were regularly joined to Europe and Asia were Egypt, North Africa, and even parts of sub-Saharan Africa.

Only gradually and fitfully did the divisions of the world that we take for granted today take shape. The peoples inhabiting the northwestern part of the Afro-Eurasian landmass did not see themselves as European Christians, and hence as a distinctive cultural entity, until the Middle Ages drew to a close in the twelfth and thirteenth centuries. Islam did not arise and extend its influence throughout the middle zone of the Afro-Eurasian landmass until the eighth and ninth centuries. And, finally, the peoples living in what we today term the Indian subcontinent did not feel a strong sense of their own cultural and political unity until the Delhi Sultanate of the thirteenth and fourteenth centuries and the Mughal Empire, which emerged at the beginning of the sixteenth century, brought political unity to that vast region. As a result, we use the terms South Asia, Vedic society, and India in place of Indian subcontinent for the premodern part of our narrative, and we use Southwest Asia and North Africa to refer to what today is designated as the Middle East. In fact, it is only in the period from 1000 to 1300 that some of the major cultural areas that are familiar to us today truly crystallized.

WORLDS TOGETHER,
WORLDS APART

FIFTH EDITION

Before You Read This Chapter

Go to inQuizitive to see what you know & learn what you've missed.

GLOBAL STORYLINES

- The universalizing religion of Islam, based on the message of the prophet Muhammad, originates on the Arabian Peninsula and spreads rapidly across Afro-Eurasia.

- The expanding Tang dynasty in East Asia consolidates its bureaucracy, struggles with religious pluralism, and extends its influence into central and East Asia.

- Christianity splits over religious and political differences, leading to a divide between Roman Catholicism in the west and Greek Orthodoxy in the east.

9

New Empires and Common Cultures, 600–1000 CE

FOCUS QUESTIONS

- Why did a universal religion arise in the Arabian Peninsula at the beginning of the seventh century CE, and how do its origins compare with those of other religions covered in this book (Judaism, Buddhism, and Christianity)?

- How and where did Islam, Buddhism, and Christianity spread in the period 600–1000 CE?

- What were the organizational structures of the Abbasids, Tang China, and Christendom?

- What were the forces of opposition and change within the Islamic, Tang, and Christian worlds?

- In what ways did the interactions between religion, empire, and commercial exchange affect developments across Afro-Eurasia during this period?

In 754 CE, the Muslim caliph (ruler) al-Mansur decided to relocate his capital city. Islam was barely a century old, yet it was flourishing under its second dynasty, the Abbasids. Al-Mansur wanted to relocate power away from Damascus (the capital of Islam's first dynasty) to the Abbasids' home region on the Iranian plateau to signal its new dawn. After traveling the length of the Tigris and Euphrates Rivers in search of a perfect site, the caliph decided to build his capital near an unimposing village called Baghdad.

He had good reasons for this selection. The site lay between Mesopotamia's two great rivers at the juncture of the canals that linked them. It was also a powerful symbolic location: close to the ancient capital of the Sasanian Empire, Ctesiphon, where the Arch of Khusro was still standing. It was also the site of earlier Sumerian and Babylonian power. By building at Baghdad, al-Mansur could reaffirm Mesopotamia's centrality in the world and exalt the universalist ambitions of Islam. Within five years of laying the first brick, towering walls surrounded what soon became known as the "round city," so named because of the way in which the different segments radiated out from the administrative and religious center.

Al-Mansur's choice had enduring effects. As the new capital of Islam, Baghdad also became a vital crossroads for commerce. Overnight, the city exploded into a bustling world entrepôt. Chinese goods arrived by land and sea; commodities from Inner Eurasia flowed in over the Silk Road; and cargo-laden camel caravans wound across Baghdad's western desert, linking the capital with Syria, Egypt, North Africa, and southern Spain. In effect, the unity that the Abbasids imposed from Baghdad intensified the movement of peoples, ideas, innovations, and commodities.

Baghdad's eminence and prosperity reflected its role as the center of the Islamic world. Yet, while Islam was gaining ground in central Afro-Eurasia, Chinese might was surging in East Asia—powerfully under the Tang—and Christianity was striving to extend its domains and add to its converts. Unquestionably, however, the two imperial powerhouses of this period were Islam and Tang China, and they are the focus of this chapter.

RELIGION AND EMPIRE

How religion and empire connect can vary in important ways. For example, as we will see in this chapter, Islam and Tang China were manifestly different worlds. The Islamic state had a universalizing religious mission: to bring humankind under the authority of the religion espoused by the Prophet Muhammad. In contrast, the Tang had no such grandiose religious aspirations, and while the ruling elite supported religious pluralism within China, they did not use Buddhism to expand their control into areas outside China. Instead, the Tang rulers expected that their neighbors would emulate Chinese institutions and pay tribute as symbols of respect to the greatness of the Tang Empire. With Islam's warriors, traders, and scholars crossing to Europe, Chinese influences taking deeper root in East Asia, and Christendom extending itself across Europe, religion, empire, and commercial exchange once again intertwined to serve as the social foundation across much of Afro-Eurasia.

Given the surge of religious energy across Afro-Eurasia, it was perhaps only a matter of time before a prophetic figure would arise among the Arabs. Christianity and Buddhism were laying claim to universal truths, spreading their faiths across wide geographical areas outside their places of origin, and competing groups now had to speak the language of universal religion. Only the Tang dynasty resisted the universalizing faiths, as Confucianism and Daoism withstood the upsurge of Chinese Buddhism—revealing that China would follow a different path by maintaining past traditions. In the seventh century CE, Arab peoples would become the makers of their own universal faith, which would join and jostle with predecessors in Afro-Eurasia.

THE ORIGINS AND SPREAD OF ISLAM

Islam began inside Arabia. Despite its remoteness and sparse population, in the sixth century CE, Arabia was feeling the effects of exciting outside currents: long-distance trade, imperial politics, and especially religious debate. As early as the the fourth century CE (see Current Trends in World History on p. 293 of Chapter 8), inhabitants in the state of Himyar (present-day Yemen) had embraced Judaism, only to see their territory conquered by Ethiopian Christians in 525 CE. In addition to establishing a state in the southeastern tip of the Arabian Peninsula, Christianity was making deep inroads into Arab societies, sending out missionaries eastward into southwestern Asia, where many Arabs lived. They established a notably strong following in northern Arabia. Also, commodities from Egypt, Syria, and Iraq circulated in local Arabian markets, and Arabs joined in the Byzantine and Sasanian military and civil bureaucracies. Thus, while one of the world's most universalizing faiths would be born in a remote region of Southwest Asia, Islam was quickly in a position to take advantage of the dynamic trade routes and to adapt imperial political institutions in Southwest Asia, the Iranian Plateau, and North Africa as it spread its faith and shaped its political empire.

Mecca, in the Hijaz (the western region of the Arabian Peninsula, bordering the Red Sea), was not an imposing place. A pre-Islamic poet wrote that its "winter and summer are equally intolerable. No waters flow . . . [and there is] not a blade of grass on which to rest the eye; no, nor hunting. [Here there are] only merchants, the most despicable of professions" (Peters, p. 23). Hardly more than a village of simple mud huts, Mecca's inhabitants sustained themselves less as traders than as caretakers of a revered sanctuary called the Kaaba. They regarded this collection of unmortared rocks piled on top of one another as the dwelling place of deities, whom the polytheistic Meccans worshipped. It was in this remote region that one of the world's major prophets was born, and the universalizing faith he founded soon spread from Arabia through the trade routes stretching across Southwest Asia and North Africa.

A Vision, a Text

In the early life of Muhammad, little suggested that momentous events would soon occur. Born in Mecca around 570 CE into a well-respected tribal family, he enjoyed only moderate success as a trader. Then came a revelation, which would convert this broker of commodities into a proselytizer of a new faith. In 610 CE, while Muhammad was on a month-long spiritual retreat

Mecca. *At the great mosque at Mecca, which many consider the most sacred site in Islam, hundreds of thousands of worshippers gather for Friday prayers. Many are performing their religious duty to go on a pilgrimage to the holy places in the Arabian Peninsula.*

in a cave near Mecca, he believed that God came to him in a vision and commanded him to recite these words:

> Recite in the Name of the Lord who createth,
>
> Createth man from a clot
>
> Recite: And thy Lord is the most Bounteous who teacheth by the pen
>
> Teacheth man that which he knew not.

Further revelations followed. The early ones were like the first: short, powerful, emphasizing a single, all-powerful God (Allah), and full of instructions for Muhammad's fellow Meccans to carry this message to nonbelievers. The words were eminently memorable, an important feature in an oral culture where poetry recitation was the highest art form. Muhammad's early preaching had a clear message. He urged his small band of followers to act righteously, to set aside false deities, to submit themselves to the one and only true God, and to care for the less fortunate—for the Day of Judgment was imminent. Muhammad's most insistent message was the oneness of God, a belief that has remained central to the Islamic faith ever since.

These teachings, compiled into an authoritative version after the Prophet's death, constituted the foundational text of Islam: the Quran. Its 114 chapters, known as suras, occur in descending order of length; the longest has 300 verses and the shortest, a mere 3. Accepted as the very word of God, they were believed to flow without flaw through God's perfect instrument, the Prophet Muhammad. (See Primary Source: The Quran: Two Suras in Praise of God.) Like the Jewish Torah, the Christian Bible, and other foundational texts, this one proclaimed the tenets of a new

faith to unite a people and to expand its spiritual frontiers. Its message already had universalist elements, though how far it was to be extended, whether just to the tribal peoples living in the Arabian Peninsula or well beyond, was not at all clear at first.

Muhammad believed that he was a prophet in the tradition of Moses, other Hebrew prophets, and Jesus and that he communicated with the same God that they did. As we have seen, Christian and Jewish communities existed in the Arabian Peninsula at this time. The city of Yathrib (later called Medina) held a substantial Jewish community. Just how deeply Muhammad understood the tenets of Judaism and Christianity is difficult to determine, but his professed indebtedness to their tradition is a part of Islamic belief.

The Move to Medina

In 622 CE, Muhammad and a small group of followers, opposed by Mecca's leaders because of their radical religious tenets and their challenge to the ruling elite's authority, escaped to Medina. Known as the *hijra* ("breaking off of relations" or "departure"), the perilous 200-mile journey yielded a new form of communal unity: the *umma* ("band of the faithful"). So significant was this moment that Muslims date the beginning of the Muslim era from this year.

Medina thus became the birthplace of a new faith called Islam ("submission"—in this case, to the will of God) and a new community called Muslims ("those who submit"). The city of Medina had been facing tribal and religious tensions, and by inviting Muhammad and his followers to take up residence there, its elders hoped that his leadership and charisma would

The Quran: Two Suras in Praise of God

These two suras from the Quran are relatively short, but they convey some of the essence of Muhammad's message. The Quran opens with a sura known as the fatiha ("of the opening"), which in its powerfully prayerlike quality lends itself to frequent recitation. Sura 87, "The Most High," provides a deeper insight into the nature of humanity's relationship with God.

THE FATIHA

In the name of God the beneficent, the merciful.
Praise be to God, Lord of the worlds,
The beneficent, the merciful.
Owner of the day of judgement,
You (alone) do we worship. You (alone) do we ask for help.
Show us the straight path,
The path of those whom You have favored; not the (path) of those who earn Your anger nor of those who go astray.

(1.1–1.7)

THE MOST HIGH

In the name of God the beneficent, the merciful.
Praise the name of your Lord the most high,
Who creates, then disposes;
Who measures, then guides;
Who brings forth the pasturage,
Then turns it to russet stubble.
We shall make you read (O Muhammad) so that you shall not forget
Except that which God wills. He knows the disclosed and that which still is hidden;
And We shall ease your way to the state of ease.
Therefore remind (men), for of use is the reminder.
He who fears will heed,
But the most wretched will flout it,
He who will be flung to the great fire
In which he will neither die nor live.
He is successful who grows,
And remembers the name of his Lord, so prays.
But you prefer the life of the world
Although the hereafter is better and more lasting.
This is in the former scrolls,
The scrolls of Abraham and Moses.

(87.1–87.19)

QUESTIONS FOR ANALYSIS

- What themes do these passages reveal about Islam's view of the relationship between God and mortals?
- Do you find any similarities to the tenets of Judaism and Christianity as you have encountered them in this book?

Source: "Sura 1," and "Sura 87," *The Norton Anthology of World Religions: Islam*, ed. Jane Dammen McAuliffe, trans. Marmaduke Pickthall (New York: W. W. Norton & Company, 2015), pp. 86, 119–120.

bring peace and unity to their city. Early in his stay, Muhammad promulgated a document, the Constitution of Medina, requiring the community's people to refer all disputes to God and him. Now the residents were expected to replace traditional family, clan, and tribal affiliations with loyalty to Muhammad as the one and true Prophet of God. From Medina the faithful broadcast their faith and their mission, at first mainly by military means, to the recalcitrants of Mecca and then to all of Arabia and then later to the entire world. In this way, Islam joined Christianity in seeking to bring the whole known world under its authority.

Over time, the core practices and beliefs of every Muslim would crystallize as the **five pillars of Islam**. Muslims were expected to (1) *adhere to and repeat* the phrase that there is no God but God and that Muhammad was His Prophet; (2) *pray* five times daily facing Mecca; (3) *fast* from sunup until sundown during the month of Ramadan; (4) *make a pilgrimage* to Mecca at least once in a lifetime if their personal resources permitted; and (5) *pay alms* in the form of taxation that would alleviate the hardships of the poor. These clear-cut expectations gave the imperial system that would soon develop a doctrinal and legal structure and a broad appeal to diverse populations.

Difficulties in Documentation

Few data can be gleaned about Muhammad and the evolution of Islam from Arabic-Muslim sources known to have been written in the seventh century CE. Non-Muslim sources, especially Christian and Jewish texts, while often unsympathetic to Muhammad and early Islam, are nonetheless more abundant and contain useful data on the Prophet and the early messages of Islam. Questions have been raised based on these sources about Muhammad's birth place, his relationship to the most powerful of the Quraysh clans during his stay in Mecca, even the date of his death. A number of non-Muslim sources, for example, contend that the Prophet did not die, as Muslim tradition holds, in 632 CE, but was alive in 634 CE, leading a military campaign into Palestine. Many of these sources, as well as the Quran itself, stress the eschatological content of Muhammad's preachings and the actions of his early followers, arguing (1) that Muhammad believed that the hour of judgment was near and (2) that it was only later, during the middle of the Umayyad period in the eighth century CE, that Islam lost its end-of-the-world emphasis and settled into a long-term religious and political system.

The only Muslim source that we have on Muhammad and early Islam is the Quran itself, which, according to Muslim tradition, was compiled, with variations, during the caliphate of Uthman (r. 644–655). Once again, recent scholarship has questioned this claim, suggesting a later date, sometime in the early eighth century CE, for the standardization of the Quran. Some scholars even contend that the text by then had additions and redactions to Muhammad's message. The Quran, in fact, is singularly quiet on some of the most important events in Muhammad's life. It mentions Muhammad's name only four times. Nor do the struggles with the Quraysh in Mecca or his flight to Medina appear. Instead, scholars are dependent on biographies of Muhammad, one of the first of which was compiled by Ibn Ishaq (704–767 CE), a work not available to present scholarship but used by later Muslim authorities, notably Ibn Hisham (d. 833 CE), who wrote *The Life of Muhammad*, and Islam's most illustrious historian, Muhammad Ibn al-Jarir al-Tabari (838–925 CE). Although these two later works come from the ninth and tenth centuries CE, Muslim tradition ever since has held these sources to be reliable on Muhammad's early life and the evolution of Islam after the death of the Prophet.

Muhammad's Successors and the Expanding *Dar al-Islam*

In 632 CE, in his early sixties, the Prophet is believed to have passed away. Islam might have withered without its leader, but the movement remained vibrant thanks to the energy of the early followers—especially Muhammad's first four successors, the "rightly guided caliphs." The Arabic word *khalīfa* means "successor," and in this context it referred to Muhammad's successors as political rulers over Muslim peoples and the expanding state. Their breakthrough was to institutionalize the new faith. They set the new religion on the pathway to imperial greatness and linked religious uprightness with territorial expansion, empire building, and an appeal to all peoples.

Now Islam's expansive spiritual force galvanized its political authority. But what kind of polity would this be? Driven by religious fervor and a desire to acquire the wealth of conquered territories, Muslim soldiers embarked on military conquests and sought to found a far-reaching territorial empire. This expansion of the Islamic state was one aspect of the struggle that they called *jihad*. From the outset, Muslim religious and political leaders divided the world into two units: the *dar al-Islam* (or the world of Islam) and the *dar al-harb* (the world of warfare), seeking nothing less than world dominion. Within fifteen years, Muslim soldiers had grasped Syria, Egypt, and Iraq—centerpieces of the former Byzantine and Sasanian Empires that now became pillars undergirding an even larger Islamic empire. Mastery of desert warfare and inspired military leadership yielded these astonishing exploits, as did the exhaustion of the Byzantine and Sasanian Empires after generations of warfare.

The Byzantines saved the core of their empire by pulling back to the highlands of Anatolia, where they had readily defensible frontiers. In contrast, the Sasanians gambled all on a final effort: they hurled their remaining military resources against the Muslim armies, only to be crushed. Having lost Iraq and unable to defend the Iranian plateau, the Sasanian Empire passed out of existence. The result: Islam acquired political foundations within a generation of its birth.

The Battle of Badr. *This image depicts the battle of Badr, which took place in 624 CE and marked the beginning of Muhammad's reconquest of Mecca from his new base in the city of Medina.*

Creating an empire and stabilizing it were two different things. We have seen some come and go, such as Alexander's. Others had more stamina. How would Islam fare? A political vacuum opened in the new and growing Islamic empire with the assassination of Ali, the last of the "rightly guided caliphs." Ali, an early convert to Islam, was a fierce leader in the early battles for expansion. The Umayyads, a branch of the Quraysh, laid claim to Ali's legacy. Having been governors of the province of Syria under Ali, this first dynasty moved the core of Islam out of Arabia to the Syrian city of Damascus. They also introduced a hereditary monarchy to resolve leadership disputes. These adaptable, cosmopolitan traders ruled from Damascus until the Abbasids overthrew them in 750 CE.

The Abbasid Revolution

As the Umayyad dynasts spread Islam beyond Arabia, some peoples resented the rulers' high-handed ways. In particular, they believed that their continuing discrimination despite their conversion to Islam was humiliating and unfair. The Arab conquerors enslaved large numbers of non-Arabs in the course of their conquests. These slaves could only lose their servile status through manumission. Even so, the non-Arab freedpeople found that they, too, were still regarded as lesser persons in spite of living in Arab households and becoming Muslims, so dominant were ethnic Arabs within a still Arab-dominated Islamic world. This situation existed even though the Arabs totaled about 250,000 to 300,000 during the Umayyad era, while non-Arab populations were 100 times as populous, totaling between 25 and 30 million. The area where protest against Arab domination reached a crescendo was in the east, notably in Khurasan, where most of the Arab conquerors did not live separate from the local populations in garrison cities (as was commonplace elsewhere) but were in close contact and intermarried local, ethnically different women. One of the early leaders of Iranian protest movements in this region was Abu Muslim, whose message about Islam was that it was a universal religion, open equally to all groups. He stated: "I am a man from among the Muslims, and I do not trace my descent to any group to the exclusion of any other. . . . My only ancestry is Islam" (Hoyland, p. 206).

Even though opponents assassinated Abu Muslim, they did not silence his message. A coalition of dissidents emerged under a movement harkening back to Abbas ibn al-Muttalid (566–653 CE), an uncle of the Prophet, hence called the Abbasid movement and claiming descent from the Prophet. Soon disgruntled provincial authorities and their military allies, as well as non-Arab converts, joined the movement. After amassing a sizable military force, the Abbasid coalition trounced the Umayyad ruler in 750 CE. Thereafter, the center of the caliphate shifted to Iraq (at Baghdad; recall the opening anecdote about al-Mansur), signifying the eastward sprawl of the faith and its empire. It also represented a success for non-Arab groups within Islam without eliminating Arab influence at the dynasty's center—the capital, Baghdad, in Arabic-speaking Iraq. This process changed the nature of the emerging empire. For as the political center of Islam moved out of Arabia to Syria (at Damascus) and then with the Abbasids to Baghdad, ethnic and geographical diversity replaced what had been ethnic purity. Thus, even as the universalizing religion strove to create a common spiritual world, it became more diverse within its political dimensions.

Not only did the Abbasids open Islam to Persian peoples, but they also embraced Greek and Hellenistic learning, Indian science, and Chinese innovations. In this fashion, Islam, drawing its original impetus from the teachings and actions of a prophetic figure, followed the trajectory of Christianity and Buddhism and became a faith with a universalist message and appeal. It owed much of its success to its ability to merge the contributions of vastly different geographical and intellectual territories into a rich yet unified culture. (See Map 9.1.)

THE CALIPHATE An early challenge for the Abbasid rulers was to determine how traditional, or "Arab," they could be and still rule so vast an empire. They chose to keep the bedrock political institution of the early Islamic state—the **caliphate** (the line of political leaders reaching back to Muhammad). Signifying both the political and spiritual head of the Islamic community, this institution had arisen as the successor to Muhammad's shining leadership. Although the caliphs exercised political and spiritual authority over the Muslim community, they did not inherit Muhammad's prophetic powers. Nor were they authorities in religious doctrine. That power was reserved for religious scholars, called *ulama*; some of these men were schooled in Islamic law, others were experts in Quranic interpretation, and still others were religious thinkers.

Abbasid rule reflected borrowed practices from successful predecessors. The caliphs' leadership style was a mixture of Persian absolute authority and the royal seclusion of the Byzantine emperors who lived in palaces far removed from their subjects. As the empire expanded, it became increasingly decentralized politically, enabling wily regional governors and competing caliphates in Spain and Egypt to grab power. The political result was an Islamic world shot through with multiple centers of power, nominally led by a weakened Abbasid caliphate. Even as Islam's political center diffused, though, its spiritual center remained fixed in Mecca, where many of the faithful gathered to circle the kaaba and to reaffirm their devotion to Islam as part of their pilgrimage obligation.

THE ARMY The Abbasids, like all rulers, relied on force to integrate their empire. For imperial Islam (as for the Romans), exercising military power required marshaling warriors and soldiers from across Afro-Eurasia.

How "Arab" should the Muslim armies be? In the early stages, leaders had conscripted military forces from local Arab populations, creating citizen armies. But as Arab populations settled down in garrison cities, the Abbasid rulers turned to professional soldiers from the empire's peripheries. Now they recruited from Turkish-speaking communities in central Asia and from the non-Arab, Berber-speaking peoples of North and West Africa. Their reliance on foreign—that is, non-Arab—military personnel represented a major shift in the Islamic world. Not only did the change infuse the empire with dynamic new populations, but soon these groups gained political authority (just as the "barbarians" had done in the last centuries of the Roman Empire; see Chapters 6 and 8). Having begun as an Arab state and then incorporated strong Persian influence, the Islamic empire now embraced Turkish elements from the pastoral belts of central Asia.

ISLAMIC LAW (THE *SHARIA*) AND THEOLOGY

In the Abbasid period, not just the caliphate but also Islamic law took shape. The **sharia** stands as the crucial foundation of Islam. It covers all aspects of practical and spiritual life, providing legal principles for marriage contracts, trade regulations, and religious prescriptions such as prayer, pilgrimage rites, and ritual fasting. It reflects the work of generations of religious scholars, rather than soldiers, courtiers, and bureaucrats. And it has remained vital throughout the Muslim world, independent of empires, to the present day.

Early Muslim communities prepared the ground for the *sharia,* endeavoring (guided by the Quran) to handle legal matters in ways that they thought Muhammad would have wanted. However, because the Quran mainly addressed family concerns, religious beliefs, and social relations (such as marriage, divorce, inheritance, dietary restrictions, and treatment of women) but not other legal questions, local judges exercised their own judgment where the Quran was silent. The most influential early legal scholar was an eighth-century CE Palestinian-born Arab, al-Shafi'i, who wanted to make the empire's laws entirely Islamic. He insisted that Muhammad's laws as laid out in the Quran, in addition to his sayings and actions as written in later reports (*hadith*), provided all the legal guidance that Islamic judges needed.

The triumph of scholars such as al-Shafi'i was deeply significant: it placed the *ulama,* the Muslim scholars, at the heart of Islam. *Ulama,* not princes and kings, became the lawmakers, insisting that the caliphs could not define religious law. Only the scholarly class could interpret the Quran and determine which *hadith* were authentic. The *ulama*'s ascendance opened a sharp division within Islam: between the secular realm of the caliphs and the religious sphere of judges, experts on Islamic jurisprudence, teachers, and holy men.

GENDER IN EARLY ISLAM

Pre-Islamic Arabia was one of the last regions in Southwest Asia where patriarchy had not triumphed. Instead, men still married into women's families and moved to those families' locations, as was common in tribal communities. Some women engaged in a variety of occupations and even, if they became wealthy, married more than one husband. But contact with the rest of Southwest Asia, where men's power over women prevailed, was already altering women's status in the Arabian Peninsula before the birth of Muhammad.

Muhammad's relations with women reflected these changes. As a young man, he married a woman fifteen years his senior—Khadija, an independent trader—and took no other wives before she died. It was Khadija to whom he went in fear following his first revelations. She wrapped him in a blanket and assured him of his sanity. She was also his first convert. Later in life, however, he took younger wives, some of whom were widows of his companions, and insisted on their veiling (partly as a sign of their modesty and privacy). He married his favorite wife, Aisha, when she was only nine or ten years old. An important figure in early Islam, she was the daughter of Abu Bakr, who became the first caliph after Muhammad's death. She became a major source for collecting Muhammad's sayings.

Khadija. *The importance of women to the founding of Islam is apparent in this Ottoman miniature, which depicts Khadija (left) bearing witness to Gabriel (center) as he conveys God's will to Muhammad (right). Both wife and prophet are veiled in accordance with hadiths promoting female modesty and prohibiting representations of Muhammad, respectively.*

By the time Islam reached Southwest Asia and North Africa, where strict gender rules and women's subordinate status were entrenched, the new faith was adopting a patriarchal outlook. Muslim men could divorce freely; women could not. A man could take four wives and numerous concubines; a woman could have only one husband. Well-to-do women, always veiled, lived secluded from male society. Still, the Quran did offer women some protections. Men had to treat each wife with respect if they took more than one. Women could inherit property (although only half of what a man inherited). Infanticide was taboo. Marriage dowries went directly to the bride rather than to her guardian, indicating women's independent legal standing. And while a woman's adultery drew harsh punishment, its proof required eyewitness testimony. The result was a legal system that reinforced men's dominance over women but empowered magistrates to oversee the definition of male honor and proper behavior.

The Blossoming of Abbasid Culture

The arts flourished during the Abbasid period, a blossoming that left its imprint throughout society. Within a century, Arabic had superseded Greek as the Muslim world's preferred language for poetry, literature, medicine, science, and philosophy. Like Greek, it spread beyond native speakers to become the language of the educated classes.

Arabic scholarship now made significant contributions, including the preservation and extension of Greek and Roman thought and the transmission of Greek and Latin treatises to Europe. Scholars at Baghdad translated the principal works of Aristotle; essays by Plato's followers; works by Hippocrates, Ptolemy, and Archimedes; and the medical treatises of Galen, using these works to extend their understanding of the natural world. To house such manuscripts, patrons of the arts and sciences—including the caliphs—opened magnificent libraries.

The Muslim world absorbed scientific breakthroughs from China and other areas, incorporated the use of paper from China, adopted siege warfare from China and Byzantium, and applied

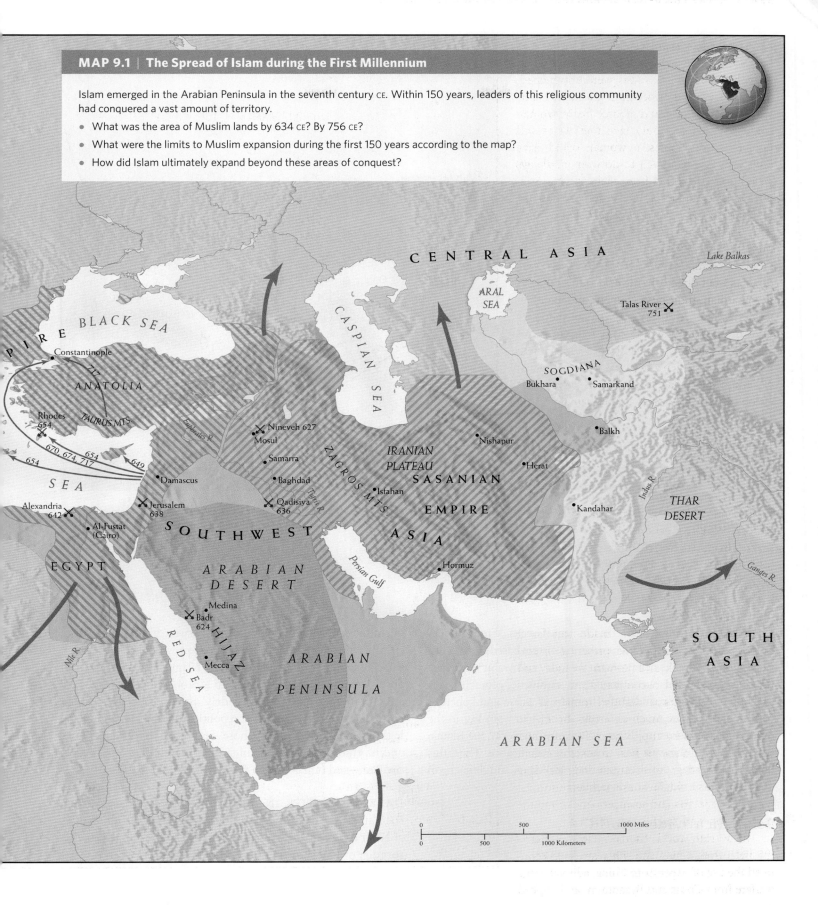

MAP 9.1 | The Spread of Islam during the First Millennium

Islam emerged in the Arabian Peninsula in the seventh century CE. Within 150 years, leaders of this religious community had conquered a vast amount of territory.

- What was the area of Muslim lands by 634 CE? By 756 CE?
- What were the limits to Muslim expansion during the first 150 years according to the map?
- How did Islam ultimately expand beyond these areas of conquest?

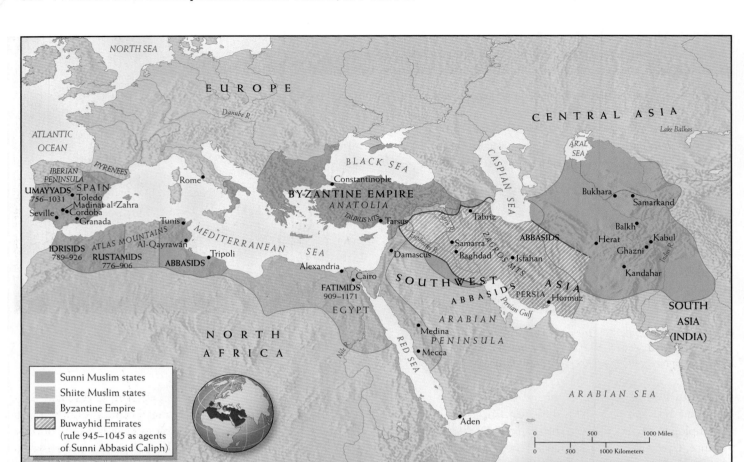

MAP 9.2 | Political Fragmentation in the Islamic World, 750–1000 CE

By 1000 CE, the Islamic world was politically fractured and decentralized. The Abbasid caliphs still reigned in Baghdad, but they wielded very limited political authority. Looking at the map, first point to Baghdad and then point out all the areas under Abbasid control.

- What are the regions where major Islamic powers emerged?
- What areas were Sunni versus Shiite?
- Why were the Abbasids unable to sustain political unity in the Islamic world?

knowledge of plants from the ancient Greeks. From Indian sources, scholars borrowed a numbering system based on the concept of zero and units of ten—what we today call Arabic numerals. Arab mathematicians were pioneers in arithmetic, geometry, and algebra, and they expanded the frontiers of plane and spherical trigonometry. Since much of Greek science had been lost in the west and later was reintroduced via the Muslim world, the Islamic contribution to the west was of immense significance. Thus, this intense borrowing, translating, storing, adding to, and diffusing of written works brought worlds together.

Islam in a Wider World

As Islam spread and became decentralized, it generated dazzling and often competitive dynasties in Spain, North Africa, and points farther east. Each dynastic state revealed the Muslim talent for achieving high levels of artistry far from its heartland. As more peoples came under the roof provided by the Quran, they invigorated a broad world of Islamic learning and science. But growing diversity led to a problem: Islam's political structures could not hold its widely dispersed believers under a single regime. Although its political system shared many legal elements (especially those controlled by Islamic texts and its enforcers), in terms of secular power Islam was deeply divided—and remains so to this day. (See Map 9.2.)

DAZZLING CITIES IN SPAIN One extraordinary Muslim state arose in Spain under Abd al-Rahman III, also known as al-Nasir li-din Allah (the Victorious; r. 912–961 CE), the successor ruler of a Muslim kingdom founded there over a century earlier. Abd al-Rahman III brought peace and stability to a violent frontier region where civil conflict had disrupted commerce and

The Great Mosque of Cordoba. *The great mosque of Cordoba was built in the eighth century CE by the Umayyad ruler Abd al-Rahman I and added to by other Muslim rulers, including al-Hakim II (who succeeded Abd al-Rahman III), considered by many historians to have been the most powerful and effective of the Spanish Umayyad caliphs.*

intellectual exchange. His evenhanded governance promoted amicable relations among Muslims, Christians, and Jews, and his diplomatic relations with Christian potentates as far away as France, Germany, and Scandinavia generated prosperity across western Europe and North Africa. He expanded and beautified the capital city of Cordoba, and his successor made the Great Mosque of Cordoba one of Spain's most stunning sites.

The Great Mosque of Cordoba, known in Spanish as la Mezquita, is the oldest standing Muslim building on the Iberian Peninsula. It is a stirring tribute to the architectural brilliance and religious zeal of Iberia's Muslims. Conceived of in 785 CE by the Umayyad ruler Abd al-Rahman I, it was finished within a year of the laying of the foundations. Abd al-Rahman I commanded that it be built in the form of a perfect square. Its most striking features were alternating red and white arches, made of jasper, onyx, marble, and granite and fashioned from materials from the Roman temple and other buildings in the vicinity. These huge double arches hoisted the ceiling to 40 feet and filled the interior with light and cooling breezes. Around the doors and across the walls, Arabic calligraphy proclaimed Muhammad's message and asserted the superiority of Arabic as God's chosen language.

A CENTRAL ASIAN GALAXY OF TALENT The other end of the Islamic empire, 8,000 miles east of Spain, enjoyed an equally spectacular cultural flowering. In a territory where Greek culture had once sparkled and where Sogdians had become leading intellectuals, Islam was now the dominant faith and the source of intellectual ferment.

The Abbasid rulers in Baghdad delighted in surrounding themselves with learned men from this region. They promoted and collected Arabic translations of Persian, Greek, and Sanskrit manuscripts, and they encouraged central Asian scholars to enhance their learning by moving to Baghdad. One of their protégés, the Islamic cleric al-Bukhari (d. 870 CE), was Islam's most dedicated collector of *hadith,* which provided vital knowledge about the Prophet's life.

Others made notable contributions to science and mathematics. Al-Khwarizmi (c. 780–850 CE) modified Indian digits into Arabic numerals and wrote the first book on algebra. The renowned Abbasid philosopher al-Farabi (d. 950 CE), from a Turkish military family, also made his way to Baghdad, where he studied eastern Christian teachings. Although he considered himself a Muslim, he thought good societies would succeed only if their rulers implemented political tenets espoused in Plato's *Republic*. He championed a virtuous "first chief" to rule over an Islamic commonwealth in the same way that Plato had favored a philosopher-king.

In the eleventh century, the Abbasid caliphate began to decline, devastated by climatic change (see Chapter 10) and weakened from overextension and the influx of outsider groups (the same problems the Roman Empire had faced). Scholars no longer trekked to the court at Baghdad. Yet the region's intellectual vitality remained strong, for young men of learning found patrons among local rulers. Consider Ibn Sina, known in the west as Avicenna (980–1037 CE). He grew to adulthood in Bukhara, practiced medicine in the courts of various Islamic rulers, and spent his later life in central Persia. Schooled in the Quran, Arabic secular literature, philosophy, geometry, and Indian and Euclidean mathematics, Ibn Sina was a master of many disciplines. His *Canon of Medicine* stood as the standard medical text in both Southwest Asia and Europe for centuries.

Ibn Sina. *Ibn Sina was a versatile scholar, most famous for his* Canon of Medicine.

TRADE AND ISLAM IN SUB-SAHARAN AFRICA Islam also crossed the Sahara Desert and penetrated well into Africa, carried by traders and scholars (see Map 9.3); there merchants exchanged weapons and textiles for gold, salt, and slaves. Trade did more than join West Africa to North Africa. It also generated prodigious wealth, which allowed centralized political kingdoms to develop. The most celebrated was Ghana, which lay at the terminus of North Africa's major trading routes. (See Primary Source: Ghana as Seen by a Muslim Observer in the Eleventh Century.)

Seafaring Muslim traders carried Islam into East Africa via the Indian Ocean. There is evidence of a small eighth-century CE Islamic trading community at Lamu, along the northern coast of present-day Kenya; and by the mid-ninth century CE, other coastal trading communities had sprung up. They all exported ivory and, possibly, slaves. On the island of Pate, off the coast of Kenya, the inhabitants of Shanga constructed the region's first mosque. This simple structure was replaced 200 years later by a mosque capable of holding all adult members of the community when they gathered for Friday prayers. By the tenth century, the East African coast featured a mixed African-Arab culture. The region's evolving Bantu language absorbed Arabic words and before long gained a new name, Swahili (derived from the Arabic plural of the word meaning "coast"). In sub-Saharan Africa as in North Africa and Asia, Islam promoted trade and elevated the status of merchants, who were themselves important agents for spreading their faith.

Opposition within Islam: Shiism and the Rise of the Fatimids

Islam's whirlwind rise generated internal tensions from the start. It is hardly surprising that a religion that extolled territorial conquests and created a large empire in its first decades would also spawn dissident religious movements that challenged the existing imperial structures. Muslims shared a reverence for a basic text and a single God, but often they had little else in common. Religious and political divisions only grew deeper as Islam spread into new corners of Afro-Eurasia. Once the charismatic Prophet died, believers disagreed over who should take his place and how to preserve authority. Strains associated with selecting the first four caliphs after Muhammad's death left a legacy of protest; to this day, they represent the greatest challenge facing Islam's efforts to create a unified culture.

SUNNIS AND SHIITES The most powerful opposition movement arose in North Africa, lower Iraq, and the Iranian plateau. The questions that fueled disagreements were who should succeed the Prophet, how the succession should take place, and who should lead Islam's expansion into the wider world. The vast majority of Muslims today are **Sunnis** (from the Arabic word meaning "tradition"). They accept that the political succession to the Prophet through the four rightly guided caliphs and then to the Umayyad and Abbasid dynasties was the correct one. Dissidents, such as the Shiites, contest this version.

Shiites ("members of the party of Ali"), among the earliest dissidents, felt that the proper successors should have been Ali, who had married the Prophet's daughter Fatima, and his descendants. Ali was one of the early converts to Islam and one of the band of Meccans who had migrated with the Prophet

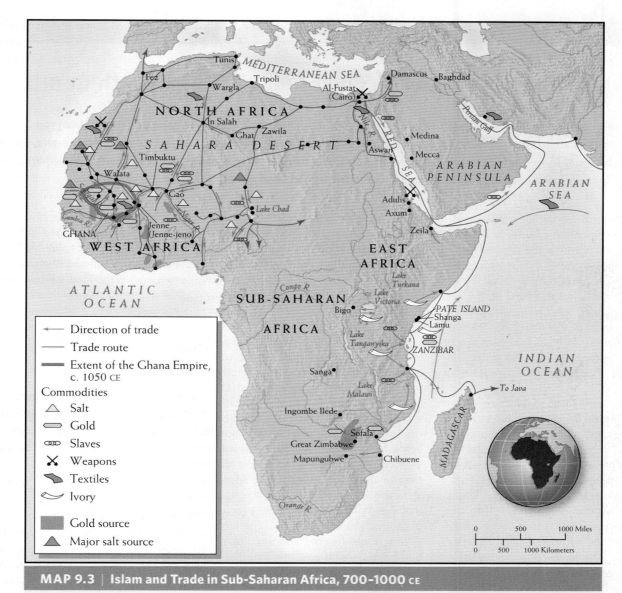

MAP 9.3 | Islam and Trade in Sub-Saharan Africa, 700–1000 CE

Islamic merchants and scholars, not Islamic armies, carried Islam into sub-Saharan Africa.

- Trace the trade routes in Africa, being sure to follow the correct direction of trade.
- According to the map key and icons, what commodities were Islamic merchants seeking below the Sahara?
- How did trade and commerce lead to the geographical expansion of the Islamic faith?

to Medina. The fourth of the rightly guided caliphs, he ruled over the Muslim community from 656 to 661 CE, dying at the hands of an assassin who struck him down as he was praying in a mosque in Kufa, Iraq. Shiites believe that Ali's descendants, whom they call *imams,* have religious and prophetic power as well as political authority—and thus should enjoy spiritual primacy.

Shiism appealed to groups whom the Umayyads and Abbasids had excluded from power; it became Islam's most potent dissident force and created a permanent divide within Islam. Shiism was well established in the first century of Islam's existence. Over time the Sunnis and Shiites diverged even more than the early political disputes would have indicated. Both groups had their own versions of the *sharia*, their own collections of *hadith*, and their own theological tenets.

FATIMIDS After 300 years of struggling, the Shiites finally seized power. Repressed in Iraq and Iran, Shiite activists made their way to North Africa, where they joined with dissident Berber groups to topple several rulers. In 909 CE, a Shiite religious and

Ghana as Seen by a Muslim Observer in the Eleventh Century

The following excerpt is from an eleventh-century manuscript written by a Muslim serving under the Umayyads in Spain. Its author, Abdullah Abu Ubayd al-Bakri, produced a massive general geography and history of the known world, as did many Muslim scholars of the period. This manuscript has special value because it provides information about West Africa, a region in which the Spanish rulers had great interest and into which Islam had been spreading for several centuries.

Ghana is the title of the king of the people. The name of the country is Aoukar. The ruler who governs the people at the present time—the year 460 AH (after the Hijra and 1067-68 CE)—is called Tenkamein. He came to the throne in 455 AH. His predecessor, who was named Beci, began his reign at the age of 85. He was a prince worthy of great praise as much for his personal conduct as for his zeal in the pursuit of justice and his friendship to Muslims. . . .

Ghana is composed of two towns situated in a plain. The one inhabited by Muslims is large and contains twelve mosques, in which the congregants celebrate the Friday prayer. All of these mosques have their imams, their muezzins, and their salaried readers. The city possesses judges and men of great erudition. . . . The city where the king resides is six miles away and carries the name el-Ghaba, meaning "the forest." The territory separating these two locations is covered with dwellings, constructed out of rocks and the wood of the acacia tree. The dwelling of the king consists of a chateau and several surrounding huts, all of which are enclosed by a wall-like structure. In the ruler's town, close to the royal tribunal, is a mosque where Muslims come when they have business with the ruler in order to carry out their prayers. . . . The royal interpreters are chosen from the Muslim population, as was the state treasurer and the majority of the state ministers. . . .

The opening of a royal meeting is announced by the noise of a drum, which they call a *deba*, and which is formed from a long piece of dug-out wood. Upon hearing the drumming, the inhabitants assemble. When the king's coreligionists [people of the same religion] appear before him, they genuflect and throw dust on their heads. Such is the way in which they salute their sovereign. The Muslims show their respect for the king by clapping their hands. The religion of the peoples is paganism and fetishism. . . . The land of Ghana is not healthy and has few people. Travelers who pass through the area during the height of the agricultural season are rarely able to avoid becoming sick. When the grains are at their fullest and are ready for harvesting is the time when mortality affects visitors.

The best gold in the land comes from Ghiarou, a town located eighteen days' journey from the capital. All of the gold found in the mines of the empire belongs to the sovereign, but the sovereign allows the people to take gold dust. Without this precaution, the gold would become so abundant that it would lose much of its value. . . . It is claimed that the king owns a piece of gold as large as an enormous rock.

QUESTIONS FOR ANALYSIS

- From this excerpt, how much can you learn about the kingdom of Ghana? Try drawing a sketch of the region based on the description in the second paragraph.
- What influence did Islam have in the empire? What aspects of the excerpt reveal the extent of Islam's acceptance?
- What elements of Ghana most interested the author?

Source: Abou-Obeïd-el-Bekri, *Description de l'Afrique septentrionale*, revised and corrected edition, translated by [William] Mac Guckin de Slane (Paris: A. Maisonneuve, 1965), pp. 327–31; translated from the French by Robert Tignor.

military leader, Abu Abdallah, overthrew the Sunni ruler there. Thus began the Fatimid regime.

After conquering Egypt in 969 CE, the Fatimids set themselves against the Abbasid caliphs of Baghdad, refusing to acknowledge their legitimacy and claiming to speak for the whole Islamic world. The Fatimid rulers established their capital in a new city that arose alongside al-Fustat, the old Umayyad capital. They called this place al-Qahira (or Cairo), "the Victorious," and promoted its beauty. Early on they founded a place of worship and learning, Al-Azhar Mosque, which attracted scholars from all over Afro-Eurasia and spread Islamic learning outward; they also built other elegant mosques and centers of learning. The Fatimid regime lasted until the late twelfth century, though its rulers made little headway in persuading the Egyptian population to embrace their Shiite beliefs. Most of the population remained Sunnis.

By 1000 CE, Islam, which had originated as a radical religious revolt in a small corner of the Arabian Peninsula, had grown into

Djinguereber Mosque. *This grand mosque was built in Timbuktu, Mali, at the height of the kingdom's power. Built by Mansa Musa in the fourteenth century, the mosque speaks to the depth and importance of Islam's roots in the Malian kingdom.*

Al-Azhar Mosque. *The mosque of al-Azhar is Cairo's most important ancient mosque. Built in the tenth century by the Fatimid conquerors and rulers of Egypt, it quickly became a leading center for worship and learning, frequented by Muslim clerics and admired in Europe.*

a vast political and religious empire. It had become the dominant political and cultural force in the middle regions of Afro-Eurasia. Like its rival in this part of the world, Christianity, it aspired to universality. But unlike Christianity, it was linked from its outset to political power. Muhammad and his early followers created an empire to facilitate the expansion of their faith, while their Christian counterparts inherited an empire when Constantine embraced their faith. A vision of a world under the jurisdiction of Muslim caliphs, adhering to the dictates of the *sharia,* drove Muslim armies, merchants, and scholars to territories thousands of miles away from Mecca and Medina. Yet the impulse to expand ran out of energy at the fringes of Islam's reach, creating political fragmentation within the Muslim world and leaving much of western Europe and China untouched. But it also had important internal consequences: Muslims were no longer the minority within their own lands, owing to the conversion of Christians, Jews, and other populations under Muslim emperors.

THE TANG STATE

The short-lived Sui dynasty (589–618 CE) and the more durable Tang dynasty (618–907 CE) expanded the territory that they controlled into central and East Asia, thus paralleling Islam's explosion out of Arabia and throughout Afro-Eurasia. Once again the landmass had two centers of power, as Islam replaced the Roman Empire in counterbalancing the power and wealth of China.

This bipolar world differed significantly from that of the Roman and Han Empires: in the centuries since their waning, Eurasian and African worlds had drawn much closer through trade, conversion, and regular political contacts. Now the two

powerhouses competed for dominance in central Asia, sharing influences and even mobile populations that weaved back and forth across porous borders between them.

China was both a recipient of foreign influences and a source of influences on its neighbors. It was becoming the hub of East Asian integration. Like the Umayyads and the Abbasids, the Tang dynasty, recovering the territory and confidence of the Han Empire, promoted a cosmopolitan culture. Under its rule, Buddhism, medicine, and mathematics from India gave China's chief cities an international flavor. Buddhist monks from Bactria; Greeks, Armenians, and Jews from Constantinople; Muslim envoys from Samarkand and Persia; Vietnamese tributary missions from Annam; nomadic chieftains from the Siberian plains; officials and students from Korea; and monkish visitors from Japan all rubbed elbows in the streets of two of China's largest cities, Chang'an and Luoyang. Ideas also traveled eastward—notably to Korea and Japan, where Daoism and Buddhism made inroads. Similarly, Chinese statecraft, as expressed through the Confucian classics, struck the early Koreans and Japanese as the best model for their own state building.

Territorial Expansion under the Tang Dynasty

China had faced a long period of political fragmentation (see Chapter 8) before Tang rulers restored Han models of empire building. Their claims that an imperial system could outperform small states found a receptive audience in a populace fatigued by internal chaos. The Tang dynasty expanded China's boundaries and reestablished its dominance in central and East Asia.

Green Revolutions in the Islamic World and Tang China, 300–600 CE

World historians often focus on the more famous Columbian Exchange to talk about how the sharing of foods between regions of the world created revolutions in diet. The Afro-Eurasian world underwent a food revolution of its own between 300 and 600 CE. New crops, especially food crops, leaped across political and cultural borders during this period, offering expanding populations more diverse and nutritious diets and the ability to feed increased numbers. Such was true of the Islamic world and Tang China in the eighth century CE. Now, however, it was India that replaced Mesopotamia as the source of a dazzling array of new cultigens. Most of them originated in Southeast Asia, made their way to India, and dispersed throughout the Muslim world and into China. These crops included new strains of rice, taro, sour oranges, lemons, limes, and most likely coconut palm trees, sugarcane, bananas, plantains, and mangoes. Sorghum and possibly cotton and watermelons arrived from Africa. Only the eggplant was indigenous to India. Although these staples spread quickly to East Asia, their westward movement was slower. Not until the Muslim conquest of Sindh in northern India in 711 CE did territories to the west fully discover the crop innovations pioneered in Southeast Asia.

India fascinated the Arabs, and they exploited its agricultural offerings to the hilt. Soon a revolution in crops and diet swept through the Muslim world. Sorghum supplanted millet and the other grains of antiquity because it was hardier, had higher yields, and required a shorter growing season. Citrus trees added flavor to the diet and provided refreshing drinks during the summer heat. Increased cotton cultivation led to a greater demand for textiles.

For over 300 years, farmers from northwest India to Spain, Morocco, and West Africa made impressive use of the new crops. They increased agricultural output, slashed fallow periods, and grew as many as three crops on lands that formerly had yielded one. (See Map 9.4.) As a result, farmers could feed larger communities; even as cities grew, the countryside became more densely populated and even more productive.

The same agricultural revolution that was sweeping through South Asia and the Muslim world also took East Asia by storm. China received the same crops that Muslim cultivators were carrying westward. Rice was critical. New varieties entered from the south, and groups migrating from the north (after the collapse of the Han Empire) eagerly took them up. Soon Chinese farmers became the world's most intensive wet-field rice cultivators. Early- and late-ripening seeds supported two or three plantings a year. Champa rice, introduced from central Vietnam, was especially popular for its drought resistance and rapid ripening.

Because rice needs ample water, Chinese hydraulic engineers went into the fields to design water-lifting devices, which peasant farmers used to construct hillside rice paddies. They also dug more canals, linking rivers and lakes (see Map 9.5) and even drained swamps, alleviating the malaria that had long troubled the region. Their efforts yielded a booming and constantly moving rice frontier.

QUESTIONS FOR ANALYSIS

- Historians think of the eighteenth century as having produced an agricultural revolution. Are we justified in using the same term for this earlier period?

- How did the new crops change diets and contribute to population growth?

Explore Further

Watson, Andrew. *Agricultural Innovation in the Early Islamic World: The Diffusion of Crops and Farming Techniques, 700–1100* (1983).

A sudden change in the course of the Yellow River (not the first such environmental calamity; see Chapter 7) caused extensive flooding on the North China plain and set the stage for the emergence of the Tang dynasty at the expense of the Sui. (See Map 9.5 for a view of the extent of the Sui dynasty.) Revolts ensued as the population faced starvation. Li Yuan, the governor of a province under the Sui dynasty, marched on Chang'an and took the throne for himself in 618 CE. He promptly established the Tang dynasty and began building a strong central government by doubling the number of government offices. By 624 CE, the initial steps of establishing the Tang dynasty were complete. But the fruits of these gains slipped into the hands of Li Yuan's ambitious son Li Shimin, who forced his father to abdicate and took the throne in 627 CE.

With a large and professionally trained army capable of defending far-flung frontiers and squelching rebellious populations, the Tang built a military organization of aristocratic cavalry and peasant soldiers. The cavalry regularly clashed on the northern steppes with encroaching nomadic peoples, who also fought on horseback; at its height the Tang military had some 700,000 horses. At the same time, between 1 and 2 million peasant soldiers garrisoned the south and toiled on public works projects.

Much like the Islamic forces, the Tang's frontier armies increasingly relied on pastoral nomadic soldiers from the Inner

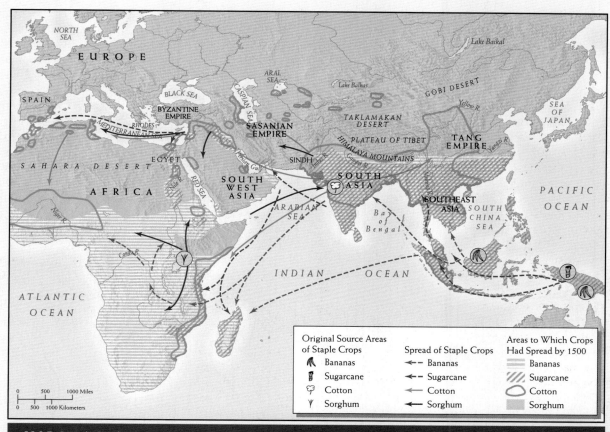

MAP 9.4 | Agricultural Diffusion in the First Millennium

The second half of the first millennium saw a revolution in agriculture throughout Afro-Eurasia. Agriculturalists across the landmass increasingly cultivated similar crops.

- Where did most of the cultigens originate? In what direction and where did most of them flow?
- What role did the spread of Islam and the growth of Islamic empires (see Map 9.1) play in the process?

Eurasian steppe. Notable were the Uighurs, Turkish-speaking peoples who had moved into western China and by 750 CE constituted the empire's most potent military force. These hard-riding and hard-drinking warriors galvanized fearsome cavalries, fired longbows at distant range, and wielded steel swords and knives in hand-to-hand combat. The Tang military also pushed the state into Tibet, the Red River valley in northern Vietnam, Manchuria, and Bohai (near the Korean peninusla).

By 650 CE, as Islamic armies were moving toward central Asia, the Tang were already the region's new colossus. At its height, Tang armies controlled more than 4 million square miles of territory—an area as large as the entire, by now politically

fragmented, Islamic world in the ninth and tenth centuries. The Tang benefited from South China's rich farmlands, brought under peasant cultivation by draining swamps, building an intricate network of canals and channels, and connecting lakes and rivers to the rice lands. The state thereby was able to collect taxes from roughly 10 million families, representing 57 million individuals. Taxes that took the form of agricultural labor propelled the expansion of cultivated frontiers throughout the south.

In spite of the Abbasid Empire's precocious spread, China in 750 CE was the most powerful, most advanced, and best administered empire in the world. (See Map 9.6.) Korea and Japan recognized its superiority in every material aspect of life.

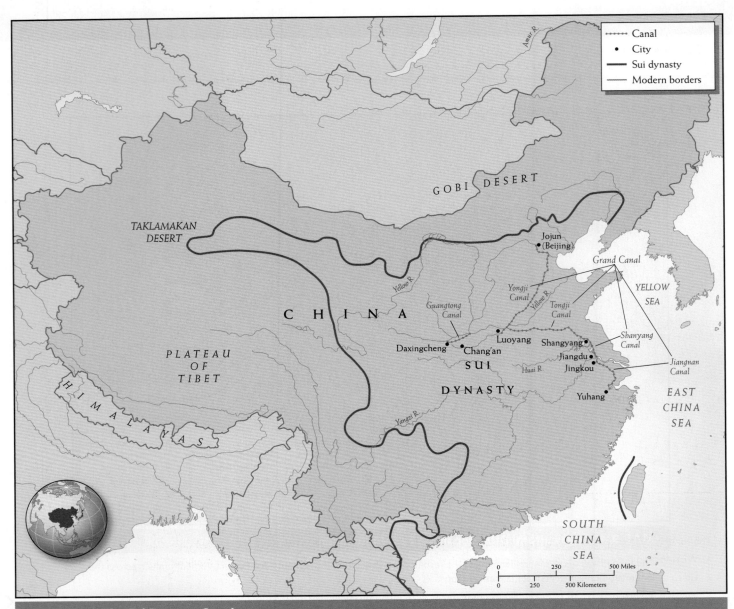

MAP 9.5 | The Sui Dynasty Canals

China, like the Islamic world, experienced a population explosion during this period.

- Where are the Sui dynasty canals on the map and the two areas showing population concentration?
- Why do you think the population concentrations are located along the canals?
- What other roles might the canals have played in addition to fostering population growth in this period within China?

Muslims were among the people who arrived at Chang'an to pay homage. Persians, Armenians, and Turks brought tribute and merchandise via the busy arteries of the Silk Road or by sea, and other travelers and traders came from Southeast Asia, Korea, and Japan. This network of routes was rarely traversed the entire length by a single person, however. It was more a chain of entrepôts than an early version of an interstate.

The peak of Chinese power occurred just as the Abbasids were expanding into Tang portions of central Asia. Rival Muslim forces drove the Tang from Turkistan in 751 CE at the Battle of Talas River, and their success emboldened groups such as the Sogdians and Tibetans to challenge the Tang in the west. As a result, the Tang gradually retreated into the old heartlands along the Yellow and Yangzi Rivers. They even saw their capital fall

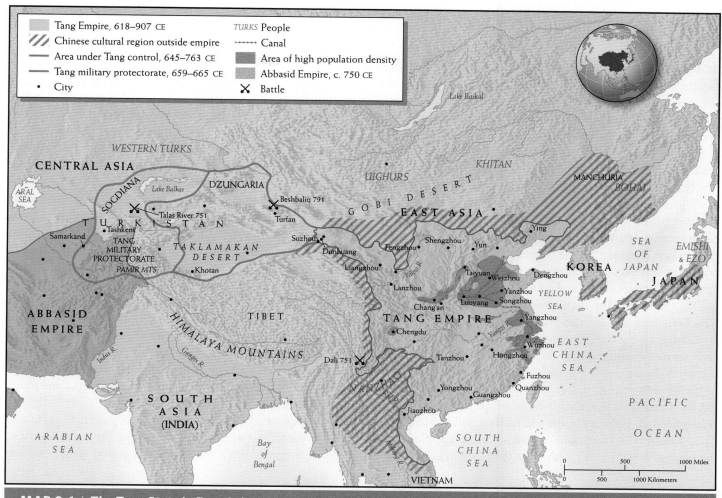

Legend:

- Tang Empire, 618–907 CE
- Chinese cultural region outside empire
- Area under Tang control, 645–763 CE
- Tang military protectorate, 659–665 CE
- • City
- TURKS People
- ••••• Canal
- Area of high population density
- Abbasid Empire, c. 750 CE
- ✗ Battle

MAP 9.6 | The Tang State in East Asia, 750 CE

The Tang dynasty, at its territorial peak in 750 CE, controlled a state that extended from central Asia to the East China Sea.

- What foreign areas are under Tang control? What areas were heavily influenced by Tang government and culture?
- How can we tell from the map that China was undergoing an economic revolution during the Tang period?
- How did the Tang maintain order and stability in such a large, dynamic realm?

to invading Tibetans and Sogdians. Thereafter, misrule, court intrigues, economic exploitation, and popular rebellions weakened the empire, even though it held on for over a century more until northern invaders toppled it in 907 CE.

Organizing an Empire

The Tang Empire, a worthy successor to the Han, ranks as one of China's great dynastic polities. Although its rulers emulated the Han in many ways (for example, by compiling a legal code based on the Han's), they also introduced new institutions.

The heart of the Tang state was the magnificent capital city of Chang'an, the population of which reached 1 million, half of

whom lived within its impressive city walls and half on the outside. The outer walls enclosed an immense area, 6 miles along an east-west axis and 5 miles from north to south. Internal security arrangements made it one of the safest urban locales for its age. Its more than 100 quarters were separated from each other by interior walls with gates that were closed at night, after which no one was permitted on the streets, which were patrolled by horsemen, until the gates reopened in the morning. As befitted a city that was in the western region of China and in close contact with central Asia, Chang'an had a large foreign population, estimated at one-third of its total, and a diverse religious life. Zoroastrian fires burned as worshippers sacrificed animals and chanted temple hymns. Nestorian Christians from Syria found a welcoming community, and not to be outdone, the Buddhists boasted that they had ninety-one of their own temples in Chang'an in 722 CE.

CONFUCIAN ADMINISTRATORS The fruits of agriculture and the day-to-day control of the Tang Empire required an efficient and loyal civil service. Whereas a shared spiritual commitment to Islam held together the multilingual, multiethnic, and even multireligious Islamic empire, the Tang found other ways to integrate remote territories and diverse groups. Their efforts, building on past practice, produced an empire-wide political culture based on Confucian teachings and classically educated elites.

Chinese integration began at the top. Entry into the ruling group required knowledge of Confucian ideas and all of the commentaries on the Confucian classics. It also required skill in the intricate classical Chinese language, in which this literature was written. A deep familiarity with these texts was as crucial in forging a Chinese cultural and political solidarity as understanding the Quran and the *sharia* was for the Abbasid state or the New Testament for Christian Europe and the Byzantine Empire.

Reinforcing the Tang state were the world's first fully written **civil service examinations**. These examinations, which tested literary skills and the Confucian classics, were the primary route to the top echelons of power and the ultimate means of uniting the Chinese state. Candidates for office, whom local elites recommended, gathered in the capital triennially to take qualifying exams. They had been trained since the age of three in the classics and histories, either by their families—especially mothers—or in Buddhist temple schools. Most failed the grueling competition, but those who were successful underwent further trials to evaluate their character and determine the level of their appointments. New officials were selected from the pool of graduates on the basis of social conduct, eloquence, skill in calligraphy and mathematics, and legal knowledge. (See Primary Source: The Pressures of Maintaining Empire by Examination.) When Emperor Li Shimin observed the new officials obediently parading out of the examination hall, he slyly noted, "The heroes of the empire are all in my pocket!" (Miyazaki, p. 13). Overall, the civil service system gave rise in China to the perennial belief in the value of a classically trained meritocracy (rule by persons of talent), which has lasted into modern times.

Having assumed the mandate of heaven (see Chapter 4), the Tang rulers and their supporters sought to establish a code of moral values for the whole empire. Building on Han dynasty models, they expanded the state school in the capital into an empire-wide series of select schools that accepted only fully literate candidates for the civil examinations. They also allowed the use of Daoist classics as texts for the exams, believing that the early Daoists represented another important stream of ancient wisdom. Ultimately, the Tang amalgamated this range of texts, codes, and tests into a common intellectual and moral credo for the governing classes.

Although official careers were in theory open to anyone of proven talent, in practice they were closed to certain groups. Despite Empress Wu's prominence (see next page), women

Christianity in China. *As subjects of the largest Christian church of the ninth century CE, Nestorian priests made a lasting impression on the Tang Empire, including this mural of their Palm Sunday procession in Xinjiang, China.*

Tang Official. *Tang officials were selected through competitive civil examinations in order to limit the power of Buddhist and Daoist clerics. This painted clay figure of a Tang official circa 717 CE was excavated in 1972.*

The Pressures of Maintaining Empire by Examination

Young and old competed equally in the Tang examination halls. The rituals of success were alluring to youths, while the tortures of failure weighed heavily on older competitors still seeking an elusive degree. For all, the tensions of seeing the posted list of successful candidates—following years of preparation for young boys and even more years of defeat for old men—were intensely personal responses to success or failure. The few who passed would look back on that day with relief and pride.

In the Southern Court they posted the list. (The Southern Court was where the Board of Rites ran the administration and accepted documents. All prescribed forms together with the stipulations for each [degree] category were usually publicized here.) The wall for hanging the list was by the eastern wall of the Southern Court. In a separate building a screen was erected which stood over ten feet tall, and it was surrounded with a fence. Before dawn they took the list from the Northern Court to the Southern Court where it was hung for display.

In the sixth year of Yuanhe [811 CE] a student at the University, Guo Dongli, broke through the thorn hedge. (The thorn hedge was below the fence. There was another outside the main gate of the Southern Court.) He then ripped up the ornamental list [*wenbang*]. It was because of this that afterwards they often came out of the gateway of the Department [of State Affairs] with a mock list. The real list was displayed a little later.

QUESTIONS FOR ANALYSIS

- Why were the stakes so high in the civil examinations? What happened to those who failed?
- Was the Tang civil examination system an open system that tested talent—that is, a meritocracy?
- Can you relate to the candidates' anxiety in terms of your own experiences—for example, waiting for college acceptance letters or your year-end grade point average?

Source: Wang Dingbao (870–940 CE), quoted in Oliver J. Moore, *Rituals of Recruitment in Tang China* (Leiden: Brill, 2004), p. 175.

were not permitted to serve, nor were sons of merchants, nor those who could not afford a classical education. Over time, Tang civil examinations forced aristocrats to compete with commoner southern families, whose growing wealth gave them access to educational resources that made them the equals of the old elites. Through examinations, this new elite eventually outdistanced the sons of the northern aristocracy in the Tang government by out-studying them.

The system underscored education as the primary avenue for success. Even impoverished families sought the best classical education they could afford for their sons. Although few succeeded in the civil examinations, many boys and even some girls learned the fundamentals of reading and writing. Classically literate mothers, for example, helped educate their sons. In fact, the Buddhists played a crucial role in extending education across society: as part of their charitable mission, their temple schools introduced many children to primers based on classical texts. Buddhist monks would never admit that many in their own ranks had initially hoped to become Confucian officials,

but in reality quite a few entered the clergy only after not qualifying for or failing the civil examinations.

CHINA'S FEMALE EMPEROR Not all Tang power brokers were men. The wives and mothers of emperors also wielded influence in the court—usually behind the scenes, but sometimes publicly. The most striking example is the Empress Wu, who dominated the court in the late seventh and early eighth centuries CE. Usually vilified in Chinese accounts, she deftly exploited the examination system to check the power of aristocratic families and consolidated courtly authority by creating groups of loyal bureaucrats, who in turn preserved loyalty to the dynasty at the local level.

Born into a noble family, Wu Zhao played music and mastered the Chinese classics as a young girl. By age thirteen, because she was witty, intelligent, and beautiful, she was recruited to Li Shimin's court and became his favorite concubine. She also fell in love with his son. When Li Shimin died, his son assumed power and became the Emperor Gaozong. Wu became the

Empress Wu. *When she seized power in her own right as Empress Wu, Wu Zhao became the first and only female ruler in Chinese history.*

new emperor's favorite concubine and gave birth to the sons he required to succeed him. As the mother of the future emperor, Wu enjoyed heightened political power. Subsequently, she took the place of Gaozong's Empress Wang by accusing her of killing Wu's newborn daughter. Gaozong believed Wu and married her.

After Gaozong suffered a stroke, Wu Zhao became administrator of the court, a position equal to the emperor's. She allegedly created a reign of terror via her secret police, who spied on her opposition and eliminated those who stood in her way. Following her husband's death in 684 CE, she expanded the military and recruited her ministers from civil examination candidates to oppose her enemies at court. After deposing two of her sons as emperors, she made herself emperor of a fifteen-year new dynasty (r. 690–705 CE), the "Zhou dynasty," the only female ruler in Chinese history.

Wu ordered scholars to write biographies of famous women, and she empowered her mother's clan by assigning high political posts to her relatives. Later, she moved the capital from Chang'an to Luoyang, She elevated Buddhism over Daoism as the favored state religion, invited the most gifted Buddhist scholars to her capital at Luoyang, built Buddhist temples, and subsidized spectacular cave sculptures. In fact, Chinese Buddhism achieved its highest officially sponsored development in this period.

EUNUCHS Tang rulers protected themselves, their possessions, and especially their women, with loyal and well-compensated men, many of whom were **eunuchs** (surgically castrated as youths and thus sexually impotent). By the late eighth century CE, more than 4,500 eunuchs were entrenched in the Tang Empire's institutions, wielding significant power not only within the imperial household but also at court and beyond.

The Chief Eunuch controlled the military. Through him, the military power of court eunuchs extended to every province and garrison station in the empire, forming an all-encompassing network. In effect, the eunuch bureaucracy mediated between the emperor and the provincial governments.

Under Emperor Xianzong (r. 806–820 CE), eunuchs acted as a third pillar of the government, working alongside the official bureaucracy and the imperial court. By establishing clear career patterns for eunuchs that paralleled those in the civil service, Xianzong sparked a striking rise in their levels of literacy and their cultural attainments. And yet, they remained the rivals of most officials. By 838 CE, the delicate balance of power between throne, eunuchs, and civil officials had evaporated. Eunuchs became an unruly political force in late Tang politics, and their competition for influence produced political instability.

An Economic Revolution

In Tang China, just as in the Abbasid caliphate, political stability fueled remarkable economic achievements. Highlighting China's success were rising agricultural production based on an egalitarian land allotment system, an increasingly fine handicrafts industry, a diverse commodity market, and a dynamic urban life.

The earlier short-lived Sui dynasty had started this economic progress by building canals, especially the Grand Canal, reunifying the north and south (see again Map 9.5). The Tang continued by centering their efforts on the Grand Canal and the Yangzi River, which flows from west to east. These waterways aided communication and transport throughout the empire and helped raise living standards. The south grew richer, largely through the backbreaking labor of immigrants from the north. Fertile land along the Yangzi became China's new granary, and areas south of the Yangzi became its demographic center. (See Current Trends in World History: Green Revolutions in the Islamic World and Tang China, 300–600 CE.)

Chinese merchants took advantage of the Silk Road to trade indirectly with India and the Islamic world; but when rebellions in northwest China and the rise of Islam in central Asia jeopardized the land route, the "silk road by sea" became the avenue of choice. Via such local exchanges from all over Asia and Africa, merchant ships arrived in South China ports bearing intoxicating cargoes of spices, medicines, and jewelry traded for Chinese silks and porcelain (see again Map 9.6). Chang'an became the richest city in the world, with its million or so residents including foreigners of every description. Rather than long-distance trade, what really drove the economic boom in the oasis states was the Tang and Islamic military presence. The integration between China and central Asia brought not only safety but also new customers.

In the large cities of the Yangzi delta, bronze, pottery, and clothing workshops proliferated. Their reputations spread far and wide for the elegance of their wares, which included rich brocades (silk fabrics), fine paper, intricately printed woodblocks,

The Tang Court. Left: *This tenth-century painting of elegant ladies of the Tang imperial court enjoying a feast and music tells us a great deal about the aesthetic tastes of elite women in this era. It also shows the secluded "inner quarters," where court ladies passed their daily lives far from the hurly-burly of imperial politics.* Right: *Castrated males, known as eunuchs, guarded the harem and protected the royal family of Tang emperors. By the late eighth century CE, eunuchs were fully integrated into the government and wielded a great deal of military and political power.*

unique iron casts, and exquisite porcelains. Art collectors all across Afro-Eurasia especially valued Tang "tricolor pottery," fired up to 900°C (1,652°F) and metallurgically decorated with brilliant hues of yellow, green, white, brown, and blue. Meanwhile, Chinese artisans transformed locally grown cotton into highest-quality clothing. The textile industry prospered as painting and dyeing technology improved, and superb silk products generated significant tax revenue. Such Chinese luxuries dominated the localized networks that connected to Southwest Asia, Europe, and Africa via the Silk Road and the Indian Ocean. (See Analyzing Global Developments: Islam and the Silk Trade: Adapting Religion to Opulence.)

Accommodating World Religions

The early Tang emperors tolerated remarkable religious diversity. Nestorian Christianity, Zoroastrianism, and Manichaeanism (a radical Christian sect) had entered China from Persia during the time of the Sasanian Empire. Islam came later. These spiritual impulses—together with Buddhism and the indigenous teachings of Daoism and Confucianism—spread throughout the Tang Empire and at first were widely used to enhance state power.

THE GROWTH OF BUDDHISM Buddhism, in particular, thrived under Tang rule. Initially, Emperor Li Shimin distrusted

Buddhist monks because they avoided serving the government and paying taxes. Yet after Buddhism gained acceptance as one of the "three ways" of learning—joining Daoism and Confucianism—Li endowed huge monasteries, sent emissaries to India to collect texts and relics, and commissioned Buddhist paintings and statuary. Caves along the Silk Road, such as those at Dunhuang, provided ideal venues for monks to paint the inside walls where religious rites and meditation took place. Soon the caves boasted bright color paintings and massive statues of the Buddha and the bodhisattvas.

ANTI-BUDDHIST CAMPAIGNS By the mid-ninth century CE, the proliferation and growing influence of hundreds of thousands of Buddhist monks and nuns threatened China's Confucian and Daoist leaders. They attacked Buddhism, arguing that its values conflicted with native traditions.

One of the boldest attacks came from the Confucian scholar-official Han Yu, who represented the rising literati from the south. His memorial against Buddhism, in 819 CE, protested the emperor's plan to bring a relic of the Buddha to the capital for exhibition. Striking a note that would have been inconceivable under the early Tang's cosmopolitanism, Han Yu attacked Buddhism as a foreign doctrine of barbarian peoples who were different in language, culture, and knowledge. These objections earned him exile to the malaria-infested southern province of Guangdong.

Yet, two decades later the state began suppressing Buddhist monasteries and confiscating their wealth, fearing that religious

One of the Four Sacred Mountains. *This monastery on Mount Song is famous because in 527 CE, an Indian priest named Bodhidharma arrived there to initiate the Zen school of Buddhism in China.*

loyalties would undermine political ones. Increasingly intolerant Confucian scholar-administrators argued that the Buddhist monastic establishment threatened the imperial order. They claimed that members of the unmarried clergy were conspiring to destroy the state, the family, and the body.

Piecemeal measures against the monastic orders gave way in the 840s CE to open persecution. Emperor Wuzong, for instance, closed more than 4,600 monasteries and destroyed 40,000 temples and shrines. More than 260,000 Buddhist monks and nuns endured a forced return to secular life, after which the state parceled out monastery lands to taxpaying landlords and peasant farmers. To expunge the cultural impact of Buddhism, classically trained literati revived ancient prose styles and the teachings of Confucius and his followers. Linking classical scholarship, ancient literature, and Confucian morality, they constructed a cultural fortress that reversed the early Buddhist successes in China.

Ultimately, the Tang era represented the triumph of homegrown ideologies (Confucianism and Daoism) over a foreign universalizing religion (Buddhism). In addition, by permanently breaking apart huge monastic holdings, the Tang made sure that no religion would rival its power. Successor dynasties continued to keep religious establishments weak and fragmented, although Confucianism maintained a more prominent role within society as the basis of the ruling classes' ideology and as a quasi-religious belief system for a wider portion of the population. As a result, within China persistent religious pluralism remained, even including Buddhism, which continued to be important in the face of dynastic persecution.

The Fall of Tang China

China's deteriorating economic conditions in the ninth century CE led to peasant uprisings, some even led by unsuccessful examination candidates. These revolts eventually brought down the dynasty. Power-hungry eunuchs also contributed to the demise of the Tang, as did pressures from Muslim incursions into the western regions of the Tang Empire and Sogdian and Tibetan pressures in the northwest. By the tenth century CE, China had fragmented into regional states and entered a new but much shorter era of decentralization. The Song dynasty that emerged in 960 CE could not unify the Tang territories, and even the Mongols, invading steppe peoples, were able to restore the glory of the Han and Tang Empires only for a century.

EARLY KOREA AND JAPAN

Chinese influence, both direct and indirect, had reached into Korea for more than a millennium and later into Japan—but not without local resistance and the flourishing of entirely indigenous and independent political and religious developments. (See Map 9.7.) Here, too, religion contributed to the strengthening of the political power of elites, and lively commercial exchanges brought new prosperity to large segments of the population. The decline of Tang power in central Asia after 750 CE caused its rulers and merchants to look toward Southeast Asia and other parts of East Asia, including the lands of the Yellow

Sea and the Sea of Japan. Buddhism also spread into these territories, bringing a more flexible and less distinctly Chinese influence, although Confucianism also proved well tailored to the needs of Japan, Korea, and Vietnam.

Early Korea

By the fourth century CE, three independent states had emerged on the Korean Peninsula. Chinese influence had increasingly penetrated the peninsula and had become a decisive element in Korean history from at least the third century BCE. Korea remained divided into "Three Kingdoms" until 668 CE, when one of these states, Silla, led a movement to prevent Chinese domination, gaining control over the entire peninsula and unifying it.

UNIFICATION UNDER THE SILLA Unification enabled the Koreans to establish an autonomous government. Their opposition to the Chinese did not deter them from modeling their government on the Tang imperial state. The Silla rulers dispatched annual emissaries bearing tribute payments to the Chinese capital and regularly sent students and monks. As a result, literary Chinese became the written language of Korean elites—not their vernacular (just as Latin did among diverse populations in medieval Europe). Chinese influence especially convinced the Silla state to organize its court and the bureaucracy and to build its capital city of Kumsong in imitation of the Tang capital of Chang'an.

In spite of Chinese influences, the loyalty of most non-Chinese Koreans was to their kinship groups. These early Koreans believed that birth, not displays of learned achievement, should be the source of influence in religious and political life. Korean holy men and women (known today as shamans) interceded with gods, demons, and ancestral spirits and remained prominent in local village life.

Silla's fortunes were entwined with the Tang's to such an extent that once the Tang declined, Silla also began to fragment. But Silla never established a full-blown Tang-style government. That would happen later under the Koryo dynasty (935–1392 CE).

THE KORYO DYNASTY The Koryo dynasty (from which the country's modern name derives) began to construct a new cultural identity by enacting a bureaucratic system, which replaced the archaic tribal system that the Silla had maintained. The Koryo went beyond earlier Silla reforms and fully used Tang-style civil service examinations for selecting semi-official military elites who would govern at court and in the provinces. The heirs of Wang Kon, who founded the dynasty, consolidated control over the peninsula and strengthened its political and economic foundations by following the Tang's bureaucratic and land allotment systems.

During this period, Korea, like Tang China itself, suffered continual harassment from northern tribes such as the Khitan.

To escape the realities of this troubled period, Koryo artisans anxiously carved wooden printing blocks drawn from the Buddhist literary works as an offering to the Buddha to protect them from invading enemies—but in vain. The Korean royal family at the time was under siege, and they hoped that the woodblocks would elicit a change in fortune. The scriptures were hidden away in a single temple and when rediscovered represented the most comprehensive and intact version of Buddhist literature written in the Chinese script.

Early Japan

Like Korea, Japan also felt China's influences, and it responded by thwarting some of these influences and accommodating others simultaneously. But Japan enjoyed added autonomy: it was an archipelago of islands, separated from the mainland although internally fragmented. In the mid-third century CE, a warlike group arrived by sea from Korea and imposed their military and social power on southern Japan. These conquerors—known as the "Tomb Culture" because of their elevated burial sites— unified Japan by extolling their imperial ancestors and maintaining their social hierarchy. They also introduced a belief in the power of female shamans, who married into the imperial clans and became rulers of early Japanese kinship groups.

Chinese dynastic records describe the early Japanese, with whom imperial China had contact in this period, as a "dwarf" people who maintained a rice and fishing economy. Japanese farmers also mastered Chinese-style sericulture: the production of raw silk by raising silkworms.

The Yamato Emperors and Shinto Origins of the Japanese Sacred Identity

In time, the complex aristocratic society that developed within the Tomb Culture gave rise to a Japanese state on the Yamato plain in the region now known as Nara, south of Osaka. Becoming the ruling faction in this area, the Yamato clan incorporated native Japanese as well as Korean migrants. Clan leaders also elevated their own belief system that featured ancestor worship into a national religion known as Shinto. (Shinto means "the way of the deities.") Shinto beliefs derived from the early Japanese groups and held that after death a person's soul (or spirit) became a Shinto *kami,* or local deity, provided that it was nourished and purified through proper rituals and festivals. Before the imperial Yamato clan became dominant, each clan had its own ancestral deities; but after 500 CE, all Japanese increasingly worshipped the Yamato ancestors, whose origins went back to the fourth-century CE Tomb Culture. Other regional ancestral deities were later subordinated to the Yamato deities, who

Islam and the Silk Trade: Adapting Religion to Opulence

The Silk Road emerged from the localized industries and commercial networks of the Han, Kushan, Parthian, and Roman Empires in the first century BCE. The greatest volume of trade along this network took place over short distances, from one oasis to the next. It was not until centuries later, after the collapse of these states, that the golden age of Afro-Eurasian trade arose with new, powerful players. Tang China inherited the Han monopoly on silk production, while the Byzantine Empire utilized its Roman resources to develop its own silk weaving industry. Yet, a major threat to these monopolies appeared in the seventh century CE, when the first Islamic empire, the Umayyad Caliphate (661–750 CE), built a vast, state-run textile industry to exert influence over its newly conquered cities. Not only did the establishment of textile factories throughout the empire keep the working classes in line, but the luxury textiles produced were incentives for the elite of newly conquered territories (many of which were wealthy and were more sophisticated than the Arab tent culture of early Islamic caliphs) to submit to Muslim rule.

Tensions arose between this opulent lifestyle and the Muslim way of life, which forbade its adherents from wearing silk. The political, social, and religious authority that the Islamic silk trade lent the caliphate, however, was crucial to its unity and longevity. What's more, the Islamic silk industry was rapidly expanding, with no limits in sight, unlike Byzantine and Tang silk, which were restricted by their respective emperors. And so this textile-centered culture proliferated in an unbridled fashion, eventually infiltrating even religious rituals. The Abbasid Caliphate (750–1258 CE) became one of the wealthiest medieval states, and its capital, Baghdad, the most cosmopolitan. To illustrate the sheer extent of the impact that the Islamic silk trade had on the values of its people, the following table is a record of the goods that Caliph Harun al-Rashid, upon whom several *Arabian Nights* stories are based, left behind upon his death in 809 CE.

Source: Xinru Liu, *The Silk Road in World History* (New York: Oxford University Press, 2010).

QUESTIONS FOR ANALYSIS

- Looking back at Map 6.3 and assuming that the exports of each region remained relatively constant throughout the history of the Silk Road, with which cities and empires did the Abbasid Empire conduct most of its trade? The least? What might account for these differences?
- What can this table tell us about the values and activities of a caliph circa 800 CE? What, if anything, does the inventory reveal about the values and activities of the non-elite or working classes?
- What kind of evidence from contemporary Tang China or western Christendom would allow you to draw comparable conclusions to arguments that can be constructed from al-Rashid's inventory?

Textiles: Silk Items	
4,000	silk cloaks, lined with sable and mink
1,500	silk carpets
100	silk rugs
1,000	silk cushions and pillows
1,000	cushions with silk brocade
1,000	inscribed silk cushions
1,000	silk curtains
300	silk brocade curtains
Everyday Textile Items	
4,000	small tents with their accessories
150	marquees (large tents)

claimed direct lineage from the primary Shinto deity Amaterasu, the sun goddess and creator of the sacred islands of Japan.

PRINCE SHOTOKU AND THE TAIKA POLITICAL REFORMS After 587 CE, the Soga kinship group—originally from Korea but by 500 CE a minor branch of the Yamato imperial family—became Japan's leading family and controlled the Japanese court through intermarriage. Soon, they were attributing their cultural innovations to their own Prince Shotoku (574–622 CE), a direct descendant of the Soga and thus of the Yamato imperial family as well.

Contemporary Japanese scribes claimed that Prince Shotoku, rather than Korean immigrants, introduced Buddhism to Japan and that his illustrious reign sparked Japan's rise as an exceptional island kingdom. Shotoku promoted both Buddhism and Confucianism, thus enabling Japan, like its neighbor China, to be accommodating to numerous religions. Although earlier Korean immigrants had laid the groundwork for the growth of these views, Shotoku was credited with introducing these faiths into the native religious culture, Shinto. The prince also had ties with several Buddhist temples modeled on Tang pagodas and halls; one of these, in Nara (Japan's first imperial capital),

Luxury Textile Items	
4,000	embroidered robes
500	pieces of velvet
1,000	Armenian carpets
300	carpets from Maysan (present-day east Iraq)
1,000	carpets from Darabjird (present-day Darab, Iran)
500	carpets from Tabaristan (southern coast of the Caspian sea)
1,000	cushions from Tabaristan

Fine Cotton Items and Garments	
2,000	drawers of various kinds
4,000	turbans
1,000	hoods
1,000	capes of various kinds
5,000	kerchiefs of different kinds
10,000	caftans (long robes)
4,000	curtains
4,000	pairs of socks

Fur and Leather Items	
4,000	boots lined with sable and mink
4,000	special saddles
30,000	common saddles
1,000	belts

Metal Goods	
500,000	dinars (cash)
2,000	brass objects of various kinds
10,000	decorated swords
50,000	swords for the guards and pages (ghulam)
150,000	lances
100,000	bows
1,000	special suits of armor
10,000	helmets
20,000	breast plates
150,000	shields
300	stoves

Aromatics and Drugs	
100,000	mithqals of musk (1 mithqual = 4.25 grams)
100,000	mithqals of ambergris (musky perfume ingredient)
	Many kinds of perfume
1,000	baskets of India aloes

Jewelry and Cut Gems	
	Jewels valued by jewelers at 4 million dinars
1,000	jeweled rings

Fine Stone and Metal Vessels	
1,000	precious porcelain vessels, now called Chinaware
1,000	ewers

is Horyuji Temple, the oldest surviving wooden structure in the world. Its frescoes include figures derived from the art of Iran and central Asia. They are a reminder that within two centuries, Buddhism had dispersed its visual culture along the full length of the Silk Road—from Afghanistan to China and then on to Korea and the island kingdom of Japan.

Political integration under Prince Shotoku did not mean political stability, however. In 645 CE, the Nakatomi clan seized the throne and eliminated the Soga and their allies. Via inter-marriage with imperial kin, the Nakatomi became the new spokesmen for the Yamato tradition. Thereafter, Nakatomi no Kamatari (614–669 CE) enacted a series of reforms, known as the Taika Reforms, which reflected Confucian principles of government allegedly enunciated by Shotoku. These reforms enhanced the power of the ruler, no longer portrayed simply as an ancestral kinship group leader but now depicted as an exalted "emperor" (tenno) who ruled by the mandate of heaven, as in China, and exercised absolute authority.

MAHAYANA BUDDHISM AND THE SANCTITY OF THE JAPANESE STATE Religious influences continued to flow into Japan, contributing to spiritual pluralism while bolstering

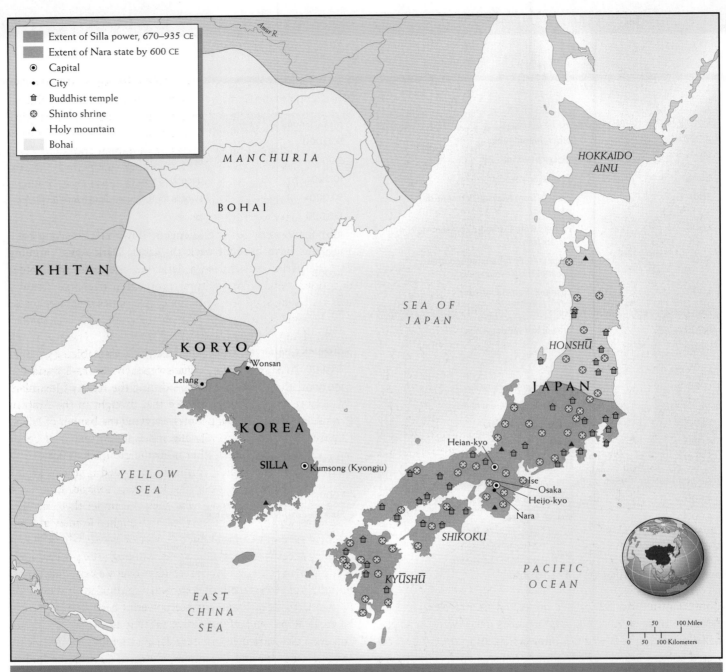

Legend:
- Extent of Silla power, 670–935 CE
- Extent of Nara state by 600 CE
- ⊙ Capital
- • City
- ⌂ Buddhist temple
- ⊛ Shinto shrine
- ▲ Holy mountain
- Bohai

MAP 9.7 | Borderlands: Korea and Japan, 600–1000 CE

The Tang dynasty held great power over the emerging Korean and Japanese states, although it never directly ruled either region.

- Based on the map, what connections do you see between Korea and Japan and the Tang Empire?
- To what extent did Korea and Japan adopt Tang customs during this period?

the Yamato rulers. Although Prince Shotoku and later Japanese emperors turned to Confucian models for government, they also dabbled in occult arts and Daoist purification rituals. In addition, the Taika edicts promoted Buddhism as the state religion of Japan. Although the imperial family continued to support native Shinto traditions, association with Buddhism gave the Japanese state extra status by lending it the prestige of a universal religion whose appeal stretched to Korea, China, and India.

State-sponsored spiritual diversity led native Shinto cults to formalize a creed of their own. Indeed, the introduction of

Creation Myth. *Tsukioka Yoshitoshi (1839–1892) depicted Japan's creation myth in* Amaterasu Appearing from the Cave. *To lure Amaterasu, the goddess of the sun, out so that light would return to the world, the other gods performed a ribald dance.*

Confucianism and Buddhism motivated Shinto adherents to assemble their diverse religious practices into a well-organized belief system to compete for followers. Shinto priests now collected ancient liturgies, and Shinto rituals (such as purification rites to ward off demons and impurities) gained recognition in the official Department of Religion.

Although the Japanese welcomed the Buddhist faith, they did not fully accept the traditional Buddhist view that the state was merely a vehicle to propagate moral and social justice for the ruler and his subjects. Instead, the Japanese saw their emperor (the embodiment of the state) as an object of worship, a sacred ruler, one in a line of luminous Shinto gods, a supreme *kami*—a divine force in his own right. Thus, Buddhism as imported from China and Korea changed in Japan to serve the interests of the state (much as Christianity served the interests of European monarchs and Islam served Islamic dynasties).

THE EMERGENCE OF EUROPEAN CHRISTENDOM

European historians previously labeled the period discussed in this chapter as the Dark Ages. In their opinion, cultural, political, and economic decline followed the fall of the Roman Empire. More recently, however, historians have marshaled evidence of significant advances in every avenue of human endeavor. Their findings have resulted in a new name for this period in European history—Late Antiquity, a label that stresses both political and cultural continuities between Rome and its successor states and new dynamic institutions.

Few revisions go unchallenged, however. Environmental historians have brought back the label "Dark Ages," arguing that the period was indeed a dark one, the result of a colder and drier climate. Agricultural production declined, famines occurred year after year, and infectious diseases spread across Afro-Eurasia. This harsher climate between 400 and 900 CE caused dying and morbidity on a large scale. There is much evidence for this assertion other than that assembled by climatologists. To begin with, a plague swept across Afro-Eurasia and decimated the Byzantine Empire during the reign of Justinian. Even more important is evidence that drought in the Arabian Peninsula led Arab tribal peoples, carrying the banner of Islam, to pour out of their severely affected lands in search of better lands and a better life, as other nomadic groups had done.

In these bleak times, Christianity provided a crucial source of unity in much the same fashion that Abbasid Islam and Tang China offered to those who sheltered under their imperial umbrellas. In the fifth century CE, the mighty Roman military machine gave way to a multitude of warrior leaders whose principal allegiances were local affiliations. Although the political ideal of the Roman Empire cast a vast shadow over western Europeans, the inheritor of the mantle of Rome was a spiritual institution—the Roman Catholic Church—whose powerful head, the pope, was based in Rome and whose universalizing agents—missionaries and monks—carried its message far and wide. (See Map 9.8.) In eastern Europe and Byzantium, a form of Christianity known as Greek Orthodoxy prevailed. Thus, the realm of Christendom, made up of Western Roman Catholicism and Greek Orthodoxy, dominated all of Europe, except for parts of the Iberian Peninsula and parts of Asia, and served to unify the lives of millions.

Charlemagne's Fledgling Empire

Far removed from the old centers of high culture, Charlemagne (r. 768–814 CE), king of the Franks in northern Europe, expanded his western European kingdom through constant warfare and plunder. In 802 CE, Harun al-Rashid, the ruler of Baghdad, sent

Prince Shotoku Taishi. *Shotoku was instrumental in the establishment of Buddhism in Japan, although his actual historical role was overstated. Left: In this hanging scroll painting from the early fourteenth century, he is idealized as a sixteen-year-old son, holding an incense censer and praying for the recovery of his sick father, the Emperor Yomei (r. 585–587 CE). Right: The main hall of the Horyuji Temple in Nara, Japan.*

the gift of an elephant to Charlemagne. The elephant caused a sensation among the Franks, who saw the gift as an acknowledgment of Charlemagne's power. In fact, Harun often sent rare beasts to distant rulers as a gracious reminder of his own formidable power. In his eyes, Charlemagne's "empire" was a minor principality.

This was an empire that Charlemagne ruled for over forty years, often traveling 2,000 miles a year on campaigns of plunder and conquest. He ultimately controlled much of western Europe, which was a significant accomplishment; yet compared with the Islamic world's rulers, he was a political lightweight. His empire had a population of less than 15 million; he rarely commanded armies larger than 5,000; and he had a rudimentary tax system. At a time when the palace quarters of the caliph at Baghdad covered nearly 250 acres, Charlemagne's palace at Aachen was merely 330 by 655 feet. Baghdad itself was almost 40 square miles in area, whereas there was no "town" outside the palace at Aachen. It was little more than a large country house set in open countryside, close to the Ardennes woods, where Charlemagne and his Franks loved to hunt wild boar on horseback.

He and his men were representatives of the warrior class that dominated post-Roman western Europe. For a time, Roman rule had imposed an alien way of life in this rough world. After that empire faded, however, war became once again the duty and joy of the aristocrat. Buoyed up by their chieftains' mead—a heavy beer made with honey, "yellow, sweet and ensnaring"— young men eagerly followed their lords into battle "among the war horses and the blood-stained armor" (Aneirin, ll. 102, 840).

And although the Franks vigorously engaged in trade, that trade was based on war. In fact, Europe's principal export at this time was Europeans, and the massive sale of prisoners of war financed the Frankish empire. From Venice, which grew rich

from its role as middleman, captives were sent as slaves across the sea to Alexandria, Tunis, and southern Spain. The main victims of this trade were Slavic-speaking peoples, tribal hunters and cultivators from eastern Europe. It is this trade that gave us our modern term *slave* (from *Slav*) for persons bought and sold as items of merchandise.

Yet this seemingly uncivilized and inhospitable zone offered fertile ground for Christianity to sink down roots. Although its worldwide expansion did not occur for centuries, its spiritual conquest of European peoples established institutions and fired enthusiasms that would later drive believers to carry its message to faraway lands.

Christianity in Western Europe

Charlemagne's empire was unquestionably primitive when compared with the Islamic empire or the Tang Empire of China. What made it significant was its location. Far removed from the old centers of high culture, it was a political system of the borderlands. It featured an expansionist Christianity that drew energy from its rough frontier mentality. Indeed, Christianity now entered a world profoundly different from the Mediterranean cities in which it had taken form.

AUGUSTINE AND THE UNIVERSAL CATHOLIC CHURCH
Christians of the west felt that theirs was the one truly universal religion. (See Primary Source: Christendom on the Edge: A View of Empire in Ireland.) Their goal was to bring rival groups into a single "catholic" church that was replacing a political unity lost in western Europe when the Roman Empire fell.

MAP 9.8 | Christendom, 600–1000 CE

The end of the first millennium saw much of Europe divided between two versions of Christianity, each with different traditions.

- Locate Rome and Constantinople on the map, the two seats of power in Christianity.
- According to the map, what were the two major regions where Christianity held sway?
- In what directions did Latin Christianity and Orthodox Christianity spread?
- Why do you suppose the Catholic Church, based in Rome, was successful in expanding to the west, but not to the east?
- Why do you suppose Orthodox Christianity, based in Constantinople, expanded into eastern Europe, but not into the west?

As far back as 410 CE, reacting to the Goths' sack of Rome, the Christian bishop Augustine of Hippo (a seaport in modern Algeria) had laid down the outlines of this belief. His book *The City of God* assured contemporary Christians that the barbarian takeover happening around them was not the end of the world. The "city of God" would take earthly shape in the form of the Catholic Church, and the Catholic Church was not just for Romans—it was for all times and for all peoples, "in a wide world which has always been inhabited by many differing peoples, that have so many different customs and languages, so many different forms of organization and so many languages, and who have had so many different religions"

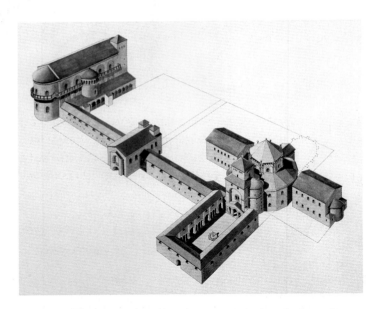

Charlemagne's Palace and Chapel. *Though not large by Byzantine or Islamic standards, Charlemagne's palace and chapel were heavy with symbolic meaning. A royal hall for banqueting in Frankish, "barbarian" style was linked by a covered walkway to the imperial domed chapel, which was meant to look like a miniature version of the Hagia Sophia of Constantinople. Outside the chapel was a courtyard, like the one outside the shrine of Saint Peter at Rome.*

(Augustine, 14.1). Only one organization would bring them all to paradise: the Catholic Church.

Several developments gave rise to this attitude. First, the arrival of Christianity in northern Europe had provoked a cultural revolution. Preliterate societies now encountered a sacred text—the Bible—in a language that seemed utterly strange. Latin had become a sacred language, and books themselves were vehicles of the holy. The bound codex (see Chapter 8), which had replaced the clumsy scroll, was still a messy object. It had no divisions between words, no punctuation, no paragraphs, no chapter headings. Readers who knew Latin as a spoken language could understand the script. But Irishmen, Saxons, and Franks could not, for they had never spoken Latin; hence the care lavished in the newly Christian north on the Latin scriptures. The few parchment texts that circulated there were carefully prepared with words separated, sentences correctly punctuated and introduced by uppercase letters, and chapter headings provided. They were far more like this textbook than anything available to Romans at the height of the empire.

Second, those who produced the Bibles were starkly different from ordinary men and women. They were monks and nuns. Christian **monasticism** had originated in Egypt, but it suited the missionary tendencies of Christianity in northern Europe particularly well. (The words *monastic* and *monk* come from the Greek *monos*, "alone": a man or a woman who chooses to live alone, without the support of marriage or family.) Monasticism

placed small groups of men and women in the middle of societies with which they had nothing in common. It appealed to a deep sense that the very men and women who had little in common with "normal" people were best suited to mediate between believers and God. Laypersons (common believers, not clergy) gave gifts to the monasteries and offered them protection. In return, they gained the prayers of monks and nuns and the reassurance that although they themselves were warriors and men of blood, the monks' and nuns' intercessions would keep them from going to hell. Payment for human sin, the atoning power of Jesus's crucifixion, and the efficacy of monastic prayers were significant theological emphases for Roman Catholics.

MONKS, NUNS, AND POPES With the spread of monasticism, Christianity in the west took a decisive turn. In Muslim (as in Jewish) societies, religious leaders emphasized what they had in common with those around them: many Islamic

Celtic Bible. *Unlike the simple codex of early Christian times, the Bible came to be presented in Ireland and elsewhere in the northern world as a magical book. Its pages were filled with mysterious, intricate patterns, which imitated on parchment the jewelry and treasure for which early medieval warlords yearned.*

Christendom on the Edge: A View of Empire in Ireland

A young Christian Briton of Roman citizenship who lived near Hadrian's Wall experienced the pull of Christianity around 400 CE. Captured by Irish slave raiders as a teenager, Patricius spent six years herding pigs on the Atlantic coast of Mayo. He escaped but years later returned to convert his former captors to Christianity. He believed that in making the fierce Irish Christians, he also made them "Romans." He thus brought Christianity to the Atlantic edge of the known world. Patricius is remembered today as Saint Patrick.

16 But after I reached Ireland, well, I pastured the flocks every day. . . . I would even stay in the forests and on the mountain and would wake to pray before dawn in all weathers, snow, frost, rain. . . .

17 And it was in fact there that one night while asleep I heard a voice saying to me: 'You do well to fast, since you will soon be going to your home country;' and again, very shortly after, I heard this prophecy: 'See, your ship is ready.' And it was not near at hand but was perhaps two hundred miles away, and I had never been there and did not know a living soul there. And then I soon ran away and abandoned the man with whom I had been for six years . . . till I reached the ship.

23 And again a few years later I was in Britain with my kinsfolk. . . . And it was there that I saw one night in a vision a man coming as it were from Ireland . . . with countless letters, and he gave me one of them, and I read the heading of the letter, 'The Voice of the Irish,' and as I read these opening words aloud, I imagined at that very instant that I heard the voice of those who were beside the forest of Foclut which is near the western sea; and thus they cried, as though with one voice: 'We beg you, holy boy, to come and walk again among us.'

Source: *St. Patrick: His Writings and Muirchu's Life,* edited and translated by A. B. E. Hood (London: Phillimore, 1978), pp. 41, 44–46, 50.

QUESTIONS FOR ANALYSIS

- What does this passage reveal about life in the Celtic worlds?
- How many voices or visions does Patricius experience in this passage? What other religious figure in this chapter also had a vision or a revelation?
- Based on your reading, how do St. Patrick's spiritual experiences compare with those of rulers and priests in the older Christian communities of Rome and Constantinople?

---

scholars, theologians, and mystics were married men just like the public, even merchants and courtiers. In the Christian west, the opposite was true: warrior societies honored small groups of men and women (the monks and nuns) who were utterly unlike themselves: unmarried, unfit for warfare, and intensely literate in an incomprehensible tongue. Even their hair looked different. Unlike warriors, these men were close-shaven; by contrast, the Orthodox clergy of the Eastern Roman Empire grew long, silvery beards (signifying wisdom and maturity; not, as in the west, the warrior's masculine strength). Catholic monks and priests shaved their heads as well.

The Catholic Church of northern Europe owed its missionary zeal to the same principles that explained the spread of Buddhism: it was a religion of monks, whose communities represented an otherworldly alternative to the warrior societies of the time. By 800 CE, most regions of northern Europe held great monasteries, many of which were far larger than the local villages. Supported by thousands of serfs, donated by kings and local warlords, the monasteries became powerhouses of prayer that kept the regions safe. Northern Christianity also gained new ties to an old center: the city of Rome. The Christian bishop of Rome had always enjoyed much prestige. But being only one bishop among many, he often took second place to his peers in Alexandria, Antioch, and Constantinople. Though people spoke of him with respect as pope, many others shared that title.

By 800 CE, this picture had changed. As believers looked down from the distant north, they saw only one pope left in western Europe: Rome's pope. The papacy as we know it arose because of the fervor with which the Catholic Church of western Europe united behind one symbolic center, represented by the popes at Rome and the desire of new Christians in northern borderlands to find a religious leader for their hopes.

Charlemagne recognized this desire very well. In 800 CE, he went out of his way to celebrate Christmas Day by visiting the shrine of Saint Peter at Rome. There, Pope Leo III acclaimed him as the new "emperor" of the west. The ceremony ratified the aspirations of an age. A "modern" Rome—inhabited by popes, famous for shrines of the martyrs, and protected by a "modern" Christian monarch from the north—was what Charlemagne's subjects wanted.

Vikings and Christendom

Vikings from Scandinavia exposed the weakness of Charlemagne's Christian empire. When Harun's elephant died in 813 CE, one year before Charlemagne himself, the Franks viewed the elephant's death as an omen of coming disasters. The great beast keeled over when his handlers marched him out to confront a Viking army from Denmark. In the next half-century, Charlemagne's empire of borderland peoples met its match on the widest border of all: that between the European landmass and the mighty Atlantic. (See Map 9.9.)

The Vikings' motives were announced in their name, which derives from the Old Norse *vik,* "to be on the warpath." The **Vikings** sought to loot the now-wealthy Franks and replace them as the dominant warrior class of northern Europe. It was their turn to extract plunder and to sell droves of slaves across the water. They succeeded because of a deadly technological advantage: ships of unparalleled sophistication, developed by Scandinavian sailors in the Baltic Sea and the long fjords of Norway. Light and agile, with a shallow draft, they could penetrate far up the rivers of northern Europe and even be carried overland from one river system to another. Under sail, the same boats could tackle open water and cross the unexplored wastes of the North Atlantic.

In the ninth century CE, the Vikings set their ships on both courses. They emptied northern Europe of its treasure, sacking the great monasteries along the coasts of Ireland and Britain and overlooking the Rhine and the Seine—rivers that led into the heart of Charlemagne's empire. At the same time, Norwegian adventurers colonized the uninhabited island of Iceland, and then Greenland. By 982 CE, they had even reached North America and established a settlement at L'Anse aux Meadows on the Labrador coast. Recent aerial reconnaissance suggests a second Viking settlement in North America roughly 300 miles south of L'Anse aux Meadows. Viking goods have been found as far west as the Inuit settlements of Baffin Island to the north of Hudson Bay, carried there along trading routes by Native Americans.

The consequences of this spectacular reach across the ocean to America were short-lived, but the penetration of eastern Europe had lasting effects. Supremely well equipped to traverse long river systems, the Vikings sailed east along the Baltic and then turned south, edging up the rivers that cross the watershed of central Russia. Here the Dnieper, the Don, and the Volga begin to flow south into the Black Sea and the Caspian. By opening this link between the Baltic and what is now Kiev in modern Ukraine, the Vikings created an avenue of commerce that linked Scandinavia and the Baltic directly to Constantinople and Baghdad. And they added yet more slaves: Muslim geographers bluntly called this route "The Highway of the Slaves."

On reaching the Black Sea, the Vikings made straight for Constantinople. In 860 CE, more than 200 Viking longships gathered ominously in the straits of the Bosporus, beneath the walls of Constantinople. What they found was not Charlemagne's rustic Aachen, but a proud city with a population exceeding 100,000 surrounded by well-engineered late Roman walls.

The Vikings had come up against a state hardened by battle. For two centuries the empire of "East Rome," centered in Constantinople, had held Islamic armies at bay. From 640 to 840 CE, they faced almost yearly campaigns launched by the Islamic

The Coronation of Charlemagne. *This is how the coronation of Charlemagne at Rome in 800 CE was remembered in medieval western Europe. This painting stresses the fact that it was the pope who placed the crown on Charlemagne's head, thereby claiming him as a ruler set up by the Catholic Church for the Catholic Church. But in 800 CE, contemporaries saw the pope as recognizing the fact that Charlemagne had already deserved to be emperor. The rise of the papacy to greater prominence and power in later medieval Europe caused this significant "re-remembering" of the event.*

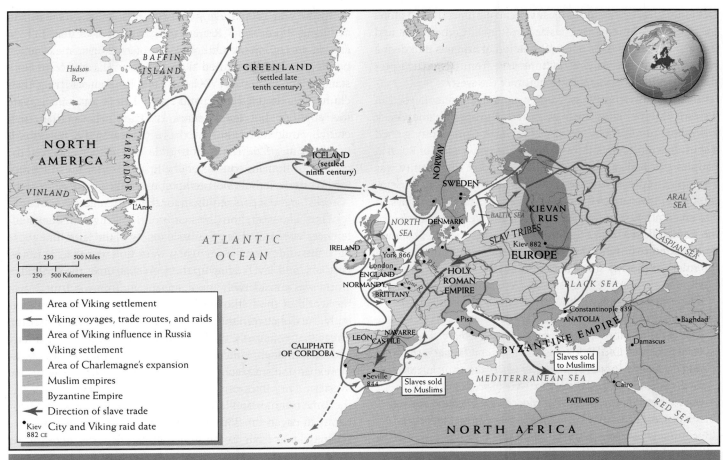

MAP 9.9 | The Age of Vikings and the Slave Trade, 800–1000 CE

Vikings from Scandinavia dramatically altered the history of Christendom.

- In what directions did the Vikings carry out their voyages, trade routes, and raids?
- What were the geographical limits of the Viking explorations in each direction?
- In what direction did the slave trade move, and what role did the Vikings and the Holy Roman emperors play in expanding the slave trade?

empire of Damascus and Baghdad, powerhouses that grew to be ten times greater than their own. For years on end, Muslim armies and navies came within striking distance of Constantinople. Each time they failed, outmaneuvered by highly professional generals and blocked by a skillfully constructed line of fortresses that controlled the roads across Anatolia. The Christian empire of East Rome fought the caliphs of Baghdad to a draw. The Viking fleet was even less suited to assault Constantinople, as the empire of "East Rome" had a deadly technological advantage in naval warfare: Greek fire, a combination of petroleum and potassium that, when sprayed from siphons, would explode in a great sheet of flame on the water. A previous emperor had used it to destroy the Muslim fleet as it lay at anchor within sight of Constantinople. Now, a century and a half later, the experience and weaponry of East Rome were too much for the Vikings, and their raid was a spectacular failure.

Despite their inability to take Byzantium, the Vikings asserted an enduring influence through their forays across the North Atlantic, their brutal interactions with Christian communities in northern Europe, and their expansion into eastern Europe, especially the slave trade they facilitated there.

Greek Orthodox Christianity in the East

In the long run, the sense of having outlasted so many military emergencies bolstered the morale of East Roman Christianity and led to its unexpected flowering. Not just Constantinople but Justinian's glorious church, the Hagia Sophia—its heart—had survived. That great building and the solemn Greek liturgy that reverberated within its domed spaces symbolized the branch of Christianity that dominated the east: **Greek Orthodoxy**. Greek

Orthodox theology held that Jesus became human less to atone for humanity's sins, as emphasized in Roman Catholicism, and more to facilitate *theosis*, a transformation of humans into divine beings. This was a truly distinct message from that which predominated in the Roman Catholicism of the west.

In the tenth century, as Charlemagne's empire collapsed in western Europe, large areas of eastern Europe became Greek Orthodox, not Catholic. As a result, Greek Christianity gained a spiritual empire in Southwest Asia. The conversion of Russian peoples and Balkan Slavs to Greek Orthodox Christianity was a complex process. It reflected a deep admiration for Constantinople on the part of Russians, Bulgarians, and other Slavs. It was an admiration as intense as that of any western Catholic for the Roman popes. This admiration amounted to awe, as shown by the famous story of the conversion to Greek Christianity of the rulers of Kiev (descendants of Vikings):

> The envoys reported[,]. . . . "We went among the Germans [the Catholic Franks] and we saw them performing many ceremonies in their churches; but we beheld no glory there. Then we went to Greece [in fact, to Constantinople and Hagia Sophia], and the Greeks led us to the edifices where they worship their God, and we knew not whether we were in heaven or on earth. For on earth there is no such splendor or such beauty, and we are at a loss to describe it. . . . [W]e can not forget that beauty. (Cross and Sherbowitz-Westor, p. 111)

By the year 1000, there were two Christianities: the new and confident "borderland" **Roman Catholicism** of western Europe and an ancient Greek Orthodoxy, protected against extinction by the iron framework of a "Roman" state inherited from Constantine and Justinian. Western Catholics believed that their church was destined to expand everywhere. East Romans were less euphoric but more tenacious. They believed that their church would forever survive the regular ravages of invasion. It was a significant difference in attitude, and neither side liked the other. East Romans considered the Franks barbarous and grasping; Western Catholics contemptuously called the East Romans "Greeks" and condemned them for their "Byzantine" cunning.

Thus, like Islam, the Christian world was divided. But its differences were not about the basic tenets of the faith, like those of Shiite and Sunni Islam. They were differences in heritage, customs, and levels of civilization. At that time, the Orthodox world was considerably more ancient and more cultured than the world of the Catholic west. And it dealt with Islam differently. At Constantinople, eastern Christianity held off Muslim forces that constantly threatened the integrity of the great city and its Christian hinterlands. In the west, by contrast, Muslim expansionism reached all the way to the Iberian Peninsula. Western Christendom, led by the Roman papacy, did not feel the same intimidation from Islam. It set about spreading Christianity to pagan tribes in the north, and it began to contemplate retaking lands from the Muslims.

Monasticism. Left: *The great monasteries of the age of Charlemagne, such as the St. Gallen Monastery, were like Roman legionary settlements. Placed on the frontiers of Germany, they were vast stone buildings, around which entire towns would gather. Their libraries, the largest in Europe, were filled with parchment volumes, carefully written out and often lavishly decorated in a "northern," Celtic style. Right: Monasticism was also about the lonely search for God at the very end of the world, which took place in these Irish monasteries on the Atlantic coast. The cells, made of loose stones piled in round domes, are called "beehives."*

Oseberg Ship. *The Viking ship was a triumph of design. It could be rowed up the great rivers of Europe, and at the same time, its sail could take it across the Atlantic.*

CONCLUSION

The period 600–1000 CE saw heightened movement across cultural boundaries as well as an insistence on the distinctiveness of individual societies. Commodities, technological innovations, ideas, merchants, adventurers, and scholars traveled from one end of Afro-Eurasia to the other and up and down coastal Africa. Spreading religion into new frontiers accompanied this mercantile activity. The proximity of the period's two powerhouses—Abbasid Islam and Tang China—facilitated the dynamic movement.

Despite the intermixing of peoples, ideas, and goods across Afro-Eurasia, new political and cultural boundaries were developing that would split this landmass in ways it could never have imagined. The most important dividing force was religion, as Islam challenged and slowed the spread of Christianity and as Buddhism challenged the ruling elite of Tang China. As a consequence, Afro-Eurasia's major cultural zones began to compete in terms of religious and cultural doctrines. The Islamic Abbasid Empire pushed back the borders of the Tang Empire. But the conflict grew particularly intense between the Islamic and Christian worlds, where the clash involved faith as well as frontiers.

The Tang Empire revived Confucianism, insisting on its political and moral primacy as the foundation of a new imperial order, and it embraced the classical written language as another unifying element. By doing so, the Tang counteracted universalizing foreign religions—notably Buddhism but also Islam—spreading into the Chinese state. The same adaptive strategies influenced new systems on the Korean Peninsula and in Japan.

In some circumstances, faith followed empire and relied on rulers' support or tolerance to spread the word. This was the

Jelling Stone. *Carved on the side of this great stone, Christ appears to be almost swallowed up in an intricate pattern of lines. For the Vikings, complicated interweaving like serpents or twisted gold jewelry was a sign of majesty: hence, in this, the first Christian monument in Denmark, Christ is part of an ancient pattern of carving, which brought good luck and victory to the king.*

case especially in East Asia. At the opposite extreme, empire followed faith—as in the case of Islam, whose believers endeavored to spread their empire in every conceivable direction. The Islamic empire and its successors represented a new force: expanding political power backed by one God whose instructions were to spread his message. In the worlds of Christianity, a common faith absorbed elements of a common culture (shared books, a language for learned classes). But in the west, political rulers never overcame inhabitants' intense allegiance to local authority.

While universalizing religions expanded and common cultures grew, debate raged within each religion over foundational principles. In spite of the diffusion of basic texts in "official" languages, regional variations of Christianity, Islam, and Buddhism proliferated as each belief system spread. The period from 600 to 1000 CE demonstrated that religion, reinforced by prosperity and imperial resources, could bring peoples together in unprecedented ways. But it could also, as the next chapter will illustrate, drive them apart in bloodcurdling confrontations.

FOCUS ON: *Faith and Empire*

The Islamic Empire

- Warriors from the Arabian Peninsula defeat Byzantine and Sasanian armies and establish an Islamic empire stretching from Morocco to South Asia.

- The Abbasid state takes over from the Umayyads, crystallizes the main Islamic institutions of the caliphate and Islamic law, and promotes cultural achievements in religion, philosophy, and science.

- Disputes over Muhammad's succession lead to a deep and enduring split between Sunnis and Shiites.

Tang China

- The Tang dynasty dominates East Asia and exerts a strong influence on Korea and Japan.

- Tang rulers balance Confucian and Daoist ideals with Buddhist thought and practice.

- A common written language and shared philosophy, rather than a universalist religion, integrate the Chinese state.

Christian Europe

- Monks, nuns, and Rome-based popes spread Christianity throughout western Europe.

- Constantinople-based Greek Orthodoxy survives the spread of Islam.

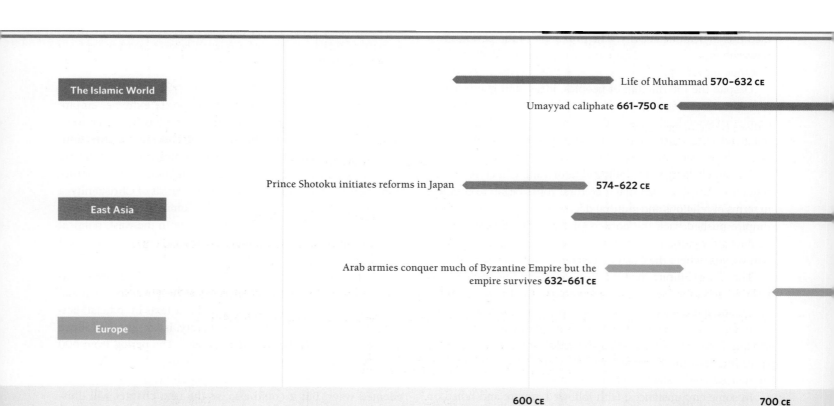

The Islamic World

Life of Muhammad **570–632 CE**

Umayyad caliphate **661–750 CE**

East Asia

Prince Shotoku initiates reforms in Japan **574–622 CE**

Arab armies conquer much of Byzantine Empire but the empire survives **632–661 CE**

Europe

600 CE

700 CE

1. **Describe** the origins and basic beliefs of Islam, including Muhammad, the Quran, and the five pillars of Islam. To what extent does this tradition fit the model for a universal religion?

2. **Analyze** the successes and failures of Islamic leaders in creating one large empire to govern Islamic communities. What opponents challenged this goal? How did the empire's expansion require a balancing act between political powers (such as the caliphate) and religious authority (such as the *ulama* and *sharia* law)?

3. **Evaluate** the impact of the spread of Islam on Afro-Asian societies. How did the large Islamic empire shape the movement of peoples, ideas, innovations, and commodities?

4. **Describe** the Tang dynasty's attempts to restore political unity to East Asia. What roles did the army, civil service examinations, and eunuchs play in Tang political organization? How did Tang leaders react to the growth of universal religions within their realm?

5. **Explain** how the Tang interacted with foreign ideas (including Zoroastrianism, Christianity, and Buddhism) and influenced other polities (as in Korea and Japan).

6. **Describe** the state structure that emerged in Korea and Japan during this era. How did other developments in Afro-Eurasia, such as the spread of universal religions, shape these new states?

7. **Identify** some of the distinctive features of Christendom in western, northern, and eastern Europe.

8. **Compare and contrast** the spread of Islam, Buddhism, and Christianity. What was the geographical range of each religious community? How did each religion gain new converts?

9. **Examine** the similarities and differences between the organizational structures of the Abbasids, Tang China, and Christendom.

10. **Compare and contrast** the forces of opposition and change within the Islamic, Tang, and Christian worlds.

11. **Analyze** the Vikings' impact on world history during this era, both in Europe and beyond. How did they shape developments in the Christian world especially?

12. **Explore** the ways in which the interaction between religion, empire, and commercial exchange affected developments across Afro-Eurasia during this period.

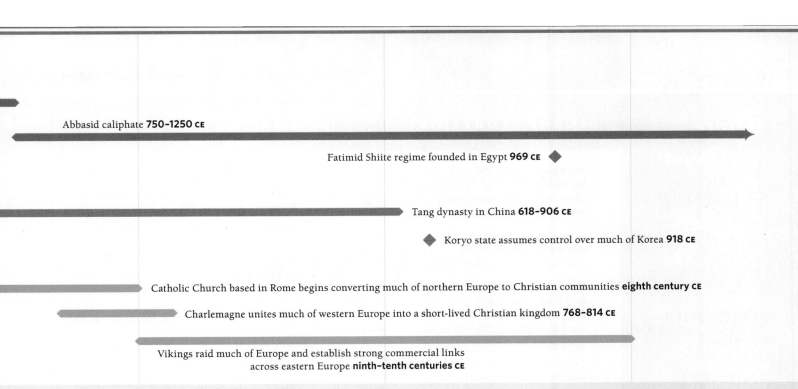

Abbasid caliphate **750–1250 CE**

Fatimid Shiite regime founded in Egypt **969 CE**

Tang dynasty in China **618–906 CE**

Koryo state assumes control over much of Korea **918 CE**

Catholic Church based in Rome begins converting much of northern Europe to Christian communities **eighth century CE**

Charlemagne unites much of western Europe into a short-lived Christian kingdom **768–814 CE**

Vikings raid much of Europe and establish strong commercial links across eastern Europe **ninth–tenth centuries CE**

800 CE   **900 CE**   **1000 CE**

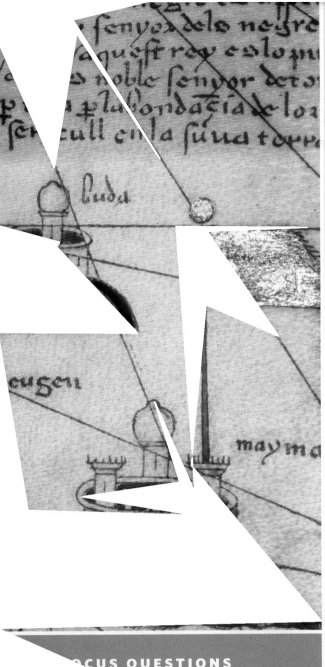

10

Becoming "The World," 1000–1300 CE

FOCUS QUESTIONS

- What technological advances occurred during this period, especially in ship design and navigation, and how did they facilitate the expansion of Afro-Eurasian trade?

- What types of social and political forces shaped the Islamic world, India, China, and Europe at this time? To what degree did these forces integrate cultures and geographical areas?

- How did sub-Saharan Africa compare with the Americas in terms of internal integration and external interactions?

- In what ways did the Mongol Empire influence peoples and places within Afro-Eurasia?

In the late 1270s, two Christian monks, Bar Sāwmā and Markōs, voyaged into the heart of Islam. They were not Europeans. They were Uighurs, a Turkish people of central Asia, many of whom had converted to Christianity centuries earlier. Sent by the mighty Mongol ruler Kubilai Khan as he prepared to become the first formally recognized emperor of China's Yuan dynasty, the monks were supposed to worship at the temple in Jerusalem. But the Great Khan also had political ambitions. He was eager to conquer Jerusalem, held by the Muslims. Accordingly, he dispatched the monks as agents to make alliances with Christian kings in the area and to gather intelligence about his potential enemy in Palestine.

By 1280, conflict and conquest had transformed many parts of the world. But friction was simply one manifestation of cultures brushing up against one another. More important was trade. Indeed, Bar Sāwmā and Markōs lingered at the magnificent trading hub of Kashgar in what is now western China, where caravan routes converged in a market for jade, exotic spices, and precious silks. Later, at Baghdad, the monks parted ways. Bar Sāwmā visited Constantinople (where the king gave him gold and silver), Rome (where he met with the pope at the shrine of Saint Peter), and Paris (where he saw that city's vibrant university) before deciding to return to China, where the Christians of the east awaited his reports. In the end, neither monk ever returned. Yet their voyages exemplified the criss-crossing of people, money, and goods along the trade routes and sea-lanes that connected the world's regions. For just as religious conflict was a hallmark of this age, so was a surge in trade, migration, and global exchange.

The period brought to a climax many centuries of human development, and it ushered in a new, very long cycle of cultural interaction from which emerge three interrelated themes. First, trade was shifting from land-based routes to sea-based routes. Coastal trading cities began to dramatically expand. Second, intensified trade and linguistic and religious integration generated the world's four major cultural "spheres," whose inhabitants were linked by shared institutions and beliefs: the Islamic world, India, China, and Europe. Not all cultures turned into "spheres," though. In the Americas and sub-Saharan Africa, there was not the same impulse to integrate regions, which remained more fragmented but thrived nonetheless. Third, the rise of the Mongol Empire represented the peak in the long history of ties and tensions between settled and mobile peoples. From China to Persia and as far as eastern Europe, the Mongols ruled over much land in the world's major cultural spheres. Each of these three themes contributes to an understanding of how Afro-Eurasia became a "world" unified through trade, migration, and even religious conflict.

DEVELOPMENT OF MARITIME TRADE

Innovations at Sea

By the tenth century CE, sea routes were eclipsing land networks for long-distance trade. Improved navigational aids, refinements in shipbuilding, better mapmaking, and new legal arrangements and accounting practices made shipping easier and slashed the costs of seaborne trade. The numbers testify to the maritime revolution: while a porter could carry about 10 pounds over long distances, and animal-drawn wagons could move 100 pounds over small distances, the Arab dhows plying the Indian Ocean were capable of transporting up to 5 tons of cargo. (Dhows are ships with triangle-shaped sails, called lateens, that allow the best use of the monsoon trade winds on the Arabian Sea and the Indian Ocean.) As a result, some coastal ports, like Mogadishu in eastern Africa, became vast transshipment centers for a thriving trade across the Indian Ocean.

A new navigational instrument spurred this boom: the needle compass. This Chinese invention initially identified promising locations for houses and tombs, but eleventh-century sailors from Guangzhou (anglicized as Canton) used it to find their way on the high seas. The device spread rapidly. Not only did it allow sailing under cloudy skies, but it also improved mapmaking. And it made all the oceans, including the Atlantic, easier to navigate.

Dhow. *This modern dhow in the harbor of Zanzibar displays the characteristic triangle sail. The triangle sail can make good use of the trade wind monsoon and thus has guided dhows on the Arabian Sea since ancient times.*

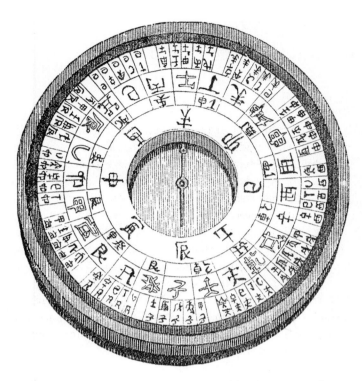

Antique Chinese Compass. *Chinese sailors from Canton started to use needle compasses in the eleventh century. By the thirteenth century, needle compasses were widely used on ships in the Indian Ocean and were starting to appear in the Mediterranean.*

Now shipping became less dangerous. Navigators relied on lateen-rigged dhows between the Indian Ocean and the Red Sea, heavy junks in the South China Sea, and Atlantic "cogs," which linked Genoa to locations as distant as the Azores and Iceland. They also enjoyed the protection of political authorities, such as the Song dynasts in China, in guiding the trading fleets in and out of harbors. The Fatimid caliphate in Egypt, for instance, profited from maritime trade and defended merchant fleets from pirates. Armed convoys of ships escorted commercial fleets and regularized the ocean traffic. The system soon spread to North Africa and southern Spain. Most of these shipping firms were family based, and they sent young men of the family, sometimes servants or slaves, to work in India. Wives in Cairo could expect gifts from their husbands to arrive with the fleet.

Changes in navigation ushered in the demise of overland routes. Silk Road merchants eventually gave up using camel trains, caravansaries (inns for travelers), and oasis hubs as they switched to the sea-lanes. The shift took centuries, but overland routes and camels were no match for multiple-masted cargo ships.

Global Commercial Hubs

Long-distance trade spawned the growth of commercial cities. (See Map 10.1.) These cosmopolitan **entrepôts** served as transshipment centers where ships could drop anchor and merchants could find lodging, exchange commodities, and replenish supplies. Their locations between borders or in ports enabled merchants to link diverse peoples commercially. Beginning in the late tenth century CE, regional centers became major anchorages of the maritime trade: in the west, the Egyptian port cities of Alexandria and Cairo; in the east, the Chinese city of Quanzhou; in the Malaysian Archipelago, the city of Melaka; and near the tip of the Indian Peninsula, the port of Kollam (often anglicized as Quilon). These hubs thrived under the political stability of dynasts who recognized that the free-for-all of trade and market life would generate wealth for them through taxes collected on cargoes.

Cairo and Alexandria were the Mediterranean's main maritime commercial centers. Cairo was home to numerous Muslim and Jewish trading firms, and Alexandria was their lookout post on the Mediterranean. It was through Alexandria that Europeans acquired silks from China and Spanish silks headed to eastern Mediterranean markets along with olive oil, glassware, flax, corals, and metals. Gemstones and aromatic perfumes poured in from India. Also changing hands were minerals and chemicals for dyeing or tanning and raw materials such as timber and bamboo. The real novelties were paper and books. Hand-copied Bibles, Talmuds, Qurans, legal and moral works, grammars in various languages, and Arabic books became the first best-sellers of the Mediterranean.

The Islamic legal system prevalent in Egypt promoted a favorable business environment. Legal specialists got around the rule that might have brought commerce to a halt—the *sharia's* (see Chapter 9) prohibition against earning interest on loans. With the clerics' blessing, Muslim traders formed partnerships between those who had capital to lend and those who needed money to expand their businesses: owners of capital entrusted their money or commodities to agents who, after completing their work, returned the investment and a share of the profits to the owners—and kept the rest as their reward. The English word *risk* derives from the Arabic *rizq,* the extra allowance paid to merchants in lieu of interest.

In China, the Song government set up offices of Seafaring Affairs in three major ports: Canton, Quanzhou, and an area near present-day Shanghai in the Yangzi Delta. In return for a portion of the taxes, these offices registered cargoes, sailors, and traders, while guards kept a keen eye on the traffic. Arabs, Persians, Jews, and Indians, as well as Chinese, traded at Quanzhou, and some stayed on to manage their businesses. Perhaps as many as 100,000 Muslims lived there during the Song dynasty. A mosque from this period is still standing. Hindu traders living in Quanzhou worshiped in a Buddhist shrine where statues of Hindu deities stood alongside those of Buddhist gods.

Because of its strategic location and proximity to Malayan tropical produce, Melaka became a key cosmopolitan city.

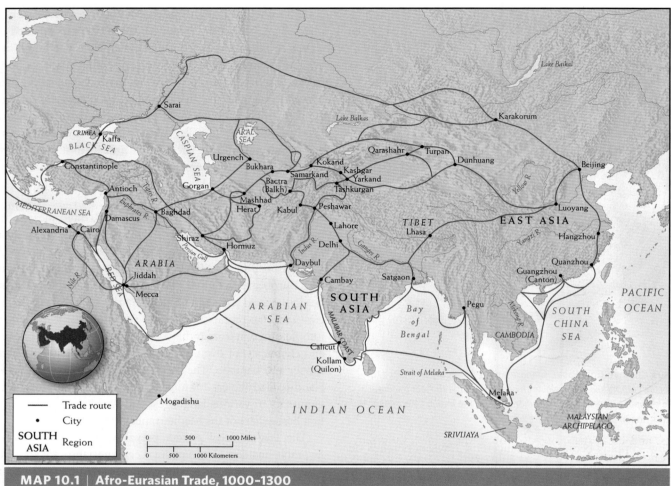

MAP 10.1 | Afro-Eurasian Trade, 1000–1300

During the early second millennium, Afro-Eurasian merchants increasingly turned to the Indian Ocean to transport their goods.

- Locate the global hubs of Kollam, Alexandria, Cairo, Melaka, and Quanzhou on this map.
- What regions do each of these global hubs represent?
- Based on the map, why would sea travel have been preferable to overland travel?
- According to the text, what revolutions in maritime travel facilitated this development?

During peak season, Southeast Asian ports teemed with colorfully dressed Indian, Javanese, and Chinese merchants and sailors selling their goods, purchasing return cargo, and waiting for the winds to change so they could reach their next destination. Local artisans hawked batik handicrafts, and money-grubbing traders converged from all over Asia to flood the markets with their merchandise and to search for pungent herbs, aromatic spices, and agrarian staples to ship out.

In the tenth century CE, South India likewise supported a nerve center of maritime trade. Many Muslim traders settled in Malabar, on the southwest coast of the Indian Peninsula, and Kollam became a cosmopolitan hub. Dhows delivered goods from the Red Sea and Africa. Chinese junks unloaded silks and porcelain and picked up passengers and commodities for East Asian markets. Muslim traders shipped horses from Arab countries to India and the southeast islands, where kings viewed them as symbols of royalty. There was even trade in elephants and cattle from tropical countries, though most goods were spices, perfumes, and textiles. Personal relationships were key. When striking a deal with a local merchant, a Chinese trader would mention his Indian neighbor in Quanzhou and that family's residence in Kollam.

Global commercial hubs relied on friendship and family to keep their businesses thriving across religious and regional divides. Whether in India, Melaka, China, or Egypt, each bustling port teemed with a cosmopolitan mix of peoples,

The Islamic World in a Time of Political Fragmentation | 361

Mazu. *As much as sailors used compasses, they could still appeal for divine help—as these Quanzhou sailors did in seeking protection at the shrine of Mazu, the goddess of seafarers. According to legend, before assuming godhood Mazu had performed many miracles. Her temple became prominent after 1123, when Quanzhou's governor survived a storm at sea while returning from Korea. After that, sailors and their families burned incense for the goddess and prayed for her aid in keeping them safe at sea.*

goods, and ideas that flowed through the growing maritime networks, thanks to improved ships and better navigational tools.

THE ISLAMIC WORLD IN A TIME OF POLITICAL FRAGMENTATION

While the number of Muslim traders began to increase in commercial hubs from the Mediterranean to the South China Sea, it was not until the ninth and tenth centuries CE that Muslims became a majority within their own Abbasid Empire (see Chapter 9). From the outset, Muslim rulers and clerics dealt with large non-Muslim populations, even as these groups were converting to Islam. Rulers accorded non-Muslims religious toleration as long as the non-Muslims accepted Islam's political dominion. Jewish, Christian, and Zoroastrian communities were free to choose their own religious leaders and to settle internal disputes in their own religious courts. They did, however, have to pay a special tax, the *jizya*, and defer to their rulers. While tolerant, Islam was an expansionist, universalizing faith. Intense proselytizing—especially by Sufi merchants—carried the sacred word to new frontiers and, in the process, reinforced the spread of Islamic institutions that supported commercial exchange. (See Primary Source: The Merchants of Egypt.)

Environmental Challenges and Fragmentation

Whereas western Europe experienced a climatic dark age between 500 and 900 CE (see Chapter 9), severe conditions—freezing temperatures and lack of rainfall—afflicted the eastern Mediterranean and the Islamic lands of Mesopotamia, the Iranian plateau, and the steppe region of central Asia in the late eleventh and early twelfth centuries. The Nile's low water levels devastated Egypt, the breadbasket for much of the area. No less than one-quarter of the summer floods that normally brought sediment-enriching deposits to Egypt's soils and guaranteed abundant harvests were utter failures in this period. Turkish nomadic pastoralists poured out of the steppe lands of central Asia, driven by drought, in search of better lands, wreaking political and economic havoc everywhere they invaded.

The Seljuk Turks entered the Iranian plateau in 1029, bringing an end to the magnificent cultural flourishing of the first half of the eleventh century (see Chapter 9). Seljuk warriors invaded Baghdad in 1055, establishing a nomadic state in Mesopotamia over a once powerful Abbasid state that now lacked the resources to defend its lands and its peoples, weakened by famines and pestilence. The invaders destroyed institutions of learning and public libraries and looted the region's antiquities. Nor was the Byzantine Empire spared.

The Merchants of Egypt

The most comprehensive collection of eleventh- and twelfth-century commercial materials from the Islamic world comes from a repository, known as a geniza, connected to the Jewish synagogue in Cairo. (It was the custom of the Jewish community to preserve, in a special storeroom, all texts that mention God.) These papers, a rich source of information about the Jewish community in Egypt at that time, touch on all manner of activities: cultural, religious, judicial, political, and commercial. The following letter is addressed to Joseph ibn 'Awkal, one of Egypt's leading merchants in the eleventh century.

Dear and beloved elder and leader, may God prolong your life, never take away your rank, and increase his favors and benefactions to you.

I inform you, my elder, that I have arrived safely. I have written you a letter before, but have seen no answer. Happy preoccupations—I hope. In that letter I provided you with all the necessary information.

I loaded nine pieces of antimony (kohl), five in baskets and four in complete pieces, on the boat of Ibn Jubār—may God keep it; these are for you personally, sent by Mūsā Ibn al-Majjānī. On this boat, I have in partnership with you—may God keep you—a load of cast copper, a basket with (copper) fragments, and two pieces of antimony. I hope God will grant their safe arrival. Kindly take delivery of everything, my lord.

I have also sent with Banāna a camel load for you from Ibn al-Majjānī and a camel load for me in partnership with you—may God keep you. He also carries another partnership of mine, namely, with 'Ammār Ibn Yijū, four small jugs (of oil).

With Abū Zayd I have a shipload of tin in partnership with Salāma al-Mahdawī. Your share in this partnership with him is fifty pounds. I also have seventeen small jugs of s[oap]. I hope they arrive safely. They belong to a man [called . . .] r b. Salmūn, who entrusted them to me at his own risk. Also a bundle of hammered copper, belonging to [a Muslim] man from the Maghreb, called Abū Bakr Ibn Rizq Allah. Two other bundles, on one is written Abraham, on the other M[. . .]. I agreed with the shipowner that he would transport the goods to their destination. I wish my brother Abū Nasr—may God preserve him—to take care of all the goods and carry them to his place until I shall arrive, if God wills.

Please sell the tin for me at whatever price God may grant and leave its "purse" (the money received for it) until my arrival. I am ready to travel, but must stay until I can unload the tar and oil from the ships.

Please take care of this matter and take from him the price of five skins (filled with oil). The account is with Salāma.

Al-Sabbāgh of Tripoli has bribed Bu 'l-'Al ā the agent, and I shall unload my goods soon.

Kindest regards to your noble self and to my master [. . . and] Abu 'l-Fadl, may God keep them.

QUESTIONS FOR ANALYSIS

- List all the different kinds of commodities that the letter talks about.
- How many different people are named as owners, partners, dealers, and agents?
- What does the letter reveal about the ties among merchants and about how they conducted their business?

Source: Letters of Medieval Jewish Traders, translated with introductions and notes by S. D. Goitein (Princeton, NJ: Princeton University Press, 1973), pp. 85–87.

Constantinople, once with a population of 1 million, saw its numbers dwindle to 200,000 by the late eleventh century; yet it was still Europe's largest city.

Political Divisions

These environmental challenges also caused Islam's political institutions to fragment just when it appeared that Shiism would be the vehicle for uniting the Islamic world. The Fatimid Shiites had established their authority over Egypt and much of North Africa (see Chapter 9), and the Abbasid state in Baghdad was controlled by a Shiite family, the Buyids. Each group created universities, in Cairo and Baghdad, respectively, ensuring that leading centers of higher learning were Shiite. But divisions also sapped Shiism, as Sunni Muslims began to challenge Shiite power and establish their own strongholds. In Baghdad, the Buyid family surrendered to a group of Sunni strongmen in 1055. A century later, the last of the Shiite Fatimid rulers gave way to a new Sunni regime in Egypt (see Map 10.2).

The new strongmen were mainly Turks. Their people had been migrating into the Islamic heartland from the Asian

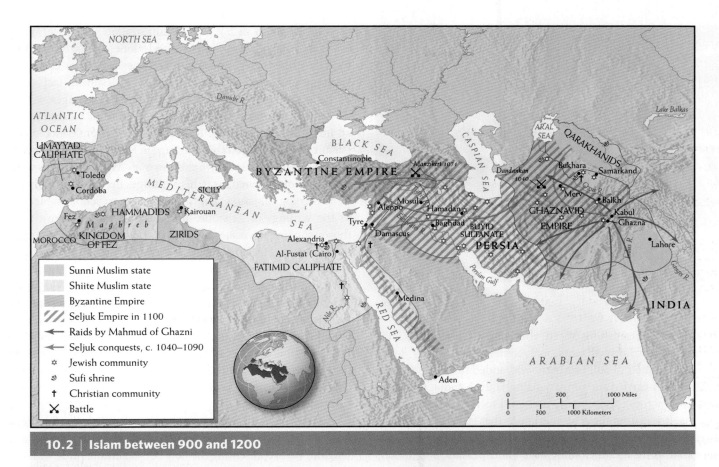

10.2 | Islam between 900 and 1200

The Muslim world experienced political disintegration in the first centuries of the second millennium.

- According to the map key, what were the two major types of Muslim states in this period and what were the two major empires?
- What were the sources of instability in this period according to the map?
- As Islam continued to expand in this period, what challenges did it face?

steppes since the eighth century CE, bringing superior military skills and an intense devotion to Sunni Islam. Once established in Baghdad, they founded outposts in Syria and Palestine and then moved into Anatolia after defeating Byzantine forces in 1071. But this Turkish state also crumbled, as tribesmen quarreled for preeminence.

By the thirteenth century, the Islamic heartland had fractured into three regions. In the east (central Asia, Iran, and eastern Iraq), the remnants of the old Abbasid state persevered. Caliphs succeeded one another, still claiming to speak for all of Islam yet deferring to their Turkish military commanders. In the core of the Islamic world—Egypt, Syria, and the Arabian Peninsula—where Arabic was the primary tongue, military men of non-Arab origin held the reins of power. Farther west in North Africa, Arab rulers prevailed, but the influence of Berbers, some from the northern Sahara, was extensive. Islam was a vibrant faith, but its political systems were splintered.

The Spread of Sufism

Even in the face of political splintering, Islam's spread was facilitated by a popular form of the religion, highly mystical and communal, called **Sufism**. The term *Sufi* comes from the Arabic word for wool (*suf*), which many of the early mystics wrapped themselves in to mark their penitence. Seeking closer union with God, they also performed ecstatic rituals, such as repeating over and over again the name of God. In time, groups of devotees gathered to read aloud the Quran and other religious tracts. Sufi mystics' desire to experience God's love found ready expression in poetry. Most admired of Islam's mystic poets was Jalal al-Din Rumi (1207–1273), spiritual founder of the Mevlevi Sufi order that became famous for the ceremonial dancing of its whirling devotees, known as dervishes.

Although many *ulama* (scholars) despised the Sufis and loathed their seeming lack of theological rigor, the movement

Dervishes. *Today, the whirling dance of dervishes is a tourist attraction, as shown in this picture from the Jerash Cultural Festival in Jordan. Though Sufis in the early second millennium were not this neatly dressed, the whirling dance was an important means of reaching union with God.*

spread with astonishing speed and offered a unifying force within Islam. Sufism's emotional content and strong social bonds, sustained in Sufi brotherhoods, added to its appeal. Sufi missionaries carried the universalizing faith to India, to Southeast Asia, across the Sahara Desert, and to many other distant regions. It was from these brotherhoods that Islam became truly a religion of the people. As trade increased and more converts appeared in the Islamic lands, urban and peasant populations came to understand the faith practiced by the political, commercial, and scholarly upper classes even while they remained attached to their Sufi brotherhood ways. Over time, Islam became even more accommodating, embracing Persian literature, Turkish ruling skills, and Arabic-language contributions in law, religion, literature, and science.

What Was Islam?

Buoyed by Arab dhows on the high seas and carried on the backs of camels following commercial networks, Islam had been transformed from Muhammad's original goal of creating a religion for Arab peoples. By 1300, its influence spanned Afro-Eurasia and enjoyed multitudes of non-Arab converts. (See Map 10.3.) It attracted urbanites and rural peasants alike, as well as its original audience of desert nomads. Its extraordinary universal appeal generated an intense Islamic cultural flowering around 1000 CE.

Some people worried about the preservation of Islam's true nature as, for example, Arabic ceased to be the language of many Islamic believers. True, the devout read and recited the Quran in its original tongue, as the religion mandated. But Persian was now the language of Muslim philosophy and art, and Turkish

was the language of law and administration. Moreover, Jerusalem and Baghdad no longer stood alone as Islamic cultural capitals. Other cities, housing universities and other centers of learning, promoted alternative versions of Islam. In fact, some of the most dynamic thought came from Islam's fringes.

At the same time, diversity fostered cultural blossoming in all fields of high learning. Indicative of the prominence of the Islamic faith and the Arabic language in thought was the legendary Ibn Rushd (1126–1198). Known as Averroës in the west, where scholars pored over his writings, he wrestled with the same theological issues that troubled western scholars. Steeped in the writings of Aristotle, Ibn Rushd became Islam's most thoroughgoing advocate for the use of reason in understanding the universe. His knowledge of Aristotle was so great that it influenced the thinking of the Christian world's leading philosopher and theologian, Thomas Aquinas (1225–1274). Above all, Ibn Rushd believed that faith and reason could be compatible. He also argued for a social hierarchy in which learned men would command influence akin to Confucian scholars in China or Greek philosophers in Athens. Ibn Rushd believed that the proper forms of reasoning had to be entrusted to the educated class—in the case of Islam, the *ulama*—who would serve the common people.

Equally powerful works appeared in Persian, which by now was expressing the most sophisticated ideas of culture and religion. Best representing the new Persian ethnic pride was Abu al-Qasim Firdawsi (920–1020), a devout Muslim who believed in the importance of pre-Islamic Sasanian traditions. In the epic poem *Shah Namah,* or *Book of Kings,* he celebrated the origins of Persian culture and narrated the history of the Iranian highland peoples from the dawn of time to the Muslim conquest. As part of his effort to extol a pure Persian culture, Firdawsi attempted to compose his entire poem in Persian, unblemished by other languages and even avoiding Arabic words.

The Islamic world's achievements in science were truly remarkable. Its scholars were at the pinnacle of scientific knowledge throughout the world in this era. In truth, the "Islamic sciences"—law, study of the Quran, traditions of the Prophet (*hadith*), theology, poetry, and the Arabic language—held primacy among the learned classes. In contrast, "foreign sciences" (later called the natural sciences in Europe) were held in lower esteem. Even so, Ibn al-Shatir (1304–1375), working on his own in Damascus, produced non-Ptolemaic models of the universe that later researchers noted were mathematically equivalent to those of Copernicus. Even earlier, the Maragha school of astronomers (1259 and later) in western Iran had produced a non-Ptolemaic model of the planets. Some historians of science believe that Copernicus must have seen an Arabic manuscript written by a thirteenth-century Persian astronomer that contained a table of the movements of the planets. In addition,

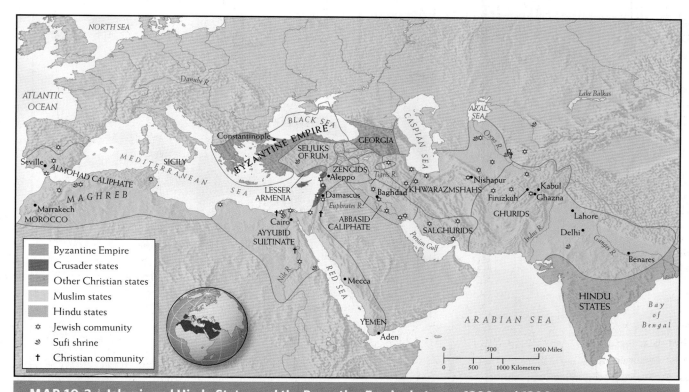

MAP 10.3 | Islamic and Hindu States and the Byzantine Empire between 1200 and 1300

Islam continued to expand after the thirteenth century.

- Where were its largest and most important gains according to the map?
- How did other religions fare under Islamic rule in this period?
- How was Islam able to continue to expand in this period?

scholars in the Islamic world produced works in medicine, optics, and mathematics as well as astronomy that were in advance of the achievements of Greek and Roman scholars.

By the fourteenth century, Islam had achieved what early converts would have considered unthinkable. No longer a religion of a minority of peoples living among Christian, Zoroastrian, and Jewish communities, it had become the people's faith. The agents of conversion were mainly Sufi saints and Sufi brotherhoods—not the *ulama,* whose exhortations had little impact on common people. The Sufis had carried their faith far and wide to North African Berbers, to Anatolian villagers, and to West African animists who believed that things in nature have souls. Ibn Rushd worried about the growing appeal of what he considered an "irrational" piety. But his message failed, because he did not appreciate that Islam's expansionist powers rested on its appeal to common folk. While the *sharia* was the core of Islam for the educated and scholarly classes, Sufism spoke to ordinary men and women.

During this period, Islam became one of the four cultural spheres that would play a major role in world history. Islam became the majority religion of most of the inhabitants of Southwest Asia and North Africa, Arabic became the everyday language for most people, and the Turks began to establish themselves as the dominant rulership force, ultimately creating the Ottoman Empire, which would last into the twentieth century. The Islamic world became integral in transregional trade and the creation and maintenance of knowledge.

INDIA AS A CULTURAL MOSAIC

Trade and migration affected India, just as it did the rest of Asia and Africa. As in the case of Islam, India's growing cultural interconnections and increasing prosperity produced little political integration. Under the canopy of Hinduism it remained a cultural mosaic; Islamic faith now joined others to make the region even more diverse. (See Map 10.4.) India illustrates how cross-cultural integration can just as easily preserve diversity as promote internal unity.

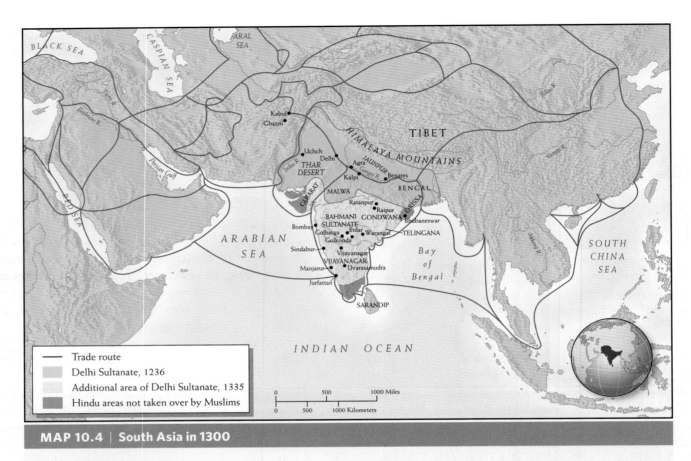

MAP 10.4 | South Asia in 1300

As the fourteenth century began, India was a blend of many cultures. Politically, the Turkish Muslim regime of the Delhi Sultanate dominated the region.

- Use the key to the map to identify the areas dominated by the Delhi Sultanate.
- How do you suppose the trade routes helped to spread the Muslims' influence in India?
- Now use the key to find the Hindu areas. Based on your reading, what factors accounted for Hinduism's continued appeal despite the Muslims' political power?

With its pivotal location along land- and sea-based routes, India became an intersection for the trade, migration, and culture of Afro-Eurasian peoples. With 80 million inhabitants in 1000 CE, it had the second-largest population in the region, not far behind China's 120 million. (See Analyzing Global Developments: Growth in the World Population to 1340.) Turks ultimately spilled into India as they had the Islamic heartlands, bringing their newfound Islamic beliefs. But the Turkish newcomers encountered an ethnic and religious mix of which they were just one part.

Before the Turks arrived, India had been splintered among rival chiefs called *rajas*. These leaders gained support from high-caste Brahmans by doling out land grants to them. Since much of the land was uncultivated, the Brahmans first built temples, then converted the indigenous hunter-gatherer peoples to the Hindu faith, and finally taught the converts how to cultivate the land. In this way the Brahmans simultaneously spread their

faith and expanded the agrarian tax base for themselves and the rajas. They also repaid the rajas' support by compiling elaborate genealogies for them and endowing them with legitimizing ancestries. In return, the rajas demonstrated that they, too, were well versed in Sanskrit culture and were prepared to patronize artists and poets. Ultimately, many of the warriors and their heirs became Indian rajas.

Invasions and Consolidations

When the Turkish warlords began entering India, South Asia's rulers, the rajas, had neither the will nor the resources to resist them after centuries of fighting off invaders. The most powerful and enduring of the Turkish Muslim regimes of northern India was the **Delhi Sultanate** (1206–1526), whose rulers brought political integration but also strengthened the cultural

Hindu Temple. *When Buddhism started to decline in India, Hinduism was on the rise. Numerous Hindu temples were built, many of them adorned with ornate carvings like this small tenth-century temple in Bhubaneshwar, in eastern India.*

of Arab traders. The Delhi Sultanate was a rich and powerful regime that brought political integration but did not enforce cultural homogeneity.

What Was India?

During the eleventh, twelfth, and thirteenth centuries, India became the most diverse and, in some respects, most tolerant region in Afro-Eurasia. India in this era arose as an impressive but fragile mosaic of cultures, religions, and ethnicities.

When the Turks arrived, the local Hindu population, having had much experience with foreign invaders and immigrants, assimilated these intruders as they had done earlier peoples. Before long, the newcomers thought of themselves as Indians who, however, retained their Islamic beliefs and steppe ways. They continued to wear their distinctive trousers and robes and flaunted their horse-riding skills. At the same time, the local population embraced some of their conquerors' ways, donning the tunics and trousers that characterized central Asian peoples.

Diversity and cultural mixing became most visible in the multiple languages that flourished in India. Although the sultans spoke Turkish languages, they regarded Persian literature as a high cultural achievement and made Persian their courtly and administrative language. Meanwhile, most Hindu subjects spoke local languages, followed their caste regulations, and practiced diverse forms of Hindu worship. The rulers did what Muslim rulers in Southwest Asia and the

diversity and tolerance that were a hallmark of the Indian social order. Sultans recruited local artisans for building projects, and palaces and mosques became displays of Indian architectural tastes adopted by Turkish newcomers. But the sultans did not force their subjects to convert, so South Asia never became an Islamic-dominant region. Nor did they display much interest in the flourishing commercial life along the Indian coast, permitting these areas to develop on their own and allowing Persian Zoroastrian traders to settle around modern-day Mumbai (Bombay). Farther south, the Malabar coast became the preserve

Lodi Gardens. *The Lodi dynasty was the last dynasty of the Delhi Sultanate. Lodi Gardens, the cemetery of Lodi sultans, placed central Asian Islamic architecture in an Indian landscape, thereby creating a scene of "heaven on the earth."*

Mediterranean did with Christian and Jewish communities living in their midst: they collected the *jizya* tax and permitted communities to worship as they saw fit and to administer their own communal law.

Ultimately, Islam in India proved that it did not have to be a conquering religion to prosper. Although Buddhism had been in decline there for centuries, it, too, became part of the cultural intermixing of these centuries. As Vedic Brahmanism evolved into Hinduism (see Chapter 8), it absorbed many Buddhist doctrines and practices, such as *ahimsa* (nonkilling) and vegetarianism. The two religions became so similar that Hindus simply considered the Buddha to be one of their deities—an incarnation of the great god Vishnu. Many Buddhist moral teachings mixed with and became Hindu stories.

Once the initial disruptive effects of the Turkish invasions were absorbed, India remained a highly diverse and tolerant region during this period. Most important, it emerged as one of the four major cultural spheres, enjoying a tremendous level of integration as Turkish-Muslim rulership and their traditions and practices successfully blended into the native Hindu society, leading to a more integrated and peaceful India.

Vishnu. *In addition to the Buddha, the four-armed Vishnu has nine other avatars, some of whom are portrayed at his feet in this tenth-century sandstone sculpture.*

SONG CHINA: INSIDERS VERSUS OUTSIDERS

The preeminent world power in 1000 CE was still China, despite its recent turmoil. Once dampened, the turbulence yielded to a long era of stability and splendor that made China a regional engine of Afro-Eurasian prosperity. In 907 CE, the Tang dynasty splintered into regional kingdoms, mostly led by military generals. In 960 CE, one of these generals ended the fragmentation, reunified China, and assumed the mandate of heaven for the Song dynasty (960–1279). (See Maps 10.5 and 10.6.) Ultimately, a nomadic group, the Jurchen (ancestors of the Manchu, who would rule China from the seventeenth until the twentieth century), would bring the Song dynasty to an end, but not before Song influence had fanned out into Southeast Asia, helping to create new identities in the political systems there.

Economic Progress

China, like India and the Islamic world, participated in Afro-Eurasia's powerful long-distance trade. Chinese merchants were as energetic as their Muslim and Indian counterparts. Yet China's commercial successes could not have occurred without the country's strong agrarian base—especially its vast wheat, millet, and rice fields, which fed a population that reached 120 million. Agriculture benefited from breakthroughs in metalworking that produced stronger iron plows, which the Song harnessed to sturdy water buffalo to extend the agricultural frontier.

Manufacturing also flourished. In 1078, for example, total Song iron production reached between 75,000 and 150,000 tons, roughly the equivalent of European iron production in the early eighteenth century. The Chinese piston-driven bellows that provided forced air for furnaces were of a size unsurpassed until the nineteenth century. Also, in the early tenth century, Chinese alchemists mixed saltpeter with sulfur and charcoal to produce a product that would burn and that could be deployed on the battlefield: gunpowder. Song entrepreneurs were soon inventing a remarkable array of incendiary devices that flowed from their mastery of techniques for controlling explosions and high heat. Moreover, artisans produced increasingly light, durable, and exquisitely beautiful porcelains. Before long, their porcelain (now called "china") was the envy of all Afro-Eurasia. Also unspooling from the artisans' hands were vast amounts of clothing and handicrafts, made from the fibers grown by Song farmers. In effect, the Song Chinese oversaw the world's first manufacturing revolution, producing finished goods on a large scale for consumption far and wide.

MONEY AND INFLATION Expanding commerce transformed the role of money and its wide circulation. By now the

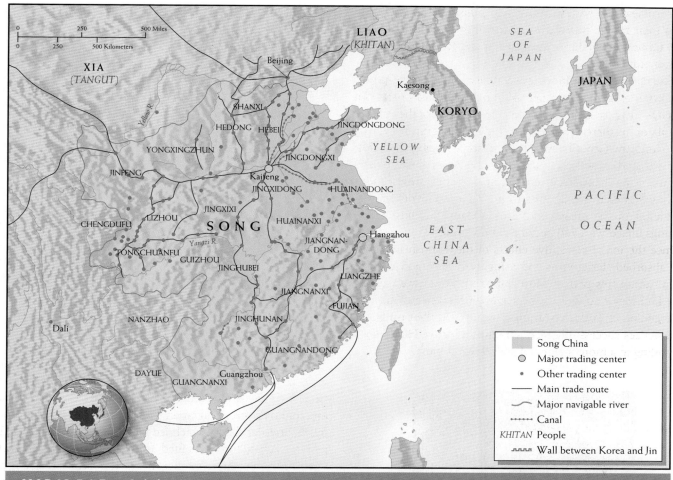

MAP 10.5 | East Asia in 1000

Several states emerged in East Asia between 1000 and 1300, but none were as strong as the Song dynasty in China.

- Using the key to the map, try to identify the factors that contributed to the Song state's economic dynamism.
- What external factors kept the Song dynasty from completely securing its reign?
- What factors drove the Chinese commercial revolution in this period?

Song government was annually minting nearly 2 million strings of currency, each containing 1,000 copper coins. In fact, as the economy grew, the supply of metal currency could not match the demand. One result was East Asia's thirst for gold from East Africa. At the same time, merchant guilds in northwestern Shanxi developed the first letters of exchange, called **flying cash**. These letters linked northern traders with their colleagues in the south. Before long, printed money had eclipsed coins. Even the government collected more than half its tax revenues in cash rather than grain and cloth. The government also issued more notes to pay its bills—a practice that ultimately contributed to the world's first case of runaway inflation.

New Elites

Song emperors ushered in a period of social and cultural vitality. They built on Tang institutions by expanding a central bureaucracy of scholar-officials chosen through competitive civil service examinations. Zhao Kuangyin, or Emperor Taizu (r. 960–976 CE), himself administered the final test for all who had passed the highest-level palace examination. In subsequent dynasties, the emperor was the nation's premier examiner, symbolically demanding oaths of allegiance from successful candidates. By 1100, these ranks of learned men had accumulated sufficient power to become China's new ruling elite.

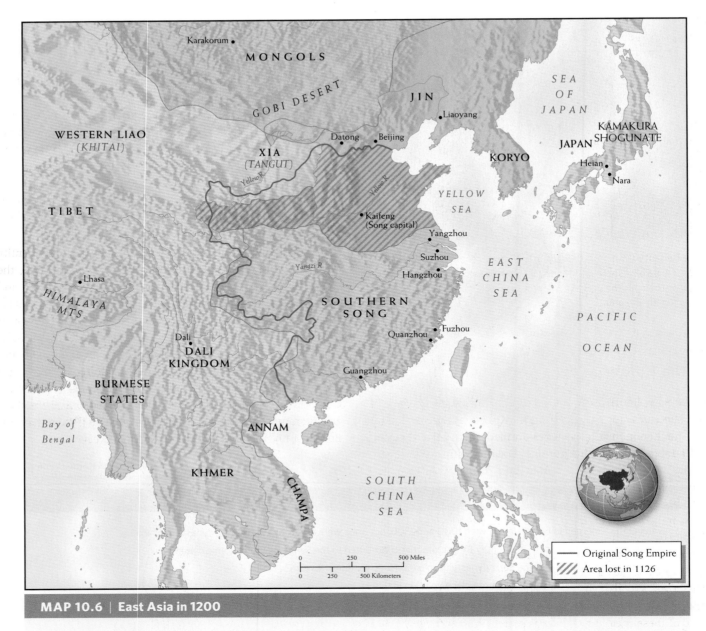

MAP 10.6 | East Asia in 1200

The Song dynasty regularly dealt with "barbarian" neighbors.

- What were the major "barbarian" tribes during this period?
- Approximately what percentage of Song China was lost to the Jin in 1126?
- How did the "barbarian" tribes affect the Han Chinese identity in this period?

Expansion of the civil service examination system was crucial to a shift in power from the still powerful hereditary aristocracy to a less wealthy but more highly schooled class of scholar-officials. Consider the career of the Northern Song reformer Wang Anshi (1021–1086), who ascended to power from a commoner family outside of Hangzhou in the east. He owed his success to gaining high marks in Song state examinations—a not insignificant achievement, for in nearby Fujian Province alone, of the roughly 18,000 candidates who gathered triennially to take the provincial examination, over 90 percent failed! After gaining the emperor's ear, Wang eventually challenged the political and cultural influence of the old Tang dynasty elites from the northwest.

Song Dynasty Coin. *The Song dynasty's rapid economic development led to the use of vast amounts of metal currency, including many copper coins like this one. The hole in the center meant that the coins could be strung together in groups.*

Negotiating with Nomads on the Borderlands

As the Song flourished, nomads on the outskirts eyed the Chinese successes closely. To the north, Khitan, Tungusic, Tangut, and Jurchen nomadic societies formed their own dynasties and adopted Chinese institutions. Located within the "greater China," as defined by the Han and Tang dynasties, these non-Chinese nomads saw China proper as an object of both conquest and emulation.

In military power the Song dynasts were relatively weak. Despite their sophisticated weapons, they could not match their enemies on the steppe when the latter united against them. Steel tips improved the arrows that the Song soldiers shot from their crossbows, and flamethrowers and "crouching tiger catapults" sent incendiary bombs streaking into their enemies' ranks. But none of these breakthroughs was secret. Warrior neighbors on the steppe mastered the new arts of war more fully than did the Song dynasts themselves.

China's strength as a manufacturing powerhouse made economic diplomacy an option, so the Song relied on "gifts" and generous trade agreements with the borderlanders. For example, after losing North China to the Khitan Liao dynasty, the Song agreed to make annual payments of 100,000 ounces of silver and 200,000 bolts of silk. The treaty allowed them to live in relative peace for more than a century. Securing peace meant emptying the state coffers and then printing more paper money. The resulting inflation added economic instability to military weakness, making the Song an easy target when Jurchen invaders made their final assault.

What Was China?

Paradoxically, the increasing exchange between outsiders and insiders within China hardened the lines that divided them and gave residents of China's interior a highly developed sense of themselves as a distinctive people possessing a superior culture. Exchanges with outsiders nurtured a "Chinese" identity among those who considered themselves true insiders and referred to themselves as Han. Driven south from their ancient homeland in the eleventh century, they grew increasingly suspicious and resentful toward the outsiders living in their midst. They called these outsiders "barbarians" and treated them accordingly.

Vital in crystallizing this sense of a distinct Chinese identity was print culture. Of all Afro-Eurasian societies in 1300, the Chinese were the most advanced in their use of printing and book publishing and circulation. Moreover, their books established classical Chinese as the common language of educated classes in East Asia. The Song government used its plentiful supply of paper to print books, especially medical texts, and to distribute calendars. The private publishing industry also expanded. Printing houses throughout the country produced Confucian classics, works on history, philosophical treatises, and literature—all of which figured in the civil examinations. Buddhist publications, too, were available everywhere.

Wang Anshi. *He owed his rise from a commoner family to a powerful position as a reformer to the Song state examinations.*

Chinese and Barbarian. *After losing the north, the Han Chinese grew resentful of outsiders. They drew a dividing line between their own agrarian society and the nomadic warriors, calling them "barbarians." Such identities were not fixed, however. Chinese and so-called barbarians were mutually dependent.*

In many respects, the Song period represented China's greatest age. China's resources, its huge population base coupled with a strong agrarian economy, and its strong foreign trade and diplomatic relations made it the most wealthy among the four major cultural spheres; its common language and its transfer of power to nonhereditary Confucian scholars made it the most unified. The country's bureaucracy was the largest in the world, totaling between 200,000 and 300,000 civil servants during the Song period, of whom 20,000 were high officials. No society had larger cities or a more urbanized population. In mid-Song times, an estimated 5 percent of its people lived in cities. The capital, Kaifeng, had a population of 1 million; 30 cities varied in size from 40,000 to 100,000 or more; 60 cities had about 15,000 residents; and 400 cities, mainly county seats and smaller prefectural centers, had populations ranging between 4,000 and 5,000.

Yet in spite of its great wealth, immense population, highly developed bureaucracy, and powerful military forces, the Han Chinese never felt secure from the strong nomadic pastoralists who inhabited the western and northern frontiers. The construction of walls in the north and military outposts along the frontiers never seemed to afford complete protection. Especially when dynastic regimes weakened, China was vulnerable to invasion and conquest by these well-armed tribal confederacies. They moved south into China proper whenever the Chinese dynasty faltered and environmental conditions drove the militarily skilled nomads in search of better lives.

CHINA'S NEIGHBORS ADAPT TO CHANGE

Feeling the pull of China's economic and political gravity, cultures around China consolidated their own internal political authority and defined their own identities in order to keep from being swallowed up. At the same time, they increased their commercial transactions.

The Rise of Warriors in Japan

Japan, like China, laid many political and cultural foundations for its later development in the three centuries between 1000 and 1300. Not only did its leaders distance themselves from Chinese influences, but they also developed a strong sense of their islands' distinctive identity. Even so, the long-standing dominance of Chinese ways remained apparent at virtually every level of Japanese society and was most pronounced at the imperial court in the capital city of Heian, present-day Kyoto. (See Primary Source: The Tale of Genji.) The city itself, founded in 795 CE, was modeled after the former Tang Chinese capital city of Chang'an.

Outside Kyoto, however, a less China-centered way of life existed and began to impose itself on the center. Here, local notables, mainly military leaders and large landowners, began to challenge the imperial court for dominance. These military adventurers nevertheless elected to keep the Japanese emperors and their court at Kyoto in office even while stripping them of real power; Japan continued to have an emperor residing at the imperial city of Kyoto right down to 1868, when the Meiji restoration took place (see Chapter 17).

The emergence of these military men marked the arrival of an important new social group in Japanese society—the warriors, or samurai. In lightweight leather armor, these expert horsemen defended their private estates with remarkable long-range bowmanship and superbly crafted single-edged long steel swords, lethal for close combat in warfare. The warriors also brought an idealization of their martial ethics, with an emphasis on loyalty, self-discipline, and a simple life tied to the land, which helped to shape Japanese society until recent times.

By the beginning of the fourteenth century, Japan had multiple sources of political and cultural power: an endangered and declining aristocracy; an imperial family with prestige but little authority; powerful landowning notables based in the provinces; and a rising and increasingly ambitious class of samurai. This yielded a combustible mix of refined high culture in the capital versus a warrior ethos in the provinces. Such a mix produced social intrigue in politics and led different provincial factions to vie with one another for preeminence.

The Tale of Genji

Lacking a written language of their own, Heian aristocrats adopted classical Chinese as the official written language while continuing to speak Japanese. Men at the court took great pains to master the Chinese literary forms, but Japanese court ladies were not expected to do so. Lady Murasaki Shikibu, the author of The Tale of Genji, hid her knowledge of Chinese, fearing that she would be criticized. In the meantime, the Japanese developed a native syllabary (a table of syllables) based on Chinese written graphs. Using this syllabary, Murasaki kept a diary in Japanese that gave vivid accounts of Heian court life. Her story— possibly the world's first novel—relates the adventures of a dashing young courtier named Genji. In the passage below, Genji evidently speaks for Murasaki in explaining why fiction can be as truthful as a work of history in capturing human life and its historical significance.

Genji . . . smiled, and went on: "But I have a theory of my own about what this art of the novel is, and how it came into being. To begin with, it does not simply consist in the author's telling a story about the adventures of some other person. On the contrary, it happens because the storyteller's own experience of men and things, whether for good or ill—not only what he has passed through himself, but even events which he has only witnessed or been told of—has moved him to an emotion so passionate that he can no longer keep it shut up in his heart. Again and again something in his own life or in that around him will seem to the writer so important that he cannot bear to let it pass into oblivion. There must never come a time, he feels, when men do not know about it. That is my view of how this art arose.

"Clearly then, it is no part of the story-teller's craft to describe only what is good or beautiful. Sometimes, of course, virtue will be his theme, and he may then make such play with it as he will. But he is just as likely to have been struck by numerous examples of vice and folly in the world around him, and about them he has exactly the same feelings as about the pre-eminently good deeds which he encounters: they are more important and must all be garnered in. Thus anything whatsoever may become the subject of a novel, provided only that it happens in this mundane life and not in some fairyland beyond our human ken.

"The outward forms of this art will not of course be everywhere the same. At the court of China and in other foreign lands both the genius of the writers and their actual methods of composition are necessarily very different from ours; and even here in Japan the art of storytelling has in course of time undergone great changes. There will, too, always be a distinction between the lighter and the more serious forms of fiction. . . . So too, I think, may it be said that the art of fiction must not lose our allegiance because, in the pursuit of the main purpose to which I have alluded above, it sets virtue by the side of vice, or mingles wisdom with folly. Viewed in this light the novel is seen to be not, as is usually supposed, a mixture of useful truth with idle invention, but something which at every stage and in every part has a definite and serious purpose."

QUESTIONS FOR ANALYSIS

- According to this passage, what motivates an author to write a story (that is, fiction)?
- Genji feels it is appropriate for a writer to address not only "what is good or beautiful" but also "vice and folly." What explanation does he give? Do you agree?

Source: *Sources of Japanese Tradition*, compiled by Ryūsaku Tsunoda, William Theodore de Bary, and Donald Keene (New York: Columbia University Press, 1964), vol. 1, pp. 177–79.

Southeast Asia: A Maritime Mosaic

Southeast Asia, like India, now became a crossroads of Afro-Eurasian influences. Its sparse population of probably around 10 million in 1000 CE—tiny compared with that of China and India—was not immune to the foreign influences riding the sea-lanes into the archipelago. The Malay Peninsula became home to many trading ports and stopovers for traders shuttling between India and China, because it connected the Bay of Bengal and the Indian Ocean with the South China Sea. (See Map 10.7.)

Indian influence had been prominent both on the Asian mainland and in island portions of Southeast Asia since 800 CE, but Islamic expansion into the islands after 1200 gradually superseded these influences. Only Bali and a few other islands far to the east of Malaya preserved their Brahmanic-Vedic religious

Heiji Rebellion. *This illustration from the Kamakura Shogunate (1185–1333) depicts a battle during the Heiji Rebellion, which was fought between rival subjects of the cloistered emperor Go-Shirakawa in 1159. Riding in full armor on horseback, the fighters on both sides are armed with devastating long bows.*

origins. Elsewhere in Java and Sumatra, Islam became the dominant religion. In Vietnam and northern portions of mainland Southeast Asia, Chinese cultural influences and northern schools of Mahayana Buddhism were especially prominent.

During this period, Cambodian, Burmese, and Thai peoples founded powerful mixed polities along the Mekong, Salween, Chao Phraya, and Irrawaddy River basins of the Asian mainland. Important Vedic and Buddhist kingdoms emerged here as political buffers between the strong states in China and India and brought stability and further commercial prosperity to the region.

Consider the kingdom that ruled Angkor in present-day Cambodia. With their capital in Angkor, the Khmers (889–1431) created the most powerful and wealthy empire in Southeast Asia. Countless water reservoirs enabled them to flourish on the great plain to the west of the Mekong River after the loss of eastern territories. Public works and magnificent temples dedicated to the revived Vedic gods from India went hand in hand with the earlier influence of Indian Buddhism. Eventually, the Khmer kings united adjacent kingdoms and extended Khmer influence to the Thai and Burmese states along the Chao Phraya and Irrawaddy Rivers.

Angkor Wat. *Mistaken by later European explorers as a remnant of Alexander the Great's conquests, the enormous temple complexes built by the Khmer people in Angkor borrowed their intricate layout and stupa architecture from the Brahmanist Indian temples of the time. (A stupa is a moundlike structure containing religious relics.) As the capital, Angkor was a microcosm of the world for the Khmer, who aspired to represent the macrocosm of the universe in the magnificence of Angkor's buildings and their geometric layout.*

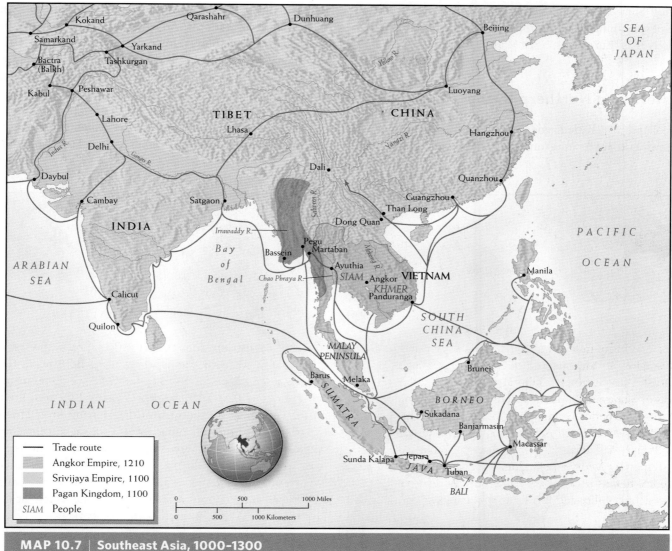

MAP 10.7 | Southeast Asia, 1000–1300

Cross-cultural influences affected Southeast Asian societies during this period.

• What makes Southeast Asia unique geographically compared with other regions of the world?

• Based on the map, why were the kingdoms of Southeast Asia exposed to so many cross-cultural influences?

• In this chapter, the term *mosaic* describes both South and Southeast Asia. Compare Map 10.4 with this map, and explain how the mosaic of Southeast Asia differed from the mosaic of India.

One of the greatest temple complexes in Angkor exemplified the Khmers' heavy borrowing from Vedic Indian architecture. Angkor aspired to represent the universe in the magnificence of its buildings. As signs of the ruler's power, the pagodas, pyramids, and terra-cotta friezes (ornamented walls) presented the life of the gods on earth. The crowning structure of the royal palace was the magnificent temple of Angkor Wat, possibly the largest religious structure ever built. In ornate detail and with great artistry, its buildings and statues represented the revival of the Hindu pantheon within the Khmer royal state.

CHRISTIAN EUROPE

Europe from 1000 to 1300 was a region of strong contrasts. Intensely localized power was balanced by a shared sense of Europe's place in the world, especially with respect to Christian identity. Some inhabitants even began to believe in the existence of something called "Europe" and increasingly referred to themselves as "Europeans." (See Map 10.8.)

Western and Northern Europe

The collapse of Charlemagne's empire had exposed much of northern Europe to invasion, principally from the Vikings, and left the peasantry with no central authority to protect them from local warlords. Armed with deadly weapons, these strongmen collected taxes, imposed forced labor, and became the unchallenged rulers of society. Within this growing warrior aristocracy, northern France led the way. The Franks (later called Frenchmen) were the trendsetters of eleventh- and twelfth-century western Europe.

The most important change was the peasantry's subjugation to these strongmen, many of whom became large landholders.

MAP 10.8 | Latin Christendom in 1300

Catholic Europe expanded geographically and integrated culturally during this era.

- According to this map, into what areas did western Christendom successfully expand?
- What factors contributed to the growth of a widespread common culture and shared ideas?
- How did long-distance trade shape the history of the region during this time?

Previously, well-to-do peasants had carried arms as "free" men. The moment the farmers lost the right to carry arms, they were no longer free. They slipped back to being mere agricultural laborers. Each peasant toiled under the authority of a landholding lord, who controlled every detail of his or her life. This was the basis of a system now called **manorialism**.

This landholding manorial class emerged around the Mediterranean basin as the Roman Empire declined in the west and the Byzantine Empire rose in the east. In both regions, important individuals in the imperial bureaucracies were granted land in payment for their service. Many turned the imperial system's large supply of slaves as well as free peasants into dependent workers serving on their estates. Estates valued self-sufficiency, and most became bipartite: the land, owned by the lord, was divided into two units. The lord held one unit, a demesne, on which the peasants had labor, tax, and other service obligations to the lord. The other consisted of small holdings farmed by peasant families for themselves. Estates also had fisheries, mills, and mineral rights. Lords constructed their homes or manors in the villages. Some were large and ornate, though the majority were modest. Many of the wealthy owners preferred to reside in large cities and turned the management of the estate over to administrators.

In lands distant from the Mediterranean, notably England, France, and Germany, manorial villages emerged out of tribal lands. These lands, originally held by chiefs, were distributed to churches and important officials. Here, too, the bipartite division of the land occurred, and here, too, though some estates were huge, nearly two-thirds of the estates were 500 acres or less.

The manorial system provided the economic and territorial foundations of this era. Political and social ties, which formed the basis of what we call **feudalism**, also bound different classes of peoples together. Feudal societies essentially had three orders: those who prayed (the clergy), those who fought (the lords), and those who toiled (the peasants). Each had obligations to the others. Lords were expected to provide protection for peasants and clerics, while clerics promoted an ethical and holy life for all. Peasants provided society's sustenance. What we might call the classic form of feudalism existed only in England, Sicily, and the Holy Land, those lands conquered by Norman warriors in the tenth century CE from their base in Normandy, France. Here, powerful landholding lords, including kings, gave some of their lands to other freemen, called vassals, in return for fealty, or loyalty, and military service. The grant of land was called a fief, and over time these lands, held by the vassals, became private estates that could be passed on to heirs. Elsewhere in Europe, feudal arrangements were not so clear-cut. The handing over of lands from nobles to subordinates, the so-called vassals, was not accompanied by formal ceremonies, the taking of oaths, and the swearing of fealty, as was the case in regions under Norman authority. Nor were the lands held by vassals always known as fiefs, and even the nobles' ownership of these lands was often disputed.

Assured of control of the peasantry, feudal lords and their vassals watched over an agrarian breakthrough—which fueled a commercial transformation that drew Europe into the rest of the global trading networks. Lordly protection and more advanced metal tools like axes and plows, combined with heavier livestock to pull plows through the root-infested sods of northern Europe, led to massive deforestation. Above this clearing activity stood castles, built by powerful lords and sometimes by strong vassals to ensure their regional autonomy. Their threatening presence also enabled lords to collect rents and tithes (shares of crops, earmarked as "donations" for the church) from the peasantry. In this blunt way, the feudal and manorial systems harnessed agrarian energy to their own needs. The population of western

The Bayeux Tapestry. *This tapestry was allegedly prepared by Queen Matilda, wife of William the Conqueror, and her ladies to celebrate the successful invasion of England in 1066. It shows the fascination of the entire "feudal" class, even women, with war. Great horses, tightly meshed chain mail, long shields, and stirrups all made such cavalry warfare possible.*

Olavinlinna Castle. *This castle in Finland was the easternmost extension of a "western" feudal style of rule through great castles. It was built at the very end of the Baltic, to keep away the Russians of Novgorod.*

Europe as a whole leaped forward, most spectacularly in the north. As a result, northern Europe, from England to Poland, ceased to be an underdeveloped "barbarian" appendage of the Mediterranean.

Eastern Europe

Nowhere did pioneering peasants develop more land than in the wide-open spaces of eastern Europe, the region's land of opportunity. Between 1100 and 1200, some 200,000 farmers emigrated from Flanders (in modern Belgium), Holland, and northern Germany to eastern frontiers. Well-watered landscapes covered with vast forests filled up what are now Poland,

the Czech Republic, Hungary, and the Baltic states. "Little Europes," whose castles, churches, and towns echoed the landscape of France, now replaced economies that had been based on gathering honey, hunting, and the slave trade. For 1,000 miles along the Baltic Sea, forest clearings dotted with new farmsteads and small towns edged inward from the coast up the river valleys.

The social structure here was a marriage of convenience between migrating peasants and local elites. The area offered the promise of freedom from the feudal lords' arbitrary justice and imposition of forced labor. Even the harsh landscape of the eastern Baltic (where the sea froze every year and impenetrable forests blocked settlers from the coast) was preferable to life in the feudal west. For their part, the elites of eastern Europe—the nobility of Poland, Bohemia, and Hungary and the princes of the Baltic—wished to live well, in the "French" style. But they could do so only if they attracted workers to their lands by offering newcomers a liberty that they had no hope of enjoying in the west.

The Russian Lands

In Russian lands, western settlers and knights met an eastern brand of Christian devotion. This world looked toward Byzantium, not Rome or western Europe. Russia was a giant borderland between the steppes of Eurasia and the booming centers of Europe. Its cities lay at the crossroads of overland trade and migration, and Kiev became one of the region's greatest cities. Standing on a bluff above the Dnieper River, it straddled newly opened trade routes. With a population exceeding 20,000, including merchants from eastern and western Europe

Saint Sophia Cathedral, Novgorod. *The cathedral of Novgorod (like that of Kiev) was called Hagia Sophia. It was a deliberate imitation of the Hagia Sophia of Constantinople, showing Russia's roots in a glorious Roman/Byzantine past that had nothing to do with western Europe.*

The Birch Bark Letters of Novgorod

The city of Novgorod was a vibrant trading center with a diverse population. From 1951 onward, Russian archaeologists in Novgorod have excavated almost 1,000 letters and accounts scratched on birch bark and preserved in the sodden, frequently frozen ground. Reading them, we realize how timeless people's basic concerns can be.

First, we meet the merchants. Many letters are notes by creditors of the debts owed to them by trading partners. The sums are often expressed in precious animal furs. They contain advice to relatives or to partners in other cities:

> Giorgii sends his respects to his father and mother: Sell the house and come here to Smolensk or to Kiev: for the bread is cheap there.

Then we meet neighborhood disputes:

> From Anna to Klemiata: Help me, my lord brother, in my matter with Konstantin. . . . [For I asked him,] "Why have you been so angry with my sister and her daughter. You called her a cow and her daughter a whore. And now Fedor has thrown them both out of the house."

There are even glimpses of real love. A secret marriage is planned:

> Mikiti to Ulianitza: Come to me. I love you, and you me. Ignato will act as witness.

And a poignant note from a woman was discovered in 1993:

> I have written to you three times. What is it that you hold against me, that you did not come to see me this Sunday? I regarded you as I would my own brother. Did I really offend you by that which I sent to you? If you had been pleased you would have torn yourself away from company and come to me. Write to me. If in my clumsiness I have offended you and you should spurn me, then let God be my judge. I love you.

QUESTIONS FOR ANALYSIS

- What does the range of people writing on birch bark tell us about these people?
- Think of the messages you send to friends and relatives today. Even if texting and e-mailing seem centuries distant from writing on birch bark, can you relate in any way to these ancient letter writers?

Source: A. V. Artsikhovskii and V. I. Borkovski, *Novgorodskie Gramoty na Bereste,* 11 vols. (Moscow: Izd-vo Akademii nauk SSSR, 1951–2004), document nos. 424, 531, 377, and 752.

and Southwest Asia, South Asia, Egypt, and North Africa, Kiev was larger than Paris—larger even than the much-diminished city of Rome.

Kiev looked south to the Black Sea and to Constantinople. Under Iaroslav the Wise (1016–1054), it became a small-scale Constantinople on the Dnieper. A stone church called St. Sophia stood (as in Constantinople) beside the imperial palace. With its distinctive "Byzantine" domes, it was a miniature Hagia Sophia (see Chapter 8). Its highest dome towered 100 feet above the floor, and its splendid mosaics depicting Byzantine saints echoed the religious art of Constantinople. But the message was political as well, for the ruler of Kiev was cast in the mold of the emperor of Constantinople. He now took the title *tsar* from the ancient Roman name given to the emperor, Caesar. From this time onward, *tsar* was the title of rulers in Russia.

The Russian form of Christianity replicated the Byzantine style of churches all along the great rivers leading to the trading cities of the north and northeast. These were not agrarian centers, but hubs of expanding long-distance trade. (See Primary Source: The Birch Bark Letters of Novgorod.) Each city became a small-scale Kiev and a smaller-scale echo of Constantinople. The Orthodox religion looked to Byzantium's Hagia Sophia rather than the Catholic faith associated with the popes in Rome. Russian Christianity remained the Christianity of a borderland—vivid oases of high culture set against the backdrop of vast forests and widely scattered settlements. Like the agricultural manors of western Europe, these Russian cities demonstrated the highly localized nature of power in Europe during this period.

What Was Christian Europe?

Christianity in this era—primarily the Roman Catholicism of the west, but also the Orthodoxy of the east—became a universalizing faith that transformed the region that was becoming known as "Europe." The Christianity of post-Roman Europe had been a religion of monks, and its most dynamic centers were great monasteries. Members of the laity were expected to revere and support their monks, nuns, and clergy, but not to imitate them. By 1200, all this had changed. The internal colonization of western Europe—the clearing of woods and founding of villages—ensured that parish churches arose in all but the wildest landscapes. Their spires were visible and their bells were audible from one valley to the next. Church graveyards were the only places where good Christians could be buried; criminals' and outlaws' bodies piled up in "heathen" graves outside the cemetery walls.

Now the clergy reached more deeply into the private lives of the laity. Marriage and divorce, previously considered family matters, became a full-time preoccupation of the church. And sin was no longer an offense that just "happened"; it was a matter that every person could do something about. Regular confession to a priest became obligatory for all Catholic, western Christians. The followers of Francis of Assisi (1182–1226) emerged as

Saint Francis of Assisi. *In this fresco by the Renaissance artist Giotto, Saint Frances of Assisi is seen renouncing his earthly wealth and embarking on a life of poverty. Saint Francis founded the order that took his name, the Franciscan Order, and promoted his principles of a life of poverty, devotion to the teachings of Jesus Christ, and concern for the poor.*

an order of preachers who brought a message of repentance. Their listeners were to weep, confess their sins to local priests, and strive to be better Christians. Franciscans instilled in the hearts of all believers a Europe-wide Catholicism based on daily remorse and daily contemplation of the sufferings of Christ and his mother, Mary. From Ireland to Riga and Budapest, Catholic Christians came to share a common piety.

UNIVERSITIES AND INTELLECTUALS Vital to the creation of Europe's Christian identity was the emergence of universities, for it was during this era that Europe acquired its first class of intellectuals. Since the late twelfth century, scholars had gathered in Paris, where they formed a *universitas*—a term borrowed from merchant communities, where it denoted a type of union. Those who belonged to the *universitas* enjoyed protection by their fellows and freedom to continue their trade. Similarly protected by their own "union," the scholars of Paris began wrestling with the new learning from Arab lands. When the bishop of Paris forbade this undertaking, they simply moved to the Left Bank of the Seine, so as to place the river between themselves and the bishop's officials, who lived around the Notre Dame Cathedral.

Those scholars were called schoolmen because of the halls—*scholae* in Latin—in which they taught. Their philosophy, scholasticism, sought to render the Christian tradition totally intelligible: God and his creation were penetrable by human reason; they made sense; so did the Bible and the traditions of the church. Teaching took the form of commentaries on the Bible and on the laws of the church (canon law). The aim was to explain every passage in the Bible so that its message could be preached with confidence. The day's teaching began with theology and the Bible—for the mind was freshest in the morning! But this community now involved rational discussions of science, astronomy, and medicine. The greatest poet of the age, the Italian Dante Alighieri (1265–1321), reflects this new expansive view of the universe. In his *Divine Comedy* (1307), he imagined a journey to heaven through hell and purgatory in which every stage—from the punishments of hell through purgatory to the fullness of joy in heaven—reflected the supreme wisdom of God, which human reason could understand and enjoy.

The scholars' ability to organize themselves gave them an advantage that their Arab contemporaries lacked. For all his genius, Ibn Rushd had to spend his life courting the favor of individual monarchs to protect him from conservative fellow Muslims, who frequently burned his books. Ironically, European scholars congregating in Paris could quietly absorb the most persuasive elements of Arabic thought, like Ibn Rushd's. Yet they endeavored to prove that Christianity was the only religion that fully met the aspirations of all rational human beings. Such was the message of many scholars, including the great intellectual Thomas Aquinas, who wrote *Summa contra Gentiles* (Summary of Christian Belief against Non-Christians) in 1264.

Chinese—struggled to define itself. Interestingly, if Ibn Battuta and Marco Polo had been able to travel in the "unknown" worlds—the African hinterlands, the Americas, and Oceania—they would have witnessed to varying degrees similar phenomena and challenges.

Marco Polo. *This medieval painting shows the caravan of Marco Polo's father and uncle crossing Asia.*

Explore Further

Battuta. *The Travels of Ibn Battuta,* translated by H. A. R. Gibb (2002).

Polo, Marco. *The Travels of Marco Polo,* edited by Manuel Komroff, translated by William Marsden (1926).

the high seas. He also used improved navigation technology to enable his ships to sail into deep waters; yet his invasions of Japan from Korea failed in 1274 and 1281. The ill-fated Javanese expedition was his last.

MONGOLS IN THE ISLAMIC WORLD In the thirteenth century, Mongol tribesmen streamed out of the steppes, crossing the whole of Asia and entering the eastern parts of Europe. Möngke Khan, a grandson of Chinggis, made clear the Mongol aspiration for world domination: he appointed his brother Kubilai to rule over China, Tibet, and the northern parts of India; and he commanded another brother, Hulagu, to conquer Iran, Syria, Egypt, Byzantium, and Armenia.

When Hulagu reached Baghdad in 1258, he encountered a feeble foe and a city that was a shadow of its former glorious self. Merely 10,000 horsemen faced his army of 200,000 soldiers, who were eager to acquire the booty of a wealthy city. Even before the battle had taken place, Baghdadi poets were composing elegies for their dead and mourning the defeat of Islam.

The slaughter was vast. Hulagu himself boasted of taking the lives of at least 200,000 people. The Mongols pursued their adversaries everywhere. They hunted them in wells, latrines, and sewers and followed them into the upper floors of buildings, killing them on rooftops until, as an Iraqi historian observed, "blood poured from the gutters into the streets. . . . The same happened in the mosques" (Lewis, pp. 82–83). In a few weeks of sheer terror, the venerable Abbasid caliphate was demolished. Hulagu's forces showed no mercy to the caliph himself, who was rolled up in a carpet and trampled to death by horses, his blood soaked up by the rug so it would leave no mark on the ground. With Baghdad crushed, the Mongol armies pushed on to Syria, slaughtering Muslims along the way.

The world experienced considerable human population growth during the first millennium of the Common Era in spite of occasional downturns, such as in Asia and Europe between 200 CE and 600 CE that were the result of climate change, movement of peoples, and the decline of the Roman and Han Empires. Overall, however, an upward trajectory occurred, though it averaged out to a mere 0.06 percent per year. For the period from 1750 to 1950, that percentage increased to a little more than 0.5 percent per year, and since 1950, the number has risen to 1.75 percent per year. Even so, as we will see in the next chapter, the major populations in the Afro-Eurasian landmass were terrified by the loss of life that accompanied the spread of the Black Death across this immense area. Since the Afro-Eurasian recovery from the Black Death, the world's population has been on a steady increase, spectacularly so in the twentieth century, the result of more abundant food supplies, more accurate knowledge of the spread of diseases and a resulting control of epidemic diseases, and a general rise in the standards of living.

Regional Human Population (in millions)						
Year	Asia	Europe	Africa	Americas	Oceania	World
400 BCE	97	30	17	8	1	153
1 CE	172	41	26	12	1	252
200	160	55	30	11	1	257
600	136	31	24	16	1	208
1000	154	41	39	18	1	253
1200	260	64	48	26	2	400
1340	240	88	80	32	2	442

Source: Massimo Livi-Bacci, *A Concise History of World Population* (Malden, MA: Wiley-Blackwell, 2012), p. 25.

QUESTIONS FOR ANALYSIS

- Why was the rate of population growth so limited in premodern times?
- Comparing the population size of the regions in 1340, what do the numbers tell us about where the largest share of wealth and power resided? How does this compare with earlier eras in the chart?
- Why was the population of the Americas in 1340 so small considering its large territorial size?
- Why were the peoples living in the Afro-Eurasian landmass so vulnerable to epidemic diseases in the fourteenth century?
- How do changes in global population relate to the developments tracked in this chapter: a maritime revolution; a more integrally connected Africa; a thriving Abbasid caliphate; and an expanding Mongol Empire?

The Collapse of Mongol Rule

In the end, the Mongol Empire reached its outer limits. In the west, the Egyptian Mamluks stemmed the advancing Mongol armies and prevented Egypt from falling into their hands. In the east, the waters of the South China Sea and the Sea of Japan foiled Mongol expansion into Java and Japan. And in the northwest, Mongol armies moved through Ukraine and went to the border of Poland. Yet they proved better at conquering than governing. They struggled to rule their vast possessions in makeshift states. Bit by bit, they yielded control to local administrators and dynasts who governed as their surrogates. There was also chronic feuding among the Mongol dynasts themselves. In China and Persia, Mongol rule collapsed in the fourteenth century. Ultimately, the Mongols would meet a deadly adversary more brutal than they were—the plague of the fourteenth century (see Chapter 11).

Mongol conquest reshaped Afro-Eurasia's social landscape. Islam would never again have a unifying authority like the caliphate or a powerful center like Baghdad. China, too, was divided and changed, but in other ways. The Mongols introduced Persian, Islamic, and Byzantine influences on China's architecture, art, science, and medicine. The Yuan policy of benign tolerance also brought elements from Christianity, Judaism, Zoroastrianism, and Islam into the Chinese mix. The Mongol thrust led to a great opening, as fine goods, traders, and technology flowed from China to the rest of the world in ensuing centuries. Finally, the Mongol conquests, somewhat like those of Alexander the Great in an earlier age (see Chapter 5), encouraged an Afro-Eurasian interconnectedness, but on a scale that the huge landmass had not known before and would not experience again for hundreds of years. Out of conquest and warfare would come centuries of trade, migration, and increasing contact between Africa, Europe, and Asia.

Mongols on Horseback. *Even after the Mongols became the rulers of China, the emperors remembered their steppe origin and maintained the skills of horse-riding nomads. This detail from a thirteenth/fourteenth-century silk painting shows Kubilai Khan hunting.*

CONCLUSION

Between 1000 and 1300 CE, Afro-Eurasia was forming large cultural spheres. As trade and migration spanned longer distances, these spheres prospered and became more integrated. In central Afro-Eurasia, Islam was firmly established, its merchants, scholars, and travelers acting as commercial and cultural intermediaries as they spread their universalizing faith. As seaborne trade expanded, India, too, became a commercial crossroads. Merchants in its port cities welcomed traders arriving from Arab lands to the west, from China, and from Southeast Asia. China also boomed, pouring its manufactures into trading networks that reached throughout Eurasia and North Africa and even Sub-Saharan Africa. Christian Europe had two centers, both of which were at war with Islam. In the east, Byzantium was a formidable empire with a resplendent and unconquerable capital city, Constantinople, in many ways the pride of Christianity. In the west, the Catholic papacy had risen from the ashes of the Roman Empire and sought to extend its ecclesiastical authority over Rome's territories in western Europe.

Neither the Americas nor sub-Saharan Africa saw the same degree of integration, but trade and migration in these areas had profound effects. Certain African cultures flourished as they encountered the commercial energy of trade on the Indian Ocean. Africans' trade with one another linked coastal and interior regions in an ever more integrated world. American peoples also built cities that dominated cultural areas and thrived through trade. American cultures shared significant features: reliance on trade, maize, and the exchange of goods such as shells and precious feathers. And larger areas honored the same spiritual centers.

By 1300, trade, migration, and conflict were connecting Afro-Eurasian worlds in unprecedented ways. When Mongol armies swept into China, into Southeast Asia, and into the heart of Islam, they applied a thin coating of political integration to these widespread regions and built on existing trade links. At the same time, most people's lives remained quite local, driven by the need for subsistence and governed by spiritual and governmental representatives acting at the behest of distant authorities.

Still, locals noticed the evidence of cross-cultural exchanges everywhere—in the clothing styles of provincial elites, such as Chinese silks in Paris or Quetzal plumes in northern Mexico; in enticements to move (and forced removals) to new frontiers; in the news of faraway conquests or advancing armies. Worlds were coming together within themselves and across territorial boundaries, while remaining apart as they sought to maintain their own identity and traditions. In Afro-Eurasia especially, as the movement of goods and peoples shifted from ancient land routes to sea-lanes, these contacts were more frequent and far-reaching. Never before had the world seen so much activity connecting its parts. Nor within them had there been so much shared cultural similarity—linguistic, religious, legal, and military. By the time the Mongol Empire arose, the regions composing the globe were those that we now recognize as the cultural spheres of today's world.

FOCUS ON: *Foundational Cultural Spheres*

The Islamic World

- Islam undergoes a burst of expansion, prosperity, and cultural diversification but remains politically fractured.

- Arab merchants and Sufi mystics spread Islam over great distances and make it more appealing to other cultures, helping to transform Islam into a foundational world.

- Islam travels across the Sahara Desert; the powerful gold- and slave-supplying empire of Mali arises in West Africa.

China

- The Song dynasty reunites China after three centuries of fragmented rulership, reaching into the past to reestablish a sense of a "true" Chinese identity as the Han through a widespread print culture and denigration of outsiders.

- Agrarian success and advances in manufacturing—including the production of both iron and porcelain—fuel an expanding economy, complete with paper money.

India

- India remains a mosaic under the canopy of Hinduism despite cultural interconnections and increasing prosperity.

- The invasion of Turkish Muslims leads to the Delhi Sultanate, which rules over India for three centuries, strengthening cultural diversity and tolerance.

Christian Europe

- Catholicism becomes a "mass" faith and helps to create a common European cultural identity.

- Feudalism organizes the elite-peasant relationship, while manorialism forms the basis of the economy.

- Europe's growing confidence is manifest in the Crusades and the reconquering of Iberia, an effort to drive Islam out of Christian lands.

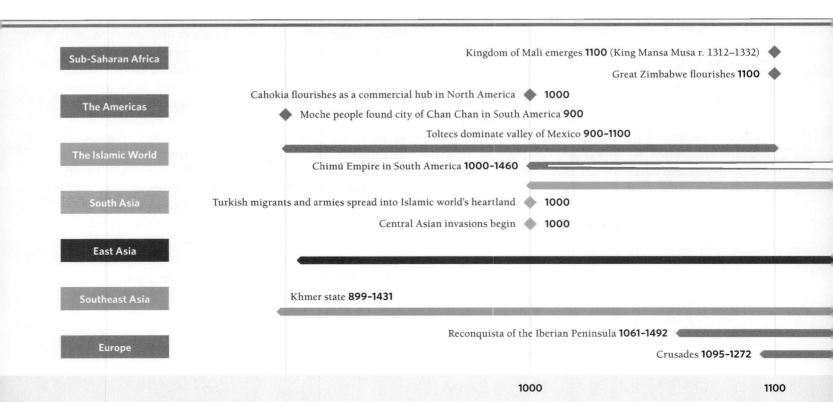

Sub-Saharan Africa

Kingdom of Mali emerges **1100** (King Mansa Musa r. 1312–1332) ◆

Great Zimbabwe flourishes **1100** ◆

The Americas

Cahokia flourishes as a commercial hub in North America ◆ **1000**

◆ Moche people found city of Chan Chan in South America **900**

Toltecs dominate valley of Mexico **900–1100**

The Islamic World

Chimú Empire in South America **1000–1460**

South Asia

Turkish migrants and armies spread into Islamic world's heartland ◆ **1000**

Central Asian invasions begin ◆ **1000**

East Asia

Southeast Asia

Khmer state **899–1431**

Europe

Reconquista of the Iberian Peninsula **1061–1492**

Crusades **1095–1272**

1000   1100

STUDY QUESTIONS

1. **Explain** how specific technological advances, especially in ship design and navigation, facilitated the expansion of Afro-Eurasian trade. In what ways did global commercial hubs in Egypt, China, Melaka, and India reflect revolutions in maritime transportation and foster commercial contact regionwide?

2. **Analyze** the social and political forces that shaped the Islamic world, India, China, and Europe at this time. **Evaluate** the degree to which these forces integrated cultures and geographical areas.

3. **Identify** environmental and political forces that contributed to fragmentation within the Islamic world. **Describe** the cultural forces that enabled diverse Islamic communities to achieve a uniform regional identity.

4. **Discuss** the impact of Muslim Turkish invaders on India. To what extent did India remain distinct from the Islamic world in this era?

5. **Explain** how economic and manufacturing developments, coupled with political developments, cemented the power of the Song dynasty. How did Song interactions with nomads and neighbors lead to distinctive identities for both the Song and their neighbors?

6. **Compare and contrast** cultural and political developments in Korea, Japan, and Southeast Asia during this era. **Analyze** the influence of other regional cultures on these societies.

7. **Describe** how Christianity expanded its geographical reach during this era; **evaluate** the roles of manorialism and feudalism, universities, and the Crusades in contributing to Europe's identity as a fragmented yet distinctive cultural sphere.

8. **Identify** the areas of sub-Saharan Africa that were parts of the larger Afro-Eurasian world by 1300. **Explain** how contact with other regions shaped political and cultural developments in sub-Saharan Africa.

9. **Analyze** the extent to which American peoples established closer contact with each other. How extensive were these contacts compared with those in the Afro-Eurasian world? Compared with those in sub-Saharan Africa?

10. **Describe** the empire that the Mongols created in the thirteenth century. How did their policies promote greater contact among the various regions and peoples of Afro-Eurasia? **Contrast** the expansion of Hulagu into the west with that of Kubilai Khan into the east.

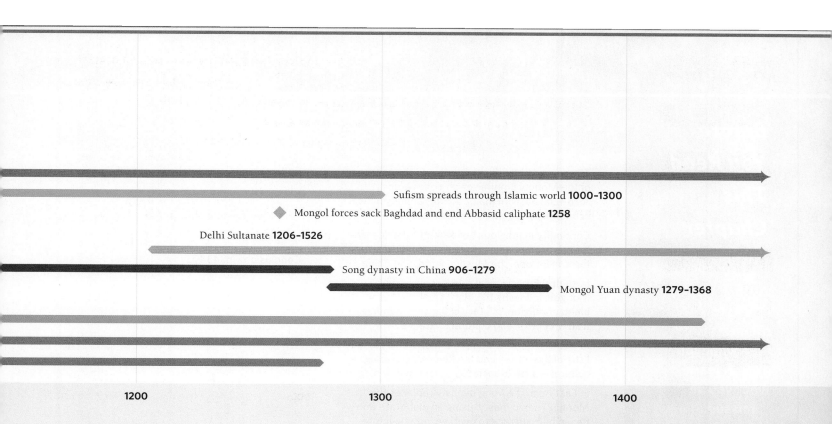

Sufism spreads through Islamic world **1000–1300**

Mongol forces sack Baghdad and end Abbasid caliphate **1258**

Delhi Sultanate **1206–1526**

Song dynasty in China **906–1279**

Mongol Yuan dynasty **1279–1368**

1200　　　　　　　　1300　　　　　　　　1400

11

Crises and Recovery in Afro-Eurasia, 1300–1500

FOCUS QUESTIONS

- What were the nature and origins of the crises that spanned Afro-Eurasia during the fourteenth century? How extensive were their effects, locally and transregionally?

- In what ways did religious belief systems maintain continuity from the fourteenth through the fifteenth centuries?

- How similar and different were the ways in which regional rulers in postplague Afro-Eurasia attempted to construct unified states? What were their greatest successes?

- How did the art and architecture of different regions reflect political realities, and what themes communicate these messages to viewers?

- In what different ways did the Iberian kingdoms, the Ottoman, Safavid, and Mughal Empires, the Ming dynasty, and European political systems extend their territory and regional influence?

When Mongol armies besieged the Genoese trading outpost of Caffa on the Black Sea in 1346, they not only damaged trading links between East Asia and the Mediterranean but also unleashed a devastating disease: the bubonic plague. Defeated Genoese merchants and soldiers withdrew, inadvertently taking the germs with them aboard their ships. By the time they arrived in Messina, Sicily, half the passengers were dead. The rest were dying. People waiting on shore for the ships' trade goods were horrified at the sight and turned the ships away. Desperately, the captains went to the next port, only to face the same fate. Despite these efforts at isolation, Europeans could not keep the plague (called the Black Death) from reaching their shores. As it spread from port to port, it eventually contaminated all of Europe, killing nearly two-thirds of the population.

This story illustrates the disruptive effects of the Mongol invasion from which the bubonic plague originated and the long-distance trade routes the Mongol Empire imposed on societies. The invasions left behind a series of khanates ruled by local warlords, rather than a centralized state. But they also ushered in an age of intensified cultural and political contact, and the channels of exchange—the land trails and sea-lanes of human voyagers—became accidental conduits for deadly microbes. These germs devastated societies far more decisively than did Mongol warfare. They were the real "murderous hordes" of world history, infecting people from every community, class, and culture. So staggering was the Black Death's toll that population densities did not recover for 200 years. Most severely affected were regions that the Mongols had brought together: settlements and commercial hubs along the old Silk Road and around the Mediterranean and South China Seas. While segments of the Indian Ocean trading world experienced death and disruption, South Asian societies, which had escaped the Mongol conquest, also escaped the great loss of life and political disruptions associated with the Black Death.

This chapter explores the ways in which Afro-Eurasian peoples restored what they thought was valuable from the old while discarding what they felt had failed them in favor of radically new institutions and ideas. The recovery had striking similarities across Afro-Eurasia. Societies reaffirmed their most deeply held and long-standing beliefs, though in a modified form. Chinese elites relied on Confucian tenets and dynastic institutions to revive their devastated communities. In the societies of India, Iran, and Turkey, new rulers turned to Islam for solace in peoples' suffering and hope for the future. Europeans also looked to their traditions. New monarchies, the forerunners of European nation-states, rose to provide leadership, while scholars looked to the Greek and Roman past for cultural and political inspiration.

Radically new political institutions and ideas appeared all across Afro-Eurasia in the aftermath of the Black Death. What historians have called the "Renaissance" captivated the European learned elite and sent its practitioners in search of the scholarship of the Greeks and Romans. They used this inspiration to produce a cultural flourishing in the arts, literature, architecture, and political and financial institutions. While recognizing the new mindsets that appeared in these centuries, this chapter also stresses continuity. Considering how grievously people suffered and how many had died, it is surprising that so much of the old—particularly religious beliefs and institutions— survived the aftermath of the Black Death. Rulers altered but did not transform inherited traditions. What was truly new and would prove enduring was a group of imperial dynasties that emerged all across Afro-Eurasia.

COLLAPSE AND CONSOLIDATION

Although the Mongol invasions overturned political systems, the plague devastated society itself. The pandemic killed millions, disrupted economies, and threw communities into chaos. Rulers could explain to their people the assaults of "barbarians," but it was much harder to make sense of an invisible enemy. Many concluded that mass death was God's wish and humankind's punishment. However, the upheaval gave ruling groups the opportunity to consolidate power by making dynastic matches through marriage, establishing new armies and taxes, and creating new systems to administer their states.

The Black Death

The spread of the **Black Death** was the fourteenth century's most significant historical development. (See Map 11.1.) Originating in Inner Asia, the disease stemmed from a combination of bubonic, pneumonic, and septicemic plague strains, and it caused a staggering loss of life. Among infected populations, death rates ranged from 25 to 65 percent.

How did the Black Death spread so far? One explanation may lie in climate changes. A cooler climate—what scholars refer to as the "Little Ice Age"—may have weakened populations and left them vulnerable to disease. In Europe, for instance, beginning around 1310, harsh winters and rainy summers shortened the growing season and ruined harvests. Here, exhausted soils no longer supplied the resources required by growing urban and rural populations, while nobles squeezed the peasantry in an effort to maintain their luxurious lifestyle. The ensuing European famine lasted from 1315 to 1322, during which time millions died of starvation or of diseases against which the malnourished population had little resistance. This climate change and famine was a factor in the Black Death that soon followed. Another climate-related factor in the spread of the plague occurred in East Asia: here, the drying up of the central Asian steppe borderlands, where bubonic plague had existed for centuries, forced rodents out of their usual dwelling places and pressed pastoral peoples, who carried the strains, to move closer to settled agricultural communities. So, it is thought, began the migration of microbes.

What spread the germs across Afro-Eurasia was the Mongols' trading network. The first outbreak in a heavily populated region occurred in the 1320s in southwestern China. From there, the disease spread through China and then took its death march along the major trade routes. The main avenue of transmission was across central Asia to the Crimea and the Black Sea and from there by ship to the Mediterranean Sea and the Italian city-states. Secondary routes were by sea: one from China to the Red Sea, and another across the Indian Ocean, through the Persian Gulf, and into the Fertile Crescent and Iraq. All routes terminated at the Italian port cities, where ships with dead and dying men aboard arrived in 1347. From there, what Europeans called the Pestilence or the Great Mortality engulfed the western end of the landmass.

The Black Death struck an expanding Afro-Eurasian population, made vulnerable because its members had no immunity to the disease and because its major realms were thoroughly

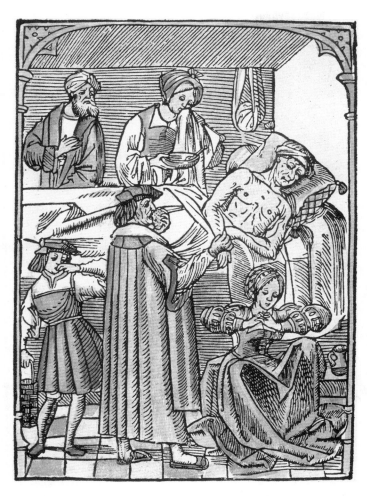

Plague Victim. *The plague was highly contagious and after a series of grotesque symptoms quickly resulted in death. Here the physician and his helper cover their noses, most likely in attempt to block out the unbearable stench emanating from the patient's boils.*

connected through trading networks. Rodents, mainly rats, carried the plague bacilli that caused the disease. Fleas transmitted the bacilli from rodent to rodent, as well as to humans. The epidemic was terrifying, for its causes were unknown at the time. Infected victims died quickly—sometimes overnight—and in great agony, coughing up blood and oozing pus and blood from ugly black sores the size of eggs. Some European sages attributed the ravaging of their societies to an unusual alignment of Saturn, Jupiter, and Mars. Many believed that God was angry with humankind. One Florentine historian compared the plague to the biblical Flood and believed that the end of humankind was imminent. Everywhere in Afro-Eurasia peoples of all classes had no explanation for the dying and often acted in ways that would be considered reprehensible or outrageous in normal times.

PLAGUE IN CHINA China was ripe for the plague's pandemic. Its population had increased significantly under the Song

dynasty (960–1279) and subsequent Mongol rule. But by 1300, hunger and scarcity began to spread as resources stretched thin. A weakened population was especially vulnerable to plague. For seventy years, the Black Death ravaged China and shattered the Mongols' claim to a mandate from heaven. In 1331, plague may have killed 90 percent of the population in Bei Zhili (modern Hebei) Province. From there it spread throughout other provinces, reaching Fujian and the coast at Shandong. By the 1350s, most of China's large cities suffered severe outbreaks.

The reign of the last Yuan Mongol rulers was a time of utter chaos. Even as the Black Death was engulfing large parts of China, bandit groups and dissident religious sects were undercutting the state's power. As in other realms devastated by the plague, popular religious movements foretold impending doom. Most prominent was the **Red Turban Movement**, which took its name from its soldiers' red headbands. This movement blended China's diverse cultural and religious traditions, including Buddhism, Daoism, and other faiths. Its leaders emphasized strict dietary restrictions, penance, and ceremonial rituals in which the sexes freely mixed, and made proclamations that the world was drawing to an end.

PLAGUE IN THE ISLAMIC WORLD The plague devastated parts of the Muslim world as well. The Black Death reached Baghdad by 1347, perhaps carried there by an Azerbaijani army that besieged the city. By the next year, the plague had overtaken Egypt, Syria, and Cyprus; one report from Tunis records the death of more than 1,000 people a day in that North African city. Animals, too, were afflicted. One Egyptian writer commented: "The country was not far from being ruined. . . . One found in the desert the bodies of savage animals with the bubos under their arms. It was the same with horses, camels, asses, and all the beasts in general, including birds, even the ostriches" (Dols, p. 156). In the eastern Mediterranean, the plague left much of the Islamic world in a state of near political and economic collapse. The great Arab historian Ibn Khaldun (1332–1406), who lost his mother and father and a number of his teachers to the Black Death in Tunis, underscored the sense of desolation: "Cities and buildings were laid waste, roads and way signs were obliterated, settlements and mansions became empty, dynasties and tribes grew weak," he wrote. "The entire world changed" (p. 67). (See Primary Source: Qalandar Dervishes in the Islamic World.)

PLAGUE IN EUROPE In Europe, the Black Death first ravaged the Italian Peninsula; then it seized France, the Low Countries (present-day Netherlands, Belgium, and Luxembourg), the Holy Roman Empire, and Britain in its deathly grip. The overcrowded and unsanitary cities were particularly vulnerable. Bremen lost at least 8,000 souls, perhaps two-thirds of its population; Hamburg, another port city, at least as

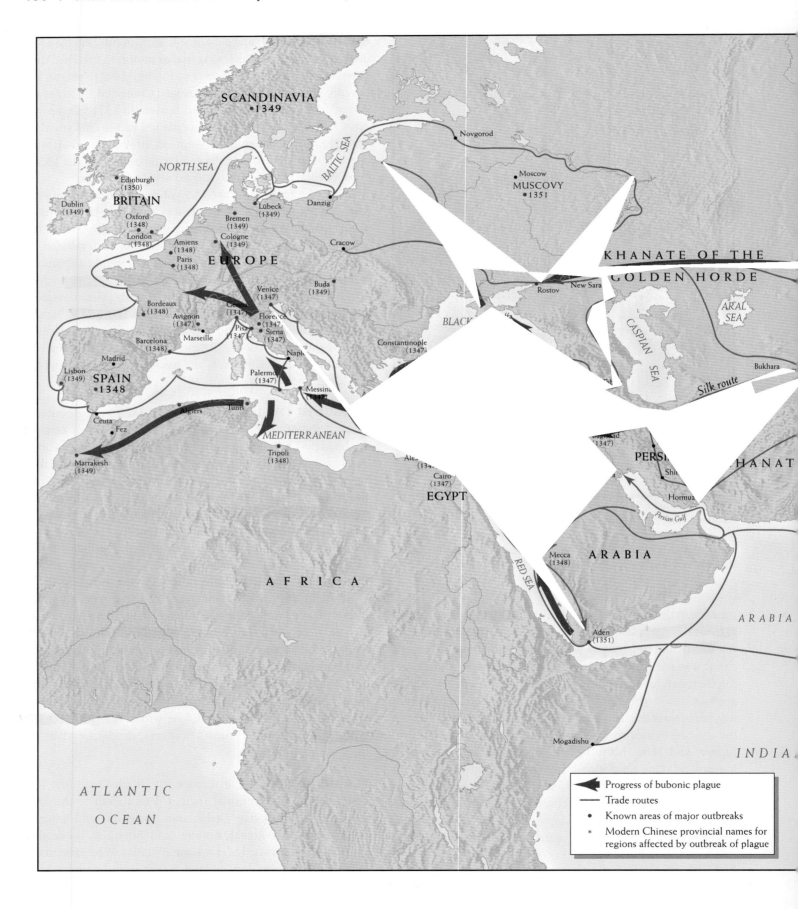

MAP 11.1 | The Spread of the Black Death

The Black Death was an Afro-Eurasian pandemic of the fourteenth century.

- What was the origin point of the Black Death?
- What were the main trade routes that allowed the Black Death to spread across Afro-Eurasia?
- Can you explain why certain parts of Afro-Eurasia were more severely affected than others?

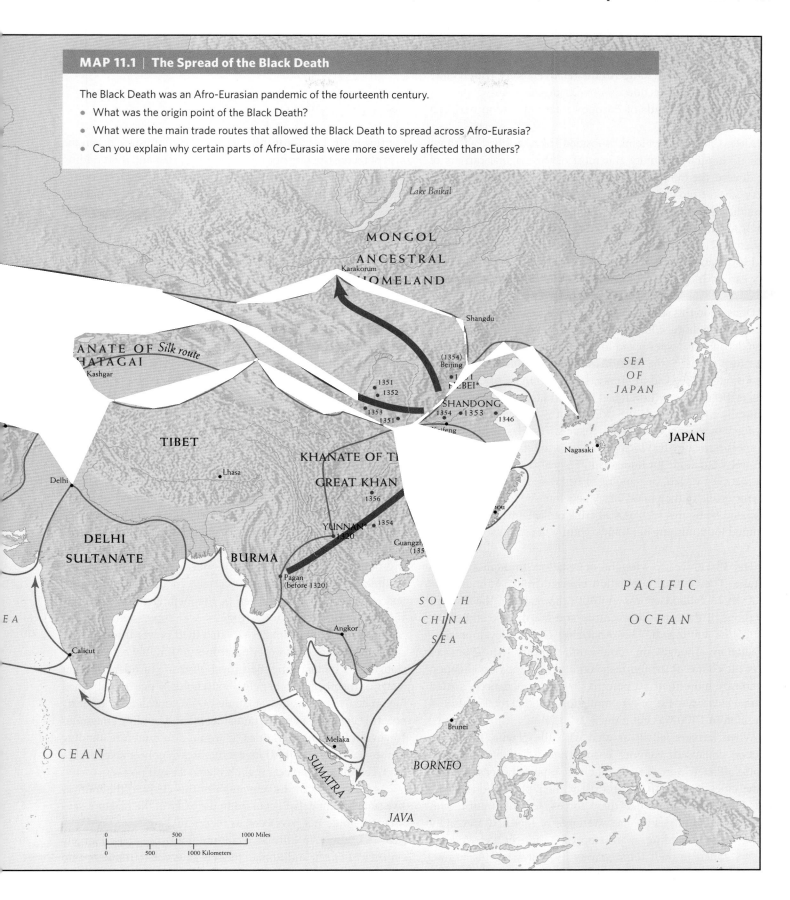

many. The poor, sleeping in crowded quarters, were especially at risk. But master bakers, bankers, and aristocrats died too, unless they were able to flee to the relatively safer countryside in time to escape infection. No one had seen dying on such a scale. Nearly two-thirds of Europe's total population perished between 1346 and 1353.

After 1353, the epidemic subsided, having killed all those with no natural immunity and most of the original carriers of the disease, the European black rat. But the plague would return every seven years or so for the rest of the century, as well as sporadically through the entire fifteenth century, killing the young and those who had managed to escape exposure in the first epidemic. The European population continued to decline, until by 1450 many areas had only one-quarter the number of a century earlier. Indeed, it took three centuries to return to population levels that existed prior to the Black Death.

Disaster on this scale had enduring psychological, social, economic, and political effects. Many individuals turned to pleasure, even debauchery, determined to enjoy themselves before it came their turn to die. Some blamed Jews for unleashing the plague, even though Jews died in numbers equal to those of Christians. Others, believing the church had lost God's favor, sought consolidation in more individualized forms of piety, such as extreme fasting or worshiping in private chapels. The Flagellants were so sure that humanity had incurred God's wrath that they whipped themselves to atone for human sin. They also bullied communities that they visited, demanding to be housed, clothed, and fed. Characteristic of the period was a new intensity of private piety, exhibited by figures such as Catherine of Siena, who was widely admired for punishing her body to purify her soul.

The Black Death wrought devastation throughout Afro-Eurasia. The Chinese population plunged from 115 million in 1200 to 75 million or less in 1400, the result of the Mongol invasions of the thirteenth century and the disease and disorder of the fourteenth. (See Analyzing Global Developments: Population Changes in Fourteenth-Century Afro-Eurasia.) Over the course of the fourteenth century, Europe's population shrank by more than 50 percent. In the most densely settled Islamic territory—Egypt—a population that had totaled around 6 million in 1400 was cut in half.

When farmers fell ill or died with the plague, food production collapsed. Famines ensued and killed off survivors. Worse afflicted were the coastal cities, especially coastal ports. Some cities lost up to two-thirds of their populations. Refugees from urban areas fled their homes, seeking security and food in the countryside. The shortages of food led to rapidly rising prices, hoarding, work stoppages, and unrest. Political leaders added to their unpopularity by repressing the unrest. Everywhere regimes collapsed. The Mongol Empire, which had held so much of Eurasia together commercially and politically, collapsed. Thus, the way was prepared for experiments in state building, religious beliefs, and cultural achievements.

Rebuilding States

Starting in the late fourteenth century, Afro-Eurasians began the task of reconstructing both their political order and their trading networks. (By then the plague had subsided, though it continued to afflict peoples for centuries.) The rebuilding of military and civil administrations—no easy task—also required political legitimacy. Rulers needed to revive confidence in themselves and their political systems, which they did by fostering beliefs and rituals that confirmed their legitimacy and by increasing their control over subjects.

The form that power took in most places was a political institution well known to Afro-Eurasians for centuries: the **dynasty**, the hereditary ruling family that passed control from one generation to the next. Dynasties sought to establish their legitimacy in three ways. First, ruling families insisted that their power derived from a divine calling: Ming emperors in China claimed for themselves what previous dynasts had asserted—the "mandate of heaven"—while European monarchs claimed to rule by "divine right." From their base in Anatolia, Ottoman warrior-princes asserted that they now carried the banner of Islam. In these ways, ruling households affirmed that God or the heavens intended for them to hold power. The new Safavid regime on the Iranian plateau embraced a Shiite form of governance. Second, leaders squelched squabbling among potential heirs by establishing clear rules about succession to the throne. Many European states tried to standardize succession by passing titles to the eldest male heir, but in practice there were countless complications and quarrels. In the Islamic world, successors could be designated by the incumbent or elected by the community; here, too, struggles over succession were frequent. Third, ruling families elevated their power through conquest or alliance—by ordering armies to forcibly extend their domains or by marrying their royal offspring to rulers of other states or members of other elite households. Once it established legitimacy, the typical royal family would consolidate power by enacting coercive laws and punishments and sending emissaries to govern far-flung territories. It would also establish standing armies and new administrative structures to collect taxes and to oversee building projects that proclaimed royal power.

As we will see in the remainder of this chapter, the innovative state building that occurred in the wake of the plague's devastation would not have been as successful had it not drawn on older traditions. In Europe, a cultural flourishing based largely on ancient Greek and Roman models gave rise to thinkers who proposed novel views of governance. The peoples of the Islamic world held fiercely to their religion as two successor states—the

Population Changes in Fourteenth-Century Afro-Eurasia

Famine, warfare, and disease led to vast population declines all across Afro-Eurasia in the fourteenth century. The Mongols were instrumental players in spreading disease across the landmass, starting in China and moving westward along land- and sea-based trading routes toward the Mediterranean World and ultimately northern Europe. (See Map 11.1.) While the effects of these destructive forces were felt across the Afro-Eurasian landmass, some states and regions were less affected than others. The population data in the table come from the best historical studies of the last forty years and are based on painstaking archival research. They serve as one of the best ways for us to gain historical insight into this tumultuous century.

QUESTIONS FOR ANALYSIS

- In what regions or cities does population loss seem to have been lower? Higher? What might account for those variations in the death rate?
- How do the losses in urban areas compare with the losses in the region where those urban areas are located? What might that comparison suggest about the impact of fourteenth-century disasters on urban versus other populations?
- Why do you think the population decline was more severe and widespread in Europe than in Asia?
- In what ways was the great loss of population in Europe and China a turning point in their histories?

Location	Earlier Population Figures	Later Population Figures	Percent Change
By Region			
Europe	80 m [a] in 1346	30 m in 1353	−60%
Asia	230 m in 1300	235 m in 1400	+2%
Islam	(regional data are not available)		
By Country			
Spain	6 m in 1346	2.5 m in 1353	−60%
Italy	10 m in 1346	4.5 m in 1363	−55%
France	18 m in 1346	7.2 m in 1353	−60%
England	6 m in 1346	2.25 m in 1353	−62.5%
China	115 m in 1200	75 m in 1400	−35%
Japan	9.75 m in 1300	12.5 m in 1400	+28%
Korea	3 m in 1300	3.5 m in 1400	+17%
India	91 m in 1300	97 m in 1400	+6.5%
By City			
London	100,000 in 1346	37,000 in 1353	−62.5%
Florence	92,000 in 1346	37,250 in 1353	−59.5%
Siena	50,000 in 1346	20,000 in 1353	−60%
Bologna	50,000 in 1346	27,500 in 1353	−45%
Cairo	500,000 in 1300	300,000 in 1400	−40%
Damascus	80,000 in 1300	50,000 in 1400	−37%

[a] m = millions

Sources: Ole J. Benedictow, *The Black Death, 1346–1353: The Complete History* (2004); Michael Dols, *The Black Death in the Middle East* (1974); Colin McEvedy and Richard Jones, *Atlas of World Population History* (1978). Ping-ti Ho, *Studies on the Population of China, 1368–1953* (1959).

Ottoman Empire and the Safavid state—absorbed numerous Turkish-speaking groups. A third Islamic state—the Mughal Empire—drew on local traditions of religious and cultural tolerance as its rulers built a new regime on the foundations of the weakened Delhi Sultanate (see Chapter 10). The Ming, having failed in their attempts to control northern Vietnam and Korea, renounced the expansionist Mongol legacy and emphasized a return to Han rulership, consolidating control of Chinese lands and concentrating on internal markets rather than overseas trade. Many of these regimes lasted for centuries, promoting political institutions and cultural values that became deeply embedded in the fabric of their societies.

ISLAMIC DYNASTIES

The devastation of the Black Death followed hard on the heels of the Mongol destruction of Islam's most important city, Baghdad (see Chapter 10), and eliminated Islam's old political order. Nonetheless, these two catastrophes prepared the way for new Islamic states to emerge. Although the Arabic-speaking peoples remained vital, still at the heart of Islam geographically, they now had to cede authority to Persian and Turkish political leaders. Persians and Turks had embraced Islam and had made their cultural, intellectual, and military influence felt well before the Mongol invasions and the Black Death. Now they became

Qalandar Dervishes in the Islamic World

The Qalandar dervish order sprang up in Damascus, Syria, and Egypt in the thirteenth century and spread rapidly throughout the Islamic world. In reaction to the period's widespread unrest, its members renounced the world and engaged in highly individualistic practices as they moved from place to place. The educated elite, however, criticized them as ignorant hypocrites living on alms obtained from gullible common folk. One of their practices was chiromancy, or palm reading. In this excerpt, Giovan Antonio Manavino, a European observer of Ottoman society, gives an obviously biased account of the Qalandars, whom he called the torlaks.

Dressed in sheepskins, the *torlaks* [Qalandars] are otherwise naked, with no headgear. Their scalps are always clean-shaven and well rubbed with oil as a precaution against the cold. They burn their temples with an old rag so that their faces will not be damaged by sweat. Illiterate and unable to do anything manly, they live like beasts, surviving on alms only. For this reason, they are to be found around taverns and public kitchens in cities. If, while roaming the countryside, they come across a well-dressed person, they try to make him one of their own, stripping him naked. Like Gypsies in Europe, they practice chiromancy, especially for women who then provide them with bread, eggs, cheese, and other foods in return for their services.

Amongst them there is usually an old man whom they revere and worship like God. When they enter a town, they gather around the best house of the town and listen in great humility to the words of this old man, who, after a spell of ecstasy, foretells the descent of a great evil upon the town. His disciples then implore him to fend off the disaster through his good services. The old man accepts the plea of his followers, though not without an initial show of reluctance, and prays to God, asking him to spare the town the imminent danger awaiting it. This time-honored trick earns them considerable sums of alms from ignorant and credulous people.

> ## QUESTIONS FOR ANALYSIS
>
> - Describe the way the Qalandar dervishes dressed, where they congregated, and how they obtained food. How did their lifestyle reflect the turmoil of the times?
> - Why do you think the Qalandars chose individualistic practices rather than communal living?
> - Why do you think Manavino is so critical of the Qalandars?

Source: Ahmet T. Karamustafa, "Dervish Groups in the Ottoman Empire, 1450–1550," from *God's Unruly Friends: Dervish Groups in the Islamic Later Middle Period, 1200–1550* (Salt Lake City: University of Utah Press, 1994), pp. 6–7.

Islam's most effective rulers. The world that they dominated occupied a vast geographical triangle. It stretched from Anatolia in the west to Khurasan in the east and to the southern apex at Baghdad.

The Ottomans, the Safavids, and the Mughals emerged as the dominant states in the Islamic world in the early sixteenth century. They exploited the rich agrarian resources of the Indian Ocean regions and the Mediterranean Sea basin, and they benefited from a brisk seaborne and overland trade. By the mid-sixteenth century, the Mughals controlled the northern Indus River valley; the Safavids occupied Persia; and the Ottomans ruled Anatolia, the Arab world, and much of southern and eastern Europe.

Despite sharing core Islamic beliefs, each empire had unique political features. The most powerful, the **Ottoman Empire**,

occupied the pivotal area between Europe and Asia. The Ottomans embraced a Sunni view of Islam, while adopting traditional Byzantine ways of governance and trying new ways of integrating the diverse peoples of their expanding territories. The Safavids, though adherents of the Shiite vision of Islam, were at the same time ardently devoted to the pre-Islamic traditions of Persia (present-day Iran). Unlike the Ottomans, their rulers were not so effective at expanding beyond their Persian base. The Mughals ruled over the wealthy but divided realm that is much of today's India, Pakistan, and Bangladesh; here they carried even further the region's religious and political traditions of assimilating Islamic and pre-Islamic Indian ways. Their wealth and the decentralization of their domain made the Mughals constant targets for internal dissent and eventually for external aggression.

The Ottoman Empire

The rise of the Ottoman Empire owed as much to innovative administrative techniques and religious tolerance as to military strength. Although the Mongols considered Anatolia to be a borderland region of little economic importance, their military forays against the Anatolian Seljuk Turkish state in the late thirteenth century brought political turmoil bordering on chaos, but opened up the region to new political forces. The ultimate victors here were the Ottoman Turks. They transformed themselves from warrior bands roaming the borderlands between Islamic and Christian worlds into rulers of a settled state and, finally, into sovereigns of a far-flung, highly bureaucratic empire. (See Map 11.2.)

Many modern Western-trained historians have portrayed the early Ottoman state as a plundering regime, engaged in rape and slaughter and carrying out campaigns of massive devastation by galvanizing their zealous warriors to terrorize local populations. They did indeed have stern and disciplined warriors, known as *ghazis*, whose commitment to Islam and their leaders was boundless. Even so, what enabled the Ottoman leaders to triumph in a region of widespread disorder was their ability to form alliances with previously hostile divergent ethnic and religious communities. Their first chief, Osman (r. 1299–1326), and his son Orhan (r. 1326–1362) were Sunni Muslims—but proved skilled at working with those who held different religious beliefs, such as Byzantine leaders, Kurds, Sufi dervish orders, and Shiites. By constructing eclectic political institutions possessing enormous elasticity, they succeeded in offering not merely toleration to diverse populations but opportunities to exercise power and gain wealth. Theirs was a hybrid state, which welcomed Christian supporters as fervently as Muslims. Hence, they prevailed over other Turkic competitors and transformed their small principality in northwestern Anatolia during the fourteenth century into the preeminent state in Anatolia. The principal characteristics of the early Ottoman state were inclusivity, resilience, and syncretism. Their takeover of the city of Bursa in 1404 marked an ascendancy in Anatolia that now threatened the very existence of the once powerful, now greatly weakened Byzantine Empire. Other Turkic warrior bands, which like the Ottomans lived off the land and fought for booty under charismatic military leaders, ultimately failed in their quest for power because they had little regard for other groups such as artisans, merchants, bureaucrats, and clerics, whose support was essential in the Ottoman rise.

THE CONQUEST OF CONSTANTINOPLE The empire's spectacular territorial expansion into Europe and eventually the Arab world was at heart a military affair. To recruit followers, the Ottomans promised wealth and glory to new subjects. This was an expensive undertaking, but territorial expansion generated financial and administrative rewards. Moreover, by spreading the spoils of conquest and lucrative administrative positions, rulers bought off potentially discontented subordinates. Still, without military might, the Ottomans would not have enjoyed the successes associated with the brilliant reigns of Murad II (r. 1421–1451) and his aptly named successor, Mehmed the Conqueror (r. 1451–1481).

Mehmed's most stunning triumph was the conquest of Constantinople, an ambition for Muslim rulers ever since the birth of Islam. Mehmed left no doubt that this was his primary goal. Indeed, shortly after his coronation, he vowed to capture the capital of the Byzantine Empire, a city of immense strategic and commercial importance. He exclaimed early in his reign that Constantinople was "an island in the midst of an Ottoman ocean." His desire to take the city "never left his tongue" (Faroqhi, p. 23). Mehmed knew this feat would require a large and well-armed fighting force, for the heavily fortified city had kept Muslims at bay for almost a century. First he built a fortress of his own, on the European bank of the Bosporus Strait,

The Fall of Constantinople. *The use of heavy artillery in the fifty-three-day siege of Constantinople was instrumental to the Ottoman victory. At the center of this Turkish miniature is one such cannon, possibly of Hungarian origin, which required hundreds of men and oxen to transport and secure outside the city walls.*

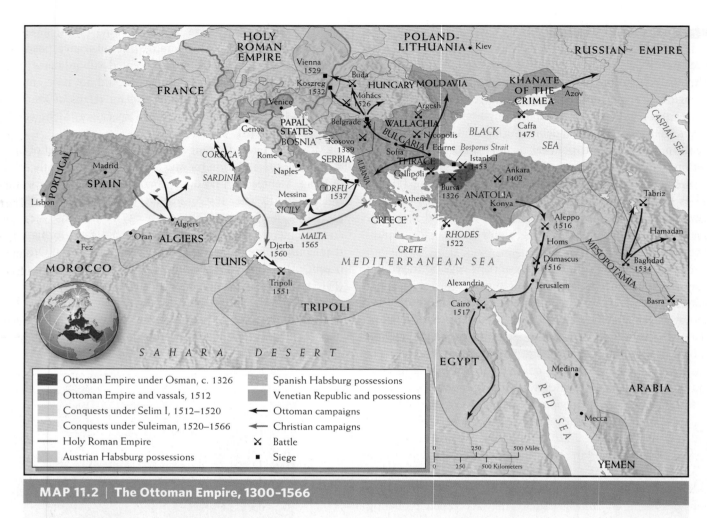

MAP 11.2 | The Ottoman Empire, 1300–1566

This map charts the expansion of the Ottoman state from the time of its founder, Osman, through the reign of Suleiman, the empire's most illustrious ruler.

- Identify the earliest part of the empire under Osman. Then identify all the areas of conquest under Suleiman. Against whom did the Ottomans fight between the years 1326 and 1566?
- What were the geographical limits of the empire?
- According to your reading, how did Ottoman rulers promote unity among such a diverse population?

to prevent European vessels from reaching the capital. Then, by promising his soldiers free access to booty and portraying the city's conquest as a holy cause, he amassed a huge army that outnumbered the defending force of 7,000 by more than tenfold. For forty days his troops bombarded Constantinople's massive walls with artillery that included enormous cannons built by Hungarian and Italian engineers. On May 29, 1453, Ottoman troops overwhelmed the surviving soldiers and took the ancient Roman and Christian capital of Byzantium—which Mehmed promptly renamed Istanbul.

Although Christians generally portrayed the "fall" of Constantinople as an insult and a disaster, in fact the Muslim conquest had cultural benefits for western Europe. Many Christian survivors fled to ports in the west, bringing with them classical and Arabic manuscripts previously unknown in Europe. The well-educated, Greek-speaking émigrés generally became teachers and translators, thereby helping to revive Europeans' interest in classical antiquity and spreading knowledge of ancient Greek (which had virtually died out in medieval times). These manuscripts and teachers would play a vital role in Europe's Renaissance.

THE TOOLS OF EMPIRE BUILDING Mehmed made Istanbul the Ottoman capital, adopting Byzantine administrative practices to unify his enlarged state and incorporating many of Byzantium's powerful families into it. From Istanbul, Mehmed and his successors would continue their expansion, eventually seizing all of Greece and the Balkan region. As a result, Ottoman navies increasingly controlled sea-lanes in the eastern Mediterranean, curtailing European access to the rich ports that handled the lucrative caravan trade. By the late fifteenth century, Ottoman forces menaced another of Christendom's great capitals, Vienna, and European merchants feared that never again would they obtain the riches of Asia via the traditional overland route.

Having penetrated the heartland of Christian Byzantium, under Selim (r. 1512–1520) and Suleiman (r. 1520–1566), the Ottomans turned their expansionist designs to the Arab world. During the latter's reign, the Ottomans reached the height of their territorial expansion, with Suleiman himself leading thirteen major military campaigns and many minor engagements. An exceptional military leader, Suleiman was an equally gifted administrator. His subjects called him "the Lawgiver" and "the Magnificent" in recognition of his attention to civil bureaucratic efficiency and justice for his people. His fame spread to Europe, where he was known as "the Great Turk." Under Suleiman's administration, the Ottoman state ruled over 20 to 30 million people. By the time Suleiman died, the Ottoman Empire bridged Europe and the Arab world. Istanbul by then was a dynamic imperial hub, dispatching bureaucrats and military men to oversee a vast domain.

Ottoman dynastic power was, however, not only military; it also rested on a firm religious foundation. The sultans combined a warrior ethos with an unwavering devotion to Islam. Describing themselves as the "shadow of God" on earth, they claimed to be caretakers for the welfare of the Islamic faith and assumed the role of protectors of the holy cities on the Arabian Peninsula and in Jerusalem after the conquests in the Arab world. They devoted substantial resources to the construction of elaborate mosques and to the support of Islamic schools throughout the empire and to extend the borders of Islam. Thus, the Islamic faith helped to unite a diverse and sprawling imperial populace, with the sultan's power fusing the sacred and the secular.

ISTANBUL AND THE TOPKAPI PALACE Istanbul reflected the splendor of this awesome empire. After the Ottoman

The Suleymaniye Mosque. *Built by Sultan Suleiman to crown his achievements, the Suleymaniye Mosque was designed by the architect Sinan to dominate the city. Four tall minarets called the faithful to prayer.*

conquest, the sultans' engineers rebuilt the city's crumbling walls, while their architects redesigned homes, public buildings, baths, inns, and marketplaces to display the majesty of Islam's new imperial center. To crown his achievements, Suleiman ordered the construction of the Suleymaniye Mosque, which sat opposite the Hagia Sophia. The latter, a domed Byzantine cathedral, was formerly the most sacred of Christian cathedrals, the largest house of worship in all of Christendom, but Suleiman had it turned into a mosque. Moreover, the Ottoman dynasts welcomed (indeed, forcibly transported) thousands of Muslims and non-Muslims to the city and revived Istanbul as a major trading center. Within twenty-five years of its conquest, its population more than tripled; by the end of the sixteenth century, 400,000 people regularly swarmed through its streets and knelt in its mosques, making it the world's largest city outside China.

Istanbul's **Topkapi Palace** reflected the Ottomans' view of governance, the sultans' emphasis on religion, and the continuing influence of Ottoman familial traditions—even in the administration of a far-flung empire. Laid out by Mehmed II, the palace complex reflected a vision of Istanbul as the center of the world. As a way to exalt the sultan's magnificent power, architects designed the complex so that the buildings containing the imperial household nestled behind layers of outer courtyards in a mosaic of mosques, courts, and special dwellings for the sultan's harem.

The growing importance of Topkapi Palace as the command post of the empire represented a crucial transition in the history of Ottoman rulers. Not only was the palace the place where future bureaucrats received their training; it was also the place where the chief bureaucrat, the grand vizier, carried out the day-to-day running of the empire. Whereas the early sultans had led their soldiers into battle personally and had met face-to-face with their kinsmen, the later rulers withdrew into the sanctity of the palace, venturing out only occasionally for grand ceremonies. Still, every Friday, subjects queued up outside the palace to introduce their petitions, ask for favors, and seek justice. If they were lucky, the sultans would be there to greet them—but they did so behind grated glass, issuing their decisions by tapping on the window. The palace thus projected a sense of majestic, distant wonder, a home fit for commanders of the faithful.

And Topkapi was indeed a home for the increasingly sedentary sultan and his harem. Among his most cherished quarters were those set aside for women. At first, women's influence in the Ottoman polity was slight. But as the realm consolidated, women became a powerful political force. The harem, like the rest of Ottoman society, had its own hierarchy of rank and prestige. At the bottom were slave women; at the top were the sultan's mother and his favorite consorts. As many as 10,000 to 12,000 women inhabited the palace, often in cramped quarters. Those who had the ruler's ear conspired to have him favor their own children, which made for widespread intrigue. When a sultan died, the entire retinue of women would be sent to a distant palace poignantly called the Palace of Tears, because the women who occupied it wept at the loss of the sultan and their own banishment from power.

DIVERSITY AND CONTROL The fact that the Ottoman Empire endured into the twentieth century owed much to the ruling elite's ability to gain the support and employ the talents of exceedingly diverse populations. After all, neither conquest nor conversion eliminated cultural differences in the empire's distant provinces. Thus, for example, the Ottomans' language policy was one of flexibility and tolerance. Although Ottoman

The Topkapi Palace. *A view of the inner courtyard of the seraglio, where the sultan and his harem lived.*

Turkish was the official language of administration, Arabic was the primary language of the Arab provinces, the common tongue of street life. Within the empire's European corner, the sounds and cadences of various languages continued to prevail. From the fifteenth century onward, the Ottoman Empire was more multilingual than any of its rivals.

In politics, as in language, the Ottomans showed flexibility and tolerance. The imperial bureaucracy permitted extensive regional and religious autonomy. In fact, Ottoman military cadres perfected a technique for absorbing newly conquered territories into the empire by parceling them out as revenue-producing units among loyal followers and kin. Regional appointees could collect local taxes, part of which they earmarked for Istanbul and part of which they pocketed for themselves. (This was a common administrative device for many world dynasties ruling extensive domains.)

Like other empires, the Ottoman state was always in danger of losing control over its provincial rulers. Local rulers—the group that the imperial center allowed to rule locally—found that great distances enabled them to operate independently from central authority. These local authorities kept larger amounts of tax revenues than Istanbul deemed proper. So, to clip local autonomy, the Ottomans established a corps of infantry soldiers and bureaucrats (called janissaries) who owed direct allegiance to the sultan. The system at its high point involved a conscription of Christian youths from the empire's European lands. This conscription, called the *devshirme*, required each village to hand over a certain number of males between the ages of eight and eighteen. Uprooted from their families and villages, selected for their fine physiques and good looks, these young men were converted to Islam and sent to farms to build up their bodies and learn Turkish. A select few were moved on to Topkapi Palace to learn Ottoman military, religious, and administrative techniques. Some of these men—such as the architect Sinan, who designed the Suleymaniye Mosque—later enjoyed exceptional careers in the arts and sciences. Recipients of the best education available in the Islamic world, trained in Ottoman ways, instructed in the use of modern weaponry, and shorn of all family connections, the *devshirme* recruits were prepared to serve the sultan (and the empire as a whole) rather than the interests of any particular locality or ethnic group.

Thus, the Ottomans established their legitimacy via military skills, religious backing, and a loyal bureaucracy. They artfully balanced the decentralizing tendencies of the outlying regions with the centralizing forces of the imperial capital. Relying on a careful mixture of faith, patronage, and tolerance, the sultans curried loyalty and secured political stability. Indeed, so strong and stable was the political system that the Ottoman Empire dominated the coveted and highly contested crossroads between Europe and Asia for many centuries.

The *Devshirme*. *A miniature painting from 1558 depicts the* devshirme *system of taking non-Muslim children from their families in the Balkan Peninsula as a human tribute in place of cash taxes, which the poor region could not pay. The children were educated in Ottoman Muslim ways and prepared for service in the sultan's civil and military bureaucracy.*

The Safavid Empire in Iran

The Ottoman dynasts were not the only rulers to extend Islam's political domain. In Persia, too, a new empire arose in the aftermath of the Mongols. The legitimacy of the Safavid Empire, like that of the Ottoman, rested on an Islamic foundation. But the Shiism espoused by Safavid rulers was quite different from the Sunni faith of the Ottomans, and these contrasting religious visions shaped distinct political systems.

In the western part of central Asia, the khanate of Chagatai, one of four governments created by the Mongols (see again Map 11.1), slipped into decline at the end of the thirteenth century. With no power dominating the area, the region fell into disorder, with warrior chieftains squabbling for preeminence. Adding to the volatility were various populist Islamic movements, some of which urged followers to withdraw from society or to parade around without clothing. Among the more prominent movements was a Sufi brotherhood led by Safi al-Din (1252–1334), which gained the backing of religious adherents and Turkish-speaking warrior bands. However, his successors, known as Safaviyeh or Safavids, embraced Shiism.

A RELIGIOUS SHIITE STATE The Safavid aspirants to power had their origins among Turkic Sufi groups in eastern Anatolia and Azerbaijan. The Ottoman takeover of most of Anatolia turned these regions into conflict zones between the Ottomans and the Safavids, but Ottoman power also forced the communities living there to find a new location. This they did in the Iranian plateau, rallying support from tribal groups in badly devastated parts of Persia and promising good governance. Forsaking their Sufi origins in this new land, they also steeped themselves in the separatist sacred tradition of Shiism. As a result, of the three great Islamic empires, the Safavid state became the most single-mindedly religious, persecuting those who did not follow its Shiite form of Islam. The most dynamic of Safi al-Din's successors, Ismail (r. 1501–1524), required that the call to prayer announce that there is no God but Allah, that Muhammad is His prophet, and that Ali is the successor of Muhammad. Rejecting his advisers' counsel to tolerate the Sunni creed of the majority of the city's population, Ismail made Shiism the official state religion. He offered the people a choice between conversion to Shiism or death, exclaiming at the moment of conquest that "with God's help, if the people utter one word of protest, I will draw the sword and leave not one of them alive" (Savory, p. 29). In 1502, Ismail proclaimed himself the first shah of the Safavid Empire. (*Shah* is the Persian word for king or leader, a title that many other cultures adopted as well.) Under Ismail and his successors, the Safavid shahs restored Persian sovereignty over the entire region traditionally regarded as the homeland of Persian speakers. (See Map 11.3.)

In the hands of the Safavids, Islam assumed an extreme and often militant form. The Safavids revived the traditional Persian idea that rulers were ordained by God, believing the shahs to be divinely chosen. Some Shiites even went so far as to affirm that there was no God but the shah. Moreover, Persian Shiism fostered an activist clergy who (in contrast to Sunni clerics) saw themselves as political and religious enforcers against any heretical authority. They compelled Safavid leaders to rule with a sacred purpose. Because the Safavids did not tolerate diversity, unlike the Ottomans, they never had as expansive an empire. Whatever territories they conquered, the Safavids ruled much more directly, based on central—and theocratic—authority. They also succeeded in transforming Iran, once a Sunni area, into a Shiite stronghold, a change that has endured down to the present.

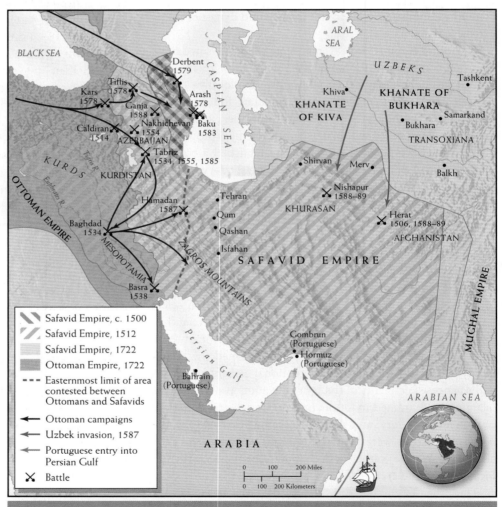

MAP 11.3 | **The Safavid Empire, 1500–1722**

The Safavid Empire rose to prominence alongside the Ottoman state.

- Locate the area where it originated. With which empire did the Safavids fight the most battles?
- Why were most of the battles limited to the regions of Azerbaijan, Kurdistan, and Mesopotamia?
- What were the geographical and political limits on the growth of the Safavid Empire?

The Delhi Sultanate and the Early Mughal Empire

A quarter century after the Safavids seized power in Persia, another Islamic dynasty, the Mughals, emerged in South Asia. Like the Ottomans and Safavids, the Mughals created a regime destined to last for many centuries. But unlike those other empires, the Mughals did not replace a Mongol regime. Instead, they erected their state on the foundations of the old Delhi Sultanate, which had come into existence in 1206. Although spared the devastating effects of the Mongols and the Black Death, nonetheless the peoples of India had to deal with an invading nomadic force every bit as destructive as the Mongols: the warriors of Timur, or Tamerlane. His military forays crushed the Delhi Sultanate

Raid on Delhi. *Timur's swift raid on Delhi in 1398 was notable for the death and destruction it caused. This sixteenth-century miniature captures the plunder and violence.*

and opened the way for a new, even more powerful regime. (See Chapter 10 for more on the Delhi Sultanate.)

RIVALRIES, RELIGIOUS REVIVAL, AND THE FIRST MUGHAL EMPEROR A wave of religious revival followed in the wake of Timur's conquests. Bengal broke away from Delhi and soon embraced a Sufi form of mystical Islam, emphasizing personal union with God. Here, too, a special form of Hinduism, called Bhakti Hinduism, put down deep roots. Its devotees preached the doctrine of divine love. In the Punjab, previously a core area of the Delhi Sultanate, a new religion known as Sikhism came into being. Sikhism largely followed the teachings of Nanak (1469–1539). Although born a Hindu, he was inspired by Islamic ideals and called on his followers to renounce the caste system and to treat all believers as equal before God. (See Primary Source: Nanak's Teachings in India.)

Following Timur's attack, rival kingdoms and sultanates asserted their independence. The Delhi Sultanate became a mere shadow of its former self, just one of several competing powers in northern India. Out of this political chaos emerged a Turkish prince, Babur (the "Tiger"), invited in 1526 by the governor of the Punjab to restore order. A great-grandson of Timur, Babur traced his lineage to both the Turks and the Mongols (he was said to be a descendant of Chinggis Khan). For years, Babur had longed to conquer India. Massing an army of Turks and Afghans armed with matchlock cannons, he easily breached the wall of elephants put together by defenders of the sultan. Delhi fell, and the Delhi Sultanate came to an end. Babur proclaimed himself emperor and spent the next few years snuffing out the remaining resistance to his rule. (See Map 11.4.) Thus, he laid the foundation of the Mughal Empire, the third great Islamic dynasty (discussed in detail in Chapter 12).

By the sixteenth century, then, the Islamic heartland had seen the emergence of three new empires. Their differences were obvious, especially in the religious sphere. The Ottomans were Sunni Islam's most fervent champions, determined to eradicate the Shiite heresy on their border, where an equally determined Persian Safavid dynasty sought to expand the realm of Shiism. In contrast to these dynasties' sectarian religious commitments, the Mughals of India, drawing on well-established Indian traditions of religious and cultural tolerance, were open-minded toward non-Muslim believers and sectarian groups within the Muslim community. Yet, the political similarities of these imperial dynasties were equally clear-cut. Although these states did not hesitate to go to war against each other, they shared similar styles of rule. All established their legitimacy via military prowess, religious backing, and a loyal bureaucracy. This combination of spiritual and military weaponry enabled emperors, espousing Muhammad's preachings, to claim vast domains. Moreover, their religious differences did not prevent the movement of

Nanak's Teachings in India

Nanak (1469–1539), generally recognized as the founder of Sikhism, lived in northern India and participated in the religious discussions that were prominent at the time. As in western Europe and Islamic Southwest Asia, this was a period of political turmoil and intense personal introspection. The following excerpts demonstrate Nanak's views on the failings of the age and his use of Islamic and Hindu ideas to elaborate a unique spiritual perspective. Nanak stressed the unity of God, an emphasis that reflected Islamic influences. Nonetheless, his insistence on the comparative unimportance of prophets ran counter to Islam, and his belief in rebirth was strictly Hindu.

There is but one God, whose name is true,
   the Creator, devoid of fear and enmity,
   immortal, unborn, self-existent; God the
   great and bountiful. Repeat His Name.

Numberless are the fools appallingly blind;
Numberless are the thieves and devourers
   of others' property;
Numberless are those who establish their
   sovereignty by force;
Numberless the cutthroats and murderers;
Numberless the liars who roam about
   lying;
Numberless the filthy who enjoy filthy gain;
Numberless the slandered who carry
   loads of calumny on their heads;
Nanak thus described the degraded.
So lowly am I, I cannot even once be a sac-
   rifice unto Thee. Whatever pleaseth
   Thee is good.
O Formless One, Thou art ever secure.

The Hindus have forgotten God, and are
   going the wrong way.

They worship according to the instruction
   of Narad.
They are blind and dumb, the blindest of
   the blind.
The ignorant fools take stones and worship them.
O Hindus, how shall the stone which itself
   sinketh carry you across?

What power hath caste? It is the reality
   that is tested.
Poison may be held in the hand, but man
   dieth if he eat it.
The sovereignty of the True One is known
   in every age. He who obeyeth God's
   order shall become a noble in His
   court.

Those who have meditated on God as the
   truest of the true have done real worship and are contented;
They have refrained from evil, done good
   deeds, and practiced honesty;

They have lived on a little corn and water,
   and burst the entanglements of the
   world.
Thou art the great Bestower; ever Thou
   givest gifts which increase a quarterfold.
Those who have magnified the great God
   have found Him.

QUESTIONS FOR ANALYSIS

- Identify all the "numberless" groups that Nanak lists. What range of social classes do they represent? How does this enumeration reflect the tumultuous times?
- What criticisms of Hindu worship does Nanak raise?
- What lines reveal his belief in rebirth?
- How does Nanak expect true believers to behave?

Source: "Nanak's Teachings in India." In William Theodore de Bary, *Sources of Indian Tradition* (New York: Columbia University Press, 1958), pp. 536–38.

goods, ideas, merchants, and scholars across political and religious boundaries—even across the most divisive boundary of all, that between Sunni Iraq and Shiite Persia.

WESTERN CHRISTENDOM

No region suffered more from the Black Death than western Christendom, and no region made a more spectacular comeback. From 1100 to 1300, Europe had enjoyed a surge in population, economic growth, and significant technological and intellectual progress, only to see these achievements halted in the fourteenth century by famine and the Black Death. Europeans responded by creating new political and cultural forms. New dynasties arose, and a cultural flourishing called the Renaissance revived Europe's connections with its Greek and Roman past and produced masterpieces in art, architecture, and other forms of thought.

Reactions and Revolts

The Black Death brought with it social and economic disorder that challenged the political order. The massive death toll and

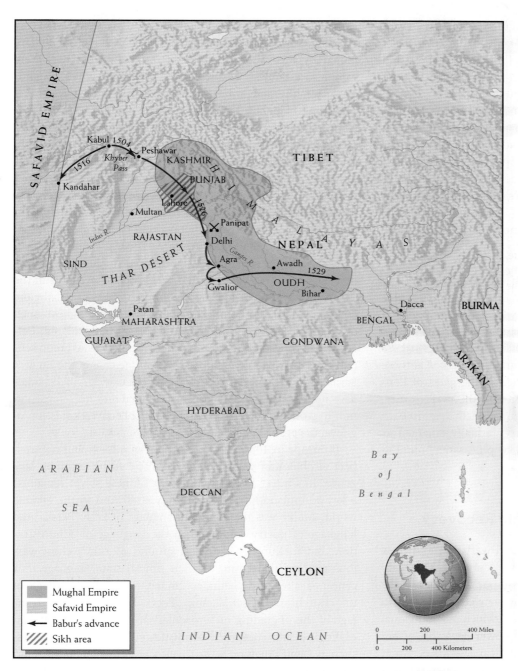

MAP 11.4 | The Mughal Empire, 1530

Compare the Mughal state with the other major Asian empires of this period, notably the Ottoman, Safavid, and Ming states (see Maps 11.2, 11.3, and 11.6).

- What geographical characteristic distinguished the Mughal state at this time from the others?
- Where in the landmass did the new state arise, and what effect do you think its place of origin had on the nature of Mughal rule?
- Based on its geographical location, to what religious traditions did the Mughals need to be sensitive?

the suddenness with which the disease struck also prompted survivors to ask questions about the major institution uniting Christendom, the Catholic Church. Even before the plague arrived, the late medieval western Church had found itself divided at the top (at one point there were three popes) and challenged from below, both by individuals critical of the extravagant lifestyles of some clergymen and by increasing demands on the clergy and church administration. Now the Black Death raised questions about God's relationship to humankind and the Catholic Church's role as God's appointed mediator on earth: Could sinful mortals ever find mercy from a vengeful God, and could an already overstretched and self-interested Church lead them to salvation? Facing challenges to its right to define religious doctrine and practices, the Church responded by demanding strict obedience to the true faith. This entailed the persecution of heretics, Jews, Muslims, homosexuals, prostitutes, and "witches." But the Church also reacted to society's suffering during this period, expanding its charitable and bureaucratic functions, providing alms to the urban poor, and registering births, deaths, and economic transactions. Its responses reassured many that God—and the church—had not abandoned true Christians and shored up the power of religious authorities.

Persecution and administration, however, cost money. Indeed, the needs as well as the extravagances of the clergy spurred certain questionable money-making tactics. One was the selling of indulgences (certificates that reduced one's time in purgatory, where souls continued the repentance that would eventually make them fit for heaven). This sort of unconventional fund-raising, and the growing gap between the church's promises and its ability to bring Christianity into people's everyday lives, more than the persecutions, eventually sparked the Protestant Reformation (see Chapter 12).

At the same time, the high death toll of the fourteenth and fifteenth centuries emboldened those who survived to seek higher wages or reductions in their feudal obligations. When landlords resisted or kings tried to impose new taxes, there were uprisings, including a 1358 peasant revolt in France that was dubbed the Jacquerie (the term derived from "Jacques Bonhomme," a name that contemptuous masters used for all peasants). Armed with only knives and staves, the peasantry went on a rampage, killing hated nobles and clergy and burning and looting all the property they could get their hands on. At issue was the peasants' insistence that they should no longer be tied to their land or have to pay for the tools they used in farming.

A better-organized uprising took place in England in 1381. Although the English Peasants' Revolt began as a protest against a tax levied to raise money for a war on France, it was also fueled by postplague labor shortages: serfs demanded the freedom to move about, and free farmworkers called for higher wages and lower rents. When landlords balked at these demands, aggrieved peasants assembled at the gates of London. The protesters demanded abolition of the feudal order, but the king ruthlessly suppressed them. Nonetheless, in both France and England, a free peasantry gradually emerged as labor shortages made it impossible to keep peasants bound to the soil.

State Building and Economic Recovery

Out of the chaos of famine, disease, and warfare, the diverse peoples of Europe found a political way forward. This path involved the formation of centralized monarchies, much as the Ottomans, Safavids, Mughals, and Ming were accomplishing in Asia. (A **monarchy** is a political system in which one individual holds supreme power and passes that power on to his or her next of kin.) Consolidation of these political systems occurred sometimes through strategic marriages but more often through warfare, both between local princely families and with local aristocratic allies and foreign mercenaries. Many of these dynasties fell as a result of civil war or conquest, but some, like the Tudors in England and the Valois in France, consolidated considerable power. In central Europe, one family, the Habsburgs, established a powerful and long-lasting dynasty. This family provided emperors for the Holy Roman Empire from 1440 to 1806. The Holy Roman Empire included territory that would later be divided into separate states such as the Netherlands, Germany, Austria, Belgium, and Croatia, and it also incorporated parts of present-day Italy, Poland, and Switzerland. Yet the Habsburg monarchs never succeeded in restoring an integrated

empire to western Europe (as Chinese dynasts had done by claiming the mandate of heaven). Indeed, although hereditary monarchy was Europe's dominant form of governance, there were also a number of oligarchic republics in which a handful of wealthy and influential voters selected their leaders, a sprinkling of political systems ruled by archbishops or other clergymen, and many "free" towns, surrounded by walls and protective of their special privileges.

Those who sought to rule the emerging states faced numerous obstacles. For example, rival claimants to the throne financed private armies. Also, the clergy demanded and received privileges and often meddled in politics themselves. The church's huge landholdings and exemptions from taxation made it, too, a formidable economic powerhouse. Towns—many of which had the right to rule themselves—refused to submit to rulers' demands. And once the printing press became available in the 1460s, printers circulated anonymous pamphlets criticizing the court and the clergy. Some states had consultative bodies—such as the Estates General in France, the Cortes in Spain, and Parliament in England—in which princes formally asked representatives of their people for advice and, in the case of the English Parliament, for consent to new forms of taxation. Such bodies gave no voice to most nonaristocratic men and no representation to women. But they did allow the collective expression of grievances against high-handed policies.

If Europe in 1450 had no central government and no prospect of obtaining political unity, it also had no common language. In China, the written literary Chinese script remained a key administrative tool for the dynasts. And in the Islamic world, Arabic was the common language of faith, Persian the language of poetry, and Turkish the language of administration. But in Europe, Latin lost ground as rulers chose various regional dialects to be their official state language. For centuries afterward, Latin continued to be the language of the church and of scholarship. Poets, however, took advantage of the upgrading of vernacular languages such as Italian or English and composed sophisticated poetic masterpieces, such as Dante Alighieri's *The Divine Comedy* or, later, Edmund Spenser's *The Faerie Queen*.

Despite, or perhaps because of, Europe's political fragmentation, new economic initiatives began to take hold, as the English and Flemish competed to expand cloth production and German and Dutch merchants extended their trading networks in the North Sea. Economic recovery was swiftest in southern Europe, where trade with Southwest Asia enriched merchants and subsidized the flourishing of luxury industries, such as glass-making in Venice. Although they remained small compared with Asian cities such as Istanbul or Beijing, Europe's towns rebounded quickly from the Black Death, particularly in Italy, the Netherlands, and along the North Sea coast. (See Map 11.5.) New prosperity and the influx of Christian

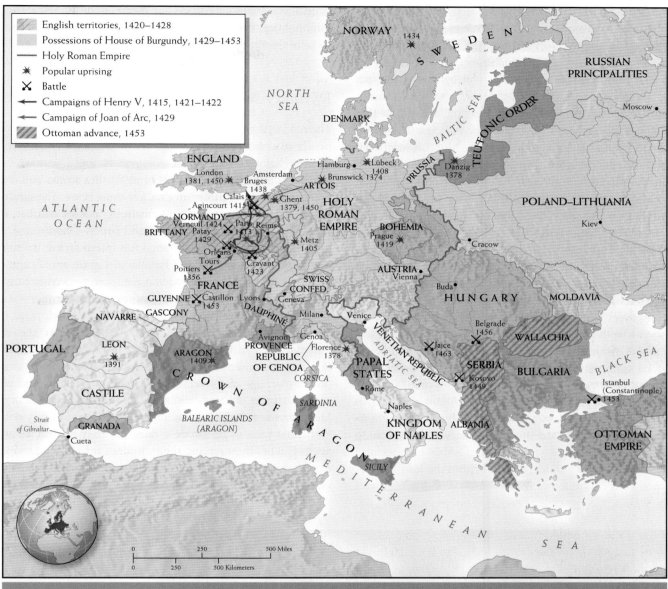

MAP 11.5 | Europe, 1400–1500

Europe was a region divided by dynastic rivalries during the fifteenth century.

- Locate the most powerful regional dynasties on the map: Portugal, Castile, Aragon, France, England, and the Holy Roman Empire. Where did the heaviest fighting occur?

- Why do you think one state was the scene for so many battles?

- On the basis of this map, predict which European territories and political systems would become powerful in subsequent centuries and which would not.

exiles from Istanbul into Italian city-states such as Venice and Florence led to a cultural flowering known as the Renaissance (discussed shortly). In northern and western Europe, the process took longer. In England and France, in particular, internal feuding, regional warfare, and religious fragmentation delayed recovery for decades (see Chapter 12).

Political Consolidation and Trade in Portugal

Portugal's fortunes demonstrate how political stabilization and the emergence of a stronger state could be useful in the revival of trade. After the chaos of the fourteenth century, Spain,

England, and France followed the Portuguese example and established national monarchies. In Spain and Portugal, warfare against Muslims would help unite Christian territories, and Mediterranean trade would add valuable income to state coffers.

Through the fourteenth century, Portuguese Christians devoted themselves to fighting the Moors, who were Muslim occupants of North Africa, the western Sahara, and the Iberian Peninsula. Decisive in this struggle was the Portuguese decision to cross the Strait of Gibraltar and seize the Moorish Moroccan fortresses at Ceuta, in North Africa: their ships could now sail between the Mediterranean and the Atlantic without Muslim interference. With that threat diminished, the Portuguese perceived their neighbor, Castile (part of what is now Spain), as their chief foe. Under João I (r. 1385–1433) the Castilians were defeated, and the monarchy could seek new territories and trading opportunities in the North Atlantic and along the West African coasts. João's son Prince Henrique, known later as Henry the Navigator, further expanded the family's domain by supporting expeditions down the coast of Africa and offshore to the Atlantic islands of the Madeiras and the Azores. The west and central coasts of Africa and the islands of the North and South Atlantic, including the Cape Verde Islands, São Tomé, Principe, and Fernando Po, soon became Portuguese ports of call.

The Portuguese monarchs granted the Atlantic islands to nobles as hereditary possessions on condition that the grantees colonize them, and soon the colonizers were establishing lucrative sugar plantations. In gratitude, noble families and merchants threw their political weight behind the king. Subsequent monarchs continued to reduce local elites' authority and to ensure smooth succession for members of the royal family. This political consolidation enabled Portugal to thrive in the wake of the Black Death.

Dynasty Building and Reconquest in Spain

The road to dynasty in Spain was arduous. Medieval Spain comprised rival kingdoms that quarreled ceaselessly. Also, Spain lacked religious uniformity: Muslims, Jews, and Christians lived side by side in relative harmony, and Muslim armies still occupied strategic areas in the south. Over time, however, marriages and the formation of kinship ties among nobles and between royal lineages yielded a new political order. One by one, the major houses of the Spanish kingdoms intermarried, culminating in the fateful wedding of Isabella of Castile and Ferdinand of Aragon. Thus, Spain's two most important provinces were joined, and Spain became a state to be reckoned with.

THE UNION OF CASTILE AND ARAGON By the time Isabella and Ferdinand married in 1469, Spain was recovering from the miseries of the fourteenth century. This was more than a marriage of convenience. Castile was wealthy and populous; Aragon enjoyed an extended trading network in the Mediterranean. Together, the monarchs brought unruly nobles and distant towns under their domain. They topped off their achievements by marrying their children into other European royal families—especially the Habsburgs, central Europe's most powerful dynasty.

Renaissance Fortifications.
This image of Belmonte Castle in Castile, Spain, built by Don Juan de Pacheco in 1456, shows just how much money and material European nobles were willing to invest to protect their centers of power.

The new rulers also sent Christian armies south to push Muslim forces out of the Iberian Peninsula. By the mid-fifteenth century, only Granada, a strategic lynchpin overlooking the straits between the Mediterranean and the Atlantic, remained in Muslim hands. After a long and costly siege, Christian forces captured the fortress there in January 1492. This was a victory of enormous symbolic importance, as joyous, to Christians, as the fall of Constantinople was depressing. Many people in Spain thumped their chests in pride, unaware or unconcerned that at the same time Ottoman armies were conquering large sections of southeastern Europe.

THE INQUISITION AND WESTWARD EXPLORATION

Just as the Safavid rulers had tried to stamp out all non-Shiite forms of Islam within their domains, so Isabella and Ferdinand sought to drive all non-Catholics out of Spain. Terrified by Ottoman incursions into Europe, in 1481 they launched the **Inquisition**, taking aim especially against *conversos*—converted Jews and Muslims—whom they suspected were Christians only in name. When Granada fell, the crown ordered the expulsion of all Jews from Spain; after 1499, a more tolerant attempt to convert the Moors by persuasion gave way to forced conversion—or emigration. This lack of tolerance meant that Spain, like other European states in this era, became increasingly homogenous. With fewer groups vying for influence within their territories, rulers turned their attention outward, fueling rivalries among the various European states.

Confident in the stability of their state, by late 1491 the Spanish monarchs were willing to listen to a Genoese navigator whose pleas for patronage they had previously rejected. Christopher Columbus promised them unimaginable riches that could finance their military campaigns and bankroll a crusade to liberate Jerusalem from Muslim hands. Off he sailed with a royal patent that guaranteed the monarchs a share of all he discovered. Soon the Spanish economy was reorienting itself toward the Atlantic, and Spain's merchants, missionaries, and soldiers were preparing for conquest and profiteering in what had been, just a few years before, a blank space on the map.

The Struggles of France and England and the Success of Small States

Warfare and strategic marriages allowed the Portuguese and Spanish monarchies to consolidate state power and to lay the foundations for revived commerce. But by no means were all states immediately successful. In France and England, the great age of European monarchy had yet to dawn.

When French forces finally pushed the English back across the English Channel in the Hundred Years' War (1337–1453), the French House of Valois began a slow process of consolidating royal power. Although diplomatic marriages helped the French crown expand its domain, two more centuries of royal initiatives and civil war were required to tame the powerful nobility. In England, even thirty years of civil war between the houses of Lancaster and York did not settle which one would take the throne. Both families in this War of the Roses ultimately lost out to the Tudors, who seized the throne in 1485.

Even where stable states did arise, they were fairly small compared with the Ottoman and Ming Empires. In the mid-sixteenth century, Portugal and Spain, Europe's two most expansionist states, had populations of 1 million and 9 million, respectively. England, excluding Wales, was a mere 3 million in 1550. Only France, with 17 million, had a population close to the Ottoman Empire's 20 to 30 million. And these numbers paled in comparison with Ming China's population of nearly 200 million in 1550 and Mughal India's 110 million in 1600.

But in Europe, small was advantageous. Portugal's relatively small population meant that the crown had fewer groups to instill with loyalty. Also, in the world of finance, the most successful merchants were those inhabiting the smaller Italian city-states and, a bit later, the cities of the northern Netherlands. The Florentines developed sophisticated banking techniques, created extensive networks of agents throughout Europe and the Mediterranean, and served as bankers to the popes. Venetian merchants enjoyed a unique role in the exchange of silks and spices from the eastern Mediterranean. It was in these prosperous city-states that the Renaissance began.

The Renaissance

Just as the Ming harkened back to Han Chinese traditions and the Ottomans looked to Sunni Islam to point the way forward, so European elites looked to their own traditions for guidance as they rebuilt after the devastation of the plague. They found inspiration in ancient Greek and Roman ideas. Europe's political and economic revival also included a powerful outpouring of cultural achievements, led by Italian scholars and artists and financed by bankers, churchmen, and nobles. Much later, scholars coined the word **Renaissance** ("rebirth") to characterize the expanded cultural production of the Italian city-states, France, the Low Countries, England, and the Holy Roman Empire in the period 1430–1550. What was being "reborn" was ancient Greek and Roman art and learning— knowledge that could illuminate a world of expanding horizons and support the rights of people other than clergymen or kings to exert power in it. Although the Renaissance was largely funded by popes and Christian monarchs, it broke the medieval church's monopoly on answers to the big questions and opened the way for secular forms of learning and a more human-centered understanding of the cosmos.

THE ITALIAN RENAISSANCE The Renaissance, ironically, was all about the new—new exposure, that is, to the old classical texts and ancient art and architectural forms. Although some Greek and Roman texts were known in Europe and the Islamic world, the fall of Constantinople and the invention of the printing press made others accessible to western scholars for the first time. Scholars now realized that the pre-Christian Greeks and Romans had known more: more about how to represent and care for the human body; more about geography, astronomy, and architecture; more about how to properly govern states and armies. It was no longer enough to understand Christian doctrine and to trust medieval authorities; one had to accurately retranslate the original sources, which required the learning of languages and of history. This dive backward into ancient Greece and Rome became known as **humanism**, the aspiration to know more about the human experience beyond what the Christian scriptures offered. Humanism was a powerful tool in the hands of those who knew how to use it. Several women, including the celebrated Italian humanist Laura Cereta (1469–1499), used their learning and rhetorical skills to defend the equality of male and female intellects at a time in which both the church and society as a whole believed women scholars to be freaks of nature. (See Primary Source: A Renaissance Defense of Human Equality.)

Wealthy families, powerful rulers, and the Catholic Church were the sponsors of Renaissance achievement. For example, by the 1480s, the Medici family had been patronizing art based on ancient models for three generations. The Medicis were bankers but also influential political players in Florence and Rome. The family contributed greatly to making Florence one of the showplaces of Renaissance art and architecture as well as the center stage for early Renaissance philosophy. Cosimo de' Medici (1389–1464) funded the completion of the sumptuous duomo (cathedral) of Florence, topped by the architect Brunelleschi's masterful dome, the largest built since antiquity. Cosimo's grandson, Lorenzo the Magnificent, supported many of the great Renaissance artists, including Leonardo da Vinci, Sandro Botticelli, and Michelangelo Buonarroti.

The artists who flourished in Florence, Rome, and Venice embraced their own form of humanism. For them, the return to ancient sources meant reviving the principles of the Roman architect Vitruvius and the imitation of nude classical sculpture. Their masterpieces, like Leonardo's *Last Supper* or Michelangelo's *David*, used the technique of perspective and classical treatments of the body to give vivacity and three-dimensionality to paintings and sculptures—even religious ones. Raphael's madonnas portrayed the Virgin Mary as a beautiful individual and not just as a symbol of chastity; similarly, Michelangelo's Sistine Chapel ceiling gave Adam the beautiful body of a Greek god so that viewers could appreciate the glory of the Creation. Of course, these artists also hoped to draw attention to their own achievements, and they were not disappointed. For soon northern European princes, too, sought out both ancient artifacts and the modern artists and humanists who could bring this inspiring new style to their courts.

THE RENAISSANCE SPREADS In the sixteenth century, a series of crises on the Italian Peninsula—including the sacking

Renaissance Masterpieces. Left: *Leonardo da Vinci's* The Last Supper *depicts Christ's disciples reacting to his announcement that one of them will betray him.* Right: *Michelangelo's* David *stands over 13 feet high and was conceived as an expression of Florentine civic ideals.*

A Renaissance Defense of Human Equality

Laura Cereta (1469–1499) was fortunate to have been the daughter of well-educated parents, her father a highly placed lawyer and her mother a successful businesswoman. But it was Laura who devoted herself at a young age to obtaining a deeply humanist education, provided at first at the convent in her home town of Brescia, Italy, and then pursued by intense self-discipline once she had become her father's assistant (at age 12) and after her early marriage (at age 15). As a young woman she became widely known among Renaissance scholars for her learning. This achievement, however, embroiled her in a controversy that had been raging for decades about whether or not intelligent women were freaks of nature. Cereta responded to this line of thought with anger and disdain.

In the following letter to a fictional correspondent—but meant to denounce men such as the medieval writer Boccaccio, who had ridiculed women's intellects—Cereta uses her extensive knowledge of the ancient world and her rhetorical brilliance to denounce those who, in praising her exceptional talents, showed contempt for others of her "race." She invokes figures from Near Eastern and classical antiquity to show that there have always been women who were learned and wise. Notice, too, that the pursuit of the good that Cereta recommends does not involve the church; although she was a pious Christian, Cereta here recommends that individuals pursue secular knowledge rather than devote themselves to religious duties or to prayer.

To Bibolo Semproni
January 13, 1488

Your complaints are hurting my ears, for you say publicly and quite openly that you are not only surprised but pained that I am said to show this extraordinary intellect of the sort one would have thought nature would give to the most learned of men—as if you had reached the conclusion, on the facts of the case, that a similar girl had seldom been seen among peoples of the world. You are wrong on both counts, Semproni, and now that you've abandoned the truth, you are going to spread information abroad that is clearly false.

. . . My cause itself is worthy; I am impelled to show what great glory that noble lineage which I carry in my own breast has won for virtue and literature—a lineage that knowledge, the bearer of honors, has exalted in every age. For the possession of this lineage is legitimate and sure, and it has come all the way down to me from the continuance of a more enduring race.

We have read that the breast of Ethiopian Sabba, imbued with divinity, solved the prophetic riddles of the Egyptian king Solomon. . . . The enduring fame of Inachan Isis will flourish, for she alone of the Argive goddesses revealed to the Egyptians her own alphabet for reading. But Zenobia, an Egyptian woman of noble erudition, became so learned not only in Egyptian but also in Latin and Greek literature that she wrote the histories of barbarian and foreign peoples. . . . Those little Greek women Phyliasia and Lasthenia were wonderful sources of light in the world of letters and they filled me with new life because they ridiculed the students of Plato, who frequently tied themselves in knots over the snare-filled sophistries of their arguments.

All history is full of such examples. My point is that your mouth has grown foul because you keep it sealed so that no arguments can come out of it that might enable you to admit that nature imparts one freedom to all human beings equally—to learn. But the question of my exceptionality remains. And here choice alone, since it is the arbiter of characters, is the distinguishing factor. For some women worry about the styling of their hair, the elegance of their clothes, and the pearls and other jewelry they wear on their fingers. Others love to say cute little things, to hide their feeling behind a mask of tranquility, to indulge in dancing, and lead pet dogs around on a leash. But those women for whom the quest for the good represents a higher value restrain their young spirits and ponder better plains. They harden their bodies with sobriety and toil, they control their tongues, they carefully monitor what they hear, they ready their minds for all-night vigils. . . . For knowledge is not given as a gift but by study. For a mind free, keen, and unyielding in the face of hard work always rises to the good, and desire for learning grows in depth and breadth.

QUESTIONS FOR ANALYSIS

- Why is Cereta upset that she is seen as exceptional?
- How does she counter claims that women are not equal to men in intelligence?
- What recommendations does she have for women who want to pursue "the quest for the good"?

Source: Laura Cereta, *Collected Letters of a Renaissance Feminist*, transcribed, translated and edited by Diana Robin (Chicago: University of Chicago Press, 1997), pp. 76–79.

of Rome in 1527 by troops under the control of the Holy Roman Empire—and increasing economic prosperity in other parts of Europe helped to spread Renaissance culture throughout Europe. Philip II of Spain, for example, purchased more than 1,000 paintings during his reign; Henry IV of France and his queen, Marie de' Medici, invested a fortune in renovating the Louvre, building a new royal residence at Fontainebleau, and hiring Peter Paul Rubens to paint grand canvases. Courtiers built up-to-date palaces and invited scholars to live on their estates; Dutch, German, and French merchants also patronized the arts. All wanted their sons to be educated in the humanistic manner. Some families and religious institutions offered women access to the new learning, and some men encouraged their sisters, daughters, and wives to expand their horizons. The well-educated nun Caritas Pirckheimer (1467–1532), for example, exchanged learned letters and books with male humanists in the German states. Studying Greek, Latin, and ancient rhetoric did not make the commercial elite equal to the aristocrats, or women equal to men, but this sort of education did enable some non-nobles to obtain social influence and to criticize the ruling elites.

THE REPUBLIC OF LETTERS Since political and religious powers were not united in Europe (as they were in China and the Islamic world), scholars and artists could play one side against the other or, alternatively, could suffer both clerical and political persecution. Michelangelo completed commissions for the Medicis, for the Florentine Wool Guild, and for Pope Julius II. Peter Paul Rubens painted for the courts of France, Spain, England, and the Netherlands, as well as selling paintings on the open market. These two painters, renowned for showing a great deal of flesh, frequently offended conservative church officials, but their secular patrons kept them in oils. The Dutch scholar Desiderius Erasmus was able to ridicule the church because he had the patronage of English, Dutch, and French supporters. Other scholars used their learning to defend the older elites: for example, numerous lawyers and scholars continued to work for the popes, defending the papacy.

The search for patrons and the flight from persecution, especially after the Reformation, made Europe's educated elite increasingly cosmopolitan (as it had in China and the Islamic empires). Scholars met one another in royal palaces and cultural centers such as Florence, Antwerp, and Amsterdam. Seeking specialized information or rare books, they formed what was known as "the republic of letters"—a network of correspondents who were more interested in individual knowledge or talent than in noble titles or clerical rank. In this way, the Renaissance knitted together the European elite. This did not mean, however, that a consensus emerged about who should rule.

POWER AND THE RENAISSANCE THEORIZING ABOUT WAR The Renaissance was not only an embrace of the arts and sciences of this world, but also a vehicle that enabled the more direct study of worldly power. Close reading of the ancient histories of Sallust, Livy, and Caesar emboldened scholars to address more forthrightly the conditions under which power could be maintained or undermined. New forms of governance were invented—and older forms buttressed. The Florentines pioneered a form of civic humanism under which all citizens were to devote themselves to defending the state against tyrants and foreign invaders; according to this view, the state would reward their civic virtue by ensuring their liberty. Yet it was also a Florentine, Niccolò Machiavelli, who wrote the most famous treatise on authoritarian power, *The Prince* (1513). Machiavelli argued that political leadership was not about obeying God's rules but about mastering the amoral means of modern statecraft. Holding and exercising power were ends in themselves, he claimed; civic virtue was merely a pretense on the part of those (like the Medici family he knew so well) who simply wanted to keep the upper hand.

In his own lifetime, Machiavelli was even more renowned for his essay *The Art of War* (1521). Here, the Florentine humanist argued that Roman military tactics, including the deploying of trained, armed citizens, would make for a more trustworthy army than the use of mercenary soldiers. The enrollment of a broadly based citizenry in the defense of the state, he insisted, would also make for political stability. His advice was hardly practicable in a Europe in which monarchs put little trust in their fellow nobles and even less in their subjects, but his ideas circulated widely and would gradually catch on and inspire military reforms in the Dutch Republic and during the Thirty Years' War (see Chapter 13). And he made little of the use of artillery, although the cannon had been used in European siege warfare since at least the 1420s; the Portuguese had already mounted them on oceangoing ships and had begun to use them to blast open South Asian ports. Machiavelli's fellow humanist Niccolò Tartaglia noticed the upsurge in cannon usage and produced an important treatise on ballistics, in which mathematics was first applied to the trajectory of projectiles. But neither of these was as influential as a wave of publications devoted to proper fortification designs, written by specialized military engineers who, for the first time, advocated the construction of defenses not to be pleasing to the eye but to best absorb the force of modern cannons. Thus began a long-lasting battle between military architects seeking to construct invincible defenseworks and artillery makers seeking to destroy them.

Like artistic and early manufacturing techniques, European military technologies diffused across the continent through conflict between states. Europeans learned much by observing one another at close range, especially during the many wars that marked the fifteenth and sixteenth centuries. As princes began to orient themselves more and more to obtaining and preserving power in this world, they began to value subjects who could build sturdy fortifications or more effectively mix gunpowder (a Chinese invention in widespread use in Europe by 1400). By the sixteenth century, many had also formed what were essentially standing armies and had begun to invest heavily in improved fortifications, not only for their castles but for their cities of residence as well. But like the church's new worldly activities, these princely activities also cost a great deal of money and demanded an expansion of state operations. In orienting the elite toward both ancient ideas and this-worldly power, in this way, too, the Renaissance revolutionized both European culture and politics—even if it could not unify the states and peoples who cultivated it.

MING CHINA

Like the Europeans, the Chinese saw their stable worldview and political order crumble under the cataclysms of human and bacterial invasions. Moreover, like the Europeans, people in China had long regarded outsiders as "barbarians." Together, the Mongols and the Black Death upended the political and intellectual foundations of what had appeared to be the world's most integrated society. The Mongols brought the Yuan dynasty to power; then the plague devastated China and prepared the way for the emergence of the Ming dynasty.

Ruled by ethnically Han Chinese, the Ming dynasty defined itself against its foreign predecessors. Ming emperors sought to reinforce everything Chinese. In particular, they supported China's vast internal agricultural markets in an attempt to minimize dependence on merchants and foreign trade.

Restoring Order

In the chaotic fourteenth century, as plague and famine ravaged China and as the Mongol Yuan dynasty collapsed, only a strong military movement capable of overpowering other groups could restore order. That intervention began at the hands of a poor young man who had trained in the Red Turban Movement: Zhu Yuanzhang. He was an orphan from a peasant household in an area devastated by disease and famine and a former novice at a Buddhist monastery. At age twenty-four, Zhu joined the Red Turbans, after which he rose quickly to become a distinguished commander. Eventually, his forces defeated the Yuan and drove the Mongols from China.

It soon became clear that Zhu had a much grander design for all of China than the ambitions of most warlords. When he took the important city of Nanjing in 1356, he renamed it Yingtian ("In response to Heaven"). Buoyed by subsequent successful military campaigns, twelve years later Zhu (r. 1368–1398) proclaimed the founding of the Ming ("brilliant") dynasty. Soon thereafter, his troops met little resistance when they seized the Yuan capital of Beijing, causing the Mongol emperor to flee to his homeland in the steppe. It would, however, take Zhu almost another twenty years to reunify the entire country.

Centralization under the Ming

Zhu and successive Ming emperors had to rebuild a devastated society from the ground up. Although in the past China had experienced natural catastrophes, wars, and social dislocation,

The Forbidden City. *The Yongle Emperor relocated the capital to Beijing, where he began the construction of the Forbidden City, or imperial palace. The palace was designed to inspire awe in all who saw it.*

the plague's legacy was devastation on an unprecedented scale. It left the new rulers with the formidable challenge of rebuilding the great cities, restoring respect for ruling elites, and reconstructing the bureaucracy.

IMPERIAL GRANDEUR AND KINSHIP The rebuilding began under Zhu, the Hongwu ("expansive and martial") Emperor, whose extravagant capital at Nanjing reflected imperial grandeur. When the dynasty's third emperor, the Yongle ("perpetual happiness") Emperor, relocated the capital to Beijing, he flaunted an even more grandiose style. Construction here mobilized around 100,000 artisans and 1 million laborers. The city had three separate walled enclosures. Inside the outer city walls sprawled the imperial city; within its walls lay the palace city, the Forbidden City. Traffic within the walled sections navigated through boulevards leading to the different gates, above which imposing towers soared. The palace compound, where the imperial family resided, had more than 9,000 rooms. Anyone standing in the front courts, which measured more than 400 yards on a side and boasted marble terraces and carved railings, would gasp at the sense of awesome power. That was precisely the effect the Ming emperors wanted (just as the Ottoman sultans did in building Topkapi Palace).

Marriage and kinship buttressed the power of the Ming imperial household. The dynasty's founder married the adopted daughter of a leading Red Turban rebel (her father, according to legend, was a convicted murderer), thereby consolidating his power and eliminating a threat. Empress Ma, as she was known, became the Hongwu Emperor's principal wife and was praised for her compassion. Emerging as the kinder face of the regime, she tempered the harsh and sometimes cruel disposition of her spouse. He had numerous other consorts as well, including Korean and Mongol women, who bore him twenty-six sons and sixteen daughters (similar to, although on smaller scale than, the sultan's harem at Topkapi Palace).

BUILDING A BUREAUCRACY Faced with the challenge of reestablishing order out of turmoil, the Hongwu Emperor initially sought to rule through his many kinsmen by giving imperial princes generous stipends, command of large garrisons, and significant autonomy in running their domains. However, when the princes' power began to threaten the court, the emperor slashed their stipends, reduced their privileges, and took control of their garrisons. No longer dependent on these men, he established an imperial bureaucracy beholden only to him and to his successors. These officials won appointments through their outstanding performance on a reinstated civil service examination.

In addition, the Hongwu Emperor took other steps to install a centralized system of rule. He assigned bureaucrats to oversee the manufacture of porcelain, cotton, and silk products as well as tax collection. He reestablished the Confucian school system as a means of selecting a cadre of loyal officials (not

Chinese Irrigation. *Farmers in imperial China used sophisticated devices to extract water for irrigation, as depicted in this illustration from the Yuan Mongol period.*

The Hongwu Emperor's Proclamation

This proclamation by the founder of the Ming dynasty, the Hongwu Emperor (r. 1368–1398), reveals how he envisioned reconstructing the devastated country as his own personal project. He sought a return to austerity by denouncing the morally corrosive effect of money and material possessions, and he especially distrusted his officials. Although frustrated in his efforts, the Hongwu Emperor nonetheless set the tone for the centralization of power in the person of the emperor.

To all civil and military officials:

I have told you to refrain from evil. Doing so would enable you to bring glory to your ancestors, your wives and children, and yourselves. With your virtue, you then could assist me in my endeavors to bring good fortune and prosperity to the people. You would establish names for yourselves in Heaven and on earth, and for thousands and thousands of years, you would be praised as worthy men.

However, after assuming your posts, how many of you really followed my instructions? Those of you in charge of money and grain have stolen them yourselves; those of you in charge of criminal laws and punishments have neglected the regulations. In this way grievances are not redressed and false charges are ignored. Those with genuine grievances have nowhere to turn; even when they merely wish to state their complaints, their words never reach the higher officials. Occasionally these unjust matters come to my attention. After I discover the truth, I capture and imprison the corrupt, villainous, and oppressive officials involved. I punish them with the death penalty or forced labor or have them flogged with bamboo sticks in order to make manifest the consequences of good or evil actions. . . .

Alas, how easily money and profit can bewitch a person! With the exception of the righteous person, the true gentleman, and the sage, no one is able to avoid the temptation of money. But is it really so difficult to reject the temptation of profit? The truth is people have not really tried.

Previously, during the final years of the Yuan dynasty, there were many ambitious men competing for power who did not treasure their sons and daughters but prized jade and silk, coveted fine horses and beautiful clothes, relished drunken singing and unrestrained pleasure, and enjoyed separating people from their parents, wives, and children. I also lived in that chaotic period. How did I avoid such snares? I was able to do so because I valued my reputation and wanted to preserve my life. Therefore I did not dare to do these evil things. . . .

In order to protect my reputation and to preserve my life, I have done away with music, beautiful girls, and valuable objects. Those who love such things are usually "a success in the morning, a failure in the evening." Being aware of the fallacy of such behavior, I will not indulge such foolish fancies. It is not really that hard to do away with these tempting things.

QUESTIONS FOR ANALYSIS

- What criticisms does the Hongwu Emperor level against the Mongol Yuan, whose rule he overthrew?
- What crimes does he accuse his own officials of committing, and what punishments does he carry out?
- Why would this Chinese emperor issue a decree that focuses on defining moral behavior?

Source: Patricia Buckley Ebrey (ed.), *Chinese Civilization: A Sourcebook,* Second Edition, revised and expanded (New York: The Free Press, 1993), pp. 205–6.

unlike the Ottoman janissaries and administrators). He also set up local networks of villages to rebuild irrigation systems and to supervise reforestation projects to prevent flooding—with the astonishing result that the amount of land reclaimed nearly tripled within eight years. Historians estimate that the Hongwu Emperor's reign oversaw the planting of about 1 billion trees, including 50 million sterculia, palm, and varnish trees around Nanjing. Their products served in building a maritime expedition fleet in the early fifteenth century. For water control, 40,987 reservoirs underwent repairs or new construction.

Now the imperial palace not only projected the image of a power center; it *was* the center of power. Every official received his appointment by the emperor through the Ministry of Personnel. The Hongwu Emperor also eliminated the post of prime minister (he executed the man who held the post) and henceforth ruled directly. Ming bureaucrats literally lost their seats and had to kneel before the emperor. In one eight-day period, the Hongwu Emperor reputedly reviewed over 1,600 petitions dealing with 3,392 separate matters. The drawback, of course, was that he had to keep tabs on this immense system, and his bureaucrats were not always up to the task. Indeed, the Hongwu Emperor constantly juggled personal and impersonal forms of authority, sometimes fortifying the administration, sometimes undermining it lest it become too autonomous. In due course, he nurtured a bureaucracy far more extensive than those of the Islamic empires. The Ming thus established the most highly centralized system of government of all the monarchies of this period. (See Primary Source: The Hongwu Emperor's Proclamation.)

Religion under the Ming

Just as the Ottoman sultans projected themselves as Muslim rulers, calling themselves the shadow of God, and European monarchs claimed to rule by divine right, so the Ming emperors enhanced their legitimacy by drawing on ancient Chinese religious traditions. Citing the mandate of heaven, the emperor revised and strengthened the elaborate protocol of rites and ceremonies that had undergirded dynastic power for centuries. As well as underscoring the emperor's centrality, official rituals (such as those related to the gods of soil and grain) reinforced political and social hierarchies.

Under the guise of "community" gatherings, rites and sacrifices solidified the Ming order by portraying the rulers as the moral and spiritual benefactors of their subjects. On at least ninety occasions each year, the emperor engaged in sacrificial rites, providing symbolic communion between the human and the spiritual worlds. These lavish festivities reinforced the ruler's image as mediator between otherworldly affairs of the gods and worldly concerns of the empire's subjects. The message was clear: the gods were on the side of the Ming household.

As an example of religious rituals reinforcing hierarchies, the emperor sanctioned official cults that were either civil or military and further distinguished as great, middle, or minor as well as celestial, terrestrial, or human categories. Official cults, however, often conflicted with local faiths. In this regard, they revealed the limits of Ming centralism. Consider Dongyang, a hilly interior region. As was common in Ming China, the people of Dongyang supported Buddhist institutions. Guan Yu, a legendary martial hero killed centuries earlier, was enshrined in a local Buddhist monastery there. But he was also worshipped as part of a state cult. Herein lay the problem: the state cult and the Buddhist monastery were separate entities, and imperial law held that the demands of the state cult prevailed over those of the local monastery. So the state-appointed magistrates in Dongyang kept a watchful eye on local religious leaders, although the magistrates refrained from tampering directly in the monastery's affairs. Although the imperial government insisted that people honor their contributions to the state, Dongyang's residents delivered most of their funds to the Buddhist monks. So strong were local sentiments that even the officials siphoned revenues to the monastery.

Ming Deities. *A pantheon of deities worshipped during the Ming, demonstrating the rich religious culture of the period.*

Ming Rulership

Religious sources of political power were less essential for the Ming dynasty than for the Islamic dynasties. Conquest and defense helped establish the realm, and bureaucracy kept it functioning. The empire's large scale (see Map 11.6) required a remarkably complex administration. To many outsiders (especially Europeans, whose region was in a state of constant war), Ming stability and centralization appeared to be political wizardry.

In terms of the structures underlying Ming power, the usual dynastic dilemmas were present. The emperor wished to be seen as the special guardian of his subjects. He wanted their

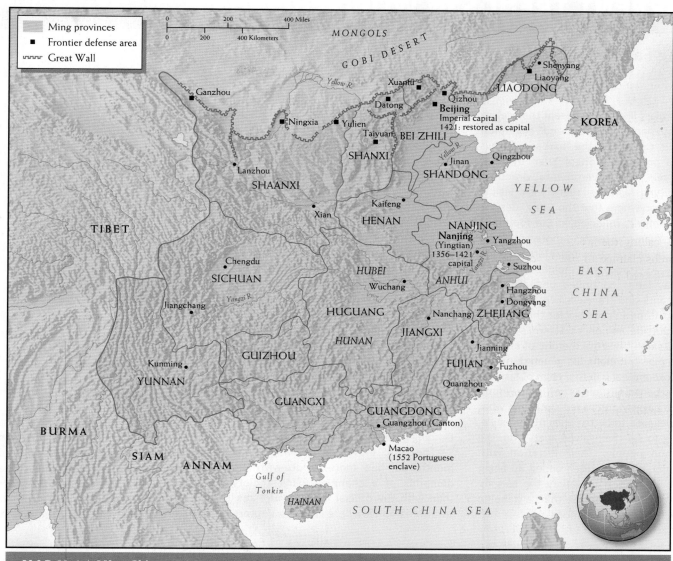

MAP 11.6 | Ming China, 1500s

The Ming state was one of the largest empires at this time—and the most populous. It had a long seacoast and even longer internal borders.

- What were the two Ming capitals, and what were the three main seaport trading cities?
- According to the map, where did the Ming rulers expect the greatest threat to their security?
- From your reading, how did the Ming rulers view foreign contact and exchange during this period?

allegiance as well as their taxes and labor. But during hard times, poor farmers were reluctant to provide resources—taxes or services—to distant officials. For these reasons alone, the Hongwu Emperor preferred to entrust management of the rural world to local leaders, whom he appointed as village chiefs, village elders, or tax captains. (In fact, a popular Chinese proverb was "The mountain is high and the emperor is far away.") Within these communities, the dynasty created a social hierarchy based on age, sex, and kinship. While women's labor remained critical for the village economy, the government reinforced a

gender hierarchy by promoting women's chastity and constructing commemorative arches for widows who refrained from remarrying. The Ming thus produced a more elaborate system for classifying and controlling its subjects than did the other Afro-Eurasian dynasties. But individuals also sought to define themselves by dressing in ways that expressed their own view of their place in the social order. (See Current Trends in World History: Ming Fashion.)

The Ming Empire, like the European and Islamic states, also faced periodic unrest and rebellion. Rebels often proclaimed

Ming Fashion

Ming rulers liked to represent themselves as custodians of the "civilized" Han traditions, in contrast to the "barbarian" ways of the previous Mongol Yuan dynasty. However, from governmental practices to clothing fashions, there were visible signs everywhere that the Ming, despite their rhetoric, followed in the footsteps of the Yuan and became more and more linked to an ever-growing, interconnected world. As trade with neighboring and faraway lands continued unabated and merchants and travelers kept moving, it proved to be impossible for the Ming to keep outside influences at arm's length. At the same time, the rhetoric of a return to the Han traditions did generate moves to invoke antiquity in the realm of fashion. Status-conscious elites with newfound wealth eagerly purchased clothes in what they believed to be the ancient Han style, hoping to set themselves apart from the common people. Their flirtation with antiquity, however, often ended up being more reinvention to satisfy the surging demands of the market than a genuine return to earlier conventions.

Founder Zhu Yuanzhang set the tone of the Ming by trying to rid the country of the close-fitting tunics worn by the Mongols. He advocated instead the wearing of the reputedly Tang-style garment of earlier times. While this measure did meet with some success, the vibrant clothing sector was hardly free of its fascination with the "exotic," such as horsehair skirts from Korea for men. A rare commodity when they first arrived, probably via trade missions, by the late fifteenth century, local weavers had become so skilled in making these skirts and consumers so eager to obtain them that craftsworkers were caught stealing the tails of horses to satisfy the soaring demand for the raw materials. Indeed, undoubtedly to the chagrin of the first Ming emperor and his descendants, much of the Yuan style and even terminology in both male and female clothing persisted during the Ming era.

The retro movement in fashion, as mentioned, had more to do with the demands of a changing Ming society than with the official advocacy for restorationism. Nowhere was this more

An example of headwear used by Ming officials, reputedly following the style of earlier dynasties. The beams attached to the crown of the cap indicate the official's rank, so the cap is known as a "beamed cap."

apparent than in the myriad styles of hats for men—a convenient yet highly visible way to make a statement in social standing. Invoking the names of earlier dynasties, there were the Han cap, the Jin cap, the Tang cap, and so on. The most interesting, however, was the Chunyang hat,

their own brand of religious beliefs, just as local elites resented central authority. Outright terror helped stymie threats to central authority. In a massive wave of carnage, the Hongwu Emperor slaughtered anyone who posed a threat to his authority, from the highest of ministers to the lowliest of scribes. From 1376 to 1393, four of his purges condemned close to 100,000 subjects to execution.

Yet, despite the emperor's immense power, the Ming Empire remained undergoverned. Indeed, as the population multiplied, there were too few loyal officials to handle local affairs. By the sixteenth and early seventeenth centuries, for example, some 10,000 to 15,000 officials shouldered the responsibility of managing a population exceeding 200 million people. Nonetheless, the Hongwu Emperor bequeathed to his descendants a set of tools for ruling that drew on subjects' direct loyalty to the emperor and on the intricate workings of an extensive bureaucracy. His legacy enabled his successors to balance local sources of power with the needs of dynastic rulership.

Trade and Exploration

In the fourteenth century, China began its economic recovery from the devastation of disease and political turmoil. Gradually, political stability allowed trade to revive. Now the new dynasty's merchants reestablished China's preeminence in long-distance commercial exchange. Chinese silk and cotton textiles, as well as fine porcelains, ranked among the world's most coveted luxuries. Wealthy families from Lisbon to Kalabar loved to wash their hands in delicate Chinese bowls and to flaunt fine wardrobes made from bolts of Chinese dyed linens and smoothly spun silk. When a Chinese merchant ship sailed into port, trading partners and onlookers crowded the docks to watch the unloading of precious cargoes. Although Ming rulers' support for overseas ventures wavered and eventually declined, this period saw important developments in Chinese trade and exploration.

During the Ming period, Chinese traders based in ports such as Hangzhou, Quanzhou, and Guangzhou (Canton) were

The "paddy-field gown" for women might have had its origins in Buddhist robes.

which allegedly drew upon both Han and Tang styles in its design but had actually become a symbol of the so-called new and strange fashion that so often attracted commentary in Ming writings. In fact, it was favored by the young, who had nothing but disdain for ancient styles!

Nor was the rage for fashion reserved for men only or even for just the privileged. As one Ming writer lamented, perhaps with a hint of exaggeration: "Nowadays the very servant girls dress in silk gauze, and the singsong girls look down on brocaded silks and embroidered gowns." Respectable women, we are told, looked to the clothing and style of the courtesans of the prosperous southern region of the country for ideas and inspiration for fashion. Indeed, much of our visual knowledge of Ming womens' clothing comes from paintings likely of highly trained courtesans or those female "entertainers" ubiquitous in Ming urban centers. These paintings reveal the different and consistently evolving styles of clothing for Ming women, including the "paddy-field gown"—which might have owed its origins to Buddhist robes—that were the focus of much criticism from those who frowned on the growing penchant for the exotic, the strange, the outrageous, and the irreverent in the realm of fashion. If nothing else, this debate about clothing certainly tells us that despite the often conservative

stance and policies of the Ming regime, the everyday life of many Ming subjects was a constant exercise in negotiating the multiple impacts of both the old and the new as well as the familiar and the foreign in different arenas of their rapidly changing society.

QUESTIONS FOR ANALYSIS

- Why did the elite cultivate an "ancient" Han style?
- Can you think of "retro" styles popular today? What do they say about the people who cultivate them?
- How do we know about changes in women's fashion in the Ming era? Are there any dangers in using these sources to understand the dress of all Ming women?

Explore Further

Finnane, Antonia. *Changing Clothes in China: Fashion, History, Nation* (2008).

as energetic as their Muslim counterparts in the Indian Ocean. These ports were home to prosperous merchants and the point of convergence for vast sea-lanes. Leaving the mainland ports, Chinese vessels carried precious wares to offshore islands, the Pescadores, and Taiwan. From there they sailed on to the ports of Kyūshū, the Ryūkyūs, Luzon, and maritime Southeast Asia. As entrepôts for global goods, East Asian ports flourished. Former fishing villages developed into major urban centers.

The Ming dynasty viewed overseas expansion with suspicion, however. The Hongwu Emperor feared that too much contact with the outside world would cause instability and undermine his rule. In fact, he banned private maritime commerce in 1371. But enforcement was lax, and by the late fifteenth century, maritime trade once again surged. Because much of the thriving business took place in defiance of official edicts, it led to constant friction between government officials and maritime traders. Although the Ming government ultimately agreed to issue licenses for overseas trade in the mid-sixteenth century, its

policies continued to vacillate. To Ming officials, the sea represented problems of order and control rather than opportunities.

THE EXPEDITIONS OF ZHENG HE One spectacular exception to the Ming's attitude toward maritime trade was a series of officially sponsored expeditions in the early fifteenth century. It was the ambitious Yongle Emperor who took the initiative. One of his loyal followers was a Muslim whom the Ming army had captured as a boy. The youth was castrated and sent to serve at the court (as a eunuch, he could not continue his family line and so theoretically owed sole allegiance to the emperor). Given the name **Zheng He** (1371–1433), he grew up to be an important military leader. The emperor entrusted him with venturing out to trade, collect tribute, and display China's power to the world.

From 1405 to 1433, Zheng He commanded the world's greatest armada and led seven naval expeditions. His larger ships stretched 400 feet in length (Columbus's *Santa Maria* was 85 feet), carried hundreds of sailors on four tiers of decks, and

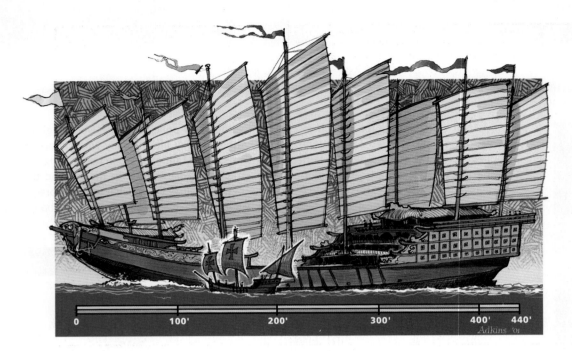

Zheng He's Ship. *A testament to centuries of experience in shipbuilding and maritime activities, the largest ship in Zheng He's armada in the early fifteenth century was about five times the length of Columbus's Santa Maria (pictured next to Zheng's ship) and had nine times the capacity in terms of tonnage. It had nine staggered masts and twelve silk sails, all designed to demonstrate the grandeur of the Ming Empire.*

maneuvered with sophisticated rudders, nine masts, and watertight compartments. The first expedition set sail with a flotilla of 62 large ships and over 200 lesser ones. All 28,000 men aboard pledged to promote Ming glory.

Zheng He and his entourage aimed to establish tributary relations with far-flung territories—from Southeast Asia to the Indian Ocean ports, to the Persian Gulf, and to the east coast of Africa. (See Map 11.7.) These expeditions did not seek territorial expansion, but rather control of trade and tribute. Zheng traded for ivory, spices, ointments, exotic woods, and even some wildlife, including giraffes, zebras, and ostriches. He also used his considerable force to intervene in local affairs, exhibiting China's might in the process. If a community refused to pay tribute, Zheng's fleet would attack it. He encouraged rulers or envoys from Southeast Asia, India, Southwest Asia, and Africa to visit his homeland. When local rulers were uncooperative, Zheng might seize them and drag them all the way to China to face the emperor, as he did the rulers of Sumatra and Ceylon.

As spectacular as they were, Zheng's accomplishments could not survive the changing tides of events at home. Although many items gathered on his voyages delighted the court, most were not the stuff of everyday commerce. The expeditions were glamorous but expensive, and in 1424, when the Yongle Emperor died, they lost their most enthusiastic patron. Moreover, by the mid-fifteenth century, there was a revival of military threats from the north. At that time, the Ming court was shocked to discover that during a tour of the frontiers, the emperor had been captured and held hostage by the Mongols. Recalling how the maritime-oriented Song dynasty had been overrun by invaders from the north (see Chapter 10), Ming officials withdrew imperial support for seagoing ventures and instead devoted their energies to overland

ventures and defense. Thus, Zheng's expeditions came to a complete halt in 1433. Never again did the Ming undertake such large-scale maritime ventures, although individual merchants, of course, returned to their profitable coastal trade routes.

The Chinese decision to forgo overseas ventures after 1433 was momentous. Although China remained the wealthiest, most densely settled region of the world with the most fully developed state structure and thriving market, the empire's wariness of overseas projects deprived merchants and would-be explorers of vital support in an age when others were beginning to look outward and across the oceans.

CONCLUSION

How could all the dying and devastation that came with the Black Death not have transformed the peoples of Afro-Eurasia? Much did change, but certain underlying ideals and institutions endured. What changed were mainly the political regimes, which took the blame for the catastrophes. The Delhi Sultanate, the Abbasid Empire, and the Yuan dynasty collapsed. In contrast, universal religions and wide-ranging cultural systems persisted even though they underwent vast transformations. The Ming dynasts in China set the stage for a long tenure by claiming, as had previous rulers, the mandate of heaven and stressing China's place at the center of their universe. A strict Shiite version of Islam emerged in Iran, while a fervent form of Sunni Islam found its champion in the Ottoman Empire. In Europe, national monarchies appeared in Spain, Portugal, France, and England. Debilitated by death and disorder, the Catholic Church recovered its centrality, though some Europeans, too, began to

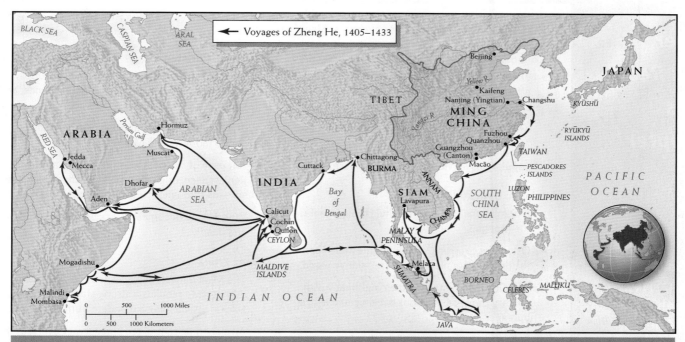

MAP 11.7 | Voyages of Zheng He, 1405–1433

Zheng He's voyages are some of the most famous in world history. Many historians have speculated about how history might have been different if the Chinese emperors had allowed the voyages to continue.

- For how many years did Zheng's voyages last?
- How far did Zheng's voyages take him?
- Why did Chinese expeditions not have the same impact as European voyages of exploration toward the end of the fifteenth century?

satisfy their spiritual longings in ways that went beyond traditional practices.

The new states and empires had notable differences. These were evident in the ambition of a Ming warlord who established a new dynasty, the military expansionism of Turkish households bordering the Byzantine Empire, the unifying vision of Mughal rulers in northern India, and the desire of various European rulers to consolidate power. But interactions among peoples also mattered: an eagerness to reestablish and expand trade networks and a desire to convert unbelievers to "the true faith"—be it a form of Islam, a variant of Hinduism, an exclusive Christianity, or a local type of Buddhism.

The dynasties all faced similar problems. They had to establish legitimacy, ensure smooth succession, deal with religious groups, and forge working relationships with nobles, townspeople, merchants, and peasants. Yet each state developed distinctive traits as a result of political innovation, traditional ways of ruling, and borrowing from neighbors. European monarchies achieved significant internal unity, often through warfare and in the context of a cultural Renaissance. Ottoman rulers perfected techniques for ruling an ethnically and religiously diverse empire: they moved military forces swiftly, allowed local communities a degree of political and religious autonomy, and trained a bureaucracy dedicated to the Ottoman and Sunni Islamic way of life. The Ming dynasty fashioned an imperial system based on a Confucian-trained bureaucracy and intense subordination to the emperor so that it could manage a mammoth population. The rising monarchies of Europe, the Shiite regime of the Safavids in Persia, and the Ottoman state all blazed with religious fervor and sought to eradicate or subordinate the beliefs of other groups.

The new states displayed unprecedented political and economic powers. All demonstrated military prowess, a desire for stable hierarchies and secure borders, and a drive to expand. Each legitimized its rule via dynastic marriage and succession, state-sanctioned religion, and administrative bureaucracies. Each supported vigorous commercial activity. The Islamic regimes, especially, engaged in long-distance commerce and, by conquest and conversion, extended their holdings.

For western Christendom, the Ottoman conquests were decisive. They provoked Europeans to establish commercial connections to the east, south, and west. The consequences of their new toeholds would be momentous—just as the Chinese decision to turn *away* from overseas exploration and commerce marked a turning point in world history. Both decisions were instrumental in determining which worlds would come together and which would remain apart.

FOCUS ON: *Crisis and Recovery in Afro-Eurasia*

Collapse and Consolidation

- Bubonic plague originates in Inner Asia and afflicts people from China to Europe.

- Climate change and famine leave people vulnerable, while commerce facilitates the spread of disease.

- The plague kills 25 to 65 percent of infected populations and leaves societies in turmoil.

Islamic Dynasties

- Ottoman, Safavid, and Mughal Empires replace the Mongols.

- Ottomans overrun Constantinople and become the primary Sunni regime in the Islamic world.

- The Ottomans establish their legitimacy with military prowess, religious backing, and a loyal bureaucracy.

- Sultans manage decentralizing tendencies of outlying provinces with flexibility and tolerance, relying on religious faith, patronage, and bureaucracy.

- Safavid and Mughal regimes arise in Iran and South Asia.

Western Christendom

- New dynastic monarchies that claim to rule by divine right appear in Portugal, Spain, France, and England.

- The Inquisition takes aim against *conversos*—converted Jews and Muslims.

- A rebirth of classical learning, known as the Renaissance, originates in Italian city-states and spreads throughout western Europe.

- War making becomes more scientific, expensive, and deadly.

Ming China

- The Ming dynasty replaces the Mongol Yuan dynasty and rebuilds a strong state from the ground up, claiming a mandate from heaven.

- An elaborate, centralized bureaucracy oversees the revival of infrastructure and long-distance trade.

- The emperor and bureaucracy concentrate on developing internal markets and overland trade at the expense of overseas commerce.

Islamic World

Osman begins Ottoman Empire **1299**

The Black Death arrives in Baghdad **1347** ◆

Western Christendom

Black Death reaches Italian port cities ◆ **1347**

Peasant revolts in England and France **1358–1381** ◀━━━━━

East Asia

Black Death reaches China **1320** ◆

The Hongwu Emperor founds Ming dynasty **1368** ◆

1300   1350

1. **Explain** how the Black Death, or bubonic plague, spread throughout Afro-Eurasia. What human activity facilitated its diffusion?

2. **Describe** the long-term consequences of bubonic plague for the Afro-Eurasian world. What were the plague's social, political, and economic ramifications in various parts of the landmass?

3. **Identify** the three main Islamic dynasties that emerged after the bubonic plague. How were they similar, and how were they different?

4. **Analyze** the ways in which the Ming dynasty centralized its power in China in the fourteenth and fifteenth centuries. What political innovations did it pursue, and what traditions did it sustain? **Compare** Chinese efforts at bureaucratic centralization with those of the Ottomans.

5. **Describe** the goals of the Ming dynasty's maritime exhibitions. Why did the government later abandon them?

6. **Compare and contrast** the ways in which regional rulers in post-plague Afro-Eurasia attempted to construct unified states. **Identify** their greatest successes.

7. **Explain** why the bubonic plague undermined the feudal order of the Catholic Church. How did regional monarchs in Europe capitalize on this development?

8. **Identify** the ways in which religious belief systems maintained continuity from the fourteenth through the fifteenth centuries.

9. **Describe** the key features of the Renaissance in Europe. How did the Renaissance spread and change?

10. **Discuss** how the art and architecture of different regions reflected the political realities of this period. **Identify** themes that communicated these messages to viewers.

11. **Analyze** the role of philosophical and religious developments—both elite movements, like humanism in Europe, and popular movements, like the Red Turban Movement in China—in politics from 1300 to 1500, and **explain** how they provided both continuity and change in each society.

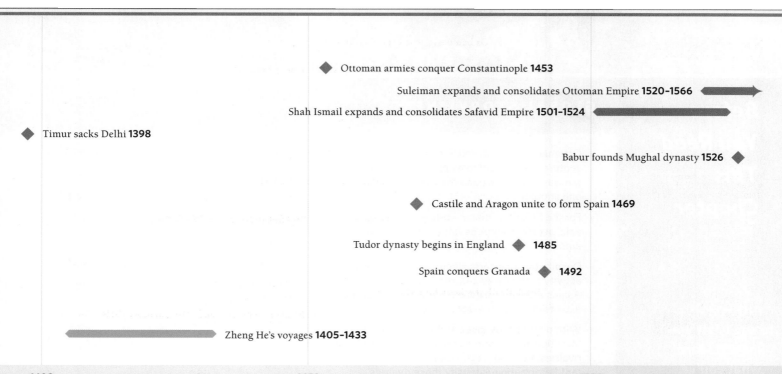

Ottoman armies conquer Constantinople **1453**

Suleiman expands and consolidates Ottoman Empire **1520–1566**

Shah Ismail expands and consolidates Safavid Empire **1501–1524**

Timur sacks Delhi **1398**

Babur founds Mughal dynasty **1526**

Castile and Aragon unite to form Spain **1469**

Tudor dynasty begins in England **1485**

Spain conquers Granada **1492**

Zheng He's voyages **1405–1433**

| 1400 | 1450 | 1500 |

Before You Read This Chapter

Go to INQUIZITIVE to see what you know & learn what you've missed.

GLOBAL STORYLINES

- Ottoman expansion and Portuguese overseas ventures begin a complex process that changes the way peoples around the world interact with one another.

- For the first time, major world empires are oceanic, overseas empires rather than continental empires.

- Despite the long-term significance of European activity in the Americas, most Africans and Asians are barely aware of the Americas or the expansion of long-distance trade.

- Within Europe, dynastic states concentrate attention and resources on their own internal rivalries. Religious revolts, especially the Protestant Reformation, intensify those rivalries.

- Asian empires thrive in the sixteenth century, thanks to commercial expansion and political consolidation.

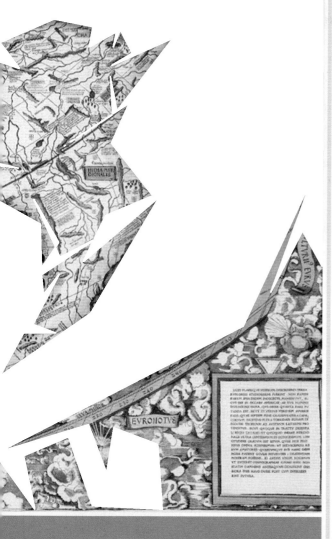

12

Contact, Commerce, and Colonization, 1450–1600

FOCUS QUESTIONS

- What were the broad patterns in world trade after 1450? How were the major features of world trade in Asia, the Americas, Africa, and Europe alike and different?

- What factors enabled Europeans to increase their trade relationships with Asian empires in the fifteenth and sixteenth centuries? How significant was each factor?

- How similar and different were the practices and the impact of European explorers in Asia and the Americas?

- Within the Afro-Eurasian polities, what types of social and political relationships developed during this period? What were the sources of conflict?

- In what ways did European colonization of the Americas affect African and Amerindian peoples? How did those groups respond?

At the time of Christopher Columbus's birth in 1451, the great world power on the rise was neither Spain nor Portugal, but the Ottoman Empire. For the Ottomans, unlike the other major Asian empires, the fifteenth and sixteenth centuries marked a period of frenzied territorial expansion in the Mediterranean as well as the Indian Ocean. The Ottomans were eager to fulfill what they considered to be Islam's primary mission: world dominion. Sultans Bayezid II (r. 1481–1512), Selim I (r. 1512–1520), and Suleiman the Magnificent (r. 1520–1566) continued the conquests of Mehmed the Conqueror and led the thrust into Arab lands and the Indian Ocean even while pressing ahead in Europe. Indeed, Selim I boasted that "he was the ruler of the east and the west" (Ozbaran, p. 64).

The sultans drew on the talents of two high officials, Ibrahim Pasha, grand vizier and briefly governor of Egypt, and Piri Reis, an Ottoman admiral and arguably the age's most accomplished cartographer. Piri Reis's researches into the Indian Ocean, an area previously unknown to the Ottomans, were vital to the Ottoman entry into this region. Not only did he produce a map of the world, but in 1526 he presented to Sultan Suleiman a masterpiece of geography and cartography known as

The Book of the Sea. The book was compendious in its research, drawing on ten Arab sources as well as four Indian maps obtained from Portuguese sources and offering full information on the geography of the world. This learned cartographer had consulted one of Columbus's maps and included a chart outlining Ferdinand Magellan's circumnavigation of the globe, completed in 1522, and information on the travels of Vasco da Gama. The Ottomans by now had become a world power, and a worldly one, and their armada dwarfed that of all others at the time. It consisted of seventy-four ships, including twenty-seven large and small galleys and munitions ships, mounted with cannons. The fleet transported 20,000 men, including 6,500 janissaries.

As they turned their attention to conquest of the Red Sea, the Arabian Peninsula, and North Africa, reestablishing under their own control trade routes disrupted by the Mongols and the Black Death, the Ottomans forced others seeking shares in South and East Asian luxuries to seek new sea passages. One of these was a pesky European state known as Portugal, which was also making inroads into South Asia. Entering the Indian Ocean essentially as well-armed pirates, the Portuguese gave the Ottomans no cause for alarm. After all, it was not Ottoman territory the Portuguese were contesting, and the Ottomans, looking westward, had bigger fish to fry.

Vasco da Gama's rounding of the Cape of Good Hope in 1498 nonetheless marked a turning point in world history. His entrance into the Indian Ocean and the subsequent Portuguese attempt to establish domination over the region's strategically located port cities gave Europeans their first toeholds in Asia. When the Portuguese pulled off a major naval victory against an Ottoman attempt to take the South Asian Portuguese-controlled port city of Diu in 1538, the Ottomans lost interest in the region, leaving it to the Portuguese—and later the Spanish, Dutch, English, and French—to exploit. No one could have predicted, in 1538, that European conquests of a few South Asian trading cities were particularly significant, compared with the Ottomans' relentless annexations of large territories, including great stretches of southeastern Europe.

Even more unpredictable, though nonetheless consequential, was an accidental discovery made by the Genoese ship captain Christopher Columbus. Seeking to circumvent Ottoman power in the eastern Mediterranean, Columbus opened up a "New World" about which Afro-Eurasians had no previous knowledge. In his wake, for the first time since the Ice Age migrations, peoples again moved from Afro-Eurasian landmasses to the Americas. So did animals, plants, commercial products, and—most momentous—deadly germs. Again, the Ottomans or Chinese might have been the ones to stumble on the Americas, but they were occupied with their own massive and prosperous empires. It was the Europeans who became empire builders of a different kind, creating overseas empires that disrupted the cultures and economies of millions and transformed their own cultures and societies in the process.

Despite the significance of Europeans' activity in the Americas, most Africans and Asians, and even most peoples indigenous to the Americas, remained, for decades or even centuries, barely aware of the importance of Columbus's discovery. As the chapter demonstrates, Asian empires in Ottoman-controlled lands and in India and China continued to flourish after recovering from the Black Death, and the Ottomans continued to focus on their own conquests. Nor did most Europeans pay much attention to events in the Americas, for they were grappling with a religious revolt—the Protestant Reformation—in their own backyard. Imperial conquests, whether Ottoman or European, reshaped old worlds. But trade, both along its older Asian routes and in its linking of Europe and the Americas, was also crucial in generating both productive and volatile new cultural syntheses.

THE OLD EXPANSIONISM AND THE NEW

Ottoman expansion overland continued as European expansion overseas began. Both caused important global shifts in the organization of polities as well as in patterns of trade. The two were interconnected, as increasing Ottoman control in the eastern Mediterranean motivated Portuguese and Spanish explorers to turn toward the Atlantic in hopes of reaching the rich trading posts of China and the Indian Ocean by another route. Ottoman expansion was made possible by the Ottomans' domination of Afro-Eurasian trade routes as they recovered in the wake of the Black Death, and it was marked by the sultanate's cooptation of local elites and a relatively tolerant attitude toward other peoples and religions. It was so successful that by 1529, the Ottomans had conquered Egypt and were knocking on the doors of Vienna. But their expansionism was not endless, running up against the powerful resistance of the Shiite Safavid regime in Persia. Nor, though they were now unquestionably *the* great power in Mediterranean shipping and the Afro-Eurasian caravan trades, did Ottoman trading methods or goods change all that much. Older forms of imperial expansion and long-distance trade worked well for them, and they stuck to them.

For the Europeans, in contrast, expansion overseas was quite new and experimental. Born from a position of weakness, Portuguese and Spanish exploration and expansion benefited greatly from unexpected accidents: first, that Columbus found a "New World" rather than the "Old World" he hoped to reach, and second, tragically, that European pathogens killed or greatly weakened Amerindian populations, making conquest and settlement possible. Expansion across the Atlantic entailed, first, the military conquest of the rich empires of the Aztecs

Chinese Porcelain Bowl. *This Dutch still-life painting features an imported Chinese porcelain bowl, demonstrating Europeans' appreciation for East Asian craftsmanship as well as their dependence on long-distance trade for the acquisition of such coveted luxury goods.*

and the Incas and the scramble to locate and exploit gold and silver deposits. But the Europeans stayed, coopting some local elites but also inventing new forms of landholding and resource extraction. The importation of thousands, and then millions, of African slaves to form a new, fully subservient labor force was also a tragic and inhumane innovation that transformed both global commerce and the Atlantic ecosystem.

Both the new expansionism and the old knitted worlds together that had previously been apart or only loosely interconnected. Together they laid the foundations for a new chapter in world history. But we must not forget that even in the midst of this global transformation, the peoples of each continent continued to focus on local, and often religious, struggles closer to their everyday lives.

OTTOMAN EXPANSION

Having built the period's most powerful military forces and armed with the latest maps and scientific instruments, the Ottomans began the sixteenth century in possession of Constantinople and great swaths of southeastern Europe and Anatolia. During the sultanate of Suleiman the Magnificent (r. 1520–1566), Ottoman forces carried the empire southward into Egypt, eastward to the Iranian borderlands, and westward into Europe. By 1550, the Ottoman Empire stretched from Hungary and the Crimea in the north to the Arabian Peninsula in the south, from Morocco in the west to the contested border with Safavid Iran in the east. (See Map 12.1.)

The Multiethnic Ottoman Elite

The institutions that early sultans had established in the fifteenth century—the devshirme system involving the seizing of young recruits for service in the Ottoman military and civil bureaucracies, the rise of the janissaries in the military's front ranks, and the replacement of powerful landholding families in Anatolia with individuals of proven loyalty to the state—became more pronounced during the sixteenth, seventeenth, and eighteenth centuries. As it spread, the Ottoman Empire encountered more and more ethnic and religious groups, incorporating them into the Ottoman hierarchy. Those who were willing to serve could rise high. Of the fifteen grand viziers who held that position between 1453 and 1515, eight were drawn from Byzantine and Balkan nobility, four were from the devshirme system, and only three were of Muslim Turkish descent. Others were not forced to convert but left largely to govern their own communities, as well as pay hefty taxes to their Turkish overlords.

Ottoman Conquests in Egypt

The conquest of Syria and Egypt in 1516–1517 was decisive in allowing Ottoman leaders to regard their Sunni state as the preeminent Muslim empire from that moment forward, even enabling some sultans to call themselves caliphs. Egypt became

The Catalan Atlas. *This 1375 map shows the world as it was then known. Not only does it depict the location of continents and islands, but it also includes information on ancient and medieval tales, regional politics, astronomy, and astrology.*

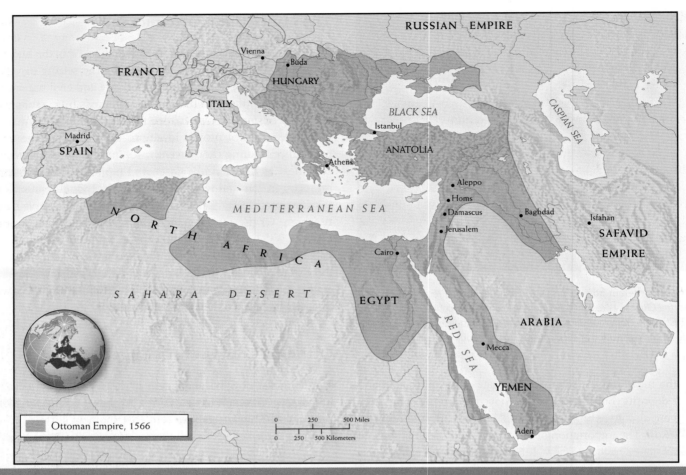

MAP 12.1 | The Ottoman Empire at the Middle of the Sixteenth Century

This map shows the expansive area controlled by the Ottoman Empire by the middle of the sixteenth century. Note the very close proximity of the Ottoman borders to the Habsburg capital of Vienna.

- What territories did the Ottomans add to their empire in the sixteenth century?
- Why did they aspire to take over Vienna, and why did they fail?
- Was the Ottoman Empire reaching its outermost limits?
- Why did the Ottomans venture so aggressively into the Red Sea and the Indian Ocean in the sixteenth century?

the Ottomans' most lucrative and important acquisition, the breadbasket of the empire and the province that provided Istanbul with the largest revenue stream. But the conquest was no easy matter. The Mamluk rulers resisted mightily, losing a bloody battle in 1516 at Marj Dabiq, north of Aleppo, after which, according to Ibn Iyas, the Arab chronicler of the age, "the battlefield was strewn with corpses and headless bodies and faces covered with dust and grown hideous." Nor did the conquest of Egypt prove any easier, for the Mamluks were determined to hold on to their most precious possession. Emotions ran high, for both sides prided themselves on being warrior states. Decapitation of enemies was common practice. In revenge for the Mamluk beheading of their fallen soldiers, the Ottoman troops plundered, raped, and killed an estimated 10,000 residents of

Cairo. The destruction, wrote Ibn Iyas, was such as "to strike terror into the hearts of man and its horrors to unhinge their reason" (Salmon, pp. 45, 111).

Ottoman Expansionism Stalls in Iran

The conquest of Constantinople and the Arab lands transformed the Ottoman Empire, creating a Muslim majority in an empire once mainly populated by conquered Christians and enabling Ottoman sultans to see themselves as heirs of a long line of empires that had ruled over these regions.

Yet on the eastern front, in conflicts with the Safavid Empire, the Ottomans encountered their earliest military failures and their most determined foe, an enemy state that plagued the Ottoman Empire until its collapse early in the eighteenth century (see Chapter 13). The Safavid state had arisen as a result of Turkic tribesmen migrating from eastern Anatolia and Azerbaijan to the Iranian plateau, where they established a zealous Shiite state (see Chapter 11). Their leaders continued to seek support and to spread their faith among the dispossessed in Ottoman-ruled Syria and Anatolia, near to the Safavid borders, and even sent agents into these areas to stir up discontent against the Ottomans. Selim II sought to defeat the Safavids, mustering a powerful force of 100,000 armed with muskets, which the Safavid force of 80,000 did not have. Selim's victory at the Battle of Chaldiran in 1514 was entirely predictable, and he had his forces sack the Safavid capital at Tabriz. His victory was short lived, however, for he could not persuade his troops to bivouac there through the harsh winter. After his troops withdrew, the Safavid rulers returned. Similar conflicts proved equally unsuccessful, failing to unseat a politically and religiously antagonist state.

In reality, the bitter conflict between Safavids and Ottomans intensified the religious commitments of both sides. The Ottomans, who had begun as a flexible ethnic and religious state dealing openly with Christian and Jewish groups and heterodox Muslims, now became the champions of Sunni Islam. By the same token, the Safavids, who had been Sufis and had migrated from eastern Anatolia, now embraced their Shiite commitments even more firmly.

The Ottomans in Europe

Blocked from further eastward expansion by the Safavids, the Ottomans were on the march westward, into Europe. Having taken Constantinople in 1453, Sultan Mehmed II took Athens in 1458 and set in motion plans to conquer Italy, though that project lapsed after his death. The Ottomans also added large swaths of Balkan territory, cutting into the Venetians' empire, and coveted commercial and naval regions in the Black Sea. The Turks then turned to North Africa and Egypt, succeeding in bringing coastal areas as well as Egypt under their dominion by 1550. This allowed them to exert more control than ever over commerce in the Mediterranean and to capture many European ships, often turning their crews into slaves or hostages for ransom, and spreading fear of "the Turk" across Christendom.

The Ottomans' encroachment into central Europe was equally terrifying for Europeans. Just at the time Martin Luther's reformers were stirring up trouble inside the Holy Roman Empire, the Turks were slicing off large sections of its easternmost territories. In the 1520s, the Ottomans seized what is today Serbia, as well as sections of Hungary, and in 1529 they threatened the Habsburg capital, Vienna. Although winter weather forced Suleiman to retreat, he ultimately took Budapest in 1541, and Turkish armies marched on into Transylvania. With little success, a series of popes sought to unite a Christendom now divided by the Reformation against the Turkish "infidels." In 1571, in a moment of rare unity, a coalition of European princes destroyed much of the Ottoman navy in the Battle of Lepanto, near the western coast of Greece. This weakened the Turkish striking force in the Mediterranean, but the Ottomans continued to dominate the area and exert control over most of southeastern Europe for centuries.

Ottoman conquests in southeastern and central Europe resulted in the subordination of Christians and Jews to Muslim rule. The Ottomans allowed minority religious communities in their provincial borderlands a large measure of self-administration. Some Turks moved into these areas, and some Christians converted to Islam, but little economic

Ottoman Attack. *In 1480, at the height of their naval strength, a huge Ottoman army besieged the island of Rhodes, one of the most prized territories held by the Venetian Republic. After a brutal battle, the Christian Hospitaller Knights, whose ships are pictured in the foreground, narrowly managed to defeat the Turkish invaders (whose tent-camp is pictured here, outside the walls of the port city of Otrano). But the Ottomans would return in 1521–1522, and this time would conquer the island.*

development occurred and most people remained poor peasants. Ottoman control, which lasted for centuries in places like Bosnia, left a multiethnic legacy, including large populations of Muslims in areas reconquered by the Habsburg Empire. Thus, the Ottomans, too, from the eastern end of the Mediterranean, became key players in the transformation of Europe's religious as well as economic and political history in the age of Da Gama and Columbus.

EUROPEAN EXPLORATION AND EXPANSION

The Muslim conquest of Constantinople and the Ottoman expansion into the Mediterranean sent shock waves through Christendom and prompted Europeans to probe unexplored links to the east. That entailed looking south and west—and venturing across the seas. (See Map 12.2.) Taking the lead were the Portuguese, whose search for new routes to Asia led them first to Africa, then the Canary Islands, and then into the Indian Ocean. Using New World silver and new military and maritime technology as their tickets to entry, the Portuguese in the fifteenth and sixteenth centuries broke into lucrative Indian Ocean networks, although they remained minor go-betweens or irksome pirates in a world still dominated by Arab, Persian, Indian, and Chinese merchants. It would be a century or more before their toeholds were firmly established.

The Portuguese in Africa and Asia

Europeans had long believed that Africa was a storehouse of precious metals. In fact, a fourteenth-century map, the Catalan Atlas, depicted a single black ruler controlling a vast quantity of gold in the interior of Africa. Thus, as the price of gold skyrocketed during and after the Black Death, ambitious men ventured southward in search of this commodity and its twin, silver. The first Portuguese sailors expected to find giants and Amazons, savages and cannibals. Sailors' stories and myths, indeed, would continue to shape their view of the places and peoples they would encounter. But the first intrepid adventurers did not allow their fears of the world they anticipated encountering to overcome their ambitions.

NAVIGATION AND MILITARY ADVANCES Innovations in maritime technology and information from Arab mariners and ancient Greek texts helped Portuguese sailors navigate the treacherous waters along the African coast. The carrack, a three- or four-masted ship, worked well on bodies of water like the Mediterranean; the caravel, with specially designed triangular sails, could nose in and out of estuaries and navigate

Caravel. *Caravels became the classic vessel for European exploration. They had many decks and plenty of portholes for cannons, could house a large crew, and had lots of storage for provisions, cargo, and booty.*

unpredictable currents and winds. By using highly maneuverable caravels and perfecting the technique of tacking (sailing into the wind rather than before it), the Portuguese advanced far along the West African coast. In addition, newfound expertise with the compass and the astrolabe helped them determine latitude. And they participated eagerly in the development of the Renaissance arts of war (see Chapter 11), adapting the new artillery technologies so that smaller cannons could be mounted on ships and used to bombard ports and rival navies—or merchant vessels.

SUGAR AND SLAVES Africa and the islands along its coast soon proved to be far more than a stop-off en route to India or a source of precious metals. Africa became a valued trading area, and its islands were prime locations for growing sugarcane—a crop that had exhausted the soils of Mediterranean islands, where it had been cultivated since the twelfth century. Along what they called the Gold Coast, the Portuguese established many fortresses and ports of call.

After seizing islands along the West African coast, the Portuguese introduced sugarcane cultivation on large plantations and exploited slave labor from the African mainland. The Madeira, Canary, and Cape Verde archipelagoes became laboratories for plantation agriculture, for their rainfall and fertile soils made them ideally suited for growing sugarcane. And because it took droves of workers to cultivate, harvest, and process sugarcane, a ready supply of slave labor enabled Portugal and Spain to build sizable plantations in their first formal colonies (regions under the political control of another country). In the 1400s, these islands saw the beginnings of a system of plantation agriculture built on slavery that would travel across the Atlantic in the following century.

COMMERCE AND CONQUEST IN THE INDIAN OCEAN

Having established plantation colonies on West Africa's outlying islands, Portuguese seafarers ventured into the Indian Ocean and inserted themselves into its thriving commerce. In Asia, Portugal never wanted to rule directly or to establish colonies. Rather, its seaborne empire adapted to local circumstances in order to exploit Asian commercial networks and trading systems.

The first Portuguese mariner to reach the Indian Ocean was Vasco da Gama (1469–1524). Like Columbus, da Gama was relatively unknown before his extraordinary voyage commanding four ships around the Cape of Good Hope at the southern tip of Africa. He explored Africa's eastern coast, and found neither savages nor impoverished lands in need of European assistance, but instead a network of commercial ties spanning the Indian Ocean, as well as skilled Muslim mariners who knew the currents, winds, and ports of call. Da Gama took on board a Muslim pilot at Malindi for instruction in navigating the Indian Ocean's winds and currents. He then sailed for the Malabar coast in southern India, one of the region's most important trading areas, arriving in 1498. Da Gama was briefly taken hostage near Calicut but was eventually allowed to leave India with a valuable cargo of spices and silks.

To the Portuguese, who traded in the name of their crown, commercial access was worth fighting for. Although da Gama lost more than half his crew on the difficult voyage back to Lisbon, he had proved the feasibility—and profitability—of trade via the Indian Ocean. When he returned to Calicut in 1502 with a larger crew, he asserted Portuguese supremacy by acting the pirate, boarding all twenty ships in the harbor and cutting off the noses, ears, and hands of their sailors. Then he burned the ships with the mutilated sailors on board. The Portuguese repeated their show of force in strategic locations, especially the three naval choke points: Aden, at the base of the Red Sea; Hormuz, in the Persian Gulf; and Melaka, at the tip of the Malay Peninsula. Once established in key ports, the Portuguese attempted to take over the trade or, failing this, to tax local merchants. Although they did not hold Aden for long, they solidified control in Sofala, Kilwa, and other important ports on the East African coast; in Goa and Calicut, in India; and in Macao, in southern China. From these strongholds, the Portuguese soon commanded the most active sea-lanes of the Indian Ocean. (See again Map 12.2; see also Primary Source: Portuguese Views of the Chinese.)

The Portuguese did not seek to interrupt the flow of luxuries among Asian and African elites in the Indian Ocean; rather, their naval captains simply kept a portion of the profits for themselves. The Portuguese introduced a pass system that required ships to pay for *cartazes*—documents identifying the ship's captain, size of the ship and crew, and its cargo. The Portuguese were unable to impose this system on Indian Ocean rulers and powerful merchants, but minor players and outsiders calculated it was cheaper to pay what were essentially bribes rather than risk losses at sea from the Portuguese fleet. The Portuguese were also active in the spice trade, and Lisbon gradually eclipsed Italian ports, such as Venice, that had previously been prime entrepôts (commercial hubs for long-distance trade) for Asian goods. But they found it even more lucrative to enter the spice trade *within* the Indian Ocean world, where there were wealthier customers to serve. Only with the discovery of the Americas and the conquest of Brazil did Portugal become an empire with large overseas colonies. For this to transpire, mariners would have to traverse the Atlantic Ocean itself.

THE ATLANTIC WORLD

Crossing the Atlantic was a feat of monumental importance in world history. It did not occur, however, with an aim to discover new lands. Columbus had wanted to voyage into the "Ocean Sea" so as to open a more direct—and more lucrative—route to Japan and China. Fired by their victory at Granada, Ferdinand and Isabella had agreed to finance his trip, hoping for riches to bankroll a crusade to liberate Jerusalem from Muslim hands. Just as Columbus had no idea he would find a "New World," Spain's monarchs (not to mention its merchants, missionaries, and soldiers) never dreamed that soon they would be preparing for conquest and profiteering in what had been, just a few years before, a blank space on their maps. (Thus the term *New World*, as applied to the Americas, reflects the Europeans' view that anything previously unknown to them was "new," even if it had existed and supported societies long before European explorers arrived on its shores.)

Columbus's voyages, in opening new sea-lanes in the Atlantic, set the stage for an epochal transformation in world history. As news of his voyages spread through Europe, ambitious mariners prepared to sail west. European rivalries, for trade and prestige, sharpened. By 1550, many of Europe's powers were scrambling, not just for a share of Indian Ocean action but also for spoils from the Atlantic.

But the opening of new trade routes for Europeans was less important for world history than the biological consequences of the first contacts between Europeans and Amerindians. In Africa and Asia, long-standing patterns of trade had yielded the development of shared immunities. But Amerindian populations, in

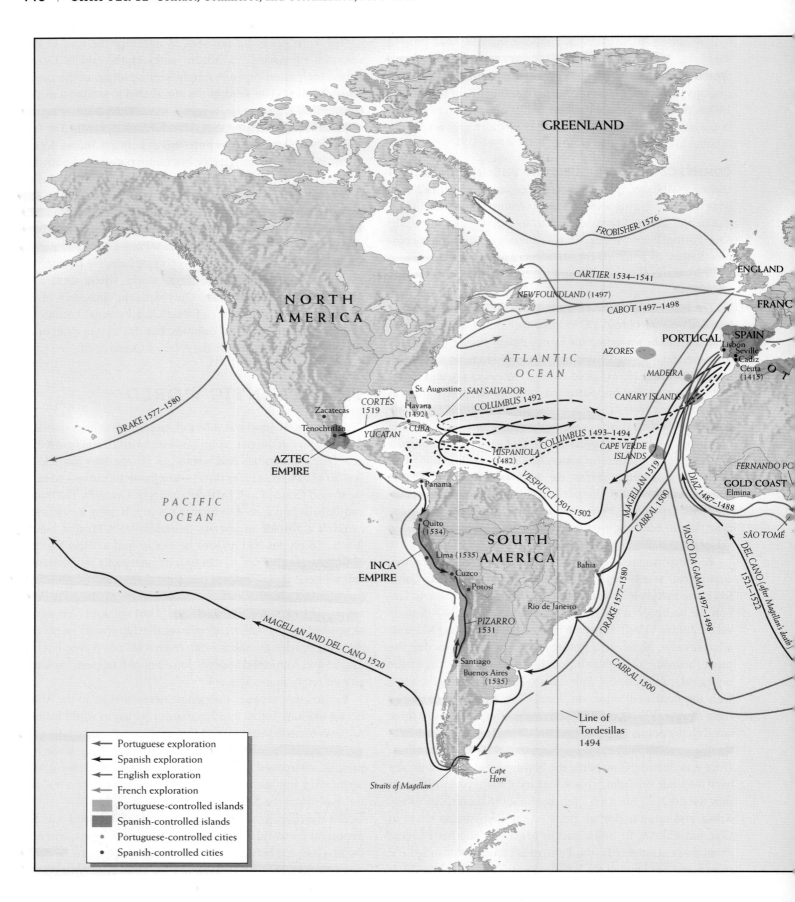

GREENLAND

NORTH AMERICA

ATLANTIC OCEAN

FROBISHER 1576

CARTIER 1534–1541

ENGLAND

NEWFOUNDLAND (1497)

CABOT 1497–1498

FRANC

PORTUGAL   SPAIN

Lisbon
Seville
Cadiz
Ceuta
(1415)

AZORES

MADEIRA

CANARY ISLANDS

COLUMBUS 1492

St. Augustine   *SAN SALVADOR*

Havana
(1492)

CUBA

YUCATAN

CORTÉS 1519

Zacatecas

Tenochtitlán

AZTEC EMPIRE

HISPANIOLA (1482)

COLUMBUS 1493–1494

CAPE VERDE ISLANDS

FERNANDO PO

GOLD COAST
Elmina

VESPUCCI 1501–1502

MAGELLAN 1519

CABRAL 1500

DIAZ 1487–1488

SÃO TOMÉ

DRAKE 1577–1580

PACIFIC OCEAN

Panama

Quito (1534)

Lima (1535)

Cuzco

Potosí

SOUTH AMERICA

INCA EMPIRE

Bahia

Rio de Janeiro

PIZARRO 1531

DRAKE 1577–1580

VASCO DA GAMA 1497–1498

DEL CANO (after Magellan's death) 1521–1522

CABRAL 1500

MAGELLAN AND DEL CANO 1520

Santiago

Buenos Aires (1535)

Line of Tordesillas 1494

Straits of Magellan

Cape Horn

←	Portuguese exploration
←	Spanish exploration
←	English exploration
←	French exploration
	Portuguese-controlled islands
	Spanish-controlled islands
•	Portuguese-controlled cities
•	Spanish-controlled cities

MAP 12.2 | European Exploration, 1420–1580

In the fifteenth and sixteenth centuries, sailors from Portugal, Spain, England, and France explored and mapped the coastline of most of the world.

- What empire to the east prevented Europeans from expanding trade routes by land?
- Trace the voyages that started from Portugal, and then trace the voyages that started from Spain.
- Why did Portuguese explorers concentrate on Africa and the Indian Ocean, whereas their Spanish counterparts focused on the Americas?
- What does the map tell us about the different patterns of exploration in the New World versus those in the Indian Ocean and the South China Sea?

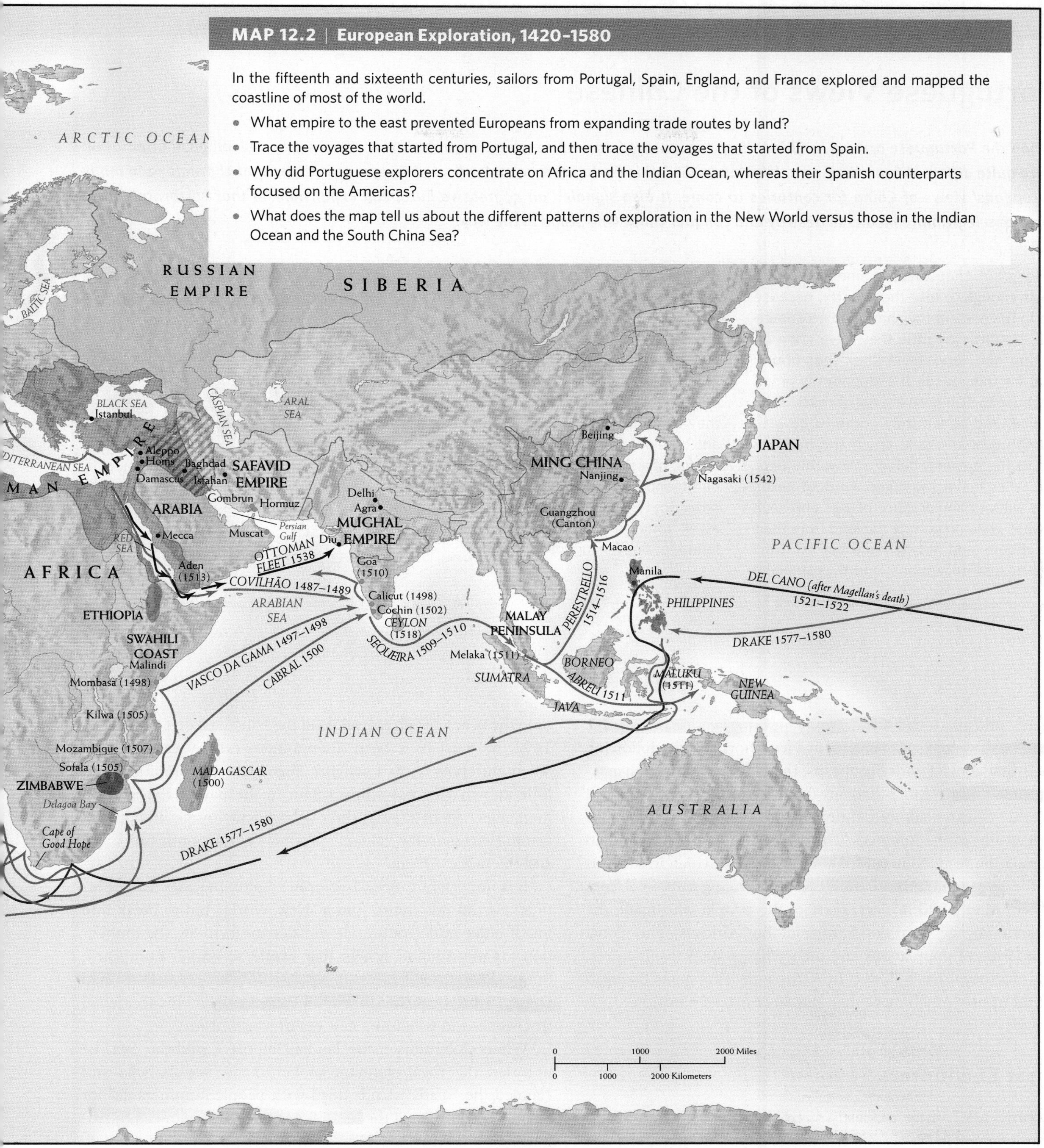

ARCTIC OCEAN

BALTIC SEA

RUSSIAN EMPIRE

SIBERIA

BLACK SEA
Istanbul

ARAL SEA

CASPIAN SEA

MEDITERRANEAN SEA

OTTOMAN EMPIRE

Aleppo
Homs
Damascus
Baghdad
Istahan
SAFAVID EMPIRE

ARABIA

Mecca

RED SEA

Gombrun
Hormuz
Muscat
Persian Gulf

Delhi
Agra
MUGHAL EMPIRE
Diu

Beijing

MING CHINA
Nanjing

JAPAN

Nagasaki (1542)

Guangzhou
(Canton)

Macao

PACIFIC OCEAN

AFRICA

ETHIOPIA

SWAHILI COAST
Malindi

Mombasa (1498)

Kilwa (1505)

Mozambique (1507)

Sofala (1505)

ZIMBABWE

Delagoa Bay

Cape of
Good Hope

Aden
(1513)

OTTOMAN FLEET 1538

COVILHÃO 1487–1489

ARABIAN SEA

VASCO DA GAMA 1497–1498

CABRAL 1500

Goa
(1510)

Calicut (1498)
Cochin (1502)
CEYLON
(1518)

SEQUEIRA 1509–1510

MALAY PENINSULA

Melaka (1511)

SUMATRA

JAVA

PERESTRELLO 1514–1516

ABREU 1511

BORNEO

Manila

PHILIPPINES

MALUKU
(1511)

NEW GUINEA

DEL CANO (after Magellan's death)
1521–1522

DRAKE 1577–1580

MADAGASCAR
(1500)

INDIAN OCEAN

DRAKE 1577–1580

AUSTRALIA

| 0 | | 1000 | | 2000 Miles |
| 0 | 1000 | | 2000 Kilometers | |

Portuguese Views of the Chinese

When the Portuguese arrived in China, they encountered an empire whose organizational structure and ideological orientation were quite different from their own. Written in 1517, this Portuguese report reflects misrepresentations that characterized many Europeans' views of China for centuries to come. It also signaled an aggressive European expansionism that celebrated brute force as a legitimate means to destroy and conquer those who stood in the way.

God grant that these Chinese may be fools enough to lose the country; because up to the present they have had no dominion, but little by little they have gone on taking the land from their neighbors; and for this reason the kingdom is great, because the Chinese are full of much cowardice, and hence they come to be presumptuous, arrogant, cruel; and because up to the present, being a cowardly people, they have managed without arms and without any practice of war, and have always gone on getting the land from their neighbors, and not by force but by stratagems and deceptions; and they imagine that no one can do them harm. They call every foreigner a savage; and their country they call the kingdom of God.

Whoever shall come now, let it be a captain with a fleet of ten or fifteen sail. The first thing will be to destroy the fleet if they should have one, which I believe they have not; let it be by fire and blood and cruel fear for this day, without sparing the life of a single person, every junk being burnt, and no one being taken prisoner, in order not to waste the provisions, because at all times a hundred Chinese will be found for one Portuguese.

Source: *Letters from Canton*, translated and edited by D. Ferguson, *The Indian Antiquary* 31 (January 1902), in J. H. Parry, *European Reconnaissance: Selected Documents* (New York: Walker, 1968), p. 140.

QUESTIONS FOR ANALYSIS

- What do you think was the main purpose of this report?
- How could this observer's views be so inaccurate?
- What is the irony in the comment "They call every foreigner a savage," followed by instructions to destroy, burn, and not spare "the life of a single person"?

---

their world apart, had no immunity for Eurasian diseases such as smallpox, typhus, and cholera; in a few short decades following their first contact with Europeans, these groups suffered a catastrophic decline. More than any other factor, the spread of "Old World" diseases allowed Europeans to conquer and colonize vast swaths of the Americas. The devastation of the Amerindian population resulted in severe labor shortages, which in turn led to the large-scale introduction of slave laborers imported from Africa. After 1500, in fact, most of the people who made the Atlantic voyage were not Europeans but Africans. The global reordering of populations and the exchange of crops, cultures, and microbes that followed from these developments changed world history much more than did any European explorer.

First Encounters

In early 1492, three modestly sized ships set sail from Spain. They stopped in the Canary Islands for supplies and repairs and cast off into the unknown. When the expedition leader stepped onto the beach of San Salvador (in the Bahamas) on October 12, 1492, he must have been disappointed: where were the rich Asian entrepôts he had sought? This leader, an ambitious but little-known Genoese ship captain in the pay of the Spanish monarchs, would attempt three subsequent voyages in hopes of gaining access to the valuable products of the South China Sea and the Indian Ocean.

It is important to see Christopher Columbus as a man of his time. He did not aim to find a "New World" but to break into much older trade routes. He did not mean to lay the foundation for the Atlantic system that would so enrich Europeans, but to generate revenues to cover the conquest of Muslim-ruled Granada and the reconquest of the Holy Land. Yet his accidental discoveries did usher in a new era in world history.

When Columbus made landfall in the Caribbean Sea, he unfurled the royal standard of Ferdinand and Isabella and claimed the "many islands filled with people innumerable" for Spain. It is fitting that the first encounter with Caribbean inhabitants, in this case the Tainos, drew blood. Columbus noted, "I showed them swords and they took them by the edge and

Columbus. *As Columbus made landfall and encountered Indians, he planted a cross to indicate the spiritual purpose of the voyage and read aloud a document proclaiming the sovereign authority of the king and queen of Spain. Quickly, he learned that the Spanish could barter for precious stones and metals.*

through ignorance cut themselves." The Tainos had their own weapons but did not forge steel and thus had no knowledge of such sharp edges.

For Columbus, the Tainos' naivety in grabbing his sword symbolized the childlike primitivism of these people, whom he would mislabel "Indians" because he thought he had arrived off the coast of Asia. In Columbus's view, the Tainos had no religion, but they did have at least some gold (found initially hanging as pendants from their noses). Likewise, Pedro Alvares Cabral, a Portuguese mariner whose trip down the coast of Africa in 1500 was blown off course across the Atlantic, wrote that the people of Brazil had all "the innocence of Adam." He also noted that they were ripe for conversion and that the soils "if rightly cultivated would yield everything." But, as with Africans and Asians, Europeans also developed a contradictory view of the peoples of the Americas. From the Tainos, Columbus learned of another people, the Caribs, who (according to his informants) were savage, warlike cannibals. For centuries, these contrasting images—innocents and savages—structured European (mis)understandings of the native peoples of the Americas.

We know less about what the Indians thought of Columbus or other Europeans on their first encounters. Certainly, the Europeans' appearance and technologies inspired awe. The Tainos fled into the forest at the approach of European ships, which they thought were giant monsters; others thought they were floating islands. European metal goods, especially weaponry, struck them as otherworldly. The strangely dressed white

men seemed godlike to some, although many Indians soon abandoned this view. The Amerindians found the newcomers different not for their skin color (only Europeans drew the distinction based on skin pigmentation) but for their hairiness. Indeed, the Europeans' beards, breath, and bad manners repulsed their Indian hosts. The newcomers' inability to live off the land also stood out.

In due course, the Indians realized that the strange, hairy people bearing metal weapons meant to stay and force the Amerindian population to labor for them. But by then it was too late. The explorers had become **conquistadors** (conquerors).

First Conquests

First contacts between peoples gave way to dramatic conquests in the Americas. After his first voyage, Columbus claimed that on Hispaniola (present-day Haiti and the Dominican Republic) "he had found what he was looking for"—gold. That was sufficient to persuade the Spanish crown to invest in larger expeditions and to seek to conquer this promising new territory. Whereas Columbus first sailed with three small ships and 87 men, ten years later the Spanish outfitted an expedition with 2,500 men. Exploration now yielded to warfare and exploitation.

Between 1492 and 1519, the Spanish conquerors of Hispaniola experimented with institutions of colonial rule over local populations. Ultimately, they created a model that the rest of the New World colonies would adapt. But the Spaniards faced Indian resistance. As early as 1494, starving Spaniards raided and pillaged Indian villages. When the Indians revolted, Spanish soldiers replied with punitive expeditions and began enslaving them to work in mines extracting gold. As the crown systematized grants (*encomiendas*) to the conquistadors for control over Indian labor, a rich class of ***encomenderos*** arose who enjoyed the fruits of the system. Although the placer gold mines soon ran dry, the model of granting favored settlers the right to coerce Indian labor endured. In return, those who received the labor rights paid special taxes on the precious metals that were extracted. Thus, both the crown and the *encomenderos* benefited from the extractive economy. The same cannot be said of the Amerindians, who perished in great numbers from disease, dislocation, malnutrition, and overwork.

Not all Europeans celebrated the pillaging. Dominican friars protested the abuse of the Indians, seeing them as potential converts who were equal to the Spaniards in the eyes of God. In 1511, Father Antonio Montesinos accused the settlers of barbarity: "By what right and with what justice do you keep these poor Indians in such cruel and horrible servitude?" Dissent and debate would be a permanent feature of Spanish colonialism in the New World.

The Aztec Empire and the Spanish Conquest

As Spanish colonists saw the bounty of Hispaniola dry up, they set out to discover and conquer new territories. Finding their way to the mainlands of the American landmasses, they encountered larger, more complex, and more militarized societies than those they had overrun in the Caribbean.

On the mainland, great civilizations had arisen centuries before, boasting large cities, monumental buildings, and riches based on wealthy agrarian societies. In both Mesoamerica, starting with the Olmecs (see Chapter 5), and the Andes, starting with the Chimú (see Chapter 10), large polities had laid the foundations for subsequent Aztec and Inca Empires. These empires were powerful. But they also represented the evolution of states and commercial systems untouched by Afro-Eurasian developments; as worlds apart, they were unprepared for the kind of assaults that European invaders had perfected. In pre-Columbian Mesoamerica and then the Andes, warfare was more ceremonial, less inclined to wipe out enemies than to make them tributary subjects. As a result, the wealth of these empires made them irresistible to outside conquerors, whose habits of war they could never have foreseen.

AZTEC SOCIETY In Mesoamerica, the ascendant Mexicas had created an empire known to us as Aztec. Around Lake Texcoco, Mexica cities grew and formed a three-city league in 1430, which then expanded through the valley of central Mexico to incorporate neighboring peoples. Gradually, the **Aztec Empire** united numerous small, independent states under a single monarch who ruled with the help of counselors, military leaders, and priests. By the late fifteenth century, the Aztec realm may have embraced 25 million people. Tenochtitlán, the primary city, situated on an immense island in Lake Texcoco, ranked among the world's largest.

Tenochtitlán spread in concentric circles, with the main religious and political buildings in the center and residences radiating outward. The city's outskirts connected a mosaic of floating gardens producing food for urban markets. As the city grew, clan-like networks evolved, and powerful families married their children to each other or found nuptial partners among the prominent families of other important cities. (Certain ruling houses in Europe were solidifying alliances in much the same way at this time; see Chapter 11.) Not only did this practice concentrate power in the great city, but it also ensured a pool of potential successors to the throne. Soon a lineage emerged to create a corps of "natural" rulers.

Holding this stratified order together was a shared understanding of the cosmos. But unlike European and most Asian cosmologies, Aztecs saw the natural order as intrinsically unstable. They believed that the universe was prone to recurring

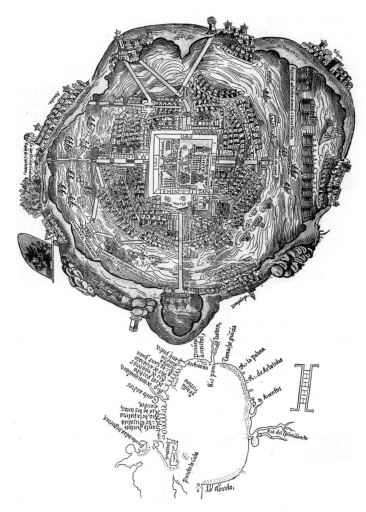

Tenochtitlán. *At its height, the Aztec capital, Tenochtitlán, was as populous as Europe's largest city. As can be seen from this map, it spread in concentric circles, with the main religious and political buildings in the center and residences radiating outward.*

cycles of disaster that would eventually end in apocalypse. Such an unstable cosmos exposed mortals to repeated creations and destructions of their world. It was the priesthood's job to balance a belief that history was destined to run in cycles with a faith that mortals could influence the gods, and their own fate, through religious rituals. These rituals also legitimized the Aztec power structure by portraying the emperor and the elite as closer to the gods than the lower orders.

Ultimately, Aztec power spread through much of Mesoamerica, but the empire's constant wars and conquests deprived it of stability. In successive military campaigns, the Aztecs subjugated their neighbors, feeding off plunder and then forcing subject peoples to pay tribute of crops, gold, silver, textiles, and other goods that financed Aztec grandeur. Such conquests also provided a constant supply of humans for sacrifice, because the Aztecs believed that the great god of the sun required human hearts to keep on burning and blood to replace that given by the gods to moisten the earth through rain. Priests escorted captured warriors up the temple steps and tore out their hearts, offering their lives and blood as a sacrifice to the sun god. Allegedly, between 20,000 and 80,000 men, women, and children were slaughtered in a single ceremony in 1487, with the four-person-wide line of victims stretching for over two miles. In this marathon of bloodletting, knife-wielding priests collapsed from exhaustion and surrendered their places to fresh executioners.

Those whom the Aztecs sought to dominate did not submit peacefully. From 1440, the empire faced constant turmoil as subject peoples resented Aztec domination, and independent peoples—such as the Tlaxcalans to the east and Tarascans (or Purépecha) to the west—waged war to preserve their independence and fiercely resisted incorporation into the Aztec's tributary empire. To pacify the realm, the Aztecs diverted more and more men and money into a mushrooming military. By the time the electoral committee chose Moctezuma II as emperor in 1502, divisions among elites and pressures from the periphery placed the Aztec Empire under extreme stress.

CORTÉS AND CONQUEST Not long after Moctezuma became emperor, news arrived from the coast of strange sightings of floating mountains (ships) bearing pale, bearded men and monsters (horses and dogs). Moctezuma consulted with his ministers and soothsayers, wondering if these men were the god Quetzalcoátl and his entourage. The people of Tenochtitlán saw omens of impending disaster. Moctezuma sank into despair, hesitating over what to do. He sent emissaries bearing jewels and prized feathers; later he sent sorcerers to confuse and bewitch the newcomers. But he did not prepare for any military engagement. After all, Mesoamericans had no idea of the interlopers' destructive potential in weaponry and germs.

Aboard one of the ships was Hernán Cortés (1485–1547), a former law student from one of the Spanish provinces. He would become the conquistador that all subsequent conquerors tried to emulate, just as Columbus was the model explorer. For a brief time, Cortés was an *encomendero* in Hispaniola; but when news arrived of a potentially wealthier land to the west, he set sail with over 500 men, eleven ships, sixteen horses, and artillery.

When the expedition arrived near present-day Veracruz, Cortés acquired two translators, including the daughter of a local Indian noble family. The daughter, who became known as Doña Marina, was a "gift" to the triumphant Spaniards from the ruler of the Tabasco region (a rival to the Aztecs). Fluent in several languages, Doña Marina displayed such linguistic skills and personal charm that she soon became Cortés's lover and

Cortés Meets Mesoamerican Rulers. Left: *This colonial image depicts the meeting of Cortés (second from right) and Moctezuma (seated on the left), with Doña Marina serving as an interpreter and informer for the Spanish conquistador. Notice at the bottom what are likely Aztec offerings for the newcomer.* Right: *This detail from a twentieth-century Mexican mural depicts the meeting of Cortés and the king of Tlaxcala (enemy of the Aztecs). As Mexicans began to celebrate their mixed-blood heritage, Doña Marina (in the middle) became the symbolic mother of the first mestizos.*

Cortés Approaches Tenochtitlán

When the Spanish conquered the Aztec Empire, they defeated a mighty power. The capital, Tenochtitlán, was probably the same size as Europe's biggest city. Glimpsing Tenochtitlán in 1521, Hernán Cortés marveled at its magnificence. But to justify his acts, he claimed to be bringing civilization and Christianity to the Aztecs. Note the contrast between Cortés's admiration for Tenochtitlán and his condemnation of Indian beliefs and practices—as well as his claim that he abolished cannibalism, something the Aztecs did not practice (although they did sacrifice humans).

This great city of Tenochtitlán is built on the salt lake.... It has four approaches by means of artificial causeways.... The city is as large as Seville or Cordoba. Its streets ... are very broad and straight, some of these, and all the others, are one half land, and the other half water on which they go about in canoes.... There are bridges, very large, strong, and well constructed, so that, over many, ten horsemen can ride abreast.... The city has many squares where markets are held.... There is one square, twice as large as that of Salamanca, all surrounded by arcades, where there are daily more than sixty thousand souls, buying and selling.... [I]n the service and manners of its people, their fashion of living was almost the same as in Spain, with just as much harmony and order; and considering that these people were barbarous, so cut off from the knowledge of God and other civilized peoples, it is admirable to see to what they attained in every respect....

It happened ... that a Spaniard saw an Indian ... eating a piece of flesh taken from the body of an Indian who had been killed.... I had the culprit burned, explaining that the cause was his having killed that Indian and eaten him, which was prohibited by Your Majesty, and by me in Your Royal name. I further made the chief understand that all the people ... must abstain from this custom.... I came ... to protect their lives as well as their property, and to teach them that they were to adore but one God ... that they must turn from their idols, and the rites they had practised until then, for these were lies and deceptions which the devil ... had invented.... I, likewise, had come to teach them that Your Majesty, by the will of Divine Providence, rules the universe, and that they also must submit themselves to the imperial yoke, and do all that we who are Your Majesty's ministers here might order them....

Source: *Letters of Cortés*, translated by Francis A. MacNutt (New York: G. P. Putnam, 1908), pp. 244, 256–57.

QUESTIONS FOR ANALYSIS

- What does Cortés's report tell us about the city of Tenochtitlán?
- Why does Cortés justify his actions to the degree that he does?
- Cortés writes, "I came ... to protect their lives as well as their property." Based on your reading of the chapter text, would you say he accomplished these objectives?

ultimately revealed several Aztec plots against the tiny Spanish force. Doña Marina subsequently bore Cortés a son, who is considered one of the first mixed-blooded Mexicans (mestizos).

With the assistance of Doña Marina and other native allies, Cortés marched his troops to Tenochtitlán. Upon entering, he gasped in wonder that "this city is so big and so remarkable" that it was "almost unbelievable." In a letter home, one of his soldiers wrote, "It was all so wonderful that I do not know how to describe this first glimpse of things never heard of, seen or dreamed of before."

How was this tiny force to overcome an empire of many millions with an elaborate warring tradition? Crucial to Spanish conquest was their alliance, negotiated through translators, with Moctezuma's enemies—especially the Tlaxcalans. After decades of yearning for release from the Aztec yoke, the Tlaxcalans and other Mesoamerican peoples embraced Cortés's promise of help. The Spaniards' second advantage was their method of warfare. The Aztecs were seasoned fighters, but they fought to capture, not to kill. Nor were they familiar with gunpowder or sharp steel swords. Although outnumbered, the Spaniards killed their foe with abandon, using superior weaponry, horses, and war dogs. The Aztecs, still unsure who these strange men were, allowed Cortés to enter their city. With the aid of the Tlaxcalans and a handful of his own men, in 1519 Cortés captured Moctezuma, who became a puppet of the Spanish conqueror. (See Primary Source: Cortés Approaches Tenochtitlán.)

Within two years, the Aztecs realized that the newcomers were not gods, and they staged an uprising that forced Cortés to retreat and regroup. This time, with the Tlaxcalans' help, he chose to defeat the Aztecs completely. He ordered the building

The Conquest of the Aztecs. *Diego Rivera's twentieth-century representation of the fall of Tenochtitlán (left) emphasizes the helplessness of the Aztecs to the ruthless and technologically superior Spanish soldiers. Though the Aztecs outnumber the Spanish in this portrayal, their faces are obscured in postures of grief and suffering, unlike their counterparts in the sixteenth-century illustration of the same event (right). Painted by a converted Indian and based on indigenous oral histories, it shows the Aztec warriors in a glory of their own, as well as the cruel fact that they were forced to fight other Indians who had sided with the Spanish.*

of boats to sail across Lake Texcoco to bombard the capital with artillery. Even more devastating was the spread of smallpox, brought by the Spanish, which ran through the soldiers and commoners like wildfire. The total number of Aztec casualties may have reached 240,000. As Spanish troops retook the capital, they found it in ruins, with a population too weak to resist. The last emperor, Cuauhtémoc, himself faced execution, thereby ending the royal Mexica lineage. The Aztecs lamented their defeat in verse: "We have pounded our hands in despair against the adobe walls, for our inheritance, our city, is lost and dead." Cortés became governor of the new Spanish colony, renamed "New Spain." He promptly allocated *encomiendas* to his loyal followers and dispatched expeditions to conquer the more distant Mesoamerican provinces.

The Mexica experience taught the Spanish an important lesson: an effective conquest had to be swift—and it had to remove completely the symbols of legitimate authority. Their winning advantage, however, was disease. The Spaniards unintentionally introduced germs that made their subsequent efforts at military conquest much easier.

The Incas

The other great Spanish conquest occurred in the Andes, where Quechua-speaking rulers, called Incas, had established an impressive polity. By the mid-fifteenth century, the **Inca Empire** controlled a vast domain incorporating 4 to 6 million people and running from what is now Chile to southern Colombia. At its center was the capital, Cuzco, with the magnificent fortress of Sacsayhuaman as its head. Built of huge boulders, the citadel was the nerve center of a complex network of strongholds that held the empire together.

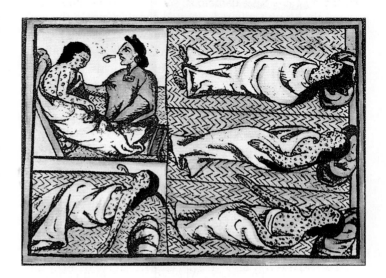

Disease and Decimation of Indians. *The real conqueror of Native Americans was not so much guns as germs. Even before Spanish soldiers seized the Aztec capital, germs had begun decimating the population. The first big killer was smallpox, recorded here by an Indian artist.*

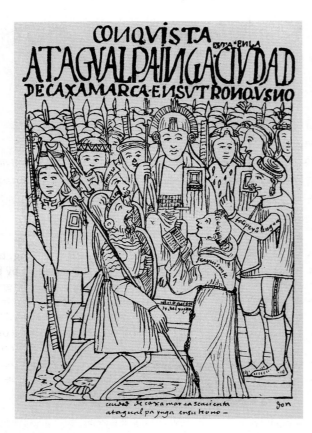

Pizarro and the Incas. *This illustration is by the Andean native Guaman Poma, whose circa 1587 epic of the conquest of Peru depicted many of the barbarities of the Spanish. Here we see the conquistador Pizarro and a Catholic priest appealing to Atahualpa—before betraying and then killing him.*

But the Incas were internally split. Lacking a clear inheritance system, the empire suffered repeated convulsions. In the early sixteenth century, the struggle over who would succeed Huayna Capac, the ruler, was especially fierce. Huáscar, his "official" son, took Cuzco (the capital), while Atahualpa, his favored son, governed the province of present-day Ecuador. Open conflict might have been averted were it not for Huayna's premature death. His killer was probably smallpox, which swept down the trade routes from Mesoamerica into the Andes (much as the bubonic plague had earlier spread through Afro-Eurasian trade routes; see Chapter 11). With the father gone, Atahualpa declared war on his brother, crushed him, forced him to witness the execution of all his supporters, and then killed him and used his skull as a vessel for maize beer.

When the Spaniards arrived in 1532, they wandered into an internally divided empire, a situation they quickly learned to exploit. Francisco Pizarro, who led the Spanish campaign, had been inspired by Cortés's victory and yearned for his own glory. Commanding a force of about 600 men, he invited Atahualpa to confer at the town of Cajamarca. There he laid a trap.

As columns of Inca warriors and servants covered with colorful plumage and plates of silver and gold entered the main square, the Spanish soldiers were awed. Writing home, one recalled, "many of us urinated without noticing it, out of sheer terror." But Pizarro's plan worked. His guns and horses shocked the Inca forces. Atahualpa himself fell into Spanish hands, later to be decapitated. Pizarro's conquistadors overran Cuzco in 1533 and then vanquished the rest of the Inca forces, a process that took decades in some areas.

Silver

For the first Europeans in the Americas, the foremost measure of success was the gold and silver that they could hoard for themselves and their monarchs. But in plundering massive amounts of silver, the conquistadors introduced it to the world's commercial systems, an act that electrified them. In the twenty years after the fall of Tenochtitlán, conquistadors took more precious metals from Mexico and the Andes than all the gold accumulated by Europeans over the previous centuries. (See Map 12.6 on p. 469.)

Having looted Indian coffers, the Spanish entered the business of mining directly, opening the Andean Potosí mines in 1545. Between 1560 and 1685, Spanish America sent 25,000 to 35,000 tons of silver annually to Spain. From 1685 to 1810, this sum doubled. The two mother lodes were Potosí, in present-day Bolivia, and Zacatecas, in northern Mexico. Silver brought bounty not only to the crown but also to privileged families based in Spain's colonial capitals; thus, private wealth funded the formation of local aristocracies.

Silver. *Silver was an important discovery for Spanish conquerors in Mesoamerica and the Andes. Conquerors expanded the custom of Inca and Aztec labor drafts to force the natives to work in mines, often in brutal conditions.*

Silver, the Devil, and Coca Leaf in the Andes

When Spanish colonists forced thousands of Andean Indians to work in the silver mines of Potosí, they permitted the chewing of coca leaves (which are now used to extract cocaine). Chewing the leaves gave Indians a mild "high," alleviated their hunger, and blunted the pain of hard work and deteriorating lungs. The habit also spread to some Spaniards. In this document, Bartolomé Arzáns de Orsúa y Vela, a Spaniard born in Potosí in 1676, expresses how important coca was to Indian miners and how harmful it was for Spaniards who fell under its spell. By the time the author wrote his observations in the late seventeenth century, the use of the coca leaf had become widespread.

I wish to declare the unhappiness and great evil that, among so many felicities, this kingdom of Peru experiences in possessing the coca herb. . . . No Indian will go into the mines or to any other labor, be it building houses or working in the fields, without taking it in his mouth, even if his life depends on it. . . .

Among the Indians (and even the Spaniards by now) the custom of not entering the mines without placing this herb in the mouth is so well established that there is a superstition that the richness of the metal will be lost if they do not do so. . . .

The Indians being accustomed to taking this herb into their mouths, there is no doubt that as long as they have it there they lose all desire to sleep, and since it is extremely warming, they say that when the weather is cold they do not feel it if they have the herb in their mouths. In addition, they also say that it increases their strength and that they feel neither hunger nor thirst; hence these Indians cannot work without it.

When the herb is ground and placed in boiling water and if a person then takes a few swallows, it opens the pores, warms the body, and shortens labor in women; and this coca herb has many other virtues besides. But human perversity has caused it to become a vice, so that the devil (that inventor of vices) has made a notable harvest of souls with it, for there are many women who have taken it—and still take it—for the sin of witchcraft, invoking the devil and using it to summon him for their evil deeds. . . .

With such ferocity has the devil seized on this coca herb that—there is no doubt about it—when it becomes an addiction it impairs or destroys the judgment of its users just as if they had drunk wine to excess and makes them see terrible visions; demons appear before their eyes in frightful forms. In this city of Potosí it is sold publicly by the Indians who work in the mines, and so the harm arising from its continued abundance cannot be corrected; but neither is that harm remediable in other large cities of this realm, where the use and sale of coca have been banned under penalties as severe as that of excommunication and yet it is secretly bought and sold and used for casting spells and other like evils.

Would that our lord the king had ordered this noxious herb pulled up by the roots wherever it is found. . . . Great good would follow were it to be extirpated from this realm: the devil would be bereft of the great harvest of souls he reaps, God would be done a great service, and vast numbers of men and women would not perish (I refer to Spaniards, for no harm comes to the Indians from it).

QUESTIONS FOR ANALYSIS

- Why would the Spaniards ban the sale of the coca herb everywhere except Potosí?
- Why would Bartolomé believe that no harm would come to the Indians for taking the coca herb?
- How does this document reveal the central role of the Catholic Church in Spanish colonial thinking? Find several words and phrases that express this outlook.

Source: Bartolomé Arzáns de Orsúa y Vela, "Claudia the Witch," in *Tales of Potosí*, edited by R. C. Padden. Trans. Morillas F. M. López (Providence, NH: Brown University Press, 1975), pp. 117–121.

Colonial mines epitomized the Atlantic world's new economy. They relied on an extensive network of Indian labor, at first enslaved, subsequently drafted. Here again, the Spanish adopted Inca and Aztec practices of requiring labor from subjugated villages: each year, village elders selected a stipulated number of men to toil in the shafts, refineries, and smelters. Under the Spanish, the digging, hauling, and smelting taxed human limits to their capacity—and beyond. Those unfortunate enough to be sent underground pounded the rock walls with chisels and hammers, releasing silicon dust. Miners could not help but breathe in the toxic dust, which created lesions and made simply inhaling seem like swallowing broken glass. (See Primary Source: Silver, the Devil, and Coca Leaf in the Andes.) Mortality rates were appalling. But the miners' sufferings reaped huge profits and significant consequences for the Europeans. The Spanish pumped so much New World silver into global commercial networks that they caused painful price inflation in Europe and transformed Europe's relationship to all its trading partners, especially those in China and India. (For more on Spain's tributary empire in the New World, see p. 468.)

The defeat of the New World's two great empires gave Europeans the means to extract human and material wealth from the Americas. In time, as Europeans settled in to stay, it also gave Europeans a market for their own products—goods that found little favor in Afro-Eurasia—and opened a new frontier that the Europeans could colonize as staple-producing provinces. At first, however, most Europeans took little notice of the Atlantic frontiers opening before them. They were, after all, embroiled in a continent-wide series of religious and political conflicts that would divide Christendom itself, as it turns out, forever.

RELIGIOUS TURMOIL IN EUROPE

In the sixteenth century, most European rulers and their subjects were focused on Europe or on Ottoman threats to the east, and not on the New World to their west. Their lives and belief systems were being turned upside down by the religious split within the Catholic Church known as the Reformation and by the wars that followed it. Religious fragmentation exacerbated already-existing dynastic rivalries and encouraged states to further centralize their bureaucracies and build up their military forces. Some of those military forces had to be used to keep the Ottomans at bay, for in this period, as we have seen, the Ottomans were making significant inroads into eastern and southern Europe.

The Reformation

Like the Renaissance, the **Protestant Reformation** in Europe began as a movement devoted to returning to ancient sources—in this case, to biblical scriptures. But it was also provoked by long-simmering dissatisfaction with the Catholic Church that came from below. Long before Martin Luther came on the scene, some scholars and believers had despaired of the church's ability to satisfy their longings for deeper, more individualized religious experience. In the fourteenth and fifteenth centuries, the church hierarchy continued to oppose reforms such as allowing laypersons to read the scriptures for themselves, as it feared heresies and challenges to its authority would arise. The church was right: for when political circumstances and the arrival of the printing press permitted Luther to avoid a heretic's death and to expand the campaign for reform, he paved the way for a "Protestant" Reformation that split Christendom for good.

MARTIN LUTHER CHALLENGES THE CHURCH The opening challenge to the authority of the pope and the Catholic Church originated in the **Holy Roman Empire**, the sprawling, loosely centralized, multiethnic empire that covered much of central and eastern Europe. When the Reformation commenced, the Holy Roman Empire was under the rule of the Habsburg prince Charles V, who inherited three great kingdoms: that of Spanish monarchs Isabella and Ferdinand (including their New World holdings), that of Holy Roman Emperor Maximilian I (in central Europe), and that of Burgundy and the Netherlands. Charles's transatlantic empire, although larger than any before or since, was not destined to last. By the time of his death (1556), it had been shattered, largely by the ideas of a stubborn and rhetorically gifted professor of theology named **Martin Luther** (1483–1546).

Initially a pious Catholic believer, Luther nonetheless believed that mortals were so given to sin that none would ever be worthy of salvation. In 1516, Luther found an answer to his quest for salvation in reading Paul's Letters to the Romans: since no human acts could be sufficient to earn admittance to heaven, individuals could only be saved by their faith in God's grace. God's free gift of forgiveness, Luther believed, did not depend on taking sacraments or performing good deeds. This faith, moreover, was something Christians could obtain just from reading the Bible—rather than by having a priest tell them what to believe. Finally, Luther concluded that Christians did not need mediators to speak to God for them; all were, in his eyes, priests, equally bound by God's laws and obliged to minister to one another's spiritual needs.

These became the three main principles that launched Luther's reforming efforts: (1) belief that faith alone saves, (2) belief that the scriptures alone hold the key to Christian truth, and (3) belief in the priesthood of all believers. But other things motivated Luther as well: corrupt practices in the church, such as the keeping of mistresses by monks, priests, and even popes; and the selling of indulgences, certificates that would supposedly shorten the buyer's time in purgatory. In the 1510s, clerics were hawking indulgences across Europe in an effort to raise money for the sumptuous new Saint Peter's Basilica in Rome.

In 1517, Luther formulated ninety-five statements, or theses, and posted them on the doors to the Wittenberg cathedral, hoping to stir up his colleagues in debate. Before long, his theses made him famous—and bolder in his criticisms. In a widely circulated pamphlet called *On the Freedom of the Christian Man* (1520), he upbraided "the Roman Church, which in past ages was the holiest of all" for having "become a den of murderers beyond all other dens of murderers, a thieves' castle beyond all other thieves' castles, the head and empire of every sin, as well as of death and damnation." As Luther's ideas spread, Pope Leo X and the Habsburg emperor, Charles V, demanded that Luther take back his criticisms and theological claims. When he refused, he was declared a heretic and avoided being burned at the stake only by the intervention of a powerful German prince who let Luther hole up in his castle.

Luther wrote many more pamphlets attacking the church and the pope, whom he now described as the anti-Christ. In 1525, he attacked another aspect of Catholic doctrine by marrying a former nun, Katharina von Bora. In Luther's view, God approved of human sexuality within the bonds of marriage, and encouraging marriage for both the clergy and the laity was the only way to prevent illicit forms of sexual behavior. Luther also translated the New Testament from Latin into German so that laypersons could have direct access, without the clergy, to the word of God. This act spurred many other daring scholars across Europe to undertake translations of their own, and it encouraged the Protestant clergy to teach children (and adults) to read their local languages.

OTHER "PROTESTANT" REFORMERS Luther's doctrines won widespread support. The renewed Christian creed appealed to commoners as well as elites, especially in communities that resented rule by Catholic "outsiders" (like the Dutch, who resented being ruled by Philip II, a Habsburg prince who lived in Spain). Thus, the reformed ideas took particularly firm hold in the German states, France, Switzerland, Scandinavia, the Low Countries, and England.

Some zealous reformers, like **Jean Calvin** (1509–1564), in France, modified Luther's ideas. To Luther's emphasis on the individual's relationship to God, Calvin added a focus on preaching and moral discipline, which he believed was best applied by autonomous religious communities. In Geneva, Switzerland, he became the leading force in a city-state republic governed by Calvinist clergymen, who banned entertainments such as the theater and gambling and saw to it that all citizens attended church and learned to read. Calvin's belief that morally righteous persons should be free to govern themselves emboldened political and religious dissenters to challenge the church and to seek more religious and political independence for their followers, who were known as Puritans in England, Presbyterians in Scotland, and Huguenots in France, the places where (in addition to Switzerland and the Netherlands) Calvinism was most popular. In contrast, those who remained loyal to the original Protestant cause now described themselves as Lutherans.

In England, Henry VIII (r. 1509–1547) and his daughter Elizabeth (r. 1558–1603) crafted a moderate reformed religion—a "middle way"—called Anglicanism, which retained many Catholic practices and a hierarchy topped by bishops. (American followers later called themselves Episcopalians, from the Latin word for bishop, *episcopus*.) Although Anglican rule was imposed on Ireland, most nonelite Irish remained Catholic. The Scots maintained a fierce devotion to their Presbyterian Church, ensuring a measure of religious diversity within the British Isles. In England, as with the rest of Europe, more radical Protestant sects, such as the Anabaptists and Quakers, also developed. While all Protestants were opposed to Catholicism and distrustful of the papal hierarchy, these different

Protestant Reformation.
Following Luther's lead, many reformers created inexpensive pamphlets to increase the circulation of their message. Pictured here is a woodcut from one such pamphlet, which shows Luther and his followers fending off the corrupt Pope Leo X.

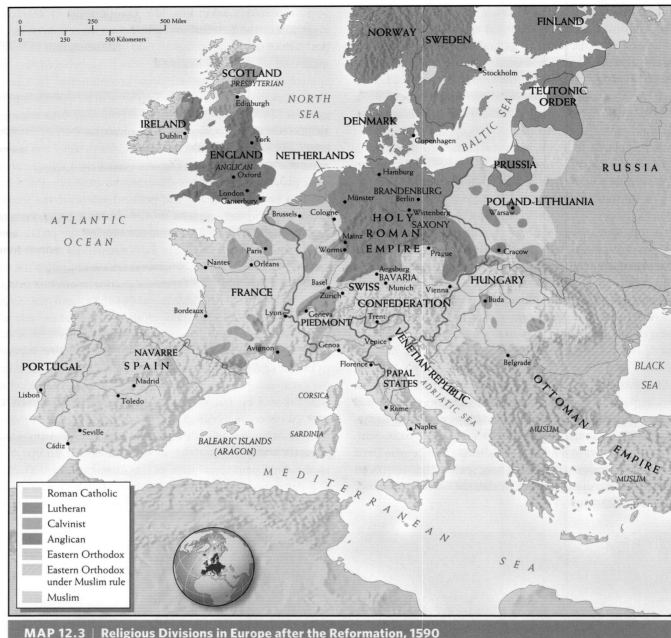

MAP 12.3 | Religious Divisions in Europe after the Reformation, 1590

In the sixteenth century, the Protestant Reformation divided western Europe. In eastern Europe, the Ottomans controlled territories inhabited by Eastern Orthodox Christians as well as some Jewish communities.

- Within the formerly all-Catholic Holy Roman Empire, what Protestant groups took hold?
- Looking at the map, can you identify any geographical patterns in the distribution of Protestant communities?
- In what regions would you expect Protestant-Catholic tensions to be the most intense?

communities sometimes developed animosities toward one another as well. (See Map 12.3.)

COUNTER-REFORMATION AND PERSECUTION The Catholic Church responded to Luther and Calvin by embarking on its own renovation, which became known as the **Counter-Reformation**. At the Council of Trent in northern Italy, whose twenty-five sessions stretched from 1545 to 1563, Catholic leaders reaffirmed most church doctrines, including papal supremacy, the holiness of all seven sacraments, the clergy's distinctive role, and the insistence that priests, monks, and nuns remain celibate. But the council also enacted reforms and adopted some of the Protestants' tactics in an effort to win back European believers and to spread the Church's message abroad. The reformed Catholics carried their message overseas—especially through an order established by Ignatius Loyola (1491–1556). Loyola founded a brotherhood of priests, the Society of Jesus, or **Jesuits**, dedicated to the revival of the Catholic Church. From bases in Lisbon, Rome, Paris, and elsewhere in Europe, the Jesuits opened missions as far as South and North America, India, Japan, and China.

Yet the Vatican continued to use repression and persecution to combat what it regarded as heretical beliefs. Priests in Augsburg performed public exorcisms, seeking to free Protestant parishioners from possession by "demons." The Index of Prohibited Books (a list of books and theological treatises banned by the Catholic Church) and the medieval Inquisition (which began around 1184 CE) were weapons against those deemed the church's enemies. But the proliferation of printing presses and the spread of Protestantism made it impossible for the Catholic Counter-Reformation to turn back the tide leading toward increased autonomy from the papacy.

Both Catholics and Protestants persecuted witches. Between about 1500 and 1700, up to 100,000 people, mostly women, were accused of being witches. Many were tried, tortured, burned at the stake, or hanged. Older women, widows, and nurses were vulnerable to charges of cursing or poisoning babies. Other charges included killing livestock, causing hailstorms, and scotching marriage arrangements. People also believed that weak and susceptible women might have sex with the devil or be tempted to do his bidding. Clearly, neither the Reformation—nor the Catholic response to it—made Europe a more tolerant society. Indeed, the Reformation split European society deeply as both Catholics and Protestants promoted their faiths.

Religious Warfare in Europe

Religious reform led Europe into another round of ferocious wars. Their ultimate effect was to weaken the Holy Roman Empire and strengthen the English, French, and Dutch. Already in the 1520s, the circulation of books presenting Luther's ideas sparked peasant revolts across central Europe. Some peasants, hoping that Luther's assault on the church's authority would help liberate them, rose up against repressive feudal landlords. In contrast to earlier wars, in which one noble's retinue fought a rival's, the defense of the Catholic mass and the Protestant Bible brought crowds of simple folk to arms. Now wars between and within central European states raged for nearly forty years as Holy Roman Emperor Charles V tried to force the Lutheran genie back into the bottle.

In 1555, the exhausted Charles V gave up the fight. He agreed to allow the German princes the right to choose Lutheranism or Catholicism as the official religion within their domains (Calvinism was still outlawed). In 1556, he abdicated and divided his realm between his younger brother Ferdinand and his son Philip. Ferdinand (r. 1556–1564) became Holy Roman Emperor and the head of the Austrian Habsburg dynasty, which ruled the Austrian, German, and central European territories that straddled the Danube. Philip II (r. Spain 1556–1598)

St. Bartholomew's Day Massacre. *An important wedding between French Catholic and Huguenot families in Paris was scheduled for August 24, 1572, St. Bartholomew's Day. But instead of reconciliation, that day saw a massacre, as Catholics tried to stamp out Protestantism in France's capital city.*

received Spain, Belgium, the Netherlands, southern Italy, and the New World possessions. Philip also inherited the Portuguese throne (from his mother), giving his Spanish Habsburg house a monopoly on Atlantic commerce.

Charles V's concessions were supposed to enable the Catholic powers to suppress Protestantism and make peace on the continent. This strategy failed. Religious conflicts led to civil wars in France and a revolt against Spanish rule in the Netherlands, which finally ended, after nearly a hundred years of conflict, with Spain conceding the Calvinist Netherlands its independence. In 1588, the Spanish further embroiled themselves in conflict with Protestant powers by sending a mighty armada of 130 ships and almost 20,000 men into the English Channel in retaliation for English privateers' plundering of Spanish ships. But England amassed even more vessels and succeeded in handing the Spanish a humiliating and costly defeat. Spain's entanglement in these conflicts depleted the fortune it had made from New World silver mines, and its decline opened the way for the Dutch and English to extend their trading networks into Asia and the New World. By the middle of the seventeenth century the center of power in Europe had shifted decisively to the north—and to the non-European power in the eastern Mediterranean, the Ottoman Empire.

THE REVIVAL OF THE ASIAN ECONOMIES

By the time the Ottomans were seizing Constantinople, the economies clustered around the Indian Ocean and China Sea had begun a vigorous revival. This economic renewal would be linked to political developments as Asian empires expanded and consolidated their power. The Mughal ruler, Akbar, and the Ottoman sultan, Suleiman the Magnificent (see Chapter 11), were equally effective and esteemed rulers. The Ming dynasty's elegant manufactures enjoyed worldwide renown, and its ability to govern highly diverse peoples led outsiders to consider China the model imperial state. The Ming, like the Mughals, seemed unconcerned with the increasing appearance of foreigners, including Europeans bearing silver, although both regimes confined European traders to port cities. If anything, the arrival of European sailors and traders in the Indian Ocean strengthened trading ties across the region and enhanced the political power and expansionist interests of Asia's imperial regimes.

The Revival of the Ottoman Caravan Trade

Seaborne commerce eclipsed but did not eliminate overland caravan trading at this time. In fact, along some routes, overland commerce thrived. One well-trafficked route linked the Baltic Sea, Muscovy, the Caspian Sea, the central Asian oases, and

Akbar Hears a Petition. *In keeping with the multiethnic and multireligious character of Akbar's empire, the image reflects the diversity of peoples seeking to have their petitions heard by the Mughal emperor.*

China. Other land routes carried goods to the ports of China and the Indian Ocean; from there, they crossed to the Ottoman Empire's heartland and went by land farther into Europe.

Of the many entrepôts that sprang up, none enjoyed more spectacular success than Aleppo, in Syria. Located at the end of caravan routes from India and Baghdad, Aleppo soon overshadowed its Syrian rivals, Damascus and Homs. A vital supply point for Anatolia and the Mediterranean cities, Aleppo by the late sixteenth century was the most important commercial center in southwest Asia. Here, successful merchants of the type celebrated in the stories of *The Thousand and One Nights* were revered. The caravans gathered on the city's edge, where animals were hired, tents sewn, and saddles and packs arranged. Large caravans involved 600 to 1,000 camels and up to 400 men;

smaller parties required no more than a dozen animals. A good leader was essential. Only someone who knew the difficult desert routes and enjoyed the confidence of nomadic Bedouin tribes (which provided safe passage for a fee) could hope to make the journey profitable.

Ottoman authorities took a keen interest in this trade, since it generated considerable tax revenue. To facilitate the caravans' movement, the government maintained refreshment and military stations along the route. But gathering so many traders, animals, and cargoes could also attract marauders, especially desert tribesmen. To prevent raids, authorities and merchants offered cash payments to tribal chieftains as "protection money"—a small price to pay to protect the caravan trade, whose revenues ultimately supported imperial expansion.

Prosperity in Ming China

China's economic dynamism was the crucial ingredient in Afro-Eurasia's global economic revival following the devastation wrought by the Black Death. External trade revived and then expanded in the sixteenth century. But China's vast internal economy was also a mainspring of the country's economic expansion. Reconstruction of the Grand Canal opened a major artery that allowed food and riches from the economically vibrant Lower Yangzi area to reach the capital region of Beijing. Cities were hubs of economic activity, but periodic markets also proliferated in many rural areas, as commercialization gathered pace and increasingly shaped the everyday life of the inhabitants of Ming China. Urban manufacturing surged, but even more important was the spread of rural handicraft industries, where the majority of spinners and weavers were women.

Along China's elaborate trading networks flowed silk and cotton textiles, rice, porcelain ceramics, paper, and many other products. The Ming's initial concern about the potentially disruptive effects of trade did not dampen this activity, and efforts to curb overseas commerce (following Zheng He's voyages; see Chapter 11) were largely unsuccessful. Indeed, the prohibition of maritime trade was officially repealed in 1567, benefiting coastal regions in particular. (See Map 12.4.)

While Chinese silks and porcelain were esteemed across Afro-Eurasia, what did foreign buyers have to trade with the Chinese? The answer is silver, which became an important stimulant to the Ming economy and essential to the Ming monetary system. Whereas their predecessors had used paper money, Ming consumers and traders mistrusted anything other than silver or gold for commercial dealings. However, China did not produce sufficient silver for its growing needs—a situation that foreigners learned to exploit. Indeed, silver and other precious metals were about the only commodities for which the Chinese would trade their precious manufactures. Through most of the sixteenth century, China's main source of silver was Japan. After the 1570s, however, the Philippines, under the control of the Spanish, became a gateway for New World silver. According to one estimate, one-third of all silver mined in the Americas wound up in Chinese hands. This influx fueled China's phenomenal economic expansion, providing further impetus to its maritime trade. (See Primary Source: A Ming Official on Maritime Trade.)

One measure of greater prosperity under the Ming was its population surge. By the mid-seventeenth century, China's population probably accounted for more than one-third of the total world population. Although 90 percent of Chinese people lived in the countryside, large numbers filled the cities. Beijing, the capital, had perhaps a million inhabitants. Cities offered diversions ranging from literary and theatrical societies to schools of learning, religious societies, urban associations, and manufactures from all over the empire. The elegance and material prosperity of Chinese cities dazzled European visitors. One Jesuit missionary described Nanjing, the secondary capital, as surpassing all other cities "in beauty and grandeur. . . . It is literally filled with palaces and temples and towers and bridges. . . . There is a gaiety of spirit among the people who are well mannered and nicely spoken."

Urban prosperity fostered entertainment districts where people could indulge themselves anonymously. Some Ming women found a place here as refined entertainers and courtesans; others as midwives, poets, sorcerers, and matchmakers. Female painters, mostly from scholar-official families, emulated males who used the home and garden for creative pursuits. The expanding book trade also accommodated women, who were writers as well as readers, not to mention literary characters and archetypes (especially of Confucian virtues). But Chinese women made their greatest fortunes inside the emperor's Forbidden City as healers, consorts, and power brokers.

To be sure, Ming rule faced a variety of problems, from piracy along the coasts to ineptness in the state. Corruption and perceptions of social decay elicited even more criticism. Consider Wang Yangming, a government official and scholar of neo-Confucian thought who urged commitment to social action. Arguing for the unity of knowledge and action, he claimed that one's own thoughts and intuition, rather than observations and external principles (as earlier neo-Confucian thinkers had emphasized), could provide the answers to problems. His more radical followers suggested that women were equal to men intellectually and should receive a full education—a position that earned these radicals banishment from the elite establishment. But even as such new ideas and the state's weaknesses created discord, Ming society remained commercially vibrant. This vitality survived the dynasty's fall in 1644, laying the foundation for increased population growth and territorial expansion in subsequent centuries.

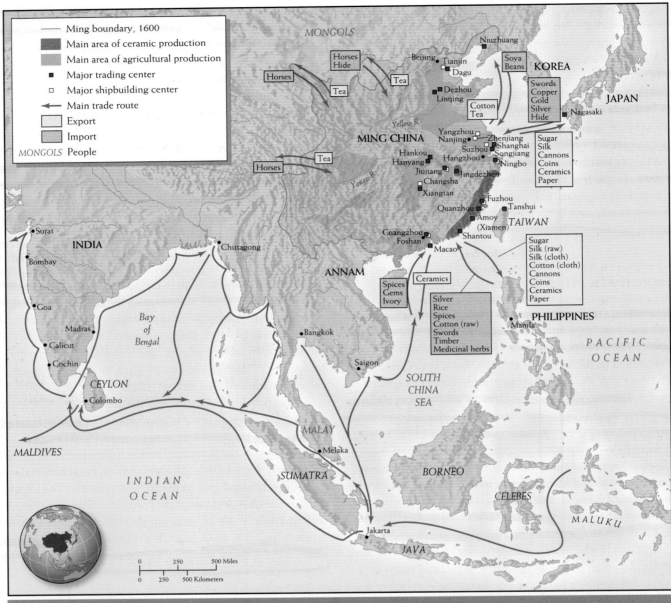

MAP 12.4 | Trade and Production in Ming China

The Ming Empire in the early seventeenth century was the world's most populous state and arguably its wealthiest.

- According to this map, what were the main items involved in China's export-import trade, and what were some of the regions that purchased its exports?
- In what way does the activity represented on this map indicate why China was the world's leading importer of silver at this time?
- Locate the major trading and shipbuilding centers, and then explain how important the export trade was to the Ming Empire's prosperity.

The Revival of Indian Ocean Trade

China's economic expansion occurred within the revival of Indian Ocean trade. In fact, many of the same merchants seeking trade with China developed a brisk commerce that tied the whole of the Indian Ocean together. As a result, ports in East Africa and the Red Sea again enjoyed links with coastal cities of India, South Asia, and the Malay Peninsula. Muslims dominated this trade.

In dealing with China, Indian merchants faced the same problem as Europeans and West Asians: they had to pay with silver. So they became as dependent on gaining access to silver as others who were courting Chinese commerce. But unlike Chinese merchants, Islamic traders, including Indian Muslims,

A Ming Official on Maritime Trade

This text was written by a sixteenth-century Ming official whose family fortune benefited greatly from the textile industry. Despite his own family background, in this excerpt he reveals some degree of ambivalence, typical of the scholar-official elite, about the accumulation of mercantile wealth in Ming society. Also interesting, however, is the author's argument in favor of the expansion of maritime trade, which he saw as more of an opportunity than a threat, in contrast to many of his contemporaries. The commercial transactions along the southeast coast were distinctly different, he argued, from the overland trade with the country's northern neighbors. He also urged the government to avoid overtaxing the merchants.

Money and profit are of great importance to men. They seek profit, they suffer by it, yet they cannot forget it. They exhaust their bodies and spirits, run day and night, yet they still regard what they have gained as insufficient. Those who become merchants eat fine food and wear elegant clothes. They ride on beautifully caparisoned, double-harnessed horses—dust flying as they race through the streets and the horses' precious sweat falling like rain. Opportunistic persons attracted by their wealth offer to serve them. Pretty girls in beautiful long-sleeved dresses and delicate slippers play stringed and wind instruments for them and compete to please them. Merchants boast that their wisdom and ability are such as to give them a free hand in affairs. They believe that they know all the possible transformations in the universe and therefore can calculate all the changes in the human world, and that the rise and fall of prices are under their command. . . .

Some people say that the southeast sea foreigners have invaded us several times so they are not the kind of people with whom we should trade. But they should realize that the southeast sea foreigners need Chinese goods and the Chinese need their goods. If we prohibit the natural flow of this merchandise, how can we prevent them from invading us? I believe that if the sea trade was opened, the trouble with foreign pirates would cease. . . . Moreover, China's exports in the northwest trade come from the national treasury. Whereas the northwest foreign trade ensures only harm, the sea trade provides us with only gain. How could those in charge of the government fail to realize the distinction?

Turning to taxes levied on Chinese merchants, though these taxes are needed to fill the national treasury, excessive exploitation should be prohibited. Merchants from all areas are ordered to stop their carts and boats and have their bags and cases examined whenever they pass through a road or river checkpoint. Often the cargoes are overestimated and thus a falsely high duty is demanded. . . .

QUESTIONS FOR ANALYSIS

- According to this official, what are the benefits of maritime trade?
- What reservations does he have about increasing trade with foreigners?
- To what extent is this official in favor of China's adopting what we would call "free trade"?

Source: Chinese Civilization: A Sourcebook, 2nd ed., edited by Patricia Buckley Ebrey (New York: The Free Press, 1993), pp. 216–218.

in the region's commercial hubs did not obey one overarching political authority. This gave them considerable autonomy from political affairs and allowed them to occupy strategic positions in long-distance trade. Meanwhile, rulers all along the Indian Ocean enriched themselves with customs duties while flaunting their status with exotic goods. For glorifying sovereigns and worshipping deities, luxuries such as silks, porcelains, ivory, gold, silver, diamonds, spices, frankincense, myrrh, and incense were in high demand. Thus, the Indian Ocean trade connected a vast array of consumers and producers long before Europeans arrived on the scene.

Of the many port cities supporting Indian Ocean commerce, Melaka was key, located on the Malaysian Peninsula at a choke point between the Indian Ocean and the South China Sea. Lacking a hinterland of farmers to support it, Melaka thrived as an entrepôt for world traders, thousands of whom resided in the city or passed through it. Indeed, Melaka's merchants were a microcosm of the region's diverse commercial community. Arabs, Indians, Armenians, Jews, East Africans, Persians, and eventually western Europeans established themselves there to profit from the commerce that flowed in and out of the port.

India was the geographical and economic center of the trade routes connected by port cities. With a population expanding as rapidly as China's, its large cities (such as Agra, Delhi, and Lahore) each boasted nearly half a million residents. India's

Caravanserai. *As trade routes throughout the Ottoman Empire bustled with lucrative deals, roadside inns called caravanserais offered shrewd merchants and their helpers rest and refreshment. This illustration of a caravanserai comes from the 1581 travel journal of Venetian envoy Jacopo Soranzo.*

manufacturing center, Bengal, exported silk and cotton textiles and rice throughout South and Southeast Asia. Like China, India had a favorable trade balance with Europe and West Asia (they were exporting more than they were importing), exporting textiles and pepper (a spice that Europeans prized) in exchange for silver.

Mughal India and Commerce

The **Mughal Empire** ruled over the hub of the Indian Ocean trade in India. It became one of the world's wealthiest empires just when Europeans were establishing sustained connections with India. These connections, however, only touched the outer layer of Mughal India, one of Islam's greatest regimes. Established in 1526, it was a vigorous, centralized state whose political authority encompassed most of modern-day India. During the sixteenth century, it had a population of between 100 and 150 million.

The Mughals' strength rested on their military power (see Chapter 11). The dynasty's founder, Babur, had introduced horsemanship, artillery, and field cannons from central Asia, and gunpowder had secured his swift military victories over northern India. Under his grandson, Akbar (r. 1556–1605), the empire enjoyed expansion and consolidation that continued (under his own grandson, Aurangzeb) until it covered almost all of India. (See Map 12.5.) Known as the "Great Mughal," Akbar was skilled not only in military tactics but also in the art of alliance making. Deals with Hindu

chieftains through favors and intermarriage also undergirded his empire.

The Mughals derived their imperial power not only from military strength but also from their flexible attitude toward the realm's diverse peoples, especially in spiritual affairs. Akbar was a Muslim, but his regime did not rely on an Islamic sectarian ideology for its legitimation. He projected a new image of the emperor that stressed his earthly political and military prowess as much as his role as a guide in divine affairs. He was a philosopher-king. In keeping with this image, the imperial court welcomed advocates of different religions. Brahman, Jain, Zoroastrian, and Muslim scholars, along with Jesuit priests, who traveled from the new Portuguese settlements, gathered in his court for learned discussions. Akbar and his successor, Jahangir, believed that the universal truths of religion existed across traditions. Accordingly, their use of Islam and its symbols in imperial culture and architecture was never exclusionary; they coexisted with the subcontinent's diverse cultural and religious heritage. This tolerant imperial policy stood in stark contrast to the sharp religious conflict in contemporary Europe. But underlying the Mughals' pluralistic attitude was the history of Islam in India. It did not expand and spread as a religion of conquest. Rather, conversions occurred and an Indian Islam took shape gradually over centuries as the people of the subcontinent engaged creatively with the rulers' religion, interpreting it according to their own cultural traditions. In this sense, the erudite discussions on comparative religion in the Mughal court recognized the ground-level reality of India's plural religious and cultural context. This earned it widespread legitimacy.

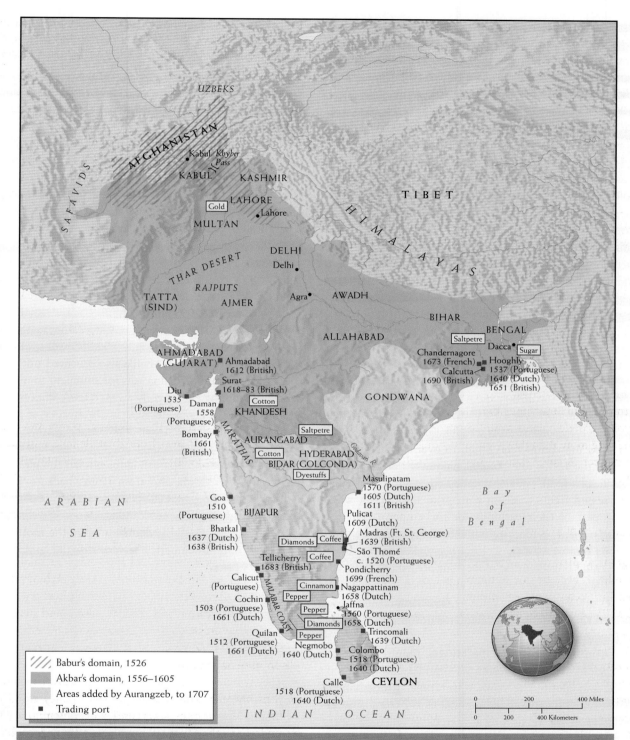

MAP 12.5 | Expansion of the Mughal Empire, 1556–1707

Under Akbar and Aurangzeb, the Mughal Empire expanded and dominated much of South Asia. Yet, by looking at the trading ports along the Indian coast, one can see the growing influence of Portuguese, Dutch, French, and English interests.

- Look at the dates for each port, and identify which traders came first and which came last.
- Compare this map with Map 12.2 (showing the earlier period 1420–1580). To what extent do the trading posts shown here reflect increased European influence in the region?
- How would these European outposts have affected Mughal policies?

Akbar's court benefited from commercial expansion in the Indian Ocean. Although the Mughals possessed no ocean navy, merchants from Mughal lands used overland routes and rivers to exchange Indian cottons, tobacco, saffron, betel leaf, sugar, and indigo for Iranian melons, dried fruits, nuts, silks, carpets, and precious metals or for Russian pelts, leathers, walrus tusks, saddles, and chain mail armor. Every year, Akbar ordered 1,000 new suits stitched of the most exquisite material. His harem preened in fine silks dripping with gold, brocades, and pearls. Carpets, mirrors, and precious metals adorned nobles' households and camps, while perfume and wine flowed freely. Soldiers, servants, and even horses and elephants sported elaborate attire.

During the sixteenth century, expanded trade with Europe brought more wealth to the Mughal polity, while the empire's strength limited European incursions. Although the Portuguese occupied Goa and Bombay on the Indian coast, they had little presence elsewhere and dared not antagonize the Mughal emperor. In 1578, Akbar recognized the credentials of a Portuguese ambassador and allowed a Jesuit missionary to enter his court. Thereafter, commercial ties between Mughals and Portuguese intensified, but merchants were still restricted to a handful of ports. In the 1580s and 1590s, the Mughals ended the Portuguese monopoly on trade with Europe by allowing Dutch and English merchantmen to dock in Indian ports.

Akbar used the commercial boom to overhaul his revenue system. Until the 1560s, the Mughal state relied on a network of decentralized tribute collectors called *zamindars*. These collectors possessed rights to claim a share of the harvest while earmarking part of their earnings for the emperor. But the Mughals did not always receive their agreed share and the peasants resented the high levies, so local populations resisted. As flourishing trade bolstered the money supply, Akbar's officials monetized the tax assessment system and curbed the *zamindars'* power. After other centralizing reforms, increased imperial revenues helped finance military expeditions and the extravagant beautification of Akbar's court.

Centered in northern India, the Mughal Empire used surrounding regions' wealth and resources—military, architectural, and artistic—to glorify the court. Over time, the enhanced wealth caused friction among Indian regions and even between merchants and rulers. Yet as long as merchants relied on rulers for their commercial gains, and as long as rulers balanced local and imperial interests, the realm remained unified and kept Europeans on the outskirts of society.

Asian Relations with Europe

As actors in the world of Asian commerce, Europeans were very much the newest, and weakest, kids on the block. Europeans' overseas expansion had originally looked toward Asia in hopes of acquiring greater access to luxury goods such as silk and spices. It took some time for them to acquire access to these markets. But silver, followed by maritime and military advances and state-backed trading companies, offered Europeans the opportunity to gradually insert themselves into the Eurasian luxury trade.

The Portuguese blazed the way as collectors of customs duties from Asian traders and, after 1557, as transshippers of Chinese porcelain and silks from the coastal enclave of Macao (see again Map 12.4). The Portuguese also dominated the silver trade from Japan. Envying Portuguese profits, the Spanish, English, and Dutch also ventured into Asian waters. With its monopoly on American silver, Spain enjoyed a competitive advantage. In 1565, the first Spanish trading galleon reached the Philippines; in 1571, after capturing Manila and making it a colonial capital, the Spanish established a brisk trade with China. Each year, ships from Spain's colonies in the Americas crossed the Pacific to Manila, bearing cargoes of silver. They returned carrying porcelain and silks for well-to-do European consumers. Merchants in Manila also procured silks, tapestries, and feathers from the China seas for shipment to the Americas, where the mining elite eagerly awaited these imports.

The year 1571 was decisive in the history of the modern world, for in that year Spain inaugurated a trade circuit that made good on Magellan's earlier achievement of circumnavigating the globe. As Spanish ships circled the globe from the New World to China and from China back to Europe, the world became commercially interconnected. Silver solidified the linkage, being the only foreign commodity for which the Chinese had an insatiable demand. From the mother lodes of the Andes and Mesoamerica, silver made the commerce of the world go round.

Macao. *This Chinese painting depicts the Portuguese enclave of Macao, on the southern border of China, around 1800.*

Other Europeans, too, wanted their share of Asia's wealth. The English and the Dutch reached the South China Sea late in the sixteenth century. Captain James Lancaster made the first English voyage to the East Indies between 1591 and 1594. Five years later, 101 English subscribers pooled their funds and formed a joint-stock company (an association in which each member owns shares of capital). This English East India Company soon won a royal charter granting it exclusive rights to import East Indian goods. Soon the company displaced the Portuguese in the Arabian Sea and the Persian Gulf. Doing a brisk trade in indigo, saltpeter, pepper, and cotton textiles, the English East India Company eventually acquired control of ports on both coasts of India—Fort St. George (Madras; 1639), Bombay (1661), and Calcutta (1690).

Still, Europeans trading in Asia remained dependent on local power brokers and commercial traders. The number of European settlers was miniscule, their cultural inroads few. Trade in Asia continued, largely in Asian hands, and focused on older routes. Although Europeans came to control some small coastal enclaves, they did not have large colonial lands to rule. Things were very different in the Atlantic world, where conquest, settlement, and trade brought with it previously unknown plants, people, products—and pathogens.

COMMERCE AND COLONIZATION IN THE ATLANTIC WORLD

The Spanish, it was once said, came to the Americas for God, gold, and glory. Fittingly, gold (and silver) took precedence on this list. Those precious metals brought glory to conquistadors, enriched Spanish coffers, and helped to finance the spiritual conquests that Catholic missionaries undertook in the Americas. The products of American mines also soon found their way into global trading circuits, giving Europeans a commodity with which to purchase African slaves and Asian goods.

The flow of peoples to the Americas and products from the Americas transformed economies—and, even more, transformed environments—across the world. Those who came to the Americas carried devastating diseases that killed tens of millions of Amerindians. The newcomers also brought horses, cattle, pigs, wheat, grapevines, and sugarcane. In exchange, they learned about crops such as potatoes and corn that would fuel a population explosion across Afro-Eurasia. Historians call this hemispheric transfer of animals, plants, people, and pathogens in the wake of Columbus's voyages the **Columbian exchange**. Over time, these transfers would change the demography and the diets of both the New and the Old Worlds.

The Columbian Exchange

The first and most profound effect of the Columbian exchange was a destructive one: the decimation of the Amerindian population by European diseases. (See Analyzing Global Developments: The European Conquest of the Americas and Amerindian Mortality.) For millennia, the isolated populations of the Americas had been cut off from Afro-Eurasian microbe migrations. Africans, Europeans, and Asians had long interacted, sharing disease pools and gaining immunities; in this sense, the Amerindians were indeed "worlds apart."

Sickness spread from almost the moment the Spaniards arrived. Even Cortés took note. "Their excretions," he wrote to the Spanish emperor, "were the sort of filth that thin swine pass which have been fed on nothing but grass." Amerindian accounts of the fall of Tenochtitlán recalled the smallpox epidemic more vividly than the fighting. Even worse, no sooner had smallpox done its work than Indians faced a second pandemic: measles. Then came pneumonic plague and influenza. As each wave retreated, it left a population more emaciated than before, even less prepared for the next wave. The scale of death remains unprecedented: imported pathogens wiped out up to 90 percent of the Amerindian population. A century after smallpox arrived on Hispaniola in 1519, no more than 5 to 10 percent of the island's population were left alive. Diminished and weakened by disease, Amerindians could not resist European settlement and colonization of the Americas. Thus were Europeans the unintended beneficiaries of a horrifying catastrophe.

As time passed, all sides adopted new forms of agriculture from one another. Indians taught Europeans how to grow potatoes and corn, crops that would become staples all across Afro-Eurasia. The Chinese found that they could grow corn in areas too dry for rice and too wet for wheat, while corn replaced, at first by fits and starts, Africa's major food grains, sorghum, millet, and rice, to become the continent's principal food crop by the twentieth century. (See Current Trends in World History: Corn and the Rise of Slave-Supplying Kingdoms in West Africa.) Europeans also took away tomatoes, beans, cacao, peanuts, tobacco, and squash, while exporting livestock such as cattle, swine, and horses to the New World. The environmental effects of the introduction of livestock to the Americas were manifold. In the highland regions north of the valley of central Mexico (where Native Americans had once maintained irrigated, highly productive agricultural estates), Spanish settlers opened up large herding ranches. An area that had once produced corn and squash now supported herds of sheep and cattle. Without natural predators, these animals reproduced with lightning speed, destroying entire landscapes with their hoofs and their foraging.

As Europeans cleared trees and other vegetation for ranches, mines, or plantations, they undermined the habitats of many

The European Conquest of the Americas and Amerindian Mortality

If the fourteenth century was an age of dying across Afro-Eurasia, the sixteenth century saw even higher mortality rates in the Americas. As a result of European conquest, the exposure to virulent diseases, and the hyperexploitation of their labor under miserable conditions, the Native American populations saw their numbers reduced by 85 percent. The numbers themselves, however, are highly controversial and have sparked intense debates. Some scholars believe that no reliable numbers can be found for the population of the Americas when Europeans first arrived. Others have used a range of methods and data sources to establish population figures, including European firsthand accounts from that period, archaeological and anthropological evidence, estimates of the maximum population size of people the land can contain indefinitely (carrying capacity), and projections built backward from more recent censuses. These estimates vary widely from as little as 8 million to as high as more than 100 million.

Area	Population in 1492	Later Populations	Mortality Rates
The Americas	53.9 m[a]	8 m in 1650	85%
The Caribbean			
Hispaniola	1.0 m	extinct by 1600	100%
The other islands	2.0 m	extinct by 1600	100%
Mexico	17.2 m	3.5 m in 1600	80%
The Andes	15.0 m	3.0 m in 1650	80%
Central America	5.63 m	1.12 m in 1700	80%
North America	3.79 m	1.5 m in 1700	60%
		250,000 in 1900	84%

[a]m = millions.

QUESTIONS FOR ANALYSIS

- Imagine yourself a historical demographer. How would you attempt to estimate the population of the Americas in 1492?
- What effect did European conquest and Amerindian dying have on the polities and religious beliefs of the Native Americans?

- Why do you think Native American population growth never recovered from the initial encounter with Europeans as Afro-Eurasian population growth eventually recovered from the Black Death?

Sources: Suzanne Austin Alchon, *A Pest in the Land: New World Epidemics in a Global Perspective* (2003); David Noble Cook, *Born to Die: Disease and New World Conquest, 1492 to 1650* (1998); William M. Denevan, *The Native Populations of the Americas in 1492* (1992); David Henige, *Numbers from Nowhere: The Amerindian Contact Population Debate* (1998); "La Catastrophe Demographique," *L'Histoire*, no. 322 (July–August 2007):17; Thornton, Russell, *American Indian Holocaust: A Population History since 1492* (1987), p. xvii.

---

indigenous mammals and birds. On the islands of the West Indies, described by Columbus as "roses of the sea," the Spanish chopped down lush tropical and semitropical forests to make way for sugar plantations. Before long, nearly all of the islands' tall trees as well as many shrubs and ground plants were gone, and residents lamented the absence of birdsong. Over ensuing centuries, the flora and fauna of the Americas took on an increasingly European appearance—a process that the historian Alfred Crosby has called ecological imperialism. At the same time, the interactions between Europeans and Amerindians would continue to shape societies on both sides of the Atlantic.

Spain's Tributary Empire

Like the Europeans who sailed into the Indian Ocean to join existing commercial systems, the Spaniards sought to exploit the wealth of indigenous empires without fully dismantling them.

Those Native Americans who survived the original encounters could be harnessed as a means to siphon tribute payments to the new masters. Spain could thereby extract wealth without extensive settlement. In Mexico and Peru, conquistadors decapitated native communities but left much of their social and economic structure intact—including networks of tribute. But unlike the European penetration of the Indian Ocean, the occupation of the New World went beyond the control of commercial outposts. Instead, European colonialism in the Americas involved laying claim to large amounts of territory—and ultimately the entire landmass. (See Map 12.6.) We should be careful, however, not to mistake the expansive claims made by European empires in the Americas with actual control of the territory. Through the fifteenth and sixteenth centuries—and as we will see in Chapter 13, through the seventeenth and eighteenth—Amerindians still maintained their dominion over much of the Americas, even as disease continued to diminish their numbers.

Map legend:

Aztec Empire, 1519
Inca Empire, 1525
AZTEC People
Spanish settlement
To 1640
To 1750
Frontier lands, 1750
Portuguese settlement
To 1640
To 1750
Frontier lands, 1750
Gold Commodity

MAP 12.6 | The Spanish and Portuguese Empires in the Americas, 1492–1750

This map examines the growth of the Spanish and Portuguese Empires in the Americas over two and a half centuries.

- Identify the natural resources that led the Spaniards and Portuguese to focus their empire building where they did.
- What were the major export commodities from these colonized areas?
- Looking back to Map 12.2, why do you think Spanish settlement covered so much more area than Portuguese settlement?
- According to your reading, how did the production and export of silver and sugar shape the labor systems that evolved in both empires?

Corn and the Rise of Slave-Supplying Kingdoms in West Africa

New World varieties of corn spread rapidly throughout the Afro-Eurasian landmass soon after the arrival of Columbus in the Americas. Its hardiness and fast ripening qualities made it more desirable than many of the Old World grain products. In communities that consumed large quantities of meat, it became the main product fed to livestock.

Corn's impact on Africa was as substantial as it was in the rest of Eurasia. Seeds made their way to western regions more quickly than regions south of the Sahara along two routes: via European merchants calling into ports along the coast and via West African Muslims returning across the Sahara after participating in the pilgrimage. The first evidence of corn cultivation in sub-Saharan Africa comes from a Portuguese navigator who identified the crop being grown on the island of Cape Verde in 1540. By the early seventeenth century, corn was replacing millet and sorghum as the main grain being grown in many West African regions and was destined to transform the work routines and diets of the peoples living in the region's tropical rain forests all the way from present-day Sierra Leone in the east to Nigeria in the west. In many ways, this area, which saw the rise of a group of powerful slave-supplying kingdoms in the eighteenth century—notably, Asante, Dahomey, Oyo, and Benin—owed its prosperity to the cultivation of this New World crop. (See Chapter 14 for a fuller discussion of these states.)

The tropical rain forests of West and central Africa were thick with trees and ground cover in 1500. Clearing them so that they could support intensive agriculture was exhausting work, requiring enormous outlays of human energy and time. Corn, a crop first domesticated in central Mexico 7,000 years ago, made this task possible. It added much-needed carbohydrates to the carbon-deficient diets of rain forest dwellers. In addition, as a crop that matured more quickly than those that were indigenous to the region (millet, sorghum, and rice) and required less labor, it yielded two harvests in a single year. Farmers also cultivated cassava, another New World native, which in turn provided households with more carbohydrate calories. Yet corn did more than produce more food per unit of land and labor. Households put every part of the plant to use: grain, leaves, stalks, tassels, and roots were all made to serve useful purposes.

Thus, at the very time that West African groups were moving southward into the rain forests, European navigators were arriving along the coast with new crops. Corn gave communities of cultivators the caloric energy to change their forest landscapes, expanding the arable areas. In a select few of these regions, enterprising clans emerged to dominate the political scene, creating centralized kingdoms like Asante, in present-day Ghana; Dahomey, in present-day Benin; and Oyo and Benin,

---

Within their colonial heartlands, Spanish masters fused traditional tribute taking with their own innovations to make villagers deliver goods and services. But because the Spanish authorities also bestowed *encomiendas*, those favored individuals could demand labor from their lands' Indian inhabitants—for mines, estates, and public works. Whereas Aztec and Inca rulers had used conscripted labor to build up their public wealth, the Spaniards did so for private gain.

Most Spanish migrants were men; very few were women. One, Inés Suárez, reached the Indies only to find her husband, who had arrived earlier, dead. She then became mistress of the conquistador Pedro de Valdivia, and the pair worked as a conquering team. Initially, she joined an expedition to conquer Chile as Valdivia's domestic servant, but she soon became much more—nurse, caretaker, adviser, and guard, having uncovered several plots to assassinate her lover. Suárez even served as a diplomat between warring Indians and Spaniards in an effort to secure the conquest. Later, she helped to rule Chile as the wife of Rodrigo de Quiroga, governor of the province. Admittedly, hers was an exceptional story. More typical were women who foraged for food, tended wounded soldiers, and set up European-style settlements.

However, there were too few Spanish women to go around, so Spanish men consorted with local women—despite the crown's disapproval. From the onset of colonization, Spaniards also married into Indian families. After conquering the Incas, Pizarro himself wedded an Inca princess, thereby (or so he hoped) inheriting the mantle of local dynastic rule. As a result of intermarriages, mestizos became the fastest-growing segment of the population of Spanish America.

Spanish migrants and their progeny preferred towns to the countryside. Ports excepted, the major cities of Spanish America were the former centers of Indian empires. Mexico City took shape on the ruins of Tenochtitlán; Cuzco arose from the razed Inca capital. In their architecture, economy, and most intimate aspects, the Spanish colonies adopted as much as they transformed the worlds they encountered.

in present-day Nigeria. These elites transformed what had once been thinly settled environments into densely populated states, with elaborate bureaucracies, big cities, and large and powerful standing armies.

There was much irony in the rise of these states, which owed so much of their strength to the linking of the Americas with Afro-Eurasia. The armies that they created and the increased populations that the new crops allowed were part and parcel of the Atlantic slave trade. That which the Americas gave with one hand (new crops), it took back with the other (warfare, captives, and New World slavery).

Corn Plantation. *This nineteenth-century engraving by famed Italian explorer Savorgnan de Brazza shows women of the West African tribe Bateke working in corn plantations. De Brazza would later serve as the governor general of the French colony in the Congo.*

QUESTIONS FOR ANALYSIS

- What were the major effects of growing corn in West Africa?
- How did the growing of corn reshape the history of the Atlantic world during this period?

Explore Further

McCann, James. *Maize and Grace: Africa's Encounter with a New World Crop, 1500–2000* (2005).

Portugal's New World Colony

No sooner did Europeans—starting with the Portuguese and Spanish—venture into the seas than they carved them up to prevent a free-for-all. The Treaty of Tordesillas of 1494, drawn up by the pope, had foreseen that the non-European world—the Americas, Africa, and Asia—would be divided into spheres of interest between Spain and Portugal. Yet the treaty was unenforceable. No less interested in immediate riches than the Spanish, the Portuguese were disappointed by the absence of tributary populations and precious metals in the areas set aside for them. What they did find in Brazil, however, was abundant, fertile land on which favored persons received massive royal grants. These estate owners governed their plantations like feudal lords (see Chapter 10).

COASTAL ENCLAVES Hemmed in along the coast, the Portuguese created enclaves. Unlike the Spanish, they rarely intermarried with Amerindians, most of whom had fled or had died

from imported diseases. Failing to find established cities, the colonists remained in more dispersed settlements. By the late seventeenth century, Brazil's white population was 300,000.

The problem was where to find labor to work the rich lands. Lacking a centralized government to deal with the labor shortage, initially the Portuguese settlers tried to enlist the dispersed indigenous population; but when recruitment became increasingly coercive, Indians turned on the settlers, whom they perceived to be interlopers. Some fought. Others fled to the vast interior. Reluctant to pursue the Indians inland, the Portuguese hugged their beachheads, extracting brazilwood (the source of a beautiful red dye) and sugar from their enclaves.

African slaves became the solution to this labor problem. What had worked for the Portuguese on sugarcane plantations in the Azores and other Atlantic islands now found application on their Brazilian plantations. Especially in the northeast, in the Bay of All Saints, the Atlantic world's first sugar-producing commercial center appeared.

Mission São Miguel. *The Jesuits were avid missionaries in the Spanish and Portuguese Empires and often tried to shelter native peoples from conquistadors and labor recruiters. Missions, like this one, in the borderlands between Brazil and Spanish colonies were targets of attack from both sides.*

SUGAR PLANTATIONS Along with silver, sugar emerged as the most valuable export from the Americas. It also was decisive in rearranging relations between peoples around the Atlantic. Cultivation of sugarcane had originated in India, spread to the Mediterranean region, and then reached the coastal islands of West Africa. The Portuguese transported the West African model to Brazil, and other Europeans took it to the Caribbean. (See again Map 12.6.) By the early seventeenth century, sugar had become a major export from the New World. By the eighteenth century, its production required continuous and enormous transfers of labor from Africa, and its value surpassed that of silver as an export from the Americas to Europe.

At first, most Brazilian sugar plantations were fairly small, employing between 60 and 100 slaves. But they were efficient enough to create an alternative model of empire, one that resulted in full-scale colonization and dislocation of the existing population. The slaves lived in wretched conditions: their barracks were miserable, and their diets were insufficient to keep them alive under backbreaking work routines. Moreover, these slaves were disproportionately men. As they rapidly died off, the only way to ensure replenishment was to import more Africans. This model of settlement relied on the transatlantic flow of slaves.

Beginnings of the Transatlantic Slave Trade

As European demand for sugar increased, the slave trade expanded. Although African slaves were imported into the Americas starting in the fifteenth century, the first direct voyage carrying them from Africa to the Americas occurred in 1525. The transatlantic slave trade began modestly in support of one commodity, sugar. From the time of Columbus until 1820, more than five times as many Africans as Europeans moved to the Americas: approximately 2 million Europeans (voluntarily) and 12 million Africans (involuntarily) crossed the Atlantic—though the especially high mortality rate for Africans meant that only 10 million survived to reach New World shores.

First to master long-distance seafaring, the Portuguese also led the way in human cargo. Trade in slaves grew steadily throughout the sixteenth century, then surged in the seventeenth and eighteenth centuries (see Chapter 13). Initially, all European powers participated—Portuguese, Spanish, Dutch, English, and French. Eventually, New World merchants in both North and South America also established direct trade links with Africa.

Well before European merchants arrived off its western coast, Africa had known long-distance slave trading. In fact, the overall number of Africans sold into captivity in the Muslim world exceeded that of the Atlantic slave trade. Moreover, Africans maintained slaves themselves. African slavery, like its American counterpart, was a response to labor scarcities. In many parts of Africa, however, slaves did not face permanent servitude. Instead, they were assimilated into families, gradually losing their servile status and swelling the size and power of their adopted lineage-based groups.

With the additional European demand for slaves to work New World plantations alongside the ongoing Muslim slave trade, pressure on the supply of African slaves intensified. Only a narrow band stretching down the spine of the African landmass, from present-day Uganda and the highlands of Kenya to Zambia and Zimbabwe, escaped the impact of Asian and European slave traders.

Within Africa, the social and political consequences were not fully evident until the great age of the slave trade in the eighteenth century, but already some economic consequences were clear. The overwhelming trend was to further limit Africa's population. Indeed, African laborers fetched high enough prices to more than cover the costs of their capture and transportation across the Atlantic.

By the late sixteenth century, important pieces had fallen into place to create a new Atlantic world, one that could not have been imagined a century earlier. This was the three-cornered **Atlantic system**, with Africa supplying labor, the Americas land and minerals, and Europeans the technology and military power to hold the system together. If observers at the time counted the Ottomans or the Ming as the greatest world powers, in the longer run the wealth flows to Europe and the slave-based development of the Americas would tip the world balance of power in Europe's favor.

CONCLUSION

In this multicentered world of the fifteenth and sixteenth centuries, Europe was a poor cousin, embroiled in religious warfare. It was the Ottoman Empire that was on the rise. The Ottomans, like the Ming in China and the Mughals in India, built wealthy, multiethnic empires and thriving trade networks. But Ottoman inroads in the Mediterranean spurred European merchants and mariners to seek alternative routes to Asia. Breaking into the Indian Ocean trade, the Portuguese had some success; Spanish silver gave more Europeans access to these rich markets. But Asian empires did not lose their autonomy. On the contrary, they absorbed Europeans—and their silver—into their own networks.

But the incorporation into Afro-Eurasian history of a "New World" after Columbus's voyages was an event of monumental significance. In the Americas, Europeans found riches. Mountains of silver and rivers of gold helped them break into Asian markets. Europeans also found opportunities for conquest and colonization, which in turn transformed their own realm as rivals fought over the spoils.

Thus, two conquests characterize this age of increasing world interconnections. Ottoman expansionism drove Europeans to find new links to Asia, demonstrating Islam's pivotal role in shaping modern world history. In turn, the Spanish conquest of the Aztecs and the Incas gave Europeans access to silver, which bought them an increased presence in Asian trading networks. Yet this remained a world whose regions were not yet fully entangled, with many of its peoples still living in ecosystems little touched by these global developments.

Amerindians also played an important role, as Europeans sought to conquer their lands, exploit their labor, and confiscate their gold and silver. Sometimes local people worked with Europeans, sometimes under Europeans, sometimes against Europeans—and sometimes none were left to work at all. Then Europeans brought in African laborers, compounding the calamity of the encounter with the tragedy of slavery. Out of the catastrophe of contact, a new oceanic system arose to link Africa, America, and Europe. This was the Atlantic system. Unlike the tributary and trading orders of the Indian Ocean and China seas, the Atlantic Ocean supported a system of formal imperial control and settlement of distant colonies and profoundly transformed economies, agricultural practices, and environments across the globe. These catastrophes and exchanges would be foundational for the ways in which worlds connected and collided in the following centuries.

FOCUS ON: *Regional Impacts of European Colonization and Trade*

Europe

- Portugal creates a trading empire in the Indian Ocean and the South China Sea.

- Spain and Portugal establish colonies in the Americas, discover silver, and establish export-oriented plantation economies.

- The Protestant Reformation breaks out in northern and western Europe, splitting the Catholic Church.

The Americas

- Millions of Amerindians, lacking immunity to European diseases, perish across the Americas.

- Spanish conquest and disease destroy the two greatest Native American empires in Mexico (the Aztecs) and Peru (the Incas).

Africa

- Trade in African captives fuels the Atlantic slave trade, which furnishes labor for European plantations in the Americas.

Asia

- Asian empires—the Mughals in India, the Ming in China, the Safavids in Iran, and the Ottomans in western Asia and the eastern Mediterranean—barely notice the Americas but profit economically from enhanced global trade.

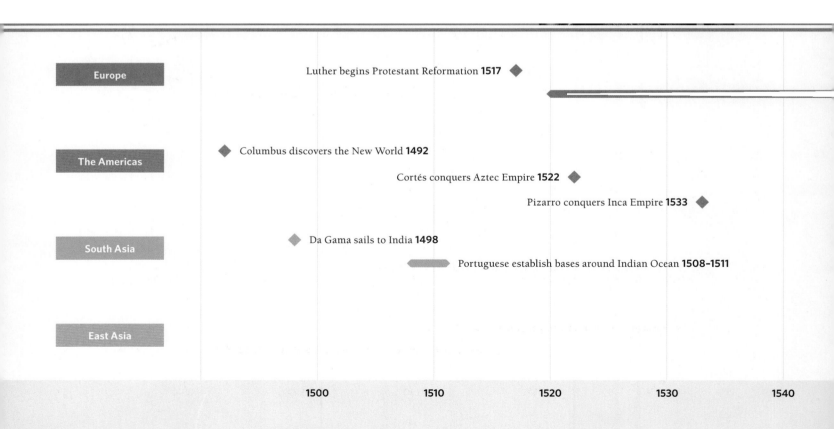

1. **Identify** the broad patterns in world trade after 1450. **Compare** the major features of this trade in Asia, the Americas, Africa, and Europe.

2. **Identify** the factors that enabled Europeans to increase their trade relationships with Asian empires during this period, and **evaluate** the significance of each factor.

3. **Describe** the obstacles to consolidating power in the Aztec and Inca Empires before the arrival of European conquistadors.

4. **Compare** the practices and the impact of European explorers in Asia and the Americas.

5. **Explain** the role of silver in transforming global trade patterns during the sixteenth century. Which regions and dynasties benefited from the increased use of silver for monetary transactions?

6. **Describe** the types of social and political relationships that developed within Afro-Eurasian polities during this period, and **identify** the sources of conflict.

7. **Compare and contrast** political and commercial developments in the Mughal and Ming dynasties during the sixteenth century. How did the expansion of global commerce affect each region?

8. **Explain** the environmental consequences of the first contacts between Europeans and Amerindians. What consequences did the Columbian exchange have on regions both beyond the Atlantic world and within it?

9. **Compare and contrast** Spain's "tributary empire" in the Americas with Portugal's "seaborne empire" in the Indian Ocean. Why did these empires pursue such different strategies?

10. **Analyze** the ways in which European colonization of the Americas affected African and Amerindian peoples. **Discuss** how those groups responded.

11. **Explain** the transformation of the African slave trade during this period. What role did the growth of sugar plantations play?

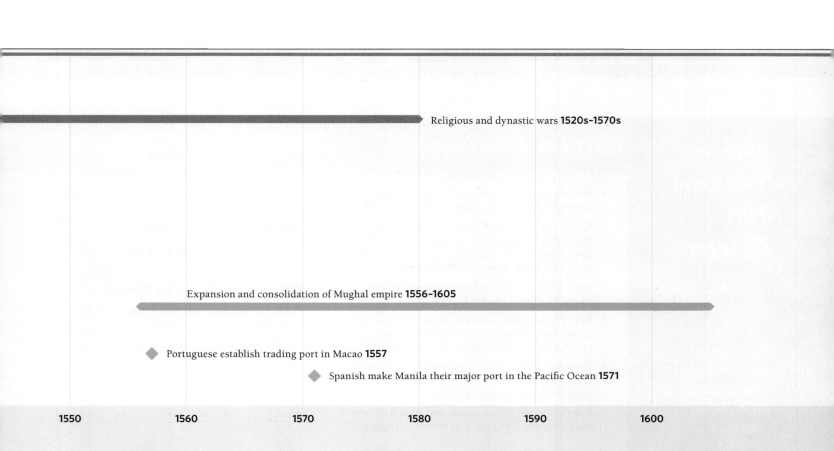

Religious and dynastic wars **1520s–1570s**

Expansion and consolidation of Mughal empire **1556–1605**

Portuguese establish trading port in Macao **1557**

Spanish make Manila their major port in the Pacific Ocean **1571**

| 1550 | 1560 | 1570 | 1580 | 1590 | 1600 |

Before You Read This Chapter

Go to INQUIZITIVE to see what you know & learn what you've missed.

GLOBAL STORYLINES

- Transoceanic trade networks create vast wealth and new kinds of inequality.
- A sharp drop in global temperatures produces the Little Ice Age, which leads to warfare, disease, famine, and dying on a scale comparable in some areas to that of the Black Death.
- Silver begins to tilt the balance of wealth and power from Asia toward Europe.
- New World sugar also accelerates the shift of power in the Atlantic world from the Spanish and Portuguese to the British and French.
- European merchants and African leaders radically increase the volume and violence of the slave trade, destabilizing African societies.
- Rulers in India, China, Japan, and Russia enlarge their empires, while Muslim empires struggle.

CHAPTER OUTLINE

13

Worlds Entangled, 1600–1750

FOCUS QUESTIONS

- What were the major steps in the integration of global trade networks in the seventeenth and eighteenth centuries?

- What effects did the Little Ice Age have on different parts of the world?

- How did the Atlantic slave trade change African societies socially and politically?

- What effect did New World silver and increased trade have on Asian empires?

- How was the impact of trade and religion on state power in various regions alike and different?

- What was the significance of European consumption of goods (like tobacco, textiles, and sugar) for the global economy?

The leading Ottoman intellectual of the sixteenth century, Mustafa Ali, was a gloomy man, convinced that the Ottoman Empire had slipped into an irreversible decline. He lived during difficult times. Islam was approaching its one-thousandth year (1000 After Hijra, AH, or 1591–1592 in the Julian calendar). Many *ulama* and high-level bureaucrats believed that the apocalypse was imminent, a day of judgment when those who were virtuous would be rewarded and those who were evil would be punished. Although Mustafa Ali did not believe that the end of the world was likely, he did think that the time was ripe for assessing not only the history of the Ottomans from their founding to the present but also the whole of human history. He began his magnum opus, *The Essence of History*, in the year when many thought that the world would end (1591). Indeed, the signs at the time were unfavorable for Ottoman success even though the first half of the century had witnessed the conquest of Egypt and the reign of Suleiman the Magnificent and the Lawgiver, arguably the most successful of the sultans. By century's end, however, the empire was losing territory to its main European adversaries, the Habsburgs, the Venetians, and the Russians; military rioting had occurred in protest against payments in debased

Stimulants, Sociability, and Coffeehouses

While armies, travelers, missionaries, and diseases have breached the world's main political and cultural barriers, commodities have been the least respectful of the lines that separate communities. It has been difficult for ruling elites to curtail the desire of their populations to dress themselves in fine garments, to possess jewelry, and to consume satisfying food and drink no matter where these products may originate. The history of commodities, thus, is a core area for world historical research, for products span cultural barriers and connect peoples over long distances. As the world's trading networks expanded in the seventeenth and eighteenth centuries, merchants in Europe, Asia, Africa, and the Americas distributed many new commodities. By far the most popular were a group of stimulants—coffee, cocoa, sugar, tobacco, and tea—all of which (except for sugar) were addictive and also produced a sense of well-being. Previously, many of these products had been grown in isolated parts of the world: the coffee bean in Yemen, tobacco and cocoa in the New World, and sugar in Bengal. Yet, by the seventeenth century, in nearly every corner of the world, the well-to-do began to congregate in coffeehouses, consuming these new products and engaging in sociable activities.

Coffeehouses everywhere served as locations for social exchange, political discussions, and business activities. Yet they also varied from cultural area to cultural area, reflecting the values of the societies in which they arose.

The coffeehouse first appeared in Islamic lands late in the fifteenth century. As coffee consumption caught on among the wealthy and leisured classes in the Arabian Peninsula and the Ottoman Empire, local growers protected their

Coffee. *Coffee drinkers at an Ottoman banquet.*

silver coinage, a result of the import of vast quantities of New World silver; and uprisings against the empire were widespread in eastern Anatolia.

Historians now know that many of these problems stemmed from the cold spell that descended on the entire world at this time. Present-day scholars have labeled the seventeenth century the Little Ice Age. This sharp drop in global temperatures, lasting between 1620 and 1680, laid waste to agricultural and pastoral lands and spread hunger and famines worldwide. A double-edged global crisis ensued. Just as global empires ramped up their competition, they squeezed their peasants for resources to pay for warfare. At the same time, global cooling meant that peasants produced less food and surpluses. Across much of Afro-Eurasia, the result was a wave of suffering, peasant unrest, and political upheaval.

Mustafa Ali captured the sentiments of this age well: "Prosperity had turned to famine, the government careers had become confused, venality was rampant, and the military class was being overrun by *re'aya* [tax-paying subjects]" (Fleischer, p. 8). Even more apocalyptical were his poems. Here his view was that "in the social sphere the world is upside down; the *ulama* are no longer learned or pious; the pillars of the state are fiends and lions; the truly learned are disdained and dismissed and government service now brings pain and poverty rather than pride and wealth. The plague destroying the world is moral as well as physical, for bribery and corruption are the order of the day" (p. 134).

In spite of the turmoil, the period 1600–1750 saw the world's oceans give way to booming sea-lanes for global trading networks. Sugar flowed from Brazil and the Caribbean, spices from Southeast Asia, cotton textiles from India, silks from China, and silver from Mesoamerica and the Andes. New World silver was crucial to these networks: it gave Europeans a commodity to exchange with Asians, and it tilted the balance of wealth and power in a westerly direction across Afro-Eurasia.

Imperial expansion and transoceanic trade, like climate change, spread across the entire globe. Europeans conquered and colonized more of the Americas, the demand for African slaves to work New World plantations leaped upward, and global trade intensified. Conquest, colonization, and commerce created riches for some but also provoked bitter rivalries. In the Americas, Spain and Portugal faced new competitors—primarily England and France. With religious tensions added to the mix, the stage was set for decades of bloody warfare in Europe and advantage by monopolizing its cultivation and sale and refusing to allow any seeds or cuttings from the coffee tree to be taken abroad.

Despite some religious opposition, coffee spread into Egypt and throughout the Ottoman Empire in the sixteenth century. Ottoman bureaucrats, merchants, and artists assembled in coffeehouses to trade stories, read, listen to poetry, and play chess and backgammon. Indeed, so deeply connected were coffeehouses with literary and artistic pursuits that people referred to them as schools of knowledge.

From the Ottoman territories, the culture of coffee drinking spread to western Europe. The first coffeehouse in London opened in 1652, and within sixty years the city claimed no fewer than 500 such establishments. In fact, the Fleet Street area of London had so many that the English essayist Charles Lamb commented, "The man must have a rare recipe for melancholy who can be dull in Fleet Street." Although coffeehouses attracted people from all levels of society, they especially appealed to the new mercantile and professional classes as locations where stimulating beverages like coffee, cocoa, and tea promoted lively conversation. Here, too, opponents claimed that excessive coffee drinking destabilized the thinking processes and even caused conversions to Islam. But against such opposition, the pleasures of coffee, tea, and cocoa prevailed. These bitter beverages in turn required liberal doses of the sweetener sugar. A smoke of tobacco topped off the experience. In this environment of pleasure, patrons of the coffeehouses indulged their addictions, engaged in gossip, conducted business, and talked politics.

QUESTIONS FOR ANALYSIS

- What factors drove the consumption of stimulants like coffee on a global scale?
- What other commodities from earlier in world history played a similar role? Were there differences in the underlying factors, such as scale of consumption, between the different periods?

Explore Further

Hattox, Ralph S. *Coffee and Coffeehouses: The Origins of a Social Beverage in the Medieval Near East* (1985).

the Americas. At the same time, rulers in India, China, and Japan enlarged their empires, while Russia's tsars incorporated Siberian territories into their domain. Meanwhile, the Ottoman, Safavid, and Mughal dynasties, though resisting most European intrusions, faced shocks from an increasingly entangled world.

GLOBAL COMMERCE AND CLIMATE CHANGE

In spite of the worldwide trauma brought on by the plunge in temperatures, global trade flourished during this period. Sugar, silver, and slaves were the primary items, promoted equally by merchant groups and the rulers and commoners of sponsoring nations. Increasing economic ties brought new products into world markets: furs from French North America, sugar from the Caribbean, tobacco from British colonies on the American mainland, coffee from Southeast and Southwest Asia, and slaves from West and central Africa. (See Current Trends in World History: Stimulants, Sociability, and Coffeehouses; see also Map 13.1.)

Closer economic contact enhanced the power of certain states and destabilized others. It bolstered the legitimacy of England and France, and it prompted strong local support of new rulers in Japan and parts of sub-Saharan Africa. With rising powers came rising competition, friction, and warfare. Governments had to squeeze more resources from trade and agriculture, a practice that spurred protest and open rebellions during the Little Ice Age, when civil wars and social unrest swept through much of the world. England, France, and Japan faced mass peasant uprisings. In the Ottoman state, rebellions almost brought the empire to its knees; the Safavid regime foundered and then collapsed; the Ming dynasty gave way to the Qing. In India, rivalries among princes and merchants eroded the Mughals' authority, compounding the instability caused by peasant uprisings.

Another result of the plunge in temperatures was a flight from marginal agricultural lands into the cities. The world had never experienced such massive urbanization: 2.5 million Japanese lived in cities, roughly 10 percent of the population, and in Holland, over 200,000 lived in ten cities close to Amsterdam. But city officials were ill equipped to deal with the influx. Disease swept through overcrowded houses, and fire ravaged whole districts. London had an excess of 228,000 deaths over births,

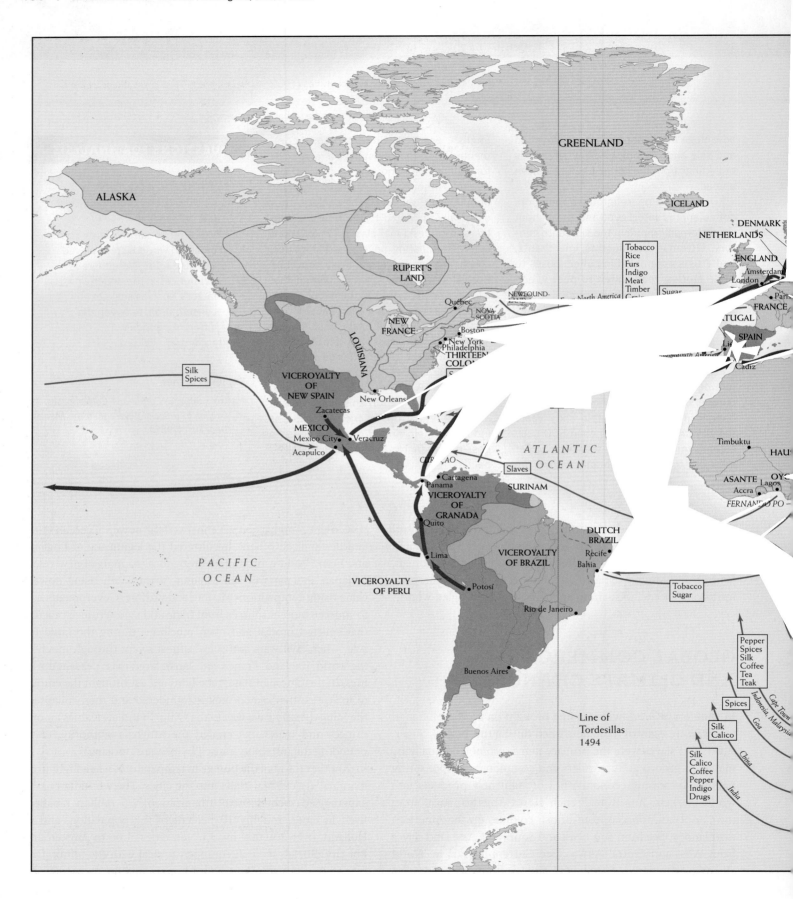

ALASKA

GREENLAND

ICELAND

DENMARK

NETHERLANDS

ENGLAND
Amsterdam
London

FRANCE
Paris

PORTUGAL

SPAIN
Lisbon
Cadiz

RUPERT'S
LAND

Québec
NOVA
SCOTIA

NEWFOUND-
LAND

North America

Boston
New York
Philadelphia

NEW
FRANCE

LOUISIANA

THIRTEEN
COLONIES

Tobacco
Rice
Furs
Indigo
Meat
Timber
Grain

Sugar

Silk
Spices

VICEROYALTY
OF
NEW SPAIN

Zacatecas

MEXICO
Mexico City   Veracruz
Acapulco

New Orleans

ATLANTIC
OCEAN

Timbuktu

Slaves

CURAÇAO

Cartagena
Panama

SURINAM

VICEROYALTY
OF
GRANADA

Quito

ASANTE   OYO
Accra   Lagos

FERNANDO PO

PACIFIC
OCEAN

Lima

DUTCH
BRAZIL

Recife

VICEROYALTY
OF BRAZIL

Bahia

VICEROYALTY
OF PERU

Potosí

Río de Janeiro

Tobacco
Sugar

Pepper
Spices
Silk
Coffee
Tea
Teak

Buenos Aires

Spices

Cape Town

Indonesia, Malaysia

Goa

China

Silk
Calico

Silk
Calico
Coffee
Pepper
Indigo
Drugs

Line of
Tordesillas
1494

India

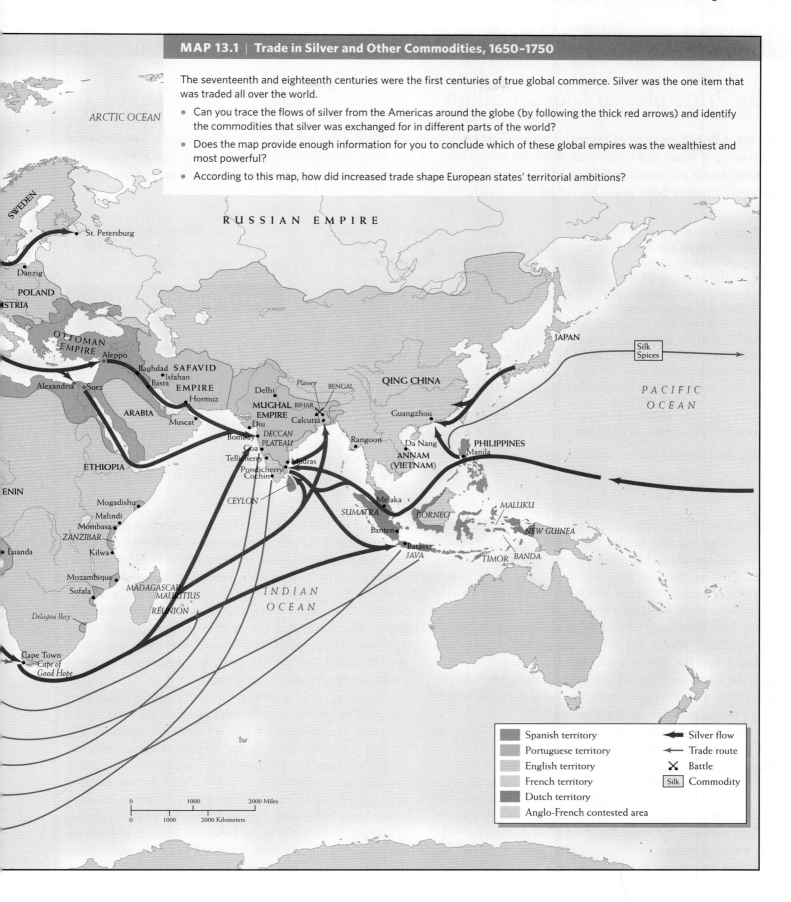

MAP 13.1 | Trade in Silver and Other Commodities, 1650–1750

The seventeenth and eighteenth centuries were the first centuries of true global commerce. Silver was the one item that was traded all over the world.

- Can you trace the flows of silver from the Americas around the globe (by following the thick red arrows) and identify the commodities that silver was exchanged for in different parts of the world?

- Does the map provide enough information for you to conclude which of these global empires was the wealthiest and most powerful?

- According to this map, how did increased trade shape European states' territorial ambitions?

ARCTIC OCEAN

RUSSIAN EMPIRE

SWEDEN
St. Petersburg
Danzig
POLAND
ISTRIA
OTTOMAN EMPIRE
Aleppo
Baghdad
Isfahan
Basra
Alexandria
Suez
Hormuz
ARABIA
Muscat
ETHIOPIA
BENIN
Mogadishu
Malindi
Mombasa
ZANZIBAR
Luanda
Kilwa
Mozambique
Sofala
MADAGASCAR
MAURITIUS
RÉUNION
Delagoa Bay
Cape Town
Cape of Good Hope

SAFAVID EMPIRE
Delhi
Plassey
BENGAL
MUGHAL EMPIRE
BIHAR
Diu
Calcutta
Bombay
Goa
DECCAN PLATEAU
Tellicherry
Pondicherry
Cochin
Madras
CEYLON
Rangoon

QING CHINA
JAPAN
Guangzhou
Da Nang
ANNAM (VIETNAM)
PHILIPPINES
Manila

Silk
Spices

PACIFIC OCEAN

Melaka
SUMATRA
BORNEO
Banten
Batavia
JAVA
MALUKU
NEW GUINEA
TIMOR
BANDA

INDIAN OCEAN

Legend:
- Spanish territory
- Portuguese territory
- English territory
- French territory
- Dutch territory
- Anglo-French contested area
- Silver flow
- Trade route
- X Battle
- Silk — Commodity

0 1000 2000 Miles
0 1000 2000 Kilometers

The Principles of Mercantilism

In 1757, a British commercial expert by the name of Malachy Postlethwayt published a commercial dictionary, **The Universal Dictionary of Trade and Commerce.** *Under the entry "trade," he set forth "some maxims relating to trade that should seem to be confirmed in the course of this work." The first five convey the economic philosophy of mercantilism and the importance that countries attached to the acquisition of precious metals.*

I. That the lasting prosperity of the landed interest depends upon foreign commerce.

II. That the increase of the wealth, splendour, and power of Great Britain and Ireland depends upon exporting more in value of our native produce and manufactures than we import of commodities from other nations and bringing thereby money into the kingdom by means of freight by shipping.

III. That domestic and foreign trade, as they are the means of increasing national treasure, of breeding seamen, and of augmenting our mercantile and royal navies they necessarily become the means of our permanent prosperity and of the safety and preservation of our happy constitution.

IV. That the constant security of the public credit and the payment of interest and principal of the public creditors depend upon the prosperous state of our trade and navigation.

V. That gold and silver is the measure of trade, and that silver is a commodity and may be exported, especially in foreign coin as well as any other commodity.

QUESTIONS FOR ANALYSIS

- According to this reading, whom does mercantilism serve?
- What are the key tenets of mercantilism?
- Why is silver more important than gold in trade?

Source: Malachy Postlethwayt, *The Universal Dictionary of Trade and Commerce*, vol. 2 (1757), p. 792.

---

yet continued to grow through in-migration. Hardly an escape from rural poverty, city dwellers had inordinately high mortality rates, what one scholar has called "the graveyard effect" (Parker, *Global Crisis*, p. 58).

Transformations in global relations began in the Atlantic, where the extraction and shipment of gold and silver siphoned wealth from the New World (the Americas) to the Old World (Afro-Eurasia). Mined mainly by coerced Amerindians and delivered into the hands of merchants and monarchs, silver from the Andes and Mesoamerica boosted the world's supply. In addition, a boom in gold production made Brazil the world's largest producer of that metal at this time.

American mining exports were so lucrative for Spain and Portugal that other European powers wanted a share in the bounty, so they, too, launched colonizing ventures in the New World. Although these latecomers found few precious minerals, they devised other ways to extract wealth, for the Americas had fertile lands on which to cultivate sugarcane, cotton, tobacco, indigo, and rice. The New World also had fur-bearing wildlife, whose pelts were prized in Europe. Better still from the colonizers' perspective, it was easy and inexpensive to produce and transport the New World crops and skins.

If silver quickened the pace of global trade, sugar transformed the European diet. First domesticated in Polynesia, sugar was not central to European diets before the New World plantations started exporting it. Previously, Europeans had used honey for sweetener, but they soon became insatiable consumers of sugar. Between 1690 and 1790, Europe imported 12 million tons of sugar—approximately 1 ton for every African enslaved in the Americas. Public tooth pulling became a popular entertainment (for spectators!) in cities like Paris, and tooth decay became a leading cause of death for Europeans.

No matter what products they supplied, colonies were supposed to provide wealth for their "mother countries"— according to exponents of mercantilism, the economic theory that drove European empire builders. **Mercantilism** saw the world's wealth as fixed: any one country's wealth came at the expense of other countries. The theory further assumed that overseas possessions existed solely to enrich European motherlands because it measured imperial power according to the hoard of treasure in the crown's coffers. To bulk up the treasury, motherlands were supposed to export more goods than they imported and thereby sustain trade surpluses. Thus, colonies should ship more "value" to the mother country than they received in return. (See Primary Source: The Principles of Mercantilism.) In addition, colonies were supposed to be closed to competitors, lest foreign traders drain precious resources from an empire's exclusive domain. As the mother country's monopoly over its colonies' trade generated wealth for royal treasuries, European states grew rich enough to wage almost unceasing wars against one another. Ultimately, mercantilists believed, as did the English philosopher Thomas Hobbes (1588–1679), that "wealth is power and power is wealth."

The mercantilist system required an alliance between the state and its merchants. Mercantilists understood economics and politics as interdependent, with the merchant needing the monarch to protect his interests and the monarch relying on the merchant's trade to enrich the state's treasury. **Chartered companies**, such as the Virginia Company (English) and the East India Companies (Dutch and English), were visible examples of the collaboration between the state and the merchant classes. European monarchs awarded these firms monopoly trading rights over vast areas. These policies and institutions of mercantilism augmented the competition among European empires for markets, colonies, and spoils, and this escalated the penetration into colonial interiors and wars between empires.

The Little Ice Age

Global cooling occurred unevenly around the world. In some places, the effect of falling temperatures, shorter growing seasons, and irregular precipitation patterns was felt as early as the fourteenth century. But the impact of the **Little Ice Age** reached further and deeper in the seventeenth century. What caused this climate change is a matter of debate. But a combination of low sunspot activity, changing ocean currents, and volcanic eruptions that filled the atmosphere with dust shocked an increasingly integrated world. While the seventeenth century was especially severe, the cold lasted well into the next century and in parts of North America into the nineteenth. The Thames River and Dutch canals froze over, which led to famous paintings of people skating on Dutch ponds and lakes. So did the waters separating Sweden from Denmark, which allowed Swedish armies to march right across to Copenhagen. In West Africa, colder and drier conditions saw an advance of the Sahara Desert, leading to repeated famines in the Senegambia region. In addition, Timbuktu and the region around the Niger bend suffered their greatest famines in the seventeenth century. It was still so cold in the early nineteenth century that the English novelist Mary Shelley and her husband spent their summer vacation indoors in Switzerland telling each other horror stories, which inspired Shelley to write *Frankenstein*. Climate change brought mass suffering because harvests failed. In China, the orange groves of Jiangxi Province had to be abandoned after constant and widespread freezing; rice fields, which need a wet spring, went dry. Famine spread across Afro-Eurasia.

There were also political consequences. As droughts, freezing, and famine spread across Afro-Eurasia, herding societies invaded settled societies. Starving peasants rose up against their lords and rulers. Political divides opened up. On the continent of Europe, the Thirty Years' War raged out of control, stoked by farmers' anger (see later in this chapter). Although the war was deeply influenced by religious and national conflicts, it owed much to the decline of food production. In the Americas, indigenous populations were already suffering grievously from the previous

Winter Landscape. *Hendrik Avercamp was one of the most prolific Dutch painters of the seventeenth century. He often painted skaters on frozen ponds, lakes, and canals. This painting is from around 1608, when the Little Ice Age was at its most intense, and shows skaters on one of the large frozen-over canals in Amsterdam.*

Woodlands Indians. *This late sixteenth-century drawing by John White, a pioneer settler on Roanoke Island, off the coast of North Carolina, depicts the Indian village of Secoton in eastern Virginia. In contrast to the great empires that the Spanish conquered in the Valley of Mexico and in the Andes, the Indians whom English, French, and Dutch colonizers encountered in the woodlands of eastern North America generally lived in villages that were politically autonomous entities.*

centuries' plagues. But the long cold snap brought more mayhem. Tensions between Iroquois and Huron rose in the Great Lakes region of North America. Civil war between Portugal and Spain in Europe wreaked havoc in Iberian colonies and led to invasion and panic. According to the bishop of Puebla, in Mexico, "the whole monarchy trembled and shook, since Portugal, Catalonia, the East Indies, the Azores and Brazil had rebelled." In the viceregal capital of New Spain, "apprehension and panic" seized the city (Parker, *Global Crisis,* p. 461). The Ottomans faced a crippling revolt, while in China the powerful Ming regime could

not deal with the climate shock. It was invaded, as was so often the case when pastures turned to dust, by Manchurian peoples from beyond the Great Wall. They installed a new regime, the Qing dynasty. Indeed, Thomas Hobbes, England's notable political philosopher and author of a classic work of political theory, *Leviathan,* summed up the age: "Man's natural state, before they came together into society, was war; and not simply war, but the war of every man against every other man" (Parker, *Global Crisis,* p. 567). He went on to add famously that "the life of man (is) solitary, poor, nasty, brutish, and short" (p. xxiii)

The Little Ice Age had a devastating impact on populations. It is hard, however, to separate the victims of starvation from the victims of war, since warfare aggravated starvation and famine contributed to war. But in continental Europe, the Thirty Years' War carried off an estimated two-thirds of the total population, on a par with the impact of the Black Death (see Chapter 11). Elsewhere, estimates were closer to one-third. Not until the twentieth century did the world again witness such extensive warfare. For some Afro-Eurasian regimes, the global crisis led to collapse and decline; for others, it became an opportunity for renewal and reinvention.

EXCHANGES AND EXPANSIONS IN NORTH AMERICA

Freezing temperatures and warfare in Europe did not prevent England, France, and Holland from joining Spain and Portugal in the rush to reap riches from American colonies and to take a greater share of global commerce. As rulers in England, France, and Holland granted monopolies to merchant companies, they began to dominate the settlement and trade of new colonies in the Americas. (See Map 13.2.) Although the search for precious metals or water routes to Asia had initially spurred many of these enterprises, the new colonizers learned that only by exploiting other resources could their claims in the Americas generate profits. Also, differences among New World societies required rethinking the character of colonies within mercantilist regimes.

In their colonies along the Atlantic seaboard, the English established one model for new colonies in the Americas. Although these territories failed to yield precious metals or a waterway across the continent, they boasted land suitable for growing numerous crops. Within the English domain, different climates and soils made for very different agricultural possibilities: wheat, rye, barley, and oats from the Middle Colonies (Pennsylvania, New York, New Jersey, and Delaware), tobacco from Virginia and North Carolina, and rice and indigo from farther south. But all the English colonies shared a common feature: population growth led to greater demand for farmlands, which put pressure on Amerindian holdings. The Little

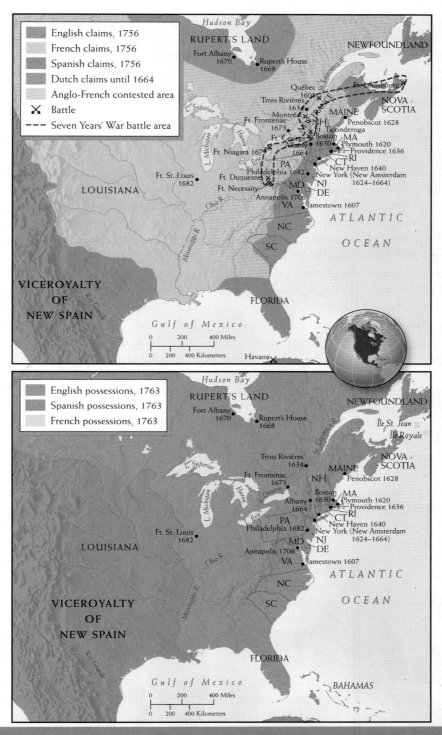

MAP 13.2 | Colonies in North America, 1607–1763

France, England, and Spain laid claim to much of North America at this time.

- Where was each of these colonial powers strongest before the outbreak of the Seven Years' War in 1756? (See p. 514 for a discussion of the Seven Years' War.)

- Which empire gained the most North American territory, and who lost the most at the end of the war in 1763?

- How do you think Native American peoples reacted to the territorial arrangements agreed to by Spain, France, and England at the Treaty of Paris, which ended the war?

Ice Age exacerbated the stress, because shorter growing seasons diminished harvests. Thus, more acreage had to be cultivated to support the colonies' surging population in North America, which meant more lands taken from Amerindians. The result: a souring of relations between Amerindians and colonists. In 1675, which colonists described as a "year without a summer," ferocious wars broke out between Amerindians and English colonists in Virginia and New England. Similar pressures ignited other conflicts throughout the seventeenth and eighteenth centuries and led to the dispossession of Amerindians from lands between the Atlantic Ocean and the Appalachian Mountains.

By contrast, Dutch and French colonies rested not on the expulsion of indigenous peoples, but on dependence on them. Holland's North American venture, however, proved short-lived, as the English took over New Netherland and renamed it New York in 1664. French claims were more enduring and extended across a vast swath of the continent, encompassing eastern Canada, the Great Lakes, and the Mississippi Valley.

Trade between Europeans and Amerindians

Crucial to the trade between Europeans and Amerindians in northern North America was the beaver, an animal for which Amerindian peoples previously had little use. In response to the Europeans' interest, one local Euro-American hunter heard an Amerindian say, "The beaver does everything perfectly well; it makes kettles, hatchets, swords, knives, bread; in short it makes everything." As long as there were beavers to be trapped, trade between the Europeans and their Indian partners flourished.

The distinctive aspect of the fur trade was the Europeans' utter dependence on Amerindian know-how. After all, trapping required familiarity with the beaver's habits and habitats, which Europeans lacked. This reliance especially forced French traders who ventured farther into the continent's interior to adapt to Indian ways. Responding to Amerindian desires to use trade as an instrument to cement familial bonds, the French gave gifts, participated in Amerindian diplomatic rituals, and even married into Indian families. As a result, *métis* (French-Amerindian offspring) played an important role in New France as interpreters, traders, and guides. Thus, the French colonization of the Americas—owing to their reliance on Amerindians as trading partners, military allies, and mates—rested more on cooperation than conquest, especially compared with the empires built by their Spanish and English rivals.

Over the long run, Europeans' trade in guns, alcohol, and trinkets gave them power advantages. It set off a crippling arms race between Amerindians and depletion of beaver stocks. But through the seventeenth and into the middle of the eighteenth century, the majority of lands in the interior of the North American continent remained firmly in Amerindian hands, despite the European empires' expansive claims. On the Great Plains in the center of North America, some Indian peoples lost ground to newcomers, but here the winners were other Indian groups. On the northern plains, the Lakotas, who had migrated westward onto the grasslands, emerged as the most successful expansionists. Coming eastward, the Comanches reigned across a vast swath of the southern plains. These and other invaders displaced existing indigenous societies from some lands, added to their ranks by capturing and often enslaving large

The Fur Trade. *For Europeans in northern North America, no commodity was as important as beaver skins. For the French especially, the fur trade determined the character of their colonial regime in North America. For Indians, it offered access to European goods, but overhunting depleted resources and provoked intertribal conflicts.*

numbers of people (especially females), and enriched themselves by their raiding and through their control over trading. The control that the Comanches asserted extended not only over other Amerindians whom they captured and whose horses they plundered, but also over would-be European colonizers. From the eastern Plains almost to the Pacific Ocean, with the exception of a few enclaves of European settlement, it was Amerindians who largely determined where Europeans could go, stay, and trade. Thus, while early eighteenth-century maps drawn by European empire makers divvied up North America principally among British, French, and Spanish realms, the reality on the ground mocked these imperial pretentions.

There was considerable irony in the fact that Spanish colonizers had empowered the Plains Amerindians. The Spanish, after all, had brought horses to the Americas, and it was the acquisition of these animals that revolutionized Amerindian life and enabled the expansions occurring on the Great Plains. Recognizing the role that horses played in their conquests, the Spanish had tried to keep them out of Indian hands. They failed. Raiders targeted horses. Once introduced into Amerindian circuits, the animals dispersed and flourished on the grasses of the Plains. So did the Indians who had greatest access to horses and who most decisively adapted to equestrianism. On horseback, Amerindians could kill bison much more effectively, which encouraged some groups to forsake farming for hunting and

other groups, like the Lakotas and Comanches, to move onto the Plains in pursuit of buffalo. Astride horses, Amerindians also gained military superiority over more sedentary peoples, whose villages and cornfields were vulnerable to mobile forces.

Not all prospered, however, and certainly not all equally. The gains of nomadic equestrians often came at the expense of those who remained wedded to a mixture of horticulture and hunting. Within horse cultures, new inequalities materialized. More successful raiders and hunters not only earned greater honor but also acquired more horses. And with more horses usually came higher status and more wives. At the same time, the status of women generally declined in the transition from horticultural to hunting societies. Their burdens, however, did not, as there were now more buffalo waiting to be turned by women into the products that sustained Plains Amerindian life.

The Plantation Complex in the Caribbean

As late as 1670, the most populous English colony was not on the North American mainland, but on the Caribbean island of Barbados. Because sugar was so desirable, from the mid-seventeenth century onward the English- and French-controlled islands of the Caribbean replicated the Portuguese sugarcane plantations of Brazil; sugar became a quintessential mercantilist commodity.

Tobacco. *The cultivation of tobacco saved the Virginia colony from ruin and brought prosperity to increasing numbers of planters. The spread of tobacco plantations also pushed Indians off their lands and led planters to turn to Africa for a labor force.*

All was not sweet here, however. Because no colonial power held a monopoly, competition to control the region—and sugar production—was fierce. The resulting turbulence did not simply reflect imperial rivalry; it also reflected labor arrangements in the colonies. Because the indigenous populations had been wiped out in Columbus's wake (see Chapter 12), owners of Caribbean estates looked to Africa to obtain workers for their plantations.

Sugar was a killing crop. So deadly was the hot, humid environment in which sugarcane flourished (as fertile for disease as for sugarcane) that many sugar barons spent little time on their plantations. Management fell to overseers, who worked their slaves to death. Despite having immunity to yellow fever and malaria from their homeland's similar environment, Africans could not withstand the regimen. Inadequate food, atrocious living conditions, and filthy sanitation added to their miseries. Moreover, plantation managers treated their slaves as nonhumans: for example, on the first day all new slaves suffered branding with the planter's seal. One English gentleman commented that slaves were like cows, "as near as beasts may be, setting their souls aside."

Slaves Cutting Cane. *Sugar was the preeminent agricultural export from the New World for centuries. Owners of sugarcane plantations relied almost exclusively on African slaves to produce the sweetener. Labor in the fields was especially harsh, as slaves worked in the blistering sun from dawn until dusk. This image shows how women and men toiled side by side.*

More than disease and inadequate rations, the work itself was decimating. Average life expectancy was three years. Six days a week, slaves rose before dawn, labored until noon, ate a short lunch, and then worked until dusk. At harvest time, 16-hour days saw hundreds of men, women, and children bent over to cut the sugarcane and transport it to refineries, sometimes seven days per week. Under this brutal schedule, slaves occasionally dropped dead from exhaustion.

Amid disease and toil, the enslaved coped and resisted as they could. The most dramatic expression of resistance was violent revolt. A more common form was flight. Seeking refuge from overseers, thousands of slaves took to the hills—for example, to the remote highlands of Caribbean islands or to Brazil's vast interior. Those who remained on the plantations resisted via foot dragging, pilfering, and sabotage.

Caribbean settlements and slaveholdings were not restricted to any single European power. But it was the latecomers—the Dutch, the English, and especially the French—who concentrated on the West Indies and who grew wealthy and powerful. (See Map 13.3.) The English took Jamaica from the Spanish in 1655 and made it the premier site of Caribbean sugar by the 1740s. When the French seized half of Santo Domingo in the 1660s (renaming it Saint-Domingue, which is present-day Haiti), they created one of the wealthiest societies based on slavery of all time. This French colony's exports eclipsed those of all the Spanish and English Antilles combined. The capital, Port-au-Prince, was one of the richest cities in the Atlantic world. The colony's merchants and planters built immense mansions worthy of the highest European nobles. Thus, the Atlantic system benefited elite Europeans, who amassed new fortunes by exploiting the colonies' natural resources and the African slaves' labor. The American trade also laid the financial foundations and the heightened consumer demands that were crucial for Europe's late eighteenth- and early nineteenth-century industrial revolution (see Chapter 15).

THE SLAVE TRADE AND AFRICA

Although the slave trade began in the mid-fifteenth century, only in the seventeenth and eighteenth centuries did the numbers of human exports from Africa begin to soar and feed mercantilist regimes. (See Map 13.4.) By 1820, four slaves had crossed the Atlantic for every European. (See Analyzing Global Developments: The Atlantic Trade in Slaves from Africa (1501–1900).) At the same time, the departure of so many inhabitants depopulated and destabilized many parts of Africa.

Capturing and Shipping Slaves

Merchants in Europe and the Americas prospered as the slave trade soared, but their fortunes depended on trading and

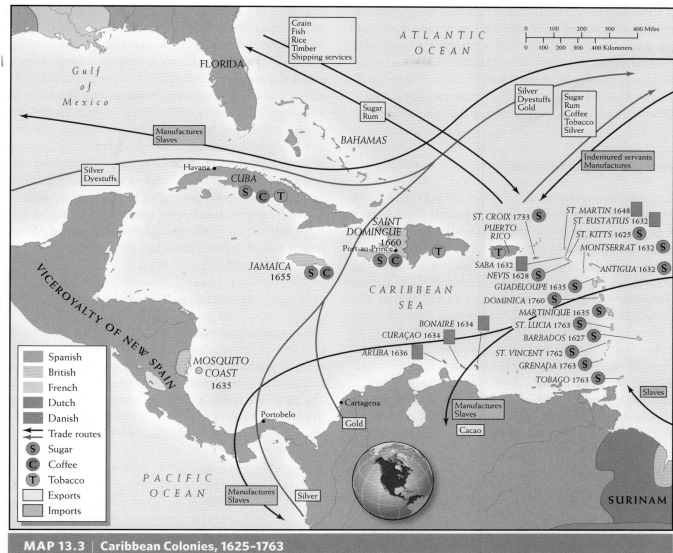

MAP 13.3 | Caribbean Colonies, 1625–1763

The Caribbean was a region of expanding trade in the seventeenth and eighteenth centuries.

- What were its major exports and imports?
- Who were its main colonizers and trading partners?
- From your reading, how did the transformation of this region shape other societies in the Atlantic world?

political networks in Africa. Because European slave traders feared African diseases, mainly malaria, they confined themselves to the coast, where they supplied powerful interior states with firearms with which to conquer other indigenous peoples and ship their defeated adversaries to the slavers.

Before the Europeans' arrival, Africa had an existing system of slave commerce, mainly flowing across the Sahara to North Africa and Egypt and eastward to the Red Sea and the Swahili coast of East Africa. From the Red Sea and Swahili coast destinations, Muslim and Hindu merchants shipped slaves to ports around the Indian Ocean. However, the number of these slaves could not match the volume destined for the Americas once plantation agriculture

began to spread. Indeed, 12.5 million Africans departed for forcible enslavement and shipment to Atlantic ports from the early fifteenth century until 1867, when the last voyage took place.

Now the slave ports along the African coast became gruesome entrepôts. Many captives perished before losing sight of Africa. Stuck in vast holding camps where disease and hunger were rampant, the slaves were then forced aboard vessels in cramped and wretched conditions. These ships waited for weeks to fill their holds while their human cargoes wasted away belowdecks. Crew members tossed dead Africans overboard as they loaded on other Africans from the shore. When the cargo was complete, the ships set sail. In their wake, crews continued to dump bodies.

Most died of gastrointestinal diseases leading to dehydration. Smallpox and dysentery were also scourges. Either way, death was slow and agonizing. Because high mortality led to lost profits, slavers learned to carry better food and more fresh water as the trade became more sophisticated. Still, when slave ships finally reached New World ports, they reeked of disease and excrement. (See Primary Source: Olaudah Equiano on the Atlantic Crossing.)

Slavery's Gender Imbalance

In moving so many Africans to the Americas, the slave trade played havoc with the ratios of men to women in both places because most slaves shipped to the Americas were males. European slave traders sought well-formed and strong males between the ages of 10 and 25, even though many plantation owners came to realize that females of the same age worked as hard as males. Although the numbers indicate Europeans' preferences for male laborers, they also reflect African slavers' desire to keep female slaves, primarily for household work. The gender imbalance made it difficult for slaves to reproduce in the Americas. So planters and slavers had to return to Africa to procure more captives—especially for the Caribbean islands, where slaves' death rates were so high.

Male slaves outnumbered females in the New World, but in the slave-supplying regions of Africa, women outnumbered men. Female captives were especially prized in Africa because of their traditional role in the production of grains, leathers, and cotton. Indeed, the Atlantic slave trade made the role of those women who remained in Africa even more essential for ensuring the subsistence of children and the aged. Moreover, the slave trade reinforced the traditional practice of polygyny—allowing relatively scarce men to take several wives. But in some states, notably the slave-supplying kingdom of Dahomey, on the West African coast, women managed to assert power because of their large numbers and heightened importance. In fact, Dahomean women became so deeply involved in succession disputes that their intrigues could make the difference between winning and losing political power. Ultimately, though, the fact that some women rose to power in a few societies did not diminish the destabilizing effects of the Atlantic slave trade or the chaos that slave raiding and slave trading had on the relations among African states.

Africa's New Slave-Supplying Polities

Africans did not passively let captives fall into the arms of European slave buyers; instead, local political leaders and merchants were energetic suppliers. This activity promoted the growth of centralized political systems, particularly in West African rain forest areas. The trade also shifted control of wealth away from households owning large herds or lands to those who profited from the capture and exchange of slaves—urban merchants and warrior elites.

 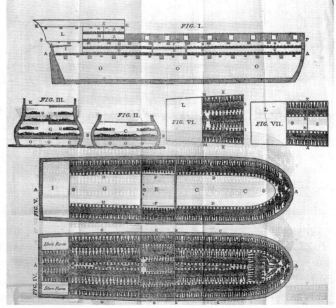

The Slave Trade. Left: *Africans were captured in the interior and then bound and marched to the coast. Note that there is only one woman among the men (and a couple of children), reflecting the gender imbalance among those captured. Right: After reaching the coast, the captured Africans would be crammed into the holds of slave vessels, where they suffered grievously from overcrowding and unsanitary conditions. Long voyages were especially deadly. If the winds failed or ships had to travel longer distances than usual, many of the captives would die en route to the slave markets across the ocean.*

Olaudah Equiano on the Atlantic Crossing

The most compelling description of the horrifying conditions that captives endured on the African coast as they awaited the arrival of slaving ships and the perils of the Atlantic crossing came from the pen of a former slave, Olaudah Equiano (c. 1745–1797). After purchasing his freedom and becoming a skilled writer, Equiano published The Interesting Narrative of the Life of Olaudah Equiano, or Gustavus Vassa, the African, Written by Himself *(1789). An instantaneous best-seller, within ten years the book saw nine English editions and appeared in American, Dutch, German, Russian, and French editions. Although some critics have questioned the authenticity of Equiano's birth and early life in Africa, the scholarly consensus remains that he was indeed born in Igboland (in the eastern part of present-day Nigeria) and made the voyage across the Atlantic after his capture at age nine.*

The first object which saluted my eyes when I arrived on the coast was the sea, and a slave ship, which was then riding at anchor, and waiting for its cargo. These filled me with astonishment, which was soon converted into terror when I was carried on board. I was immediately handled and tossed up to see if I were sound by some of the crew; and I was now persuaded that I had gotten into a world of bad spirits, and that they were going to kill me. Their complexions too differing so much from ours, their long hair, and the language they spoke, (which was very different from any I had ever heard) united to confirm me in this belief. Indeed such were the horrors of my views and fears at the moment, that, if ten thousand worlds had been my own, I would have freely parted with them all to have exchanged my condition with that of the meanest slave in my own country. When I looked round the ship too and saw a large furnace or copper boiling, and a multitude of black people of every description chained together, every one of their countenances expressing dejection and sorrow, I no longer doubted of my fate; and, quite overpowered with horror and anguish, I fell motionless on the deck and fainted. When I recovered a little I found some black people about me, who I believed were some of those who brought me on board, and had been receiving their pay; they talked to me in order to cheer me, but all in vain. I asked them if we were not to be eaten by those white men with horrible looks, red faces, and loose hair. They told me I was not . . . .

In a little time after, amongst the poor chained men, I found some of my own nation, which in a small degree gave ease to my mind. I inquired of these what was to be done with us; they gave me to understand we were to be carried to these white people's country to work for them. I then was a little revived, and thought, if it were no worse than working, my situation was not so desperate: but still I feared I should be put to death, the white people looked and acted, as I thought, in so savage a manner; for I had never seen among any people such instances of brutal cruelty; and this not only shewn towards us blacks, but also to some of the whites themselves . . . .

At last, when the ship we were in had got in all her cargo, they made ready with many fearful noises, and we were all put under deck, so that we could not see how they managed the vessel. But this disappointment was the least of my sorrow. The stench of the hold while we were on the coast was so intolerably loathsome, that it was dangerous to remain there for any time, and some of us had been permitted to stay on the deck for the fresh air; but now that the whole ship's cargo were confined together, it became absolutely pestilential. The closeness of the place, and the heat of the climate, added to the number in the ship, which was so crowded that each had scarcely room to turn himself, almost suffocated us. This produced copious perspirations, so that the air soon became unfit for respiration, from a variety of loathsome smells, and brought on a sickness among the slaves, of which many died, thus falling victims to the improvident avarice, as I may call it, of their purchasers. This wretched situation was again aggravated by the galling of the chains, now become insupportable; and the filth of the necessary tubs [latrines], into which the children often fell, and were almost suffocated. The shrieks of the women, and the groans of the dying, rendered the whole a scene of horror almost inconceivable.

QUESTIONS FOR ANALYSIS

- The slave trade involved capturing Africans from various parts of the interior of the continent. Which lines in the reading give evidence of this?
- Equiano's book came out in 1789 in the midst of a campaign to abolish the slave trade. Considering the formality of his language, what type of audience do you suppose he was seeking to reach?
- Why would this book describing the horrors of the slave trade have appeared only in the late 1700s, even though such brutal conditions had been existing for more than two centuries?

Source: Olaudah Equiano, *The Interesting Narrative of the Life of Olaudah Equiano, or Gustavus Vassa, the African, Written by Himself,* A Norton Critical Edition, edited by Werner Sollors (New York: Norton, 2001), pp. 38–41.

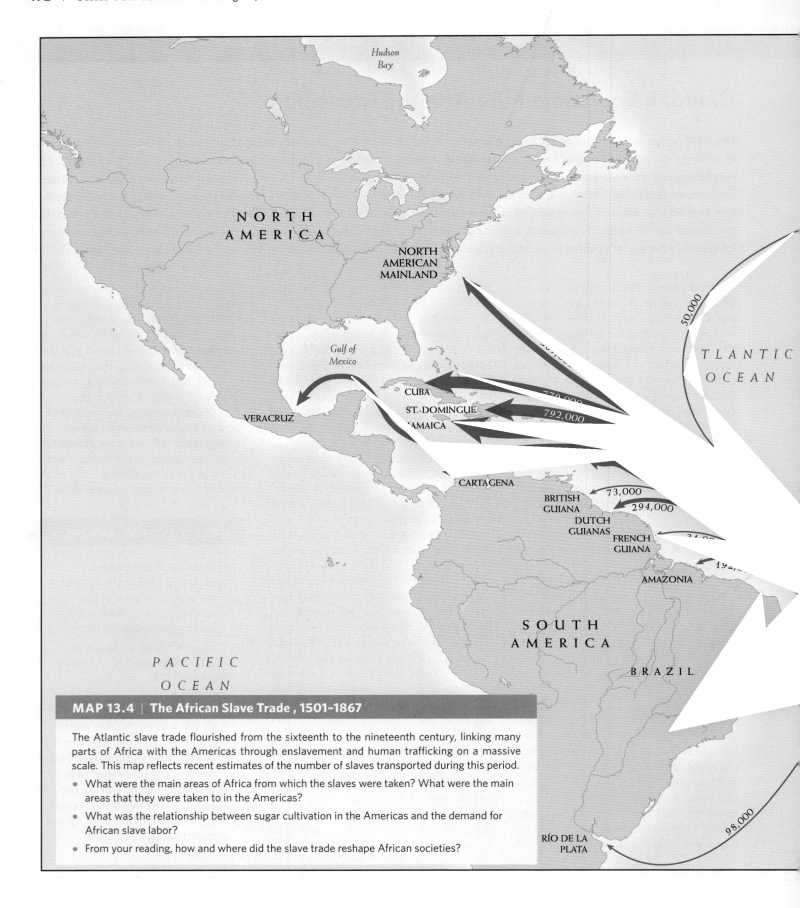

Hudson Bay

NORTH AMERICA

NORTH AMERICAN MAINLAND

Gulf of Mexico

CUBA

ST.-DOMINGUE

JAMAICA

VERACRUZ

CARTAGENA

BRITISH GUIANA

DUTCH GUIANAS

FRENCH GUIANA

AMAZONIA

SOUTH AMERICA

BRAZIL

PACIFIC OCEAN

ATLANTIC OCEAN

RÍO DE LA PLATA

50,000

770,000

792,000

73,000

294,000

98,000

MAP 13.4 | The African Slave Trade , 1501–1867

The Atlantic slave trade flourished from the sixteenth to the nineteenth century, linking many parts of Africa with the Americas through enslavement and human trafficking on a massive scale. This map reflects recent estimates of the number of slaves transported during this period.

- What were the main areas of Africa from which the slaves were taken? What were the main areas that they were taken to in the Americas?

- What was the relationship between sugar cultivation in the Americas and the demand for African slave labor?

- From your reading, how and where did the slave trade reshape African societies?

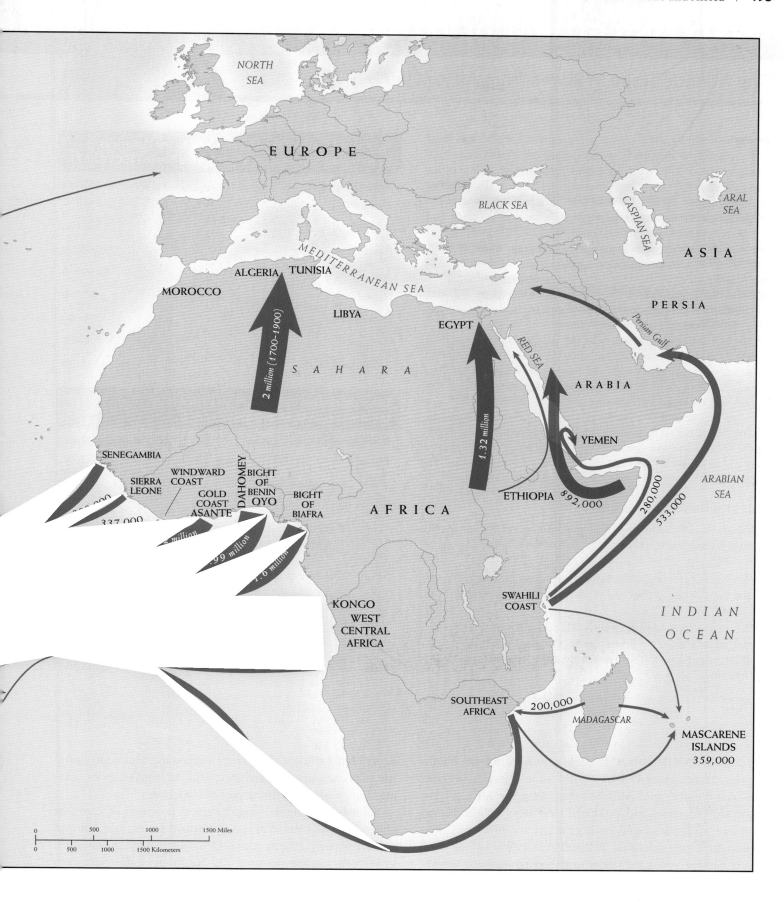

NORTH
SEA

EUROPE

BLACK SEA

CASPIAN
SEA

ARAL
SEA

ASIA

MEDITERRANEAN SEA

MOROCCO

ALGERIA TUNISIA

LIBYA

EGYPT

PERSIA

Persian Gulf

RED SEA

ARABIA

2 million (1700-1900)

S A H A R A

1.32 million

YEMEN

SENEGAMBIA

SIERRA
LEONE

WINDWARD
COAST

GOLD
COAST
ASANTE

DAHOMEY

BIGHT
OF
BENIN
OYO

BIGHT
OF
BIAFRA

337,000

million

.99 million

1.6 million

A F R I C A

ETHIOPIA

892,000

280,000

533,000

*ARABIAN
SEA*

KONGO
WEST
CENTRAL
AFRICA

SWAHILI
COAST

I N D I A N

O C E A N

SOUTHEAST
AFRICA

200,000

MADAGASCAR

MASCARENE
ISLANDS
359,000

0	500	1000	1500 Miles
0	500	1000	1500 Kilometers

The Atlantic Trade in Slaves from Africa (1501–1900)

The world's leading slave traders were also the world's most important maritime powers during the period from 1501 to 1900. The following tables focus on which countries transported these slaves and where they ended up. The Spanish and Portuguese established the first European empires in the Americas and created the model for the early slave trade. But northern European powers like Great Britain and France, reflecting their growing strength in maritime commerce, dominated the Atlantic slave trade between 1642 and 1808. In the final phase of the Atlantic slave trade, 1808–1867, the northern European powers and the United States disengaged from the trade, allowing the Portuguese and the Spanish once again to dominate the trade now centered largely on Cuba and Brazil.

In recent decades, scholars of the Atlantic slave trade have created the Trans-Atlantic Slave Trade Database, which can be accessed at the Voyages Web site (www.slavevoyages.org). Constructed from nearly 35,000 documented voyages during this period, this database incorporates roughly 80 percent of the slave ventures that set out for Africa to obtain slaves from all around the Atlantic world during this era. Through painstaking research, historians have been able to reconstruct the Atlantic world slave trade and offer a clear insight into the experiences of all those involved and the impact of this trade on the global economy during four centuries.

QUESTIONS FOR ANALYSIS

- Which countries were the most heavily invested in the Atlantic slave trade based on the data in the first table? How do you know?
- What was the relationship between the slave-trading countries and the colonies in the New World based on the entries in both tables?
- Why is the total number of slaves traded different from the number of slaves that disembarked? Did you expect the differences between these two numbers to be greater than they are? If so, why?

Source: David Eltis and David Richardson, *Atlas of the Transatlantic Slave Trade* (2010).

Number of Slaves Taken from Africa to the Americas by Nationality of Vessels That Carried Them (1501–1867)

Vessel Nationality	Number of Slaves
Portugal/Brazil	5,849,300
Great Britain	3,259,900
France	1,380,970
Spain/Uruguay	1,060,900
Netherlands	555,300
United States	305,800
Baltic States	110,400
Total Atlantic World	**12,522,570**

Disembarkation of Slaves from Africa to the Americas (1501–1900)

Disembarking Country/Colony	Number of Slaves
Brazil (Portugal)	4,720,000
Smaller Caribbean islands (mix)	1,750,000
Jamaica (Spain then Great Britain)	1,000,000
Saint-Domingue (Spain then France)	792,000
Cuba (Spain)	779,000
Spanish Caribbean mainland	390,000
United States	389,000
Dutch Guiana	294,000
Amazonia	142,000
Total	**10,703,000**

THE KONGO KINGDOM In some parts of Africa, the booming slave trade wreaked havoc as local leaders feuded over control of the traffic; mercantilist rivalry along the African coast disrupted old states and produced new ones. In the Kongo kingdom, civil wars raged for over a century after 1665, and captured warriors were sold as slaves. As members of the royal family clashed, entire provinces saw their populations vanish. Most important to the conduct of war and the control of trade were firearms and gunpowder, which made the capturing of slaves highly efficient. Moreover, kidnapping became so prevalent that cultivators worked their fields bearing weapons, leaving their children behind in guarded stockades.

Some leaders of the Kongo kingdom fought back. Consider Queen Nzinga (1583–1663), a masterful diplomat and a shrewd military planner. Having converted to Christianity, she managed to keep Portuguese slavers at bay during her long reign. Even after Portuguese forces defeated her troops in battle, she conducted effective guerrilla warfare into her sixties.

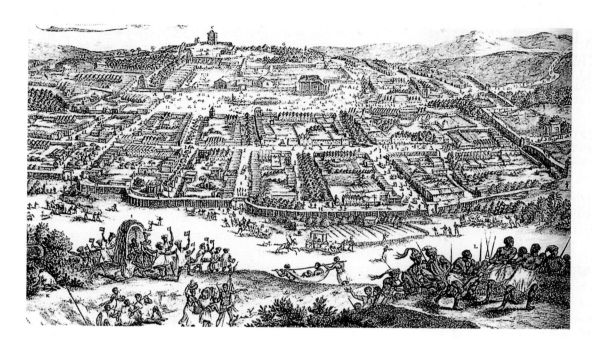

The Port of Loango. *Partly as a result of the profits of the slave trade, African rulers and merchants were able to create large and prosperous port cities such as Loango (pictured here), which was on the western coast of south-central Africa.*

Consider also the Christian visionary Dona Beatriz Kimpa Vita. Born in the Kongo in 1684 and baptized as a Christian, at age twenty she claimed to have received visions from St. Anthony of Padua. She believed that she died every Friday and was transported to heaven to converse with God, returning to earth on Monday to broadcast God's commands to believers. Her message aimed to end the Kongo civil wars and re-create a unified kingdom. Although she gained a large following, she failed to win the support of leading political figures. In 1706, she was captured and burned at the stake.

OYO, ASANTE, AND OTHER GROUPS As some African merchants and warlords sold other Africans, their commercial success enabled them to consolidate political power and grow wealthy. Their wealth financed additional weapons, with which they subdued neighbors and extended political control. Among the most durable new polities was the Asante state, which arose in the West African tropical rain forest in 1701 and expanded through 1750. This state benefited from its access to gold, which it used to acquire firearms (from European traders) to raid nearby communities for servile workers. From its capital city at Kumasi, the state eventually encompassed almost all of present-day Ghana. Main roads spread out from the capital like spokes of a wheel, each approximately twenty days' travel from the center. Through the Asante trading networks, African traders bought, bartered, and sold slaves, who wound up in the hands of European merchants waiting in ports with vessels carrying manufactured products and weaponry.

Also active in the slave trade—and enriched by it—was the Oyo Empire. This territory, which straddled the main trade routes, linked tropical rain forests with interior markets of the northern savanna areas. The empire's strength rested on its impressive army brandishing weapons secured from trade with Europeans. Deploying cavalry units in the savanna and infantry units in the rain forest, the Oyo's military campaigns became annual events, only suspended so that warriors could return home for agricultural duties. Every dry season, Oyo armies marched on their neighbors to capture entire villages.

Slavery and the emergence of new political organizations enriched and empowered some Africans, but they cost Africa dearly. For the princes, warriors, and merchants who organized the slave trade, their business (like that of Amerindian fur suppliers) enabled them to obtain European goods—especially alcohol, tobacco, textiles, and guns. The Atlantic system also tilted wealth away from rural dwellers and village elders and increasingly toward port cities. Across the landmass, the slave trade thinned the population. True, Africa was spared a demographic catastrophe equal to the devastation of American Indians. The introduction of American food crops—notably maize and cassava, producing many more calories per acre than the old staples of millet and sorghum—blunted the trade's depopulating aspects. Yet some areas suffered grievously from three centuries of heavy involvement in the slave trade. The Atlantic trade enhanced the warrior class, who carried out raids for captives; the dislocations, internal power struggles, and economic hardships that followed precipitated the rise and fall of West African kingdoms.

Since the seventeenth century saw the deportation of 2 million African men, women, and children to the Americas, it is worth asking whether the Little Ice Age was a factor in the fate of these peoples. Unfortunately, information on sub-Saharan Africa is not as rich as it is for Europe and Asia. Nonetheless, what we do know, mainly from travelers' accounts, is that many of the areas from which slaves came—like Kongo, the interior of West Africa, and Senegambia—suffered from severe drought and witnessed a spike in the number of captives sold to slavers.

COMPARATIVE PERSPECTIVES ON CLIMATE CHANGE: THE OTTOMAN EMPIRE AND MING CHINA

The Little Ice Age tore asunder two of Afro-Eurasia's largest and most stable empires—the Ottoman Empire and Ming China—though in both cases other factors were also at work. One survived, and the other did not—although in both empires peasants and nomads, driven by severe famines, rose in rebellion, asserting that their rulers had failed to look after them.

The Ottomans Struggle to Maintain Power and Legitimacy

Hardest and earliest hit by climate change was the eastern Mediterranean. Here, fierce cold and endless drought brought famine and high mortality. In 1620, the Bosporus froze over, enabling residents of Istanbul to walk from the European side of the city into the Asian side. In Ottoman territories dependent on floodwaters for their well-being, such as Egypt and Iraq, food was in short supply and mortality rates skyrocketed. In addition, the import of New World silver led to high levels of inflation and a destabilized economy. Yet, in spite of the dire circumstances, the Ottomans continued their military campaigns against the Habsburgs. Banditry, nomadic invasions of settled lands, refusal to pay taxes, and ultimately outright revolt were the inevitable result.

THE CELALI REVOLT AND KÖPRÜLÜ REFORMS A revolt, begun in central Anatolia in the early sixteenth century, continued with fits and starts throughout the century and reached a crescendo at the beginning of the seventeenth century. This later full-blown uprising took its name from Sheikh Celali, who had led a rebellion in the early sixteenth century. Later rebels called themselves Celalis, looking to his life for inspiration. They united hordes of bandits and eventually challenged the sultan's authority. With a 30,000-strong army, the rebels turned much of Anatolia into a danger zone full of pillaging, looting, burning of villages, and killing. Large segments of the Ottoman population, many of whom were Shiites or turned to Shiism to express their opposition to Ottoman rule, joined the rebellion. Poised to assault Istanbul in 1607–1608, the rebels encountered the sultan's troops on the plains outside the capital and were trounced. The empire pulled back from the edge of collapse.

Although the Ottomans survived, they did so in a greatly weakened state. The empire's population, around 35 million in the 1590s, was still below that number when the first official census was carried out in 1830. Meanwhile, the European powers with access to New World colonies sprinted ahead of the Ottomans economically, militarily, and culturally.

The Ottomans did, however, experience a period of good governance in the mid- to late-seventeenth century in spite of Mustafa Ali's pessimistic predictions. New grand viziers from the Köprülü family spearheaded changes to revitalize the government. Known as the Köprülü reforms, the changes in administration reenergized the state and enabled the military to reacquire some of its lost possessions. Revenues again increased, and inflation decreased. Fired by revived expansionist ambitions, Istanbul decided to renew its assault on Christianity (see Chapter 11)—beginning with rekindled plans to seize Vienna. Although the Ottomans amassed an enormous force outside the Habsburg capital in 1683, both sides suffered heavy losses, but the Ottoman forces ultimately retreated. Under the treaty that ended the Austro-Ottoman war, the Ottomans lost major European territorial possessions, including Hungary.

Despite failing to take Vienna, the Ottoman state flourished in the first half of the eighteenth century. No event was more resplendent than the two weeks of feasting, parades, and entertainment that accompanied the circumcision of the sultan's sons in 1720. Istanbul also once again became a beehive of political activity, adorned with new palaces and mosques.

THE MAMLUKS IN OTTOMAN EGYPT A weakened Ottoman state prompted outlying provinces to assert their autonomy. Egypt led the way. Here, too, plummeting temperatures and monsoon failures leading to aridity and low Nile waters may have been factors. Egypt experienced extremely low Niles from 1641 to 1643, owing to catastrophic drought, and then such extreme cold that a Turkish traveler in the 1670s reported that everyone who could afford to wore fur-lined clothing.

In 1517, Egypt had become the Ottoman Empire's greatest conquest. The wealthiest Ottoman territory, it was an important source of revenue and initially was well governed by its Ottoman-appointed governors. Its payments to Istanbul exceeded those of any other Ottoman province. Yet, starting in the mid-seventeenth century, households modeled on the sultan's arose and increasingly asserted their independence from Istanbul. By the latter half of the eighteenth century, the dominant households were made up of **Mamluks** (Arabic for "owned" or "possessed"), military men who had ruled Egypt as an independent regime until the Ottoman conquest (see Chapter 10). Although the Ottoman forces had routed the Mamluks on the battlefield in 1517, Ottoman governors in Egypt allowed the Mamluks to reform themselves. By the second half of the eighteenth century, these military men were nearly as powerful as their ancestors had been in the fifteenth century when they ruled Egypt independently. Mamluk leaders also enhanced their power by aligning with Egyptian merchants and catering to the *ulama*. Turning the Ottoman governor in Egypt into a mere figurehead, this provincial elite kept much of the area's fiscal resources for themselves at the expense of the imperial coffers and the local peasantry.

Siege of Vienna. *This seventeenth-century painting depicts the Ottoman siege of Vienna, which began on July 14, 1683, and ended on September 12. The city might have fallen if the Polish king, John III, had not answered the pope's plea to defend Christendom and sent an army to assist German and Austrian troops in defeating the Ottomans.*

Although the Ottoman Empire survived the impact of the Little Ice Age (in contrast to the Ming dynasty in China), it emerged in a severely weakened condition. It was well on its way to becoming "the sick man of Europe," as the great European powers described the Ottoman state in the nineteenth century. The Celali revolts resulted in devastating population losses, while the repeated low Nile floods reduced food and tribute payments from Egypt to Istanbul, further weakening the Ottoman state. Not all the decline was associated with climate change, however. Heterodox and Sufi religious leaders challenged the Sunni orthodoxy of the clerical and bureaucratic classes. In Egypt and the other Arab provinces of the Ottoman Empire, local notables, notably Mamluks in Egypt and warlords and religious leaders in greater Syria, sought autonomy from Istanbul.

Ming China Succumbs to Manchu Rule

The Ming dynasty was less fortunate than the Ottomans. It did not survive. The Little Ice Age was not wholly responsible for the fall of the Ming, but it played a predominant role. Drought and freezing temperatures affected food production not only in China proper, where the Ming prevailed, but also throughout Inner China, where by the seventeenth century the Manchus of Manchuria were a rising power. The Ming capital of Beijing suffered grievously. An estimated 300,000 perished within the inner city in 1644, causing many Han Chinese to conclude that the Ming had lost the mandate of heaven.

THE MANCHUS FIND A VULNERABLE TARGET Unlike the Ottoman Empire, China's imperial state always had powerful enemies on its northern frontier, eager to take over the state apparatus and prosper by assuming control of a productive economy. By the early seventeenth century, a rising **Manchu** population, based in Inner China and unable to feed their people in Manchuria, were poised to breach the Great Wall in search of better lands. They found a Chinese government and its population in disarray from warfare and fiscal crisis. Peasant rebellions crippled central authorities. Outlaw armies swelled under charismatic leaders. The so-called "roving bands" wreaked havoc across the countryside. The most famous rebel leader, the "dashing prince," Li Zicheng, reached the outskirts of Beijing in 1644. Only a few companies of soldiers and a few thousand eunuchs stood to defend the capital's 21 miles of walls. Li Zicheng seized Beijing easily. Two days later, the emperor hanged himself. On the following day, the triumphant "dashing prince" rode into the capital and claimed the throne.

News of the fall of the Ming capital sent shock waves around the empire. One hundred and seventy miles to the northeast, where China meets Manchuria, the Ming's army's commander received the news within a matter of days.

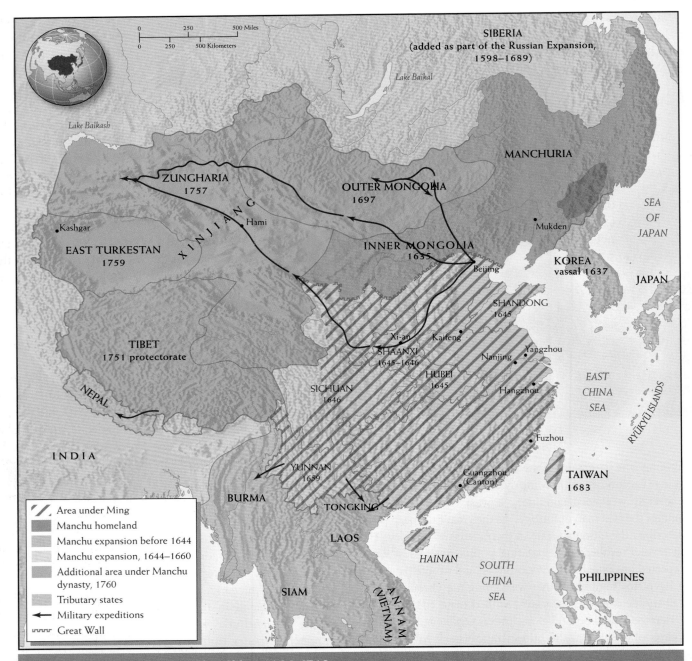

MAP 13.5 | From Ming to Qing China, 1644–1760

Qing China under the Manchus expanded its territory significantly during this period.

- Find the Manchu homeland and then the area of Manchu expansion after 1644, when the Manchus established the Qing dynasty.
- Where did the Qing dynasty expand?
- Based on the map, why do you think the Qing dynasty expanded so aggressively during this period?
- What does the location of Manchuria tell you about the historical origins of the Qing?

Tasked to defend the Ming against their Manchu neighbors, the commander knew a precarious position when he saw one. Caught between an advancing rebel army on the one side and the Manchus on the other, he made a fateful decision: he made a pact with the Manchus for their cooperation to fight the "dashing prince." In return, his new allies got the "gold and treasure" in the capital. Thus, without shedding a drop of blood, the Manchus joined the Ming forces. After years of coveting the Ming Empire, the Manchus were finally marching on Beijing. (See Map 13.5.)

Other factors besides the Little Ice Age, including some that troubled the Ottoman Empire at this time, spelled the end of the Ming dynasty. As elsewhere, the influx of silver from the New World and Japan, while at first stimulating the Chinese economy, led to severe economic dislocations. As noted in Chapter 12, Europeans used New World silver to pay for their purchases of Chinese goods. Increasing monetization of the economy, which entailed silver becoming the primary medium of exchange, bolstered market activity and state revenues at the same time.

Yet the primacy of silver had differential impacts on the Ottomans and the Chinese. In the Ottoman Empire, the influx of New World silver undermined the Ottoman ambition to create an autonomous economy. In China, silver pressured peasants, who now needed that metal to pay their taxes and purchase goods. (See Primary Source: Huang Liuhong on Eliminating Authorized Silversmiths.) When silver supplies were abundant, the peasants faced inflationary prices. But when supplies became scant, as they did over the seventeenth century because of a decline in New World mining and rising silver demand in Europe, Chinese peasants could not meet their obligations to state officials and merchants. The frustrated masses

Silver. *This seventeenth-century helmet from the Ming (1368–1633) or Qing (1644–1911) dynasty features steel, gold, silver, and textiles, all of which were vital to the Chinese economy during this century. Silver was especially important, for its large influx from Japan and the Americas led to severe economic problems, political unrest, and the overthrow of the Ming dynasty.*

thus often seethed with resentment, which quickly turned to rebellion.

Although China had prospered in the sixteenth and seventeenth centuries, regional wealth undermined the central dynasty. Local power holders increasingly defied the Ming government. Moreover, because Ming rulers discouraged overseas commerce and forbade foreign travel, they did not reap the rewards of long-distance trade. Rather, these profits went to merchants and adventurers who evaded imperial edicts. All this happened as Beijing faced mounting defense costs. The combined result of climate shock, regional opposition, and fiscal crisis brought down the Ming dynasty in 1644.

THE QING DYNASTY ASSERTS CONTROL Despite their small numbers, the Manchus overcame early resistance to their rule and oversaw an impressive expansion of their realm. The Manchus were descendants of the Jurchens (see Chapter 10). They emerged as a force early in the seventeenth century, when their leader claimed the title of khan after securing the allegiance of various Mongol groups in northeastern Asia, paving the way for their eventual conquest of China.

When the Manchus defeated Li Zicheng and seized power in Beijing, they numbered around 1 million. Assuming control of a domain that included perhaps 250 million people, they were keenly aware of their minority status. Taking power was one thing; keeping it was another. But keep it they did. In fact, during the eighteenth century, the Manchu **Qing** ("pure") **dynasty** (1644–1911) incorporated new territories, experienced substantial population growth, and sustained significant economic growth. Despite coming to power at a time of political chaos, the Manchus established a stable and long-lived imperial system in contrast to the political and economic turmoil that rocked the societies of the Atlantic world.

The key to China's relatively stable economic and geographical expansion lay in its rulers' shrewd and flexible policies. The early Manchu emperors were able administrators who knew that to govern a diverse population, they had to adapt to local ways. To promote continuity, they respected Confucian codes and kept the classic texts as the basis of the prestigious civil service examinations (see Chapter 9). Social hierarchies of age, gender, and kin—indeed, the entire image of the family as the bedrock of social organization—endured. In some areas, like Taiwan, the Manchus added new territories to existing provinces. Elsewhere, they gave newly acquired territories, like Mongolia, Tibet, and Xinjiang, their own form of local administration. Imperial envoys in these regions administered through staffs of locals and relied on native institutions. Until the late nineteenth century, the Qing dynasty showed little interest in integrating those regions into "China proper."

At the same time, Qing rulers conveyed a clear sense of their own majesty and legitimacy. Rulers relentlessly promoted

Huang Liuhong on Eliminating Authorized Silversmiths

The influx of silver into China had profound effects on its economy and government. For instance, silver became the medium for assessing taxes. In his magistrate's manual from around 1694, Huang Liuhong (Huang Liu-hung) indicated the problems that arose from involving authorized silversmiths in the payment process. The situation demonstrates how silver had become an integral part of the lives of the Chinese people.

The purpose of using an authorized silversmith in the collection of tax money is twofold. First, the quality of the silver delivered by the taxpayers must be up to standard. The authorized silversmith is expected to reject any substandard silver. Second, when the silver is delivered to the provincial treasury, it should be melted and cast into ingots to avoid theft while in transit. But, to get his commission, the authorized silversmith has to pay a fee and arrange for a guarantor. In addition, he has to pay bribes to the clerks of the revenue section and to absorb the operating expenses of his shop—rent, food, coal, wages for his employees, and so on. If he does not impose a surcharge on the taxpayers, how can he maintain his business?

There are many ways for an authorized silversmith to defraud the taxpayers. First, he can declare that the quality of the silver is not up to standard and a larger amount is required. Second, he can insist that all small pieces of silver have to be melted and cast into ingots; hence there will be wastage in the process of melting. Third, he may demand that all ingots, no matter how small they are, be stamped with his seal, and of course charge a stamping fee. Fourth, he may require a fee for each melting as a legitimate charge for the service. Fifth, he can procrastinate until the taxpayer becomes impatient and is willing to double the melting fee. Last, if the taxpayer seems naive or simple minded, the smith can purposely upset the melting container and put the blame on the taxpayer. All these tricks are prevalent, and little can be done to thwart them.

When the silver ingots are delivered to the provincial treasury, few of them are up to standard. The authorized silversmith often blames the taxpayers for bringing in silver of inferior quality although it would be easy for him to reject them at the time of melting. Powerful official families and audacious licentiates often put poor quality silver in sealed envelopes, which the authorized silversmith is not empowered to examine. Therefore, the use of an authorized silversmith contributes very little to the business of tax collection; it only increases the burden of small taxpayers.

> ### QUESTIONS FOR ANALYSIS
>
> - What are the six ways that an authorized silversmith can defraud taxpayers?
> - Why does the author suggest that the use of authorized silversmiths increases the burden of small taxpayers?
> - What reasons would the Chinese state have for maintaining such a "flawed" system?

Source: Huang Liu-hung, *A Complete Book Concerning Happiness and Benevolence: A Manual for Local Magistrates in Seventeenth Century China* (Tucson: University of Arizona Press, 1984), pp. 190–91.

patriarchal values. Widows who remained "chaste" enjoyed public praise, and women in general were urged to lead a "virtuous" life serving male kin and family. To the majority Han population, the Manchu emperor represented himself as the worthy upholder of familial values and classical Chinese civilization; to the Tibetan Buddhists, the Manchu state offered imperial patronage. So, too, with Islamic subjects. Although the Islamic Uighurs, as well as other Muslim subjects, might have disliked the Manchus' easygoing religious attitude, they generally endorsed the emperor's claim to rule.

However, insinuating themselves into an existing order and appeasing subject peoples did not satisfy the Manchu yearning to leave their imprint. They also introduced measures that emphasized their authority, their distinctiveness, and the submission of their mostly Han Chinese subjects. For example, Qing officials composed or translated important documents into Manchu and banned intermarriage between Manchu and Han (although this was difficult to enforce). Other edicts imposed Manchu ways—for example, requiring all Han males to shave their forehead and braid their hair in a queue and to wear high collars and tight jackets instead of loose Ming-style clothes.

Nothing earned the regime's disapproval more than the urban elites' indulgence in sensual pleasure. The Qing court regarded the "decadence" of the late Ming, symbolized by its famous actresses, as one of the Ming's principal failings. In 1723, the Qing banned female performers from the court and then from commercial theaters, with young boys taking female roles onstage. The Qing also tried to regulate commercial theater by

Qing Theater with Female Impersonators. *The Qing court banned women from performing in theaters, which led to the practice of using young boys in female roles.*

excluding women from the audience. The popularity of female impersonators onstage, however, brought a new cachet to homosexual relationships. A gulf began to open between the government's aspirations and its ability to police society. For example, the urban public continued to flock to performances by female impersonators in defiance of the Qing's bans.

Manchu impositions fell mostly on the peasantry, for the Qing financed their administrative structure through taxes on peasant households. In response, the peasants sought new lands to cultivate in border areas, having lost much land during the Little Ice Age. On these estates, they planted New World crops that grew well in difficult soils. This move introduced an important change in the Chinese diet: while rice remained the staple diet of the wealthy, peasants increasingly subsisted on corn and sweet potatoes.

EXPANSION AND TRADE UNDER THE QING The Qing dynasty forged tributary relations with Korea, Vietnam, Burma, and Nepal, and its territorial expansion reached far into central Asia, Tibet, and Mongolia. In particular, the Manchus confronted the Junghars of western Mongolia, who controlled much of central Asia in the mid-seventeenth century and whose predecessors had once captured an early Ming emperor. Wary of a potential alliance between the Junghars and an emerging Russia on its northern frontiers, the Qing dynasty launched successive campaigns and defeated the Junghars by the mid-eighteenth century.

While officials redoubled their reliance on an agrarian base, trade and commerce flourished. Chinese merchants continued to ply the waters stretching from Southeast Asia to Japan, exchanging textiles, ceramics, and medicine for spices and rice. Although initially the Qing state vacillated about permitting maritime trade with foreigners, it sought to regulate external commerce more formally as it consolidated its rule. In 1720, in Canton, a group of merchants formed a monopolistic guild to trade with Europeans. Although the guild disbanded in the face of opposition from other merchants, it revived after the Qing restricted European trade to Canton. The **Canton system,** established by imperial decree in 1759, required European traders to have guild merchants act as guarantors for their good behavior and payment of fees.

China, in sum, negotiated a century of climate change and political upheaval without dismantling established ways in politics and economics, much as the Ottomans did. Climate change was far from the only, or even the primary, factor in China's major political upheaval, the replacement of Ming rule with a long-lasting Qing dynasty. As in the Ottoman Empire, the influx of New World silver disrupted the economy, leading to a cycle of booms and busts. Even so, there was much continuity in the seventeenth and eighteenth centuries. At the heart of this continuity was the peasantry, who continued to practice popular faiths, cultivate crops, and stay close to fields and villages. Trade with the outside world remained marginal to overall commercial life; like the Ming, the Qing cared more about the agrarian than the commercial health of the empire, believing the former to be the foundation of prosperity and tranquility. As long as China's peasantry could keep the dynasty's coffers full,

Canton. *Not only were foreigners not allowed to trade with the Chinese outside of Canton, but they were also required to have Chinese guild members act as guarantors of their good behavior and payment of fees.*

the government was content to squeeze the merchants when it needed funds. Some historians view this practice as a failure to adapt to a changing world order, as it ultimately left China vulnerable to outsiders—especially Europeans. But this view puts the historical cart before the horse. By the mid-eighteenth century, Europe still needed China more than the other way around. For the majority of Chinese, no superior model of belief, politics, or economics was conceivable. Indeed, although the Qing had taken over a crumbling empire in 1644, a century later China was enjoying a new level of prosperity.

In both the Ottoman Empire and China, the Little Ice Age had severe effects. The Ottoman Empire barely survived, although its population losses were not recouped until well into the nineteenth century and its sense of power and legitimacy were badly shaken. In contrast, while the Ming dynasty lost out to a regime drawn from the much-despised Manchurian region, the new Qing dynasty created a stable political order, a prosperous economy, and a well-functioning social order—though one that favored those of Manchu descent. As noted previously, climate change was not the sole factor in causing these outcomes, but its role was significant.

OTHER PARTS OF ASIA IN THE SEVENTEENTH AND EIGHTEENTH CENTURIES

The other regions in Asia also experienced great difficulties brought on by the Little Ice Age. All had to cope with droughts, high winds, hailstorms, and earthquakes, but some weathered

the troubles better than others. In Iran, the Safavid regime came to an end in the seventeenth century, but here regime change was due more to ethnic diversity and ineffective rulers than to severe climatic conditions. A similar situation played out in India, which endured at least four lesser monsoons and a plethora of rebellions that led Shah Aurangzeb (r. 1658–1797) to carry out savage persecutions of non-Muslim groups. Nevertheless, Mughal monarchs, even Aurangzeb, dealt promptly and reasonably effectively with the famines, even the most severe one that ravaged the Gujarati region between 1630 and 1632. The Tokugawa regime in Japan, installed early in the sixteenth century, overcame the difficulties that the Little Ice Age presented. In fact, it experienced a century of increased agricultural productivity, rapid population growth, and impressive urbanization, mostly owing to the shrewd provincial administrators that the Tokugawa rulers appointed.

Global trading networks blossomed even more vigorously in Asia than in the Americas and Europe. China probably possessed one-fourth of the world's population and was still the wealthiest region in the world. In addition, the Europeans were less dominant in Asia than in the Americas and therefore had to content themselves as commercial intermediaries in Asia's brisk long-distance trade. They penetrated Asian markets with American silver largely because the Asians, especially the Chinese, regarded their trade goods as inferior. Nor could they conquer Asian empires or colonize vast portions of the region or enslave Asian peoples as they had Africans. The Mughal Empire continued to grow, and the Qing dynasty, which had wrested control from the Ming, significantly expanded China's borders. Still, in some places the balance of power was tilting in Europe's direction. Not only did the Ottomans' borders contract, but by the late eighteenth century, Europeans had established economic and military dominance in parts of India and much of Southeast Asia.

The Dutch in Southeast Asia

In Southeast Asia, the Dutch already enjoyed a dominant position by the seventeenth century. Although the Portuguese had seized the vibrant port city of Melaka in 1511 and the Spaniards had taken Manila in 1571, neither was able to monopolize the lucrative spice trade. To challenge them, the Dutch government persuaded its merchants to charter the Dutch East India Company (abbreviated as VOC) in 1602. Benefiting from Amsterdam's position as the most world's efficient money market with the lowest interest rates, the VOC raised ten times the capital of its English counterpart—the royal chartered English East India Company. The advantages of chartered companies were evident in the VOC's scale of operation: at its peak the company had 257 ships and employed 12,000 persons. Throughout two centuries it sent ships manned by a total of 1 million men to Asia.

Attack on Bantam. *This engraving depicts a Dutch attack on Bantam in the late seventeenth century as part of the VOC's effort to expand its empire in Southeast Asia.*

The VOC's main impact was in Southeast Asia, where spices, coffee, tea, and teak wood were key exports (see again Map 13.1). The company's objective was to secure a trade monopoly wherever it could, fix prices, and replace the indigenous population with Dutch planters. In 1619, under the leadership of Jan Pieterszoon Coen (who once said that trade could not be conducted without war nor war without trade), the Dutch swept into the Javanese port of Jakarta (renamed Batavia by the Dutch). In defiance of local rulers and English rivals, the Dutch burned all the houses, drove out the population, and constructed a fortress from which to control the Southeast Asian trade. Two years later, Coen's forces took over a cluster of nutmeg-producing islands known as Banda. The traditional chiefs and almost the entire population were killed outright, left to starve, or enslaved. Dutch planters and their slaves replaced the decimated local population and sent their produce to the VOC. The motive for such rapacious action was the huge profit to be made by buying nutmeg at a low price in the Bandanese Islands and selling it at many times that price in Europe.

With their monopoly of nutmeg secured, the Dutch went after the market in cloves. Their strategy was to control production in one region and then destroy the rest, which entailed, once again, wars against producers and traders in other areas. Portuguese Melaka soon fell to the Dutch and became a VOC outpost. Although this aggressive expansion met widespread resistance, by 1670 the Dutch controlled all of the lucrative spice trade from the Maluku islands.

Next, the VOC gained control of Bantam (present-day Banten), the largest pepper-exporting port. However, the Dutch had to share this commerce with Chinese and English competitors. Moreover, since there was no demand for European products in Asia, the Dutch had to participate more in inter-Asian trade as a way to reduce their need to make payments in precious metals. So they purchased, for example, calicoes (plain white cotton cloths) in India or copper in Japan for resale in Melaka and Java. They also diversified into trading silk, cotton, tea, and coffee, in addition to spices.

As a result of the Dutch enterprise, European outposts such as Dutch Batavia and Spanish Manila soon eclipsed old cosmopolitan cities such as Bantam. Indeed, as Europeans competed for supremacy in the borderlands of Southeast Asia, they made local societies serve their own ambitions and began replacing traditional networks with trade routes that primarily served European interests. The Dutch used Europe's traditional appetite for Southeast Asian spices like nutmeg, pepper, and cloves, to which they added coffee, tea, and teak wood, to integrate the islands of the Dutch East Indies into the global economy.

The Islamic Heartland

By the early seventeenth century, the three major Muslim empires of Afro-Eurasia, stretching from the Balkans and North Africa to South Asia, had a combined population of between 130 and 150 million. Yet, compared with Southeast Asia, they did not feel such direct effects of European intrusion. Here, trade was not as instrumental as in East Asia, and though the importation of silver was significant and destabilizing, it was not the powerful factor promoting large-scale trade with Europe that it was in China. The Islamic heartland did, however, face internal difficulties. While the Ottoman and Mughal Empires remained resilient, the Safavid Empire fell into chaos.

THE SAFAVID EMPIRE The Safavid Empire had always required a powerful, religiously inspired ruler to enforce Shiite religious orthodoxy and to hold together the realm's tribal, pastoral, mercantile, and agricultural factions. During its rise, charismatic political leadership and religious messianism had overcome the innate tendencies of the peoples living on the Iranian plateau to resist the authority of state power. The Iranian plateau consisted of vast semidesert and wooded areas surrounded by mountains and was inhabited by diverse, often hostile ethnic, linguistic, and religious communities. Moreover, a substantial percentage of the Safavid population of 8.5 million comprised nomadic peoples who bristled when confronted with centralized power. Abbas I (r. 1588–1629), the fifth Safavid shah, used the strength of his personality, his commitment to Shiism, and his talent for playing off one group against another to enhance the state's power (see Chapter 14). His successors were weaker and less charismatic, and the state foundered as eunuchs and harem women asserted their authority over that of the shahs and as tribal groups slipped away from control from the center.

By 1722, the state was under assault from within and without, and it collapsed abruptly at the hands of Afghan clansmen, who overran its inept and divided armies and besieged the capital at Isfahan (see again Map 13.1). As the city's inhabitants perished from hunger and disease, some desperate survivors ate the corpses of the deceased. After the shah abdicated, the invaders executed thousands of officials and members of the royal household. The empire limped along until 1773, when a revolt toppled the last ruler from the throne.

Even so, the Safavid period left an immense imprint on the peoples of the Iranian plateau. They continued their commitment to Shiism in a predominantly Sunni world and harkened back in admiration to their Persian historical traditions. (For a discussion of Safavid culture at its height, see Chapter 14.)

THE MUGHAL EMPIRE In contrast to the Ottomans' setbacks, the Mughal Empire reached its height in the 1600s. The period saw Mughal rulers extend their domain over almost all of India and enjoy increased domestic and international trade. But they eventually had problems governing dispersed and resistant provinces, where many villages retained traditional religions and cultures.

Before the Mughals, India had never had a single political authority. Akbar and his successors had conquered territory in the north (see Chapter 12, Map 12.5), so now the Mughals turned to the south and gained control over most of that region by 1689. As the new provinces provided additional resources, local lords, and warriors, the Mughal bureaucracy grew better at extracting services and taxes.

Indian Cotton. *European traders were drawn to India by its famed cotton textiles. This image from around 1800 shows a woman separating the cotton from the seeds; it captures the preindustrial technology of cotton production in India.*

Imperial stability and prosperity did not depend entirely on the Indian Ocean trading system. Indeed, although the Mughals profited from seaborne trade, they never undertook overseas expansion. The main source of their wealth was land rents, boosted via incentives to bring new land into cultivation. Here peasants planted, in part, New World crops like maize and tobacco. But the imperial economy also benefited from Europeans' increased demand for Indian goods and services—such as a sixfold rise in the English East India Company's textile purchases.

LOCAL AUTONOMY IN MUGHAL INDIA Eventually, Mughals were victims of their own success. More than a century of imperial expansion, commercial prosperity, and agricultural development placed substantial resources in the hands of local and regional authorities. As a result, local warrior elites became more autonomous. By the late seventeenth century, many regional leaders were well positioned to resist Mughal authority.

Thus, increased prosperity enabled distant provinces to challenge central rulers. When, under Aurangzeb (r. 1658–1707), the Mughals pushed deep into southern India, they encountered fierce opposition from the Marathas in the northwestern Deccan plateau (see again Map 13.1). To finance this expansion, Aurangzeb raised taxes on the peasants. As resentment spread, even the elite grew restive at the drain on imperial finances. Seeking support from the *ulama*, the monarch abandoned the toleration of heterodoxy and of non-Muslims that his predecessors had allowed. All this turmoil set the stage for successful peasant revolts.

Now the Indian peasants (like their counterparts in Ming China, Safavid Persia, and the Ottoman Empire) capitalized on weakening central authority to assert their independence. They, too, were feeling the effects of the Little Ice Age on their lands' productivity. Many rose in rebellions; others resorted to banditry. At this point the Mughal emperors had to accept diminished power over a loose unity of provincial "successor states." (For a discussion of Mughal culture at its height, see Chapter 14.) Most of these areas accepted Mughal control in name only, administering semiautonomous regimes through access to local resources. Yet India still flourished,

and landed elites brought new territories into agrarian production. Cotton, for instance, supported a thriving textile industry as peasant households focused on weaving and cloth production. Much of their production was destined for export as the region deepened its integration into world trading systems.

PRIVATE COMMERCIAL ENTERPRISE The Mughals themselves paid scant attention to commercial matters, but local rulers welcomed Europeans into Indian ports, striking deals with merchants from Portugal, England, and Holland. Some Indian merchants formed trading companies of their own to control the sale of regional produce to competing Europeans; others established intricate trading networks that reached as far north as Russia.

One of these companies built a trading and banking empire that demonstrated how local prosperity could undercut imperial power. This was the House of Jagat Seth, which at first specialized in shipping Bengal cloth through Asian and European merchants. Increasingly, however, most of their business in the provinces of Bengal and Bihar was tax farming, whereby they collected taxes for the imperial coffers (see again Map 13.1). The Jagat Seths maintained their own retinue of agents to gather levies from farmers while pocketing substantial profits for themselves. In this way, they and other mercantile houses grew richer and gained greater political influence over financially strapped emperors. Thus, even as global commercial entanglements enriched some in India, the effects undercut the Mughal dynasty.

Tokugawa Japan

Integration with the Asian trading system exposed Japan to new external pressures, even as the islands grappled with internal turmoil. But the Japanese dealt with these pressures more successfully than the mainland Asian empires (Ottoman, Safavid, Mughal, and Ming), which saw political fragmentation and even the overthrow of ruling dynasties. In Japan, a single ruling family emerged. This dynastic state, the **Tokugawa shogunate**, accomplished something that most of the world's other regimes did not: it regulated foreign intrusion. While Japan played a modest role in the expanding global trade, it remained free of outside exploitation.

UNIFICATION OF JAPAN During the sixteenth century, Japan had endured political instability as banditry and civil strife disrupted the countryside. Regional ruling families, called *daimyos*, had commanded private armies of warriors known as samurai. The daimyos sometimes brought order to their domains, but no one family could establish preeminence over others. Although Japan had an emperor, his authority did not extend beyond the court in Kyoto.

Ultimately, several military leaders attempted to unify Japan. One general, who became the supreme minister, arranged

Aurangzeb. *The last powerful Mughal emperor, Aurangzeb continued the conquest of the Indian subcontinent. Pictured in his old age, he is shown here with his courtiers.*

marriages among the children of local authorities to solidify political bonds. Also, to coax cooperation from the daimyos, he ordered that their wives and children be kept as semihostages in the residences they were required to maintain in Edo. After the general died, one of the daimyos, Tokugawa Ieyasu, seized power. This was a decisive moment. In 1603, Ieyasu assumed the title of shogun (military ruler), retaining the emperor in name only while taking the reins of power himself. He also solved the problem of succession, declaring that rulership would be hereditary and that his family would be the ruling household. This hereditary Tokugawa shogunate lasted until 1867.

Now administrative authority shifted from Kyoto to the site of Ieyasu's domain headquarters: the castle town called Edo, later renamed Tokyo. (See Map 13.6.) The Tokugawa built Edo out of a small earthen fortification clinging to a coastal bluff. Behind Edo lay a village in a swampy plain. In a monumental work of engineering, the rulers ordered the swamp drained, the forest cleared, many of the hills leveled, canals dredged, bridges built, the seashore extended by landfill, and a new stone castle completed. By the time Ieyasu died, Edo had a population of 150,000.

The Tokugawa shoguns ensured a flow of resources from the working population to the rulers and from the provinces to the capital. Villages paid taxes to the daimyos, who transferred resources to the seat of shogunate authority. No longer engaged in constant warfare, the samurai became administrators. Peace brought prosperity. Agriculture thrived. Improved farming techniques and land reclamation projects enabled the country's population to triple between 1550 and 1700.

FOREIGN AFFAIRS AND FOREIGNERS Internal peace and prosperity did not insulate Japan from external challenges, especially the intrusion of Christian missionaries and European traders. Initially, Japanese officials welcomed these foreigners out of an eagerness to acquire muskets, gunpowder, and other new technology. But once the ranks of Christian converts swelled, Japanese authorities realized that Christians were intolerant of other faiths, believed Christ to be superior to any authority, and fought among themselves. Trying to stem the tide, the shoguns prohibited conversion to Christianity and attempted to ban its practice. After a rebellion by converted peasants protesting high rents and taxes, the government suppressed Christianity and drove European missionaries from the country.

Even more troublesome was the lure of trade with Europeans. The Tokugawa knew that trading at various Japanese ports would pull the commercial regions in various directions, away from the capital. When it became clear that European traders preferred the ports of Kyūshū (the southernmost island), the shogunate restricted Europeans to trade only in ports under Edo's direct rule in Honshū. Then Japanese authorities expelled all European competitors. Only the Protestant (and nonmissionizing) Dutch won permission to remain in Japan, confined to an island near Nagasaki. The Dutch were allowed to unload just one ship each year, under strict supervision by Japanese authorities.

These measures did not close Tokugawa Japan to the outside world, however. Trade with China and Korea flourished, and the shogun received missions from Korea and the Ryūkyū Islands. Edo also gathered information about the outside world from the resident Dutch and Chinese (who included monks, physicians,

Edo in the Rain. *This facsimile of an ukiyo-e ("floating world") print by Hiroshige (1797–1858) depicts one of several bridges in the bustling city of Edo (later Tokyo), with Mount Fuji in the background.*

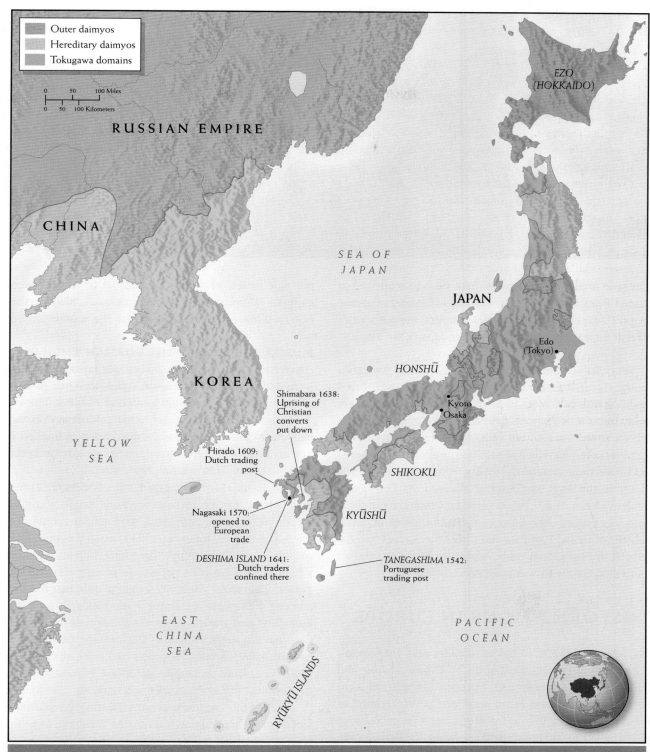

Outer daimyos
Hereditary daimyos
Tokugawa domains

0   50   100 Miles
0   50   100 Kilometers

RUSSIAN EMPIRE

CHINA

EZO (HOKKAIDO)

SEA OF JAPAN

JAPAN

Edo (Tokyo)

HONSHŪ

KOREA

Shimabara 1638:
Uprising of
Christian
converts
put down

Kyoto
Osaka

Hirado 1609:
Dutch trading
post

YELLOW SEA

SHIKOKU

Nagasaki 1570:
opened to
European
trade

KYŪSHŪ

DESHIMA ISLAND 1641:
Dutch traders
confined there

TANEGASHIMA 1542:
Portuguese
trading post

EAST CHINA SEA

PACIFIC OCEAN

RYŪKYŪ ISLANDS

MAP 13.6 | Tokugawa Japan, 1603–1867

The Tokugawa shoguns created a strong central state in Japan at this time.

- According to this map, how extensive was their control?

- What foreign states were interested in trade with Japan?

- How did Tokugawa leaders attempt to control relations with foreign states and other entities?

Portuguese Arriving in Japan. *In the 1540s, the Portuguese arrival on the islands of Japan sparked a fascination with the strange costumes and the great ships of these "southern barbarians" (so called because they had approached Japan from the south). Silk-screen paintings depicted Portuguese prowess in exaggerated form, such as in the impossible height of the fore and aft of the vessel pictured here.*

and painters). A few Japanese were permitted to learn Dutch and to study European technology, shipbuilding, and medicine (see Chapter 14). By limiting such encounters, the authorities ensured that foreigners would not threaten Japan's security.

New World silver and climate change challenged the major Asian states. Mughal rulers dealt with famines and rebellions while guiding South Asia to its greatest power and influence. China's dynastic change from the Ming to the Qing did not diminish its wealth and power, although irregular supplies of silver (glut followed by scarcity) produced inflation and altered relations between the state and outlying regions. The Ottomans expanded into the Arab world and challenged the Portuguese in the Indian Ocean, but suffered significant military and territorial losses in Europe. The Europeans established commercial footholds in South and East Asia and thrust themselves into the already brisk Indian Ocean trade, while the Dutch created an export-oriented colony in Southeast Asia.

TRANSFORMATIONS IN EUROPE

Between 1600 and 1750, religious conflict and the consolidation of dynastic power, spurred on by climate change and long-distance trade, transformed Europe. Commercial centers shifted northward, and Spain and Portugal lost ground to England and France. Farther to the north, the state of Muscovy expanded dramatically to become the sprawling Russian Empire.

Expansion and Dynastic Change in Russia

During this period, the Russian Empire became the world's largest-ever state. It gained positions on the Baltic Sea and the Pacific Ocean, and it established political borders with both the Qing Empire and Japan. These momentous shifts involved

the elimination of steppe nomads as an independent force. Culturally, Europeans as well as Russians debated whether Russia belonged more to Europe or to Asia. The answer was both.

MUSCOVY BECOMES THE RUSSIAN EMPIRE The principality of Moscow, or Muscovy, like Japan and China, used territorial expansion and commercial networks to consolidate a powerful state. Originally a mixture of Slavs, Finnish tribes, Turkic speakers, and many others, **Muscovy** expanded to become a huge empire that spanned parts of Europe, much of northern Asia, numerous North Pacific islands, and even—for a time—a corner of North America (Alaska).

Like Japan, Russia emerged out of turmoil. Three factors inspired the regime to seize territory: security concerns, the ambitions of private individuals, and religious conviction. Security concerns were foremost, as expansion was inseparable from security. Because the steppe, stretching deep into Asia, remained a highway for nomadic peoples (especially descendants of the powerful Mongols), Muscovy sought to dominate the areas south and east of Moscow. Beginning in the 1590s, Russian authorities built forts and trading posts along Siberian rivers at the same time that privateers, enticed by the fur trade, pushed even farther east. By 1639, the state's borders had reached the Pacific. Now Muscovy claimed an empire straddling Eurasia and incorporating peoples of many languages and religions. (See Map 13.7.)

Much of this expansion occurred during the colorful and violent reign of Ivan IV, known as Ivan the Terrible, a name that could also be translated as "awesome" (r. 1547–1584). A Muscovite grand prince, he restyled himself "tsar of all of the Russias," ruling in the northern reaches of a European-Asian crossroads that lacked natural borders. The many invasions and counterinvasions that had taken place in the past persuaded Ivan that the only way to achieve security against hostile neighbors was to conquer them first and then rule in an autocratic fashion. Ivan's great military victory in 1552 over the powerful Tatar Khanate,

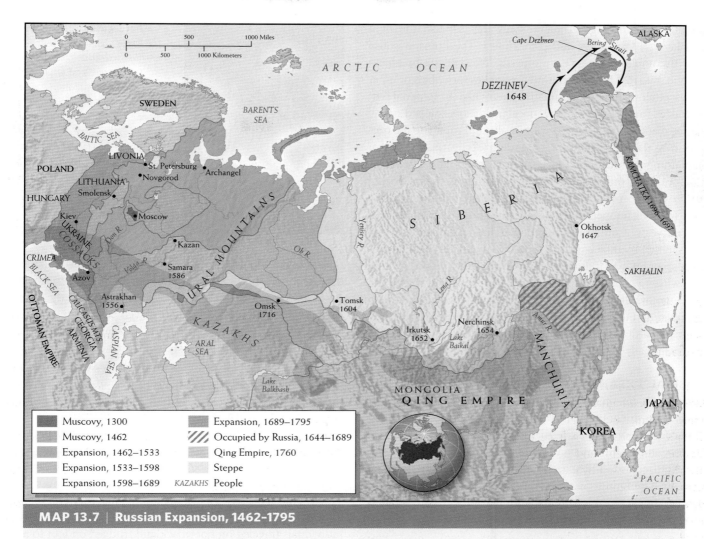

MAP 13.7 | Russian Expansion, 1462–1795

The state of Muscovy incorporated vast territories through overland expansion as it grew and became the Russian Empire. It did so in part because of its geographical position and its strategic needs.

- Using the map key, identify how many different expansions the Russian Empire underwent between 1462 and 1795 and in what directions generally.
- With what countries and cultures did the Russian Empire come into contact?
- What drove such dramatic expansion?

centered on the Volga River city of Kazan, began a transformation of his largely Orthodox, Christian, Russian-speaking realm through the incorporation of large Muslim, Turkic-speaking populations. Ivan also sponsored expeditions that led to the conquest of even vaster territories in the east, which came to be known as Siberia. His ambitions to expand in the south were blocked by the Ottoman Empire. In the northwest, despite twenty-four years of war against Sweden, Poland-Lithuania, and the Teutonic Knights of Livonia, he failed to conquer non-Russian territories on the Baltic Sea. His reign devolved into internal violence, and he even threatened to abdicate and become a monk. Ivan killed his son and heir in a violent argument, leaving the throne to

an enfeebled and childless son, so that the dynasty came to an end in 1598. Remarkably, in 1613, the various elite clans freely decided to restore autocratic rule, choosing the Romanov family.

Ivan's paradoxical reign, full of both dynamism and destruction, set Moscow on an expansionist course toward a transcontinental empire, a state of many religions, and a zealous commitment to strongly authoritarian rule. Like the Ottoman and Qing dynasts, Romanov tsars and their aristocratic supporters would retain power into the twentieth century.

ABSOLUTIST GOVERNMENT AND SERFDOM In the seventeenth and eighteenth centuries, the Romanovs created an absolutist system of government. Only the tsar had the right to make war, tax, judge, and coin money. The Romanovs also made the nobles serve as state officials. Now Russia became a despotic state that had no political assemblies for nobles or other groups, other than mere consultative bodies like the imperial senate. Indeed, away from Moscow, local aristocrats enjoyed nearly unlimited authority in exchange for loyalty and tribute to the tsar.

During this period, Russia's peasantry bore the burden of maintaining the wealth of the small nobility and the monarchy. Most peasant families gathered into communes, isolated rural worlds where people helped one another deal with plummeting Little Ice Age temperatures, severe landlords, and occasional poor harvests. Communes functioned like extended kin networks in that members reciprocated favors and chores. The typical peasant hut was a single chamber heated by a wood-burning stove with no chimney. Livestock and humans often shared the same quarters. In 1649, peasants were legally bound as serfs to the nobles and the tsar, meaning they had to perform obligatory services and deliver part of their produce to their lords. The lords essentially controlled all aspects of their serfs' lives.

IMPERIAL EXPANSION AND MIGRATION Three factors were key to Russia's becoming an empire: (1) the conquest of Siberia, which brought vast territory and riches in furs; (2) incorporation of the fertile southern steppes, known as Ukraine; and (3) victory in a prolonged war with Sweden. Peter the Great (r. 1682–1725) accomplished the victory in Sweden, after which he founded a new capital at St. Petersburg. Thereafter, Russia developed a formidable military-fiscal state bureaucracy, but the aristocracy remained predominant.

Catherine the Great. *Catherine the Great styled herself an enlightened despot, furthering the Russian Empire's adaptation of European high culture.*

Under Peter's successors, including the hard-nosed Catherine the Great, Russia added even more territory. Catherine placed her former lover on the Polish throne and subsequently, together with the Austrians and Prussians, carved up the medieval state of Poland. Her victories against the Ottomans allowed Russia to annex Ukraine, the grain-growing "breadbasket" of eastern Europe. By the late eighteenth century, Russia's grasp extended from the Baltic Sea through the heart of Europe, Ukraine, and the Crimea on the Black Sea and into the ancient lands of Armenia and Georgia in the Caucasus Mountains.

The Russian Empire was a harsh but colossal space that induced the movement of peoples within it. Many people migrated eastward, into Siberia. Some were fleeing serfdom; others were being deported for having rejected changes in the state's official Eastern Orthodox religious services. Battling astoundingly harsh temperatures and frigid Arctic winds, these individuals traveled on horseback and trudged on foot to resettle in the east. But the difficulties of clearing forested lands or planting crops in boggy Siberian soils, combined with extraordinarily harsh winters, meant that many settlers died or tried to return. Isolation was a problem, too. There was no established land route back to Moscow until the 1770s, when exiles completed the Great Siberian Post Road through the swamps and peat bogs of western Siberia. The writer Anton Chekhov later called it "the longest and ugliest road in the whole world."

Economic and Political Fluctuations in Western Europe

During this period, the European economies became more commercialized. As in Asia, developments in distant parts of the world shaped the region's economic upturns and downturns. Compounding these pressures was the continuation of dynastic rivalries and religious conflicts.

Underlying the economic and political fluctuations taking place in Europe, especially the brutal warfare of the Thirty Years'

Nenets Hunters. *Hunters of the Nenets tribe in far North Asia's treeless tundra show off their warm animal-skin clothing and self-fashioned weapons, as depicted in a 1620 engraving by Theodore de Bry, one of the first Europeans to come into contact with them.*

War, was the powerful impact of the Little Ice Age. Freezing temperatures shortened agricultural growing seasons by one to two months. The result was escalating prices for essential grain products, now in short supply. Famines and death from diseases because of malnourishment followed. Among the Europeans hardest hit at the end of the seventeenth century were the populations of France, Norway, and Sweden, where starvation took the lives of 10 percent of the population. Moreover, declining tax yields prevented European governments from offering vital services to their suffering citizens. The cooling had a few benefits, however, among which were the magnificent violins, still prized today, crafted by Antonio Stradivari (1644–1737) from the denser wood that freezing temperatures produced.

THE THIRTY YEARS' WAR For a century after Martin Luther broke with the Catholic Church (see Chapter 12), religious warfare raged in Europe. So did contests over territory, power, and trade. The **Thirty Years' War** (1618–1648) reflected all of these—a war between Protestant princes and the Catholic emperor for religious predominance in central Europe; a struggle for regional control among Catholic powers (the Spanish and Austrian Habsburgs and the French); and a bid for independence (from Spain) by the Dutch, who wanted to trade and worship as they liked.

The brutal conflict began as a struggle between Protestants and Catholics within the Habsburg Empire, but it soon became a war for preeminence in Europe. It took the lives of civilians as well as soldiers. In total, fighting, disease, and famine wiped out a third of the German states' urban population and two-fifths of their rural population. The war also depopulated Sweden and Poland. Ultimately, the Treaty of Westphalia (1648) stated, in essence, that as there was a rough balance of power between Protestant and Catholic states, they would simply have to put up with each other. The Dutch won their independence, but the war's enormous costs provoked severe discontent in Spain, France, and England. Central Europe did not recover in economic or demographic terms for more than a century.

The Thirty Years' War transformed war making. Whereas most medieval struggles had been sieges between nobles leading small armies, centralized states fielding standing armies now waged grand-scale campaigns. The war also changed the ranks of soldiers: as the conflict ground on, local enlisted men defending their king, country, and faith gave way to hired mercenaries or criminals doing forced service. Even officers, who previously obtained their stripes by purchase or royal decree, now had to earn them. Gunpowder, cannons, and handguns became standardized. By the eighteenth century, Europe's wars featured huge standing armies boasting a professional officer corps, deadly artillery, and long supply lines bringing food and ammunition to the front. The costs—material and human—of war began to soar and put added pressure on empires to expand and compete for overseas spoils.

WESTERN EUROPEAN ECONOMIES In spite of warfare's toll on economic activity, the European states enjoyed significant commercial expansion. Northern Europe gained more than did the south, however. Spain, for example, started losing ground to its rivals as the costs of defending its empire soared and merchants from northern Europe cut in on its trading networks. The weighty costs of its involvement in the Thirty Years' War dealt the Spanish economy a final, disastrous blow. Other previously robust economies also suffered under the pressures of greater economic connection and competition. Venice, for

The Thirty Years' War. *The mercenary armies of the Thirty Years' War were renowned for pillaging and tormenting the civilians of central Europe. In this engraving by Jacques Callot, the townsfolk exact revenge on some of these soldiers, hanging many, as an accompanying caption claims, "damned and infamous thieves, like bad fruit, from this tree."*

Amsterdam Stock Exchange. *The high concentration of merchants in Amsterdam naturally gave way to the world's first stock exchange in the seventeenth century. This diverse gathering of men trading stocks and preparing to participate in auctions, as depicted by renowned painter Emanuel de Witte, was a common sight throughout the Dutch Golden Age.*

example, which before the era of transoceanic shipping had been Europe's chief gateway to Asia, saw its economy decline.

As European commercial dynamism shifted northward, the Dutch led the way with innovative commercial practices and a new mercantile elite. They specialized in shipping and in financing regional and long-distance trade. Their famous *fluits-chips* carried heavy, bulky cargoes (like Baltic wood) with relatively small crews. Now shipping costs throughout the Atlantic world dropped as Dutch ships transported their own and other countries' goods. Amsterdam's merchants founded an exchange bank, established a rudimentary stock exchange, and pioneered systems of underwriting and insuring cargoes.

England and France also became commercial powerhouses, establishing aggressive policies to promote national business and drive out competitors. Consider the English Navigation Act of 1651. By stipulating that only English ships could carry goods between the mother country and its colonies, it protected English shippers and merchants—especially from the Dutch. The English subsequently launched several effective trade wars against Holland. The French, too, followed aggressive mercantilist policies and ultimately joined forces with England to invade Holland.

Economic development was not limited to port towns: the countryside, too, enjoyed breakthroughs in production. In northwestern Europe, investments in water drainage, larger livestock herds, and improved cultivation practices generated much greater yields. Also, a four-field crop rotation involving wheat, clover, barley, and turnips kept nutrients in the soil and provided year-round fodder for livestock. As a result (and as we have seen many times throughout history), increased output supported a growing urban population. By contrast, in Spain and Italy, agricultural change and population growth came more slowly.

Production rose most where the organization of rural property changed. In England, for example, in a movement known as **enclosure**, landowners took control of lands that traditionally had been common property serving local needs. Claiming exclusive rights to these lands, the landowners planted new crops or pastured sheep with the aim of selling the products in distant markets. The largest landowners put their farms in the hands of tenants, who hired wage laborers to till, plant, and harvest. Thus, in England, peasant agriculture gave way to farms run by wealthy families who exploited the marketplace to buy what they needed (including labor) and to sell what they produced. In this regard, England led the way in a Europe-wide process of commercializing the countryside.

DYNASTIC MONARCHIES: FRANCE AND ENGLAND

European monarchs had varying success with centralizing state power. In France, Louis XIII (r. 1610–1643) and especially his chief minister, Cardinal Richelieu, concentrated power in the hands of the king. After 1614, kings refused to convene the Estates-General, a medieval advisory body. Composed of representatives of three groups—the clergy (the First Estate, those who pray), the nobility (the Second Estate, those who fight), and the unprivileged remainder of the population (the Third Estate, those who work)—the Estates-General was an obstacle to the king's full empowerment. Instead of sharing power, the king and his counselors wanted him to rule free of external checks, to create—in the words of the age—an **absolute monarchy**. The ruler's authority was to be complete and his state free of bloody disorders. His rule would be lawful; but he, not his jurists, would dictate the last legal word. If the king made a mistake, only God could call him to account. Thus the French, like most Europeans, believed in the "divine right of kings," a political belief not greatly different from imperial China, where the emperor was thought to rule with the mandate of heaven.

In absolutist France, privileges and state offices flowed from the king's grace. All patronage networks ultimately linked to the king. The great palace Louis XIV built at Versailles teemed with nobles from all over France seeking favor, dressing according to the king's expensive fashion code, and attending the latest tragedies, comedies, and concerts. Just as the Japanese shogun monitored the daimyos by keeping their families in Edo, Louis XIV kept a watchful eye on the French nobility at Versailles.

The French dynastic monarchy provided a model of absolute rule for other European dynasts, like the Habsburgs of the Holy Roman Empire, the Hohenzollerns of Prussia, and the Romanovs of Muscovy. The king and his ministers controlled all public power, while other social groups, from the nobility to the peasantry, had no formal body to represent their interests. Nonetheless, French absolutist government was not as absolute as the king wished. Pockets of stalwart Protestants practiced their religion secretly in the plateau villages of central France. Peasant disturbances continued. Criticism of court life, wars, and religious policies filled anonymous pamphlets, jurists' notebooks, and courtiers' private journals. Members of the nobility also grumbled about their political misfortunes, but since the king would not call the Estates-General, they had no formal way to express their concerns.

England might also have evolved into an absolutist regime, but there were important differences between England and France. Queen Elizabeth (r. 1558–1603) and her successors used many policies similar to those of the French monarchy, such as control of patronage (to grant privileges) and elaborate court festivities. Also, refusing to share her power with a man, the "Virgin Queen" never married and exerted sole control over church, military, and aristocracy. However, the English Parliament remained an important force. Whereas the French kings did not need the consent of the Estates-General to enact taxes, the English monarchs had to convene Parliament to raise money.

Under Elizabeth's successors, fierce quarrels broke out over taxation, religion, and royal efforts to rule without parliamentary consent. Tensions ran high between Puritans (who preferred a simpler form of worship and more egalitarian church government) and Anglicans (who supported the state-sponsored, hierarchically organized Church of England headed by the king). Social and economic grievances led to civil war in the 1640s and an ultimate victory for the parliamentary army (largely Puritan)—and the beheading of King Charles I. Twelve years of government as a commonwealth without a king followed.

In 1660, the monarchy was restored, but without resolving issues of religious tolerance and the king's relation to Parliament. Charles II and his successor, James II, aroused opposition by their autocracy and secret efforts to bring England back into the Catholic fold. The conflict between an aspiring absolutist throne and Parliament's insistence on shared sovereignty and Protestant succession culminated in the Glorious Revolution of 1688–1689. In a bloodless upheaval, James II fled to France and Parliament offered the crown to William of Orange and his wife, Mary (a Protestant). The conflict's outcome established the principle that English monarchs must rule in conjunction with Parliament. Although the Church of England was reaffirmed as the official state church, Presbyterians and Jews were allowed to practice their religions. Catholic worship, still officially forbidden, was tolerated as long as the Catholics kept quiet. By 1700, then, England's nobility and merchant classes had a guaranteed

Versailles. *Louis XIV's Versailles, just southwest of Paris, was a hunting lodge that was converted at colossal cost in the 1660s–1670s into a grand royal chateau with expansive grounds. The image presented here was painted by the French artist Pierre Patel in 1688. Much envied and imitated across Europe, the palace became the epicenter of a luxurious court life that included entertainment such as plays and musical offerings, state receptions, royal hunts, boating, and gambling. Thousands of nobles at Versailles vied with each other for closer proximity to the king in the performance of court rituals.*

Queen Elizabeth of England. *This portrait (c. 1600, by the painter Robert Peake, the Elder) depicts an idealized Queen Elizabeth near the end of her long reign. The queen is pictured riding in a procession in the midst of an admiring crowd composed of the most important nobles of the realm.*

say in public affairs and assurance that state activity would privilege the propertied classes as well as the ruler.

Events in France and England stimulated much political writing. In England, Thomas Hobbes published *Leviathan* (1651), a defense of the state's absolute power over all competing forces. John Locke published *Two Treatises of Civil Government* (1689), which argued not only for the natural rights to liberty and property but also for the rights of peoples to form a government and then to disband and re-form it when it did not live up to its contract. French theorists also proposed new ways of conducting politics and making law and debated the extent to which elites could check the king. As the eighteenth century unfolded, the question of where sovereignty lay grew more pressing.

MERCANTILIST WARS The rise of new powers in Europe intensified rivalries for control of the Atlantic system. As conflicts over colonies and sea-lanes replaced earlier religious and territorial struggles, commercial struggles became worldwide wars. Across the globe, European empires constantly skirmished over control of trade and territory. English and Dutch trading companies took aim at Portuguese outposts in Asia and the Americas and then at each other. Ports in India suffered repeated assaults and counterassaults. In response, European powers built huge navies to protect their colonies and trade routes and to attack their rivals. After 1715, mercantilist wars occurred mainly outside Europe, as empires feuded over colonial possessions. Each round of warfare ratcheted up the scale and cost of fighting.

The **Seven Years' War** (known as the French and Indian War in the United States) marked the culmination of this rivalry.

Fought from 1756 to 1763, it saw Native Americans, African slaves, Bengali princes, Filipino militiamen, and European foot soldiers dragged into a contest over imperial possessions and control of the seas. Some fleets, like the French at the Battle of Quiberon Bay, were dispatched to the bottom of the ocean. Some fortresses, like Spain's Havana and France's Quebec City, fell to invaders. What sparked the war was a skirmish of British colonial troops (featuring a lieutenant colonel named George Washington) allied with Seneca warriors against French soldiers in the Ohio Valley (see Map 13.2 for North American references). In India, the war had a decisive outcome, for here the East India Company trader Robert Clive rallied 850 European officers and 2,100 Indian recruits to defeat the French (there were but 40 French artillerymen) and their 50,000 Maratha allies at Plassey. The British seized the upper hand—over everyone—in India. Not only did the British drive off the French from the rich Bengali interior, but they also crippled Indian rulers' resistance against European intruders (see Map 12.4 for India references).

The Seven Years' War changed the balance of power around the world. Britain emerged as the foremost colonial empire. Its rivals took a pounding: France lost its North American colonies, and Spain lost Florida (though it gained the Louisiana Territory west of the Mississippi in a secret deal with France). In India, as well, the French were losers and had to acknowledge British supremacy in the wealthy provinces of Bihar and Bengal. But overwhelmingly, the biggest losers were indigenous peoples everywhere. With the rise of one empire over all others, it was harder for Native Americans to play the Europeans off against each other. Maratha princes faced the same problem. Clearly, as worlds became more entangled, the gaps between winners and losers grew more pronounced.

Wealth from long-distant trade and intense warfare led to the rise of militarily powerful, monarchical states in Europe. In the long run, beginning in the eighteenth century and coming to fulfillment in the nineteenth, the most dynamic of these states, notably Britain and France, ultimately joined by a newly unified Germany, were able to dominate the great states of Afro-Eurasia economically and militarily.

CONCLUSION

A radical decline in temperatures worldwide made the seventeenth century a time of famine, dying, epidemic disease, and political turmoil that produced regime change in China, Persia, and England and threatened the rulers of the Ottoman and Mughal Empires. Yet by the 1750s, the world's regions were more economically connected than ever. The process of integrating the resources of previous worlds apart that had begun with Columbus's voyages intensified during this period. Traders shipped a wider variety of commodities—from Baltic wood to Indian cotton, from New World silver and sugar to Chinese silks and porcelain—over longer distances. People increasingly wore clothes manufactured elsewhere, consumed beverages made from products cultivated in far-off locations, and used imported guns to settle local conflicts.

Everywhere, this integration and the consumer opportunities that it made possible came at a heavy price. Nowhere was it more costly than in the Americas, where colonization and exploitation led to the expulsion of Indians from their lands and the decimation of their numbers. The cost was also very high for the millions of Africans forced across the Atlantic to work New World plantations and for the millions more who did not survive the journey.

Along with sugar, silver was the product from the Americas that most transformed global trading networks and that showed how greater entanglements could both enrich and destabilize. Although Spanish colonizers mined New World silver and shipped it to western Europe and Asia, it was Spain's main competitors in Europe that gained the upper hand in the seventeenth and eighteenth centuries. Nearly one-third of the silver from the New World ended up in China as payment for products like porcelains and silks that consumers still regarded as the world's finest manufactures. But if China's economy remained vibrant, silver did play a part in the fall of one dynasty and the rise of another. For the Ottoman, Mughal, and Safavid Empires, the influx of silver created rampant inflation and undermined their previous economic autonomy.

Certain societies coped with climate change and increased commercial exchange more successfully than others. The Safavid and Ming dynasties could not withstand the pressures; both collapsed. The Spanish, Ottoman, and Mughal Empires managed to survive but faced increasing pressure from aggressive rivals. More than any other country, England survived the travails of climate change, but witnessed the execution of a monarch (Charles I) and an autocratic Puritan government under Oliver Cromwell. By century's end, England had a new empire, a strengthened parliament, and an energetic merchant class ready to dominate global markets. For newcomers to the integrating world, the opportunity to trade helped support new dynasties. Japan and Russia emerged on the world stage. But even in these newer regimes, commerce and competition did not erase conflict. To the contrary, while the world was more together economically than ever before, greater prosperity for some hardly translated into peace for most.

The Americas

- England, France, and Holland join Spain and Portugal as colonial powers in the Americas.

- The English and French colonies in the Caribbean become the world's major exporters of sugar.

Africa

- The Atlantic slave trade increases to record proportions, creating gender imbalances, impoverishing some regions, and elevating the power of slave-supplying states.

Southeast Asia

- The Dutch East India Company takes over the major islands of Southeast Asia.

The Islamic World

- World trade destabilizes the Safavid, Ottoman, and Mughal Empires.

- The Little Ice Age destabilizes the Ottoman state and leads to a powerful but ultimately unsuccessful rebellion, the Celali revolts.

East Asia

- The Ming dynasty in China, poorly administered and suffering from the effects of climate change, loses the mandate of heaven and is replaced by the Qing.

- The Tokugawa shogunate unifies Japan and limits the influence of Europeans in the country.

Europe

- Tsarist Russia expands toward the Baltic Sea and the Pacific Ocean and becomes the largest state in the world.

- The Thirty Years' War is partly the result of a dramatic cooling of the global climate and enmity between Protestant and Catholic countries.

- Europe recovers from the Thirty Years' War (1618–1648), with Holland, England, and France emerging as economic powerhouses.

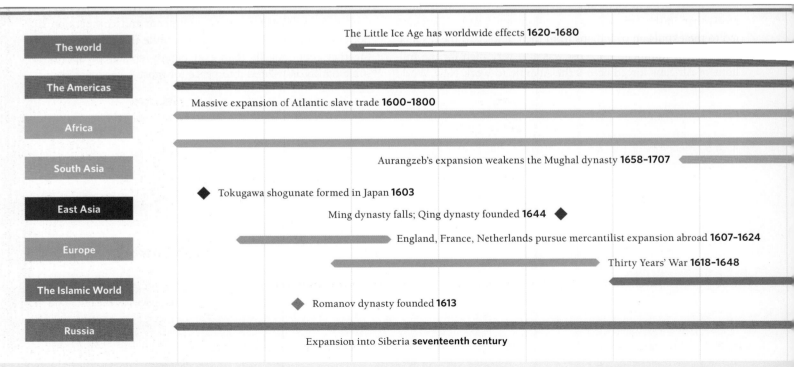

The world	The Little Ice Age has worldwide effects **1620–1680**
The Americas	
Africa	Massive expansion of Atlantic slave trade **1600–1800**
South Asia	Aurangzeb's expansion weakens the Mughal dynasty **1658–1707**
East Asia	Tokugawa shogunate formed in Japan **1603**
	Ming dynasty falls; Qing dynasty founded **1644**
Europe	England, France, Netherlands pursue mercantilist expansion abroad **1607–1624**
	Thirty Years' War **1618–1648**
The Islamic World	
	Romanov dynasty founded **1613**
Russia	Expansion into Siberia **seventeenth century**

1600   1650

KEY TERMS

STUDY QUESTIONS

1. **Identify** the main steps in the integration of global trade networks during this period, and **describe** some examples of resistance to this integration.

2. **Define** mercantilism, and **analyze** how mercantilist practices affected all regions of the Atlantic world between 1600 and 1750. Whose interests did mercantilism serve, and at whose expense?

3. **Explain** the global effects of the Little Ice Age.

4. **Describe** the plantation complex in the Caribbean. Why was it so valued by Europeans relative to other regions of the Americas?

5. **Analyze** how the Atlantic slave trade reshaped African societies socially and politically. Which regions and groups benefited from Africa's growing entanglements in global commerce?

6. **Discuss** the effect of New World silver and increased trade on Asian empires, and **compare** their different responses.

7. **Analyze** how global trade affected the Ottoman and Mughal Empires during this era. How did each regime respond to these growing entanglements?

8. **Analyze** to what extent the Tokugawa shogunate succeeded in creating a strong central government in Japan. How did it avoid the problems associated with expanding trade that many other dynasties faced at this time?

9. **Compare and contrast** the expansionist policies of the Russian state with those pursued by the British and French regimes during this period. How were they similar and how were they different?

10. **Compare and contrast** the impact of trade and religion on state power in various regions. In Europe and Asia, did certain dynasties hold an advantage over others in controlling commercial networks and using them to enrich their societies?

11. **Evaluate** how the European desire for consumer goods had an impact on the global economy at this time.

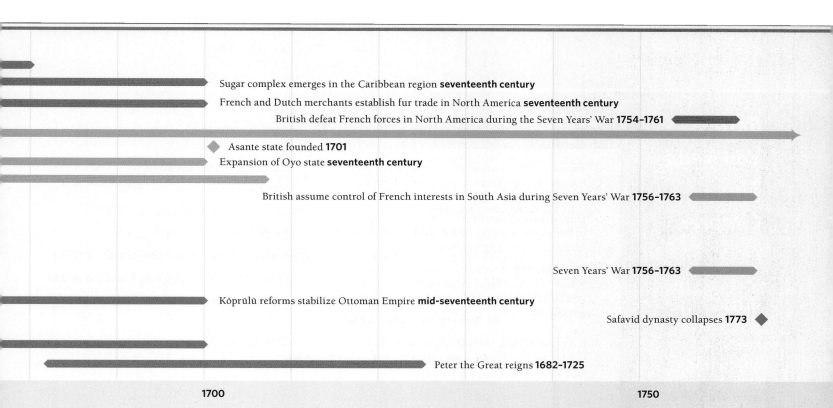

Sugar complex emerges in the Caribbean region **seventeenth century**

French and Dutch merchants establish fur trade in North America **seventeenth century**

British defeat French forces in North America during the Seven Years' War **1754–1761**

Asante state founded **1701**

Expansion of Oyo state **seventeenth century**

British assume control of French interests in South Asia during Seven Years' War **1756–1763**

Seven Years' War **1756–1763**

Köprülü reforms stabilize Ottoman Empire **mid-seventeenth century**

Safavid dynasty collapses **1773**

Peter the Great reigns **1682–1725**

1700   1750

14

Cultures of Splendor and Power, 1500–1780

FOCUS QUESTIONS

- What were the connections between cultural growth and the creation of a global market?

- In what ways did each culture in this period reflect the ideas of the state in which it was produced? How were the various cultures alike and how were they different in this regard?

- What were the different responses to foreign cultures across Afro-Eurasia in the period 1500–1780? How were they similar and how were they different?

- How did hybrid cultures emerge in the Americas, and what was the connection between these cultures and Enlightenment ideology?

- In what ways did race and cultural differences play a role in the process of global integration?

In 1664, a sixteen-year-old girl from New Spain asked her parents for permission to attend the university in the capital. Although she had mastered Greek logic, taught Latin, and become a proficient mathematician, she had two strikes against her: she was a woman, and her thinking ran against the grain of the Catholic Church. So keen was she to pursue her studies that she proposed to disguise herself as a man. But her parents denied her requests, and instead of attending university she entered a convent in Mexico City, where she spent the rest of her life. Fortunately, the convent turned out to be a sanctuary for her. There she studied science and mathematics and composed remarkable poetry. Sor (Sister) Juana Inés de la Cruz was the bard of a new world where people mixed in faraway places, where new wealth created new customs, and where new ideas began to take hold. One of her poems, "You Men," begins: "Silly, you men—so very adept / at wrongly faulting womankind, not seeing you're alone to blame / for faults you plant in woman's mind." Her poetry illustrates how new discoveries and new knowledge challenged old ways. But her life story also reflects the fierce resistance to new ways. Sor Juana's poetry enraged church authorities, who forced her to recant her words and who burned her books. Only the intervention of the viceroy's wife prevented officials from torching the nun's complete works before she died of plague in 1695.

Sor Juana's story attests to the conflicts between new ideas and old orders that occurred once the entanglements of commerce and the consolidation of empires fostered knowledge of foreign ways. On the one hand, global commerce created riches that supported the arts, architecture, and scientific ventures. On the other, experimentations in new ways caused discomfort among defenders of the old order and provoked backlashes against innovation.

This chapter explores how global commerce enriched and reshaped cultures in the centuries after the Americas ceased to be worlds apart from Afro-Eurasia. Profiting from trade in New World commodities, many rulers and merchants displayed their power by commissioning fabulous works of art and majestic palaces and sprawling plazas. These cultural splendors were meant to impress. They also demonstrated the growing connections between distant societies, reflecting how exotic, borrowed influences could blend with domestic traditions. Book production and consumption soared, with some publications finding their way around the world. The spread of books and ideas and increasing cultural contact led to experiments in religious tolerance and helped foster cultural diversity. Yet even as Europeans, who were the greatest beneficiaries of New World riches, claimed to advance new universal truths, cultural productions worldwide still showed the resilience of local traditions.

TRADE AND CULTURE

For many groups, the period's global cultural flourishing owed much to burgeoning world trade, which allowed some rulers to consolidate wealth, administration, and military power. These rulers were eager to patronize the arts as a way to legitimize their power and reflect their cultural sophistication. In Europe, monarchs known as enlightened absolutists restricted the clergy and nobility and hired loyal bureaucrats who championed the knowledge of the new age. British monarchs, though not absolutists (because they shared power with Parliament), followed suit. Mughal emperors, Safavid shahs, and Ottoman sultans glorified their regimes by bringing artists and artisans from all over the world to give an Islamic flavor to their major cities and buildings. Rulers in China and Japan also looked to artists to extol their achievements. And in Africa, the wealth garnered from slave trading underwrote cultural productions of extraordinary merit.

Of course, some rulers and polities were more eager for change than others. Moreover, certain societies—in the Americas and the South Pacific, for example—found that contact, conquest, and commerce undermined indigenous cultural life. Although Europeans and native peoples often exchanged ideas and practices, these transfers were mediated by imbalances in power.

Both Amerindians and Africans, for example, adapted to European missionizing by creating mixed forms of religious worship—but only because they were under pressure to do so. Europeans absorbed much from Native Americans and African slaves but did not share sovereignty or wealth in return.

Despite the unifying aspects of world trade, each society retained core aspects of its individuality. Ruling classes disseminated values based on cherished classical texts and long-established moral and religious principles. They used space in new ways to establish and project their power. (See Current Trends in World History: The Political Uses of Space.) They mapped geographies and wrote histories according to their traditional visions of the universe. Even as global trade drew their attention outward, societies celebrated their achievements in politics, economics, and culture with pride in their own heritages.

In 1500, the world's most dynamic cultures were in Asia, in areas profiting from the Indian Ocean and China Sea trades. It was in China and the Islamic world that the spice and luxury trades first flourished; here, too, rulers had successfully established political stability and centralized control of taxation, law making, and military force. This often involved recruiting people from diverse backgrounds and promoting secular (nonreligious) education. In the Ottoman, Ming, and Mughal Empires, for example, while older ways did not die out, both trade and empire building contributed to the spread of knowledge about distant people and foreign cultures.

CULTURE IN THE ISLAMIC WORLD

For centuries, Muslim elites had generously funded cultural development. As the Ottoman, Safavid, and Mughal Empires gained greater expanses of territory in the sixteenth and seventeenth centuries, they acquired new resources to fund more such pursuits. Rulers supported new schools and building projects, and the elite produced books, artworks, and luxury goods. Cultural life reflected the politics of empire building, as emperors and elites sought greater prestige by patronizing intellectuals and artists.

Forged under different empires, Islamic cultural and intellectual life now reflected three distinct worlds. In place of an earlier Islamic cosmopolitanism, unique cultural patterns prevailed within each empire. Although the Ottomans, the Safavids, and the Mughals shared a common faith, each developed a relatively autonomous form of Muslim culture.

The Ottoman Cultural Synthesis

By the sixteenth century, the Ottoman Empire was enjoying a remarkably rich culture that blended ethnic, religious, and linguistic elements exceeding those of previous Islamic empires.

The Ottomans' cultural synthesis accommodated both Sufis (mystics who stressed contemplation and ecstasy through poetry, music, and dance) and ultraorthodox *ulama* (Islamic jurists who stressed tradition and religious law). It also balanced the interests of military men and administrators with those of clerics. Finally, it allowed autonomy to the minority faiths of Christianity and Judaism.

LAW AND OTTOMAN CULTURAL UNITY The Ottoman world achieved cultural unity, above all, by an outstanding intellectual achievement—its system of administrative law. As the empire absorbed diverse cultures and territories, the sultans realized that the *sharia* (Islamic holy law) would not suffice because it was silent on many secular matters. Moreover, the Ottoman state needed comprehensive laws to bridge differences among the many social and legal systems under its rule. Mehmed II, conqueror of Constantinople, began the reform. By recruiting young boys, rather than noblemen, for training as bureaucrats or military men and making them accountable directly to the sultan, he fashioned a professional bureaucracy with unswerving loyalty to the ruler. Mehmed's successor, Suleiman the Magnificent and the Lawgiver, continued this work by compiling a comprehensive legal code. The code addressed subjects' rights and duties, proper clothing, and how Muslims were to relate to non-Muslims.

RELIGION AND EDUCATION A sophisticated educational system was crucial for the empire's religious and intellectual integration and for its cultural achievements. Here, too, the Ottomans tolerated difference. They encouraged three educational systems that produced three streams of talent—civil and military bureaucrats, *ulama*, and Sufi masters. The administrative elite attended hierarchically organized schools that culminated in the palace schools at Topkapi (see Chapter 11). In the religious sphere, an equally elaborate system took students from elementary schools (emphasizing reading, writing, and numbers) on to higher schools, or *madrasas* (emphasizing law, religious sciences, the Quran, and the regular sciences). These graduates became *ulama* who served as judges, experts in religious law, or teachers. Another set of schools, *tekkes*, taught the devotional strategies and religious knowledge for students to enter Sufi orders.

Each set of schools created lasting linkages between the ruling elite and the orthodox religious elite. The *tekkes*, especially, helped integrate Muslim peoples living under Ottoman rule. The value that the Ottomans placed on education was evident in the saying that "an hour of learning is worth more than a year of prayer"—and in the advances that those schooled in Ottoman institutions made in astronomy, physics, history, geography, and politics.

NEW IDEAS AND THE ARTS The Ottomans combined inherited traditions with new elements in art as well. For

Islamic Scientists. *This fifteenth-century Persian miniature shows Islamic scholars working with sophisticated navigational and astronomical instruments and reflects the importance that the educated classes in the Islamic world attached to observing and recording the regularities in the natural world. Indeed, many of Europe's advances in sailing drew on knowledge from the Muslim world.*

example, portraiture became popular after the Italian painter Gentile Bellini visited Istanbul and composed a portrait of Mehmed II. In other areas, though, the Ottomans kept their own styles. Consider the magnificent architectural monuments of the sixteenth through eighteenth centuries, including mosques, gardens, tombs, forts, and palaces: these show scant western influence. Nor were the Ottomans interested in western literature or music. They generally believed that God had given the Islamic world a monopoly on truth and enlightenment and that their military successes proved his favor.

The elites' capacity to celebrate their well-being and prosperity spread to the broader public during the so-called Tulip Period during the first half of the eighteenth century. The elite had long admired the tulip's bold colors and graceful blooms, and for centuries the flower served as the sultans' symbol. In fact, both Mehmed the Conqueror and Suleiman the Magnificent grew tulips in the most prestigious courtyards at Topkapi Palace in Istanbul. And many Ottoman warriors heading into battle wore undergarments embroidered with tulips to ensure victory. By the early eighteenth century, tulip designs appeared on tiles, fabrics, and public buildings, and authorities sponsored elaborate tulip festivals.

Ottoman Court Women. *This eighteenth-century watercolor found in Topkapi Palace, in Istanbul, shows various musical instruments being played by court women, who were often called on to provide entertainment.*

Fascination with the tulip represented a widespread delight in worldly things. Commoners, too, now celebrated life's pleasures—in coffeehouses and taverns. Indeed, Ottoman demand for luxury goods grew so extensive (seeking lemons, soap, pepper, metal tools, coffee, and wine) that a well-traveled diplomat looked askance at the supposed wealth of Europe. He wrote, "In most of the provinces [of Europe], poverty is widespread, as a punishment for being infidels. Anyone who travels in these areas must confess that goodness and abundance are reserved for the Ottoman realms" (Mazower, p. 116). Thus, despite challenges from western Europe and foreboding that their best days were behind them, the Ottomans took some foreign elements into their culture while preserving inherited ways.

Safavid Culture

The Safavid Empire in Persia (modern-day Iran) was not as long-lived as the Ottoman Empire, but it was significant for giving Shiism a home base and a location for displaying Shiite culture. The brilliant culture that emerged during the Safavid period provided a unique blend of Shiism and Persia's distinctive historical identity. It found its highest expression in the city of Isfahan, capital of the Safavid state from its creation in 1598 until the empire's end in 1722.

THE SHIITE EMPHASIS The Safavids faced a critical dilemma when they seized power. They owed their rise to the support of Turkish-speaking tribesmen who followed a populist form of Islam. But to hold on to power, the Safavid shahs needed to cultivate powerful and conservative elements of Iranian society: Persian-speaking landowners and orthodox *ulama*. Thus, they turned away from the more popular Turkish-speaking Islamic brotherhoods with their mystical and Sufi qualities and instead built a mixed political and religious system that extolled a Shiite vision of law and society and drew on older Persian imperial traditions. Even after the Safavids lost power, Shiism remained the fundamental religion of the Iranian people.

The most effective architect of a cultural life based on Shiite religious principles and Persian royal absolutism was Shah Abbas I (r. 1587–1629). The location that he chose to display the wealth and royal power of his state, its Persian and Shiite heritages, and its artistic sensibility was the new capital city of Isfahan. For this purpose the shah hired skilled artists and architects to design a city that would dwarf even Delhi and Istanbul, the other showplaces of the Islamic world. The architectural goal was to create an earthly representation of heavenly paradise.

ARCHITECTURE AND THE ARTS The Safavid shahs were unique in seeking to project both absolute authority and accessibility. For example, their dwellings were unlike those of other Afro-Eurasian rulers—such as Topkapi Palace, in Istanbul; the Citadel, in Cairo; and the Red Forts of the Mughals. Those enclosed and fortified buildings enhanced rulers' power by concealing them from their subjects. In contrast, the buildings of Isfahan were open to the outside, demonstrating the Safavid rulers' desire to connect with their people.

Isfahan's centerpiece was the great plaza next to the royal palace and the royal mosque at the capital's heart. The plaza, surrounded by elaborate public and religious buildings, measured nearly 100,000 square yards, only slightly less than Tiananmen Square, in Beijing, and seven times bigger than the plaza of San Marco, in Venice. A suitably impressed seventeenth-century English visitor noted that the plaza was 1,000 paces from north to south and 200 from east to west—far larger than the largest urban squares in London and Paris. He added that it "is without

The Ottomans and the Tulip. *From the earliest times, the Ottomans admired the beauty of the tulip. Left: Sultan Mehmed II smelling a tulip, symbol of the Ottoman sultans. Right: The Ottomans used tulip motifs to decorate tiles in homes and mosques and to decorate pottery wares, as on the plate shown here.*

doubt as spacious, as pleasant, and aromatic a market as any in the universe" (Parker, p. 206).

Other aspects of intellectual life also reflected the elites' aspirations, wealth, and commitment to Shiite principles. Safavid artists perfected the illustrated book, the outstanding example being *The King's Book of Kings*, which contains 250 miniature illustrations demonstrating artists' mastery of three-dimensional representation and their ability to harmonize different colors. Weavers produced highly ornate and beautiful silks and carpets for trade throughout the world, and artisans painted tiles in vibrant colors and created mosaics that adorned mosques and other buildings. Moreover, the Safavids developed an elaborate calligraphy that was the envy of artists throughout the Islamic world. (See Primary Source: Islamic Views of the World.) All of these works celebrated Shiite visions of the sacred while reinforcing the authority and prestige of the empire's ruling elite.

Power and Culture under the Mughals

Like the Safavids and the Ottomans, the Mughals fostered a lavish high culture, supported primarily by taxes on agriculture but reliant on silver for its currency and, at its highpoint, open to global trade. Because they ruled over a large non-Muslim population, the culture that they developed was broad and open. So highly did it value art and learning that it welcomed non-Muslims into its circle. Thus, while Islamic traditions dominated the empire's political and judicial systems, Hindus shared with Muslims the flourishing of learning, music, painting, and architecture. In this arena, aesthetic refinement and philosophical sophistication could bridge religious differences.

RELIGION Mughal rulers were flexible toward their realm's diverse peoples, especially in spiritual affairs. Though its primary

commitment to Islam stood firm, the imperial court also patronized other beliefs, displaying a tolerance that earned it widespread legitimacy. The contrast with Europe, where religious differences drove deep fractures within and between states, was stark.

The promise of an open Islamic high culture found its greatest fulfillment under the emperor Akbar (r. 1556–1605). This skillful military leader was also a popular ruler who allowed common people as well as nobles from all ethnic groups to converse with him at court. Unlike European monarchs, who tried to enforce religious uniformity, Akbar studied comparative religion and hosted regular debates among Hindu, Muslim, Jain, Parsi, and Christian theologians. His quest for universal truths outside the strict *sharia* led him to develop a religion of his own. Ultimately, he introduced at his court a "Divine Faith" (Dīn-i Ilāhī) that was a mix of Quranic, Hindu, Catholic, and other influences; it emphasized piety, prudence, gentleness, liberality, and a yearning for God.

A liberal religious attitude was not limited to Akbar's reign but remained an important feature of Mughal rule. Sufism was the most important expression of this attitude. Dara Shikoh, Emperor Shah Jahan's eldest son, for example, was an accomplished scholar of Sufism. He translated Sanskrit texts into Persian, including the Hindu text *Upanishads*, which, in turn, was translated into French and circulated in Europe. Dara Shikoh declared there was no fundamental difference between Islam and Hinduism. His open religious attitude drew the ire of the orthodox *ulama*, which pressed for the supremacy of Islamic law and upheld religious purity.

A debate between conservative and liberal attitudes also characterized Hinduism. Orthodox writers reiterated Brahman privileges and opposed the entry of women and the shudras (members of the lower caste) in the spiritual sphere. But saints of the Bhakti (devotional) sects offered a different vision. This movement, which had led to the establishment of Sikhism (see Chapter 11), swept through northern India between the fifteenth

Islamic Views of the World

Although maps give the impression of objectivity and geographical precision, they actually reveal the mapmaker's view of the world (via the way the world is arranged, names of locations, areas placed in the center or at the periphery, and accompanying text). In most cultures, official maps located their own major administrative and religious sites at the center of the universe and reflected local elites' ideas about how the world was organized.

The two maps shown here are from the Islamic world. The map of al-Idrisi, dating from the twelfth century, was a standard one of the period. Showing the world as Afro-Eurasian peoples knew it at that time, the map features only three landmasses: Africa, Asia, and Europe. The second map, made in Iran around 1700, was unabashedly Islamic: it offers a grid that measures the distance from any location in the Islamic world to the holy city of Mecca.

QUESTIONS FOR ANALYSIS

- What does each map reveal about the worldview of these Islamic societies?
- What do you think each map was used for?

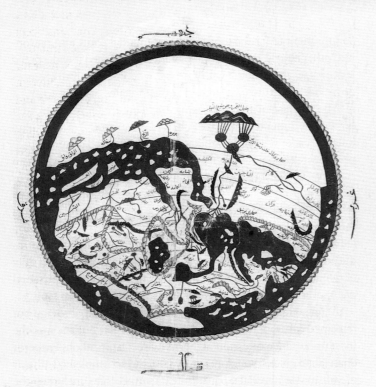

Al-Idrisi map, twelfth century

Iranian map, seventeenth century

and the seventeenth centuries. Devotion to the playful cowherd Krishna, rather than rituals officiated by Brahmans, gained popularity as the path to salvation. One famous Bhakti saint was Mirabai (1498–1547), a woman who was compelled to marry a warrior's son but preferred the company of Krishna's devotees. She composed many poems mocking marriage and asceticism. If Mirabai challenged the prohibition of women in the spiritual sphere, another Bhakti saint, Tukaram (1608–1649),

asserted the fundamental equality of human beings and challenged caste inequality. Yet another saint, Eknath (1533–1599), wrote poems that poked fun at both orthodox Hindus and Muslims and argued that true devotees of God were without caste or creed.

While Persian and Sanskrit functioned as languages of the court and the elite, the Bhakti movement addressed the common folk in regional languages. This promoted the development

Akbar Leading Religious Discussion. *This miniature painting from 1604 shows Akbar receiving Muslim theologians and Jesuits. The Jesuits (in the black robes on the left) hold a page relating, in Persian, the birth of Christ. A lively debate will follow the Jesuits' claims on behalf of Christianity.*

of Marathi, Hindi, Bengali, and other regional vernaculars. It also produced a lively engagement between Sufism and Hindu devotionalism—so much so that scholars cannot determine which tradition is the source of which particular poem. While Bhakti poetry narrated Krishna's story as a Sufi romance, some Sufi poetry began by invoking Allah before turning to Hindu imagery and themes. Sufism spread in popular culture with poetry and songs addressed to daily life, not just an esoteric union with God. Among these were songs for women, including one for those engaged in grinding food grains or spinning thread. These songs nurtured religious devotion and amplified the role of women in popular Islam. Women regularly visited Sufi shrines and prayed for divine intervention in their daily lives.

Religious life under the Mughals at both elite and popular levels presents a rich and diverse picture of dialogue and interaction between different religions, which is at odds with the image of Hindu-Muslim cultural separatism that some religious nationalists today hold.

ARCHITECTURE AND THE ARTS In architecture, too, the Mughals produced masterpieces that blended styles. This was already evident as builders combined Persian, Indian, and Ottoman elements in tombs and mosques under Akbar's predecessors. But Akbar enhanced this mixture in the elaborate city he built at Fatehpur Sikri, beginning in 1571. The buildings included residences for nobles (whose loyalty Akbar wanted), gardens, a drinking and gambling zone, and even an experimental school devoted to studying language acquisition in children. Building the huge complex took a decade, much less time than it took for construction of Louis XIV's comparable royal residence a century later at Versailles.

Akbar's descendant Shah Jahan also patronized architecture and the arts. In 1630, he ordered the building in Agra of a magnificent white marble tomb for his beloved wife, Mumtaz Mahal. Like many other women in the Mughal court, she had been an important political counselor. Designed by an Indian architect of Persian origin, this structure, the **Taj Mahal**, took twenty years and 20,000 workers to build. The 42-acre complex included a main gateway, a garden, minarets, and a mosque. The translucent marble mausoleum lay squarely in the middle of the structure, enclosed by four identical facades and crowned by a majestic central dome rising to 240 feet. The stone inlays of different types and hues, organized in geometric and floral patterns and featuring Quranic verses inscribed in Arabic calligraphy, gave the surface an appearance of delicacy and lightness. Blending Persian and Islamic design with Indian materials and motifs, this poetry in stone represents the most splendid example of Mughal high culture and the combining of cultural traditions. Like Shah Abbas's great plaza, the Taj Mahal gave a sense of refined grandeur to this empire's power and splendor. (See again Current Trends in World History: The Political Uses of Space.)

FOREIGN INFLUENCES VERSUS ISLAMIC CULTURE Under later emperors, Mughal culture remained vibrant although not quite so brilliant. François Bernier, a seventeenth-century French traveler, wrote admiringly of the broad philosophical interests of Danishmand Khan, whom the emperor Aurangzeb had appointed as governor of Delhi. According to Bernier, Khan avidly read the works of the French philosophers Gassendi and Descartes and studied Sanskrit treatises to understand different philosophical traditions. But Aurangzeb, a pious Muslim, favored Islamic arts and sciences. He dismissed many of the court's painters and musicians and in 1669 ordered that all recently built non-Islamic places of worship be torn down. In his court, intellectuals debated whether metaphysics, astronomy, medicine, mathematics, and ethics were of use in the practice of Islam. Women, at least at court, apparently were allowed to pursue the arts, for two of Aurangzeb's daughters were accomplished poets.

Well into the eighteenth century, the Mughal nobility exuded confidence and lived in unrivaled luxury. The presence of foreign scholars and artists enhanced the courtly culture, and the elite eagerly consumed exotic goods from China and

The Political Uses of Space

The use of space for political purposes is a theme we can trace across world history. It has also allowed us to look at political history in new and different ways through a cultural lens by considering the ways rulers used symbols and space to convey this sense of power. In the early modern period, many kings and emperors opted to build grand palaces to create lavish power centers from which they could project their influence over their kingdoms; petitioners and potential rivals would have to come to *them* to ask for favors or to complete their business. Monarchs sculpted these environments, creating a series of spaces, each of them open to a smaller and smaller number of the king's favorites. Both palaces and their surrounding grounds were ornate and splendid, were expensive to construct, and involved the best craftsmen and artists available, which often meant borrowing ideas and designs from neighboring cultures. Palace complexes of this type, built in Beijing, in Istanbul, and just outside of Paris, used space to project the rulers' power and to show who was boss.

The **Forbidden City of Beijing** was the earliest of these impressive sites of royal power (see illustration on p. 427). Its construction took about four years—from 1416 to 1420—although the actual name "Forbidden City" did not appear until 1576. The entrance of the city was straddled by the Meridian Gate, the tallest structure of the entire complex, which towered over all other buildings at more than 115 feet above the ground. It was from this lofty position that the emperor extended his gaze toward his empire as he oversaw various court ceremonies, including the important annual proclamation of the calendar that governed the entire country's agricultural and ritual activities. Foreign emissaries received by the court were also often allowed to use one of the passageways through the gate, where they were expected to be duly awed. As for the officials' daily audience with the emperor, they had to line up outside the Meridian Gate around 3 A.M. before proceeding to the Hall of Supreme Harmony. It was typical of the entire construction project that this impressive hall with vermilion walls and golden tiles was built at considerable cost. For the columns of the hall, fragrant hardwood had to be found in the tiger-ridden forests of the remote southwest, while the mountain forests of the south and southwest were searched for other timbers that eventually made their way to the capital through the Grand Canal.

The **Topkapi Palace**, in Istanbul, capital of the Ottoman Empire, began to take shape in 1458 under Mehmed II and underwent steady expansion over the years (see illustration on p. 414). Topkapi projected royal authority in much the same way as the Forbidden City emphasized the power of Chinese emperors: governing officials worked enclosed within massive walls, and monarchs rarely went outside their inner domain.

More than two centuries later, in the 1670s and 1680s, the French monarch Louis XIV built the **Palace of Versailles** on the site of a royal hunting lodge 11 miles from Paris, the French capital (see illustration on p. 513). This enormously costly complex was built to house Louis's leading clergymen and nobles, who were obliged to visit at least twice a year. Louis hoped that by taking wealthy and powerful men and women away from their local power bases and diverting them with entertainments, he could keep them from plotting new forms of religious schism or challenging his right to rule. Going to Versailles also allowed him to escape the pressures and demands of the population of Paris. Many European monarchs—including Russia's Peter the Great—would build palace complexes modeled on Versailles.

If in China, the Ottoman Empire, and France emperors built what were essentially private spaces in which to conduct and dominate state business, Shah Abbas (r. 1587-1629), of the Safavid Empire, chose to create a great new public space

Europe. Foreign trade also brought in more silver, advancing the money economy and supporting the nobles' sumptuous lifestyles. In addition, the Mughals assimilated European military technology: they hired Europeans as gunners and military engineers in their armies, employed them to forge guns, and bought guns and cannons from them. However, Mughal appreciation for other European knowledge and technology was limited. Thus, when a representative of the English East India Company presented an edition of Mercator's *Maps of the World* to the emperor in 1617, the emperor returned it with the remark that no one could read or understand it. The Mughals, like the Ottomans, remained supremely confident of their own cultural world.

The Islamic world drew on intellectual currents that spanned the Eurasian–North African landmass, for its centers were in Istanbul, Cairo, Isfahan, and Delhi. From Islam's founding, Muslims had looked to India and China, not to Europe, for inspiration. By the eighteenth century, the increasing wealth and power of Christian kingdoms enriched by New World colonies made those cultures more imposing. Yet even as Muslims brought a few new European elements into their cultural mix, instead. In the early seventeenth century, Shah Abbas oversaw the construction of the **great plaza at Isfahan**, a structure that reflected his desire to bring trade, government, and religion together under the authority of the supreme political leader. An enormous public mosque, the Shah Abbas Mosque, dominated one end of the plaza, which measured 1,667 feet by 517 feet. At the other end were trading stalls and markets. Along one side sat government offices; the other side offered the exquisite Mosque of Shaykh Lutfollah. If the other rulers of this era devoted their (considerable) income to creating rich *private* spaces, Shah Abbas used the vast open space of the plaza to open up his city to all comers, keeping only the Mosque of Shaykh Lutfollah for his personal use.

The royal use of space says a great deal about how monarchs in this era wished to be seen and remembered and about how they wanted to rule. While some wanted to retreat from the rest of society, Shah Abbas wanted to create an open space for trade and the exchange of ideas. World history is full of palaces and plazas (the Piazza San Marco, in Venice, might be compared to the royal plaza at Isfahan); we can still visit and admire them. But when we do, we should also remember that architecture that either opens up to the public or sets aside privileged spaces has always had political as well as cultural functions.

Isfahan. *On the great plaza at Isfahan, markets and government offices operated in close proximity to the public Shah Abbas Mosque, shown here, and the shah's private mosque. The design of this plaza represented Shah Abbas's desire to unite control of trade, government, and religion under one leader.*

QUESTIONS FOR ANALYSIS

- Choose one of the places discussed in this feature. How did the architectural layout shape the political power exercised by that space?
- How did private spaces, like the palace at Versailles, differ from public spaces, like the great plaza at Isfahan? What political goals could be accomplished by each?

Explore Further

Babaie, Sussan. *Isfahan and Its Palaces: Statecraft, Shi'ism and the Architecture of Conviviality in Early Modern Iran* (2008).

Necipoğlu, Gülru. *Architecture, Ceremonial, and Power: The Topkapi Palace in the Fifteenth and Sixteenth Centuries* (1991).

most still regarded Europeans as rude barbarians. More impressive in the eyes of elites in Persia, India, and the Ottoman Empire were the cultural splendors to be found to the east.

CULTURE AND POLITICS IN EAST ASIA

Like the Ottomans, Safavids, and Mughals, the Chinese did not need to prove the richness of their scholarly and artistic traditions. China had long been a renowned center of learning, with its emperors and elites supporting artists, poets, musicians, scientists, and teachers. But in late Ming and early Qing China, cultural flourishing owed more to a booming internal market, as the growing population and extensive commercial networks propelled the circulation of ideas as well as goods. As a result, China's cultural sphere expanded and diversified well before similar changes occurred elsewhere.

In Japan, too, prosperity promoted cultural dynamism. Because of Japan's giant neighbor across the sea, the Japanese people had always been aware of outside influences. Like the Chinese government, the Tokugawa shogunate tried to

The Taj Mahal. *A symbol of Mughal splendor, the Taj Mahal was a mausoleum that was built of white marble. Often described as poetry in stone, it was constructed under Shah Jahan as an homage to his deceased wife, Mumtaz Mahal* (right).

promote Confucian notions of a social hierarchy organized on the basis of social position, age, gender, and kin. It also tried to shield the country from egalitarian ideas that would threaten the strict social hierarchy. But the forces that undermined government control of knowledge in China proved even stronger in Japan. Here, a decentralized political system enabled different cultural influences to spread, including European ideas and practices. By the eighteenth century, in struggling to define its own identity through these contending currents, the cultural scene in Japan was more lively, open, and varied than its counterpart in China.

China: The Challenge of Expansion and Diversity

In China, the circulation of books spread ideas among the literate, and religious rituals instilled cultural values among the broader population. Advances in cartography reflected the distinctive worldview of Chinese elites.

PUBLISHING AND THE TRANSMISSION OF IDEAS Broader circulation of ideas had more to do with the decentralization of book production than with technological innovations. After all, woodblock and movable type printing had been present in China for centuries. Initially, the state had spurred book production by printing Confucian texts; but before long, the economy's increasing commercialization

weakened government controls over what got printed. Even as officials clamped down on unorthodox texts, there was no centralized system of censorship, and unauthorized opinions circulated freely.

By the late Ming era, a burgeoning publishing sector catered to the diverse social, cultural, and religious needs of educated elites and urban populations. European visitors admired the vast collections of printed materials housed in Chinese libraries, describing them as "magnificently built" and "finely adorn'd." In fact, the late Ming was an age of collections of other sorts as well. Members of the increasingly affluent elite acquired objects for display (such as paintings, ceramics, and calligraphy) as a sign of their status and refinement. Consumers could build collections by purchasing from multiple sources—from roadside peddlers to monks to gentlemen dealers—because books and other luxury goods were now more affordable. Increasingly, publishers offered a mix of wares: guidebooks for patrons of the arts, travelers, or merchants; handbooks for performing rituals, choosing dates for ceremonies, or writing proper letters; almanacs and encyclopedias; morality books; and medical manuals.

Especially popular were study aids for the civil service examination, including models for the required, highly structured eight-part essay. In 1595, Beijing reeled with scandal over news that the second-place graduate had reproduced verbatim several model essays published by commercial printers. Just over twenty years later, the top graduate plagiarized a winning essay submitted years earlier. Ironically, then, the increased circulation of knowledge led critics to bemoan a decline in real learning. Instead of mastering the classics, they charged, examination candidates were simply memorizing the work of others.

Examination hopefuls were not the only beneficiaries of the book trade, for elite women also joined China's literary culture, penetrating the formerly male-only domain as readers, writers, and editors. Anthologies of women's poetry were especially popular, not only in the market, but also, when issued in limited circulation, to celebrate the refinement of the writer's family. Men of letters soon recognized the market potential of women's writings. Some also saw women's less regularized style (usually acquired through family channels rather than state-sponsored schools) as a means to challenge stifling stylistic conformity. A few women even served as publishers themselves.

Although elite women enjoyed success in the world of culture, the period brought increasing restrictions on their lives. Remarriage of widows and premarital sex might have met with disapproval in earlier times, but now they were utterly unthinkable for women from "good" families. Ironically, the thriving publishing sector indirectly promoted the stricter morality by printing plays and novels that echoed the government's conservative attitudes. Meanwhile, footbinding (which elite women first adopted around the late Tang-Song period) spread among common people, as small, delicate feet came to signify femininity and respectability.

Chinese Civil Service Exam. *This nineteenth-century photo shows a Chinese Civil Service Examination compound. Lining the compound were cells in which candidates sat for the examination. Other than three long boards—the highest served as a shelf, the middle one as a desk, and the lowest as a seat—the cell had neither furniture nor a door. Indeed, the cells were little more than spaces partitioned on three sides by brick walls and covered by a roof; the floors were packed dirt. Generations of candidates spent three days and two nights in succession in these cells as they strove to enter officialdom.*

POPULAR CULTURE AND RELIGION Important as the book trade was, it had only an indirect impact on most men and women in late Ming China. Those who could not read well or at all absorbed cultural values through oral communication, ritual performance, and daily practices. The Ming government tried to control these channels, too. It appointed village elders as guardians of local society and instituted "village compacts" to ensure shared responsibility for proper conduct and observation of the laws.

Still, the everyday life of rural and small-town dwellers went on outside these official networks. Apart from toiling in the field, villagers participated in various religious and cultural practices, such as honoring local guardian spirits, patronizing Buddhist and Daoist temples, or watching performances by touring theater groups. Furthermore, villagers often took group pilgrimages to religious sites and attended markets in nearby towns offering restaurants, brothels, and other types of entertainment. At the marketplaces the visitors gathered news and gossip or listened to itinerant storytellers and traveling monks; such open-ended cultural activities gave audiences opportunities to reinterpret official norms to serve their own purposes and to contest the government's rules. For example, commoners could take officially approved morality tales celebrating impartial officials and use them to challenge the real-life behavior of government bureaucrats.

Popular religions that mingled various traditions also reflected late Ming cultural flourishing. Here, at the grassroots level, there was little distinction among Buddhist, Daoist, and local cults. After all, the Chinese believed in cosmic unity; and although they venerated spiritual forces, they did not consider any of them to be a Supreme Being who favored one sect over another. They believed it was the emperor, rather than any religious group, who held the mandate of heaven; the enforcement of orthodox values was more a matter of political than of religious control. Unless sects posed an obvious threat, the emperor had no reason to regulate their spiritual practices. This situation promoted religious tolerance and avoided the sectarian warfare that plagued post-Reformation Europe.

TECHNOLOGY AND CARTOGRAPHY Belief in cosmic unity did not prevent the Chinese from devising technologies to master nature's operations in this world. For example, the magnetic compass, gunpowder, and the printing press were all Chinese inventions. Moreover, Chinese technicians had mastered iron casting and produced mechanical clocks centuries before Europeans did. Chinese astronomers also compiled accurate records of eclipses, comets, novae, and meteors. In part, the emperor's needs drove their interest in astronomy and calendrical science. After all, it was his job as the Son of Heaven, and thus mediator between heaven and earth, to determine the best dates for planting, holding festivities, scheduling mourning periods, and convening judicial court sessions. The

Footbinding. *Two images of bound feet: (left) as an emblem of feminine respectability when wrapped and concealed, as on this well-to-do Chinese woman; (right) as an object of curiosity and condemnation when exposed for the world to see.*

Chinese believed that the empire's stability depended on correct calculation of these dates.

In the realm of cartography, the Chinese demonstrated most clearly their understanding of the world. Their maps encompassed elements of history, literature, and art—not just technical detail. It was not that "scientific" techniques were lacking; a map made as early as 1136 reveals that Chinese cartographers could readily draw to scale. Yet, valuing written text over visual and other forms of representation, Chinese elites did not always treat geometric and mathematical precision as the main objective of cartography. Reflecting the elites' worldview, most maps placed the realm of the Chinese emperor, as the ruler of "All under Heaven," at the center, surrounded by foreign countries. Thus, the physical scale of China and distances to other lands were distorted. Still, some of the maps cover a vast expanse: one includes an area stretching from Japan to the Atlantic, encompassing Europe and Africa. (See Primary Source: Chinese Views of the World.)

CHINESE VIEWS OF EUROPEANS Before the nineteenth century, the Chinese had incomplete knowledge about foreign lands despite a long history of contact. The empire saw itself as superior to all others (a common feature of many cultures). A Ming geographical publication portrayed the Portuguese as men who are "seven feet tall, have eyes like a cat, a mouth like an oriole, an ash-white face, thick and curly beards like black gauze, and almost red hair" (quoted in Dikötter, p. 14). Qing authors in the eighteenth century confused France with the Portugal known during Ming times, and they characterized England and Sweden as dependencies of Holland. During this period of cultural flourishing, in short, most Chinese did not feel compelled to revise their view of the world.

Cultural Identity and Tokugawa Japan

The culture that developed in Japan in this period drew on local traditions and, increasingly, foreign influences from China and Europe. Chinese cultural influence had long crossed the Sea of Japan, but under the Tokugawa shogunate there was also interest in European culture. This interest grew via the Dutch presence in Japan and via limited contact with Russians. At the same time, the study of Japanese traditions and culture surged. Thus, Tokugawa Japan engaged in a three-cornered conversation that included time-honored Chinese ways (transmitted via Korea), European teachings, and distinctly Japanese traditions.

NATIVE ARTS AND POPULAR CULTURE Until the sixteenth and seventeenth centuries, the main patrons of Japanese culture were the imperial court in Kyoto, the hereditary shogunate, religious institutions, and a small upper class. These groups developed an elite culture of theater and stylized painting. Samurai (former warriors turned bureaucrats) and daimyo (regional lords) favored a masked theater, called Noh and an elegant ritual for making tea and engaging in contemplation. In their gardens, the lords built teahouses with stages for Noh drama. These gave rise to hereditary schools of actors, tea masters, and flower arrangers. The elites also hired

Chinese Views of the World

The Chinese developed cartographical skills early in their history. A third-century map, no longer in existence, was designed to enable the emperors to "comprehend the four corners of the world without ever having to leave their imperial quarters." The *Huayi tu* (Map of Chinese and Foreign Lands) from 1136 depicted the whole world on a stone stele, including 500 place names and textual information on foreign lands. Chinese maps typically devoted more attention to textual explanations with moral and political messages than to locating places accurately. One such map, the Chinese wheel map from the 1760s, is full of textual explanations.

QUESTIONS FOR ANALYSIS

- Why do you think Chinese maps included messages that focused on moral and political themes?
- How are these maps similar to and different from the Islamic maps shown on p. 524?

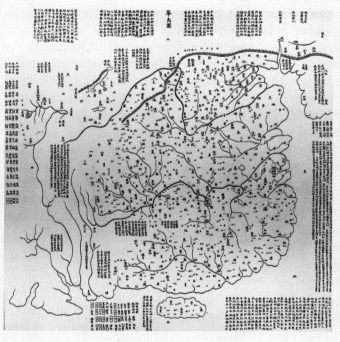

The *Huayi tu* map, 1136

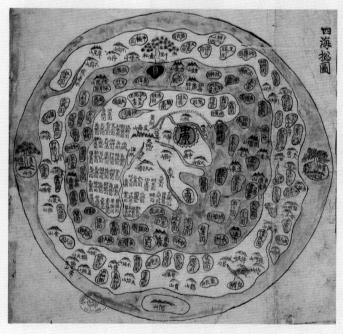

Chinese wheel map, 1760s

Sources: *Left:* The Needham Research Institute. *Right:* The British Library, London.

commoner-painters to decorate tea utensils and other fine articles and to paint the brilliant interiors and standing screens in grand stone castles. Some upper-class men did their own painting, which conveyed philosophical thoughts. Calligraphy was proof of refinement.

Alongside the elite culture arose a rougher urban one. Here, artisans and merchants could purchase, for example, works of fiction and colorful prints (often risqué) made from carved woodblocks and could enjoy the company of female entertainers known as geisha who were skilled (*gei*) in playing the three-stringed instrument (*shamisen*), storytelling, and performing;

some were also prostitutes. Kabuki—a type of theater that combined song, dance, and skillful staging to dramatize conflicts between duty and passion—became wildly popular. This art form featured dazzling acting, brilliant makeup, and sumptuous costumes.

Much popular entertainment chronicled the world of the common people rather than politics or high society. The urbanites' pleasure-oriented culture was known as "the floating world" (*ukiyo*), and the woodblock prints depicting it as *ukiyo-e* (*e* meaning "picture"). Here, the social order was temporarily turned upside down. Those usually considered inferior—actors,

Artist and Geisha at Tea. *The erotic, luxuriant atmosphere of Japan's urban pleasure quarters was captured in a new art form, the ukiyo-e, or "pictures from a floating world." In this image set in Tokyo's celebrated Yoshiwara district, several geisha flutter about a male artist.*

musicians, courtesans, and others seen as possessing low morals—became idols. Even some upper-class samurai partook of this "lower" culture. But to enter the pleasure quarters, they had to leave behind their swords, a mark of rank.

Literacy in Japan now surged, especially among men. The most popular novels sold 10,000 to 12,000 copies. In the late eighteenth century, Edo had some sixty booksellers and hundreds of book lenders. In fact, the presence of so many lenders allowed books to spread to a wider public that previously could not afford to buy them. By the late eighteenth century, as more books circulated and some of them criticized the government, officials tried to censor certain publications. The government's response testified to the uncommon power wielded by people of modest means and the relative significance of popular culture in Japan.

RELIGION AND CHINESE INFLUENCE In the realm of higher culture, China loomed large in the Tokugawa world. Japanese scholars wrote imperial histories of Japan in the Chinese style,

and Chinese law codes and other books attracted a significant readership. Some Japanese traveled south to Nagasaki to meet Zen Buddhist masters and Chinese residents there. A few Chinese monks won permission to found monasteries outside Nagasaki and to give lectures and construct temples in Kyoto and Edo.

Although Buddhist temples grew in number, they did not displace the native Japanese practice of venerating ancestors and worshipping gods in nature. Later called Shintō ("the way of the gods"), this practice boasted a network of shrines throughout the country. Shintō developed from time-honored beliefs in spirits, or *kami*, who were associated with places (mountains, rivers, waterfalls, rocks, the moon) and activities (harvest, fertility). Seeking healing or other assistance, adherents appealed to these spirits in nature and daily life through incantations and offerings. Some women under Shintō served as *mikos*, a kind of shaman with special divinatory powers.

Shintō rituals competed with a powerful strain of neo-Confucianism that issued moral and behavioral guidelines. For example, in 1762, "Greater Learning for Females" appeared—an influential text that made Confucian teachings understandable for nonscholars. In particular, it outlined social roles that stressed hierarchy based on age and gender as a way to ensure order. At the same time, merit became important in determining one's place in the social hierarchy. Doing the right thing (propriety) and being virtuous were key.

By the early eighteenth century, neo-Confucian teachings of filial piety and loyalty to superiors had become the official state creed. This philosophy legitimated the social hierarchy and the absolutism of political authorities, but it also instructed the shogun and the upper class to provide "benevolent administration" for the people's benefit. That meant taking into account petitioners' complaints and requests, whether for improved irrigation and roads or for punishment of unfair officials. Thus did Japanese culture shape state structure—and vice versa.

Reacting to the influence of Chinese Buddhism and desiring to honor their own country's greatness, some thinkers promoted intellectual traditions from Japan's past. These efforts stressed "native learning," Japanese texts, and Japanese uniqueness. In so doing, they formalized a Japanese religious and cultural tradition and denounced Confucianism and Buddhism as foreign contaminants.

EUROPEAN INFLUENCES Chinese thought was not the only outside influence to compete with revived native learning. By the late seventeenth century, Japan was also tapping other sources of knowledge. By 1670, a guild of Japanese interpreters in Nagasaki who could speak and read Dutch accompanied Dutch merchants on trips to Edo. As European knowledge spread to high circles in Edo, in 1720 the shogunate lifted its ban on foreign books. Thereafter, European ideas, called "Dutch learning," circulated more openly. Scientific, geographical, and medical texts

Kabuki Theater. *Kabuki originated among dance troupes in the environs of temples and shrines in Kyoto in the late sixteenth and early seventeenth centuries. As kabuki spread to the urban centers of Japan, the theater designs enabled the actors to enter and exit from many directions and to step out into the audience, lending the skillful, raucous shows great intimacy.*

appeared in Japanese translations and in some cases displaced Chinese texts. A Japanese-Dutch dictionary appeared in 1745, and the first official school of Dutch learning followed. Students of Dutch or European teachings remained a limited segment of Japanese society, but the demand for translations intensified.

Japan's internal debates about what to borrow from the Europeans and the Chinese illustrate the changes that the world had undergone in recent centuries. A few hundred years earlier, products and ideas generally did not travel beyond coastal regions and had only a limited effect (especially inland) on local cultural practices. By the eighteenth century, though, expanded networks of exchange and new prosperity made the integration of foreign ideas feasible and, sometimes, desirable. The Japanese did not consider the embracing of outside influences as a mark of inferiority or subordination, particularly when they could put those influences to good use. This was not the case for the great Asian land-based empires, which were eager lenders but hesitant borrowers.

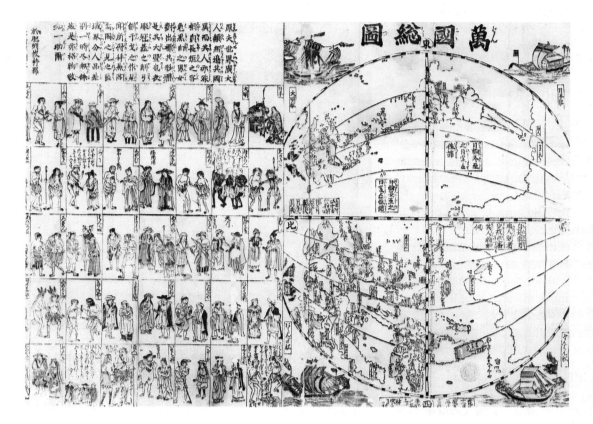

Japanese Map of the World. *Japanese maps underwent a shift as a result of encounters with the Dutch. Here, in a map dated 1671, much information is incorporated about distant lands, both cartographically on the globe and pictorially, to the left, in two-person images representing various peoples of the world in their purported typical costumes.*

AFRICAN CULTURAL FLOURISHING

The wealth that spurred artistic achievement and displays of power in the three major Islamic states and China and Japan did not bypass African states. The slave trade enriched African upper classes who sold their captives to European slavers and used their wealth to fund cultural activities and invigorate centuries-old artisanal and artistic traditions. As in the Islamic world and East Asia, African artisans maintained local forms of cultural production, such as wood carving, weaving, and metal working.

Cultural traditions in Africa varied from kingdom to kingdom, but there were patterns among them. For example, all West African elites encouraged craftsmen to produce carvings, statues, masks, and other objects that glorified the rulers' power and achievements. (Royal patrons in Europe, Asia, and the Islamic world did the same with architecture and painting.) There was also a widespread belief that rulers and their families had the gods' blessing, much as was the case in Ottoman, Safavid, Mughal, Chinese, and Japanese societies at this time. But African arts and crafts not only celebrated royal power; they also captured the energy of a universe that people believed was filled with spiritual beings. Starting in the 1500s and continuing through the eighteenth century when the slave trade reached its peak, African rulers had even more reason—and means—to support cultural pursuits. After all, as destructive as the slave trade was for African peoples, it made the slave-trading states wealthy and powerful.

The Asante, Oyo, and Benin Cultural Traditions

The kingdom of Asante led the way in cultural attainments, and the Oyo Empire and Benin also promoted rich artistic traditions. The Asante kingdom's access to gold and the revenues that it derived from selling captives undergirded its prosperity, making it the richest state in West Africa—perhaps even in the whole of sub-Saharan Africa. So deeply imbued with a desire to achieve economic success were the citizens of Asante that they accorded the highest respect to entrepreneurs who made money and surrounded themselves with retainers and slaves. The adages of the age were inevitably about becoming rich: "Money is king," "Nothing is as important as money." People who had wealth displayed it ostentatiously, wearing special garments signaling that they were persons of wealth and power. Those who could command the services of at least 1,000 subjects were entitled to wear a special cloth and to have a horsetail switch borne in front of them. Even more coveted was the right to carry the elephant-tail whip, which denoted an esteemed title.

Artisans celebrated these traditions through the crafting of magnificent seats or stools coated with gold as symbols of authority; the most ornate were reserved for the head of the Asante federation, the Asantehene, who ruled this far-flung empire from the capital city of Kumasi. By the eighteenth century, these monarchs ventured out from the secluded royal palace only on ceremonial and feast days, when they wore sumptuous silk garments featuring many dazzling colors and geometric patterns in interwoven strips. Known as Kente cloth, this fabric was worn at first only by rulers, but later on wealthy individuals were permitted to garb themselves with it. Kings also had the golden elephant tail carried in front of them, a symbol of the greatest wealth. Held aloft on these celebratory occasions were maces, spears, staffs, and other symbols of power fashioned from the kingdom's abundant gold supplies. These reminded the common people of the Asantehene's connection to the gods.

Equally resplendent were rulers of the Oyo Empire and Benin, located in the territory that now constitutes Nigeria. Elegant, refined metalwork in the form of West African bronzes reflects these rulers' awesome power and their peoples' highest esteem. The bronze heads of Ife, capital city of the Yoruba Oyo Empire, are among the world's most sophisticated artworks. According to one commentator, "Little that Italy or Greece or Egypt ever produced could be finer, and the appeal of their beauty is immediate and universal" (Tignor, p. 428). Artisans fashioned the best known of these works in the thirteenth century (before the slave trade era), but the tradition continued and became more elaborate in the seventeenth and eighteenth centuries.

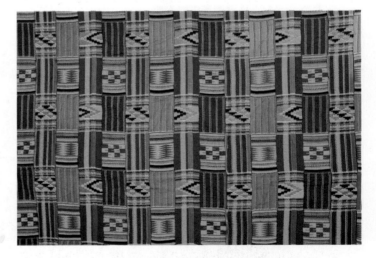

Kente Cloth. *Kente cloth originated among the Asante people and spread to other parts of West Africa. Threads of silk and cotton were interwoven to produce patterns with dazzling colors and geometric shapes. The colors represented different meanings important to the Asante peoples. Gray stood for healing and gold for royalty. Red was said to engender spiritual moods.*

Bronzes from Benin, too, displayed exquisite craftsmanship. Although historical records have portrayed Benin as one of Africa's most brutal slave-trading regimes, it also produced art of the highest order. Whether Benin's reputation for brutality was deserved or simply part of Europeans' later desire to label African rulers as "savage" in order to justify their conquest of the landmass, it cannot detract from the splendor of its artisans' creations.

Wealth acquired from the slave trade fostered cultural flourishing in Africa, notably though not exclusively in West Africa. Here, as in the Islamic world and East Asia, artisans and craftspersons drew on their own traditions. But the African artistic tradition, unlike Islamic and East Asian traditions, was little influenced by other cultures, even at a time when Africa was being drawn into global networks of exchange and political domination.

THE ENLIGHTENMENT IN EUROPE

An extraordinary cultural flowering also occurred in Europe during the seventeenth and eighteenth centuries. Ironically, its origins lay in the period of the Little Ice Age, a time of devastating religious and civil wars, events that provoked many European thinkers to turn their backs on religious strife and to develop useful ways for understanding and improving *this* world. First came "the new science," a search for stable, testable, and objective knowledge, especially in physics and astronomy. From its findings and inspiration a wider movement, the **Enlightenment**, was born. Often defined purely in intellectual terms as the spreading of faith in reason and in universal rights and laws, this era encompassed broader developments, such as the expansion of literacy, the spread of critical thinking, the improvement of agricultural productivity, and the decline of religious persecution. As literate, middle- and upper-class men and women gained confidence in being able to reason for themselves, to understand the world without calling on traditional authorities, and to publicly criticize what they found distasteful or wrong, they embraced an increasingly "enlightened" age.

Quarrels and competition between European states and increasing contact between Europe and the wider world after the sixteenth century contributed to the shaping of Enlightenment culture. Conflict at home and competition between states pushed Europeans overseas, where they became eager consumers of other peoples' goods and practices, including Amerindian trapping methods and Chinese methods of making porcelain. The European states' aspirations to modernize and build their armies generated new patronage and support for ideas that sometimes troubled religious authorities and grew increasingly dynamic and radical as they spread downward to new social groups. But the more they learned in their interactions with others, and the more they succeeded in secularizing and spreading

Ife Bronzes. *An Ife bronze from the Yoruba peoples of present-day Nigeria. This magnificent work, one of a collection of fifteen pieces, was crafted sometime between the eleventh and fifteenth centuries and discovered by an American researcher in 1939.*

Brass Oba Head. *The brass head of an Oba, or king, of Benin. The kingdom's brass and bronze work was among the finest in all of Africa.*

their ideas at home, the more European intellectuals became convinced not only that their culture was superior—for that was hardly rare—but that they had discovered a set of universal laws that applied to everyone, everywhere around the globe. (See Primary Source: European Views of the World.)

The New Science

The search for new, testable knowledge began centuries before the Enlightenment in the efforts of Nicolaus Copernicus (1473–1543) and Galileo Galilei (1564–1642) to understand the

European Views of the World

As Europeans became world travelers and traders, they needed accurate information on places and distances so they could get home as well as return to the sites they had visited. Europe's first printed map of the New World, the Waldseemüller map (produced in 1507), portrayed the Americas as a long and narrow strip of land. Asia and Africa dwarf its unexplored landmass. By the mid-seventeenth century, European maps were seemingly more objective, yet they still grouped the rest of the world around the European countries. Moreover, the effort to make world maps that served navigational purposes led to distortions (like the stretching of polar zones in the 1569 Mercator projection) that made Europe seem disproportionately large and central.

Waldseemüller map, 1507

Mercator projection, 1569

Sources: Top: Courtesy Wychwood Editions. Bottom: Rare Books Division, The New York Public Library, Astor, Lenox and Tilden Foundations.

Galileo. *Worried that the new science would undermine the Christian faith, the Catholic Church put Italian scientist Galileo on trial in 1633 for espousing heretical beliefs and condemned him to house arrest until his death in 1642.*

behavior of the heavens. These men were both astronomers and mathematicians. Making their own mathematical calculations and observations of the stars and planets, these scholars came to conclusions that contradicted age-old assumptions. By no means was trusting one's own work rather than the accepted authorities easy or without risk: when Galileo confirmed Copernicus's claims that the earth revolved around the sun, he was put on trial for heresy.

In the seventeenth century, a small but influential group of scholars committed themselves, similarly, to experimentation, calculation, and observation. They adopted a method for "scientific" inquiry laid out by the philosopher Sir Francis Bacon (1561–1626), who claimed that real science entailed the formulation of hypotheses that could be tested in carefully controlled experiments. Bacon believed that traditional authorities could never be trusted; only by conducting experiments could humans begin to comprehend the workings of nature. Bacon was chiefly wary of classical and medieval authorities, but his principle also applied to traditional knowledge that European scientists were encountering in the rest of the world. Confident of their calculations performed according to the new **scientific method**, scientists like Isaac Newton (1642–1727) defined what they believed were universal laws that applied to all matter and motion; they criticized older conceptions of nature (from Aristotelian ideas to folkloric and foreign ones) as absurd and obsolete. Thus, in his *Principia Mathematica*, Newton set forth the laws of motion—including the famous law of gravitation, which simultaneously explained falling bodies on earth and planetary motion.

It is no longer fashionable to call these changes a scientific revolution, for European thinking did not change overnight. Only gradually did thinkers come to see the natural world as operating according to inviolable laws such as gravity and inertia. But by the late seventeenth century, many rulers had developed a new interest in science's discoveries, and they established royal academies of science to encourage local endeavors. This patronage, of course, had a political function. By incorporating the British Royal Society in 1662, for example, Charles II hoped to show not only that the crown backed scientific progress but also that England's great minds backed the crown. Similar reasoning lay behind Louis XIV's founding of the French Academy of Sciences. As other rulers followed suit, the church's power over European culture—already weakened and divided by the Reformation—waned.

The new science was, at least at first, heavily theoretical. But this does not mean it lacked practical applications or appeal to wider audiences. The new math was useful for the science of ballistics, and the new astronomy for building better clocks and navigational devices, such as the chronometer. More technical sophistication necessitated, in turn, the establishment of military schools, which increasingly stressed engineering methods, made advances in surveying and mapping, and introduced a culture of meritocracy into the previously noble-dominated armies. In rural areas, landowners began to read books about crop rotation and formed societies to discuss the latest methods of animal breeding. In Italy, numerous female natural philosophers emerged, and the genre of scientific literature for "ladies" took hold. By about 1750, even artisans and journalists were applying Newtonian mechanics to their practical problems and inventions. A consensus emerged among proponents of the new science that useful knowledge came from collecting data and organizing them into universally valid systems, rather than from studying revered classical texts.

By the eighteenth century, the spread of the new science, together with expanding commerce and the relaxation, in some places, of censorship, began to give reform-minded Europeans hope that they were living in a *siècle des lumières*, or "century of light." In many places, this was still more hope than reality, as literacy was far from universal, peasants still suffered under arbitrary systems of taxation, and judicial regimes remained harsh. Most people still understood their relationship with God, nature, and other humans via Christian doctrines and local customs. But many thinkers could now hope that Thomas Hobbes's pessimism, formed in the midst of the Little Ice Age and the terrors of the seventeenth century (see Chapter 13), had been wrong and that human societies, along with the sciences, could be improved. That hope launched the movement we now call the Enlightenment.

Enlightened Thought and Its Spread

Enlightenment thinkers, called *philosophes* in France, built on the achievements of the new science, insisting that scientific reasoning could and should be used to understand human societies as well as the natural world. Thinkers such as the English scientist and political writer John Locke (1712–1704), the French writers Voltaire (1694–1778) and Denis Diderot (1713–1784), and the Scottish economist Adam Smith (1723–1790) believed in the power of human reason to criticize and improve existing institutions and practices. They claimed that oppressive governments, religious superstition, and irrational social inequalities were not ills people simply had to accept. Human beings could use their reason, Locke believed, to combat the human-made evils of intolerance and superstition. Similarly, Voltaire criticized the torture of criminals, Diderot denounced the despotic tendencies of the French kings Louis XIV and Louis XV, and Smith exposed the inefficiencies of mercantilism. Very few of these writers were political radicals or atheists (people who do not believe in any god), but their belief that Europe and the world could be improved by the universal application of law and reason made their ideas highly appealing to modernizing reformers and radical critics alike.

In general, Enlightenment thinkers distrusted institutions and conventions and argued that societies should be governed by applying reason and natural laws rather than by following traditions. The application of reason to history, Locke claimed, showed that divine-right monarchies were a myth. Early peoples had voluntarily *made* their political institutions, binding themselves to their rulers according to a "social contract." When a government became tyrannical, it violated that contract, and the people had the right to rebel and create a new contract. All men were born equal in God's eyes, Locke argued, and were equally endowed by nature with the facility to flourish; hence, they must be equal under human law. Similarly, Jean-Jacques Rousseau (1712–1778) reversed the pessimistic principle that humankind was inherently sinful and in need of a master. "Man is born good," he countered. "It is society that corrupts him." Other Enlightenment thinkers, similarly, believed that the only true inequalities among men were those produced by natural talents and education, and they criticized the European social

Colbert Presents French Scientists to Louis XIV. *In founding the Académie des Sciences in 1666, King Louis XIV hoped to show his support for the new science and win scientists' endorsement for his still rather fragile regime. Here his chief minister (and the inventor of mercantile policies), Jean-Baptiste Colbert, presents the scholars to the king. The central presence of maps and globes in the image tells us how much exploration of the world and conquest of colonies were part of this collaborative endeavor.*

order in which status was based on birth rather than on merit. Voltaire ridiculed the nobility and clergy for their stupidity, greed, and injustice. In *The Wealth of Nations,* Smith remarked that there was little difference (other than education) between a philosopher and a street porter: both were born, he claimed, with the ability to reason, and both were (or should be) free to rise in society according to their talents. Yet, Locke, Rousseau, and Voltaire did not believe that women could act as independent, rational individuals in the same way that all men, presumably, could. Although educated women like Mary Wollstonecraft and Olympe de Gouges took up the pen to protest these inequities (see Chapter 15 for further discussion), the Enlightenment did little to change women's subordinate status in European society.

The Enlightenment touched all of Europe, but to varying extents. In the Netherlands, France, and Britain, where population density and urbanization were greatest, enlightened learning spread widely; in Spain, Poland, and Russia, enlightened circles were small and barely influenced the general population. Enlightened thought flourished in commercial centers such as Amsterdam and Edinburgh and in colonial ports such as Philadelphia and Boston. As education and literacy levels rose in these cities, book sales and newspaper circulation surged. Religious literature and bibles were still the best sellers, but the widening market increasingly put scientific treatises, scandalous novels, and even pornography into readers' hands.

POPULAR CULTURE The expanding reading public grew increasingly omnivorous and increasingly difficult to police. In England, the Netherlands, and Switzerland, authorities essentially gave up censoring, and radical books and pamphlets printed there were smuggled into other markets, where they found readers of many sorts. Some of the most popular works were not from high intellectuals but from more sensationalist essayists. Pamphlets charging widespread corruption, fraudulent stock speculation, and insider trading circulated widely. Sex, too, sold well. Works like *Venus in the Cloister or the Nun in a Nightgown* racked up as many sales as the now-classic works of the Enlightenment. Bawdy and irreligious, these vulgar

Chronometer. *In the 1760s, the English clockmaker John Harrison perfected the chronometer, a timepiece mariners could use to reckon longitude while at sea. Although the Royal Society initially refused to believe that Harrison had solved this long-standing problem, Harrison's instrument made navigation so much safer and more predictable that it became standard equipment on European ships.*

best-sellers exploited consumer demand—but they also seized the opportunity to mock authority figures, such as nuns and priests. Some even dared to go after the royal family, portraying Marie Antoinette as having sex with her court confessor. In these cases, pornography—some of it even philosophical—spilled into the literary marketplace for political satire. Such works displayed the seamier side of the Enlightenment, but they also revealed a willingness (on the part of high and low intellectuals alike) to challenge established beliefs and institutions and to undermine royal and clerical authority.

New readerships generated new cultural institutions and practices. In Britain and Germany, book clubs and coffeehouses sprang up to cater to sober men of business and learning; here, aristocrats and well-to-do commoners could read news sheets or discuss stock prices, political affairs, and technological novelties. Similar noncourtly socializing occurred in Parisian salons, where aristocratic women presided. Speaking their minds more openly in these private settings than at court or at public assemblies, women here freely exchanged ideas with men. The number of female readers and writers soared, and the relatively new genre of the novel, as well as specialized women's journals, appealed especially to them.

SEEKING UNIVERSAL LAWS Inspired by the new science, many thinkers sought to discover the "laws" of human behavior, an endeavor linked with criticism of existing governments. Explaining the laws of economic relations was chiefly the work of Adam Smith, whose book *The Wealth of Nations* described universal economic laws. It became one of the most influential and long-lived of enlightened works. Smith claimed that unregulated markets in a laissez-faire economy best suited humankind because they allowed the individual's "trucking and bartering" nature to express itself fully. (Laissez-faire expresses the concept that the economy works best when it is left alone—that is, when the state does not regulate or interfere with the workings of the market.) In Smith's view, the "invisible hand" of the market, rather than government regulations, would lead to prosperity and social peace. Smith recognized growing economic gaps between "civilized and thriving" nations and "savage" ones; the latter were so miserably poor that, Smith claimed, they were reduced to infanticide, starvation, and euthanasia. Yet, he believed that until these nations learned to play by what he called nature's laws, they could not expect a happy fate. Smith was just one of many writers who felt that non-Europeans had no other choice but to follow the Enlightenment's "universal" laws.

The French *Encyclopédie* was perhaps the Enlightenment's most characteristic attempt to encompass universal knowledge. Edited by the brilliant and irreverent writer Denis Diderot, it ultimately comprised twenty-eight volumes containing essays by more than 130 intellectuals. It was extremely popular among the elite despite its political, religious, and

Salon of Madame Geoffrin. *Much of the important work—and wit—of the Enlightenment was the product of private gatherings known as salons. Often hosted, like the one depicted here, by aristocratic women, these salons also welcomed down-at-the-heels writers and artists, offering everyone, at least in theory, the opportunity to discuss the sciences, the arts, politics, and the idiocies of their fellow humans on an equal basis.*

intellectual radicalism. Its purpose was "to collect all the knowledge scattered over the face of the earth" and to make it useful to men and women in the present and future. Indeed, the *Encyclopédie* offered a wealth of information about all manner of things, including detailed descriptions and illustrations showing how to make pins and bind books. It also described the virtues of peace and the evils of tyrannical governance, the principles of geometry, and the latest advances in painting. Although it covered all parts of the world, it generally treated the non-European world as historically important and interesting, but also as unmodern and in need of an Enlightenment only known to Europeans. (See Analyzing Global Developments: How Can We Measure the Impact of an Idea?)

Consequences of the Enlightenment

The Enlightenment—or, more properly, Enlightenments, as there was much variation across Europe—was a movement with numerous ambivalent consequences, both for religious and political institutions and for Europe's relationship with the rest of the world.

RELIGION AND THE ENLIGHTENMENT Although few Enlightenment thinkers were atheists, most criticized what they perceived to be the irrational rituals, superstitions, persecutions, and expenditures defended by clergy. The Scottish philosopher and historian David Hume attacked biblical miracles, and Voltaire underscored the bloodiness of the Crusades. They insisted that the use of reason, rather than force or rote repetition of formulas,

was the best way to create a community of believers and morally good people. Their critiques of church authorities and practices were highly controversial. Some governments bowed to clerical pressure and censored the most radical books or exiled writers, but many absolutist monarchs saw an advantage in reducing the church's power and introducing at least some measure of tolerance of religious minorities into their realms.

Tolerance did not mean full civil rights—for Catholics in England, for example, or for Jews anywhere in Europe. Tolerance simply meant a loosening of religious uniformity, and the population as a whole often resented even this. Few Europeans entirely lost their faith as a result of the spread of enlightened ideas and critiques. But it is unquestionably the case that the Enlightenment succeeded in spreading the suspicion of religious authorities and the distaste for religious persecution, and it did create new forms of religious belief and practice. At the level of institutions, the Enlightenment was instrumental in laying the foundation for revolutionaries' attacks on the church and for the evolution of secular states and societies in Europe in the nineteenth century.

The application of enlightened ideas to non-European religions had ambivalent effects. On the one hand, enlightened thinkers sought information about other religions and wrote books discussing similarities between Christian and non-Christian practices and beliefs. But their imposition of enlightened categories and principles often resulted in severe misunderstandings, as differences were increasingly explained as others' "backward" refusal to evolve along European lines. For example, authors of the *Encyclopédie* portrayed Islam with

How Can We Measure the Impact of an Idea?

The single most important work of the European Enlightenment, which set out to provide an objective compendium of all human knowledge, Denis Diderot's *Encyclopédie* was very French. Of its more than 130 authors, only sixteen were foreign, and, of those sixteen, seven came from the French-speaking city of Geneva, just across the border. All of them were men. Within France, the authors came primarily from the north, especially from Paris. Noble and clerical authors weighed more heavily on the list of authors than in society at large (this had to do with literacy rates, which were much higher among the elite); most of Diderot's authors came from the Third Estate. None of those bourgeois authors had much to do with capitalism, nor did the aristocratic authors have much to do with feudalism. There were large contingents of doctors, lawyers, government officials, and skilled artisans.

We know very little about the production and diffusion of the first edition of the *Encyclopédie*, produced from 1751 to 1772 under Diderot's direction. The first four editions, in fact, were expensive luxury items, relatively unimportant in terms of diffusion. The *Encyclopédie* that circulated in prerevolutionary Europe came from cut-rate smaller format editions published between 1777 and 1782, when the final, revised version, the *Encyclopédie méthodique*, began to appear. For these later editions, thorough records have survived, raising far-reaching questions about how ideas circulated and where during the Enlightenment, at least within Europe. (We know very little about the circulation of the *Encyclopédie* beyond Europe.) Where did the writers come from, where did their ideas go, and how, if at all, did their origins influence the content and ultimate significance of their project? We include a table of key words and their classification in thematic categories from the original edition, to give a sense of its contents and priorities.

Terms	# of Appearances	Principal Categories
Commerce	5,713	Commerce, geography
Science	2,095	[Multiple categories]
Christ	1,821	Theology, holy scripture
Africa	1,772	Geography, history, natural history, botany
Slavery	238	Natural law, ethics, religion, ancient history
African slavery (*La traite des nègres*)	15	Commerce
Negro	536	Natural history, commerce
Saint-Domingue	96	Geography, botany
China	957	Agriculture, chemistry, history, natural history, geography, metaphysics, tapestry
Turk or Turkey	701	Geography, history
Muhammad	356	Theology, history, philosophy

QUESTIONS FOR ANALYSIS

- What does the diffusion of the *Encyclopédie* within France and across Europe tell us about its influence? How should we evaluate the influence of a book?
- Do you think the *Encyclopédie*'s local origins compromise its universal ambitions?
- How do you think the social origins of the contributors shaped the kinds of topics covered by the *Encyclopédie*?

Source: Robert Darnton, *The Business of Enlightenment: A Publishing History of the Encyclopédie, 1775–1800* (1979).

the same ill will that they applied to other organized religions, condemning Muhammad as an imposter and the Quran as a book stuffed with barbaric and ignorant ideas that contradicted the laws of physics. The application of these enlightened tests to non-European religions often substituted new prejudices against "backward" religions and cultures for old prejudices against non-Christians destined for hell.

THE ENLIGHTENMENT AND POLITICS Absolutist governments did not entirely reject enlightened ideas, which included ideas that were in most cases reformist or critical of religious authorities rather than directly political. Rulers, like astronomers, recognized the virtues of universality (as in a universally applicable system of taxation) and precision (as in a well-drilled army). Also, social mobility allowed more skilled bureaucrats to rise through the ranks, while commerce provided the state with new riches. The idea of collecting knowledge, too, appealed to states that wanted greater control over their subjects and to extend their reach overseas. Consider Louis XIV, who was persuaded to establish a census (though he never carried it out)

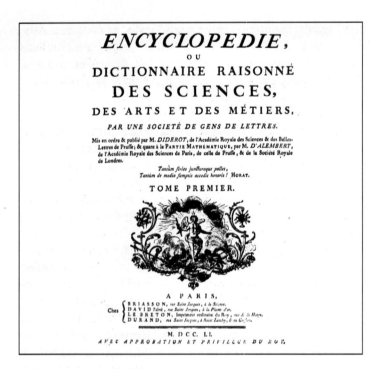

The *Encyclopédie*. *Originally published in 1751, the Encyclopédie was the most comprehensive work of learning of the French Enlightenment. Left: The title page features an image of light and reason being dispersed throughout the land. The title itself identifies the work as a dictionary, based on reason, that deals not just with the sciences but also with the arts and occupations. It identifies two of the leading men of letters (gens de lettres), Denis Diderot and Jean le Rond d'Alembert, as the primary authors of the work. Contributors to the Encyclopédie included craftsmen as well as intellectuals. Below: The detailed illustrations of a pin factory and the processes and machinery employed in pin making are from a plate in the fourth volume of the Encyclopédie and demonstrate its emphasis on practical information.*

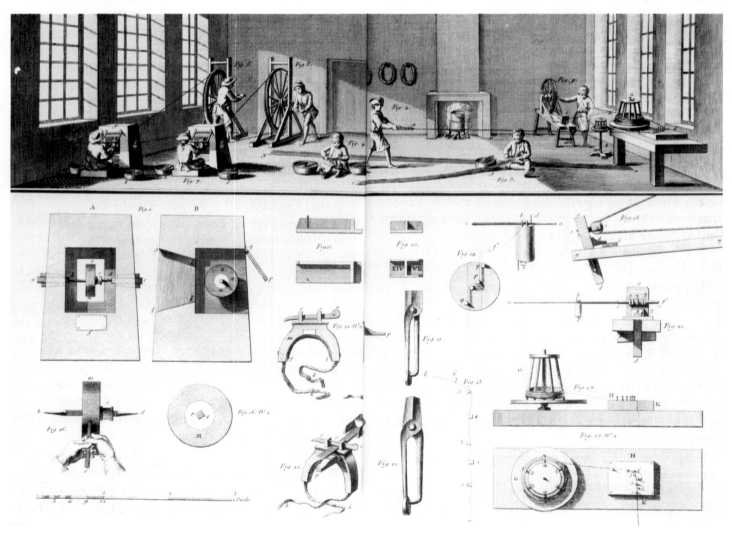

so that he could "know with certitude in what consists his grandeur, his wealth, and his strength." Many enlightened princes supported innovations in the arts and agriculture or sent scientific missions out to explore the world and plant their flags. Like the philosophes, they were convinced that the improvement of trade, agriculture, and national productivity was the right way forward, even though some also were beholden to the older values of the nobility and clergy. Merit and religious tolerance could also be useful in attempts to make states more profitable and armies more efficient. In this way, cultural efflorescence and secular state building in Europe went hand in hand.

But ideas are powerful things and could not be contained within elite circles or prevented from becoming increasingly radical. If many philosophes were themselves uncomfortable with offering liberty and equality (not to mention sovereignty) to *all* people, this was doubly true of their rulers. The Enlightenment in itself was revolutionary only in thought: but thought, too, can be powerful. In the later eighteenth century, new readerships and institutions enabled the extensive spread of concepts such as freedom of conscience, religious tolerance, and equality before the law, even to women, lower-class men, and enslaved peoples whom European elites felt might not deserve it. This was perhaps the Enlightenment's most important, if unintended, legacy.

THE ENLIGHTENMENT AND THE ORIGINS OF RACIAL THOUGHT A darker side of the Enlightenment is evident in the ways in which the new science's insistence on classification and universal natural laws led to a transformation in the idea of "race." Previously, the word *race* referred to a swift current in a stream or a test of speed or a lineage (mainly that of a royal or noble family). By the late seventeenth century, a few writers were expanding the definition to designate a European ethnic lineage, identifying, for example, the indomitable spirit and freedom-loving ethos of the Anglo-Saxon race.

The Frenchman François Bernier, who had traveled in Asia, may have been the first European to attempt to classify the world's peoples. He used a variety of criteria, including those that were to become standard from the late eighteenth century down to the present, such as skin color, facial features, and hair texture. Bernier published this work in his *New Division of the Earth by the Different Groups or Races Who Inhabit It* (1684). Later, the Swedish naturalist Carolus Linnaeus (1707–1778), the French scholar Georges Louis LeClerc, the comte de Buffon (1707–1788), and the German anatomist Johann Friedrich Blumenbach (1752–1840) also used racial principles to classify humankind.

Enlightened Europeans were not the first to remark on other peoples' distinctive—and to them, unpleasing—physical features and to see themselves as superior. Chinese elites glorified their "white" complexions against the peasants' dark skin; against the black, wavy-haired "devils" of Southeast Asia; and against the Europeans' "ash-white" pallor. Amerindians commented critically on the hairiness of European invaders. What the Enlightenment added was the drive to classify all of humankind and impose a hierarchy, one that put white Europeans on top.

Although Bernier may have begun the process, Carolus Linnaeus decisively pushed forward the project of creating a racial classification of humankind. His *Systema Naturae* (1735) sought to classify all the world's plants and animals by giving each a binomial, or two-word, name. In subsequent editions, Linnaeus perfected his system, identifying five subspecies of the mammal he called *Homo sapiens*, or "wise man." Linnaeus gave each of the continents a subspecies: *Homo europaeus*, *Homo americanus*, *Homo afer*, and *Homo asiaticus*. He added a fifth category, *Homo monstrosus*, for "wild" men and "monstrous" types. Linnaeus's classifications were based on a combination of physical characteristics that included skin color and social qualities. He characterized Europeans as light skinned and governed by laws; Asians as "sooty" and governed by opinion; indigenous American peoples as copper skinned and governed by custom; and Africans (whom he consigned to the lowest rung of the human ladder) as ruled by personal whim. Later eighteenth-century natural historians dismissed Linnaeus's fifth category, which contained mythical monstrous races and people with mental and physical disabilities, but the habit of ranking "races" and lumping together physical and cultural characteristics persisted.

In inventorying the world's peoples and assigning each group a place on the ladder of human achievement, Europeans applied their reverence for classical sculpture. Those who most resembled Greek nudes were considered the most beautiful and the most civilized and suited for world power. In his *Natural History* (1750), the comte de Buffon insisted that classical sculptures had established the proper proportion for the human form. Having divided humans into distinct "races," he determined that white peoples were the most admirable and Africans the most contemptible. It is one of the paradoxes of the Enlightenment that a movement that generated a quest for universal knowledge and spread the idea of human liberty far and wide also introduced a new form of what would be considered "scientific" racism—one marked, too, by European biases.

The European Enlightenment in Global Perspective

Europe's new science and enlightened thought arose in reaction both to Europe's expanding interaction with the rest of the world and to the period's environmental, religious, and political

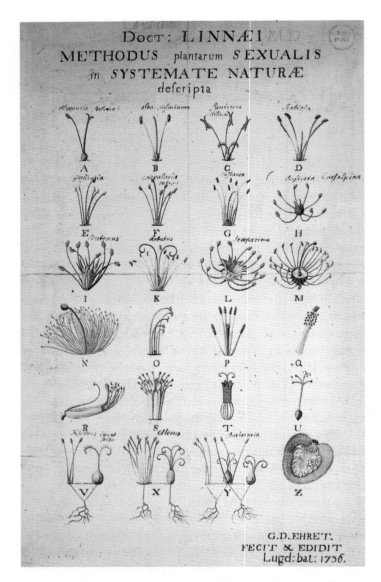

Linnaeus and Classification. *Linnaeus's famous system of plant and animal classifications, which depended on sexual forms (such as the stamen and pistil in plants), was in wide use by the end of the eighteenth century.*

even fundamentalist ways, reiterating the importance of the religious sciences, which included studies of the Quran, the sayings of the Prophet (*hadith*), the *sharia* (religious law), theology, poetry, and the Arabic language, and questioning the value of the foreign sciences and the study of the natural world. Occasional scholars were able to challenge the *ulama's* monopoly on learning and to look outward for inspiration, but such efforts relied on reformist patrons, who were not in great abundance.

Consider Ibrahim Muteferrika, a Hungarian convert to Islam who set up a printing press in Istanbul in 1729. Under the patronage of a reformist grand vizier, Muteferrika published works on science, geography, and history that drew on western findings. Encouraged by his success, Turkish intellectuals translated and published some of Europe's most influential scientific works. When Muteferrika's patron was killed, however, the *ulama* reasserted their control over education and publications and closed off this promising avenue of contact with western learning. While in Europe a diverse set of quarreling and competing churches and patrons made possible the articulation of new and more secular sciences, in Ottoman lands the older authorities and ideas could not so easily be dislodged.

China's science suffered a fundamental disadvantage compared with Europe's. It was practical and empirical rather than theoretical. Its practitioners were less inclined to mathematize the study of the natural world. Nor did they fully understand the use of the experimental method; and unlike European scientists, who fostered a mathematical and mechanistic view of the natural world, they saw all of life and nature organically. Nonetheless, starting in the late sixteenth century, Jesuit missionaries found Chinese literati and the official classes extraordinarily receptive to European breakthroughs in astronomy and mathematics. Here, it seemed, was a fruitful bridge between Europe's new science and China's ruling elites.

The two first Jesuit missionaries to reach China, Michele Ruggieri (1543–1607) and Matteo Ricci (1552–1610), arrived in China in 1582 and 1583, respectively. As was the case with many Jesuits at this time, both were brilliantly educated not just in religious and theological matters but in Europe's evolving new science. Although the Catholic Church had banned the works of Copernicus and Galileo, both men were "closet Copernicans" and believed that presenting Europe's scientific achievements to the ruling classes at the emperor's court would win them favor and facilitate conversions of many Chinese to Christianity. At the time of their arrival, China was in the midst of debates over its solar calendar, which now was out of sync with the seasons and causing difficulties coordinating ceremonial rites and rituals. Thus, Chinese officials were eager to employ Jesuit knowledge of mathematics and astronomy—based on Copernican and Galileo heliocentrism—to assist them in bringing ceremonial dates and political and economic activities into a better relationship with

chaos. But why Europe? Why not China or the Islamic world? As we have seen, Chinese and Muslim scholars could boast rich traditions of scientific and technological development and literary production. Why, then, did Chinese literati and, perhaps more important, Muslim scholars, who still had the most advanced knowledge of the natural sciences even as late as the fourteenth century, let the Europeans assume the lead in understanding the natural world? Answers are difficult to provide, but some suggestions are now coming to light.

For Islam, the rise of Sufi orders and Sufi mysticism posed a challenge to the dominance that the *ulama* believed that they should have over all fields of thought and principles of belief. The *ulama* responded to this threat in conservative, the seasons. For their part, the Jesuits participated in Confucian ceremonies, hoping to win favor with the emperor and arguing that the rites were compatible with Catholicism. But, to the Jesuits' great disappointment, the Chinese did not accept their religious and theological tenets, and the men made only a very small number of converts. When Pope Clement XI issued a papal bull in 1715 condemning the missionaries' participation in the rites, the project of cultural exchange broke down. Offended, the Jiangxi emperor, who had once been sympathetic to the Jesuits, banned Christian missionaries from practicing in China. His successor went even further, ordering the closing of all churches and the expulsion of Jesuits from China. Thus, starting in the mid-eighteenth century, the European window on China and the Chinese window on Europe were closed. China turned away from European contact, most notably Europe's new science that had once intrigued Chinese ruling classes.

Difficulties or disinterest in receiving and spreading foreign ideas in these two earlier scientific powerhouses made it impossible for them to keep pace with the European Enlightenment.

Matteo Ricci adapts to Chinese Culture. *This image depicts Jesuit father Matteo Ricci together with one of his most high-profile converts to Christianity, the scholar and official Xu Guangqi. Behind them stands a painting of the Madonna and baby Jesus with a text in literary Chinese, demonstrating Ricci's commitment to adapting Christianity and European culture to the text-oriented Chinese cultural world.*

Even more than the Ottomans, the Chinese remained a cultural world apart. The situation could not have been more different in the Americas.

CREATING HYBRID CULTURES IN THE AMERICAS

In the Americas, mingling between European colonizers and native peoples (as well as African slaves) produced hybrid cultures. But the cultural mixing grew increasingly unbalanced as Europeans imposed authority over more of the Americas. For Native Americans, the pressure to adapt their cultures to those of the colonists began from the start. Over time, Indians faced mounting pressure as Europeans insisted that their conquests were not simply military endeavors but also spiritual errands. In addition to guns and germs, all of Europe's colonizers brought Bibles, prayer books, and crucifixes with the intent of Christianizing and "civilizing" Indian and African populations in the Americas. Yet, missionary efforts produced uneven and often unpredictable outcomes. Even as Indians and African slaves adopted Christian beliefs and practices, they often retained older religious practices too.

European colonists likewise borrowed from the peoples they subjugated and enslaved. This was especially true in the sixteenth and seventeenth centuries, when the colonists' survival in the New World often depended on adapting. Before long, however, many American settlements had become stable and prosperous, and colonists preferred not to admit their past dependence on others. New hierarchies emerged, and elites in Latin America and North America increasingly followed the tastes and fashions of European aristocrats. Yet, even as they imitated Old World ways, these colonials forged identities that separated them from Europe.

Spiritual Encounters

Settlers in the New World had the military and economic power to impose their culture—especially their religion—on some indigenous peoples. While the Jesuits had little impact in China, Christian missionaries in the Americas had armies and officials to back up their insistence that Native Americans and African slaves abandon their own deities and spirits for Christ. Nonetheless, their attempts to force conversions were rarely a complete success, and some European settlers became interested in Amerindian culture.

FORCING CONVERSIONS European missionaries, especially Catholics, used numerous techniques to bring Indians within the Christian fold. Smashing idols, razing temples, and whipping backsliders all belonged to the missionaries' arsenal. Catholic orders (principally Dominicans, Jesuits, and Franciscans) also learned what they could about Indian beliefs and rituals—and then exploited that knowledge to make conversions to Christianity. For example, many missionaries demonized local gods, subverted indigenous spiritual leaders, and transformed Indian iconography into Christian symbols. But at the same time, the missionaries preserved much linguistic and ethnographic information about indigenous communities. In sixteenth-century Mexico, the Dominican friar Bernardino de Sahagún compiled an immense ethnography of Mexican ways and beliefs. In seventeenth-century Canada, French Jesuits prepared dictionaries and grammars of the Iroquoian and Algonquian languages and translated Christian hymns into Amerindian tongues.

Neither gentle persuasion nor violent coercion produced the results that missionaries desired. When conversions did occur, the resulting Christian practices were usually hybrid forms in which indigenous deities and rituals merged with Christian ones. Among Andean mountain people, for example, priestesses of local cults took the Christian name Maria to mask their secret worship of traditional deities. In other cases, indigenous communities turned their backs on Christianity and accused missionaries of bringing disease and death. Those who did convert often believed that Christian spiritual power supplemented, rather than supplanted, their own religions.

Indians Becoming Christians. *This image is from a colonial chronicle illustrated and narrated by indigenous scribes who had converted to Christianity. The picture of Indians before the conquest entering a house of prayer is intended to represent the Indians as proto-Christians.*

MIXING CULTURES More distressing to missionaries than the blending of beliefs or outright defiance were the Indians' successes in converting captured colonists, whom they often adopted (particularly women and children) as a way to replace lost kin. It deeply troubled the missionaries that many captured colonists accepted their adoptions and refused to return to colonial society when given the chance. Moreover, some other Europeans voluntarily chose to live among the Indians. Comparing the records of cultural conversion, one eighteenth-century colonist suggested that "thousands of Europeans are Indians," yet "we have no examples of even one of those Aborigines having from choice become European" (Crèvecoeur, p. 306). (Aborigines, or aboriginals, are original, native inhabitants of a region, as opposed to invaders, colonizers, or later peoples of mixed ancestry.) While this calculation may be exaggerated, it reflects the fact that Europeans who adopted Indian culture, like Christianized Indians, lived in a mixed cultural world. In fact, their familiarity with both Indian and European ways made them ideal intermediaries for diplomatic arrangements and economic exchanges.

Europeans also attempted to Christianize slaves from Africa, though many slave owners doubted the wisdom of converting persons they regarded as mere property. Sent forth with the pope's blessing, Catholic priests targeted slave populations in the American colonies of Portugal, Spain, and France. Applying many of the same techniques that missionaries used with Indian "heathens," these priests produced similarly mixed results. Often converts blended Islamic or traditional African religions with Catholicism. Converted slaves wove remembered practices and beliefs from their homeland into their American Christianity, transforming both along the way. In northeastern Brazil, for example, slaves combined the Yoruba faiths of their ancestors with Catholic beliefs, and they frequently attributed powers of African deities to Christian saints. Sometimes Christian and African faiths were practiced side by side. In Saint-Domingue, slaves and free blacks practiced *vodun* ("spirit" in the Dahomey tongue); in Cuba, *santería* ("cult of saints" in Spanish), a faith of similar origins.

Just as slaveholders feared, Christianity—especially in its hybrid forms—could inspire resistance, even revolt, among slaves. Indeed, a major runaway slave leader in mid-eighteenth-century Surinam was a Christian. Those held in bondage in the English colonies drew inspiration from Christian hymns that promised deliverance, and they embraced as their own the Old Testament story of Moses leading the Israelites out of Egypt. By the late eighteenth century, freed slaves like the Methodist Olaudah Equiano (see Chapter 13) were asserting that slavery was unjust and incompatible with Christian brotherhood.

INTERMARRIAGE AND CULTURAL MIXING Beyond the attractions of Indian cultures, Europeans mixed with Indians because there were many more men than women among the

Racial Mixing. Left: *This image shows racial mixing in colonial Mexico—the father is Spanish, the mother Indian, and the children mestizo. This is a well-to-do family, illustrating how Europeans married into the native aristocracy. Right: Here, too, we see a racially mixed family. The father is Spanish, the mother black or African, and the child a mulatto. Observe, however, the less aristocratic and markedly less peaceful nature of this family.*

colonists. Almost all the early European traders, missionaries, and settlers were men (although the British North American settlements saw more women arrive relatively early on). In response to the scarcity of women and as a way to help Amerindians accept the newcomers' culture, the Portuguese crown authorized intermarriage between Portuguese men and local women. These relations often amounted to little more than rape, but longer-lasting relationships developed in places where Indians kept their independence—as among French fur traders and Indian women in Canada, the Great Lakes region, and the Mississippi Valley. Whether by coercion or consent, sexual relations between European men and Indian women resulted in offspring of mixed ancestry. In fact, the mestizos of Spanish colonies and the métis of French outposts soon outnumbered settlers of wholly European descent.

The increasing numbers of African slaves in the Americas further complicated the mix of New World cultures. Unlike marriages between fur traders and Indian women, in which the women held considerable power because of their connections to Indian trading partners, sexual intercourse between European men and enslaved African women was almost always forced. Children born from such unions swelled the ranks of mixed-ancestry people in the colonial population. Again, however, unlike the offspring of European fur traders and Indian women, who generally found an equal place in their mothers' communities or gained power as intermediaries between their parents' cultures, the children of African women and European men generally became the enslaved property of their fathers.

Forming American Identities

Colonization of the Americas brought Europeans, Africans, and Indians into sustained contact, though the nature of the colonies and the character of the contact varied considerably. Where their dominance was strongest, European colonists imposed their ways on subjugated populations and imported what they took to be the chief attributes of the countries and cultures they had left behind. Yet Europeans were not immune to cultural influences from the groups they dispossessed and enslaved, and over time the colonists developed distinctive "American" identities. The cultures and identities of Indians and African slaves also underwent significant transformations, though often what Europeans imposed was only partially adopted.

CREOLE IDENTITIES In Spanish America, ethnic and cultural mixing produced a powerful new class, the **creoles**—persons of European descent born in the Americas. By the late eighteenth century, creoles increasingly resented the control that **peninsulars**—men and women born in Spain or Portugal but living in the Americas—had over colonial society. Creoles especially chafed under the peninsular rulers' exclusive privileges, like those that forbade creoles from trading with other colonial ports. Also, they disliked the fact that royal ministers gave most official posts to peninsulars.

In many cities of the Spanish and Portuguese Empires, reading clubs and salons hosted energetic discussions of fresh Enlightenment ideas and contributed to the growing creole identity. In one university in Peru, Catholic scholars taught their students that Spanish labor drafts and taxes on Andean natives not only violated divine justice but also offended the natural rights of free men. The Spanish crown, recognizing the role of printing presses in spreading troublesome ideas, strictly controlled the number and location of printers in the colonies. In Brazil, royal authorities banned them altogether. Nonetheless, books, pamphlets, and simple gossip allowed new notions of history and politics to circulate among literate creoles.

The global Enlightenment also inspired a quest for modern science as a basis for creole reform. The Spanish government sent Royal Botanical Expeditions composed of scientists and artists to Chile and Peru (1777–1788), New Granada (1783–1816), and New Spain (1787–1803). These campaigns collected and classified an astonishing array of flora; they also produced beautifully illustrated publications that launched an American style of natural painting, notable for documenting the richness of tropical habitats, and several new and marketable commodities that would change the shape of colonization forever.

Perhaps the most significant of these commodities was the one popularized by Celestino Mutis, a Spanish-born physician who had moved to New Granada as a young man. Mutis was fascinated by the medicinal properties of New World plants, and he oversaw the making of no less than 6,500 botanical illustrations from New Granada alone. He was especially interested in the cinchona plant, whose bark had been used by Amerindians and Jesuit missionaries for centuries to cure malaria. Mutis recognized that cinchona, or quinine, if scientifically cultivated, could be the commodity that allowed more Europeans to settle in the tropics. Committed both to the Enlightenment and to Spanish mercantilism, Mutis believed—rightly, it turned out—that his scientific efforts would improve the health of all of humanity *and* yield riches for Spanish colonies.

The botanical conquest of the New World added to the global warehouse of what Europeans and creoles knew about natural diversity. It also emboldened scientific and entrepreneurial activity in the tropics and gave Spanish American creoles a sense that they, too, were part of the "century of light" and on the side of reform and improvement.

ANGLICIZATION In one important sense, wealthy colonists in British America were similar to the creole elites in Iberian America: they, too, copied European ways. For example, they constructed "big houses" (in Virginia) modeled on the country estates of English gentlemen, imported opulent furnishings and fashions from the finest British stores, and exercised more control over colonial assemblies. Imitating the English also involved tightening patriarchal authority. In seventeenth-century Virginia, men had vastly outnumbered women, which gave women some power (widows, in particular, gained greater control over property and more choices when they remarried). During the

The Cinchona Plant. *The creole New Granada botanical expedition generated thousands of scientific illustrations of previously unknown tropical plants. One of the enlightened leaders of this expedition, Celestino Mutis, recommended the intensive cultivation of the cinchona plant, whose bark could be used to make the most effective antimalarial medicine of the day, quinine.*

eighteenth century, however, sex ratios became more equal, and women's property rights diminished as English customs took precedence. Overall, patriarchal authority was evident in family portraits, where husband-patriarchs sat or stood in front of their wives and children.

Intellectually, too, British Americans were linked to Europe. Importing enormous numbers of books and journals, these Americans played a significant role in the Enlightenment as producers and consumers of political pamphlets, scientific treatises, and social critiques. Indeed, drawing on the words of numerous Enlightenment thinkers, American intellectuals created the most famous of enlightened documents: the Declaration of Independence. It announced that all men were endowed with equal rights and were created to pursue worldly happiness. In this way, Anglicized Americans, like the creole elites of Latin America, showed themselves to be products of both European and New World encounters.

The Voyages of Captain James Cook. Left: *During his celebrated voyages to the South Pacific, Cook kept meticulous maps and diaries. Although he had little formal education, he became one of the great exemplars of enlightened learning through experience and experiment.* Right: *Kangaroos were unknown in the western world until Cook and his colleagues encountered (and ate) them on their first visit to Australia. This engraving of the animal (which unlike most animals, plants, and geographical features actually kept the name the Aborigines had given it) from Cook's 1773 travelogue,* A Voyage Round the World in the Years 1768–1771, *lovingly depicts the kangaroo's environs and even emotions.*

CAPTAIN COOK AND THE MAKING OF A NEO-EUROPEAN CULTURE IN OCEANIA

In the South Pacific, another kind of Anglicization was under way, one similarly shaped by imperialism and enlightened science. Here, even more than in Latin America, enlightened science, embodied in the voyages of Captain James Cook, had ecologically as well as culturally transformative consequences, creating replications of Europe in far distant parts of the world. The focus here is on Australia, but one could also analyze the English colonial territories of New Zealand or Canada in the same terms. Here the wiping out of local peoples and the resettlement by white Europeans—albeit many of them outcasts—created the basis for a variation on colonization marked by a greater degree of cultural transfer.

Until Europeans colonized it in the late eighteenth century, Australia was, like the Americas before Columbus, truly a world apart. Separated by water and sheer distance from other regions, Australia's main features were harsh natural conditions and a sparse population. At the time of the European colonization, the island was home to around 300,000 people, mostly hunter-gatherers. While Pacific seafarers may have ventured into the area in the past, there is little evidence that either Chinese or Muslim merchants had ever strayed that far south. Spices had drawn the Portuguese and Dutch into the South Pacific (see Chapter 13), and the Spanish, despite considerable resistance, had conquered Guam and the Mariana Islands by

1700. Both the Portuguese and the Dutch had seen the northern and western coasts of Australia, but they had found only sand, flies, and Aboriginals. Only after the scientific voyages of Captain James Cook (1728–1779) to the region in 1768–1779 did Europeans see Australia's more hospitable eastern coast and develop serious interest in colonization. Now the intrusion into **Oceania** (Australia, New Zealand, and the islands of the southwestern Pacific) presented Europeans with a previously unknown region that could serve as a laboratory for studying other peoples and geographical settings. (See Map 14.1.)

James Cook was a veteran sailor, a practitioner of the new science, and, as it turned out, an imperial transformer of worlds. Known to the Royal Society for his excellent maps and his successful attempts to combat scurvy, Cook was the ideal captain to guide the first of what would be three scholarly voyages to observe the movement of the planet Venus from the Southern Hemisphere. Besides Cook, the Royal Society sent along on this 1768 trip one of its members who was a botanist; a doctor and student of Carolus Linnaeus; and numerous artists and other scientists. The crew also carried sophisticated instruments and had instructions to keep detailed diaries. This grand data-collecting expedition returned in 1771 and was succeeded by two more. As in the case of Mutis's investigations in New Granada, Cook's voyages generated a flood of scholarly and popular publications. These featured approximately 3,000 drawings of Pacific plants, animals, birds, landscapes, and peoples never seen in Europe, all categorized according to Linnaeus's system, and most of them, with the exception of the kangaroo, given English, rather than Aboriginal, names.

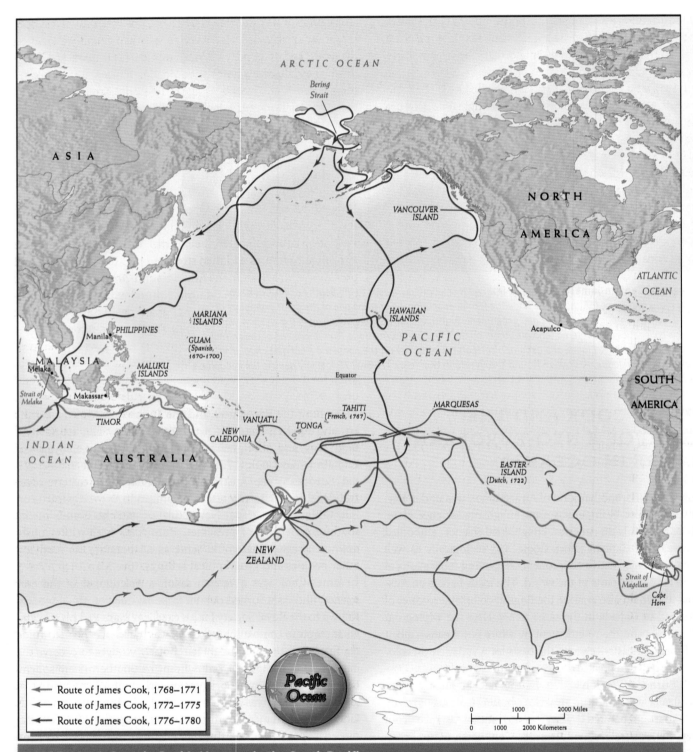

MAP 14.1 | **Captain Cook's Voyages in the South Pacific**

Captain Cook's voyages throughout the Pacific Ocean symbolized a new era in European exploration of other societies.

- According to this map, how many voyages did Cook take?
- Where did Cook explore, and what peoples did he encounter?
- According to your reading, how did Cook's endeavors symbolize "scientific" imperialism?

Beyond the voyages' scientific purposes, however, the British government assigned Cook the secret mission of finding and claiming "the southern continent" for Britain. This he accomplished no less successfully than the project of scholarly data collection, discovering raw materials useful to Britain. Extracting those materials, however, required a labor force, and the Aboriginals of Australia, like the Indians of the Americas, perished in great numbers from imported diseases. Those who survived generally fled to escape control by British masters. Thus, to secure a labor force, plans arose for grand-scale conquest and resettlement by British colonists. On his third voyage, Cook brought an astonishing array of animals and plants with which to turn the South Pacific into a European-style garden. His lieutenant later brought apples, quinces, strawberries, and rosemary to Australia; the seventy sheep imported in 1788 laid the foundations for the region's wool-growing economy. In fact, the domestication of Australia arose from the Europeans' certainty about their superior know-how and a desire to make the entire landmass serve British interests.

In 1788, a British military expedition took official possession of the eastern half of Australia. The intent was, in part, to establish a prison colony far from home. This plan belonged to the realm of "enlightened" dreams: that of ridding "civilized" society of all evils by resettling lawbreakers among the "uncivilized." The intent was also to exploit Australia for its timber and flax and to use it as a strategic base against Dutch and French expansion. In the next decades, immigration—free and forced—increased the Anglo-Australian population from an original 1,000 to about 1.2 million by 1860. Importing their customs and their capital, British settlers turned Australia into a frontier version of home, just as they had done in British America. Yet, such large-scale immigration had disastrous consequences for the surviving Aboriginals. Like the Native Americans, the original inhabitants of Australia were decimated by disease and increasingly forced westward by European settlement, with European ideas and institutions simply replacing local ones. Thus was Oceania, even more than Latin America and far more than the major land empires of Afro-Eurasia, made over in Europe's image.

In their first encounters with Pacific Islanders, most notably in the French encounters in Tahiti that predated Cook's voyages, Europeans were often welcomed by aboriginals extending hospitality and willing to trade foodstuffs and luxury goods. Accordingly, Europeans often portrayed the islands as "tropical paradises" and their light-skinned inhabitants as direct descendants of Adam and Eve. They depicted Tahitians, Hawaiians, Australians, and New Zealanders as virtuous, uncorrupted people who fit the description of the "noble savage" popularized by Jean-Jacques Rousseau. But the more they sought to dominate and the more resistance they encountered, the more Europeans abandoned their romantic view of the South Sea Islanders. Declining appreciation for their innocence was clear after 1779, when Cook himself was murdered by Hawaiians resentful of his contempt for their gods and his crew's less-than-friendly extraction of goods and treatment of local women. The news of Cook's death scandalized his homeland; the king himself, it is said, shed tears. Thereafter, Europeans began to emphasize the "savagery" of South Pacific cultures and insisted ever more urgently on the exportation of "civilized" European culture and forms of rule.

CONCLUSION

New wealth produced by commerce and state building created the conditions for a global cultural renaissance in the sixteenth, seventeenth, and eighteenth centuries. It began in the Chinese and Islamic empires and then stretched into Europe, Africa, and previous worlds apart in the Americas and Oceania. Experiments in religious tolerance encouraged cultural exchange; book production and consumption soared; grand new monuments took shape; luxury goods became available for wider enjoyment.

A striking aspect of this cultural renaissance was its unevenness. While elites and sometimes the middle classes benefited, the poor did not. They remained illiterate, undernourished, and often subjected to brutal treatment by rulers and landowners. Elite women in Europe and China increasingly joined literate society, but they gained no new rights. Urban areas also profited more from the new wealth than rural ones, so people seeking refinement flocked to the cities. Some former cultural centers, like the Italian Peninsula, lost their luster as new, more commercially and culturally dynamic centers took their place.

Among states, too, cultural inequalities were glaring. Although the Islamic and Chinese worlds confidently retained their own systems of knowing, believing, and representing, the Americas and Oceania increasingly faced European cultural pressures. Here, while hybrid practices became widespread by the late eighteenth century, European beliefs and habits predominated as the standards for judging degrees of "civilization." African cultures largely escaped this influence, though their homelands felt the impact of European expansionism through the slave trade.

From a commercial standpoint, the world was more integrated than ever before. But the exposure and cultural borrowing that global trade promoted largely reconfirmed established ways. The Chinese, for instance, still believed in the superiority of their traditional knowledge and customs. Muslim rulers, confident of Islam's primacy, allowed others to form subordinate cultural communities within their realm and adopted Europeans ideas only when doing so served their own imperial purposes. Meanwhile, the Europeans were constructing knowledge that they believed was both universal and objective, enabling mortals to master the world of nature and all its inhabitants. This view would prove consequential, as well as controversial, in the centuries to come.

FOCUS ON: *The Flourishing of Regional Cultures*

The Islamic World

- The Ottomans' unique cultural synthesis accommodates not only mystical Sufis and ultraorthodox *ulama* but also military men, administrators, and clerics.
- The Safavid state proclaims the triumph of Shiism and Persian influences in the sumptuous new capital, Isfahan.
- Mughal courtly culture values art and learning and, at its high point, welcomes non-Muslim contributions.

East Asia

- China's cultural flourishing, coming from within, is evident in the broad circulation of traditional ideas, publishing, and mapmaking.
- Japan's imperial court at Kyoto develops an elite culture of theater, stylized painting, tea ceremonies, and flower arranging.

Europe

- Cultural flourishing known as the Enlightenment yields a faith in reason and a belief in humans' ability to fathom the laws of nature and human behavior.
- European thinkers articulate a belief in unending human progress.
- Europeans expand into Australia and the South Pacific.

Africa

- Slave-trading states such as Asante, Oyo, and Benin celebrate royal power and wealth through art.

The Americas

- Even as Euro-Americans participate in the Enlightenment, their culture reflects Native American and African influences.

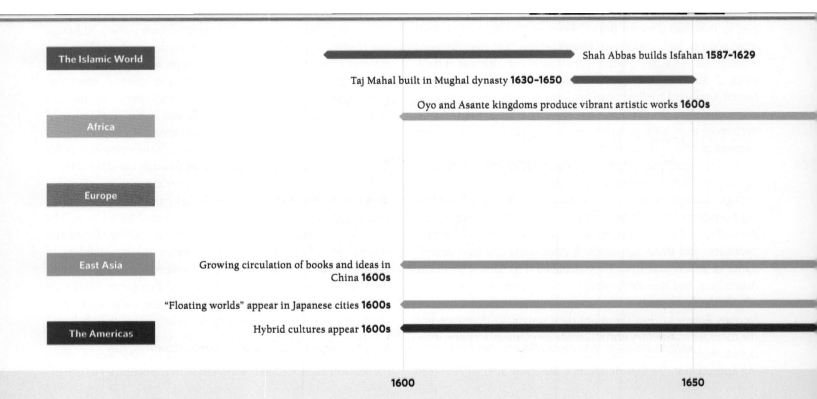

	1600	1650
The Islamic World		Shah Abbas builds Isfahan **1587–1629**
	Taj Mahal built in Mughal dynasty **1630–1650**	
Africa	Oyo and Asante kingdoms produce vibrant artistic works **1600s**	
Europe		
East Asia	Growing circulation of books and ideas in China **1600s**	
	"Floating worlds" appear in Japanese cities **1600s**	
The Americas	Hybrid cultures appear **1600s**	

creoles *p. 547*

Enlightenment p. 535

Forbidden City of Beijing p. 526

great plaza at Isfahan p. 527

Oceania p. 549

Palace of Versailles p. 526

peninsulars p. 547

philosophes p. 538

scientific method p. 537

Taj Mahal p. 525

Topkapi Palace p. 526

1. **Explain** the connections between cultural growth and the creation of a global market.

2. **Discuss** the processes that brought forth cultural syntheses in the three Islamic dynasties during this era. To what extent did European culture influence each empire?

3. **Describe** Chinese and Japanese cultural achievements during this period. How did foreign influences affect each dynasty?

4. **Define** the term *Enlightenment* as it pertained to Europe. How did Enlightenment ideas shape European attitudes toward other cultures?

5. **Describe** how hybrid cultures emerged in the Americas during this era, and **explain** the connection between these cultures and Enlightenment ideology. Did the spread of this philosophy bring communities across the Atlantic together, or did it drive them apart?

6. **Analyze** the different responses to foreign cultures across Afro-Eurasia during this period, and **identify** their similarities and differences.

7. **Describe** and **compare** how each culture in this period reflected the ideas of the state in which it was produced.

8. **Compare and contrast** European exploration of Oceania in the eighteenth century with European exploration of the Americas in the sixteenth century (see Chapter 12). How did European exploration of Oceania transform European attitudes toward non-European groups around the world?

9. **Analyze** the role that race and cultural difference played in the process of global integration.

10. **Explore** the relationship between the scientific method, concepts of racial difference, and established social hierarchies. Pay particular attention to Cook's expeditions to Oceania.

11. **Evaluate** the extent to which dynastic rulers around the world were able to control cultural developments during this period. How did new cultural developments potentially undermine local governments?

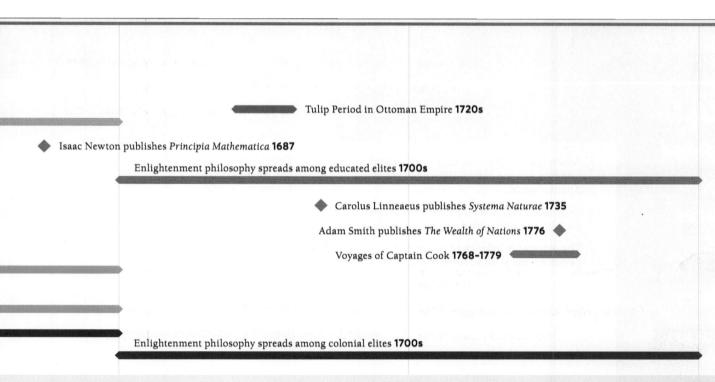

Tulip Period in Ottoman Empire **1720s**

Isaac Newton publishes *Principia Mathematica* **1687**

Enlightenment philosophy spreads among educated elites **1700s**

Carolus Linneaeus publishes *Systema Naturae* **1735**

Adam Smith publishes *The Wealth of Nations* **1776**

Voyages of Captain Cook **1768–1779**

Enlightenment philosophy spreads among colonial elites **1700s**

1700   1750   1800

Before You Read This Chapter

Go to INQUIZITIVE to see what you know & learn what you've missed.

GLOBAL STORYLINES

- A new era based on radically new ideas of freedom and the nation-state emerges in the Atlantic world.

- The industrious and industrial revolutions transform communities and the global economy.

- The worldwide balance of power shifts decisively toward northwestern Europe.

CHAPTER OUTLINE

15

Reordering the World, 1750–1850

In 1798, the French commander Napoleon Bonaparte invaded Egypt. At the time, Europeans regarded this territory as the cradle of a once-great culture, a land bridge to the Red Sea and trade with Asia, and an outpost of the Ottoman Empire. Occupying the country would allow Napoleon to introduce some of the principles of the French Revolution and to seize control of trade routes to Asia. Napoleon also hoped that by defeating the Ottomans, who ruled over Egypt, he would augment his and France's historic greatness. But events did not go as Napoleon planned, for his troops faced a resentful Egyptian population.

Although Napoleon soon returned to France and his dream of a French Egypt was short-lived, his invasion challenged Ottoman rule and threatened the balance of power in Europe. Indeed, the effect of Napoleon's actions in Africa, the Americas, and Europe, combined with the principles of the French Revolution, laid the foundations for a new era—one based on a radically new understanding of freedom as the absence of constraint, the opposition of privileges handed down by a lord or master.

The new idea of freedom first rang out across western Europe and the Americas and reverberated around the world. It destroyed the

American colonial domains of Spain, Portugal, Britain, and France, brought new nations to the stage, and challenged established elites everywhere. The impulse for change was a belief that governments should enact laws that apply to all peoples, though in practice there were exceptions (slaves, women, and colonial subjects). Free speech, free markets, and governments freely elected by freeborn men, it was thought, would benefit everyone. The idea of freedom also challenged systems like mercantilist control and chattel slavery that held empires together. In Europe and the Americas, though not elsewhere, the era also witnessed the emergence of the nation-state. This new form of political organization derived legitimacy from its inhabitants, often referred to as citizens, who, in theory if not always in practice, shared a common culture, language, and ethnicity.

Yet freedom in some corners of the globe set the stage for depriving people of freedom elsewhere and led inexorably to changes in the worldwide balance of power. Even as western Europeans lost their American colonies, they gained economic and military strength that further challenged Asian and African governments. In China, the ruling Manchus faced European pressure to permit expanded trade. In Egypt and the Ottoman Empire, reform-minded leaders tried to modernize. When the rise of Egypt threatened Europe's strategic interests in the eastern Mediterranean, the European states intervened to rein in that country's ambitions.

Underlying much of these political and social upheavals were major changes in the world economy. Countries began to produce goods less for their own population and more for people living in other places around the globe. This specialization for export markets further integrated the world. Regions in Europe began to build factories and harness new sources of energy, like coal, to make cheaper manufactured goods out of imported staples, like cotton, shipped from semitropical frontiers. But results were paradoxical. While the world became more integrated and economic growth took off, social disparities grew wider—both within and across countries. What is called "the industrial revolution" set in motion great divides between Europe and North America and the rest of the world and even within industrializing societies.

REVOLUTIONARY TRANSFORMATIONS AND NEW LANGUAGES OF FREEDOM

In the eighteenth century, the circulation of goods, people, and ideas created pressure for reform around the Atlantic world. As economies expanded, many people in Europe and the Americas felt that the restrictive mercantilist system prevented them from sharing in the new wealth and power. Similarly, an increasingly literate public called for their states to adopt just practices, including the abolition of torture and the accountability of rulers. Although elites resisted the demands for more freedom to trade and more influence in government, power holders could not stamp out these demands before they became—in several places—full-scale revolutions.

Reformers wanted to expand the franchise, to enable property holders to vote. Claims of **popular sovereignty**, the idea that political power depends on "the people," became rooted in the idea of the nation: people who share a common language, common culture, and common history. This, in turn, gave rise to the nation-state as a form of political organization. Over the course of the nineteenth century, political movements began to emphasize nationalism, the idea that peoples having a common identity and thus constituting a fully fledged nation should have states of their own, and democracy, the idea that the people, the *demos*, should choose their own representatives and be governed by them (see Chapter 16). In this chapter, we concentrate on first expressions of this new thinking in thirteen of Britain's North American colonies and in France. In both places, the "nation" and the "people" toppled their former rulers.

This chapter also concentrates on far-reaching economic developments that came in tandem with revolutionary political change. Economic reformers argued that unregulated economies would produce faster economic growth. Going well beyond the work of Adam Smith, they called for **free trade** (or **laissez-faire**), unencumbered by tariffs, quotas, and fees; free markets, which would be unregulated; and free labor, which meant using paid labor rather than slave labor. They insisted that these economic freedoms would yield more just and more efficient societies, ultimately benefiting everyone, everywhere in the world.

Yet the same elites who wanted a freer world often exploited slaves, denied women equal treatment, restricted colonial economies, and tried to forcibly open Asia's and Africa's markets to European trade and investment. In Africa, another corner of the Atlantic world, idealistic upheavals did not lead to free and sovereign peoples, but to greater enslavement.

POLITICAL REORDERINGS

Late in the eighteenth century, revolutionary ideas spread across the Atlantic world, following the trail of Enlightenment ideas about freedom and reason. (See Map 15.1.) As more newspapers, pamphlets, and books circulated in European countries and American colonies, readers began to discuss their societies' problems and to believe they had the right to participate in governance.

The slogans of independence, freedom, liberty, and equality seemed to promise an end to oppression, hardship, and inequities. In the North American colonies and in France, revolutions ultimately brought down monarchies and blossomed in republics. The examples of the United States and France soon encouraged others in the Caribbean and Central and South America to reject the rule of monarchs. In all of these revolutionary environments, new institutions—such as written constitutions and permanent parliaments—claimed to represent the people.

The North American War of Independence, 1776–1783

The American Revolution ended British rule in North America. It was the first in a series of revolutions to shake the Atlantic world, inspired by new ideas of freedom.

By the mid-eighteenth century, Britain's colonies in North America swelled with people and prosperity. Bustling port cities like Charleston, Philadelphia, New York, and Boston saw inflows of African slaves, European migrants, and manufactured goods, while agricultural staples flowed out. A "genteel" class of merchants and landowning planters dominated colonial affairs.

But with settlers arriving from Europe and slaves from Africa, land was a constant source of dispute. Large landowners struggled with independent farmers (yeomen). Sons and daughters of farmers, often unable to inherit or acquire land near their parents, moved westward, where they came into conflict with Amerindian peoples. To defend their lands, many Amerindians allied with Britain's rival, France. After losing the Seven Years' War (see Chapter 13), however, France ceded its Canadian colony to Britain to secure the return of its much more lucrative Caribbean colonies, especially Saint Domingue. This left many Amerindians no choice but to turn to Britain to help them resist the aggressive advances of land-hungry colonists. British officials did make some concessions to Indian interests, but they did not have the troops or financial strength to protect them.

ASSERTING INDEPENDENCE FROM BRITAIN Even as tensions simmered and sometimes boiled over into bloodshed on the western frontier of British North America, the situation of the British in North America still looked very strong in the mid-1760s. At that point, Britain stood supreme in the Atlantic world, with its greatest foes defeated and its empire expanding. Political revolution seemed unimaginable. And yet, a decade later, that is what occurred.

The spark came from the government of King George III, which insisted that colonists help pay for Britain's war with France and for the benefits of being subjects of the British Empire. It seemed only reasonable to King George and his ministers, faced with staggering war debts, that colonists contribute to the crown that protected them. Accordingly, the king's officials imposed taxes on a variety of commodities and tried to end the lucrative smuggling by which colonists had been evading the restrictions that mercantilism was supposed to impose on colonial trade. To the king's surprise and dismay, colonists raised vigorous objections to the new measures and protested having to pay taxes when they lacked political representation in the British Parliament. (See Primary Source: Declaring Independence.)

In 1775, resistance in the form of petitions and boycotts turned into open warfare between a colonial militia and British troops in Massachusetts. Once blood was spilled, more radical voices came to the fore. Previously, leaders of the resistance to taxation without representation had claimed to revere the British Empire while fearing its corruptions. Now calls for severing the ties to Britain became more prominent. Thomas Paine, a recent immigrant from England, captured the new mood in a pamphlet he published in 1776, arguing that it was "common sense" for people to govern themselves. Later that year, the Continental Congress (in which representatives from thirteen colonies gathered) adapted part of Payne's popular pamphlet for the Declaration of Independence.

Drawing on Enlightenment themes (see Chapter 14), the declaration written by Thomas Jefferson affirmed the people's natural rights to govern themselves. It also drew inspiration from the writings of British philosopher John Locke, notably the idea that governments should be based on a **social contract** in which the law binds both ruler and people. Locke had even

The Boston Massacre. *Paul Revere's idealized view of the Boston Massacre of March 5, 1770. In the years after the Seven Years' War, Bostonians grew increasingly disenchanted with British efforts to enforce imperial regulations. When British troops fired on and killed several members of an angry mob in what came to be called the "Boston Massacre," the resulting frenzy stirred revolutionary sentiments among the populace.*

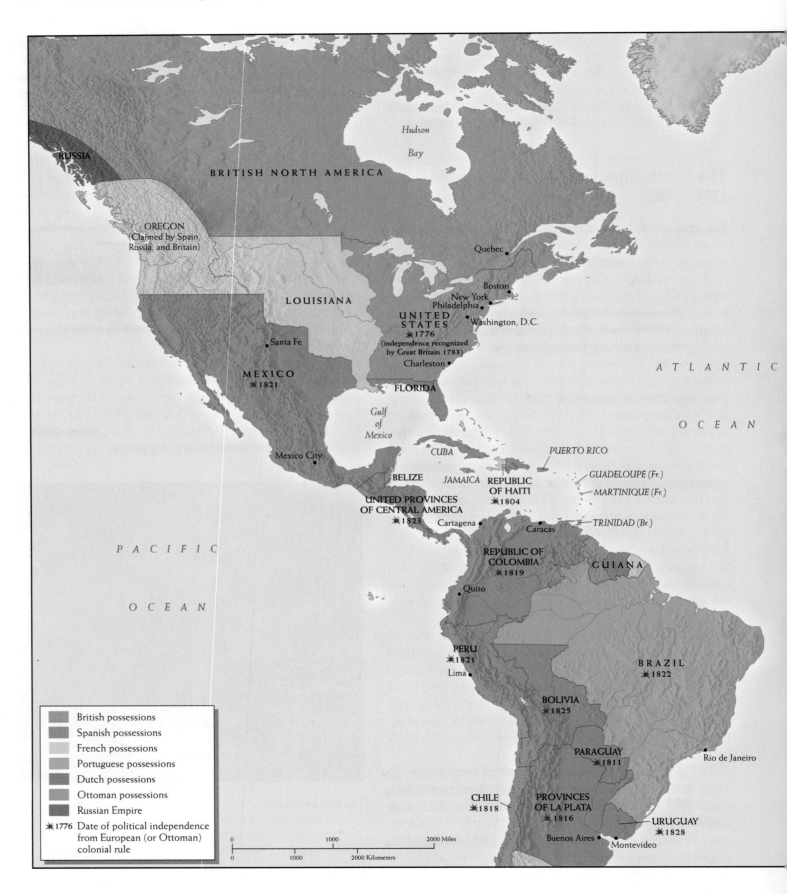

RUSSIA

BRITISH NORTH AMERICA

Hudson Bay

OREGON
(Claimed by Spain, Russia, and Britain)

Quebec

Boston
New York
Philadelphia
Washington, D.C.

LOUISIANA

UNITED
STATES
✳1776
(independence recognized
by Great Britain 1783)
Charleston

Santa Fe

MEXICO
✳1821

FLORIDA

*Gulf
of
Mexico*

Mexico City

CUBA

PUERTO RICO

BELIZE
JAMAICA
REPUBLIC
OF HAITI
✳1804

GUADELOUPE (Fr.)

MARTINIQUE (Fr.)

UNITED PROVINCES
OF CENTRAL AMERICA
✳1823

Cartagena

Caracas

TRINIDAD (Br.)

REPUBLIC OF
COLOMBIA
✳1819

GUIANA

PACIFIC

Quito

ATLANTIC

OCEAN

PERU
✳1821
Lima

BRAZIL
✳1822

OCEAN

BOLIVIA
✳1825

PARAGUAY
✳1811

Rio de Janeiro

CHILE
✳1818

PROVINCES
OF LA PLATA
✳1816

URUGUAY
✳1828

Buenos Aires
Montevideo

British possessions
Spanish possessions
French possessions
Portuguese possessions
Dutch possessions
Ottoman possessions
Russian Empire
✳1776 Date of political independence
from European (or Ottoman)
colonial rule

0   1000   2000 Miles

0   1000   2000 Kilometers

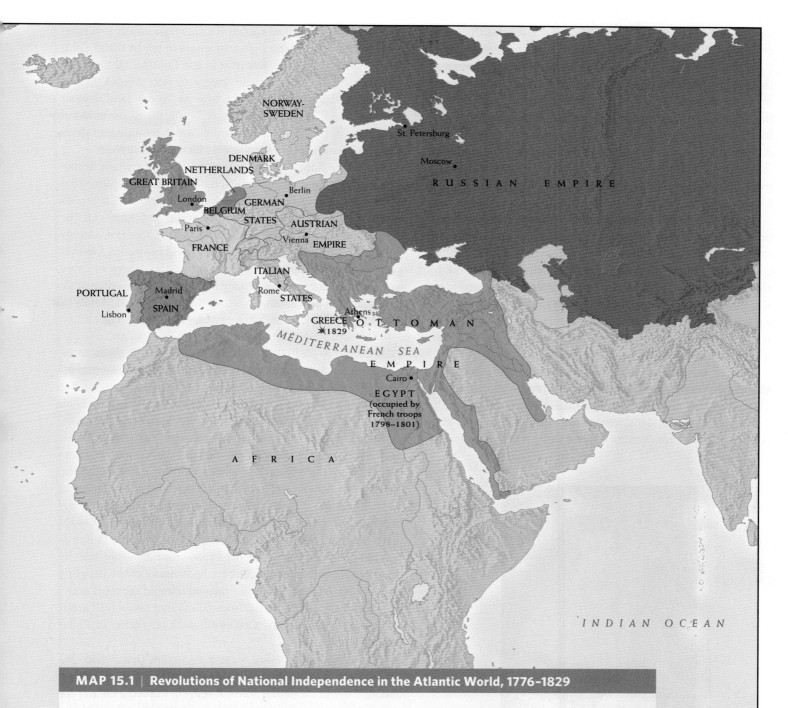

MAP 15.1 | Revolutions of National Independence in the Atlantic World, 1776–1829

Influenced by Enlightenment thinkers and the French Revolution, colonies gained independence from European powers (and in the case of Greece, from the Ottoman Empire) in the late eighteenth and early nineteenth centuries.

- Which European powers granted independence to their colonial possessions in the Americas during this period? What were the first two colonial territories to become independent in the Americas?

- Given that the second American republic arose from a violent slave revolt, why do you suppose the United States was reluctant to recognize its political independence?

- According to your reading, why did colonies in Spanish and Portuguese America obtain political independence decades after the United States won its independence?

written that the people had the right to rebel against their government if it broke the contract and infringed on their rights.

With the Declaration of Independence, the rebels announced their right to rid themselves of the English king and form their own government. But neither the Declaration of Independence nor Locke's writings explained how these colonists (now calling themselves Americans) should organize a nonmonarchical government—or how thirteen weakly connected colonies (now calling themselves states) might prevail against the world's most powerful empire. Nonetheless, the colonies soon became embroiled in a revolution that would turn the world upside down.

During their War of Independence, Americans designed new political arrangements. First, individual states elected delegates to state constitutional conventions, where they drafted written constitutions to govern the workings of their states. Second, by eliminating royal authority, the state constitutions gave extensive powers to legislative bodies, whose members "the people" would elect. But who constituted the people? That is, who had voting rights? Not women. Not slaves. Not Indians. Not even adult white men who owned no property.

Despite the limited extent of voting rights, the notion that all men are created equal overturned former social hierarchies. Thus, common men no longer automatically deferred to gentlemen of higher rank. Many women claimed that their contributions to the revolution's cause (by managing farms and shops in

Abigail Adams. *Abigail Adams was the wife of John Adams, a leader in the movement for American independence and later the second president of the United States. Abigail's letters to her husband testified to the ways in which revolutionary enthusiasm for liberty and equality began to reach into women's minds. In the spring of 1776, Abigail wrote to implore that the men in the Continental Congress "remember the ladies, and be more generous and favorable to them than your ancestors. . . . If particular care and attention is not paid to the Ladies we are determined to foment a Rebellion, and will not hold ourselves bound by any Laws in which we have no voice, or Representation."*

their husbands' absence) earned them greater equality in marriage, including property rights. In letters to her husband, John Adams, who was a representative in the Continental Congress and a champion of American independence, Abigail Adams stopped referring to the family farm as "yours" and instead called it "ours." Most revolutionary of all, many slaves sided against the revolution, for it was the British who offered them freedom—most directly in exchange for military service.

Alas, their hopes for freedom were thwarted when Britain conceded the loss of its rebellious American colonies. That improbable outcome owed to a war in which British armies won most of the major battles but could not finish off the Continental Army under the command of General George Washington. Washington hung on and held his troops together long enough to convince the French that the American cause was not hopeless and that supporting it might be a way to settle a score against the British. This they did, and with the Treaty of Paris (1783), the United States gained its independence.

BUILDING A REPUBLICAN GOVERNMENT With independence, the former colonists had to build a new government. They generally agreed that theirs was not to be a monarchy. But what it *was* to be remained through the 1780s a source of much debate, involving heated words and sometimes heated action.

Amid the political revolution against monarchy, the prospect of a social revolution of women, slaves, and artisans generated a reaction against what American elites called the "excesses of democracy." Their fears increased after farmers in Massachusetts, led by Daniel Shays, interrupted court proceedings in which the state tried to foreclose on their properties for nonpayment of taxes. The farmers who joined in Shays's Rebellion in 1786 also denounced illegitimate taxation—this time, by their state's government. Acting in the interests of the fledgling government, Massachusetts militiamen defeated the rebel army. But to save the young nation from falling into "anarchy," propertied men convened the Constitutional Convention in Philadelphia a year later.

This gathering aimed to forge a document that would create a more powerful national government and a more unified nation. After fierce debate, the convention drafted a charter for a republican government in which power would rest with representatives of the people—not a king. When it went before the states for approval, the Constitution was controversial. Its critics, known as Anti-Federalists, feared the growth of a potentially tyrannical national government and insisted on including a Bill of Rights to protect individual liberties from abusive government intrusions. Ultimately, the Constitution won ratification, and it was soon amended by the Bill of Rights.

Ratification of the Constitution and the addition of the Bill of Rights did not end arguments about the scope and power of the national government of the United States. A question

Declaring Independence

In July 1776, the Continental Congress issued a declaration of independence that announced the secession of the thirteen North American colonies from Great Britain. Principally authored by Thomas Jefferson, the document spelled out the American colonists' lengthy list of grievances against Britain that "impelled" their separation from the empire and that entitled them to international recognition. The Declaration's most famous sentence, however, addressed more universal aspirations based on natural rights: "We hold these Truths to be self-evident, that all men are created equal, that they are endowed by their Creator with certain unalienable Rights, that among these are Life, Liberty, and the pursuit of Happiness."

In the decades after 1776, the United States' declaration became a model for other colonies and provinces asserting their independence, as the documents excerpted here suggest.

The Venezuelan Declaration of Independence (July 5, 1811): It is contrary to order, impossible to the Government of Spain, and fatal to the welfare of America, that the latter, possessed of a range of country infinitely more extensive, and a population incomparably more numerous, should depend and be subject to a Peninsular Corner of the European Continent. . . . We, the Representatives of the United Provinces of Venezuela, calling on the SUPREME BEING to witness the justice of our proceedings and the rectitude of our intentions, do implore his divine and celestial help; and ratifying at the moment in which we are born to the dignity to which his Providence restores to us, the desire we have of living and dying free. . . . We, therefore, . . . DO declare solemnly to the world, that its united Provinces are, and ought to be, from the day, by act and right, Free, Sovereign, and Independent States. . . . And that this, our solemn Declaration may be held valid, firm, and durable, we hereby pledge our lives, fortunes, and sacred tie of our national honour.

The Unanimous Declaration of Independence made by the Delegates of the People of Texas (March 2, 1836): When, in consequence of such acts of malfeasance and abduction on the part of the government, anarchy prevails, and civil society is dissolved into its original elements, in such a crisis, the first law of nature, the right of self-preservation, the inherent and inalienable right of the people to appeal to first principles, and take their political affairs into their own hands in extreme cases, enjoins it as a right towards themselves, and a sacred obligation to their posterity, to abolish such government, and create another in its stead, calculated to rescue them from impending dangers, and to secure their welfare and happiness. . . . We, therefore, the delegates, with plenary powers, of the people of Texas, in solemn convention assembled, appealing to a candid world for the necessities of our condition, do hereby resolve and declare that our political connection with the Mexican nation has forever ended, and that the people of Texas do now constitute a free, sovereign, and independent republic, and are fully invested with the rights and attributes which properly belong to independent nations; and, conscious of the rectitude of our intentions, we fearlessly and confidently commit the issue to the decision of the supreme Arbiter of the destinies of nations.

A Declaration of Independence by the Representatives of the People of the Commonwealth of Liberia (July 16, 1847): We the representatives of the people of the Commonwealth of Liberia, in Convention assembled, invested with authority for forming a new government, relying upon the aid and protection of the Great Arbiter of human events, do hereby, . . . declare the said commonwealth a FREE, SOVEREIGN, AND INDEPENDENT STATE. . . . We recognize in all men, certain natural and inalienable rights: among these are life, liberty, and the right to acquire, possess, enjoy and defend property.

QUESTIONS FOR ANALYSIS

- What common elements can you identify in these declarations? Consider, in particular, the audiences at which they are aimed, the justifications for breaking free of colonial dependence they put forward, and the rights that they claim will be secured by national independence.

- What groups did the American Declaration of Independence overlook, and why?

Source: David Armitage, *The Declaration of Independence: A Global History* (Cambridge, MA: Harvard University Press, 2007), pp. 165, 199–207, 211–223.

that deeply troubled the new nation was slavery—specifically, whether a country that declared all men to be equal could tolerate a substantial slave population. Southern slaveholders, for whom slavery was a mainstay of the economy, answered that question unequivocally, and those individuals who would have preferred a different policy had to give way. In an uneasy truce, political leaders agreed not to let the debate over whether to abolish slavery escalate into a cause for disunion. As the frontier pushed westward, however, the question of which new states would or would not allow slavery sparked debates yet again. Initially, the existence of ample land postponed a confrontation. In 1800, Thomas Jefferson's election as the third president of the United States marked the triumph of a model of sending pioneers out to new lands in order to reduce conflict on old lands. In the same year, however, a Virginia slave named Gabriel Prosser raised an army of slaves to seize the state capital at Richmond and won support from white artisans and laborers for a more inclusive republic. His dream of an egalitarian revolution fell victim to white terror and black betrayal, though: twenty-seven slaves, including Prosser, went to the gallows. With them, for the moment, died the dream of a multiracial republic in which all men were truly created equal.

In a larger Atlantic world context, the American Revolution ushered in a new age based on ideas of freedom. The successful defiance of Europe's most powerful empire and the establishment of a nonmonarchical, republican form of government sent shock waves through the Americas and Europe and even into distant corners of Asia and Africa. It also helped pave the way for other revolts over the next several decades.

The French Revolution, 1789–1799

Partly inspired by the American Revolution, French men and women soon began to call for liberty, too—and the result profoundly shook Europe's dynasties and social hierarchies. Its impact, though, reached well beyond Europe, for the French Revolution, even more than the American, inspired rebels and terrified rulers around the globe.

ORIGINS AND OUTBREAK For decades, enlightened thinkers had attacked France's old regime—the court, the aristocracy, and the church—at the risk of imprisonment or exile. But by the mid-eighteenth century, discontent had spread beyond the educated few. In the countryside, peasants grumbled about having to pay taxes and tithes to the church, whereas nobles and clergy paid almost no taxes. Also, despite improved health and nutrition, peasants still suffered occasional deprivation. A combination of these pressures, as well as a fiscal crisis, unleashed the French Revolution of 1789.

The French king himself opened the door to revolution. Eager to weaken his rival, England, Louis XVI spent huge sums in support of the American rebels—and thereby overloaded the state's debt. To raise sufficient funds, Louis needed to change the structure of taxation; but to do so, he was forced to convene the Estates-General, a medieval advisory body that had not met since 1614. When the king reluctantly agreed to summon the Estates-General in 1788, his subjects rejoiced. The delegates of the clergy (the First Estate) and the aristocracy (the Second Estate) hoped to restore some of the privileges they had lost to the absolutist state. The delegates representing everyone else (the Third Estate), in contrast, believed that the time had come for taxation to be shared equally. The most forceful advocate for this position was a clergyman, Abbé Sieyès, who argued in January 1789 that the Third Estate, those who worked and paid taxes, *were* the nation; the privileged few were parasites. The terrible weather and poor harvest of 1788 also stoked discontent, as the price of bread—the foundation of the French diet—soared and many members of Sieyès's "nation" went hungry.

When the Estates-General finally assembled in late May 1789, but had not yet been convened, bread prices were painfully high. Afraid the king would crush the reform movement, delegates of the Third Estate declared themselves to be the "National Assembly," the body that should determine France's future. On July 14, 1789, a hungry and angry Parisian crowd took to the streets, looting bakeries and attacking the headquarters of the tax collectors. They stormed a medieval armory—the Bastille—that not only was an infamous prison for political prisoners but also held a large store of gunpowder. The crowd murdered the commanding officer, then cut off his head and paraded it through the streets of Paris. On this day (Bastille Day), the king made the fateful decision not to call out the army, and the capital city belonged to the crowd. As news spread to the countryside, peasants torched manor houses and destroyed municipal archives containing records of the hated feudal dues. Barely three weeks later, the French National Assembly abolished the feudal privileges of the nobility and the clergy. In the Declaration of the Rights of Man and of the Citizen, the assembly echoed the Americans' Declaration of Independence, but in more universal language.

REVOLUTIONARY CHANGES AND CONFLICTS The French Declaration laid out an array of enlightened principles that did indeed revolutionize French society and politics. It guaranteed all citizens of the French nation a new kind of liberty, defined not as a special privilege given by the king but as a freedom from constraint, including religious constraints. Against old regimes' legalized inequalities, it proclaimed equality under the law. It also ratified Sieyès's principle that sovereignty resides in the nation. These sweeping changes announced the coming

The "Tennis Court Oath." *Locked out of the chambers of the Estates-General, the deputies of the Third Estate reconvened at a nearby indoor tennis court in June 1789; there they swore an oath not to disband until the king recognized the sovereignty of a national assembly.*

of a new era of liberty, equality, and fraternity that threatened to end dynastic and aristocratic rule in Europe.

Inspired by revolutionary rhetoric, some women argued that the new principles of citizenship should include women's rights as well. In 1791, a group of women demanded the right to bear arms to defend the revolution, but they stopped short of claiming equal rights for both sexes. In their view, women would become citizens by being good revolutionary wives and mothers, not because of any natural rights. In the same year, Olympe de Gouges composed the Declaration of the Rights of Woman and the Female Citizen, proposing rights to divorce, hold property in marriage, be educated, and have public careers.

The all-male assembly did not take up these issues, believing that a "fraternity" of free *men* composed the nation. (For a statement claiming similar rights for women in Britain, see Primary Source: Mary Wollstonecraft on the Rights of Women.)

As the revolution gained momentum, deep divisions emerged. In late 1790, all clergy had to take an oath of loyalty to the new state—an action that enraged Catholics. Meanwhile, the revolutionary ranks began to splinter, as men and women argued over the revolution's proper goals. Soon a new National Convention was elected by universal manhood suffrage, meaning that all adult males could vote—the first such election in Europe. In 1792, the first French Republic was proclaimed.

Women March on Versailles. *On October 5, 1789, a group of market women, many of them fishwives (traditionally regarded as leaders of the poor), marched on the Paris city hall to demand bread. Quickly, their numbers grew, and they redirected their march to Versailles, some 12 miles away and the symbol of the entire political order. In response to the women, the king finally appeared on the balcony and agreed to sign the revolutionary decree and return with the women to Paris.*

Mary Wollstonecraft on the Rights of Women

As revolutionaries stressed the rights of "man" across the Atlantic world, Mary Wollstonecraft (1759–1797), an English writer, teacher, editor, and proponent of spreading education, resented her male colleagues' celebration of their newfound liberties. In A Vindication of the Rights of Woman *(1792), one of the founding works of modern feminism, she argued that the superiority of men was as arbitrary as the divine right of kings. For this, male progressives denounced her. The author is a "hyena in petti-coats," noted one critic. In fact, she was arguing that women had the same rights to be reasonable creatures as men and that education should be available equally to both sexes.*

I love man as my fellow; but his sceptre, real or usurped, extends not to me, unless the reason of an individual demands my homage; and even then the submission is to reason, and not to man. In fact, the conduct of an accountable being must be regulated by the operations of its own reason; or on what foundation rests the throne of God?

It appears to me necessary to dwell on these obvious truths, because females have been insulated, as it were; and while they have been stripped of the virtues that should clothe humanity, they have been decked with artificial graces that enable them to exercise a short-lived tyranny. Love, in their bosoms, taking the place of every nobler passion, their sole ambition is to be fair, to raise emotion instead of inspiring respect; and this ignoble desire, like the servility in absolute monarchies, destroys all strength of character. Liberty is the mother of virtue, and if women be, by their very constitution, slaves, and not allowed to breathe the sharp invigorating air of freedom, they must ever languish like exotics, and be reckoned beautiful flaws in nature. Let it also be remembered, that they are the only flaw.

As to the argument respecting the subjection in which the sex has ever been held, it retorts on man. The many have always been enthralled by the few; and monsters, who scarcely have shown any discernment of human excellence, have tyrannized over thousands of their fellow-creatures. Why have men of superior endowments submitted to such degradation? For, is it not universally acknowledged that kings, viewed collectively, have ever been inferior, in abilities and virtue, to the same number of men taken from the common mass of mankind—yet have they not, and are they not still treated with a degree of reverence that is an insult to reason? China is not the only country where a living man has been made a God. *Men* have submitted to superior strength to enjoy with impunity the pleasure of the moment; *women* have only done the same, and therefore till it is proved that the courtier, who servilely resigns the birthright of a man, is not a moral agent, it cannot be demonstrated that woman is essentially inferior to man because she has always been subjugated.

QUESTIONS FOR ANALYSIS

- Wollstonecraft compares men to kings and women to slaves. What are her criticisms of kings, and why does she call them "monsters"?
- In what ways are Wollstonecraft's ideas an outgrowth of Enlightenment thinking?
- Do you find Wollstonecraft's arguments compelling? Explain why or why not.

Source: Mary Wollstonecraft, *A Vindication of the Rights of Woman*, edited by Miriam Brody (New York: Penguin Books, 1792/1993), pp. 122–123.

The radicals believed that to sweep away traditional forms of inequality and oppression, they would need to destroy the old regime's entire system of thinking and ways of speaking. So they changed street names to honor revolutionary heroes, destroyed monuments to the royal family, adopted a new flag, and insisted that everyone be addressed as "citizen." They were so exhilarated by the new world they were creating that they changed time itself. Now they proclaimed time not from the birth of Christ but from the moment that the French Republic was proclaimed. Thus, September 22, 1792, became day 1 of year 1 of the new age. A new calendar was created, and the new ten months were given the names of natural phenomena. For example, the month corresponding to our November was dubbed "Brumaire," the month of fog.

But these changes also produced opposition. As antirevolutionary armies began to mass on France's borders, radicals grew increasingly afraid that internal enemies, especially clergymen and aristocrats, were conspiring against the revolution. The radicals closed the churches and imprisoned all clergy members who would not swear the oath of loyalty to the revolutionary state. These measures were deeply unpopular and stoked counterrevolutionary opposition. Louis XVI himself was accused of conspiracy, and in January 1793 he lost his head to the guillotine.

FRUCTIDOR

Le Fructidor. *In 1792, radical French revolutionaries replaced France's traditional calendar, displacing saints and holy days, and renaming the months after natural phenomena. For example, the third month of the summer quarter (corresponding to the harvest months of August and early September) was renamed Le Fructidor, based on the Latin word fructus, meaning fruit. Almanacs such as this one offered French citizens visual representations of the new dating system.*

THE TERROR After the king's execution, radicals known as Jacobins, who wanted to extend the revolution beyond France's borders, instituted the first national draft to form, by 1794, the world's largest modern army of 800,000 soldiers. Led by the lawyer Maximilien Robespierre, the Jacobins also launched the Reign of Terror to purge the nation of its internal enemies. These included aristocrats but also those who hid priests, resisted the draft, or refused to hand their grain over to revolutionary troops. Some antirevolutionary Catholics, peasants, and draft dodgers took up arms, creating civil war conditions in several parts of France. Jacobin leaders oversaw the execution of as many as 40,000 of these so-called enemies of the people.

By mid-1794, enthusiasm for Robespierre's measures had lost popular support, and Robespierre himself went to the guillotine on 9 Thermidor (July 28, 1794). His execution marked the end of the Terror. Several years later, following more political turmoil, a coup d'état brought to power a thirty-year-old general from the recently annexed Mediterranean island of Corsica.

The general, **Napoleon Bonaparte** (1769–1821), put security and order ahead of social reform. True, his regime retained many of the revolutionary changes, especially those associated with more efficient state government; but retreating from the Jacobins' anti-Catholicism, he allowed religion to be freely practiced again in France. Determined not only to reform France but also to prevail over its enemies, he retreated from republican principles. Napoleon first was a member of a three-man consulate; then he became first consul; finally, he proclaimed himself emperor. Most important, he created a civil legal code—the Napoleonic Code—that applied throughout all of France (and the French colonies, including the Louisiana Territory). By designing a law code applicable to the nation as a whole, Napoleon created a model that would be widely imitated by emerging nation-states in Europe and the Americas in the century to come.

The Napoleonic Era, 1799–1815

Determined to extend the reach of French influence, Napoleon had his armies trumpet the principles of liberty, equality, and fraternity wherever they went. Many local populations actually embraced the French, regarding them as liberators from the old order—as indeed in many cases they proved to be. Inspired by his leadership, many non-Frenchmen, including many Poles, volunteered to fight in the army. Napoleon was not surprised to face resistance from aristocrats commanding foreign armies, but he so believed that he was the great liberator that he was shocked when ordinary people rebelled against the French, as was the case in Egypt. After defeating Mamluk troops there in 1798, Napoleon soon faced a rebellious local Egyptian population.

In Portugal, Spain, and Russia, French troops also faced fierce popular resistance. Portuguese and Spanish soldiers and peasants formed bands of resisters called guerrillas, and British troops joined them to fight the French in the Peninsular War (1808–1813). In Germany and Italy, as local inhabitants grew tired of hearing that the French occupiers' ways were superior, many looked to their past for inspiration to oppose the French. Now they discovered something they had barely recognized before: *national* traditions and borders.

In Europe, Napoleon extended his empire from the Iberian Peninsula to the Austrian and Prussian borders. (See Map 15.2.) In 1812, he invaded Russia and marched his now multinational army all the way to Moscow. His forces, however, were overstretched, undersupplied, and outmaneuvered by wily Russian troops. Soon, the French were forced to retreat through battle-scarred territory, suffering grievously from Russian harassment and the harsh winter. As Napoleon fled westward, all of the major European powers united against him and

MAP 15.2 | Napoleon's Empire, 1812

Early in the first decade of the nineteenth century, Napoleon controlled almost all of Europe.

- What major states were under French control? What countries were allied to France?
- Compare this map with the European part of Map 15.1, and explain how Napoleon redrew the map of Europe. What major country was not under French control?
- According to the reading, how was Napoleon able to control and build alliances with so many states and kingdoms?

decimated what was left of his army. Forced to capitulate in 1814, Napoleon was sent into exile, but he managed to escape soon after to lead his troops one last time. At the Battle of Waterloo in Belgium in 1815, armies from Prussia, Austria, Russia, and Britain crushed his troops as they made their last stand.

In 1815, delegates from the victorious states met at the Congress of Vienna. They agreed to respect one another's borders and to cooperate in preventing future revolutions and war. They restored thrones to monarchs deposed by the French under Napoleon, and they returned France itself to the care of a new Bourbon king.

The impact of the French Revolution and Napoleon's conquests, however, was far-reaching. The stage was now set for a century-long struggle between those who wanted to restore monarchies and hierarchies as they existed before the French Revolution and those who wanted to guarantee a more liberal order based on individual rights, limited government, and free trade.

Revolution in Saint Domingue (Haiti)

The thirteen colonies in North America were not the only ones to secede from European masters. France also saw colonies break away in this age of new freedoms. This was the case in Saint Domingue, presently Haiti. Unlike most of British North

Battle of the Pyramids. *The French army invaded Egypt with grand ambitions and high hopes. Napoleon brought a large cadre of scholars along with his 36,000-man army, intending to win Egyptians to the cause of the French Revolution and to establish a French imperial presence on the banks of the Nile. This idealized portrait of the famous Battle of the Pyramids, fought on July 21, 1798, shows Napoleon and his forces crushing the Mamluk military forces.*

America, here the revolution came from the bottom rungs of the social ladder: slaves. In this Caribbean colony, freedom therefore meant not just liberation from Europe, but also emancipation from white planters. Saint Domingue therefore added a second, global dimension to the nineteenth-century struggle over personal liberties. It also posed very dramatically the question: How universal were these new rights?

The French Revolution sent shock waves through this highly prized French colony. At the time, the island's black slave population numbered 500,000, compared with 40,000 white French settlers and about 30,000 free "people of color" (individuals of mixed black and white ancestry as well as freed black slaves). Almost two-thirds of the slaves were relatively recent arrivals, brought to the colony to toil on its renowned sugar plantations, which were exceptional in their brutality. The slave population was an angry majority without local ties, producing wealth for rich absentee landlords of a different race.

The calling of the Estates-General in France in 1789 inspired white settlers in Saint Domingue, little realizing how small a minority they were and how deeply the vast slave population resented them, to demand self-government for themselves. The slaves, however, borrowed the French revolutionary slogan of liberty, equality, and fraternity to denounce their masters and to demand their freedom. Civil war erupted, and Dominican slaves fought French forces that had arrived to restore order. Finally, in 1793, the left wing of the National Convention in

Revolution in Saint Domingue. *In 1791, slaves and people of color rose up against white planters. This engraving was based on a German report on the uprising and depicts white fears of slave rebellion as much as the actual events themselves.*

Two Case Studies in Greed and Environmental Degradation

The Caribbean has four large islands, known as the Greater Antilles, each of which has a distinctive history—Cuba, Jamaica, Puerto Rico, and Hispaniola. Our discussion here is about the island of Hispaniola, which Columbus discovered in 1492 and which briefly became the center of Spain's New World empire. Later, in the seventeenth century, the French took over the smaller, western part of the island, and when political independence came to the Caribbean, the island evolved into the two present-day states of Haiti and the Dominican Republic. Although both are relatively poor countries, their present economic and social differences are markedly and surprisingly different, especially considering that they share a relatively small island.

Haiti is the poorest country in the Americas. It is 99 percent deforested, suffers from massive soil erosion, and has a government unable to provide even the most basic services of water, electricity, and education to its people. Right next door, the Dominican Republic, with a population roughly the same size as Haiti's, has five times as many cars and trucks, six times as many paved roads, seven times as many college and university graduates, and eight times as many physicians. Its citizens enjoy significantly longer life expectancy and lower infant mortality than their Haitian neighbors. The differences cry out for an explanation, and one can be found only by examining the radically different histories of the two lands.

Two hundred and fifty years ago, Haiti, which was under French colonial rule at that time and known as Saint Domingue, was the richest colony in the Americas, perhaps even the richest colony in the world, accounting for two-thirds of France's worldwide investment. In contrast, Spanish-ruled Santo Domingo, which had ceased to be of interest to the Spanish colonial elites, who had turned their attention to the more populous and resource-rich territories of Mexico and Peru, was a backwater colonial territory. Saint Domingue's extraordinary wealth came from large, white-owned sugar plantations that used a massive and highly coerced slave population. The slaves' lives were short and brutal, lasting on average only fifteen years; hence, the wealthy planter class had to replenish their labor supplies from Africa at frequent intervals.

White planters on the island were eager to amass quick fortunes so that they could sell out and return to France. Vastly outnumbered by enslaved Africans at a time when abolitionist sentiments were gaining ground in Europe and even

Toussaint L'Ouverture. *In the 1790s, Toussaint L'Ouverture led the slaves of the French colony of Saint Domingue in the world's largest and most successful slave insurrection. Toussaint embraced the principles of the French Revolution and demanded that universal rights be applied to people of African descent.*

France, more deeply committed to the ideal of equality, abolished slavery, though they also did so in an effort to restore order in the colony.

Once liberated, the former slaves took control of the island, but their struggles were not over. First they had to fight British and Spanish forces on the island. Then, after Napoleon took power in France, bringing with him a strong commitment to order and France's imperial ambitions, the French restored slavery and sent an army to suppress forces led by Toussaint L'Ouverture, a former slave. But before long, a combination of guerrilla fighters and yellow fever decimated the French army. In 1804, General Jean-Jacques Dessalines declared "Haiti" independent. (See Current Trends in World History: Two Case Studies in Greed and Environmental Degradation.)

The specter of a free country ruled by former slaves sent shudders across the Western Hemisphere and also in Britain and Spain, which had neighboring colonies with large slave populations. What if the revolt went viral? All around the Caribbean, news circulated about slave conspiracies. In Florida, fugitive slaves banded together with Seminole Indians to drive European settlers into the sea. The Haitian government contributed money and some troops to insurrectionists in South America. Charleston, South Carolina, went into a panic in 1793 when Dominican slaves were freed. As far away as Albany, New York, slaves were executed for arson. Jamaican rulers went on high alert. A version of martial law was declared in Venezuela. Thomas Jefferson, author of the Declaration of Independence and the U.S. president at the time, was also a holder of numerous slaves, and he refused circulating among slaves in the Americas, the planters' families knew that their prosperity was unlikely to last. They gave little thought to sustainable growth and were not troubled that they were destroying their environment.

Yet, the planters greeted the onset of the French Revolution in 1789 with enthusiasm. They saw an opportunity to assert their independence from France, to engage in wider trading contacts with North America and the rest of the world, and thus to become even richer. They ignored the possibility that the ideals of the French Revolution—especially its slogan of liberty, equality, and fraternity—could inspire the island's free blacks, free mulattoes, and slaves. Indeed, no sooner had the white planters thrown in their lot with the Third Estate in France than a slave rebellion broke out in Saint Domingue. From its beginnings in 1791, it led, after great loss of life to African slaves and French soldiers, to the proclamation of an independent state in Haiti in 1804, ruled by African Americans. Haiti became the Americas' second independent republican government.

Although the revolt brought political independence to its black population, it only intensified the land's environmental deterioration. Not only did sugarcane

fields become scorched battlefields, but freed slaves rushed to stake out independent plots on the old plantations and in wooded areas. In both places, the new peasant class energetically cleared the land. The small country became even more deforested, and intensive cultivation increased erosion and soil depletion. Haiti fell into a more vicious cycle of environmental degradation and poverty.

The second case study of greed leading to the destruction of the environment comes from the independent Brazilian state, where the ruling elite, having achieved autonomy from Portugal, expanded the agrarian frontier. Landowners oversaw the clearing of ancient hardwood forests so that slaves and squatters could plant coffee trees. The clearing process had begun with sugarcane in the coastal regions, but it accelerated with coffee plantings in the hilly regions of São Paulo. In fact, coffee was a worse threat to Brazil's forests than any other invader in the previous 300 years. Consider that coffee trees thrive on soils that are neither soggy nor overly dry. Therefore, planters razed the "virgin" forest, which contained a balanced variety of trees and undergrowth, and Brazil's once-fertile soil suffered rapid depletion by a single-crop industry. Within one generation, the

clear-cutting led to infertile soils and extensive erosion, which drove planters farther into the frontier to destroy even more forest and plant more coffee groves. The environmental impact was monumental: between 1788 and 1888, when slavery was abolished, Brazil produced about 10 million tons of coffee at the expense of 300 million tons of ancient forest biomass (the accumulated biological material from living organisms).

QUESTIONS FOR ANALYSIS

- Who intensified the deforestation and degradation in each story, and why did they do it?
- Why do you think deforestation increased in intensity after Haitians and Brazilians gained their autonomy/independence?

Explore Further

Diamond, Jared, and James A. Robinson (eds.). *Natural Experiments of History* (2010).

Geggus, David (ed.). *The Impact of the Haitian Revolution in the Atlantic World* (2001).

to recognize Haiti. Like other American slave owners, he worried that the example of a successful slave uprising might inspire similar revolts in the United States and elsewhere in the Americas.

The revolution in Saint Domingue therefore tilted the scales of campaigns for liberty far beyond the island. Fear of the contagion of slave revolt forced some governments to rethink the commitment to slavery altogether. The British government curtailed the expansion of plantation agriculture in Trinidad. One by one, European and American governments began to question the wisdom of importing more African slaves lest they lose control of their colonies. It was not just exalted ideals of liberty that fueled the abolitionist movement, but also the fear of what would happen if slaves rose up violently to claim rights given to other humans.

Revolutions in Spanish and Portuguese America

From North America and France, revolutionary enthusiasm spread through Spanish and Portuguese America. But unlike the colonists' war of independence that produced the United States, political upheaval in the rest of the Americas began first of all from subordinated people of color. (See Map 15.3.)

Even before the French Revolution, Andean Indians rebelled against Spanish colonial authority. In a spectacular uprising in the 1780s, they demanded freedom from forced labor and compulsory consumption of Spanish wares. After an army of 40,000 to 60,000 Andean Indians besieged the ancient capital of Cuzco and nearly vanquished Spanish

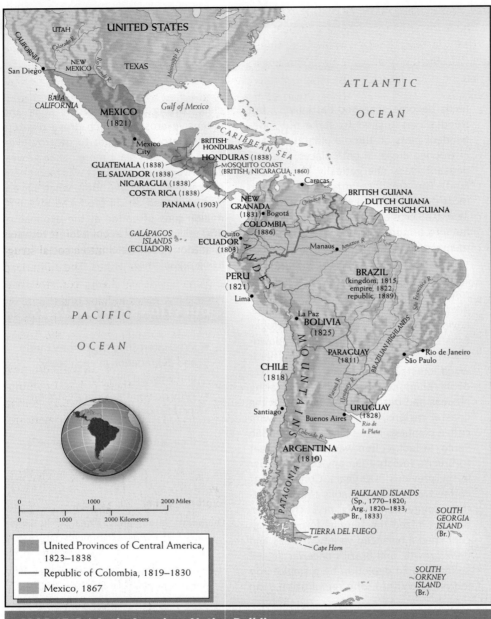

MAP 15.3 | Latin American Nation Building

Creating strong, unified nation-states proved difficult in Latin America. The map highlights this experience in Mexico, the United Provinces of Central America, and the Republic of Colombia. In each case, the governments' territorial and nation-building ambitions failed to some degree.

- During what period did a majority of the colonies in Latin America gain independence?
- Which European countries lost the most in Latin America during this period?
- According to the reading, why did all these colonies gain their independence during this time?

the independence-seeking Anglo-American colonists, lest they unleash a social revolution. Ultimately, however, the French Revolution and Napoleonic Wars shattered the ties between Spain and Portugal and their American colonies.

BRAZIL AND CONSTITUTIONAL MONARCHY Brazil was a prized Portuguese colony whose path to independence saw little political turmoil and no social revolution. In 1807, French troops stormed Lisbon, the capital of Portugal, but not before the royals and their associates fled to Rio de Janeiro, then the capital of Brazil. There they made reforms in administration, agriculture, and manufacturing, and they established schools, hospitals, and a library. In fact, the royals' migration prevented the need for colonial claims for autonomy, because with their presence Brazil was now the center of the Portuguese Empire. Furthermore, the royal family willingly shared power with the local planter aristocracy, so the economy prospered and slavery expanded.

In 1821, the exiled Portuguese king returned to Lisbon, instructing his son Pedro to preserve the family lineage in Rio de Janeiro. Soon, however, Brazilian elites rejected Portugal altogether. Fearing that colonists might topple the dynasty in Rio de Janeiro and spark regional disputes, in 1822 Pedro declared Brazil an independent empire. Shortly thereafter, he established a constitutional monarchy, which would last until the late nineteenth century. By the 1840s, Brazil had achieved a political stability unmatched in the Americas. Its socially controlled transition from colony to nation was unique in Latin America.

armies, it took Spanish forces many years to eliminate the insurgents.

After this uprising, Iberian American elites who feared their Indian or slave majorities renewed their loyalty to the Spanish or Portuguese crown. They hesitated to imitate

MEXICO'S INDEPENDENCE When Napoleon occupied Spain, he sparked a crisis in the Spanish Empire, spurring independence movements throughout the colonies. Because the ruling Spanish Bourbons fell captive to Napoleon in 1807, colonial elites in Buenos Aires (Argentina), Caracas (Venezuela), and Mexico City (Mexico) enjoyed self-rule without an emperor. Once the Bourbons returned to power in 1814 after Napoleon was crushed, creoles (American-born Spaniards) resented it when Spain reinstated peninsulars (colonial officials born in Spain). Creoles wanted to free themselves of these officials.

From 1810 to 1813, two rural priests in Mexico, Father Miguel Hidalgo and Father José María Morelos, galvanized an insurrection of peasants, Indians, and artisans. They sought an end to abuses by the elite, denounced bad government, and called for redistribution of wealth, return of land to the Indians, and respect for the Virgin of Guadalupe (who later became Mexico's patron saint). The rebellion nearly choked off Mexico City, the colony's capital, which horrified peninsulars and creoles alike and led them to support royal armies that eventually crushed the uprising.

Despite the military victory, Spain's hold on its colony weakened. Like the creoles of South America, those of Mexico identified themselves more as Mexicans and less as Spanish Americans. So when the Spanish king appeared unable to govern effectively abroad and even within Spain, the colonists considered home rule. Anarchy seemed to spread through Spain in 1820, and Mexican generals (with support of the creoles) proclaimed Mexican independence in 1821. Unlike in Brazil, Mexican secession did not lead to stability.

OTHER SOUTH AMERICAN REVOLUTIONS The loosening of Spain's grip on its colonies was more prolonged and militarized than Britain's separation from its American colonies. Venezuela's Simón Bolívar (1783–1830), the son of a merchant-planter family who was educated on Enlightenment texts, dreamed of a land governed by reason. He revered Napoleonic France as a model state built on military heroism and constitutional proclamations. So did the Argentine leader, General José de San Martín (1778–1850). Men like Bolívar, San Martín, and their many generals waged extended wars of independence against Spanish armies and their allies between 1810 and 1824. In some areas, like present-day Uruguay and Venezuela, the wars left entire provinces depopulated.

What started in South America as a political revolution against Spanish colonial authority escalated into a social struggle among Indians, mestizos, slaves, and whites. The militarized populace threatened the planters and merchants; rural folk battled against aristocratic creoles; Andean Indians fled the mines and occupied great estates. Provinces fought their neighbors. Popular armies, having defeated Spanish forces by the 1820s, fought civil wars over the new postcolonial order.

New states and collective identities of nationhood now emerged. However, a narrow elite led these political communities, and their guiding principles were contradictory. Simón Bolívar, for instance, urged his followers to become "American,"

Latin American Revolutionaries. Left: *At the center of this Juan O'Gorman mural is the Mexican priest and revolutionary Miguel Hidalgo y Costilla, who led—as O'Gorman portrays—a multiclass and multiethnic movement.* Right: *Simón Bolívar fought Spanish armies from Venezuela to Bolivia, securing the independence of five countries with the greater goal of transforming the former colonies into modern republics. Among his favorite models were George Washington and Napoleon Bonaparte, whose iconic portrait by Jacques-Louis David inspired this painting of Bolívar.*

to overcome their local identities. He wanted the liberated countries to form a Latin American confederation, urging Peru and Bolivia to join Venezuela, Ecuador, and Colombia in the "Gran Colombia." But local identities prevailed, giving way to unstable national republics. Bolívar died surrounded by enemies; San Martín died in exile. The real heirs to independence were local military chieftains, who often forged alliances with landowners. Thus, the legacy of the Spanish American revolutions was contradictory and echoed developments elsewhere around the world: the triumph of wealthy elites under a banner of liberty, yet often at the expense of poorer, nonwhite, and mixed populations.

CHANGE AND TRADE IN AFRICA

Africa also was swept up in revolutionary tides, as increased domestic and world trade—including the selling of African slaves—shifted the terms of state building across the continent. The main catalyst for Africa's political shake-up was the rapid growth and then the demise of the Atlantic slave trade. Here, in contrast to the Americas and Europe and even much of the rest of the world, ideals like liberty, equality, fraternity, and the pursuit of happiness had decidedly contrary effects. The abolition of the slave trade, which European reformers believed would lead to economic prosperity based on "legitimate trade," had the perverse effect of intensifying domestic slavery. As Africa became an exporter of raw materials rather than human beings, the hard work done on African farms and plantations—producing palm, palm kernels, peanuts, and gum for export—was done by slaves.

Abolition of the Slave Trade

Even as it enriched and empowered some Africans and many Europeans, the slave trade became a subject of fierce debate in the late eighteenth century. Some European and American revolutionaries argued that slave labor was inherently less productive than free wage labor and ought to be abolished. At the same time, another group favoring abolition of the slave trade insisted that traffic in slaves was immoral. In London they created committees, often led by Quakers, to lobby Parliament for an end to the slave trade. Quakers in Philadelphia did likewise. Pamphlets, reports, and personal narratives denounced the traffic in people. (See Primary Source: Frederick Douglass Asks, "What to the Slave Is the Fourth of July?")

In response to abolitionist efforts, North Atlantic powers moved to prohibit the slave trade. Denmark acted first in 1803, Great Britain followed in 1807, and the United States joined the campaign in 1808. Over time, the British persuaded the French and other European governments to do likewise. To enforce the ban, Britain posted a naval squadron off the coast of West Africa to prevent any slave trade above the equator and finally compelled Brazil and Cuba, the last countries to allow slavery after the end of the American Civil War, to end slave imports. After 1850, Atlantic slave shipping dropped sharply.

But up until the 1860s, even though the British had outlawed the slave trade and the Americans had agreed to cease importing slaves, slavers continued to buy and ship captives, often illegally. British squadrons that stopped these smugglers

Chasing Slave Dhows. *From being one of the major proponents of the Atlantic slave trade the British became its chief opponent, using their naval forces to suppress those European and African slave traders who attempted to subvert the injunction against slave trading. Here a British vessel chases an East African slave dhow trying to run slaves from the island of Zanzibar.*

Frederick Douglass Asks, "What to the Slave Is the Fourth of July?"

Frederick Douglass spent the first twenty years of his life as a slave. After running away in 1838, he toured the northern United States delivering speeches that attacked the institution of slavery. The publication of his autobiography in 1845 cemented his standing as a leading abolitionist. In the excerpt below, taken from an address delivered on July 5, 1852, Douglass contrasts the freedom and natural rights extolled in the Declaration of Independence and celebrated on the Fourth of July with the dehumanizing condition—and lack of freedom—of African American slaves.

Fellow-Citizens—pardon me, and allow me to ask, why am I called upon to speak here to-day? What have I, or those I represent, to do with your national independence? Are the great principles of political freedom and of natural justice, embodied in that Declaration of Independence, extended to us? and am I, therefore, called upon to bring our humble offering to the national altar, and to confess the benefits, and express devout gratitude for the blessings, resulting from your independence to us?. . .

But, such is not the state of the case. I say it with a sad sense of the disparity between us. I am not included within the pale of this glorious anniversary! Your high independence only reveals the immeasurable distance between us. The blessings in which you this day rejoice, are not enjoyed in common. The rich inheritance of justice, liberty, prosperity, and independence, bequeathed by your fathers, is shared by you, not by me. The sunlight that brought life and healing to you, has brought stripes and death to me. This Fourth of July is *yours*, not *mine. You* may rejoice, *I* must mourn. . . .

Must I undertake to prove that the slave is a man? That point is conceded already. Nobody doubts it. The slaveholders themselves acknowledge it in the enactment of laws for their government. They acknowledge it when they punish disobedience on the part of the slave. There are seventy-two crimes in the state of Virginia, which, if committed by a black man (no matter how ignorant he be) subject him to the punishment of death; while only two of these same crimes will subject a white man to the like punishment. What is this but the acknowledgment that the slave is a moral, intellectual, and responsible being. The manhood of the slave is conceded. It is admitted in the fact that southern statute books are covered with enactments forbidding, under severe fines and penalties, the teaching of the slave to read or write. When you can point to any such laws, in reference to the beasts of the field, then I may consent to argue the manhood of the slave. When the dogs in your streets, when the fowls of the air, when the cattle on your hills, when the fish of the sea, and the reptiles that crawl, shall be unable to distinguish the slave from a brute, then will I argue with you that the slave is a man!

Source: David W. Blight (ed.), *Narrative of the Life of Frederick Douglass: An American Slave, Written by Himself* (Boston: Bedford Books, 1993), pp. 141–145.

took the freed captives to the British base at Sierra Leone and resettled them there. Liberia, too, became a territory for freed captives and for former slaves returning from the Americas.

New Trade with Africa

Even as the Atlantic slave trade died down, Europeans promoted commerce with Africa. Now they wanted Africans to export raw materials and to purchase European manufactures. What Europeans liked to call "legitimate" trade aimed to raise the Africans' standard of living by substituting trade in produce for trade in slaves. West Africans responded by exporting palm kernels and peanuts. The real bonanza was in vegetable oils to lubricate machinery and make candles and in palm oil to produce soap. Africa's palm and peanut plantations were less devastating to the environment than their predecessors in the West Indies had been. There, planters had felled forests to establish sugar estates (see Chapter 12). In West Africa, where palm products became crucial exports, the palm tree had always grown wild. Although intensive cultivation caused some deforestation, the results were not as extreme as in the Caribbean. Regardless of the environmental impact, European merchants argued that by becoming vibrant export societies, Africans would earn the wealth to profitably import European wares.

SUCCESS IN THE AGE OF LEGITIMATE COMMERCE

Emerging in the age of legitimate commerce, the new trade gave rise to a generation of successful West African merchants. There were many rags-to-riches stories, like that of King Jaja of Opobo (1821–1891). Kidnapped and sold into slavery as a youngster, he started out paddling canoes carrying palm oil to coastal ports. Ultimately becoming the head of a coastal canoe house, as a merchant-prince and chief he founded the port of Opobo and could summon a flotilla of war canoes on command. Another freed slave, a Yoruba, William Lewis, made his way back to Africa and settled in Sierra Leone in 1828. Starting with a few utensils and a small plot of land, he became a successful merchant who sent his son Samuel to England for his education. Samuel eventually became an important political leader in Sierra Leone.

EFFECTS IN AFRICA Just as the slave trade shaped African political communities, its demise brought sharp adjustments. For some, it was a welcome end to the constant drainage of people. For others, it was a disaster because it cut off income necessary to buy European arms and luxury goods. Many West African regimes, like the Yoruba kingdom, collapsed once chieftains could no longer use the slave trade to finance their retinues and armies.

The rise of free labor in the Atlantic world and the dwindling foreign slave trade had an unanticipated and perverse effect in Africa. It strengthened slavery there. In some areas, by the mid-nineteenth century, slaves accounted for more than half the population. No longer did they comfortably serve in domestic employment; instead, they toiled on palm oil plantations or, in East Africa, on clove plantations. They also served in the military forces, bore palm oil and ivory to markets as porters, or paddled cargo-carrying canoes along rivers leading to the coast. In 1850, northern Nigeria's ruling class had more slaves than independent Brazil and almost as many as the United States. No longer the world's supplier of slaves, Africa itself had become the world's largest slaveholding region.

ECONOMIC REORDERINGS

Behind the political and social upheavals, profound changes were occurring in the world economy. Until the middle of the eighteenth century, global trade touched only the edges of societies, most of which produced for their own subsistence. At that time, surpluses were confined to specialty goods such as porcelains and silks, which entered trade arteries but did not change the cultures that produced them. By the middle of the nineteenth century, however, global trade was experiencing rapid growth. The export of silver and gold, mainly from the Americas, stimulated long-distance commercial exchanges, causing farmers to use their earnings to purchase the products of an increasing trade. Cities expanded as trade and industrialization brought new urban occupations into being.

Regional and Global Origins of Industrialization

Europeans were undergoing some basic changes, especially in northwestern Europe and British North America. Here, as elsewhere in the world, households had always produced mainly for themselves and made available for marketplaces only meager surpluses of goods and services. But dramatic changes occurred when family members, including wives and children, decided to work harder and longer in order to produce more for the market and purchase more in the market. In these locations, households devoted less time to leisure activities and more time to working, using the additional income from hard work to improve their standard of living. Scholars recently have come to call this change an **industrious revolution**. Beginning in the second half of the seventeenth century, it gained speed in the eighteenth century and laid the foundations for the industrial revolution of the late eighteenth and early nineteenth centuries.

MERGING SPHERES OF TRADE These local changes overlapped with the wider shifts in Europe's place in the world. The willingness to work more and an eagerness to eat more new foods, to wear better clothes, and to consume products that had once been available as luxuries only to the wealthy classes fueled regional and global trade. By the eighteenth century, separate trading spheres described in earlier chapters were merging into increasingly integrated circuits. Sugar and silver coming from the Americas were the pioneering products. By the eighteenth century, other staples joined the long-distance trading business. Tea, for instance, became a beverage of world trade. Its leaves came from China, the sugar to cut its bitterness from the Caribbean, the slaves to harvest the sweetener from Africa, and the ceramics from which to drink a proper cup from the English Midlands.

One of the most important imports to Europe and North America were cotton textiles, produced by skilled artisans in Bengal, Gujerat, and South India. These lightweight, brilliantly colorful, and easily washable textiles of an unusually high quality appealed to peoples all over the world, becoming a favorite of European populations. In addition, tobacco, raw cotton, rice, and sugar poured in from the Americas, originating mainly from large-scale slave plantations. These primary imports boosted the European standard of living and spurred institutions and industries connected to global trade, such as shipping and shipbuilding, and strong and diverse financial institutions, such as insurance companies, stock exchanges, and banks. These latter institutions were to serve the Europeans, especially the British, well during the industrial revolution. They became the instruments to channel more and more money into manufacturing enterprises.

So, Europe saw a double effect from increasing global trade: first, rising markets for cottons, linen, and silk; and second, institutions to pool capital for investment in other sectors. Cheap inputs and more efficient mass production soon gave new manufacturers the edge against Asian artisanal producers. European—and especially British—producers began to undercut Indians in their home market for textiles. In China, cheaper "Deftware" from the Netherlands and stoneware from England cut deeply into the market for Chinese porcelain. In this way, European industrialization resulted in the deindustrialization of Asia.

The state played an important role in nurturing European industries. States began to see the benefits of a strong merchant and manufacturing class: not only did manufacturing increase the wealth of nations, as Adam Smith had argued, but it created pools of money that the state could borrow in times of need. States also enacted new laws to defend the rights of private property owners and inventors, so they could reap rewards from patents and be encouraged to innovate further. If the state encouraged the making of money, it also agreed to protect those who loaned money. Capitalists could rely on the government to force debtors to honor their obligations, thus protecting lenders from risk. These measures formed a pact between merchants and the state that would make some parts of Europe and some colonies of Europe distinctive.

Nowhere was this new alliance clearer than in England. Critical for the takeoff of the English cotton manufacturing industry were tariffs against Indian textile imports. Here, the pressure came from the woolen and linen industries, which wanted to shut out their Indian competitors. The chief beneficiaries, however, would be cotton entrepreneurs. In 1701, the English Parliament passed a law against the importation of dyed or printed calicoes coming from China, India, and Persia. The state followed this act of Parliament by passing a law that fined anyone wearing printed or dyed calicoes, though Indian muslins were exempted.

SOCIAL AND POLITICAL CONSEQUENCES OF GLOBAL TRADE

The expansion of global trade had important social and political consequences. Global trading now trickled its way down from elites to ordinary folk, especially in western Europe. Even ordinary people could purchase imported goods with their earnings. Thus, the poor began to enjoy—some would say became addicted to—coffee, tea, and sugar and eventually even felt the need to use soap. European artisans and farmers purchased tools, furnishings, and home decorations. Colonial laborers also used their meager earnings to buy imported cotton cloth made in Europe from the raw cotton they themselves had picked several seasons earlier.

As new goods flowed from ever more distant corners of the globe, immense fortunes grew. To support their enterprise, traders needed new services, in insurance, bookkeeping, and the recording of legal documents. Trade helped nurture the emergence of new classes of professionals—accountants and lawyers. The new cities of the commercial revolution, hubs like Bristol, Bombay, and Buenos Aires, provided the homes and flourishing neighborhoods for a class of men and women

New Farming Technologies. *Although new technologies only gradually transformed agriculture, the spread of more intensive cultivation led to increased yields.*

known as the **bourgeoisie**: urban businessmen, financiers, and other property owners without aristocratic origins.

As Europe moved to the center of this new global economic order, one class in particular moved to the top of the social ladder: the trader-financiers. Like the merchandiser, the financier did not have to emerge from the high and mighty of Eurasia's dynasties. Consider Mayer Amschel Rothschild (1744–1812): born the son of a money changer in the Jewish ghetto of Frankfurt, Rothschild progressed from coin dealing to money changing, then from trading textiles to lending funds to kings and governments. By the time of his death, he owned the world's biggest banking operation and his five sons were running powerful branches in London, Paris, Vienna, Naples, and Frankfurt.

By extending credit, families like the Rothschilds also enabled traders to ship goods across long distances without having to worry about immediate payment. All these financial changes implied world integration through the flow of goods as well as the flow of money. In the 1820s, sizable funds amassed in London flowed to Egypt, Mexico, and New York to support trade, public investment, and, of course, speculation.

The Industrial Revolution and the British Surge

Trade and finance repositioned western Europe's relationship with the rest of the world. So did the emergence of manufacturing—a big leap in output, as was taking place in agriculture, in this case of industrial commodities. The heart of this process was a gradual accumulation and diffusion of technical knowledge. Lots of little inventions, their applications, and their diffusion across the Atlantic world gradually built up a stock of technical knowledge and practice. Historians have traditionally called these changes the **industrial revolution**, a term first used by the British economic historian Arnold Toynbee in the late nineteenth century. Although the term suggests radical and rapid economic change, the reality was much more gradual and less dramatic than originally believed. Yet the term still has great validity, for the major economic changes that occurred in Britain, northwestern Europe, and North America catapulted these countries ahead of the rest of the world in industrial and agricultural output and standard of living.

MANUFACTURING AND THE COTTON TEXTILE INDUSTRY Nowhere was this industrial revolution more evident than in Britain. Britain had a few natural advantages, like large supplies of coal (for cheap carbon-based energy) and iron (for cheap and durable metal). It also had a political and social environment that allowed merchants and industrialists to invest heavily while also expanding their internal and international markets. But the cost of labor in Britain was relatively high, the result of the industrious revolution. For the British to outsell competitors in India and China, they would have to replace expensive workers with cheap energy and sufficient capital to purchase labor-saving machines.

In addition to its coal and iron reserves, by the eighteenth century Britain could boast an abundance of inventors and entrepreneurs. Few were university educated or conversant in the ideas of the Enlightenment, though some were. What was key to their success was their experimental and observational practices, a popularization of scientific methods to develop new technologies. This included intrepid young artisans, who were literate and numerate enough to lead the way in inventing laborsaving devices like steam engines and mechanical spinners, crucial inventions for the cotton textile industry.

The first problem tackled by these artisanal innovators was that of how to pump water out of coal mining shafts. Using steam to make smooth rotary power, they created a cheaper and more efficient energy source than a horse or river could provide. Coal and steam were also polluting and not renewable, which would create longer-term problems. But for the moment, they fueled the industrial revolution. Once rotary power was connected to spinning and weaving devices, the capacity to produce low-cost, high-volume cloth took off. Steam allowed factories to locate farther away from earlier energy sources and in swelling cities, where these units of production could grow in scale without driving up production costs. What followed was a cascade of smaller, but important, innovations. In this fashion, mechanical production eclipsed manual production that was the basis of textile production in the rest of the world.

A good example of how the alliance of the inventor with the investor furthered the industrial revolution was the advent of the steam engine. Such engines burned coal to boil water; the resulting steam drove mechanized devices. While several tinkerers worked on the device, the most famous was James Watt (1736–1819) of Scotland, who managed to separate steam condensers from piston cylinders. This enabled pistons to stay hot and run constantly. Watt joined forces with the industrialist Matthew Boulton, who marketed the steam engine and set up a laboratory where Watt could refine his device. The steam engine catalyzed a revolution in transportation. Steam-powered engines also improved sugar refining, pottery making, and other industrial processes, generating more products at lower cost than when workers had made them by hand.

In a dramatic way, cotton became Britain's dominant industry in the nineteenth century. Even in the middle of the eighteenth century, India's cotton textile industry had dwarfed Britain's. Factories in Bengal produced 85 million pounds of yarn per year compared with 3 million in England. At the time, cotton production was entirely a hand industry, but a series of macro inventions—James Hargreaves's spinning jenny, Richard Arkwright's water frame, and Samuel Crompton's combination

A Cotton Textile Mill in the 1830s. *The region of Lancashire became one of the major industrial hubs for textile production in the world. By the 1830s, mills had made the shift from artisanal work to highly mechanical mass production. Among the great breakthroughs was the discovery that cloth could be printed with designs, such as paisley or calico (as in this image), and marketed to middle-class consumers.*

of the jenny and the water frame into the "mule"—enabled the British to produce yarns that rivaled India's in durability, quality, and beauty. The difference? The British product was much cheaper because it relied on fewer workers. In contrast to India, where one person, usually a woman, produced yarn on a hand-held spinning wheel, in England and Scotland one person could operate a jenny, a water frame, and finally a mule and produce seventy times what a single hand-operated wheel could yield. Crompton's spectacular mule worked in pairs overseen by a single minder with the help of two boys to roll out fabric in large quantities. The largest carried up to 1,320 spindles and was as long as 150 feet. These macro inventions became the tools of the first industrial factories.

By the 1830s, Britain's dominance of world markets was unrivaled. In this decade, British cotton textile mills employed 425,000 workers and accounted for 16 percent of jobs in British manufacturing. To sustain the output of fabric, Britain's boom required imported raw cotton from Brazil, Egypt, India, and the United States. Most raw cotton for British factories had come from colonial India until 1793, when the American inventor Eli Whitney (1765–1825) patented a "cotton gin" that separated cotton seeds from fiber. After that, cotton farming spread so quickly in the southern United States that by the 1850s it was producing more than 80 percent of the world's cotton supply. In turn, every black slave in the Americas and many Indians in British India were wearing cheap, British-produced cotton shirts. In less than a century, India had gone from exporting fine textiles to Britain to exporting raw cotton, while imports of British cloth drove thousands of Bengali artisan weavers out of business. The Indian economy suffered doubly because even its cotton producers had to compete against new suppliers. Thus did the industrial revolution transform the balance of world economic power.

A NEW ECONOMIC ORDER It is important to note that the industrial revolution did not always result in the creation of large-scale industries. The large factory was rare in manufacturing. Indeed, the largest employers at the time were the slave plantations of the Americas that produced the staples for industrial consumption. Small-scale production remained the norm, mass production the exception. Small-scale production simply became more efficient through innovations in techniques and machinery. The silks of Lyon, cutlery of Solingen, calicoes of Alsace, and cottons of Pawtucket, Rhode Island, were all products of small firms in heavily industrialized belts.

One of the great mysteries of the industrial revolution was why China, the home of inventors of astronomical water clocks and gunpowder, did not become an epicenter of industrial production. There are three reasons. First, China did not foster experimental science of the kind that allowed Watt to stumble onto the possibility of steam or Hargreaves, Arkwright, and Crompton to invent spinning jennies. Chinese authorities discouraged the partnership of inventors and investors. Experimentation, testing, and the links between thinkers and investors were a distinctly Atlantic phenomenon. The Qing, like the Mughal and Ottoman dynasties, swept the great minds into the bureaucracy and reinforced the old agrarian system based on peasant exploitation and tribute. Second, unlike the Europeans, Chinese rulers saw little need to engage in overseas expansion or establish trading outposts in faraway lands in search of riches. The agrarian dynasties of China and India neither showered favors on local merchants nor effectively shut out interlopers. This made them vulnerable to cheap manufactured imports from European traders backed by their governments extolling the virtues of free trade. Third, China did not have ready access to cheap sources of fuel. China's coal deposits lay in the northwest, but merchants and trading hubs were in the southeast.

Cheap carbon gave British manufacturers a comparative advantage. And once ahead of the industrial game, British manufacturers could drive their Asian competitors out of business.

It is important to emphasize, however, that British inventions took hold elsewhere in Europe and in the British colonies. The British lead did not last forever. France and Belgium scrambled to catch up. By the end of the nineteenth century, German industrialists were eclipsing British leaders. The ability for Europeans and North Americans to close the British gap further underscores the importance of the political and economic obstacles faced by Chinese and other entrepreneurs in this age of fast-paced change.

The effects of British and then European and North American industrialization were profound. Historically, Europe had a trade imbalance with partners to the east—furs from Russia and spices and silks from Asia. It made up for this with silver from the Americas. But the new economic order meant that by the nineteenth century, western Europe not only had manufactures like textiles to export to the world; it also had capital. One of Europe's biggest debtors was none other than the sultan of the Ottoman Empire, whose tax system could not keep up with the daunting expenditures necessary to keep the realm together. More and more, Asian, African, and American governments found themselves borrowing from Europe's financiers just as their people were buying industrial products from Europe and selling their primary products to European consumers and producers.

Working and Living

The industrial revolution brought more demanding work routines—not only in the manufacturing economies of western Europe and North America but also on the farms and plantations of Asia and Africa. Although the European side of the story is better known, cultivators throughout the rest of the world toiled harder and for longer hours.

URBAN LIFE AND WORK ROUTINES Increasingly, Europe's workers made their living in cities. London, Europe's largest city in 1700, saw its population nearly double over the next century to almost 1 million. By the 1820s, population growth was even greater in the industrial hubs of Leeds, Glasgow, Birmingham, Liverpool, and Manchester. (See Map 15.4 and Analyzing Global Developments: Town and Countryside, Core and Periphery in the Nineteenth Century.) By contrast, in the Low Countries (Belgium and the Netherlands) and France, where small-scale, rural-based manufacturing flourished, the shift to cities was less extreme.

For most urban dwellers, cities were not healthy places. Water that powered the mills, along with chemicals used in dyeing, went directly back into waterways that provided drinking water. Overcrowded tenements shared just a few outhouses. Most European cities as late as 1850 had no running water, no garbage pickup, no underground sewer system. The result was widespread disease. (In fact, no European city at this time had as clean a water supply as the largest towns of the ancient Roman Empire once had.)

Often families were forced to send women and children outside the home to work. Their wages, usually less than half those paid to adult male workers, helped families survive but exposed these workers, too, to the dangers and hardships of working in factories or mines. Most worked shifts of 12 or more hours at a time, making it impossible for children to obtain the kind of education that might have made escape from the working class possible. Orphans and inhabitants of workhouses—places where debtors, drunks, or those accused of immoral behavior were sent—were treated essentially as slave labor.

Changes in work affected the understanding of time. Most farmers' workloads had followed seasonal rhythms, but after 1800, industrial settings imposed a rigid concept of work discipline and time. To keep the machinery operating, factory and mill owners installed huge clocks and used bells or horns to signify the workday's beginning and end. Employers also measured output per hour and compared workers' performance. Josiah Wedgwood, a maker of teacups and other porcelain, installed a Boulton & Watt steam engine in his manufacturing plant and made his workers use it efficiently. He rang a bell at 5:45 in the morning so employees could start work as day broke. At 8:30 the bell rang for breakfast, at 9:00 to call them back, and at 12:00 for a half-hour lunch; it last tolled when darkness put an end to the workday. Sometimes, though, factory clocks were turned back in the morning and forward at night, falsely extending the exhausted laborers' workday.

Despite higher production, industrialization imposed numbing work routines and paltry wages. Worse, however, was having no work at all. As families abandoned their farmland and depended on wages, being idle meant having no income. Periodic downturns in the economy put wage workers at risk, and many responded by organizing protests. In 1834, the British Parliament centralized the administration of all poor relief and deprived able-bodied workers of any relief unless they joined a workhouse, where working conditions resembled those of a prison.

SOCIAL PROTEST AND EMIGRATION While entrepreneurs accumulated private wealth, the effects of the industrial revolution on working-class families raised widespread concern. In the 1810s in England, groups of jobless craftsmen, called Luddites, smashed the machines that had left them unemployed. In 1849, the English novelist Charlotte Brontë

MAP 15.4 | Industrial Europe around 1850

By 1850, much of western Europe was industrial and urban, with major cities linked to one another through a network of railroads.

• According to this map, what natural resources contributed to the growth of the industrial revolution? What effects did it have on urban population densities?

• Explain how the presence of an extensive railroad system helped to accelerate industrialization.

• According to your reading, why were the effects of the industrial revolution more rapidly apparent in Great Britain and in northwestern Europe?

Town and Countryside, Core and Periphery in the Nineteenth Century

The textile industry was by far the most dynamic sector of the world economy in the nineteenth century. It was dependent on cotton, whose production was labor-intensive but required relatively little capital investment and benefited little from economies of scale. In the first half of the century, cotton was primarily produced by slaves in the southern United States. By the late 1850s, the United States accounted for 77 percent of the cotton consumed in Britain, for 90 percent in France, and for about 92 percent in Russia. After the U.S. Civil War and subsequent slave emancipations, sharecroppers continued to produce the crop, though cotton production began to flourish in Brazil, Egypt, West Africa, and India.

Wheat, on the other hand, was the basic staple of European and Mediterranean diets well into the nineteenth century, and it remains vitally important. Before the advent of railroads, most wheat was consumed locally. In the second half of the century, however, vast quantities of wheat came onto world markets as railroads spread through the Midwest of the United States and the plains of central and eastern Europe. Grown on large, capital-intensive farms, that wheat—as well as rye, corn, millet, and other grains—fed radically expanding European and American industrial cities and factory towns, linking them to rich agricultural hinterlands and contributing unwittingly to the economic volatility of the nineteenth century. Here we chart the fortunes of two of the most important commodities of the nineteenth-century world—cotton and wheat—against the growth of cities and railroads.

QUESTIONS FOR ANALYSIS

- Which countries appear to have been the most dynamic? Pay attention to relative change over time—not only in the biggest cities and most extensive rail networks but also in those growing the fastest.
- How did the growth of railroads and cities vary by country? What does this tell us about the relationship between economic core regions and their peripheries and about patterns of inequality more generally?
- How did the extension of railroads, along with the economic integration they fostered, influence patterns of inequality worldwide?

Population of Major Cities (in thousands)

	1800	1830	1850	1880	1900
Alexandria	15		60	231	320
Delhi		150	152	173	209
Rio de Janeiro	43	125	166	360	523
London	1,117		2,685	4,770	6,586
Paris	576		1,053	2,269	2,714
Moscow	250		365	748	989
New York City	60	161	340	847	1,478
Tokyo	457			824	1,819

Population Estimates (in thousands)

	1800	1825	1850	1875	1900
Egypt	3,854	4,541	4,752	6,961	10,186
India	255,000	257,000	285,000	306,000	
Brazil			7,678	9,930	17,438
England	8,893	12,000	17,928	22,712	32,528
France	27,349	30,462	35,783	36,906	38,451
Russia	35,500	52,300	68,500	90,200	132,900
America	5,297	11,252	23,261	45,073	76,094
Japan	25,622	26,602	27,201	25,037	44,359

Output of Cotton (in thousand metric tons)

	1800	1825	1850	1875	1900
Egypt				132	293
India			12	533	536
America	17	121	484	1,050	2,120

Wheat Production (in thousand metric tons)

	1825	1850	1875	1900
France	4,580	6,600	7,550	8,860
Russia			53	136
America		2,722	8,546	16,302

Length of Open Railway Lines (in kilometers)

	1825	1850	1875	1900
Egypt		1,184	1,410	2,237
India		32	10,527	39,834
Brazil		14	1,801	15,316
England	43	9,797	23,365	30,079
France	17	2,915	19,351	38,109
Russia	27	501	19,029	53,234
America	37	14,518	119,246	311,160
Japan		29	62	6,300

Source: S. Beckert, "Emancipation and Empire: Reconstructing the Worldwide Web of Cotton Production in the Age of the American Civil War," *The American Historical Review* 109, no. 5 (December 2004): 1405–1438; B. R. Mitchell, *International Historical Statistics: Africa, Asia, and Oceania, 1750–2005, International Historical Statistics: The Americas, 1750–2005,* and *International Historical Statistics: Europe, 1750–2005* (London: Palgrave Macmillan, 2007).

A Model Textile Mill. *Distressed by the terrible working conditions of nineteenth-century textile mills, Welsh industrialist and reformer Robert Owen sought to create humane factories. From maintaining the orderliness of the factory floor to posting work rules on the walls, Owen's reforms saw significant improvements in the health and morale of his workers. Nonetheless, he would continue to employ children in his factories, like most of his contemporaries.*

published a novel, *Shirley*, depicting the misfortunes caused by the power loom. Charles Dickens described a mythic Coketown to evoke pity for the working class in his 1854 classic *Hard Times*. Both Elizabeth Gaskell, in England, and Émile Zola, in France, described the hardships of women whose malnourished children were pressed into the workforce too early. Gaskell and Zola also highlighted the hunger, loneliness, and illness that prostitutes and widows endured. These social advocates sought protective legislation for workers, including curbing child labor, limiting the workday, and, in some countries, legalizing prostitution for the sake of monitoring the prostitutes' health.

Some people, however, could not wait for legislative reform. Thus, the period saw unprecedented emigration, as unemployed workers or peasants abandoned their homes to seek their fortunes in America, Canada, and Australia. During the Irish Potato Famine of 1845–1849, at least 1 million Irish citizens left their country (and a further million or so died) when fungi attacked their subsistence crop. Desperate to escape starvation, they booked cheap passage to North America on ships so notorious for disease and malnutrition that they earned the name "coffin ships." Those who did survive faced discrimination in their new land, for many Americans feared that the immigrants would drive down wages or create social unrest.

The industrial revolution produced wealth on an unprecedented scale, but that wealth was unevenly distributed. Inequalities existed both within societies and between them. Free trade had at first led to the creation of small firms, but over time, the most productive workshops expanded into massive, dynamic, creative, and unstable industrial corporations.

PERSISTENCE AND CHANGE IN AFRO-EURASIA

Western Europe's military might, its technological achievements, and its economic strength represented a threat to the remaining Afro-Eurasian empires. Across the continent, western European merchants and industrialists sought closer economic and (in some cases) political ties. They did so in the name of gaining "free" access to Asian markets and products. In response, Russian and Ottoman rulers modernized their military organizations and hoped to achieve similar economic strides while distancing themselves from the democratic principles of the French Revolution. The Chinese Empire remained outside the orbit of European power until the first Opium War of the early 1840s forced the Chinese to acknowledge their military weaknesses. Thus, changes in the Atlantic world unleashed new pressures around the globe, though with varying degrees of intensity.

Revamping the Russian Monarchy

Russian rulers responded to the pressures by strengthening their traditional authority through modest reforms and the suppression of domestic opposition. Tsar Alexander I (r. 1801–1825) was fortunate that Napoleon committed several blunders and lost his formidable army in the Russian snows. Yet the French Revolution and its massive, patriotic armies struck at the heart of Russian political institutions, which rested upon a huge peasant population laboring as serfs. The tsars could no longer easily justify their absolutism by claiming that enlightened despotism was the most advanced form of government, since a new model, rooted in popular sovereignty and the concept of the nation, had arisen.

In December 1825, when Alexander died unexpectedly and childless, there was a question over succession. Some of the Russian officers launched a patriotic revolt, hoping to convince Alexander's brother Constantine to take the throne and to guarantee a constitution in place of a more conservative brother, Nicholas. The Decembrists, as the proponents of Constantine were called, came primarily from elite families and were familiar with western European life and institutions. A few Decembrists wanted to establish a constitutional monarchy to replace Russia's despotism; others favored a tsar-less republic and the abolition of serfdom. But the officers' conspiracy failed to win over conservative landowners and bureaucrats, who believed in the tsar's divine right to rule and did not want to see serfdom abolished. As Constantine, too, supported Nicholas's claim to power, Nicholas (r. 1825–1855) became tsar and brutally suppressed the insurrectionists.

Russia's rulers and upper classes had always both feared and been inspired by western examples. They continued to borrow western technology and modes of administration but held at bay western ideas and practices of liberty through censorship and the promotion of a distinctly Russian identity. In trying to maintain absolutist rule, Nicholas and his successors portrayed the monarch's family as the ideal historical embodiment of the nation with direct ties to the people. Nicholas himself prevented rebellion by expanding the secret police, enforcing censorship, conducting impressive military exercises, and maintaining serfdom. And in the 1830s, he introduced a conservative ideology that stressed religious faith, hierarchy, and obedience. Although in 1861 a new tsar, Alexander II, would finally abolish serfdom, throughout the nineteenth century Russia remained the most conservative of the great powers.

Reforming Egypt and the Ottoman Empire

Unlike Russia, where Napoleon's army had reached Moscow, the Ottoman capital in Istanbul never faced a threat by French troops. Still, Napoleon's invasion of Egypt shook the Ottoman Empire. Even before this trauma, imperial authorities faced the challenge posed by increased trade with Europe and the greater presence of European merchants and missionaries. In addition, many non-Muslim religious communities in the sultan's empire wanted the European powers to advance their interests. In the wake of Napoleon, who had promised to remake Egyptian society, reformist energies swept from Egypt to the center of the Ottoman domain. (See Primary Source: An Egyptian Intellectual's Reaction to the French Occupation of Egypt.)

REFORMS IN EGYPT In Egypt, far-reaching changes came with **Muhammad Ali**, a skillful, modernizing ruler. After the French withdrawal in 1801, Muhammad Ali (r. 1805–1848) won a chaotic struggle for supreme power in Egypt and aligned himself with influential Egyptian families. Yet he looked to revolutionary France for a model of modern state building. As with Napoleon (and Simón Bolívar in Latin America), the key to his hold on power was the army. With the help of French advisers, the modernized Egyptian army became the most powerful fighting force in the Middle East.

Muhammad Ali also reformed education and agriculture. He established a school of engineering and opened the first modern medical school in Cairo under the supervision of a French military doctor. And his efforts in the countryside made Egypt one of the world's leading cotton exporters. A summer crop, cotton required steady watering when the Nile's irrigation waters were in short supply. So Muhammad Ali's public works department, advised by European engineers, deepened the irrigation canals

Decembrists in St. Petersburg. *Russians energetically participated in the coalition that defeated Napoleon, but the ideas of the French Revolution greatly appealed to the educated upper classes, including aristocrats of the officer corps. In December 1825, at the death of Tsar Alexander I, some regimental officers staged an uprising of about 3,000 men, demanding a constitution and the end of serfdom. But Nicholas I, the new tsar, called in loyal troops and brutally dispersed the "Decembrists," executing or exiling their leaders.*

An Egyptian Intellectual's Reaction to the French Occupation of Egypt

In the 1798 invasion of Egypt, Napoleon Bonaparte attempted to win rank-and-file Egyptian support against the country's Mamluks, who were the most powerful group in Egypt at the time, though the country was still under the authority of the Ottoman sultan. Bonaparte portrayed himself as a liberator and invoked the ideals of the French Revolution, as he had done with great success all over Europe. His Egyptian campaign did not succeed, however, and local opposition was bitter. The chronicler Abd al-Rahman al-Jabarti has left one of the most perceptive accounts of these years.

On Monday news arrived that the French had reached Damanhur and Rosetta [in the Nile Delta]. . . . They printed a large proclamation in Arabic, calling on the people to obey them. . . . In this proclamation were inducements, warnings, all manner of wiliness and stipulations. Some copies were sent from the provinces to Cairo and its text is:

In the name of God, the Merciful, the Compassionate. There is no God but God. He has no son nor has He an associate in His Dominion.

On behalf of the French Republic which is based upon the foundation of liberty and equality, General Bonaparte, Commander-in-Chief of the French armies makes known to all the Egyptian people that for a long time the Sanjaqs [its Mamluk rulers] who lorded it over Egypt have treated the French community basely and contemptuously and have persecuted its merchants with all manner of extortion and violence. Therefore the hour of punishment has now come.

Unfortunately, this group of Mamluks . . . have acted corruptly for ages in the fairest land that is to be found upon the face of the globe. However, the Lord of the Universe, the Almighty, has decreed the end of their power.

O ye Egyptians . . . I have not come to you except for the purpose of restoring your rights from the hands of the oppressors and that I more than the Mamluks serve God. . . .

And tell them also that all people are equal in the eyes of God and the only circumstances which distinguish one from the other are reason, virtue, and knowledge. . . . Formerly, in the lands of Egypt there were great cities, and wide canals and extensive commerce and nothing ruined all this but the avarice and the tyranny of the Mamluks.

[Al-Jabarti then challenged the arguments in the French proclamation and portrayed the French as godless invaders, inspired by false ideals.] They follow this rule: great and small, high and low, male and female are all equal. Sometimes they break this rule according to their whims and inclinations or reasoning. Their women do not veil themselves and have no modesty. . . . Whenever a Frenchman has to perform an act of nature he does so where he happens to be, even in full view of people, and he goes away as he is, without washing his private parts after defecation. . . .

His saying "[all people] are equal in the eyes of God" the Almighty is a lie and stupidity. How can this be when God has made some superior to others as is testified by the dwellers in the Heavens and on Earth? . . .

So those people are opposed to both Christians and Muslims, and do not hold fast to any religion. You see that they are materialists, who deny all God's attributes. . . . May God hurry misfortune and punishment upon them, may He strike their tongues with dumbness, may He scatter their hosts, and disperse them.

> ## QUESTIONS FOR ANALYSIS
>
> - When the proclamation speaks of "the fairest land that is to be found upon the face of the globe," what land is it referring to?
> - Why do you think Napoleon's appeals to the ideals of the French Revolution failed with Egyptians?
> - Why does al-Jabarti claim that the invaders are godless even though the proclamation clearly suggests otherwise?

Source: Abd al-Rahman al-Jabarti, *Al-Jabarti's Chronicle of the First Seven Months of the French Occupation of Egypt*, translated by S. Moreh (Leiden: E. J. Brill, 1975), pp. 39–40, 43, 46–47.

and constructed a series of dams across the Nile. These efforts transformed Egypt, making it the most powerful state in the eastern Mediterranean and alarming the Ottoman state and the great powers in Europe.

Muhammad Ali's modernizing reforms, however, disrupted the habits of the peasantry. After all, incorporation into the industrial world economy involved harder work (as English wage workers had discovered), often with little additional pay. Because irrigation improvements permitted year-round cultivation, Egyptian peasants now had to plant and harvest three crops instead of one or two. Moreover, the state controlled the prices of cultivated products, so peasants saw little profit from their extra efforts. Young men also faced conscription into the state's enlarged army, while whole families had to toil, unpaid, on public works projects. In addition, a state-sponsored program of industrialization aimed to put Egypt on a par with Europe: before long, textile and munitions factories employed 200,000 workers. But Egypt had few skilled laborers or cheap sources of energy, so by the time of Muhammad Ali's death in 1849, few of the factories survived.

External forces also limited Muhammad Ali's ambitious plans. At first, his new army enjoyed spectacular success. But Muhammad Ali overplayed his hand when he sent forces into Syria in the 1830s and later when he threatened Anatolia, the heart of the Ottoman state. Fearing that an Egyptian ruler might attempt to overthrow the Ottoman sultan and threaten the balance of power in the eastern Mediterranean region, the European powers compelled Egypt to withdraw from Anatolia and reduce its army.

Muhammad Ali. *The Middle Eastern ruler who most successfully assimilated the educational, technological, and economic advances of nineteenth-century Europe was Muhammad Ali, ruler of Egypt from 1805 until 1848.*

OTTOMAN REFORMS Under political and economic pressures like those facing Muhammad Ali in Egypt, Ottoman rulers also made reforms. Indeed, military defeats and humiliating treaties with Europe were painful reminders of the sultans' vulnerability. In 1805, Sultan Selim III tried to create a new infantry, trained by western European officers. But before he could bring this force up to fighting strength, the janissaries stormed the palace, killed its new officers, and deposed Selim in 1807. Over the next few decades, janissary military men and clerical scholars (*ulama*) cobbled together an alliance that continuously thwarted reformers.

Why did reform falter in the Ottoman state before it could be implemented? After all, in France and Spain the old regimes were also inefficient and burdened with debts and military losses. The French required a ferocious revolution to overturn the old order and to remove its supporters. But reform was possible only if the forces of restraint—especially old regime militaries—were weak or dismantled, as in France, where young officers like Napoleon Bonaparte emerged and reformers were strong and courageous. In the Ottoman Empire, the janissary class had grown powerful, providing the main resistance to change. Ottoman authority depended on clerical support, and the Muslim clergy also resisted change. Blocked at the top, Ottoman rulers were hesitant to appeal for popular support. Such an appeal, in the new age of popular sovereignty and national feeling, would be dangerous for an unelected dynast in a multiethnic and multireligious realm.

Mahmud II (r. 1808–1839), who acknowledged Europe's rising power, broke the political deadlock. He shrewdly manipulated his conservative opponents. Convincing some clerics that the janissaries neglected traditions of discipline and piety and promising that a new corps would pray fervently, the sultan won the *ulama*'s support and in 1826 established a European-style army corps. When the janissaries plotted their inevitable mutiny, Mahmud rallied clerics, students, and subjects. The schemers retreated to their barracks, only to be shelled by the sultan's artillery and then destroyed in flames. Thousands of other janissaries were rounded up and executed.

Like Muhammad Ali in Egypt, Mahmud brought in European officers to advise his forces. Here, too, military reform spilled over into nonmilitary areas. The Ottoman modernizers created a medical college and then a school of military sciences. To understand Europe better and to create a first-rate diplomatic corps, the Ottomans schooled their officials in European languages and had European classics translated into Turkish. As Mahmud's successors extended reforms into civilian life, this era—known as the Tanzimat, or reorganization period—saw legislation that guaranteed equality for all Ottoman subjects, regardless of religion.

The reforms, however, stopped well short of revolutionary change. For one thing, reform relied too much on the personal whim of rulers. Also, the bureaucratic and religious infrastructure remained committed to old ways. Moreover, any effort to reform the rural sector met resistance by the landed interests. Finally, the

Indian Resistance to Company Rule. *Tipu Sultan, the Mysore ruler, put up a determined resistance against the British. This painting by Robert Home shows Charles Cornwallis, the East India Company's governor, receiving Tipu's two sons as hostages after defeating him in the 1792 war. The boys remained in British custody for two years. Tipu returned to fighting the British and was killed in the war of 1799.*

merchant classes profited from business with a debt-ridden sultan. By preventing the empire's fiscal collapse through financial support to the state, bankers lessened the pressure for reform and removed the spark that had fired the revolutions in Europe. Together, these factors impeded reform in the Ottoman Empire.

Colonial Reordering in India

Europe's most important colonial possession in Asia between 1750 and 1850 was British India. Unlike in North America, the changes that the British fostered in Asia did not lead to political independence. Instead, India was increasingly dominated by the **East India Company**, which the crown had chartered in 1600. The company's control over India's imports and exports in the eighteenth and nineteenth centuries, however, contradicted British claims about their allegiance to a world economic system based on "free trade."

THE EAST INDIA COMPANY'S MONOPOLY Initially, the British, through the East India Company, tried to control India's commerce by establishing trading posts along the coast but without taking complete political control. After conquering the state of Bengal in 1757, the company began to fill its coffers and its officials began to amass personal fortunes. Even the British governor of Bengal pocketed a portion of the tax revenues. Such unbridled abuse of power caused the Bengal army, along with forces of the Mughal emperor and of the ruler of Awadh, to revolt. Although the rebels were unsuccessful, British officials left the emperor and most provincial leaders in place—as nominal rulers.

Nonetheless, the British secured the right for the East India Company to collect tax revenues in Bengal, Bihar, and Orissa and to trade free of duties throughout Mughal territory. In return, the Mughal emperor would receive a hefty annual pension. The company went on to annex other territories, bringing much of South Asia under its rule by the early 1800s. (See Map 15.5.)

To rule with minimal interference, however, required knowing the conquered society. This led to Orientalist scholarship: British scholar-officials wrote the first modern histories of South Asia, translated Sanskrit and Persian texts, identified philosophical writings, and compiled Hindu and Muslim law books. Through their efforts, the company state presented itself as a force for revitalizing authentic Hinduism and recovering India's literary and cultural treasures. Although the Orientalist scholars admired Sanskrit language and literature, they still supported English colonial rule and did not necessarily agree with local beliefs.

EFFECTS IN INDIA Maintaining a sizable military and civilian bureaucracy also required taxation. Indeed, taxes on land were the East India Company's largest source of revenue. From 1793 onward, land policies required large and small landowners alike to pay taxes to the company. As a result, large estate owners gained more power and joined with the company in determining who could own property. Whenever smaller proprietors defaulted on their taxes, the company put their properties up for auction, with the firm's own employees and large estate owners often obtaining title.

Company rule and booming trade altered India's urban geography as well. By the early nineteenth century, colonial cities

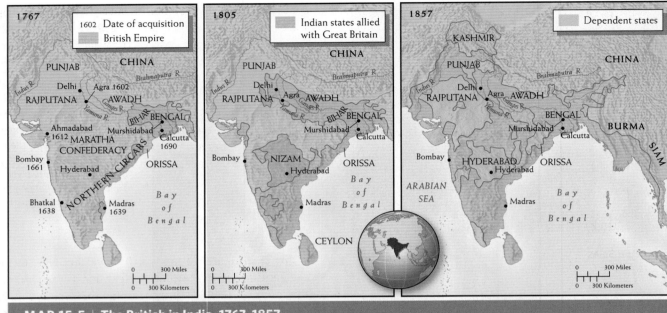

MAP 15.5 | The British in India, 1767–1857

Starting from locations in eastern and northeastern India, the British East India Company extended its authority over much of South Asia prior to the outbreak of the Indian Rebellion of 1857.

- What type of location did the British first acquire in India? How did the company expand into the interior of India and administer these possessions?
- Why did the British choose a strategy of direct rule over some areas and indirect rule over others within the larger region?

like Calcutta, Madras, and Bombay were the new centers at the expense of older Mughal cities like Agra, Delhi, Murshidabad, and Hyderabad. As the colonial cities attracted British merchants and Indian clerks, artisans, and laborers, their populations surged. Calcutta's reached 350,000 in 1820; Bombay's jumped to 200,000 by 1825. In these cities, Europeans lived close to the company's fort and trading stations, while migrants from the countryside clustered in crowded quarters called "black towns."

Back in Britain, the debts of rural Indians and the conditions of black towns generated little concern. Instead, calls for reform focused on the East India Company's monopoly: its sole access to Indian wealth and its protection of company shareholders and investors. In 1813, the British Parliament, responding to merchants' and traders' demands to participate in the Indian economy, abolished the company's monopoly over trade with India.

India now became an importer of British textiles and an exporter of raw cotton—a reversal of its traditional pattern of trade. In the past, India had been an important textile manufacturer, exporting fine cotton goods throughout the Indian Ocean and to Europe. But its elites could not resist the appeal of cheap

Calcutta. *Designated the capital of British India in 1772, Calcutta became vital to the British East India Company's activities as a main exporter of goods such as cotton and opium. The wealthy British merchants and Anglo-Indians that Calcutta attracted utterly transformed its landscape, as shown in this 1910 photograph of the Great Eastern Hotel, which was commonly hailed the "Jewel of the East." This street scene of wide paved roads, carriages, and Victorian architecture would be difficult to distinguish from one of turn-of-the-century London, were it not for the Indian figures in traditional dress.*

Packing Cotton Bales. *This 1864 engraving of the packing of cotton bales registers the shift in cotton trade between India and Britain: from being an exporter of cotton manufactures up to the eighteenth century, India became a source of raw cotton in the nineteenth century.*

British textiles. As a result, India's own industrialization stalled. In addition, the import of British manufactures caused unfavorable trade balances that changed India from a net importer of gold and silver to an exporter of these precious metals.

PROMOTING CULTURAL CHANGE Led by evangelical Christians and liberal reformers, the British did more than alter the Indian economy; they also advocated far-reaching changes in Indian culture so that its people would value British goods and culture. In 1817, James Mill, a philosopher and an employee of the East India Company, condemned what he saw as backward social practices and cultural traditions. He and his son, John Stuart Mill, argued that only dictatorial rule could bring good government and economic progress to India, whose people they considered unfit for self-rule or liberalism. (See Primary Source: James Mill on Indian Tradition.) The mood swung away from the Orientalists' respect for India's classical languages, philosophies, cultures, and texts. In 1835, the British poet, historian, and Liberal politician Lord Macaulay recommended that English replace Persian as the language of administration and that European education replace Oriental learning. This, he hoped, would produce a class that was Indian in blood and color but English in tastes and culture.

If British officials saw liberalism as an excuse for empire, Indian intellectuals saw in it a blueprint for reform. Thus, Ram Mohun Roy, an Indian reformer, locked horns with orthodox Hindus and took the lead in urging the British to abolish the practice of *sati*, by which women burned to death on the funeral pyres of their dead husbands. Roy also championed free press, unsuccessfully challenging its restriction in India by the British as a violation of universal liberal principles.

A new colonial order built with such contradictory application of liberalism was necessarily unstable. Most wealthy landowners resented the loss of their land and authority. Peasants, thrown to the mercy of the market, moneylenders, and landlords were in turmoil. Dispossessed artisans stirred up towns and cities. And merchants and industrialists chafed under the British-dominated economy. Even though India was part of a more interconnected world and thereby supported Europe's industrialization, it was doing so as a colony. As freedom expanded in Europe, exploitation expanded in India.

The Continuing Qing Empire

The Qing dynasty, which had taken power in 1644, was still enjoying prosperity and territorial expansion as the nineteenth century dawned. Its court elites accepted the dynasty's authority in spite of the fact that the Manchus were not Han Chinese but came originally from Manchuria. In this regard, Chinese upper classes were unlike most of the delegates called to the Estates-General in France in 1789, seething with resentment against the monarchy and the aristocracy.

Rice cultivation. *From hand-sowing seedlings to harvesting the grains in leech-infested waters, the process of rice cultivation was so labor-intensive that multigenerational households cropped up throughout imperial China to yield the necessary workforce.*

James Mill on Indian Tradition

James Mill was a Scottish political economist and philosopher who believed that according to the principles of utilitarianism, law and government are essential for maximizing a people's usefulness and happiness. Thus, his History of British India (1818) *criticized India's Hindu and Muslim cultures and attributed their so-called backwardness to the absence of a systematic form of law. Mill's critique was also an attack on earlier British Orientalists, whose close engagement with Indian culture and Indian texts led them to oppose interfering in traditional practices. A year after the book's publication, the East India Company appointed him as an official.*

The condition of the women is one of the most remarkable circumstances in the manners of nations. Among rude people, the women are generally degraded; among civilized people they are exalted.

. . .

Nothing can exceed the habitual contempt which the Hindus entertain for their women. Hardly are they ever mentioned in their laws, or other books, but as wretches of the most base and vicious inclinations, on whose natures no virtuous or useful qualities can be engrafted. "Their husbands," says the sacred code, "should be diligently careful in guarding them: though they well know the disposition with which the lord of creation formed them; Manu allotted to such women a love of their bed, of their seat, and of ornament, impure appetites, wrath, weak flexibility, desire of mischief, and bad conduct."

. . .

They are held, accordingly, in extreme degradation. They are not accounted worthy to partake of religious rites but in conjunction with their husbands. They are entirely excluded from the sacred books. . . .

. . .

They [the Hindus] are remarkably prone to flattery; the most prevailing mode of address from the weak to the strong, while men are still ignorant and unreflecting.

The Hindus are full of dissimulation and falsehood, the universal concomitants of oppression. The vices of falsehood, indeed, they carry to a height almost unexampled among other races of men. Judicial perjury is more than common; it is almost universal.

. . .

This religion has produced a practice, which has strongly engaged the curiosity of Europeans; a superstitious care of the life of the inferior animals. A Hindu lives in perpetual terror of killing even an insect; and hardly any crime can equal that of being unintentionally the cause of death to any animal of the more sacred species. This feeble circumstance, however, is counteracted by so many gloomy and malignant principles, that their religion, instead of humanizing the character, must have had no inconsiderable effect in fostering that disposition to revenge, that insensibility to the sufferings of others, and often that active cruelty, which lurks under the smiling exterior of the Hindu.

. . .

Few nations are surpassed by the Hindus, in the total want of physical purity, in their streets, houses, and persons. Mr. Forster, whose long residence in India, and knowledge of the country, render him an excellent witness, says of the narrow streets of Benares: "In addition to the pernicious effect which must proceed from a confined atmosphere, there is, in the hot season, an intolerable stench arising from the many pieces of stagnated water dispersed in different quarters of the town. The filth also which is indiscriminately thrown into the streets, and there left exposed, (for the Hindus possess but a small portion of general cleanliness) add to the compound of ill smells so offensive to the European inhabitants of this city."

. . .

The attachment with which the Hindus, in common with all ignorant nations, bear to astrology, is a part of their manners exerting a strong influence upon the train of their actions. "The Hindus of the present age," says a partial observer, "do not undertake any affair of consequence without consulting their astrologers, who are always Brahmans." The belief of witchcraft and sorcery continues universally prevalent.

Source: James Mill, *The History of British India* (New Delhi: Atlantic Publishers & Distributors, 1990), pp. 279, 281–282, 286–287, 288, 289, 297, 299.

QUESTIONS FOR ANALYSIS

- What did James Mill hold to be the chief indicator of a civilization's accomplishment?
- In what ways do Mill's views on India reflect a deep disagreement with British Orientalists?

EXPANDING BOUNDARIES The Qing had a talent for extending the empire's boundaries and settling frontier lands. Before 1750, they conquered Taiwan (the stronghold of remaining Ming forces), pushed westward into central Asia, and annexed Tibet. Qing troops then eliminated the threat of the powerful Junghars in western Mongolia and halted Russian efforts to take southern Siberia in the 1750s. To secure these territorial gains, the Qing encouraged settlement of frontier lands like Xinjiang. New crops from the Americas aided this process—especially corn and sweet potatoes, which grow well in less fertile soils.

Like their European counterparts, Chinese peasants were on the move. But migration occurred in Qing China for different reasons. The state-sponsored westward movement into Xinjiang, for example, aimed to secure a recently pacified frontier region through military colonization, after which civilians would follow. So peasants received promises of land, tools, seed, and the loan of silver and a horse—all with the dual objectives of producing enough food grain to supply the troops and relieve pressure on the poor and arid northwestern part of the country. These efforts brought so much land under cultivation by 1840 that the region's ecological and social landscape completely changed.

Other migrants were on the move by their own initiative. The ever-growing competition for land even drove them into areas where the Qing regime had tried to restrict migration (because of excessive administrative costs), such as Manchuria and Taiwan. As the migrants introduced their own agricultural techniques, they reshaped the environment through land reclamation and irrigation projects and sparked large population increases.

PROBLEMS OF THE EMPIRE Despite their success in expanding the empire, the Qing faced nagging problems. As a ruling minority, they took a conservative approach to innovation. And only late in the eighteenth century did they deal with rapid population growth. On the one hand, the tripling of China's population since 1300 demonstrated the realm's prosperity; on the other, a population of over 300 million severely strained resources—especially soil for growing crops and wood for fuel.

In spite of the difficulties that beset the Qing, European rulers and upper classes remained eager consumers of Chinese silks, teas, carved jade, tableware, jewelry, paper for covering walls, and ceramics. The Chinese, for their part, had little demand for most European manufactures. Trade with the Europeans continued, however, even though Emperor Qianlong famously wrote in 1793, in response to a request for more trade by Britain's king, that "as your ambassador can see for himself, we possess all things and have no use for your country's manufactures."

By the mid-nineteenth century, technological advances, such as steam-powered naval ships, strengthened European powers, and the Qing could no longer dismiss their increasing demands. The first clear evidence of an altered balance of power was a British-Chinese war over a narcotic. Indeed, the **Opium War** exposed China's vulnerability in a new era of European ascendancy.

THE OPIUM WAR AND THE "OPENING" OF CHINA Europeans had been selling staples and intoxicants in China for a long time. For example, tobacco, a New World crop, had become widely popular in China by the seventeenth century.

Opium. Left: *A common sight in late Qing China was establishments catering specifically to opium smoking. Taken from a volume condemning the practice, this picture shows opium smokers idling their day away.* Right: *Having established a monopoly in the 1770s over opium cultivation in India, the British greatly expanded their manufacture and export of opium to China to balance their rapidly growing import of Chinese tea and silk. This picture from the 1880s shows an opium warehouse in India where the commodity was stored before being transported to China.*

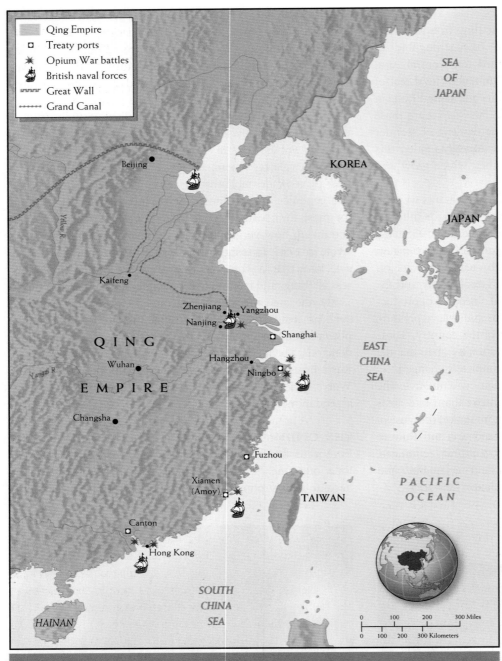

MAP 15.6 | The Qing Empire and the Opium War

The Opium War demonstrated the superiority of British military technology. Their victory granted the British control of Hong Kong and established a series of treaty ports, which gave Europeans access to Chinese trade and which were subject to the laws of designated European countries.

- How many treaty ports were there after the Opium War? What was their significance?
- How did the Opium War change relations between China and the western powers?

with tobacco. By the late eighteenth century, opium smokers with their long-stemmed pipes were conspicuous at every level of Chinese society.

Although the Qing banned opium imports in 1729, the Chinese continued to smoke the drug and import it illegally. Sensing its economic potential, the East India Company created an opium monopoly in India in 1773. The reason was a rapid growth in the company's purchase of tea. Because the Chinese showed little taste for British goods, the British had been financing their tea imports with exports of silver to China. But by the late eighteenth century, the company's tea purchases had become too large to finance with silver. Fortunately for the company, the Chinese were eager for Indian cotton and opium, and then mostly just opium.

Opium's impact on the balance of trade was devastating. In a reversal from earlier trends, silver began to flow out of instead of into China. Once silver shortages occurred, the peasants' tax burden grew heavier because they had to pay in silver (see Chapter 13). Consequently, long-simmering unrest in the countryside gained momentum. At the Qing court, some officials wanted to legalize the opium trade so as to eliminate corruption and boost revenues. (After all, as long as opium was an illegal substance, the government could not tax its traffic.) Others wanted stiffer prohibitions. In 1838, the emperor sent a special commissioner to Canton, the main center of the trade, to eradicate the influx of opium.

Though determined, the Chinese were no match for Britain's modern military technology. After a British fleet—including four steam-powered battleships—entered Chinese waters in June 1840, the warships bombarded coastal regions near Canton and sailed upriver for a short way. (See Map 15.6.) On land, Qing soldiers, some armed with imported matchlocks, fared badly against the modern artillery of British troops, many

Initially, few people would have predicted that tobacco smoking would lead to the widespread use of opium, previously used as a medicine or an aphrodisiac. But before long, people in Southeast Asia, Taiwan, and China were smoking crude opium mixed

Trade in Canton. *In this painting, we can see the hongs, the buildings that made up the factories, or establishments, where foreign merchants conducted their business in Canton. From the mid-eighteenth century to 1842, Canton was the only Chinese port open to European trade.*

of whom were Indians supplied with percussion cap rifles. Along the Yangzi River, outgunned Qing forces fought fiercely, but they were no match for British military technology. Many of the Qing soldiers killed their own wives and children before committing suicide.

FORCING MORE TRADE The Qing ruling elite capitulated, and with the 1842 Treaty of Nanjing, the British acquired the island of Hong Kong and the right to trade in five treaty ports. They also forced the Chinese to repay their costs for the war. Subsequent treaties guaranteed that the British and other foreign nationals would be tried in their own courts for crimes, rather than in Chinese courts, and would be exempt from Chinese law. Moreover, the British insisted that any privileges granted through treaties with other parties would also apply to them. Other western nations followed the British example in demanding the same right, and the arrangement thus guaranteed all Europeans and North Americans a privileged position in China.

Still, China did not become a formal colony. To the contrary, in the mid-nineteenth century, Europeans and North Americans were trading only on its outskirts. Most Chinese did not encounter the Europeans. Daily life for most people went on as it had before the Opium War. Only the political leaders and urban dwellers were beginning to feel the foreign presence and wondering what steps China might take to acquire European technologies, goods, and learning.

CONCLUSION

During the period 1750–1850, changes in politics, commerce, industry, and technology reverberated throughout the Atlantic world and, to varying degrees, elsewhere around the globe. By 1850, the world was more integrated economically, with Europe increasingly at the center.

In the Americas, colonial ties broke apart. In France, the people toppled the monarchy. Dissidents threatened the same in Russia. Such upheavals introduced a new public

vocabulary—the language of the nation—and made the idea of revolution empowering. In the Americas and parts of Europe, nation-states took shape around redefined hierarchies of class, gender, and color. Britain and France emerged from the political crises of the late eighteenth century determined to expand their borders. Their drive forced older empires such as Russia and the Ottoman state to make reforms.

As commerce and industrialization transformed economic and political power, European governments compelled others (including Egypt, India, and China) to expand their trade with European merchants. Ultimately, such countries had to participate in a European-centered economy as exporters of raw materials and importers of European manufactures. Trade underlay much of the fundamental political reorderings of this period. For North and South American colonists, having the right to trade freely in every market of the world intensified their demands for political freedom. The British fought a war with the Chinese to keep their ports open to all trade goods, including opium. European statesmen joined together to stymie Muhammad Ali's conquest of the Ottoman Empire in part because of their desire to keep eastern Mediterranean markets available to their merchants.

By the 1850s, many of the world's peoples became more industrious, producing less for themselves and more for distant markets. Through changes in manufacturing, some areas of the world also made more goods than ever before. With its emphasis on free trade, Europe began to force open new markets—even to the point of colonizing them. Gold and silver now flowed out of China and India to pay for European-dominated products like opium and textiles.

However, global reordering did not mean that Europe's rulers had uncontested control over other people or that the institutions and cultures of Asia and Africa ceased to be dynamic. Some countries became dependent on Europe commercially; others became colonies. China escaped colonial rule but was forced into unfavorable trade relations with the Europeans. In sum, dramatic changes combined to unsettle systems of rulership and to alter the economic and military balance between western Europe and the rest of the world.

FOCUS ON: *The Global Effects of the "New Ideas"*

The Atlantic World

- North American colonists revolt against British rule and establish a nonmonarchical, republican form of government.

- In the wake of the American Revolution, the French citizenry proclaims a new era of liberty, equality, and fraternity and executes opponents of the revolution, notably the king and queen of France.

- Napoleon's French Empire extends many principles of the French Revolution throughout Europe.

- In the midst of the French Revolution, Haitian slaves throw off French rule, abolish slavery, and create an independent state.

- Napoleon's invasion of Iberia frees Portuguese and Spanish America from colonial rule.

- The British lead a successful campaign to abolish the Atlantic slave trade and promote new sources of trade with Africa.

- An industrial revolution spreads outward from Britain to a few other parts of the Atlantic world.

- The Russian monarchy strengthens its power through modest reforms and suppression of rebellion.

Africa, India, and Asia

- In Egypt, a military leader, Muhammad Ali, modernizes the country and threatens the political integrity of the Ottoman Empire.

- The British East India Company increasingly dominates the Indian subcontinent.

- The Qing Empire persists despite major European encroachments on its sovereignty.

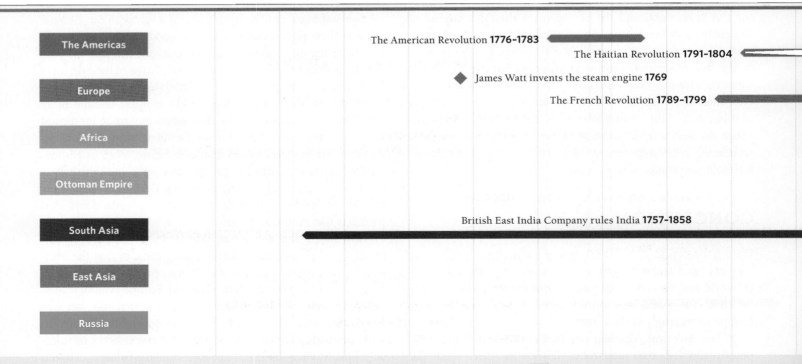

The Americas

Europe

Africa

Ottoman Empire

South Asia

East Asia

Russia

The American Revolution **1776–1783**

The Haitian Revolution **1791–1804**

James Watt invents the steam engine **1769**

The French Revolution **1789–1799**

British East India Company rules India **1757–1858**

1750   1775

1. **Describe** the new ideas of freedom, and **explain** how they differed from earlier understandings of this term.

2. **Discuss** the political and social revolutions that occurred in the Atlantic world between 1750 and 1850. What ideas inspired these changes? How well did revolutionaries implement these changes?

3. **Compare and contrast** the way Latin American peoples achieved independence with the process in the United States. How similar were their goals? How well did they achieve these goals?

4. **Analyze** Napoleon's role in spreading the ideas of political and social revolution. How did his armies spread the concept of nationalism? How did Napoleon's military pursuits affect political and social ferment in the Americas?

5. **Explain** how the Atlantic world's political and social revolution led to the end of the Atlantic slave trade. What economic, social, and political consequences did this development have on sub-Saharan Africa?

6. **Compare** political and economic developments in the Atlantic world with those in regions elsewhere around the globe in the period 1750–1850.

7. **Explain** the relationship between industrialization and the "industrious revolution." Where did the industrial revolution begin? What other parts of the Atlantic world did it spread to during this time?

8. **Identify** and **explain** the key developments that constituted the industrial revolution. **Discuss** why some parts of Europe led the way.

9. **Explore** how industrialization altered the societies that began to industrialize during this time. What impact did this process have on the environment? How were gender roles and familial relationships altered?

10. **Analyze** how the two intertwined Atlantic revolutions (political and industrial) altered the global balance of power. How did the Russian, Mughal, Ottoman, and Qing dynasties respond to this change?

11. **Compare** the responses to European influence in Egypt under Muhammad Ali, in India under the rule of the East India Company, and in China during the Opium War.

12. **Describe** patterns of global trade and economic growth, and **connect** them to political changes during the period 1750–1850.

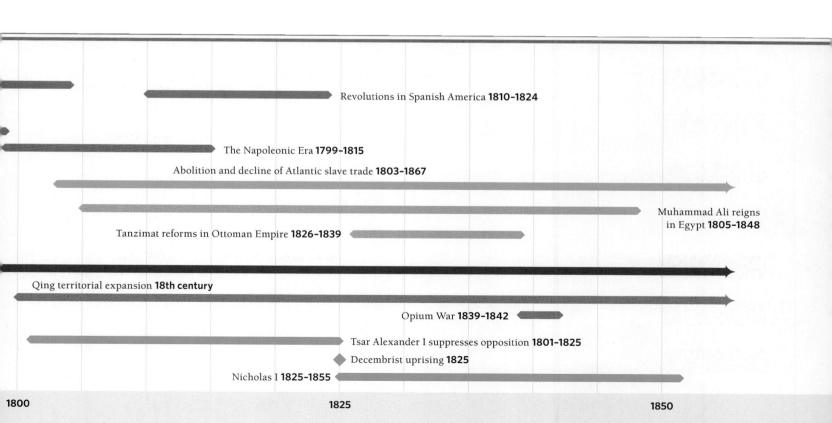

Revolutions in Spanish America **1810–1824**

The Napoleonic Era **1799–1815**

Abolition and decline of Atlantic slave trade **1803–1867**

Muhammad Ali reigns in Egypt **1805–1848**

Tanzimat reforms in Ottoman Empire **1826–1839**

Qing territorial expansion **18th century**

Opium War **1839–1842**

Tsar Alexander I suppresses opposition **1801–1825**

Decembrist uprising **1825**

Nicholas I **1825–1855**

1800   1825   1850

CHAPTER 1

Alley, Richard B., and Michael L. Bender. "Greenland Ice Cores: Frozen in Time." *Scientific American* 278 (February 1998): 80–85. A study that describes the pioneering work that astronomers and climatologists have carried out in the twentieth century to enhance our knowledge of climate change and its impact on plants and animals, including human beings.

Arsuaga, Juan Luis. *The Neanderthal's Necklace: In Search of the First Thinkers*, translated by Anthony Klatt (2002). A stimulating overview of prehistory that focuses on the Neanderthals and compares them with *Homo sapiens.*

Barham, Lawrence, and Peter Mitchell. *The First Africans: African Archaeology from the Earliest Toolmakers to Most Recent Foragers* (2008). New findings on the evolution of hominins in Africa.

Barker, Graeme. *Agricultural Revolution in Prehistory: Why Did Foragers Become Farmers?* (2006). The most recent, truly global, and up-to-date study of this momentous event in world history.

Bellwood, Peter. *First Farmers: The Origins of Agricultural Societies* (2005). A state-of-the-art global history of the origins of agriculture, including recent archaeological, linguistic, and microbiological data.

Bender, Michael L. *Paleoclimate* (2013). A definitive overview of the world's climate over the entire life of our universe, written by a renowned geoclimatologist.

Bogucki, Peter. *The Origins of Human Society* (1999). An authoritative overview of prehistory.

Brooke, John L. *Climate Change and the Course of Global History: A Rough Journey* (2014). An excellent overview of the impact of climate on history, particularly useful for the hominin period and the emergence of *Homo sapiens.*

Cauvin, Jacques. *The Birth of the Gods and the Origins of Agriculture*, translated by Trevor Watkins from the original 1994 French publication (2000). An important work on the agricultural revolution of Southwest Asia and the evolution of symbolic thinking at this time.

Cavalli-Sforza, Luigi Luca. *Genes, Peoples, and Languages*, translated by Mark Selestad from the original 1996 French publication (2000). An expert's introduction to the use of gene research for revealing new information about the evolution of human beings in the distant past.

Childe, V. Gordon. *What Happened in History* (1964). A classic work by one of the pioneers in studying the early history and evolution of human beings. Though superseded in many respects, it is still an important place to start one's reading and a work of great power and emotion.

Christian, David. *Maps of Time: An Introduction to Big History* (2004). A definitive historical work on the origins of our universe and the emergence of plant and animal life, including the hominin populations. The work synthesizes discoveries since the end of World War II that have transformed our knowledge of the universe and its peopling.

Clark, J. Desmond, and Steven A. Brandt (eds.). *From Hunters to Farmers: The Causes and Consequences of Food Production in Africa* (1984). Excellent essays on the agricultural revolution.

Coon, Carleton Stevens. *The Story of Man; from the First Human to Primitive Culture and Beyond*, 2nd ed. (1962). An important early work on the evolution of humans, emphasizing the distinctiveness of "races" around the world.

Cunliffe, Barry (ed.). *The Oxford Illustrated Prehistory of Europe* (1994). The definitive work on early European history.

Ehrenberg, Margaret. *Women in Prehistory* (1989). What was the role of women in hunting and gathering societies, and how greatly were women affected by the agricultural revolution? The author offers a number of stimulating generalizations.

Ehret, Christopher. *The Civilizations of Africa: A History to 1800* (2002). Although this is a general history of Africa, the author, a linguist and an expert on early African history, offers new information and new overviews of African peoples in very ancient times.

Fagan, Brian. *People of the Earth: An Introduction to World Prehistory* (1989). An authoritative overview of early history, widely used in classrooms.

Fage, J. D., and Roland Oliver (eds.). *The Cambridge History of Africa*, 8 vols. (1975–1984). A pioneering work of synthesis by two of the first and foremost scholars of the history of Africa. Volume 1 deals with African prehistory.

Frison, George C. *Survival by Hunting: Prehistoric Human Predators and Animal Prey* (2004). An archaeologist applies his knowledge of animal habitats, behavior, and hunting strategies to an examination of prehistoric hunting practices in the North American Great Plains and Rocky Mountains.

Gebauer, Anne Birgitte, and T. Douglas Price (eds.) *Transition to Agriculture in Prehistory* (1992). Excellent essays on the agricultural revolution, especially those written by the two editors.

Harari, Yuval Noah. *Sapiens: A Brief History of Humankind* (2015). A largely successful overview of human history from the hominins to the present.

Imbrie, John, and Katherine Palmer Imbrie. *Ice Ages and Solving the Mystery* (1979). A readable overview of the work done by geologists and climatologists on the earth's temperatures, written by two scholars who contributed to these breakthroughs.

"Inter-Group Violence among the Early Holocene Hunter-Gatherers of West Turkana, Kenya." *Nature* 529 (January 21, 2016): 394–398. Describes a spectacular discovery of the remains of hunter-gatherers who engaged in warfare.

Johnson, Donald, Lenora Johnson, and Blake Edgar. *Ancestors: In Search of Human Origins* (1999). A good overview of human evolution, with insightful essays on *Homo erectus* and *Homo sapiens.*

Jones, Steve, Robert Martin, and David Pilbeam (eds.). *The Cambridge Encyclopedia of Human Evolution* (1992). A superb guide to a wide range of subjects, crammed with up-to-date information on the most controversial and obscure topics of human evolution and early history.

Ki-Zerbo, J. (ed.). *Methodology and African Prehistory*, vol. 1 of the UNESCO *General*

History of Africa (1981). A general history of Africa, written for the most part by scholars of African descent.

Klein, Richard G., and Blake Edger. *The Dawn of Human Culture* (2002). A fine and reliable guide to the tangled history of human evolution.

Leakey, Richard. *The Origin of Humankind* (1994). A readable and exciting account of human evolution, written by the son of the pioneering archaeologists Louis and Mary Leakey, a scholar of equal stature to his parents.

Lewin, Roger. *The Origin of Modern Humans* (1993). Yet another good overview of human evolution, with useful chapters on early art and the use of symbols.

Loewe, Michael, and Edward Shaughnessy (eds.). *The Cambridge History of Ancient China: From the Origins of Civilization to 221 B.C.* (1999). A good review of the archaeology of ancient China.

Mellaart, James. *Çatal Höyük: A Neolithic Town in Anatolia* (1967). A detailed description of one of the first towns associated with the agricultural revolution in Southwest Asia.

Meredith, Martin. *Born in Africa: The Quest for Human Origins* (2011). A well-written and authoritative overview of the evolution of humankind from the earliest hominins to *Homo sapiens*.

Mithen, Steven. *The Prehistory of the Mind: The Cognitive Origins of Art and Science* (1996). A stimulating discussion of the impact of biological and cultural evolution on the cognitive structure of the human mind.

Olson, Steve. *Mapping Human History: Genes, Race, and Our Common Origins* (2003). Using the findings of genetics and attacking the racial thinking of an earlier generation of archaeologists, the author writes powerfully about the unity of all human beings.

Price, T. Douglas (ed.). *Europe's First Farmers* (2000). A discussion of the agricultural revolution in Europe.

Price, T. Douglas, and Anne Birgitte Gebauer (eds.). *Last Hunters, First Farmers: New Perspectives on the Prehistoric Transition to Agriculture* (1996). An exciting collection of essays by some of the leading scholars in the field studying the transition from hunting and gathering to settled agriculture.

Reich, David, et al. "Genome-Wide Patterns of Selection in 230 Ancient Eurasians." *Nature*, November 23, 2015, Vol. 522, published online, November 23, 2015. New DNA research on the skeletons of 230 West-Eurasians who lived between 6500 and 300 BCE shows the three waves of migrations into Europe in its distant past. These migrations came from Africa via Southwest Asia, Anatolia, and the Russian steppes.

Ruddiman, William F. *Plows, Plagues, and Petroleum: How Humans Took Control of Climate* (2005). An excellent study of how energy sources have changed over the very long run.

Sahlins, Marshall. "Notes on the Original Affluent Society." In *Man the Hunter*, edited by Richard B. Lee and Irven DeVore (1968), pp. 85–89. Sahlins coined the widely used and now famous expression "affluent society" for hunter-gatherers.

Scarre, Chris (ed.). *The Human Past: World Prehistory and the Development of Human Societies* (2005). An encyclopedia and an overview rolled up into one mammoth volume, written by leading figures in the field of early human history.

Shaw, Thurstan, Paul Sinclair, Bassey Andah, and Alex Okpoko (eds.). *The Archaeology of Africa: Food, Metals, and Towns* (1993). Research on the earliest history of human beings in Africa.

Shreeve, James. "Mystery Man." *National Geographic* 228 (October 2015): 30–57. An authoritative and up-to-date account of the extraordinary discovery of fossil remains of a hominid species, now named *Homo naledi*.

Smith, Bruce D. *The Emergence of Agriculture* (1995). How early humans domesticated wild animals and plants.

Stringer, Christopher, and Robin McKie. *African Exodus: The Origins of Modern Humanity* (1996). Detailed data on why Africa was the source of human origins and why *Homo sapiens* is a recent wanderer out of Africa.

Tattersall, Ian. *The Fossil Trail: How We Know What We Think We Know about Human Evolution* (1995). A passionately written book about early archaeological discoveries and the centrality of Africa in human evolution.

Tattersall, Ian. *The World from Beginnings to 4000 BCE* (2008). A brief up-to-date overview of humanity's early history by a leading authority.

Tattersall, Ian. *Masters of the Planet: The Search for Our Human Origins* (2012). The most recent survey of human evolution.

Van Oosterzee, Penny. *Dragon Bones: The Story of Peking Man* (2000). Describes how the late nineteenth-century unearthing of sites in China containing fossils of animals used for medicinal purposes led to the discovery of Peking Man.

Weiss, Mark L., and Alan E. Mann. *Human Biology and Behavior: An Anthropological Perspective* (1996). The authors stress the contribution that biological research has made and continues to make to unravel the mystery of human evolution.

Wrangham, Richard. *Catching Fire: How Cooking Made Us Human* (2009). The author shows how fire made it possible for humans to have a more varied and richer diet but also one that provided energy for the one organ—the brain—that consumes the most energy.

CHAPTER 2

Adams, Robert McCormick. *The Evolution of Urban Society* (1966). A classic study of the social, political, and economic processes that led to the development of the first urban civilizations.

Algaze, Guillermo. *Ancient Mesopotamia at the Dawn of Civilization* (2008). A compelling analysis of the complex environmental and social factors underlying the rise of the world's first urban culture in southern Mesopotamia.

Andrews, Carol. *Egyptian Mummies* (1998). An illustrated summary of Egyptian mummification and burial practices.

Bagley, Robert. *Ancient Sichuan: Treasures from a Lost Civilization* (2001). Describes the remarkable findings in Southwest China, particularly at Sanxingdui, which have challenged earlier accounts of the Shang dynasty's central role in the rise of early Chinese culture.

Bar-Yosef, Ofar, and Anatoly Khazanov (eds.). *Pastoralism in the Levant: Archaeological Materials in Anthropological Perspectives* (1992). Classic study of the role of nomads in the development of societies in the Levant during the Neolithic period.

Bruhns, Karen Olsen. *Ancient South America* (1994). The best basic text on pre-Columbian South American cultures.

Butzer, Karl W. *Early Hydraulic Civilization in Egypt: A Study of Cultural Ecology* (1976). The best work on how the Egyptians dealt with the Nile floods and the influence that these arrangements had on the overall organization of society.

Cunliffe, Barry. *Europe between the Oceans, 9000 BC–AD 1000* (2008). A very up-to-date and spectacularly illustrated account of early Europe.

Feng, Li. *Early China: A Social and Cultural History* (2013). An important new study on the origins of Chinese culture.

Fukuyama, Francis. *The Origins of Political Order: From Prehistoric Times to the French Revolution* (2011). A superb overview of the powerful political elements that were behind the great river-basin societies in ancient times.

Habu, Junko. *Ancient Jomon of Japan* (2004). Study of prehistoric Jomon hunter-gatherers on the Japanese archipelago that incorporates several different aspects of anthropological studies, including hunter-gatherer archaeology, settlement archaeology, and pottery analysis.

Jacobsen, Thorkild. *The Treasures of Darkness: A History of Mesopotamian Religion* (1976). Best introduction to the religious and philosophical thought of ancient Mesopotamia.

Kemp, Barry J. *Ancient Egypt: Anatomy of a Civilization* (1989). An overview of the culture of the pharaohs.

Kramer, Samuel Noah. *The Sumerians: Their History, Culture and Character* (1963). Classic study of the Sumerians and their culture by a pioneer in Sumerian studies.

Pollock, Susan. *Ancient Mesopotamia: The Eden That Never Was* (1999). An analysis of the social and economic development of Mesopotamia from the beginnings of settlement until the reign of Hammurapi.

Possehl, Gregory L. *Indus Age: The Beginnings* (1999). The second of four volumes analyzing the history of the Indus Valley civilization.

Postgate, J. N. *Early Mesopotamia: Society and Economy at the Dawn of History* (1992). A study of the economic and political development of the Sumerian civilization.

Preziosi, Donald, and L. A. Hitchcock. *Aegean Art and Architecture* (1999). One of the best general guides to the figurative and decorative art produced by the Minoans and Mycenaeans and by related early societies in the region of the Aegean.

Ratnagar, Shereen. *Understanding Harappa: Civilization in the Greater Indus Valley* (2001). Harappan site archaeological data of the last century organized into a historical narrative comprehensible to the general audience.

Ratnagar, Shereen. *Trading Encounters: From the Euphrates to the Indus in the Bronze Age*, 2nd ed. (2004). A comprehensive presentation of the evidence for the relationship between the Indus Valley and its western neighbors.

Rice, Michael. *Egypt's Legacy: The Archetypes of Western Civilization, 3000–300 BC* (1997). The author argues for the decisive influence of Egyptian culture on the whole of the Mediterranean and its later historical development.

Roaf, Michael. *Cultural Atlas of Mesopotamia and the Ancient Near East* (1990). A comprehensive compendium of the historical and cultural development of the Mesopotamian culture from the Neolithic background through the Persian Empire.

Shaw, Ian (ed.). *The Oxford History of Ancient Egypt* (2000). The most up-to-date and comprehensive account of the history of Egypt down to the Greek invasion.

Thapar, Romila. *Early India: From the Origins to AD 1300* (2002). The standard work on this period in Indian history by India's leading historian.

Thorp, Robert. *The Chinese Neolithic: Trajectories to Early States* (2005). Uses the latest archaeological evidence to describe the development of early Bronze Age cultures in North and Northwest China from about 2000 BCE.

Tignor, Robert L. *Egypt: A Short History* (2011). An overview of the history of Egypt from the rise of the pharaohs to the present.

Van de Mieroop, Marc. *The Ancient Mesopotamian City* (1997). A highly readable presentation of the earliest cities in the world.

Van de Mieroop, Marc. *A History of the Ancient Near East, ca. 3000–323 BC* (2004). An overview of the Near East in its period of historical prominence, written by an expert historian and archaeologist.

Wright, Rita P. *The Ancient Indus: Urbanism, Economy, and Society* (2010). A reconstruction of the Indus society with updated archaeological data.

CHAPTER 3

Allan, Sarah. *The Shape of the Turtle: Myth, Art and Cosmos in Early China* (1991). Explains the roles of divination and sacrifice in artistic representations of the Shang cosmology.

Allen, James P. *Middle Egyptian: An Introduction to the Language and Culture of Hieroglyphs* (2000). An introduction to the system of writing and its use in ancient Egypt.

Anthony, David W. *The Horse, the Wheel, and Language: How Bronze-Age Riders from the Eurasian Steppes Shaped the Modern World* (2007). A superb analysis of the origins and spread of the Indo-European peoples.

Arnold, Dieter. *Building in Ancient Egypt: Pharaonic Stone Masonry* (1996). Details the complex construction of monumental stone architecture in ancient Egypt.

Baines, John, and Jaromir Málek. *Atlas of Ancient Egypt* (1980). Useful compilation of information on ancient Egyptian society, religion, history, and geography.

Beal, Richard H. *The Organization of the Hittite Military* (1992). A detailed study based on textual sources of the world's first chariot-based army.

Behringer, Wolfgang. *A Cultural History of Climate* (2010). A general history of the impact of climate on many different societies.

Bell, Barbara. "The Dark Ages in Ancient History. I. The First Dark Age in Egypt," *American Journal of Archaeology*, 75 (January 1971): 1–26. An environmental analysis of the decline of the Old Kingdom and the emergence of the First Intermediate Period.

Bogucki, Peter, and Pam J. Crabtree (eds.). *Ancient Europe 8000 BC–AD 1000: Encyclopedia of the Barbarian World*, 2 vols. (2004). An indispensable handbook on the economic, social, artistic, and religious life in Europe during this period.

Bruhns, Karen Olsen. *Ancient South America* (1994). The best basic text on pre-Columbian South American cultures.

Bryant, Edwin. *The Quest for the Origins of Vedic Culture: The Indo-Aryan Migration Debate* (2001). Insight into the highly charged debate on who the Indo-European speakers were, where they originated, and where they migrated to.

Castleden, Rodney. *The Mycenaeans* (2005). One of the best current surveys of all aspects of the Mycenaean Greeks.

Chadwick, John. *The Decipherment of Linear B*, 2nd ed. (1968). Not only a retelling of the story of the decipherment of the Linear B script, but also an introduction to the actual content and function of the tablets themselves.

Cline, E. H. *Sailing the Wine-Dark Sea: International Trade and the Late Bronze Age Aegean* (1994). An excellent account of the trade and contacts between the

Aegean and other areas of the Mediterranean, Europe, and the Near East during the late Bronze Age.

Cunliffe, Barry. *Facing the Ocean: The Atlantic and Its Peoples, 8000 BC–AD 1500* (2001). An in-depth, highly useful treatment of western Europe during this period.

Cunliffe, Barry (ed.). *Prehistoric Europe: An Illustrated History* (1997). A state-of-the-art treatment of first farmers, agricultural developments, and material culture in prehistoric Europe.

Curry, Andrew. "Slaughter at the Bridge," *Science* 351 (March 25, 2016): 1384–1389. New information on a battle among hunter-gatherer warriors in northern Europe in the thirteenth century BCE.

Davis, W. V., and L. Schofield. *Egypt, the Aegean and the Levant: Interconnections in the Second Millennium BC* (1995). A discussion of the complex interactions in the eastern Mediterranean during the "international age."

Doumas, Christos. *Thera: Pompeii of the Ancient Aegean* (1983). A study of the tremendous volcanic eruption and explosion that destroyed the Minoan settlement on the island of Thera.

Drews, Robert. *Coming of the Greeks: Indo-European Conquests in the Aegean and the Near East* (1988). A good survey of the evidence for the "invasions" or "movements of peoples" that reconfigured the world of the eastern Mediterranean and Near East.

Finley, M. I. *The World of Odysseus*, 2nd rev. ed. (1977; reprint, 2002). The classic work that describes what might be recovered about the social values and behaviors of men and women in the period of the so-called Dark Ages of early Greek history.

Frankfort, Henri. *Ancient Egyptian Religion: An Interpretation* (1948; reprint, 2000). A classic study of Egyptian religion and culture during the pharaonic period.

Frayne, Douglas. *Old Babylonia Period, 2003-1595 B.C.* (1990). A standard and still useful study of this period in Babylonian history.

Jamison, Stephanie W. *Sacrificed Wife, Sacrificer's Wife: Women, Ritual, and Hospitality in Ancient India* (1996). A linguistic analysis of gender roles in Vedic literature.

Keightley, David N. *The Ancestral Landscape: Time, Space, and Community in Late Shang China, ca. 1200-1045 BC* (2000). Provides insights into the nature of royal kinship that undergirded the Shang court and its regional domains.

Kemp, Barry J. *Ancient Egypt: Anatomy of a Civilization* (2006). A definitive presentation of the history, culture, and religion of ancient Egypt.

Klein, Jacob. "The Marriage of Martu: The Urbanization of 'Barbaric' Nomads." In Meir Malul (ed.), *Mutual Influences of Peoples and Cultures in the Ancient Near East* (1996). A collection of essays written by scholars of the ancient Near East.

Kristiansen, Kristian. *Europe before History* (1998). The finest recent survey of all the major developmental phases of European prehistory.

Kuhrt, Amelie. *The Ancient Near East, c. 3000 BCE-300 CE*, 2 vols. (1995). A fundamental treatment of Egypt and Southwest Asia during these three millennia by a top scholar.

Leick, Gwendolyn (ed.). *The Babylonian World* (2007). Comprehensive presentation of the Babylonian world based on archaeology, texts, and works of art.

McIntosh, Jane. *Handbook to Life in Prehistoric Europe* (2006). Highlights the archaeological evidence that enables us to re-create the day-to-day life of different prehistoric communities in Europe.

Pines, Yuri. *The Everlasting Empire: The Political Culture of Ancient China and Its Imperial Legacy* (2012). How imperial unity became the norm in ancient China.

Preziosi, Donald, and L. A. Hitchcock. *Aegean Art and Architecture* (1999). One of the best general guides to the figurative and decorative art produced by both the Minoans and the Mycenaeans and by related early societies in the region of the Aegean.

Quirke, Stephen. *Ancient Egyptian Religion* (1992). A highly readable presentation of ancient Egyptian religion that summarizes the roles and attributions of the many Egyptian gods.

The Rigveda, the Earliest Religious Poetry of India, translated by Stephanie W. Jamison and Joel P. Bereton (2014). A new translation of the earliest literature of South Asia, correcting errors made in earlier translations.

Robins, Gay. *Women in Ancient Egypt* (1993). An interesting survey of the place of women in ancient Egyptian society.

Robins, Gay. *The Art of Ancient Egypt* (1997). The most comprehensive survey to date of the art of pharaonic Egypt.

Romer, John. *Ancient Lives: Daily Life in Egypt of the Pharaohs* (1990). A discussion of the economic and social lives of everyday ancient Egyptians.

Roth, Martha. *Law Collections from Mesopotamia and Asia Minor* (1985). An assemblage of law codes from Southwest Asia, including Hammurapi's famous legal edicts.

Sandars, N. K. *The Sea Peoples: Warriors of the Ancient Mediterranean* (1985). A readable discussion of a very complex period of Levantine history.

Simpson, William Kelly (ed.). *The Literature of Ancient Egypt: An Anthology of Stories, Instructions, and Poetry* (1972). A compilation of the most important works of literature from ancient Egypt.

Thapar, Romila. *The Past before Us: Historical Tradition of Early North India* (2013). A comprehensive evaluation of ancient Indian literature.

Thorp, Robert L. *China in the Early Bronze Age: Shang Civilization* (2005). Reviews the archaeological discoveries near Anyang, site of two capitals of the Shang kings.

Warren, Peter. *The Aegean Civilizations: From Ancient Crete to Mycenae*, 2nd ed. (1989). An excellent textual and pictorial guide to all the basic aspects of the Minoan and Mycenaean societies.

Wilson, John A. *The Culture of Ancient Egypt* (1951). A classic study of the history and culture of pharaonic Egypt.

Yadin, Yigael. *The Art of Warfare in Biblical Lands in the Light of Archaeological Discovery* (1963). A well-illustrated presentation of the machinery of war in the second and first millennia BCE.

Yoffee, Norman (ed.). *The Cambridge World History*, Vol. 3, *Early Cities in Comparative Perspective* (2014). One of nine volumes that trace world history through individual articles written by experts.

CHAPTER 4

Ahlström, Gosta W. *The History of Ancient Palestine from the Paleolithic Period to Alexander's Conquests* (1993). An excellent survey of the history of the region by a renowned expert, with good attention to the recent archaeological evidence.

Astour, Michael. "New Evidence on the Last Days of Ugarit," *American Journal of Archaeology* 69 (1965). An early and important article on the destruction of important cities in the Levant in the twelfth century BCE.

Aubet, Maria Eugenia. *The Phoenicians and the West*, 2nd ed. (2001). The basic survey of the Phoenician colonization of the western Mediterranean and Atlantic, with special attention to recent archaeological discoveries.

Behringer, Wolfgang. *A Cultural History of Climate*, translated by Patrick Camiller (2010). A summary view of the place of climate in historical change, written by an expert in historical climatology.

Benjamin, Craig (ed.). *The Cambridge World History*, Vol 4: *A World with States, Empires, and Networks, 1200 BCE–900 CE* (2015). An important overview of developments in the world, with individual chapters written by experts.

Briant, Pierre. *From Cyrus to Alexander: A History of the Persian Empire*, translated by Peter T. Daniels (2002). A complex and comprehensive history of the Persian Empire by its finest modern scholar.

Bright, John. *A History of Israel*, 4th ed. (2000). An updated version of a classic and still very useful overview of the whole history of the Israelite people down to the end of the period covered in this chapter.

Cook, John M. *The Persian Empire* (1983). An older but still useful and highly readable standard history of the Persian Empire.

Fagan, Brian. *The Long Summer: How Climate Changed Civilization* (2004). An accessible overview of the role of climate in historical change, written by one of the leading historians of ancient history and an individual who has brought together considerable evidence about climatic change and historical development.

Falkenhausen, Lothar von. *Chinese Society in the Age of Confucius (1000–250 BC): The Archaeological Evidence* (2006). A timely reassessment of early Chinese history that compares the literary texts on which it has traditionally been based with the new archaeological evidence.

Fukuyama, Francis. *The Origins of Political Order: From Prehuman Times to the French Revolution* (2011). Argues that the first real kings in Chinese history and the first real states and dynasties did not appear until the Qin and Han.

Grayson, A. Kirk. "Assyrian Civilization." In *Cambridge Ancient History,* Vol. 3, pt. 2 (1992), pp. 194–228. Examines the Assyrian and Babylonian Empires and other states of Southwest Asia from the eighth to the sixth centuries BCE.

Hornung, Erik. *Akhenaten and the Religion of Light*, translated from the German by David Lorton (1999). A brief but important biography of Egypt's most controversial pharaoh.

Hornung, Erik. *History of Ancient Egypt: An Introduction*, translated from the German by David Lorton (1999). An accessible overview of the history of ancient Egypt by a leading Egyptologist.

Isserlin, Benedikt J. *The Israelites* (1998). A well-written illustrated history of all aspects of life in the regions of the Levant inhabited by the Israelites.

Keay, John. *India: A History* (2010). A useful, readable overview of the sweep of Indian history.

Lancel, Serge. *Carthage: A History*, translated by Antonia Nevill (1997). By far the best single-volume history of the most important Phoenician colony in the Mediterranean. (The first three chapters are especially relevant to materials covered in this chapter.)

Lemche, Niels Peter. *Ancient Israel: A New History of Israelite Society* (1988). A quick, readable, and still up-to-date summary of the main phases and themes.

Lewis, Mark Edward. *Writing and Authority in Early China* (1999). A work that traces the changing uses of writing to command assent and obedience in early China.

Liverani, Mario. *The Ancient Near East: History, Society and Economy* (2014). Parts 5 and 6 are especially relevant to the materials covered in this chapter.

Liu, Guozhong. *Introduction to the Tsinghua Bamboo-Strip Manuscripts*, translated by Christopher J. Foster and William N. French (2016). An important essay on the implications of these texts for our understanding of early Western Zhou history.

Markoe, Glenn E. *Phoenicians* (2000). A thorough survey of the Phoenicians and their society as it first developed in the Levant and then expanded over the Mediterranean, with excellent illustrations of the diverse archaeological sites.

Matthews, Victor H., and Don C. Benjamin. *Social World of Ancient Israel, 1350–587 BCE* (1993). A thematic overview of the main occupational groups and social roles that characterized ancient Israelite society.

Oates, Joan, and David Oates. *Nimrud: An Assyrian Imperial City Revealed* (2001). A fine and highly readable summary of the state of our knowledge of the Neo-Assyrian Empire from the perspective of the early capital of Assurnasirpal II.

Oded, Bustenay. *Mass Deportations and Deportees in the Neo-Assyrian Empire* (1979). A detailed textual examination of the deportation strategy of the Assyrian kings.

Potts, D. T. *The Archaeology of Elam: Formation and Transformation of an Ancient Iranian State* (1999). The definitive study of the archaeology of western Iran from the Neolithic period through the Persian Empire.

Quinn, Josephine C., and Nicholas C. Vella (eds.). *The Punic Mediterranean* (2014). A valuable and readable collection of chapters on various aspects of how the Phoenician colonization of the Mediterranean led to the formation of new cultural identities.

Radner, Karen. *Ancient Assyria: A Very Short Introduction* (2015). A highly readable and up-to-date survey of all the important aspects of Assyrian government and society.

Shaughnessy, Edward L. *Sources of Western Zhou History: Inscribed Bronze Vessels* (1992). Detailed work on the historiography and interpretation of the thousands of ritual bronze vessels discovered by China's archaeologists.

Stein, Burton. *A History of India*, 2nd ed., edited by David Arnold (2010). One of the standard general histories of India, brought up to date by a leading historian of the subcontinent.

Tanner, Harold M. *China: A History* (2009). A readable and up-to-date overview of the sweep of Chinese history.

Thapar, Romila. *From Lineage to State* (1984). The only book on early India that uses religious literature historically and analyzes major lineages to reveal the transition from tribal society to state institutions.

Thapar, Romila. *The Aryan. Recasting Constructs* (2011). On the rise of the theory of an Aryan race and the beginnings of Indian history.

Tignor, Robert L. *Egypt: A Short History* (2010). A succinct treatment of the entire history of Egypt from the pharaohs to the present, with three chapters on the ancient period.

Trautmann, Thomas. *India: Brief History of a Civilization* (2011). A highly readable survey of Indian history with emphasis on its early history.

Tubb, Jonathan N. *Canaanites* (1998). The best recent survey, well illustrated, of one of the main ethnic groups dominating the culture of the Levant.

CHAPTER 5

Adams, William Y. *Nubia: Corridor to Africa* (1977). The authoritative historical overview of Nubia, the area of present-day Sudan just south of Egypt and a geographical connecting point between the Mediterranean and sub-Saharan Africa.

Allan, Sarah. *Buried Ideas: Legends of Abdication and Ideal Government in Early Chinese Bamboo-Slip Manuscripts* (2016). Four recently discovered Warring States texts challenge long-standing ideas about Chinese intellectual history.

Armstrong, Karen. *Buddha* (2001). A readable and impressive account of the life of the Buddha.

Aubet, Maria Eugenia. *The Phoenicians and the West*, 2nd ed. (2001). The basic survey of the Phoenician colonization of the western Mediterranean and Atlantic, with special attention to recent archaeological discoveries.

Barker, Graeme, and Tom Rasmussen. *The Etruscans* (1998). The most up-to-date introduction to this important pre-Roman society in the Italian peninsula, with strong emphasis on broad social and material patterns of development as indicated by the archaeological evidence.

Benjamin, Craig (ed.). *The Cambridge World History*, Vol. 4: *A World with States, Empires, and Networks, 1200 BCE–900 CE* (2015). Essays by experts on these centuries in world history. Especially important for thinking about the Axial Age is the chapter by Bjorn Wittrock, "The Axial Age in World History," pp. 101–119.

Bresson, Alain. *The Making of the Ancient Greek Economy: Institutions, Markets, and Growth in the City-States*, translated by Steven Rendall (2015). The most conceptually sophisticated and factually up-to-date account of the economic regimes of the Greek city-states.

Burkert, Walter. *Greek Religion*, translated by John Raffan (1985). The best one-volume introduction to early Greek religion, placing the Greeks in their larger Mediterranean and Near Eastern contexts.

Burns, Karen Olsen. *Ancient South America* (1994). A very useful overview of recent debates and conclusions about pre-Columbian archaeology in South America, including both the Andes and the lowland and coastal regions.

Cartledge, Paul (ed.). *The Cambridge Illustrated History of Ancient Greece* (2002). An excellent history of the Greek city-states down to the time of Alexander the Great.

Chakravarti, Uma. *The Social Dimensions of Early Buddhism* (1987). A description of the life of Buddha drawn from early Buddhist texts.

Cho-yun, Hsu. *Ancient China in Transition* (1965). An account of the political, economic, social, and intellectual changes that occurred during the Warring States period.

Coarelli, Filippo (ed.). *Etruscan Cities* (1975). A brilliantly and lavishly illustrated guide to the material remains of the Etruscans: their cities, their magnificent tombs, and their architecture, painting, sculpture, and other art.

Coe, Michael, Richard A. Diehl, David A Freidel, et al. (eds.), *The Olmec World: Ritual and Rulership* (1996). A collection of field-synthesizing articles with important illustrations, based on one of the most comprehensive exhibitions of Olmec art in the world.

Confucius. *The Analects (Lun Yü)*, translated by D. C. Lau (1979). An outstanding translation of the words of Confucius as recorded by his major disciples. Includes valuable historical material needed to provide the context for Confucius's teachings.

Eisenstadt, S. N. (ed.). *The Origins and Diversity of Axial Age Civilizations* (1986). A set of essays that develops Jaspers's concept of the Axial Age cultures.

Elman, Benjamin A., and Martin Kern (eds.). *Statecraft and Classical Learning: The Rituals of Zhou in East Asian History* (2010). Traces the long-term political rise of classical learning and state rituals in East Asia from the decline of the Eastern Zhou kingdom to the rise of later imperial dynasties in China, Japan, and Korea.

Finley, M. I., and H. W. Pleket. *The Olympic Games: The First Thousand Years* (2005). A fine description of the most famous of the Greek games; it explains how they exemplify the competitive spirit that marked many aspects of the Greek city-states.

Garlan, Yvon. *War in the Ancient World: A Social History*, translated by Janet Lloyd (1976). A discussion of the emergence of the forms of warfare, including male citizens fighting in hoplite phalanxes and the development of siege warfare, that were typical of the Greek city-states.

Garlan, Yvon. *Slavery in Ancient Greece*, translated by Janet Lloyd (1988). A treatment of the emergence, development, and institutionalization of chattel slavery in the Greek city-states.

Iliffe, John. *Africans: The History of a Continent*, 2nd ed. (2007). A first-rate scholarly survey of Africa from its beginnings, with a strong emphasis on demography.

Jaspers, Karl. *The Origin and Goal of History* (1953). The book that first developed the idea of the Axial Age.

Lancel, Serge. *Carthage: A History*, translated by Antonia Nevill (1997). By far the best single-volume history of the most important Phoenician colony in the Mediterranean.

Lewis, Mark Edward. *Sanctioned Violence in Early China* (1990). An analysis of the use of sanctioned violence as an element of statecraft from the Warring States period to the formation of the Qin and Han Empires in the second half of the first millennium BCE.

Lewis, Mark Edward. *Writing and Authority in Early China* (1999). A revisionist account of the central role of writing and persuasion in models for the invention of a Chinese world empire.

Ling, Trevor. *The Buddha: Buddhist Civilization in India and Ceylon* (1972). An overview of Buddhism in India and Ceylon.

Lloyd, G. E. R. *Early Greek Science: Thales to Aristotle* (1970). An especially clear and concise introduction to the main developments and intellectuals that marked the emergence of critical secular thinking in the early Greek world.

Lloyd, G. E. R., and Nathan Sivin. *The Way and the Word: Science and Medicine in Early China and Greece* (2002). A comprehensive rethinking of the social and political settings in ancient China and city-state Greece that contributed to the different views of science and medicine that emerged in each place.

Mote, Frederick. *Intellectual Foundations of China* (1971). An early but still useful description of the seminal figures in China's early intellectual life.

Murray, Oswyn. *Early Greece*, 2nd ed. (1993). One of the best introductions to the emergence of the Greek city-states down to the end of the Archaic Age.

Ober, Josiah. *The Rise and Fall of Classical Greece* (2015). A compelling general interpretation of the rise of the Greek city-states in the sixth and fifth centuries BCE and their subsequent demise in the fourth century.

Osborne, Robin. *Archaic and Classical Greek Art* (1998). An outstanding book that clearly explains the main innovations in Greek art, setting them in their historical context.

Osborne, Robin. *Greece in the Making, 1200–479 BC* (1999). The standard history of the whole early period of the Greek city-states characterized by an especially fine and judicious mix of archaeological data and literary sources.

Pallottino, Massimo. *The Etruscans,* rev. ed., translated by J. Cremona (1975). A fairly traditional but still classic survey of all aspects of Etruscan history and political and social institutions.

Pines, Yuri, Paul R. Goldin, and Martin Kern (eds.). *Ideology of Power and Power of Ideology in Early China* (2015). A new assessment of state ideology and political legitimation under the Eastern Zhou dynasty during the Warring States era.

Redford, Donald B. *From Slave to Pharaoh: The Black Experience of Ancient Egypt* (2004). A description of Egypt's Twenty-fifth Dynasty, which was made up of Sudanese conquerors.

Schaberg, David. *A Patterned Past: Form and Thought in Early Chinese Historiography* (2002). A comprehensive study of the intellectual content of historical anecdotes by the followers of Confucius collected around the fourth century BCE.

Schaps, David. *The Invention of Coinage and the Monetization of Ancient Greece* (2004). A new analysis that offers a broad overview of the emergence of coined money in the Near East and the eastern Mediterranean and its effects on the spread of money-based markets.

Sharma, J. P. *Republics in Ancient India, c. 1500 B.C.–500 B.C.* (1968). Relying on information from early Buddhist texts, this book first revealed that South Asia had not only monarchies but also alternative polities.

Shaw, Thurston. *Nigeria: Its Archaeology and Early History* (1978). An important introduction to the early history of Nigeria by one of that country's leading archaeologists.

Shinnie, P. L. *Ancient Nubia* (1996). An excellent account of the history of the ancient Nubians, who, we are discovering, had great influence on Egypt and on the rest of tropical Africa.

Snodgrass, Anthony. *Archaic Greece: The Age of Experiment* (1981). A good introduction to the archaeological evidence of Archaic Greece.

Taylor, Christopher, Richard Hare, and Jonathan Barnes. *Greek Philosophers* (1999). A fine, succinct, one-volume introduction to the major aspects of the three big thinkers who dominated the high period of classical Greek philosophy: Socrates, Plato, and Aristotle.

Torok, Laszlo. *Meroe: Six Studies on the Cultural Identity of an Ancient African State* (1995). A good collection of essays on the most recent work on Meroe.

Von Falkenhausen, Lothar. *Chinese Society in the Age of Confucius (100-250 BC)* (2006). The larger Chinese society under the influence of Confucian thought.

Welsby, Derek. *The Kingdom of Kush: The Napatan and Meroitic Empires* (1996). A fine book on these two important Nubian kingdoms.

CHAPTER 6

Bradley, Keith. *Slavery and Rebellion in the Roman World, 140 B.C.–70 B.C.* (1989). A description of the rise of large-scale plantation slavery in Sicily and Italy and a detailed account of the three great slave wars.

Bresson, Alain. *The Making of the Ancient Greek Economy: Markets and Growth in the City-States,* translated by Steven Rendall (2015). An up-to-date and theoretically well-informed analysis of the market economics of the Greek city-states in the Hellenistic era.

Browning, Iain. *Palmyra* (1979). A narrative of the history of the important desert city that linked eastern and western trade routes.

Casson, Lionel. *The Periplus Maris Erythraei* (1989). An introduction to a typical ancient sailing manual, this one of the Red Sea and Indian Ocean.

Casson, Lionel. *Ships and Seamanship in the Ancient World* (1995). The classic account of the ships and sailors that powered commerce and war on the high seas.

Colledge, Malcolm. *The Art of Palmyra* (1976). A well-illustrated introduction to the unusual art of Palmyra with its mixture of eastern and western elements.

Fowler, Barbara H. *The Hellenistic Aesthetic* (1989). How the artists in this new age saw and portrayed their world in new and different ways.

Green, Peter. *Alexander to Actium: The Historical Evolution of the Hellenistic Age* (1990). The best general guide to the whole period in all of its various aspects, and well illustrated.

Habicht, Christian. *Athens from Alexander to Antony,* translated by Deborah L. Schneider (1997). The authoritative account of what happened to the great city-state of Athens in this period.

Hansen, Valerie. *The Silk Road: A New History* (2012). The most recent work on the Silk Road; authoritative on the eastern terminus of this vital trade route.

Herodotus. *The Histories,* 4 volumes, translated by Tom Holland (2013). A basic work, which many scholars regard as the first world history. The translation given here was done by Brent Shaw and came from the original Greek.

Holt, Frank L. *Thundering Zeus: The Making of Hellenistic Bactria* (1999). A basic history of the most eastern of the kingdoms spawned by the conquests of Alexander the Great.

Hopkirk, Peter. *Foreign Devils on the Silk Road* (1984). A historiography of the explorations and researches on the central Asian Silk Road of the nineteenth and early twentieth centuries.

Juliano, Annette L., and Judith A. Lerner (eds.). *Nomads, Traders and Holy Men along China's Silk Road* (2003). A description of the travelers along the Silk Road in human terms, focusing on warfare, markets, and religion.

Keay, John. *India: A History* (2000). A well-written and well-researched overview of the entire history of South Asia.

Kosmin, Paul J. *The Land of the Elephant Kings: Space, Territory, and Ideology in the Seleucid Empire* (2014). The best current analysis of the relationships of Seleucid kings, both with their own subjects and, especially, with the Mauryan kingdom of India and the nomadic peoples of central Asia.

Kuzima, E. E. *The Prehistory of the Silk Road* (2008). Valuable information on the early history of the Silk Road.

Lane Fox, Robin. *Alexander the Great* (1973). Still the most readable and in many ways the sanest biography of the world conqueror.

Lewis, Naphtali. *Greeks in Ptolemaic Egypt* (1986). An account of the relationships between Greeks and Egyptians as seen through the lives of individual Greek settlers and colonists.

Liu, Xinru. *Ancient India and Ancient China* (1988). The first work to connect political and economic developments in India and China with the evolution and spread of Buddhism in the first half of the first millennium.

Liu, Xinru. *The Silk Road in World History* (2010). A study of the history of the great trade and communications route that connected the different regions of Afro-Eurasia between the third century BCE and the thirteenth century CE.

Long, Antony A. *Hellenistic Philosophy: Stoics, Epicureans, Sceptics*, 2nd ed. (1986). One of the clearest guides to the new trends in Greek philosophical thinking in the period.

Martin, Luther H. *Hellenistic Religions: An Introduction* (1987). An introduction to the principal new Hellenistic religions and cults that emerged in this period.

Mendels, Doron. *The Rise and Fall of Jewish Nationalism* (1992). A sophisticated account of the various phases of Jewish resistance in Judah to foreign domination.

Miller, James Innes. *The Spice Trade of the Roman Empire, 29 B.C. to A.D. 641* (1969). A first-rate study of the spice trade in the Roman Empire.

Pomeroy, Sarah B. *Women in Hellenistic Egypt: From Alexander to Cleopatra* (1990). A highly readable investigation of women and family in the best-documented region of the Hellenistic world.

Ray, Himanshu P. *The Wind of Change, Buddhism and the Maritime Links of Early South Asia* (1994). Ray's study of Buddhism and maritime trade stretches from the Arabian Sea to the navigations between South Asia and Southeast Asia.

Rosenfield, John. *The Dynastic Art of the Kushans* (1967). Instead of focusing on the Gandharan Buddhist art itself, Rosenfield selects sculptures of Kushan royals and those representing nomadic populations in religious shrines to display the central Asian aspect of artworks of the period.

Rostovtzeff, Michael Ivanovich. *Caravan Cities,* translated by D. and T. Talbot Rice (1932). Though published more than eight decades ago, this small volume contains accurate descriptions of the ruins of many caravan cities in modern Jordan and Syria.

Rostovtzeff, Michael Ivanovich. *The Social and Economic History of the Hellenistic World* (1941). A monumental achievement. One of the great works of history written in the twentieth century. An unsurpassed overview of all aspects of the politics and social and economic movements of the period. Despite its age, there is still nothing like it.

Schoff, Wilfred H. (ed. and trans.). *The Periplus of the Erythraean Sea* (1912). An invaluable tool for mapping the names and places from the Red Sea to Indian coastal areas during this period.

Shipley, Graham. *The Greek World after Alexander, 323–30 BC* (2000). A more up-to-date survey than Peter Green's work (above), with more emphasis on the historical detail in each period.

Thapar, Romila. *Aśoka and the Decline of the Mauryas* (1973). Using all available primary sources, including the edicts of Aśoka and Greek authors' accounts, Thapar gives the most authoritative analysis of the first (and most important) empire in Indian history.

Vainker, Shelagh. *Chinese Silk: A Cultural History* (2004). A work that traces the cultural history of silk in China from its early origins to the twentieth century and considers its relationship to the other decorative arts. The author draws on the most recent archaeological evidence to emphasize the role of silk in Chinese history, trade, religion, and literature.

Wood, Francis. *The Silk Road: Two Thousand Years in the Heart of Asia* (2004). Illustrated with drawings, manuscripts, paintings, and artifacts to trace the Silk Road to its origins as far back as Alexander the Great, with an emphasis on its importance to cultural and religious movements.

Young, Gary K. *Rome's Eastern Trade: International Commerce and Imperial Policy, 31 BC–AD 305* (2001). This study examines the taxation and profits of eastern trade from the perspective of the Roman government.

CHAPTER 7

Barbieri-Low, Anthony J., and Robin D. S. Yates. *Law, State, and Society in Early Imperial China (2 Vols): A Study with Critical Edition and Translation of the Legal Texts from Zhangjiashan Tomb No. 247* (2015). A new account of changes in Western (Former) Han dynasty law in terms of its moralization via instituting Confucianism.

Batty, Roger. *Rome and the Nomads: The Pontic-Danubian Realm in Antiquity* (2007). A comprehensive account of relations between the Roman Empire and the nomads of the western Eurasian steppelands.

Bodde, Derk. *China's First Unifier: A Study of the Ch'in Dynasty as Seen in the Life of Li Ssu (280?–208 B.C.)* (1938). A classic account of the key Legalist adviser, Li Si, who formulated the Qin policy to enhance its autocratic power.

Bowman, Alan K. *Life and Letters on the Roman Frontier: Vindolanda and Its Peoples* (1994). An introduction to the exciting discovery of writing tablets from a Roman army base in northern Britain.

Bradley, Keith. *Slavery and Society at Rome* (1994). An excellent overview of the major aspects of the slave system in the Roman Empire.

Chevallier, Raymond. *Roman Roads,* translated by N. H. Field (1976). A guide to the fundamentals of the construction, maintenance, administration, and mapping of Roman roads.

Coarelli, Fillipo (ed.). *Pompeii,* translated by Patricia Cockram (2006). A lavishly illustrated large volume that allows the reader to sense some of the wondrous wealth of the buried city of Pompeii.

Colledge, Malcolm A. R. *The Parthians* (1967). A bit dated but still a fundamental introduction to the Parthians, the major power on the eastern frontier of the Roman Empire.

Cornell, Tim. *The Beginnings of Rome: Italy and Rome from the Bronze Age to the Punic Wars, c. 2000 to 264 B.C.* (1995). The single best one-volume history of Rome through its early history to the first war with Carthage.

Cornell, Tim, and John Matthews. *Atlas of the Roman World* (1982). A history of the Roman world; much more than simply an atlas. It provides not only good maps and a gazetteer but also marvelous color illustrations and a text that guides the reader through the basics of Roman history.

Csikszentmihalyi, Mark. *Readings in Han Chinese Thought* (2006). A volume presenting a representative selection of primary sources to illustrate the growth of ideas in early imperial times; a useful introduction to the key strains of thought during this crucial period.

Dien, Albert E. "The Qin Army and Its Antecedents." In Liu Yang (ed.), *China's Terracotta Warriors: The First Emperor's Legacy* (2013). An account of the Qin army in light of its Warring States precedents.

Dixon, Suzanne. *The Roman Family* (1992). The best one-volume guide to the nature of the Roman family and family relations.

Elvin, Mark. *The Retreat of the Elephants: An Environmental History of China* (2004). A pioneering environmental history of China covering over 4,000 years of its history.

Garnsey, Peter, and Richard Saller. *The Roman Empire: Economy, Society, and Culture*, 2nd ed. (2014). A perceptive and critical introduction to three basic aspects of social life in the empire.

Giardina, Andrea (ed.). *The Romans*, translated by Lydia Cochrane (1993). Individual studies of important typical figures in Roman society, from the peasant and the bandit to the merchant and the soldier.

Goldsworthy, Adrian. *The Roman Army at War: 100 B.C.–A.D. 200* (1996). A summary history and analysis of the Roman army in action during the late Republic and early Roman Empire.

Harris, William. *Ancient Literacy* (1989). A basic survey of what is known about communication in the form of writing and books in the Roman Empire.

Hopkins, Keith. *Death and Renewal: Sociological Studies in Roman History*, vol. 2 (1983). Innovative studies in Roman history, including one of the best on gladiators and another on death and funerals.

Hopkins, Keith. *A World Full of Gods: Pagans, Jews and Christians in the Roman Empire* (1999). A somewhat unusual but interesting and provocative look at the world of religions in the Roman Empire.

Hughes, J. Donald. *Environmental Problems of the Greeks and Romans: Ecology in the Ancient Mediterranean*, 2nd ed. (2014). A much improved and expanded edition of a classic work on the environment in Greek and Roman antiquity and a state-of-the-art summary of our current knowledge.

Juliano, Annette L., and Judith A. Lerner (eds.). *Nomads, Traders and Holy Men along China's Silk Road* (2003). A description of the travelers along the Silk Road in human terms, focusing on warfare, markets, and religion.

Kern, Martin, and Michael Hunter (eds.). *The Analects. A Western Han Text?* (2013). Challenges the assumption that the Confucian *Analects* was compiled before the Han dynasty.

Knapp, Robert C. *Invisible Romans* (2011). A highly readable introduction to the lower orders of Roman imperial society: the poor, slaves, freedmen, prostitutes, gladiators, bandits, and pirates (among others).

Lewis, Mark. *The Early Chinese Empires: Qin and Han* (2007). A recent account of the rise of imperial China after the Warring States period.

Liang, Cai. *Witchcraft and the Rise of the First Confucian Empire* (2014). A new account of the rise of the Confucians at the Former (Western) Han court during the famous witchcraft trials circa 91–87 BCE.

Loewe, Michael. *The Government of the Qin and Han Empires: 221 BCE–220 CE* (2006). A useful overview of the government of the early empires of China. Topics include the structure of central government, provincial and local government, the armed forces, officials, government communications, the laws of the empire, and control of the people and the land.

Millar, Fergus. *The Emperor in the Roman World, 31 B.C.–A.D. 337* (1992). Everything you might want to know about the Roman emperor, with special emphasis on his role as the administrator of the empire.

Millar, Fergus. *The Crowd in the Late Republic* (1998). An innovative study of the democratic power of the citizens in the city of Rome itself.

Potter, David. *The Roman Empire at Bay: A.D. 180–395*, 2nd ed. (2014). A new basic text covering the later Roman Empire, including the critical transition to a Christian state.

Qian, Sima. *Records of the Grand Historian: Qin Dynasty*, 3rd ed., translated by Burton Watson (1995). The classic work of Chinese history in a readable translation. The Han dynasty's Grand Historian describes the slow rise and meteoric fall of the Qin dynasty from the point of view of the succeeding dynasty, which Sima Qian witnessed or heard of during his lifetime.

Southern, Pat. *The Roman Army: A Social and Institutional History* (2006). A guide to all aspects of the Roman army.

Vainker, Shelagh. *Chinese Silk: A Cultural History* (2004). A work that traces the cultural history of silk in China from its early origins to the twentieth century and considers its relationship to the other decorative arts. The author draws on recent archaeological evidence to emphasize the role of silk in Chinese history, trade, religion, and literature.

Wood, Francis. *The Silk Road: Two Thousand Years in the Heart of Asia* (2004). A work illustrated with drawings, manuscripts, paintings, and artifacts to trace the Silk Road to its origins as far back as Alexander the Great. The author stresses the importance of the Silk Road to cultural and religious movements.

Woolf, Greg (ed.). *The Cambridge Illustrated History of the Roman World* (2005). A good guide to various aspects of Roman history, culture, and provincial life.

Woolf, Greg. *Rome: An Empire's Story* (2012). An up-to-date narrative of the Roman empire, told according to major themes that are particularly relevant to world history.

CHAPTER 8

Bowersock, Glen W. *Empires in Collision in Late Antiquity* (2013). Brilliant, short studies of the relations between Ethiopia, Arabia, and Byzantium as a background to the origins of Islam.

Brown, Peter. *The World of Late Antiquity: From Marcus Aurelius to Muhammad, AD 150–750* (1989). A social, religious, and cultural history of the late Roman and Sasanian Empires, with illustrations and a time chart.

Brown, Peter. *The Rise of Western Christendom: Triumph and Diversity, A.D. 200–1000*, 2nd ed. (2003). The rise and spread of Christianity in Europe and Asia, with up-to-date bibliographies on all topics, maps, and time charts. Reprinted with a new introduction in 2013.

Brown, Peter. *Through the Eye of a Needle: Wealth, the Fall of Rome, and the Making of Christianity in the West, 350–550* (2012). Christianity and Roman society before and after the end of the empire.

Brown, Peter. "The Silk Road in Late Antiquity." In V. H. Maier and J. Hickman (eds.), *Reconfiguring the Silk Road* (2014). Silk Road from the perspective of its western outlets and influences.

Brown, Peter. *Treasure in Heaven: The Holy Poor in Early Christianity* (2016). On the social role of early Christian monasticism in Syria and Egypt.

Bühler, G. (trans.). *The Laws of Manu* (1886). The classic translation of one of India's most important historical, legal, and religious texts.

Canepa, Matthew P. *The Two Eyes of the Earth: Art and Ritual of Kingship between Rome and Sasanian Iran* (2009). An interesting look at how two great global powers, Rome and Iran, shared images of rulership.

Coe, Michael D. *The Maya*, 6th ed. (1999). A work by the world's most famous Mayanologist, with recent evidence, analyses, and illustrations.

Cowgill, George L. "The Central Mexican Highlands and the Rise of Teotihuacan to the Decline of Tula." In Richard Adams and Murdo Macleod (eds.), *The Cambridge History of the Native Peoples of the Americas, Vol. 2: Mesoamerica, Part 1* (2000). A thorough review of findings about urban states in central Mexico.

Fash, William L. *Scribes, Warriors and Kings: The City of Copan and the Ancient Maya* (2001). A fascinating and comprehensive study of one of the most elaborate of the Mayan city-kingdoms.

Fisher, Greg. *Between Empires: Arabs, Romans, and Sasanians in Late Antiquity* (2011). Arab, Roman, and Sasanian empires compared.

Fisher, Greg (ed.). *Arabs and Empires before Islam* (2015). A collection of up-to-date studies on the relationships of various Arab groups with imperial powers, especially Rome and Persia.

Fowden, Elizabeth Key. *The Barbarian Plain: Saint Sergius between Rome and Iran* (1999). The study of a major Christian shrine and its relations to Romans, Persians, and Arabs.

Fowden, Garth. *Empire to Commonwealth: The Consequences of Monotheism in Late Antiquity* (1993). A study of the relation between empire and world religions in western Asia.

Gombrich, Richard F., and Sheldon Pollack (eds.). *Clay Sanskrit Library* (2005–2006). All major works from the Gupta and post-Gupta periods, in both Sanskrit and English versions. During the Gupta period, classical Sanskrit literature reached its apex, with abundant drama, poetry, and folk stories.

Gordon, Charles. *The Age of Attila* (1960). The last century of the Roman Empire in western Europe, vividly illustrated from contemporary sources.

Haldon, John. *The Empire That Would Not Die: The Paradox of Eastern Rome's Survival* (2010). Incorporates much new climatological evidence.

Hansen, Valerie. *The Silk Road: A New History* (2012). A detailed history of the Silk Road, based largely on Chinese sources.

Harper, Prudence. *The Royal Hunter: The Art of the Sasanian Empire* (1978). The

ideology of the Sasanian Empire as shown through excavated hoards of precious silverware.

Heather, Peter. *The Fall of the Roman Empire: A New History of Rome and the Barbarians* (2006). A military and political narrative based on up-to-date archaeological material.

Herrmann, Georgina. *Iranian Revival* (1977). The structure and horizons of the Sasanian Empire as revealed in its monuments.

Hillgarth, Jocelyn (ed.). *Christianity and Paganism, 350–750: The Conversion of Western Europe*, rev. ed. (1986). A collection of contemporary sources.

Holcombe, Charles. *In the Shadow of the Han: Literati Thought and Society at the Beginning of the Southern Dynasties* (1994). A clear and concise account of the evolution of thought in China after the fall of the Han dynasty in 220 CE. The book presents the rise of Buddhism and Daoism as popular religions as well as elite interest in classical learning in a time of political division and barbarian conquest in North and South China.

La Vaissière, Étienne de. *Sogdian Traders: A History*, translated by James Ward (2005). A summary of historical facts about the most important trading community and its commercial networks on the Silk Road, from the early centuries CE to its demise in the ninth century CE.

Little, Lester (ed.). *Plague and the End of Antiquity: The Pandemic of 541–750* (2008). A series of debates over the nature and impact of the first great pandemic attested in global history.

Liu, Xinru, and Lynda Norene Shaffer. *Connections across Eurasia: Transportation, Communication, and Cultural Exchanges on the Silk Roads* (2007). A survey of trade and religious activities on the Silk Road.

Lopez, Ariel G. *Shenoute of Atripe and the Uses of Poverty: Rural Patronage, Religious Conflict, and Monasticism in Late Antique Egypt* (2013). Places a leading Egyptian abbot in his full social context.

Maas, Michael. *Readings in Late Antiquity: A Source Book* (1999). Well-chosen extracts that illustrate the interrelation of Romans and non-Romans and of Christians, Jews, and pagans.

Maas, Michael. *The Age of Atilla: The Cambridge Companion to the Age of Attila* (2013). Essays on this important age in the late Antique period.

Maas, Michael (ed.). *The Cambridge Companion to the Age of Justinian* (2005). A survey of all aspects of the Eastern Roman Empire in the sixth century CE.

Moffett, Samuel. *A History of Christianity in Asia*, Vol. 1 (1993). Particularly valuable on Christians in China and India.

Munro-Hay, Stuart. *Aksum: An African Civilization of Late Antiquity* (1991). The origins of the Christian kingdom of Ethiopia.

Murdock, George P. *Africa: Its Peoples and Their History* (1959). A vital introduction to the peoples of Africa and their history.

Oliver, Roland. *The African Experience: From Olduvai Gorge to the Twenty-First Century* (1999). An important overview, written by one of the pioneering scholars of African history and one of the leading authorities on the Bantu migrations.

Payne, Richard. *A State of Mixture: Christians, Zoroastrians, and Iranian Political Culture in Late Antiquity* (2015). A new view of Christianity in Sasanian Iran.

Pourshariati, Parvaneh. *The Decline and Fall of the Sasanian Empire: The Sasanian-Parthian Confederacy and the Arab Conquest of Iran* (2008). An innovative perspective on the demise of the Sasanians and the relevance of their decline for the Arab conquest of Iran.

Pregadio, Fabrizio. *Great Clarity: Daoism and Alchemy in Early Medieval China* (2006). An examination of the religious aspects of Daoism. The book focuses on the relation of alchemy to the Daoist traditions of the third to sixth century CE and shows how alchemy was integrated into the elaborate body of doctrines and practices of Daoists at that time.

Tempels, Placide. *Bantu Philosophy* (1959). A highly influential effort to argue for the underlying cultural unity of all the Bantu peoples.

Vansina, Jan. *Paths in the Rainforests: Toward a History of Political Tradition in Equatorial Africa* (1990). The best work on Bantu history.

Walker, Joel. *The Legend of Mar Kardagh: Narrative and Christian Heroism in Late Antique Iraq* (2006). Christians and Zoroastrians in northern Iraq and in Iran.

Yarshater, Ehsan. *Encyclopedia Iranica* (1982+). This encyclopedia offers countless articles dealing with all aspects of the Sasanian Empire and religion and culture in the regions between Mesopotamia and central Asia.

Zhang, Xun, *Fian Zhuan Jiaozhu* (1985) The account of a Chinese Buddhist who traveled to India to learn more about Buddhism and to bring back to China copies of important texts. The text excerpted in this chapter was done by Xinru Liu.

Zürcher, E. *The Buddhist Conquest of China: The Spread and Adaptation of Buddhism in Early Medieval China,* 3rd ed. (2007). A reissue of the classic account of the assimilation of Buddhism in China during the medieval period, with particular focus on the religious and philosophical success of Buddhism among Chinese elites in South China.

CHAPTER 9

Ahmed, Leila. *Women and Gender in Islam* (1992). A superb overview of the relations between men and women throughout the history of Islam.

Aneirin. *Y Gododdin: Britain's Oldest Heroic Poem,* edited and translated by A. O. H. Jarman (1988). A sixth-century CE Welsh text that describes the battle of the last Britons against the invading Anglo-Saxons.

Arberry, Arthur J. (trans.). Introduction to *The Koran Interpreted: A Translation* (1986). One of the most eloquent appreciations of this classical work of religion.

Augustine. *The City of God,* translated by H. Bettenson (1976). An excellent translation of Augustine's monumental work of history, philosophy, and religion.

Berkey, Jonathan P. *The Formation of Islam: Religion and Society in the Near East, 600–1800* (2005). A recent overview of the history of Islam before the modern era. It is particularly sensitive to the influence of external elements on the history of the Muslim peoples.

Bol, Peter. *This Culture of Ours: Intellectual Transitions in T'ang and Sung China* (1994). A study tracing the transformation of the shared culture of the Chinese learned elite from the seventh to the twelfth centuries.

Bowersock, G. W. *The Throne of Adulis: Red Sea Wars on the Eve of Islam* (2013). A vital study of the kingdom of Himyar, in present-day Yemen, a center of Judaism and Christianity before the rise of Islam in the Arabian Peninsula.

Brooke, John L. *Climate Change and the Course of Global History: A Rough Journey* (2014). An overview of a changing climate and its impact on historical developments.

Brown, Peter. *The Rise of Western Christendom: Triumph and Diversity, AD 200–1000,* 2nd ed. (2003). A description of the changes in Christianity in northern Europe and the emergence of the new cultures and political structures that coincided with this development.

Bulliet, Richard W. *Conversion to Islam in the Medieval Period: An Essay in Quantitative History* (1979). A study of the rate at which the populations overrun by Arab conquerors in the seventh century CE embraced the religion of their rulers.

Bulliet, Richard W. *Cotton, Climate, and Camels in the Early Islamic State* (2009). A fascinating account of the economic development on the Iranian plateau, with an emphasis on climate.

Cook, David. *Understanding Jihad* (2005). An exploration of the meaning of Jihad, a significant Muslim concept in today's world, as understood in early Islam.

Cook, Michael. *Muhammad* (1983). A brief but careful life of the Prophet that takes full account of the prolific and often controversial preexisting scholarship.

Cook, Michael. *The Koran: A Very Short Introduction* (2000). A useful overview of Islam's holy book.

Creswell, K. A. C. *A Short Account of Early Muslim Architecture,* revised and supplemented by James W. Allan (1992). The definitive treatment of the subject.

Crone, Patricia, *The Nativist Prophets of Early Islam: Rural Revolt and Local Zoroastrianism* (2012). The rise of protest movements in Islam that led to the Abbasid takeover from the Umayyads.

Cross, S. H., and O. P. Sherbowitz-Westor (trans.). *The Russian Primary Chronicle* (1953). A vivid record of the Viking settlement of Kiev, the conversion of Kiev, and the princes of Kiev in the tenth and eleventh centuries.

Donner, Fred M. *The Early Islamic Conquests* (1981). The best account of the Arab conquests in the Persian and Byzantine Empires in the seventh century CE.

Donner, Fred M. *Muhammad and the Believers at the Origins of Islam* (2010). A richly detailed study of Muhammad's prophecy and the rise of Islam during the Umayyad period.

Duncan, John. *The Origins of the Chosŏn Dynasty* (2000). A historical account of the early Korean dynasties from 900 to 1400.

Elman, Benjamin. *Precocious China: Civil Examinations, 1400–1900* (2013). Summary of civil exams in China from medieval times.

Fage, J. D. *Ghana: A Historical Introduction* (1966). A brief but authoritative history of Ghana from earliest times to the mid-twentieth century.

Fisher, Humphrey J. *Slavery in the History of Muslim Black Africa* (2001). A general history of the relations between North Africa and black Africa, focusing on one of the most important aspects of contact—the slave trade.

Fowden, Garth. *Before and after Muhammad: The First Millennium Refocused* (2014). The author sets Islam in its larger Greek and Christianity setting, part of the work of the Late Antique scholarly community.

Graham-Campbell, James. *Cultural Atlas of the Viking World* (1994). A positioning of the Vikings against their wider background in both western and eastern Europe.

Haider, Najam. *The Origins of the Shi'a: Identity, Ritual, and Sacred Space in Eighth-Century Kufah* (2011). A definitive study on the origin of Shiism.

Hawting, G. R. *The First Dynasty of Islam: The Umayyad Caliphate, A.D. 661–750* (2000). The essential scholarly treatment of Islam's first dynasty.

Herrmann, Georgina. *Iranian Revival* (1977). The structure and horizons of the Sasanian Empire as revealed in its monuments.

Hillgarth, J. N. (ed.). *Christianity and Paganism, 350–750: The Conversion of Western Europe,* rev. ed. (1986). A collection of contemporary sources.

Hodges, Richard, and David Whitehouse. *Mohammed, Charlemagne, and the Origins of Europe* (1983). A spirited comparison of Islam and the rise of Europe.

Hodgson, Marshall G. S. *The Venture of Islam: Conscience and History in a World Civilization, 3 vols.* (1977). A magnificent history of the Islamic peoples. Its first volume, *The Classical Age of Islam,* is basic reading for anyone interested in the history of the Muslim world.

Holdsworth, May. *Women of the Tang Dynasty* (1999). An account of women's lives during the Tang dynasty.

Hourani, Albert. *History of the Arab Peoples* (2002). The best overview of Arab history.

Hoyland, Robert G. *In God's Path: The Arab Conquests and the Creation of the Islamic Empire* (2015). New work that draws on non-Arabic sources to fill in gaps in Islamic historiography.

Jones, Gwynn. *The Norse Atlantic Saga* (1986). The Viking discovery of America.

Kennedy, Hugh. *The Prophet and the Age of the Caliphate: The Islamic Near East from the Sixth to the Eleventh Century* (2004). A very good recent synthesis of the rise and spread of Islam.

Lee, Peter, et al. (eds.). *Sources of Korean Tradition*, vol. 1 (1996). A unique view of Korean history through the eyes and words of the participants or witnesses themselves, as provided in translations of official documents, letters, and policies.

Levtzion, Nehemia. *Ancient Ghana and Mali* (1980). The best introduction to the kingdoms of West Africa.

Levtzion, Nehemia, and Jay Spaulding. *Medieval West Africa: Views from Arab Scholars and Merchants* (2003). An indispensable source book on early West African history.

Levy-Rubin, Milka. *Non-Muslims in the Early Islamic Empire: From Surrender to Co-existence* (2011). The exploitation of non-Muslims in early Islam and their later conversion and rise to prominence.

Lewis, Bernard. *The Middle East: Two Thousand Years of History from the Rise of Christianity to the Present Day* (1995). A stimulating introduction to an area that has seen the emergence of three of the great world religions.

Lewis, Bernard (trans.). *Islam from the Prophet Muhammad to the Capture of Constantinople*. Vol. 2: *Religion and Society* (1974). A fine collection of original sources that portray various aspects of classical Islamic society.

Lewis, David Levering. *God's Crucible: Islam and the Making of Europe, 570–1215* (2008). An exciting and well-written overview of the high period of Islamic power and cultural attainments.

Middleton, John. *The Swahili: The Social Landscape of a Mercantile Community* (2000). An exciting synthesis of the Swahili culture of East Africa.

Miyazaki, Ichisada. *China's Examination Hell* (1981). A study of China's examination system.

Nurse, Derek, and Thomas Spear. *The Swahili: Reconstructing the History and Language of an African Society, 800–1500* (1984). A work that explores the history of the Muslim peoples who lived along the coast of East Africa.

Peters, F. E. *Muhammad and the Origins of Islam* (1994). A work that explores the early history of Islam and highlights the critical role that Muhammad played in promoting a new religion and a powerful Arab identity.

Pourshariati, Parvaneh. *Decline and Fall of the Sasanian Empire* (2008). Fundamental analysis of the end of the Sasanian Empire and the reasons for the success of the Arab/Muslim invasions.

Robinson, Chase F. *The New Cambridge History of Islam*, Vol. 1: *The Formation of the Islamic World, Sixth to Eleventh Centuries* (2010). An authoritative and up-to-date six-volume overview of the history of Islam from the sixth century CE to the present.

Schirokauer, Conrad, et al. *A Brief History of Japanese Civilization*, 2nd ed. (2005). A balanced account; chapters focus on developments in art, religion, literature, and thought as well as on Japan's economic, political, and social history in medieval times.

Shoemaker, Stephen T. *The Death of a Prophet: The End of Muhammad's Life and the Beginnings of Islam* (2012). The use of non-Arabic sources to learn about Muhammad and the rise of Islam.

Smith, Julia. *Europe after Rome: A New Cultural History, 500–1000* (2005). A vivid analysis of society and culture in so-called Dark Age Europe.

Totman, Conrad. *History of Japan* (2004). A recent and readable summary of Japanese history from ancient to modern times.

Twitchett, Denis. *Financial Administration under the T'ang Dynasty* (1970). A pioneering account—based on rare Dunhuang documents that survived from medieval times in Buddhist grottoes in central Asia—of the political and economic system undergirding the Chinese imperial state.

Twitchett, Denis. *The Birth of the Chinese Meritocracy: Bureaucrats and Examinations in T'ang China* (1976). A description of the role of the written civil examinations that began during the Tang dynasty.

Whittow, Mark. *The Making of Byzantium, 600–1025* (1996). A study on the survival and revival of the Eastern Roman Empire as a major power in eastern Europe and Southwest Asia.

Wood, Ian. *The Missionary Life: Saints and the Evangelization of Europe, 400–1050* (2001). The horizons of Christians on the frontiers of Europe.

CHAPTER 10

Allsen, Thomas. *Commodity and Exchange in the Mongol Empire: A Cultural History of Islamic Textiles* (1997). A study that uses golden brocade, the textile most treasured by Mongol rulers, as a lens through which to analyze the vast commercial networks facilitated by the Mongol conquests and control.

Allsen, Thomas. *Culture and Conquest in Mongol Eurasia* (2001). A work that emphasizes the cultural and scientific exchanges that took place across Afro-Eurasia as a result of the Mongol conquest.

Bagge, Svere, Michael Gelting, and Thomas Lundkvist (eds.). *Feudalism: New Landscapes of Debate* (2011). A collection of essays on interpretations of feudalism by experts on the topic.

Bailey, Mark. *The English Manor, c. 1200–c. 1500* (2002). An important detailed study of English manorialism.

Bartlett, Robert. *The Making of Europe: Conquest, Colonization and Cultural Change, 950–1350* (1993). The modes of cultural, political, and demographic expansion of feudal Europe along its frontiers, especially in eastern Europe.

Bay, Edna G. *Wives of the Leopards: Gender, Politics, and Culture in the Kingdom of Dahomey* (1998). A work that stresses the role of women in an important West African society and dips into the early history of this area.

Beach, D. N. *Shona and Zimbabwe, 900–1850: An Outline of Shona History* (1980). A good place to start for exploring the history of Great Zimbabwe.

Bloch, Marc. *Feudal Society*, translated by L. A. Manyon (1961). The classic study of feudalism, now being criticized.

Brooks, George E. *Landlords and Strangers: Ecology, Society, and Trade in Western Africa, 1000–1630* (1993). A survey assembled from primary sources of early West African history that stresses transregional connections.

Bulliet, Richard W. *Cotton, Climate, and Camels in Early Islamic Iran* (2009). An analysis of the upswing of the Iranian plateau economy after the Muslim conquest and then its decline as a result of climate change.

Buzurg ibn Shahriyar of Ramhormuz. *The Book of the Wonders of India: Mainland, Sea and Islands*, edited and translated by G. S. P. Freeman-Greenville (1981). A collection of stories told by sailors, both true and fantastic; they help us imagine the lives of sailors of the era.

Chappell, Sally A. Kitt. *Cahokia: Mirror of the Cosmos* (2002). A thorough and vivid account of the "mound people"; it explores not just what we know of Cahokia but how we know it.

Christian, David. *A Short History of Russia, Central Asia, and Mongolia.* Vol. 1: *Inner Eurasia from Prehistory to the Mongol Empire* (1998). Essential reading for students interested in interconnections across the Afro-Eurasian landmass.

Curtin, Philip. *Cross-Cultural Trade in World History* (1984). A groundbreaking book on intercultural trade with a primary focus on Africa, especially the cross-Saharan trade and Swahili coastal trade.

Dawson, Christopher. *Mission to Asia* (1980). Accounts of China and the Mongol Empire brought back by Catholic missionaries and diplomats after 1240 CE.

Duby, Georges. *The Three Orders: Feudal Society Imagined*, translated by Arthur Goldhammer (1982). Another classic study of feudalism.

Ellenblum, Ronnie. *The Collapse of the Eastern Mediterranean: Climate Change and the Decline of the East, 950–1072* (2012). An analysis of the impact of freezing temperatures and drought on the societies of the eastern Mediterranean.

Flori, Jean. "Knightly Society." In David Luscombe and Jonathon Riley Smith (eds.), *The New Cambridge Medieval History*, Vol. 4, Part 1: *c. 1024–1198* (2004). A brilliant overview of knights in medieval times and an overview of the debate on feudalism with the author's own insightful conclusions. Other useful articles in this volume are by Susan Reynolds and by David Luscombe and Jonathon Riley Smith.

Foltz, Richard C. *Religions of the Silk Road: Overland Trade and Cultural Exchange from Antiquity to the Fifteenth Century* (1999). A study of the populations and the cities of the Silk Road as transmitters of culture across long distances.

Franklin, Simon, and Jonathan Shepherd. *The Emergence of Rus: 750–1200* (1996). The formation of medieval Russia between the Baltic and Black Seas.

Ganshof, F. L. *Feudalism*, translated by Philip Griersur (1952). Perhaps the work most often dealt with by critics of the

term *feudalism.* Simple, straightforward, easily comprehended study of feudalism.

Gibb, Hamilton A. R. *Saladin: Studies in Islamic History,* edited by Yusuf Ibish (1974). A sympathetic portrait of one of Islam's leading political and military figures.

Goitein, S. D. "New Light on the Beginnings of the Karim Merchants." *Journal of the Economic and Social History of the Orient* 1 (1957): 175–184. Goitein's description of Egyptian trade.

Goitein, S. D. *Letters of Medieval Jewish Traders* (1973). The classic study of medieval Jewish trading communities based on the commercial papers deposited in the Cairo Geniza (a synagogue storeroom) during the tenth and eleventh centuries; it explores not only commercial activities but also the personal lives of the traders around the Indian Ocean basin.

Goitein, S. D. *A Mediterranean Society: An Abridgment in One Volume,* revised and edited by Jacob Lassner (1999). A portrait of the Jewish merchant community with ties across the Afro-Eurasian landmass, based largely on the documents from the Cairo Geniza (of which Goitein was the primary researcher and interpreter).

Harris, Joseph E. *The African Presence in Asia: Consequences of the East African Slave Trade* (1971). One of the few books that looks broadly at the impact of Africans and African slavery on the societies of Asia.

Hartwell, Robert. "Demographic, Political, and Social Transformations of China, 750–1550." *Harvard Journal of Asiatic Studies* 42 (1982): 365–442. A pioneering study of the demographic changes that overtook China during the Tang and Song dynasties, which are described in light of political reform movements and social changes in this crucial era.

Historical Relations across the Indian Ocean: Report and Papers of the Meeting of Experts Organized by UNESCO at Port Louis, Mauritius, from 15 to 19 July, 1974 (1980). Excellent essays on the connections of Africa with Asia across the Indian Ocean.

Hitti, Philip. *An Arab-Syrian Gentleman and Warrior in the Period of the Crusades: Memoirs of Usāmah ibn-Munqidh* (1929). The Crusaders seen through Muslim eyes.

Hodgson, Natasha. *Women, Crusading, and the Holy Land in Historical Narrative*

(2007). A book dealing with the Crusades and focusing on the place of women in them.

Holt, P. M. *The Age of the Crusades: The Near East from the Eleventh Century to 1517* (1984). The Crusades period as seen from the eastern Mediterranean and through the lens of a leading British scholar of the area.

Huff, Toby E. *The Rise of Early Modern Science* (2009) A bold attempt to look at the rise of scientific work in the Islamic world, premodern China, and Europe, seeking to explain why the scientific revolution occurred in Europe rather than the Islamic world or China.

Hunter, Timothy (ed.). *The New Cambridge Medieval History*, Vol. 3: *c. 900–c. 1024* (1999). Comprehensive articles written by experts of this period.

Hymes, Robert, and Conrad Schirokauer (eds.). *Ordering the World: Approaches to State and Society in Sung Dynasty China* (1993). A collection of essays that traces the intellectual, social, and political movements that shaped the Song state and its elites.

Ibn Battuta. *The Travels of Ibn Battuta,* translated by H. A. R. Gibb (2002). A readable translation of the classic book, originally published in 1929.

Ibn Fadlan, Ahmad. *Ibn Fadlan's Journey to Russia: A Tenth Century Traveler from Baghdad to the Volga River,* translated with commentary by Richard Frye (2005). A coherent summary of the observations of an envoy who traveled from Baghdad to Russia.

Irwin, Robert. *The Middle East in the Middle Ages: The Early Mamluk Sultanate, 1250–1582* (1986). Egypt under Mamluk rule.

Jeppie, Shamil, and Souleymane Bachir Diagne (eds.). *The Meanings of Timbuktu* (2008). New materials on the ancient Muslim city of Timbuktu by scholars who have been preserving its manuscripts and writing about its historical importance.

Keay, John. *India: A History* (2000). A spirited and informative overview of the entire history of the South Asian subcontinent.

Lancaster, Lewis, Kikun Suh, and Chai-shin Yu (eds.). *Buddhism in Koryo: A Royal Religion* (1996). A description of Buddhism at its height in the Koryo period, when the religion made significant contributions to the development of Korean culture.

Levtzion, Nehemia, and Randall L. Pouwels (eds.). *The History of Islam in Africa* (2000). A useful general survey of the place of Islam in African history.

Lewis, Bernard (trans.). *Islam: From the Prophet Muhammad to the Capture of Constantinople* (1974). Vol. 2: *Religion and Society.* A fine collection of original sources that portray various aspects of classical Islamic society.

Lopez, Robert S. *The Commercial Revolution of the Middle Ages, 950–1350* (1976). An account focusing on the development around the Mediterranean of commercial practices such as the use of currency, accounting, and credit.

Lyons, Malcolm C., and D. E. P. Jackson. *Saladin: The Politics of the Holy War* (1984: reprint 2001). The fundamental revisionist work on one of the more important historical figures of the time.

Maalouf, Amin. *The Crusades through Muslim Eyes,* translated by Jon Rothschild (1984). The European Crusaders as seen by the Muslim world.

Marcus, Harold G. *A History of Ethiopia* (2002). An authoritative overview of the history of this great culture.

Mass, Jeffrey. *Yoritomo and the Founding of the First Bakufu: The Origins of Dual Government in Japan* (1999). A revisionist account of how the Kamakura military leader Minamoto Yoritomo established the "dual polity" of court and warrior government in Japan.

McDermott, Joseph. *A Social History of the Chinese Book: Books and Literati Culture in Late Imperial China* (2006). The history of the book in China since the Song dynasty, with comparisons to the book's role in other civilizations, particularly the European.

McEvitt, Christopher. *The Crusaders and the Christian World of the East: Rough Tolerance* (2008). Excellent work on the relations of religious groups in the Crusader kingdoms.

McIntosh, Roderik. *The Peoples of the Middle Niger: The Island of Gold* (1988). A historical survey of an area often omitted from other textbooks.

Moore, Jerry D. *Cultural Landscapes in the Ancient Andes: Archaeologies of Place* (2005). The most recent and up-to-date analysis of findings based on recent archaeological evidence, emphasizing the importance of local cultures and diversity in the Andes.

Mote, F. W. *Imperial China, 900–1800* (1999). Still the best general history of China, written by one of the world's leading Sinologists.

Niane, D. T. (ed.). *General History of Africa.* Vol. 4: *Africa from the Twelfth to the Sixteenth Century* (1984). The fourth volume of the UNESCO history of Africa with articles by experts on this period. The work features the scholarship of Africans.

Oliver, Roland (ed.). *From c. 1050 to c. 1600,* vol. 3 of *The Cambridge History of Africa,* edited by J. D. Fage and Roland Oliver (1977). Another general survey of African history. This volume draws heavily on the work of British scholars.

Peters, Edward. *The First Crusade* (1971). The Crusaders as seen through their own eyes.

Petry, Carl F. (ed.). *Islamic Egypt, 640–1517,* vol. 1 of *The Cambridge History of Egypt,* edited by M. W. Daly (1998). A solid overview of the history of Islamic Egypt up to the Ottoman conquest.

Polo, Marco. *The Travels of Marco Polo,* revised from Marsden's translation and edited by Manuel Komroff (1926). A solid translation of Marco Polo's famous account.

Popovic, Alexandre. *The Revolt of African Slaves in Iraq in the 3rd/9th Century,* translated by Leon King (1999). The account of a massive revolt against their slave masters by African slaves taken to labor in Iraq's mines and fields.

Reynolds, Susan. *Fiefs and Vassals: The Medieval Evidence Reinterpreted* (1994). The book that made the most determined attack on the concept of feudalism.

Sarris, Peter. "The Origins of the Manorial Economy: New Insights from Late Antiquity." *The English Historical Review* 119 (April 2004): 279–311. An original contribution on the origins of manorialism, based first on Egyptian papyri and extended to other parts of the Byzantine Empire and western Europe.

Scott, Robert. *Gothic Enterprise: A Guide to Understanding the Medieval Cathedral* (2003). The meaning and social function of religious building in medieval cities in northern Europe.

Shaffer, Lynda Norene. *Maritime Southeast Asia to 1500* (1996). A history of the peoples of the southeast fringe of the Eastern Hemisphere, up to the time that they became connected to the global commercial networks of the world.

Shimada, Izumi. "Evolution of Andean Diversity: Regional Formations (500 BCE–CE 600)." In Frank Salomon and Stuart Schwartz (eds.), *South America,* vol. 3 of *The Cambridge History of the Native Peoples of the Americas,* part 1, pp. 350–517 (1999). A splendid overview that contrasts the varieties of lowland and highland cultures.

Steinberg, David Joel, et al. *In Search of Southeast Asia: A Modern History* (1987). An account of the emergence of the modern Southeast Asian polities of Cambodia, Burma, Thailand, and Indonesia.

Tyerman, Christopher. *God's War: A New History of the Crusades* (2006). The balance of religious and nonreligious motivations in the Crusades.

Waley, Daniel. *The Italian City-Republics,* 3rd ed. (1988). The structures and culture of the new cities of medieval Italy.

Watson, Andrew. *Agricultural Innovation in the Early Islamic World: The Diffusion of Crops and Farming Techniques, 700–1100* (1983). An impressive study of the spread of new crops throughout the Muslim world.

West, Charles. *Reframing the Feudal Revolution: Political and Social Transformation between Marne and Moselle, c. 800–c. 1100* (2013). Big change seen through an intensely studied region.

Wickham, Chris. *Sleepwalking into a New World: The Emergence of Italian City Communes in the Twelfth Century* (2015). Origins of the city democracies of medieval Italy.

Williamson, Tom. *Shaping Medieval Landscapes: Settlement, Society, Environment* (2004). A study of the manorial system in England.

CHAPTER 11

Barkey, Karen. *Empire of Difference: The Ottomans in Comparative Perspective* (2008). A revisionist view of the rise and flourishing of the Ottoman Empire.

Benedictow, Ole J. *The Black Death, 1346–1351: The Complete History* (2004). An exhaustive statistical study of the mortality during the first years of the Black Death's arrival in Europe.

Bois, Guy. *The Crisis of Feudalism: Economy and Society in Eastern Normandy, c. 1300–1550* (1984). A good case study of a French region that illustrates the turmoil in fourteenth-century France.

Brook, Timothy. *Praying for Power: Buddhism and the Formation of Gentry Society in Late Ming China* (1994). An analysis of the role of a significant religious force in the political and social developments of the Ming.

Dardess, John. *A Ming Society: T'ai-ho County, Kiangsi, Fourteenth to Seventeenth Centuries* (1996). A work that covers the different changes and developments of a single locality in China through the centuries.

Dols, Michael W. *The Black Death in the Middle East* (1977). One of the few scholarly works to examine the Black Death outside Europe.

Dreyer, Edward. *Early Ming China: A Political History, 1355–1435* (1982). A useful account of the early years of the Ming dynasty.

Faroqhi, Suraiya N., and Kate Fleet (eds.). *The Cambridge History of Turkey*, Vol. 2: *The Ottoman Empire as a World Power, 1453–1603* (2013). An overview of this crucial period in Ottoman history, written by experts in the field.

Finkel, Caroline. *Osman's Dream: The Story of the Ottoman Empire, 1300–1923* (2005). The most authoritative overview of Ottoman history.

Hale, John. *The Civilization of Europe in the Renaissance* (1994). A beautifully crafted account of the politics, economics, and culture of the Renaissance period in western Europe.

He, Yuming. *Home and the World: Editing the "Glorious Ming" in Woodblock-Printed Books of the Sixteenth and Seventeenth Centuries* (2013). An insightful exploration of Ming society through a close look at its vibrant print culture and market for books.

Ho, Ping-ti. *Studies on the Population of China, 1368–1953* (1959). A useful overview of China's population from Ming times until the mid-twentieth century.

Hodgson, Marshall. *The Venture of Islam: Conscience and History in a World Civilization*, vol. 3 (1974). A good volume on the workings of the Ottoman state.

Hoffman, Philip T. *Why Did Europe Conquer the World?* (2015). Makes an interesting case for the importance of Europe's use of gunpowder technologies.

Itzkowitz, Norman. *Ottoman Empire and Islamic Tradition* (1972). Another good book on the Ottoman state.

Jackson, Peter. *The Delhi Sultanate* (1999). A meticulous, highly specialized political and military history.

Jackson, Peter, and Lawrence Lockhart (eds.). *The Cambridge History of Iran*, Vol. 6 (1986). A volume that deals with the Timurid and Safavid periods in Iran.

Jones, E. L. *The European Miracle* (1981). A provocative work on the economic and social recovery from the Black Death.

Kafadar, Cemal. *Between Two Worlds: The Construction of the Ottoman State* (1995). A thorough reconsideration of the origins of one of the world's great land empires.

Karamustafa, Ahmed. *God's Unruly Friends: Dervish Groups in the Islamic Later Middle Period, 1200–1550* (1994). A book that describes the unorthodox Islamic activities that were occurring in the Islamic world prior to and alongside the establishment of the Ottoman and Safavid Empires.

Levathes, Louise. *When China Ruled the Seas: The Treasure Fleet of the Dragon Throne, 1405–33* (1994). A book that provides a lively account of the Zheng He expeditions.

Lowry, Heath W. *The Nature of the Early Ottoman State* (2003). New perspectives on the rise of the Ottomans to prominence.

McNeill, William. *Plagues and Peoples* (1976). A pathbreaking work with a highly useful chapter on the spread of the Black Death throughout the Afro-Eurasian landmass.

Morgan, David. *Medieval Persia, 1040–1797* (1988). Contains an informative discussion of the Safavid state.

Peirce, Leslie. *The Imperial Harem: Women and Sovereignty in the Ottoman Empire* (1993). A work that describes the powerful place that imperial women had in political affairs.

Pirenne, Henri. *Economic and Social History of Medieval Europe* (1937). A classic study of the economic and social recovery from the Black Death.

Reid, James J. *Tribalism and Society in Islamic Iran, 1500–1629* (1983). A useful account of how the Mongols and other nomadic steppe peoples influenced Iran in the era when the Safavids were establishing their authority.

Savory, Roger. *Iran under the Safavids* (1980). A standard work on Safavid history and still useful.

Schäfer, Dagmar. *The Crafting of the 10,000 Things: Knowledge and Technology in Seventeenth-Century China* (2011). An innovative study of the philosophy of technology and crafts in the late Ming period with important implications for the global history of science.

Singman, Jeffrey L. (ed.). *Daily Life in Medieval Europe* (1999). An introductory description of the social and material world experienced by Europeans of different walks of life.

Tuchman, Barbara W. *A Distant Mirror: The Calamitous Fourteenth Century* (1978). A book that shows, in a vigorous way, how war, famine, and pestilence devastated Europeans in the fourteenth century.

Wittek, Paul. *The Rise of the Ottoman Empire* (1958). A work that contains vital insights on the emergence of the Ottoman state amid the political chaos in Anatolia.

CHAPTER 12

Axtell, James. *Beyond 1492: Encounters in Colonial North America* (1992). A wonderfully informed speculation about Indian reactions to Europeans.

Brady, Thomas A., et al. (eds.). *Handbook of European History 1400–1600: Late Middle Ages, Renaissance, and Reformation*. Vol. 1: *Structures and Assertions* (1996). A good synthetic survey of recent literature and historiographical debates.

Brook, Timothy. *Vermeer's Hat: The Seventeenth Century and the Dawn of the Global World* (2008). An interesting look at the connections forged across the globe through the works of a well-known European artist.

Burns, Bradford. *A History of Brazil* (1993). A comprehensive study of the long-term effects of the European colonization of Brazil.

Casale, Giancarlo. *The Ottoman Age of Exploration* (2010). The author places Ottoman exploration in a comparative context alongside European overseas expansion.

Cass, Victoria. *Dangerous Women: Warriors, Grannies, and Geishas of the Ming* (1999). An original study of Chinese female archetypes in memoirs, miscellanies, short stories, and novels.

Chaudhuri, K. N. *Trade and Civilisation in the Indian Ocean: An Economic History from the Rise of Islam to 1750* (1985). An excellent, comprehensive work that deals with the Indian Ocean economy and the appearance of European merchants there from the sixteenth century onward.

Clendinnen, Inga. *Aztecs: An Interpretation* (1991). Brilliantly reconstructs the culture of Tenochtitlán in the years before its conquest.

Cortés, Hernán. *Five Letters of Cortés to the Emperor, 1519–1526* (1991). Offers fascinating insights into the mind of the conqueror.

Crosby, Alfred W. *The Columbian Exchange: Biological and Cultural Consequences of 1492* (1972). A provocative discussion of the ecological consequences that followed the European "discovery" of the Americas.

Crosby, Alfred W. *Ecological Imperialism: The Biological Expansion of Europe, 900–1900* (1986). Another important work on the ecological consequences of European expansion.

Curtin, Philip. *Cross-Cultural Trade in World History* (1984). A work stressing the role of trade and commerce in establishing cross-cultural contacts.

Diamond, Jared. *Guns, Germs, and Steel: The Fates of Human Societies* (1997). An influential argument about the biological and technological determinants of how some societies took charge over others.

Díaz del Castillo, Bernal. *The Conquest of New Spain* (1963). The eyewitness account of a Spanish soldier who participated in the conquest of the Aztec Empire.

Faroqhi, Suraiya N. (ed.). *The Cambridge History of Turkey*, Vol. 3: *The Later Ottoman Empire, 1603–1839* (2008). Definitive articles on this important period in Ottoman history.

Faroqhi, Suraiya N., and Kate Fleet (eds.). *The Cambridge History of Turkey*, Vol. 2: *The Ottoman Empire as a World Power, 1453–1603* (2013). A collection of articles written by leading scholars of this crucial period in Ottoman history.

Febvre, Lucien. *The Problem of Unbelief in the Sixteenth Century: The Religion of Rabelais* (1982). A tour de force of intellectual history by the man who moved the study of the Reformation away from great men to the broader question of religious revival and mentalities.

Finkel, Caroline. *Osman's Dream: The History of the Ottoman Empire* (2005). A detailed and exhaustively researched history of the Ottomans from the origins of the Ottoman state at the end of the thirteen century to the dismantling of the empire after World War I.

Flynn, Dennis, and Arturo Giráldez (eds.). *Metals and Monies in an Emerging Global Economy* (1997). Contains several articles relating to silver and the Asian trade.

Frank, Andre Gunder. *ReOrient: Global Economy in the Asian Age* (1998). A reassessment of the role of Asia in the economic development of the world from around 1400 onward.

Glahn, Richard von. *The Economic History of China: From Antiquity to the Nineteenth Century* (2016). A masterful new survey of Chinese economic history.

Greenblatt, Stephen. *Marvelous Possessions: The Wonder of the New World* (1991). An insightful study of the ways in which Europe's encounters with the New World changed European culture.

Gruzinski, Serge. *The Conquest of Mexico* (1993). An important work on the conquest of Mexico.

Habib, Irfan. *The Agrarian System of Mughal India* (1963). One of the best studies on the subject.

Hall, Richard Seymour. *Empires of the Monsoon: A History of the Indian Ocean and Its Invaders* (1996). A very engaging journalistic account with fabulous details.

Hodgson, Marshall. *The Venture of Islam*, vols. 2 and 3 (1974). A magisterial work that includes the Indian subcontinent in its careful study of the political and cultural history of the whole Islamic world.

Hulme, Peter. *Colonial Encounters: Europe and the Native Caribbean, 1492–1797* (1986). Presents an interesting interpretation of the encounters of Europeans and Native Americans.

Lach, Donald F. *Asia in the Making of Europe*, 5 books in 3 vols. (1965–). Perhaps the single most comprehensive and innovative guide to the European voyages of discovery.

Las Casas, Bartolomé. *A Short Account of the Destruction of the Indies*, edited by Anthony Pagden (2004). The most famous book written about the conquest of the New World.

Lockhart, James, and Stuart Schwartz. *Early Latin America* (1983). One of the finest studies of European expansion in the late fifteenth century.

McCann, James. *Maize and Grace: Africa's Encounter with a New World Crop, 1500–2000* (2005). A significant study of how maize, a New World crop, became Africa's most widely grown grain.

Melville, Elinor G. K. *A Plague of Sheep: Environmental Consequences of the Conquest of Mexico* (1994). A history of the transformation of a valley in Mexico from the Aztec period to the era of Spanish rule.

Mignolo, Walter D. *The Darker Side of the Renaissance: Literacy, Territoriality, and Colonization* (1995). Uses literary theory and literary images to present provocative interpretations of the encounter of Europeans and Native Americans.

Ozbaran, Salih. *Ottoman Expansion toward the Indian Ocean in the 16th Century* (2009). An important treatment of the Ottoman entry into the Indian Ocean at a time when the Portuguese were also expanding there.

Pagden, Anthony. *European Encounters with the New World* (1993). A complex look at the deep and lasting imprint of the New World on its conquerors.

Phillips, William D., and Carla Rahn Phillips. *The World of Christopher Columbus* (1992). One of the finest studies of European expansion in the late fifteenth century.

Roper, Lyndal. *Martin Luther: Renegade and Prophet* (2016). A magisterial biography that demonstrates the ways in which Luther was a rebel but also a man of his time.

Russell-Wood, A. J. R. *The Portuguese Empire, 1415–1808* (1992). An important survey of early Portuguese exploration.

Salmon, W. H. *An Account of the Ottoman Conquest of Egypt in the Year A.H. 932 (A.D. 1516), Translated from the Third Volume of the Arabic Chronicle of Muhammad Ahmed Ibn Iyas, an Eyewitness of the Scenes He Describes* (1921). An evocative primary source on the Ottoman-Mamluk conflict.

Von Glahn, Richard. *Fountain of Fortune: Money and Monetary Policy in China, 1000–1700* (1996). Includes an excellent analysis of the history of silver in Ming China.

CHAPTER 13

Alam, Muzaffar. *The Crisis of Empire in Mughal North India* (1993). Represents the best of the scholarly interpretations on the subject.

Bay, Edna. *Wives of the Leopard: Gender, Politics, and Culture in the Kingdom of Dahomey* (1998). A useful treatment of gender issues in Dahomey.

Blackburn, Robin. *The Making of New World Slavery: From the Baroque to the Modern, 1492–1800* (1997). A good place to begin when studying African slavery and the Atlantic slave trade, it compares the early expansion of the plantation systems across the Atlantic and throughout the Americas.

Blanning, Tim. *The Pursuit of Glory: Europe, 1648-1815* (2007). An elegantly written and deeply insightful overview of European political history from the Thirty Years' War to the fall of Napoleon.

Bushkovitch, Paul. *Peter the Great* (2016). An updated version of a standard work, offering a concise overview of one of Russia's most celebrated and energetic rulers.

Calloway, Colin G. *One Vast Winter Count: The Native American West before Lewis and Clark* (2003). A sweeping survey of North American Indian histories prior to the nineteenth century.

Crossley, Pamela. *A Translucent Mirror: History and Identity in Qing Imperial Ideology* (1999). The author deals with the formation of identities such as "Manchu" and "Chinese" during the Qing period.

Dale, Stephen F. *The Muslim Empires of the Ottomans, Safavids, and Mughals* (2010). A comparative overview of Islam's three most powerful empires of the sixteenth and seventeenth centuries.

Eaton, Richard. *Essays on Islam and Indian History* (2000). A wide-ranging account that pays particular attention to Islam's social history in the subcontinent.

Eltis, David, and Richardson, David. *Atlas of the Transatlantic Slave Trade* (2010). This work contains the most up-to-date data on the Atlantic slave trade, the numbers transported, where the captives came from, and where they landed.

Fleischer, Cornell H. *Bureaucrat and Intellectual in the Ottoman Empire (1542-1600)* (1986). A probing study into Mustafa Ali, the Ottoman Empire's leading sixteenth-century intellectual.

Flynn, Dennis O., and Arturo Giraldez (eds.). *Metals and Money in an Emerging World Economy* (1997). A collection of articles about the place of silver in the world economy.

Forsyth, James. *A History of the Peoples of Siberia: Russia's North Asian Colony 1581-1990* (1992). A narrative overview of a violent history reminiscent of the western expansion of the United States.

Glahn, Richard von. *Fountains of Fortune: Money and Monetary Policy in China, 1000-1700* (1996). A discussion of the place of silver in the Chinese economy.

Halperin, Charles J. *Russia and the Golden Horde: The Mongol Impact on Medieval Russian History* (1985). A book on the rise of Muscovy, forebear of the Russian Empire, from within the Mongol realm.

Hämäläinen, Pekka. *The Comanche Empire* (2008). A book that inverts the conventional history of empires in North America by arguing that the Comanches were the most successful expansionist power in the middle of the continent during the eighteenth century.

Hartley, Janet. *Siberia: A History of the People* (2014). A vivid portrait of diverse conquerors—fur traders, Cossack adventurers, political criminals—of a region larger than almost all continents.

Hattox, Ralph S. *Coffee and Coffeehouses: The Origins of a Social Beverage in the Medieval Near East* (1985). This work shows how widespread and popular coffee consumption and coffeehouses were around the world.

Herzog, Tamar. *Frontiers of Possession: Spain and Portugal in Europe and the Americas* (2015). An exploration of how Spanish and Portuguese rulers carved up the New World, less by military action and diplomatic treaties and more by quarrels over land settlement and rights to trade and travel.

Huang, Ray. *1587, a Year of No Significance: The Ming Dynasty in Decline* (1981). An insightful analysis of the problems confronting the late Ming.

Lensen, George. *The Russian Push Toward Japan: Russo-Japanese Relations 1697-1875* (1959). A discussion of why and how Japan established its first border with another state and how Russia pursued its ambitions in the Pacific.

Lockhart, James. *The Nahuas after the Conquest* (1992). A landmark study of the social reorganization of Mesoamerican societies under Spanish rule.

Lovejoy, Paul. *Transformations in Slavery: A History of Slavery in Africa* (1983). An excellent discussion of African slavery.

Mathee, Rudi. *Persia in Crisis, Safavid Decline, and the Fall of Isfahan* (2012). A study of the disintegration of the Safavid state.

Mikhail, Alan. *Nature and Empire in Ottoman Egypt: An Environmental History* (2011). An important study of the impact of the environment on Egypt in the eighteenth century.

Monahan, Erika. *The Merchants of Siberia: Trade in Early Modern Eurasia* (2016). A stirring account of entrepreneurs battling the harshest imaginable conditions to establish trading networks connecting the far-flung territories north of the ancient Silk Road.

Moon, David. *The Plough That Broke the Steppes: Agriculture and Environment in Russia's Grasslands, 1700-1913* (2013). A bold incorporation of environmental aspects to retell the epic story of Russia's most numerous social group.

Nakane, Chie, and Shinzaburo Oishi (eds.). *Tokugawa Japan: The Social and Economic Antecedents of Modern Japan* (1990). First-rate essays on Japanese village society, urban life, literacy, and culture.

Nwokeji, G. Uko. *The Slave Trade and Culture in the Bight of Biafra: An African Society in the Atlantic World* (2010). A study of the Aro peoples of southeastern Nigeria and their use of their commercial powers to promote a vigorous trade with European slavers on the coast.

Pamuk, Sevket. *A Monetary History of the Ottoman Empire* (2000). A discussion of the place of silver in the Ottoman Empire.

Parker, Geoffrey. *Global Crisis: War, Climate Change, and Catastrophe in the Seventeenth Century* (2013). A comprehensive and exhaustively researched study of the effects of the Little Ice Age on the governments and societies of the entire world in the seventeenth century.

Parker, Geoffrey (ed.). *The Thirty Years' War* (1997). The standard account of the conflict and its outcomes.

Perdue, Peter C. *China Marches West: The Qing Conquest of Central Asia* (2005). This volume chronicles the expansion of the Qing Empire to its northwest, drawing comparisons to other colonial empires and their legacies.

Platonov, S. F. *Ivan the Terrible* (1986). Covers the controversies over Russia's infamous tsar.

Rawski, Evelyn. *The Last Emperors: A Social History of Qing Imperial Institutions* (1998). This volume explores the mechanisms and processes through which the Qing court negotiated its Manchu identity.

Reid, Anthony. *Charting the Shape of Early Modern Southeast Asia* (1999). A collection of articles by a leading historian of Southeast Asia.

Spence, Jonathan, and John Wills (eds.). *From Ming to Ch'ing: Conquest, Region, and Continuity in Seventeenth-Century China* (1979). Covers the various aspects of a tumultuous period of dynastic transition.

Subramanyam, Sanjay. *From the Tigris to the Ganges, Explorations in Connected History* (2012). A study that demonstrates that Afro-Eurasia in the seventeenth and eighteenth centuries contained a porous network of empires, cultures, and economies.

Subramanyam, Sanjay, and Muzaffar Alam. *Indo-Persian Travels in the Age of Discoveries, 1400–1800* (2012). A lively portrait of cultural exchanges between Persia, central Asia, and India as seen in travel literature.

Taylor, Alan. *American Colonies: The Settling of North America* (2001). Brings together British, French, and Spanish colonial histories and shows how the fortunes of each were entangled with one another and with those of diverse Native American peoples.

Thornton, John K. *Africa and Africans in the Making of the Atlantic World, 1400–1800* (1998). A wonderful discussion of how African slaves played a large role in the formation of the Atlantic world.

Thornton, John K. *The Kongolese Saint Anthony: Dona Beatriz Kimpa Vita and the Antonian Movement, 1684–1706* (1998). An excellent monograph on religious movements in the Kongo.

Toby, Ronald P. *State and Diplomacy in Early Modern Japan: Asia in the Development of the Tokugawa Bakufu* (1984). The author shows that the Japanese, far from being isolated from the outside world, engaged in vigorous and successful diplomacy.

Van Dusen, Nancy E. *Global Indios: The Indigenous Struggle for Justice in Sixteenth-Century Spain* (2015). A remarkable study of the ways that Spanish rulers enslaved Amerindians in the Americas and even exported them back to Europe.

Vilar, Pierre. *A History of Gold and Money* (1991). An excellent study of the development of the early silver and gold economies.

CHAPTER 14

Axtell, James. *The Invasion of America: The Contest of Cultures in Colonial North America* (1985). Discusses the strategies of Christian missionaries in converting the Indians, as well as the success of Indians in converting Europeans.

Babaie, Sussan. *Isfahan and Its Palaces: Statecraft, Shi'ism and the Architecture of Conviviality in Early Modern Iran* (2008). An overview of the city of Isfahan, as the capital of the Safavid state.

Barmé, Geremie R. *The Forbidden City* (2008). A concise introduction to the history of one of the most important physical emblems of Chinese imperial power.

Berlin, Ira. *Many Thousands Gone: The First Two Centuries of Slavery in North America* (1998). Surveys the development of African American culture in colonial North America.

Bleichmar, Daniela. *Visible Empire: Botanical Expeditions and Visual Culture in the Hispanic Enlightenment* (2012). A fascinating and beautifully illustrated history of creole botanical expeditions in the eighteenth century.

Brockey, Liam. *Journey to the East: The Jesuit Mission to China, 1579–1724* (2007). A detailed and definitive treatment of the Jesuits in China up to 1724, the year when Jesuit influence began to decline.

Brook, Timothy. *The Confusions of Pleasure: Commerce and Culture in Ming China* (1999). An insightful survey of Ming society.

Clunas, Craig. *Superfluous Things: Material Culture and Social Status in Early Modern China* (1991). A good account of the late Ming elite's growing passion for material things.

Collcutt, Martin, Marius Jansen, and Isao Kumakura. *A Cultural Atlas of Japan* (1988). A sweeping look at the many different forms of Japanese cultural expression over the centuries, including the flourishing urban culture of Edo.

Crèvecoeur, Hector St. John de. *Letters from an American Farmer*, reprinted from the orginal edition, with a prefatory note by W. P. Trent and an introduction by Ludwig Lewisohn (New York: Fox, Duffield, 1904). Powerful and informative letters of a French settler in the Americas in the eighteenth century.

Darnton, Robert. *The Business of the Enlightenment: A Publishing History of the Encyclopédie, 1775–1800* (1979). The classic study of Europe's first great compendium of knowledge.

Dash, Mike. *Tulipomania: The Story of the World's Most Coveted Flower and the Extraordinary Passions It Aroused* (1999). A global perspective on and lively account of the spread of the tulip around the world as a flower signifying both beauty and status.

Dikötter, Frank. *The Discourse of Race in Modern China* (1992). A good survey of Chinese discussions of race in the modern era.

Doniger, Wendy. *The Hindus: An Alternative History* (2009). A deeply scholarly yet accessibly written history of Hinduism that takes into account both texts and popular practices and contains a lively account of dissenting traditions.

Eaton, Richard. *Essays on Islam and Indian History* (2000). A wide-ranging account that pays particular attention to Islam's social history in the subcontinent.

Elman, Benjamin A. *On Their Own Terms: Science in China, 1550–1900* (2005). A study of the development of "native" Chinese science and how the process interacted with the introduction of western science to China over the course of three and a half centuries.

Eze, Emmanuel Chukwudi (ed.). *Race and the Enlightenment: A Reader* (1997). Readings examining the idea of race in the context of the Enlightenment.

Fleischer, Cornell. *Bureaucrat and Intellectual in the Ottoman Empire: The Historian Mustafa Ali (1540–1600)* (1986). Offers good insight into the world of culture and intellectual vitality in the Ottoman Empire.

Grafton, Anthony, April Shelford, and Nancy Siraisi. *New Worlds, Ancient Texts: The Power of Tradition and the Shock of Discovery* (1995). A concise discussion of the impact of the New World on European thought.

Gutierrez, Ramon. *When Jesus Came, the Corn Mothers Went Away: Marriage, Sexuality, and Power in New Mexico, 1500–1846* (1991). A provocative dissection of the spiritual dimensions of European colonialism in the Americas.

Harley, J. B., and David Woodward (eds.). *The History of Cartography*. Vol. 2, Book 2: *Cartography in the Traditional East and Southeast Asian Societies* (1994). An authoritative treatment of the subject.

Hart, Roger. *Imagined Civilizations: China, the West, and Their First Encounter* (2013). A treatment of the Jesuit mission to China as the first contact between Chinese and European cultures.

Horton, Robin. *Patterns of Thought in Africa and the West: Essays on Magic, Religion, and Science* (1993). Reflections on African patterns of thought and attitudes toward nature, which can help us understand African American religious beliefs and resistance movements.

Huff, Toby. *The Rise of Early Modern Science* (2003).

Huff, Toby. *Intellectual Curiosity and the Scientific Revolution: A Comparative Perspective* (2011). Huff's two books represent a sustained effort to deal with Europe's scientific revolution comparatively, asking the question why Europe and not China or the Islamic world.

Kai, Ho Yi. *Science in China, 1600-1900: Essays by Benjamin Elman* (2015). Elman, an expert on Chinese science, offers his latest word on China's scientific achievements in a context of Europe's transmission of science through the Jesuit mission.

Keene, Donald. *The Japanese Discovery of Europe: Honda Toshiaki and Other Discoverers, 1720-1798* (1952). A study of the ways Japan managed to incorporate knowledge from the outside world with the development of national traditions.

Ko, Dorothy. *Teachers of the Inner Chambers: Women and Culture in Seventeenth-Century China* (1994). Explores the lives of elite women in late Ming and early Qing China.

Lewis, Bernard. *Race and Color in Islam* (1979). Examines the Islamic attitude toward race and color.

Mazower, Mark. *Salonica, City of Ghosts: Christians, Muslims and Jews, 1430-1900* (2006). An overview of one of the most important cities of the Ottoman Empire.

Morgan, Philip D. *Slave Counterpoint: Black Culture in the Eighteenth-Century Chesapeake and Lowcountry* (1998). Describes the development of African American culture in colonial North America.

Munck, Thomas. *The Enlightenment: A Comparative Social History, 1721-1794* (2000). A wonderful survey, with unusual examples from the periphery, especially from Scandinavia and the Habsburg Empire.

Necipoglu, Gulru. *Architecture, Ceremonial, and Power: The Topkapi Palace in the Fifteenth and Sixteenth Centuries* (1991). A magnificently illustrated book that shows the enormous artistic talent that the Ottoman rulers poured into their imperial structure.

Needham, Joseph "Mathematics and Science in China and the West." In *Science and Civilisation in China*, Vol. 3, pp. 150-168 (1954). An important section of Needham's exhaustive multivolume treatment of Chinese science.

This section deals with what Needham considered the fundamental difference between Chinese and European science at the time of the scientific revolution, namely, Europe's mathematization of the natural world.

Needham, Joseph. *The Grand Tritation: Science and Society in East and West* (1969). Along with his three other entries here, Joseph Needham's efforts to understand Chinese science in relationship to Europe's new science.

Needham, Joseph. "The Evolution of Oecumenical Science: The Role of Europe and China." *Journal of Interdisciplinary Science* 1 (1976): 202-214. More from Needham on European and Chinese science.

Needham, Joseph. *Science in Traditional China: A Comparative Perspective* (1981). Needham's thoughts on Chinese science after the publication of his monumental *Science and Civilisation in China*.

Parker, Kenneth. *Early Modern Tales of the Orient: A Critical Anthology* (1999). A collection of travelers' accounts of the Near East.

Publishing and the Print Culture in Late Imperial China (Special Issue). *Late Imperial China* 17:1 (June 1996). A collection of important articles with a foreword by the French cultural historian Roger Chartier.

Qaisar, Ahsan Jan. *The Indian Response to European Technology, AD 1498-1707* (1998). A meticulous, scholarly work on this little-studied subject.

Rizvi, Athar Abbas. *The Wonder That Was India*. Vol. 2: *A Survey of the History and Culture of the Indian Sub-Continent from the Coming of the Muslims to the British Conquest, 1200-1700* (1987). A deeply learned work in intellectual history.

Safier, Neil. *Measuring the New World: Enlightenment Science and South America* (2008). Examines the ways in which European, and especially Parisian, surveyors set about gauging the curvature of the earth, starting in Quito, Ecuador. Along the way, they learned much more about local natural history, which flowed back to Paris to inform the Enlightenment.

Shapiro, Steven. *The Scientific Revolution* (1996). Still one of the most authoritative overviews of Europe's new science.

Sivan, Nathan. "Why the Scientific Revolution Did Not Take Place in China—or Didn't It?" The author questions the value of asking why China did not have

a scientific revolution even while arguing that the Chinese, in fact, did.

Smith, Bernard. *European Vision and the South Pacific* (1985). An excellent cultural history of Cook's voyages.

Smith, Richard J. *Chinese Maps: Images of "All under Heaven"* (1996). Provides a good introduction to the history of cartography in China.

Sorkin, David. *The Religious Enlightenment: Protestants, Jews, and Catholics from London to Vienna* (2008). Discusses a wide range of thinkers who were able to reconcile Enlightenment thought with religious belief.

Tignor, Robert L. "W. R. Bascom and the Ife Bronzes." *Africa: Journal of the International African Institute* 60, no. 3 (1990): 425-434. Explores controversies over issues of where antiquities of great artistic value like the Ife bronzes should reside.

Welch, Anthony. *Shah Abbas and the Arts of Isfahan* (1973). Describes the astonishing architectural and artistic renaissance of the city of Isfahan under the Safavid ruler Shah Abbas.

Whitfield, Peter. *The Image of the World: Twenty Centuries of World Maps* (1994). A good introduction to the history of cartography in different parts of the world.

Wilks, Ivor. *Forests of Gold: Essays on the Akan and the Kingdom of Asante* (1993). A study that focuses on the Asante's drive for wealth.

Zilfi, Madeline C. *The Politics of Piety: The Ottoman Ulema in the Post-Classical Age (1600-1800)* (1988). Explores the cultural flourishing that took place within the Islamic world in this period.

CHAPTER 15

Allen, Robert C. *The British Industrial Revolution in Global Perspective* (2009). The most recent and authoritative study of the industrial revolution in Britain and its implications around the world.

Anderson, Fred. *Crucible of War: The Seven Years' War and the Fate of Empire in British North America, 1754-1766* (2000). The best synthesis of the "great war for empire" that set the stage for the American Revolution.

Bayly, C. A. *Indian Society and the Making of the British Empire* (1998). A useful work on the early history of the British conquest of India.

Blackburn, Robin. *The Overthrow of Colonial Slavery, 1776–1848* (1988). Places the abolition of the Atlantic slave trade and colonial slavery in a large historical context.

Brown, Harold G. *Ending the French Revolution: Violence, Justice, and Repression from the Terror to Napoleon* (2007). Describes how the Directory and Napoleon imposed stability on France in the wake of the revolution.

Cambridge History of Egypt: Modern Egypt from 1517 to the End of the Twentieth Century, Vol. 2 (1998). Volume 2 contains authoritative essays on all aspects of modern Egyptian history, including the impact of the French invasion and the rule of Muhammad Ali.

Cassel, Par Kristoffer. *Grounds of Judgement: Extraterritoriality and Imperial Powers in Nineteenth-Century China and Japan* (2012). A study of the idea and practice of extraterritoriality within the context of the triangular relationship between China, Japan, and the West.

Chaudhuri, K. N. *The Trading World of Asia and the East India Company, 1660–1760* (1978). An authoritative economic history of the East India Company's operations.

Crafts, N. F. R. *British Economic Growth during the Industrial Revolution* (1985). A pioneering study that emphasizes a long-term, more gradual process of adaptation to new institutional and social circumstances.

de Vries, Jan. *The Industrious Revolution: Consumer Behavior and the Household Economy, 1650 to the Present* (2008). A book on the lead-up to the industrial revolution, written by the leading economic historian who coined the term *industrious revolution*.

Diamond, Jared, and James A. Robinson (eds.). *Natural Experiments of History* (2010). This book consists of eight comparative studies drawn from history, archaeology, economics, economic history, geography, and political science, covering a spectrum of approaches, ranging from a nonquantitative narrative style to quantitative statistical analyses.

Doyle, William. *The Oxford History of the French Revolution* (1990). A highly detailed discussion of the course of events.

Drescher, Seymour. *Abolition: A History of Slavery and Anti-Slavery* (2009). A recent and authoritative overview of slavery and its opponents.

Elvin, Mark. *The Retreat of the Elephants: An Environmental History of China* (2004). A study of the different ways in which China's natural environment was shaped.

Fick, Carolyn E. *The Making of Haiti: The Saint Domingue Revolution from Below* (1990). Provides a detailed account of the factors that led to the great slave rebellion on the island of Haiti at the end of the eighteenth century.

Findley, Carter. *Bureaucratic Reform in the Ottoman Empire: The Sublime Porte, 1789–1922* (1980). A useful guide to Ottoman reform efforts in the nineteenth century.

Geggus, David (ed.). *The Impact of the Haitian Revolution in the Atlantic World* (2001). A lively effort to disentangle the effects of the Haitian Revolution from those of the French Revolution.

Hevia, James. *Cherishing Men from Afar: Qing Guest Ritual and the Macartney Embassy of 1793* (1995). Offers a definitive interpretation of the nature of Sino-British conflict in the Qing period.

Hobsbawm, Eric. *Nations and Nationalism since 1780* (1990). An important overview of the rise of the nation-state and nationalism around the world.

Howe, Daniel Walker. *What Hath God Wrought: The Transformation of America, 1815–1848* (2007). A Pulitzer Prize–winning interpretation of how new technologies and new ideas reshaped the economy, society, culture, and politics of the United States in the first half of the nineteenth century.

Hunt, Lynn. *Politics, Culture and Class in the French Revolution* (1984). Examines the influence of sociocultural shifts as causes and consequences of the French Revolution, emphasizing the symbols and practice of politics invented during the revolution.

Inikori, Joseph. *Africans and the Industrial Revolution in England* (2002). Demonstrates the important role that Africa and Africans played in facilitating the industrial revolution.

Isset, Christopher Mills. *State, Peasant, and Merchant in Qing Manchuria, 1644–1862* (2007). A study of the relationships between the sociopolitical structures and peasant lives in a key region during the Qing.

James, C. L. R. *The Black Jacobins: Toussaint L'Ouverture and the San Domingo Revolution* (1938). A classic chronicle of the only successful slave revolt in history, and providing a critical portrait of their leader, Toussaint L'Ouverture.

Jones, E. L. *Growth Recurring* (1988). Discusses the controversy over why the industrial revolution took place in Europe, stressing the unique ecological setting that encouraged long-term investment.

Kinsbruner, Jay. *Independence in Spanish America* (1994). A fine study of the Latin American revolutions that argues that the struggle was as much a civil war as a fight for national independence.

Landers, Jane. *Atlantic Creoles in the Age of Revolutions* (2011). A collection of fascinating and unique portraits of Atlantic world creoles who managed to move freely and purposefully through French, Spanish, and English colonies and through Indian territory in the unstable century between 1750 and 1850.

Lieven, Dominic. *Russia Against Napoleon* (2010). Explains how outnumbered Russian forces were able to defeat the massive army that Napoleon assembled for his conquest of Russia.

Mayer, Arno J. *The Furies: Violence and Terror in the French and Russian Revolutions* (2000). A stimulating and provocative essay comparing the French and Russian Revolutions.

Mokyr, Joel. *The Lever of Riches* (1990). An important study of the causes of the industrial revolution that emphasizes the role of small technological and organizational breakthroughs.

Mokyr, Joel. *Enlightened Economy: An Economic History of Britain, 1700–1850* (2009). Perspectives on the evolution of the British economy in the era that produced the industrial revolution.

Naquin, Susan, and Evelyn Rawski. *Chinese Society in the Eighteenth Century* (1987). A survey of mid-Qing society.

Neal, Larry. *The Rise of Financial Capitalism* (1990). An important study of the making of financial markets.

Nikitenko, Aleksandr. *Up from Serfdom: My Childhood and Youth in Russia, 1804–1824* (2001). One of the very few recorded life stories of a Russian serf.

Parthasarathi, Prasannan. *Why Europe Grew Rich and Asia Did Not: Global Economic Divergence, 1600–1800* (2011). A work that places the British industrial revolution in a global context, with much emphasis on India's textile manufacturing before being superseded by British manufacturers.

Pomeranz, Kenneth. *The Great Divergence: Europe, China, and the Making of the Modern World Economy* (2000). Offers explanations of why Europe and not some other place in the world, like parts of China or India, forged ahead economically in the nineteenth century.

Rudé, George. *Europe in the Eighteenth Century* (1972). Emphasizes the rise of a new class, the bourgeoisie, against the old aristocracy as a cause of the French Revolution.

Taylor, Alan. *American Revolutions: A Continental History, 1750–1804* (2016). A sweeping interpretation of the founding of the United States that places the War of Independence in a North American perspective, bringing together the diverse revolutions that transformed societies and borders across the continent.

Wong, R. Bin. *China Transformed: Historical Change and the Limits of European Experience* (2000). Draws attention to the relative autonomy of merchant capitalists in the European dynastic states in comparison with China.

Wood, Gordon S. *Empire of Liberty: A History of the Early Republic, 1789–1815* (2009). An excellent synthesis of the history of the United States in the tumultuous years between the ratification of the Constitution and the War of 1812.

Wortman, Richard. *Scenarios of Power: Myth and Ceremony in Russian Monarchy*, 2 vols. (1995–2000). Examines how dynastic Russia confronted the challenges of the revolutionary epoch.

CHAPTER 16

Anderson, David M. *Revealing Prophets: Prophets in Eastern African History* (1995). Good discussion of the prophets in eastern Africa.

Beecher, Jonathan. *The Utopian Vision of Charles Fourier* (1983). A fine biography of this important thinker.

Boyd, Jean. *The Caliph's Sister: Nana Asma'u, 1793–1865, Teacher, Poet, and Islamic Leader* (1988). A study of the most powerful female Muslim leader in the Fulani religious revolt.

Clancy-Smith, Julia. *Rebel and Saint: Muslim Notables, Populist Protest, Colonial Encounter (Algeria and Tunisia, 1800–1904)* (1994). Examines Islamic protest movements against western encroachments in North Africa.

Clogg, Richard. *A Concise History of Greece* (1997). A good introduction to the history of Greece in its European context.

Dalrymple, William. *The Last Mughal: The Fall of a Dynasty: Delhi, 1857* (2007). A deeply researched and riveting account of Delhi during the 1857 revolt.

Danziger, Raphael. *Abd al-Qadir: Resistance to the French and Internal Consolidation* (1977). Still the indispensable work on this important Algerian Muslim leader.

Dowd, Gregory E. *A Spirited Resistance: The North American Indian Struggle for Unity, 1745–1815* (1992). Emphasizes the importance of prophets like Tenskwatawa in the building of pan-Indian confederations in the era between the Seven Years' War and the War of 1812.

Earle, Rebecca. *The Return of the Native: Indians and Myth Making in Spanish America, 1810–1930* (2007). Examines how Indian resistance and the memory of struggles over sovereignty and land shaped emerging national identities, especially in Mexico and the Andes.

Guha, Ranajit. *Elementary Aspects of Peasant Insurgency in Colonial India* (1983). Not specifically on the Great Rebellion of 1857 but includes it in its pioneering "subalternist" interpretation of South Asian history.

Hamilton, Carolyn (ed.). *The Mfecane Aftermath: Reconstructive Debates in Southern African History* (1995). Debates on Shaka's *Mfecane* movement and its impact on southern Africa.

Hiskett, Mervyn. *The Sword of Truth: The Life and Times of the Shehu Usman dan Fodio* (1994). An authoritative study of the Fulani revolt in northern Nigeria.

Johnson, Douglas H. *Nuer Prophets: A History of Prophecy from the Upper Nile in the Nineteenth and Twentieth Centuries* (1994). Deals with African prophetic and charismatic movements in eastern Africa.

Keddie, Nikki. *An Islamic Response to Imperialism: Political and Religious Writings of Sayyid Jamal ad-Din "al-Afghani"* (1968). Definitive information on the Afghani's life and influence, coupled with a translation of one of his most important essays.

Laven, David, and Lucy Riall (eds.). *Napoleon's Legacy: Problems of Government in Restoration Europe* (2000). Excellent collection of essays on Restoration politics in various states.

Mukherjee, Rudrangshu. *Awadh in Revolt 1857–58* (1984). A careful case study of the Indian Rebellion.

Omer-Cooper, J. D. *The Zulu Aftermath: A Nineteenth-Century Revolution in Bantu Africa* (1966). A good place to start in studying Shaka's *Mfecane* movement, which greatly rearranged the political and ethnic makeup of southern Africa.

Ostler, Jeffrey. *The Plains Sioux and U.S. Colonialism from Lewis and Clark to Wounded Knee* (2004). Uses the lens of colonial theory to track relations between the Sioux and the United States, offering fresh insights about the Ghost Dance movement.

Peires, J. B. (ed.). *Before and After Shaka* (1981). Discusses elements in the debate over Shaka's *Mfecane* movement.

Pilbeam, Pamela. *French Socialists Before Marx: Workers, Women and the Social Question in France* (2001). Describes the development of a variety of socialist ideas in early nineteenth-century France.

Platt, Stephen R. *Autumn in the Heavenly Kingdom: China, the West, and the Epic Story of the Taiping Civil War* (2012). A study of the Taiping from a global perspective.

Reed, Nelson. *The Caste War of Yucatan* (1964). A classic narrative of the Caste War of the Yucatán.

Restall, Matthew. *The Maya World* (1997). Describes in economic and social terms the origins of the Yucatán upheaval in southern Mexico.

Ruedy, John. *Modern Algeria: The Origins and Development of a Nation* (2005). Still the best overview of the modern political history of Algeria.

Rugeley, Terry. *Rebellion Now and Forever: Mayans, Hispanics, and Caste War Violence in Yucatán, 1800–1880* (2009). Explains the combination of economic and cultural pressures that drove the Mayas in the Yucatán to revolt in the Caste War.

Spence, Jonathan. *God's Chinese Son: The Taiping Heavenly Kingdom of Hong Xiuquan* (1996). A fascinating portrayal of the Taiping through the prism of its founder.

Sperber, Jonathan. *Karl Marx: A Nineteenth-Century Life* (2013). An engaging and authoritative biography of Marx that emphasizes his role as a radical journalist.

Stedman Jones, Gareth. *Karl Marx: Greatness and Illusion* (2016). Now the authoritative biography of the founder of communism, showing Marx's own ambivalence about what he had created.

Wagner, Rudolf. *Reenacting the Heavenly Vision: The Role of Religion in the Taiping Rebellion* (1982). A brief but insightful analysis of the religious elements in the Taiping's doctrines.

White, Richard. *The Middle Ground: Indians, Empires, and Republics in the Great Lakes Region, 1650–1815* (1991). A pathbreaking exploration of intercultural relations in North America that offers a provocative interpretation of the visions of Tenskwatawa and the efforts of Tecumseh to resist the expansion of the United States.

CHAPTER 17

Berry, Sara. *Cocoa, Custom and Socio-Economic Change in Western Nigeria* (1975). Innovative study based on interviews with local farmers that suggests that farmer enterprise and microeconomic theory better explain the spectacular growth in cocoa production than grand economic theory.

Cain, P. A., and A. G. Hopkins. *British Imperialism: Innovation and Expansion, 1688–1914* (1993). An excellent discussion of British imperialism, especially British expansion into Africa.

Clark, Christopher. *Iron Kingdom: The Rise and Downfall of Prussia, 1600–1947* (2009). Includes an excellent discussion of the rise of German nationalism and Prussian power.

Cronon, William. *Nature's Metropolis: Chicago and the Great West* (1991). Makes connections between territorial expansion, industrialization, and urban development.

Davis, John. *Conflict and Control: Law and Order in Nineteenth-Century Italy* (1988). A superb study of the north-south and other rifts after Italian political unification.

Frankel, S. Herbert. *Capital Investment in Africa: Its Course and Effects* (1938). A careful study based on a mass of detailed figures and statistics on the general economic development of states in sub-Saharan Africa.

Friesen, Gerald. *The Canadian Prairies* (1984). The most comprehensive account of Canadian westward expansion.

Gluck, Carol. *Japan's Modern Myths: Ideology in the Late Meiji Period* (1985). A study of how states fashion useful historical traditions to consolidate and legitimize their rule.

Goswami, Manu. *Producing India: From Colonial Economy to National Space* (2004). An excellent study of how political economy produced the space of India, which the nationalists claimed as a national space.

Headrick, Daniel R. *The Tools of Empire: Technology and European Imperialism in the Nineteenth Century* (1981). A useful general study of the relationship between imperialism and technology.

Herbst, Jeffrey. *States and Power in Africa: Comparative Lessons in Authority and Control* (2000). An overview of the impact of colonial rule on contemporary African states.

Heyia, James I. *English Lessons: The Pedagogy of Imperialism in Nineteenth-Century China* (2003). A study of British imperialism in Qing China as a pedagogical project and a cultural endeavor.

Hill, Polly. *The Gold Coast Cocoa Farmer: A Preliminary Survey* (1965). An early but still important study of the introduction and spread of cocoa farming in the Gold Coast.

Hine, Robert V., and John Mack Faragher. *The American West: A New Interpretive History* (2000). Presents an excellent synthesis of the conquests by which the United States expanded from the Atlantic to the Pacific.

Hobsbawm, Eric J. *Nations and Nationalism since 1780: Programme, Myth, Reality* (1993). An insightful survey of the origins and development of nationalist thought throughout Europe.

Hochschild, Adam. *King Leopold's Ghost* (1998). A full-scale, eminently readable study of Europe's most egregiously destructive colonial regime in Africa.

Judson, Peter. *The Habsburg Empire: A New History* (2016). An innovative history of the relationship between "the people" and the state in a multiethnic empire.

Lieven, Dominic. *Empire: The Russian Empire and Its Rivals* (2000). A comparison of the British, Ottoman, Habsburg, and Russian Empires.

Mackenzie, John M. *Propaganda and Empire* (1984). Contains a series of useful chapters showing the importance of the empire to Britain.

Mamdani, Mahmood. *Citizen and State: Contemporary Africa and the Legacy of Late Colonialism* (1996). A survey of the impact of European colonial powers on African political systems.

McClintock, Anne. *Imperial Leather: Race, Gender and Sexuality in the Colonial Contest* (1995). A study of the imperial relationship between Victorian Britain and South Africa from the point of view of cultural studies.

McNeil, William. *Europe's Steppe Frontier: 1500–1800* (1964). An excellent study of the definitive victory of Russia's agricultural empire over grazing nomads and independent frontier people.

Mitchell, B. R. *International Historical Statistics: Africa, Asia, and Oceania, 1750–2005* (2007). This comparative volume provides data from over two centuries for all principal areas of economic and social activity in both eastern and western Europe.

Mittler, Barbara. *A Newspaper for China? Power, Identity and Change in Shanghai's News Media, 1872–1942* (2004). An analysis of how the influential foreign-managed newspaper *Shenbao* succeeded in capturing its Chinese readership in the late Qing.

Montgomery, David. *The Fall of the House of Labor: The Workplace, the State, and American Labor Activism, 1865–1925* (1987). An excellent discussion of changes in work in the late nineteenth century.

Myers, Ramon, and Mark Peattie (eds.). *The Japanese Colonial Empire, 1895–1945* (1984). A collection of essays exploring different aspects of Japanese colonialism.

Needell, Jeffrey. *A Tropical Belle Epoque: Elite Culture and Society in Turn of the Century Rio de Janeiro* (1987). Shows the strength of the Brazilian elites at the turn of the century.

Porter, Bernard. *The Absent-Minded Imperialists: What the British Really Thought about Empire* (2004). A careful discussion of the ways in which empire changed the British—and did not.

Prakash, Gyan. *Another Reason: Science and the Imagination of Modern India* (1999). A study of how science and technology transformed the British imperial governance and unified India into a geographical unity.

Prasad, Ritika. *Tracks of Change: Railways and Everyday Life in Colonial India*

(2016). A detailed analysis of how railways transformed the everyday experience of Indians under colonial rule.

Stengers, Jean. *Combien le Congo a-t-il coûté à la Belgique?* (1957). A detailed financial accounting of how much Leopold put into the Congo and how much he took out, underscoring just how ruthlessly he exploited this possession.

Topik, Steven. *The Political Economy of the Brazilian State, 1889–1930* (1987). An excellent discussion of the Brazilian state, especially of its elites.

Walker, Mack, *German Home Towns: Community, State, and the General State, 1648–1871* (1971, 1998). A brilliant, street-level analysis of the Holy Roman Empire (the First Reich) and the run-up to the German unification of 1871 (the Second Reich).

Wasserman, Mark. *Everyday Life and Politics in Nineteenth-Century Mexico* (2000). Wonderfully captures the way in which people coped with social and economic dislocation in late nineteenth-century Mexico.

Weeks, Theodore R. *Nation and State in Late Imperial Russia: Nationalism and Russification on the Western Frontier, 1863–1914* (1996). A good discussion of the Russian Empire's responses to the concept of the nation-state.

White, Richard. *Railroaded: The Transcontinentals and the Making of Modern America* (2011). A seering exposé of the corruptions and a startling critique of the economic and environmental costs associated with the expansion of railroad lines across Canada, the United States, and Mexico.

Zarrow, Peter. *After Empire: The Conceptual Transformation of the Chinese State, 1885–1924* (2012). A history of the changing ideas regarding the Chinese state that eventually led to the abandonment of monarchical rule by the Chinese people.

CHAPTER 18

Bayly, C. A. *The Birth of the Modern World, 1780–1914: Global Connections and Comparisons* (2004). A general study of the key political, economic, social, and cultural features of the modern era in world history.

Bergère, Marie-Claire. *Sun Yat-sen* (1998). Originally published in French in 1994, this is a judicious biography of the man generally known as the father of the modern Chinese nation.

Chatterjee, Partha. *The Nation and Its Fragments* (1993). One of the most important works on Indian nationalism by a leading scholar of "Subaltern Studies."

Conrad, Joseph. *Heart of Darkness* (1899). First published in a magazine in 1899, this novella contains a searing critique of King Leopold's oppressive and exploitative policies in the Congo and was part of a growing concern for the effects that European empires were having around the world, especially in Africa.

Crosby, Alfred. *Ecological Imperialism: The Biological Expansion of Europe, 900–1900* (2nd ed., 2004). A fascinating biohistory of European imperialism.

Esherick, Joseph. *The Origins of the Boxer Uprising* (1987). The definitive account of the episode.

Esherick, Joseph. "How the Qing Became China." In Joseph W. Esherick, Hasan Kayali, and Eric Van Young (eds.), *Empire to Nation: Historical Perspectives on the Making of the Modern World* (2006). A study of the processes through which the Qing Empire became the nation-state of China.

Everdell, William R. *The First Moderns: Profiles in the Origins of Twentieth-Century Thought* (1997). A rich account of the many faces of modernism, focusing particularly on science and art.

Finnane, Antonia. *Changing Clothes in China: Fashion, History, Nation* (2008). An exploration of changing Chinese identities from the perspective of clothing.

Gay, Peter. *The Cultivation of Hatred* (1994). A provocative discussion of the violent passions of the immediate pre–Great War era.

Hochschild, Adam. *King Leopold's Ghost: A Story of Greed, Terror, and Heroism in Colonial Africa* (1998). A well-written account of the violent colonial history of the Belgian Congo under King Leopold in the late nineteenth century.

Judge, Joan. *The Precious Raft of History: The Past, the West, and the Woman Question in China* (2008). An insightful exploration of the "woman question" in China at the turn of the twentieth century.

Katz, Friedrich. *The Life and Times of Pancho Villa* (1998). An exploration of the Mexican Revolution that shows how Villa's armies destroyed the forces of Díaz and his followers.

Keddie, Nikki. *An Islamic Response to Imperialism: Political and Religious Writings of Sayyid Jamal ad-Din "al-Afghani"* (1968). Definitive information on Afghani's life and influence, coupled with a translation of one of his most important essays.

Kern, Stephen. *The Culture of Time and Space 1880–1918* (1986). A useful study of the enormous changes in the experience of time and space in the age of late industrialism in Europe and America.

Kuhn, Philip. *Chinese among Others: Emigration in Modern Times* (2008). An overview of the history of Chinese migration.

McKeown, Adam. *Melancholy Order: Asian Migration and the Globalization of Borders* (2008). An examination of global migration patterns since the mid-nineteenth century and how regulations designed to restrict Asian migration to other parts of the world led to the modern regime of migration control.

Meade, Teresa. *"Civilizing" Rio: Reform and Resistance in a Brazilian City, 1889–1930* (1997). A wonderful study of cultural and class conflict in Brazil.

Moon, David. *The Plough That Broke the Steppes: Agriculture and Environment on Russia's Grasslands, 1700–1914* (2013). An excellent environmental history of the Russian steppe.

Pick, Daniel. *Faces of Degeneration: A European Disorder, c. 1848–c. 1918* (1993). A study of Europe's fear of social and biological decline, particularly focusing on France and Italy.

Pretorius, Fransjohn (ed.). *Scorched Earth* (2001). A study of the Anglo-Boer War in terms of its environmental impact.

Saler, Michael (ed.). *The Fin de Siècle World* (2014). A comprehensive anthology of essays on turn-of-the-century politics and culture across the world.

Sarkar, Sumit. *The Swadeshi Movement in Bengal* (1973). A comprehensive study of an early militant movement against British rule.

Schorske, Carl E. *Fin-de-Siècle Vienna: Politics and Culture* (1980). The classic treatment of the birth of modern ideas and political movements in turn-of-the-century Austria.

Trachtenberg, Alan. *The Incorporation of America: Culture and Society in the Gilded Age* (1982). A provocative synthesis of changes in the American economy, society, and culture in the last decades of the nineteenth century.

Wang, David Der-wei. *Fin-de-Siècle Splendor: Repressed Modernities of Late Qing Fiction, 1849–1911* (1997). A fine work that attempts to locate the "modern" within the writings of the late Qing period.

Warren, Louis. *Buffalo Bill's America: William Cody and the Wild West Show* (2005). A superb portrait of William F. Cody, the person; of Buffalo Bill, the persona Cody (and others) created; and of the popular culture his Wild West shows brought to audiences in Europe and North America.

Warwick, Peter. *Black People and the South African War, 1899–1902* (1983). An important study that reminds readers of the crucial involvement of black South Africans in this bloody conflict.

Womack, John, Jr. *Zapata and the Mexican Revolution* (1968). A major work on the Mexican Revolution that discusses peasant struggles in the state of Morelos in great detail.

CHAPTER 19

Akcam, Taner. *The Young Turks' Crime Against Humanity: The Armenian Genocide and Ethnic Cleansing in the Ottoman Empire* (2012). An exhaustive examination of the factors that impelled the Turkish authorities to carry out ethnic cleansing against the Armenians during World War I.

Aksakal, Mustafa. *The Ottoman Road to War in 1914: The Ottoman Empire and the First World War* (2008). An important study of the personalities and factors that led the Ottomans to join with Germany and Austria-Hungary during World War I, a fateful decision that ultimately spelled the end of the Ottoman Empire.

Ambedkar, B. R. *Annihilation of Caste: The Annotated Critical Edition* (1936). Ambedkar's brilliant polemic against Gandhi on caste. With a new introduction by Arundhati Roy, this work is an essential reading for an understanding of Ambedkar's thoughts.

Anderson, Scott. *Lawrence in Arabia: War, Deceit, Imperial Folly, and the Making of the Middle East* (2013). A new and authoritative biography of T. E. Lawrence, with significant new material on British policies in the Middle East as seen through the eyes of a strong pro-Arab figure.

Bloxham, Donald. *The Great Game of Genocide: Imperialism, Nationalism, and the Destruction of the Ottoman Armenians* (2005). The definitive work on the Armenian genocide, set in a wide historical context.

Bosworth, R. J. B. *Mussolini's Italy: Life under the Dictatorship, 1915–1945* (2006). An eye-opening treatment of fascism in Italy beyond Mussolini.

Brown, Judith. *Gandhi: Prisoner of Hope* (1990). A biography of Gandhi as a political activist.

Clark, Christopher. *Sleepwalkers: How Europe Went to War* (2012). A reexamination of the crucial role of Austria-Hungary in triggering the world war.

De Grazia, Victoria, and Ellen Furlough (eds.). *The Sex of Things: Gender and Consumption in Historical Perspective* (1996). Path-breaking essays on how gender affects consumption.

Dumenil, Lynn. *The Modern Temper: America in the 1920s* (1995). A general discussion of American culture in the decade after World War I.

Fainsod, Merle. *Smolensk under Soviet Rule* (1989). The most accessible and sophisticated interpretation of the Stalin revolution in the village.

Gelvin, James. *Divided Loyalties: Nationalism and Mass Politics in Syria at the Close of Empire* (1998). Offers important insights into the development of nationalism in the Arab world.

Horne, John (ed.). *State, Society, and Mobilization during the First World War* (1997). Essays on what it took to wage total war among all the belligerents.

Horne, John (ed.). *A Companion to World War I* (2010). A collection of articles written by leading scholars of World War I; the most comprehensive and up-to-date work on this war.

Johnson, G. Wesley. *The Emergence of Black Politics in Senegal* (1971). A useful examination of the stirrings of African nationalism in Senegal.

Kennedy, David M. *Freedom from Fear: The American People in Depression and War, 1929–1945* (1999). A wonderful narrative of turbulent years.

Kershaw, Ian. *Hitler*, 2 vols. (1998–2000). A masterpiece combining biography and context.

Kimble, David. *A Political History of Ghana* (1963). An excellent discussion of the beginnings of African nationalism in Ghana.

Kotkin, Stephen. *Magnetic Mountain: Stalinism as a Civilization* (1995). Recaptures the atmosphere of a time when everything seemed possible, even creating a new world.

Kotkin, Stephen. *Stalin*. Vol. 1: *Paradoxes of Power* (2014). A sweeping history of the tsarist regime, world war, Russian Revolution, civil war, and rise of Stalin.

Lambert, Nicholas A. *Planning Armageddon: British Economic Warfare and the First World War* (2012). Mines new archives to show that the British had an aggressive plan before the war to destroy Germany financially, which the British government approved and began to enact until the United States forced them to back off.

LeMahieu, D. L. *A Culture for Democracy: Mass Communication and the Cultivated Mind in Britain between the Wars* (1988). One of the great works on mass culture.

Lyttelton, Adrian. *The Seizure of Power: Fascism in Italy, 1919–1929* (1961). Still the classic account.

Marchand, Roland. *Advertising the American Dream: Making Way for Modernity, 1920–1945* (1985). An excellent discussion of the force of mass production and mass consumption.

Mazower, Mark. *Dark Continent: Europe's Twentieth Century* (1999). A wide-ranging overview of Europe's tempestuous twentieth century.

McGirr, Lisa. *The War on Alcohol: Prohibition and the Rise of the American State* (2016). Emphasizes the power of cultural reaction against modernity that brought about Prohibition and the irony that its enforcement helped to expand the power of the modern state.

McKeown, Adam. *Melancholy Order: Asian Migration and the Globalization of Border* (2008). A major study of the vast movement of peoples around the globe between the middle of the nineteenth and middle of the twentieth centuries.

Morrow, John H., Jr. *The Great War: An Imperial History* (2004). Places World War I in the context of European imperialism.

Musgrove, Charles D. *China's Contested Capital: Architecture, Ritual, and Response in Nanjing* (2013). An exploration of how the Chinese Nationalist capital of Nanjing served as a focal point for the making of a nation and a new form of mass politics.

Nottingham, John, and Carl Rosberg. *The Myth of "Mau Mau": Nationalism in Kenya* (1966). Dispels the myths in describing the roots of nationalism in Kenya.

Pedersen, Susan. *The Guardians: the League of Nations and the Crisis of Empire* (2015). Skillfully reexamines the neglected effort to regulate the colonial world under a so-called mandate system.

Rutledge, Ian. *Enemy on the Euphrates: The British Occupation of Iraq and the Great Arab Revolt, 1914-1921* (2014). An impassioned investigation of Britain's effort to take control of the oil-rich territory of Iraq and the determined resistance of the Iraqi peoples.

Strand, David. *An Unfinished Republic: Leading by Word and Deed in Modern China* (2011). A study of how the need for popular support led to a new political culture characterized by public speaking and performance in early twentieth-century China.

Suny, Ronald Gregor. *"They can Live in the Desert but Nowhere Else": A History of the Armenian Genocide* (2015). A careful, document-based analysis of the Armenian genocide.

Taylor, Jay. *The Generalissimo: Chiang Kai-shek and the Struggle for Modern China* (2009). The first serious biographical study of Chiang Kai-shek in English, although its reliance on Chiang's own diary as a source does raise some questions of historical interpretation.

Thorp, Rosemary (ed.). *Latin America in the 1930s* (1984). An important collection of essays on Latin America's response to the shakeup of the interwar years.

Tsin, Michael. *Nation, Governance, and Modernity in China: Canton, 1900-1927* (1999). An analysis of the vision and social dynamics behind the Guomindang-led revolution of the 1920s.

Vianna, Hermano. *The Mystery of Samba* (1999). Discusses the history of samba, emphasizing its African heritage as well as its persistent popular content.

Wakeman, Frederic Jr. *Policing Shanghai, 1927-1937* (1995). An excellent account of Guomindang rule in China's largest city during the Nanjing decade.

Winter, J. M. *The Experience of World War* (1988). A comprehensive presentation of the many sides of the twentieth century.

Young, Louise. *Japan's Total Empire: Manchuria and the Culture of Wartime Imperialism* (1998). An innovative case study of Japanese imperialism and mass culture with broad implications.

Zuber, Terence. *Inventing the Schlieffen Plan: German War Planning, 1871-1914* (2002). Uses new archives to demonstrate definitively that the famed Schlieffen Plan is essentially a myth, and explains how that myth was created.

CHAPTER 20

Aburish, Said K. *Nasser: The Last Arab* (2004). A recent and impressive look at Egypt's most powerful political leader in the 1950s and 1960s.

Anderson, Jon Lee. *Che Guevara: A Revolutionary Life* (1997). A sweeping study of the radicalization of Latin American nationalism.

Austin, Granville. *The Indian Constitution: Cornerstone of a Nation*, 2nd ed. (1999). A classic study of constitution making in India.

Bayly, Christopher, and Tim Harper. *Forgotten Armies: Britain's Asian Empire and the War with Japan* (2004). A brilliant social and military history of World War II as fought and lived in South and Southeast Asia.

Chatterjee, Partha. *Nationalist Thought and the Colonial World: A Derivative Discourse* (1986). An influential interpretation of the ideological and political nature of Indian nationalism and the struggle for a postcolonial nation-state.

Cook, Alexander C. (ed.). *Mao's Little Red Book: A Global History* (2014). A look at the global impact of the Chinese Cultural Revolution through the lens of the iconic "little red book" of quotations from Mao.

Crampton, R. J. *Eastern Europe in the Twentieth Century and After*, 2nd ed. (1997). A comprehensive overview covering all Soviet-bloc countries.

Dikötter, Frank. *Mao's Great Famine: The History of China's Most Devastating Catastrophe, 1958-1962* (2010). A recent detailed account of one of the greatest human-made disasters in twentieth-century history.

Dower, John W. *Embracing Defeat: Japan in the Wake of World War II* (1999). A prize-winning study of the transformation of one of the war's vanquished.

Elkins, Caroline. *Imperial Reckoning: The Untold Story of Britain's Gulag in Kenya* (2005). A Pulitzer Prize–winning study of the brutal war to suppress the nationalist uprising in Kenya in the 1950s that ultimately led to independence for that country.

Feshbach, Murray, and Alfred Friendly Jr. *Ecocide in the USSR: Health and Nation under Siege* (1992). A crucial study of ecological disasters in the Soviet Union.

Gao Yuan. *Born Red: A Chronicle of the Cultural Revolution* (1987). A gripping personal account of the Cultural Revolution by a former Red Guard.

Gordon, Andrew (ed.). *Postwar Japan as History* (1993). Essays covering a wide range of topics on postwar Japan.

Hargreaves, John D. *Decolonization in Africa* (1996). A good place to start when exploring the history of African decolonization.

Hasan, Mushirul (ed.). *India's Partition: Process, Strategy and Mobilization* (1993). A useful anthology of scholarly articles, short stories, and primary documents on the partition of India.

Iriye, Akira. *Power and Culture: The Japanese-American War, 1941-1945* (1981). A discussion that goes beyond the military confrontation in Asia.

Jackson, Kenneth T. *Crabgrass Frontier: The Suburbanization of the United States* (1985). An insightful and influential consideration of the movement of the American population from cities to suburbs.

Jalal, Ayesha. *The Sole Spokesman: Jinnah, the Muslim League and the Demand for Pakistan* (1985). A study of the high politics leading to the violent partition of British India.

Keep, John L. H. *Last of the Empires: A History of the Soviet Union 1945-1991* (1995). A detailed overview of the core of the "Second World."

Morris, Benny. *Righteous Victims: A History of the Zionist-Arab Conflict, 1881-1999* (2000). On the Arab-Israeli War of 1948.

Pantsov, Alexander V. *Mao: The Real Story*, translated by Steven I. Levine (2012). A well-researched biography of Mao.

Patterson, James T. *Grand Expectations: The United States, 1945-1974* (1996). Synthesizes the American experience in the postwar decades.

Patterson, Thomas. *Contesting Castro* (1994). The best study of the tension between the United States and Cuba. Culminating in the Cuban Revolution, it explores the deep American misunderstanding of Cuban national aspirations.

Roberts, Geoffrey. *Stalin's Wars: From World War to Cold War, 1939-1953* (2007). A reassessment of Stalin's wartime leadership that conveys the vast scale of what took place.

Ruedy, John. *Modern Algeria: The Origins and Development of a Nation* (1992). Gives the history of the Algerian nationalist movements and provides an overview of the Algerian War of Independence.

Tignor, Robert L. *W. Arthur Lewis and the Birth of Development Economics* (2006). An intellectual biography of the Nobel Prize–winning, West Indian–born economist who proposed formulas to promote the economic development of less developed societies and then sought to implement them in Africa and the West Indies.

Wiener, Douglas R. *A Little Corner of Freedom: Russian Nature Protection from Stalin to Gorbachev* (2002). A groundbreaking book about Russian environmentalism.

Zatlin, Jonathan. *The Currency of Socialism: Money and Political Culture in East Germany* (2007). A fascinating description of how the economy of East Germany did—and did not—work.

Zubkova, Elena. *Russia after the War: Hopes, Illusions, and Disappointments, 1945–1957* (1998). Uses formerly secret archives to catalogue the devastation and difficult reconstruction of one of the war's victors.

CHAPTER 21

Collier, Paul. *The Bottom Billion: Why the Poorest Countries Fail and What Can Be Done about It* (2007). Shows that despite the world's advancing prosperity, more than a billion people have been left behind in abject poverty.

Davis, Deborah (ed.). *The Consumer Revolution in Urban China* (2000). A look at the different aspects of the recent profound social transformation of urban China.

Davis, Mike. *City of Quartz: Excavating the Future in Los Angeles* (1990). Offers provocative reflections on the recent history, current condition, and possible future of Los Angeles.

Dutton, Michael. *Streetlife China* (1999). A fascinating portrayal of the survival tactics of those inhabiting the margins of society in modern China.

Eichengreen, Barry. *Globalizing Capital: A History of the International Monetary System* (1996). An insightful analysis of how international capital markets changed in the period from 1945 to 1980.

Gourevitch, Philip. *We Wish to Inform You That Tomorrow We Will Be Killed with Our Families: Stories from Rwanda* (1999). A volume that reveals the hatreds that culminated in the Rwanda genocide.

Guillermoprieto, Alma. *Looking for History: Dispatches from Latin America* (2001). A collection of articles by the most important journalist reporting on Latin American affairs.

Han, Minzhu (ed.). *Cries for Democracy: Writings and Speeches from the 1989 Chinese Democracy Movement* (1990). A collection of documents from the events leading up to the incident in Tiananmen Square on June 4, 1989.

Herbst, Jeffrey. *States and Power in Africa: Comparative Lessons in Authority and Control* (2000). Explores the political dilemmas facing modern African polities.

Honig, Emily, and Gail Hershatter. *Personal Voices: Chinese Women in the 1980's* (1988). A record of Chinese women during a period of rapid social change.

Huang, Yasheng. *Capitalism with Chinese Characteristics: Entrepreneurship and the State* (2008). A sharp, unsentimental inside look at China's market economy and its future prospects.

Kavoori, Anandam P., and Aswin Punathambekar (eds.). *Global Bollywood* (2008). A collection of essays by leading film scholars on Indian cinema on different aspects of the processes by which the Hindi film industry became Bollywood.

Klitgaard, Robert. *Tropical Gangsters* (1990). On the intimate connections between corrupt native elites and international aid agencies.

Kotkin, Stephen. *Armageddon Averted: The Soviet Collapse, 1970–2000* (2001). Places the surprise fall of the Soviet Union in the context of the great shifts in the post–World War II order.

Macekura, Stephen. *Of Limits and Growth: The Rise of Global Sustainable Development in the Twentieth Century* (2016). Explores the rise of global environmental politics in the 1970s and 1980s and the debate about resources and climate change.

Mamdani, Mahmood. *When Victims Become Killers: Colonialism, Nativism, and the Genocide in Rwanda* (2001). Discusses the genocide in Rwanda in light of the legacy of colonialism.

Mehta, Suketu. *Maximum City: Bombay Lost and Found* (2005). Examines one of the great, and contradictory, cities in the era of globalization.

Miller, Chris. *The Struggle to Save the Soviet Economy: Mikhail Gorbachev and the Collapse of the USSR* (2016). An insightful analysis of internal debates in Moscow over rival directions for the Soviet economy and the response to Chinese reforms after 1978.

Mottahedeh, Roy. *The Mantle of the Prophet: Religion and Politics in Iran,* 2nd ed. (2008). Perhaps the best book on the 1979 Iranian Revolution and its aftermath.

Nathan, Andrew, and Perry Link. *The Tiananmen Papers* (2002). An inside look at the divisions within the Chinese elite in connection with the 1989 crackdown.

Portes, Alejandro, and Rubén G. Rumbaut. *Immigrant America,* 2nd ed. (1996). A good comparative study of how immigration has transformed the United States.

Prakash, Gyan. *Mumbai Fables* (2010). A spirited account of the rise of India's most modern city, a center of intellectual, commercial, and political vitality.

Prunier, Gerald. *Africa's World War: Congo, the Rwandan Genocide, and the Making of a Continental Catastrophe* (2009). A chilling discussion of the spillover effects of the Rwandan genocide on central, eastern, and southern Africa.

Punathambekar, Aswin. *From Bombay to Bollywood: The Making of a Global Media Industry* (2013). A study of the transformation of the Indian film industry that globalizes its content and reach.

Reinhart, Carmen, and Kenneth Rogoff. *This Time Is Different: Eight Centuries of Financial Folly* (2009). Explains the latest financial crash using historical perspective.

Ruggie, John Gerard. *Just Business: Multinational Corporations and Human Rights* (2013). Shows how even big business got into human rights advocacy.

Sikkink, Kathryn. *The Justice Cascade: How Human Rights Prosecutions Are Changing World Politics* (2011). Shows how new forms of global organizing and new social norms are changing the political rules across borders.

Stein, Judith. *Pivotal Decade: How the United States Traded Factories for Finance in the Seventies* (2010). A comprehensive study of the rise of American banking and the decline of heartland industries.

Ther, Philipp. *Europe since 1989: A History* (2016). A concise account of European integration and neoliberalism since the fall of the Berlin Wall.

Van Der Wee, Hermann. *Prosperity and Upheaval: The World Economy, 1945–1980* (1986). Describes very well the transformation and problems of the world economy, particularly from the 1960s onward.

Westad, Odd Arne. *The Global Cold War: Third World Interventions and the Making of Our Times* (2007). A genuinely global perspective on the Cold War and its consequences.

Winn, Peter. *Americas: The Changing Face of Latin America and the Caribbean* (1992). A useful portrayal of Latin America since the 1970s.

EPILOGUE

Achcar, Gilbert. *Morbid Symptoms: Relapse in the Arab Uprising* (2016). An up-to-date overview of the difficulties that the proponents of the Arab Spring encountered, with long and detailed treatments of Syria and Egypt.

Christensen, Thomas J. *The China Challenges: Shaping the Choices of a Rising Power* (2015). A survey of "China's Rise" and the challenges and choices the country faces in the contemporary world.

Cleveland, William L., and Martin Bunton. *A History of the Modern Middle East*, 6th ed. (2016). The sixth edition of an important textbook that covers the whole of the Middle East from 1800 to the present.

Cooper, Frederick. *Africa in the World: Capitalism, Empire, Nation-State* (2014). An overview of Africa's place in global history, based on the most recent scholarship.

Darwall, Rupert. *The Age of Global Warming: A History* (2013). An accessible narrative about how scientists became increasingly aware of the threat of climate change and the multinational effort to reduce carbon emissions.

Deaton, Angus. *The Great Escape: Health, Wealth, and the Origins of Inequality* (2013). An examination of the heightened degree of inequality by a Nobel Prize–winning authority who emphasizes that contemporary well-to-do individuals have largely failed to help those not so fortunate to achieve their potential.

Eichengreen, Barry. *Hall of Mirrors: The Great Depression, the Great Recessions and the Uses—and Misuses—of History* (2015). A chronicle of the financial upheaval of 2008–2009, comparing the policies and mindsets of major decision makers to the choices made in the 1930s.

Esposito, John L., Tamara Sonn, and John O. Voll. *Islam and Democracy after the Arab Spring* (2016). An analysis of the prospects of democracy in Muslim countries, with case studies of Tunisia, Egypt, and Turkey, among others.

Ferguson, James. "Seeing Like an Oil Company: Space, Security, and Global Capital in Neoliberal Africa." *American Anthropologist* 107 (2005): 377–382. A critique of James Scott's book *Seeing Like a State*, and a view of the role of oil and mining companies in Africa and their failure to promote economic growth there.

Ferguson, James. *Global Shadows: Africa in the Neo-Liberal World Order* (2006). Journal articles brought together in a book by one of the leading African anthropologists. They deal with contemporary African issues and dilemmas, placed in a global context.

Ferguson, James. *Give a Man a Fish: Reflections on the New Politics of Distribution* (2015). An analysis of social welfare programs in southern Africa, involving cash payments to the poorest members of societies, and their implications for neoliberal capitalism.

Franco, Jean. *Cruel Modernity* (2013). An examination of the cultural dimensions of Latin America's experience with recent neoliberal policies and the tensions and violence of relatively stateless societies.

Gerges, Fawaz A. *ISIS: A History* (2016). One of a series of books that explores the rise of ISIS and stresses the place of violence in building a new Islamic state.

Jaffrelot, Christophe. *Saffron Modernity in India: Narendra Modi and His Experiment with Gujarat* (2014). A political history of how Narendra Modi emerged dominant in Gujarat using anti-Muslim nationalist ideology, captured the leadership of the BJP, and built a personality cult that catapulted him as a national leader.

Judis, John. *The Populist Explosion: How the Great Recession Transformed American and European Politics* (2016). A book by a journalist and political analyst that argues that the contemporary populist upsurges on both the right and left are responses to neoliberal globalization.

Lacau, Ernest. *On Populist Reason* (2007). This dense but insightful study by a political theorist offers original philosophical views on the meaning of "the people" by examining historical examples of populism.

Lee, Soo im, and Stephen-Murphy-Shigematsu. *Japan's Diversity Dilemmas: Ethnicity, Citizenship, and Education* (2006). Still an important work that examines whether Japan can assimilate foreigners, crucial for its aging workforce, or is condemned to demographic and economic decline because of its extremely low birthrate and pride in ethnic purity.

Lepore, Jill. *The Whites of Their Eyes: The Tea Party's Revolution and the Battle over American History* (2011). A history of the American far right and the Tea Party and their imagination of a nostalgic American past.

Lynch, Marc. *The New Arab Wars: Uprisings and Anarchy in the Middle East* (2016). Brings the narrative of the Arab Spring and the ambitions of its diverse proponents up to the present.

McCants, William. *The ISIS Apocalypse: The History, Strategy, and Doomsday Vision of the Islamic State* (2015). An important study of ISIS, based on a wide reading of ISIS's publications.

Milankovic, Brian. *Global Inequality: A New Approach for the Age of Globalization* (2016). Using the most up-to-date data on worldwide incomes, the author shows how the last quarter-century has yielded a convergence in global income distribution across societies and the widening of a gap within societies.

Moubayed, Sami. *Under the Black Flag: At the Frontier of the New Jihad* (2015). A study of the rise of jihadism within the Arab world, with a concentration on Syria.

Muller, Jan-Werner. *What Is Populism?* (2016). The sharpest analysis yet of the nature and prospects of populism, especially its relations to political establishments, which it condemns but on which it depends.

Owen, Roger. *The Rise and Fall of Arab Presidents for Life, with a New Afterword* (2014). A study that examines the emergence of Arab leaders who endeavored to hold on to power for as long as they lived, with insights into the actions of those who brought many of the leaders down during the Arab Spring.

Pietz, David A. *The Yellow River: The Problem of Water in Modern China* (2015). A critical look at health and environmental issues in China today, from a historical perspective through the lens of one of its major rivers.

Radelet, Steven. *Emerging Africa: How Seventeen Countries Are Leading the Way* (2010). An Afro-optimist sees many African countries enjoying economic growth and political stability, proving that Africa can also join much of the rest of the world in achieving economic and political progress.

Radelet, Steven. *The Great Surge: The Ascent of the Developing World* (2015). An overview of the extraordinary progress that many of the countries in what once was called the Third World have achieved in economic and political successes.

Reid, Michael. *Forgotten Continent: The Battle for Latin America's Soul* (2009). A journalistic account of how Latin America grappled with market openings, new democratic forces, and the search for policies to close the gap between the haves and have-nots.

Shambaugh, David. *China Goes Global: The Partial Power* (2013). An analysis of China's role in the global arena and its impact, from economics to culture.

Trenin, Dmitri. *Should We Fear Russia?* (2016). A clear-eyed view of what contemporary Russia is and is not.

Warwick, John. *Black Flags Flying: The Rise of ISIS* (2015). A detailed account of the leadership groups within ISIS and its relationship to al-Qaeda.

Weiss, Michael, and Hassan Hassan. *ISIS: Inside the Army of Terror* (2015). An account based on interviews and wide reading of western and Arabic sources on the rise of ISIS.

Wright, Lawrence. *The Looming Tower: Al-Qaeda and the Road to 9/11* (2006). A Pulitzer Prize–winning study of the origins and evolution of al-Qaeda.

Wright, Lawrence. *The Terror Years: From al-Qaeda to ISIS* (2016). Primarily a study of the decline of the power of al-Qaeda, which created an opening for the more territorially based ISIS.

Abd al-Rahman III Islamic ruler in Spain who held a countercaliphate and reigned from 912 to 961 CE.

aborigines Original, native inhabitants of a region, as opposed to invaders, colonizers, or later peoples of mixed ancestry.

absolute monarchy Form of government where one body, usually the monarch, controls the right to tax, judge, make war, and coin money. The term *enlightened absolutists* was often used to refer to state monarchies in seventeenth- and eighteenth-century Europe.

acid rain Precipitation containing large amounts of sulfur, mainly from coal-fired plants.

adaptation Ability to alter behavior and to innovate; finding new ways of doing things.

African National Congress (ANC) Multiracial organization founded in 1912 in an effort to end racial discrimination in South Africa.

African sacred kingships Institutions that marked the centralized politics of East, West, and central Africa. The inhabitants of these kingships believed that their kings were descendants of the gods.

Afrikaners Descendants of the original Dutch settlers of South Africa; often referred to as Boers.

agones Athletic contests in ancient Greece.

Ahmosis Egyptian ruler in the southern part of the country who ruled from 1550 to 1525 BCE. Ahmosis used Hyksos weaponry—horse chariots in particular—to defeat the Hyksos themselves.

Ahura Mazda Supreme god of the Persians believed to have created the world and all that is good and to have appointed earthly kings.

AIDS (acquired immunodeficiency syndrome) Virus that compromises the ability of the infected person's immune system to ward off disease. First detected in 1981, AIDS was initially stigmatized as a "gay cancer," but as it spread to heterosexuals, public awareness about it increased. In its first two decades, AIDS killed 12 million people.

Akbarnamah Mughal intellectual Abulfazl's *Book of Akbar*, which attempted to reconcile the traditional Sufi interest in the inner life within the worldly context of a great empire.

Alaric II Visigothic king who issued a simplified code of innovative imperial law.

Alexander the Great (356–323 BCE) Leader who used novel tactics and new kinds of armed forces to conquer the Persian Empire, which extended from Egypt and the Mediterranean Sea to the interior of what is now Afghanistan and as far as the Indus River valley. Alexander's conquests broke down barriers between the Mediterranean world and Southwest Asia and transferred massive amounts of wealth and power to the Mediterranean, transforming it into a more unified world of economic and cultural exchange.

Alexandria Port city in Egypt named after Alexander the Great. Alexandria was a model city in the Hellenistic world. It was built up by a multiethnic population from around the Mediterranean world.

Al-Khwarizmi Scientist and mathematician who lived from 780 to 850 CE and is known for having modified Indian digits into Arabic numerals.

Allied Powers Name given to the alliance between Britain, France, Russia, and Italy, who fought against Germany, Austria-Hungary, and the Ottoman Empire (the Central Powers) in World War I. In World War II the name was used for the alliance between Britain, France, and America, who fought against the Axis Powers (Germany, Italy, and Japan).

allomothering System by which mothers rely on other women, including their own mothers, daughters, sisters, and friends, to help in the nurturing and protection of children.

alluvium Area of land created by river deposits.

alphabet A writing system in which each character ideally represents a single sound. The first full alphabet was developed by the Phoenicians in the mid-second millenium BCE and consists of 22 letters (all of them consonants).

American Railway Union Workers' union that initiated the Pullman Strike of 1894, which led to violence and ended in the leaders' arrest.

Amnesty International Nongovernmental organization formed to defend "prisoners of conscience"—those detained for their beliefs, race, sex, ethnic origin, language, or religion.

Amorites Name that Mesopotamian urbanites called the transhumant herders from the Arabian desert. Around 2300 BCE, the Amorites, along with the Elamites, were at the center of newly formed dynasties in southern Mesopotamia.

Amun Once insignificant Egyptian god elevated to higher status by Amenemhet (1991–1962 BCE). *Amun* means "hidden" in ancient Egyptian; the name was meant to convey the god's omnipresence.

Analects Texts that include the teachings and cultural ideals of Confucius.

anarchism Belief that society should be a free association of its members, not subject to government, laws, or police.

Anatolia Now mainly the area known as modern Turkey. In the sixth millennium BCE, people from Anatolia, Greece, and the Levant took to boats and populated the Aegean. Their small villages endured almost unchanged for two millennia.

ancestral worship Religious practice in which the living honor their dead ancestors through rituals, believing that the dead intervene with their powers on behalf of the living.

Angkor Wat Magnificent Khmer Vaishnavite temple that crowned the royal palace in Angkor. It had statues representing the Hindu pantheon of gods.

Anglo-Boer War (1899–1902) War in South Africa between the British and the Afrikaners over the gold-rich Transvaal. In response to the Afrikaners' guerrilla tactics and in order to contain the local population, the British instituted the first concentration camps. Ultimately, Britain won the conflict.

animal domestication Gradual process that occurred simultaneously with or just before the domestication of plants, depending on the region.

annals Historical records. Notable annals are the cuneiform inscriptions that record successful Assyrian military campaigns.

Anti-Federalists Critics of the U.S. Constitution who sought to defend the people against the power of the federal government and insisted on a bill of rights to protect individual liberties from government intrusion.

apartheid Racial segregation policy of the Afrikaner-dominated South African government. Legislated in 1948 by the Afrikaner National Party, it existed in South Africa for many years.

Arab-Israeli War of 1948–1949 Conflict between Israeli and Arab armies that arose in the wake of a UN vote to partition Palestine into Arab and Jewish territories. The war shattered the legitimacy of Arab ruling elites.

Aramaic Dialect of a Semitic language spoken in Southwest Asia; it became the lingua franca of the Persian Empire.

Aristotle (384–322 BCE) Philosopher who studied under Plato but came to different conclusions about nature and politics. Aristotle believed in collecting observations about nature and discerning patterns to ascertain how things worked.

Aryans Nomadic charioteers who spoke Indo-European languages and entered South Asia in 1500 BCE. The early Aryan settlers were herders.

Asante state State located in present-day Ghana, founded by Akan-speaking peoples at the end of the seventeenth century. It grew in power in the next century because of its access to gold and its involvement in the slave trade.

ascetic One who rejects material possessions and physical pleasures.

Asiatic Society Cultural organization founded by British Orientalists who supported native culture but still believed in colonial rule.

Aśoka Emperor of the Mauryan dynasty from 268 to 231 BCE. A great conqueror and unifier of India, he is said to have embraced Buddhism toward the end of his life.

Assur One of two cities on the upper reaches of the Tigris River that were the heart of Assyria proper (the other was Nineveh).

Aśvaghosa First known Sanskrit writer. He may have lived from 80 to 150 CE and may have composed a biography of the Buddha.

Ataturk, Mustafa Kemal (1881–1938) Ottoman army officer and military hero who helped forge the modern Turkish nation-state. He and his followers deposed the sultan, declared Turkey a republic, and constructed a European-like secular state, eliminating Islam's hold over civil and political affairs.

Atlantic system New system of trade and expansion that linked Europe, Africa, and the Americas. It emerged in the wake of European voyages across the Atlantic Ocean.

Atma Vedic term signifying the eternal self, represented by the trinity of deities.

Atman In the Upanishads, an eternal being who exists everywhere. The atman never perishes but is reborn or transmigrates into another life.

Attila Sole ruler of all Hunnish tribes from 433 to 453 CE. Harsh and much feared, he formed the first empire to oppose Rome in northern Europe.

Augustus Title meaning "Revered One," assumed in 27 BCE by the Roman ruler Octavian (63–14 BCE). This was one of many titles he assumed; others included *imperator*, *princeps*, and *caesar*.

australopithecines Hominin species that appeared 3 million years ago and, unlike other animals, walked on two legs. Their brain capacity was a little less than one-third that of a modern human's, or about the size of the brain capacity of today's African apes. Although not humans, they carried the genetic and biological material out of which modern humans would later emerge.

Austro-Hungarian Empire New configuration of the Austrian Empire in which Hungary received greater autonomy; established in 1867, it collapsed at the end of World War I.

authoritarianism Centralized and dictatorial form of government, proclaimed by its adherents to be superior to parliamentary democracy and especially effective at mobilizing the masses. This thinking was widely accepted in parts of the world during the 1930s.

Avesta Compilation of holy works transmitted orally by Zoroastrian priests for millennia and eventually recorded in the ninth century CE.

axial age Term often used to describe the pivotal period of the first millennium BCE, when radical thinkers across the "second-generation societies" of Afro-Eurasia—including the Greek philosophers of the Mediterranean, Zoroaster in Southwest Asia, Buddha in South Asia, and Confucius and Master Lao in East Asia—offered dramatically new ideas that challenged their times.

Axis Powers The three aggressor states in World War II: Germany, Japan, and Italy.

Aztec Empire Mesoamerican empire that originated with a league of three Mexica cities in 1430 and gradually expanded through the Central Valley of Mexico, uniting numerous small, independent states under a single monarch who ruled with the help of counselors, military leaders, and priests. By the late fifteenth century, the Aztec realm may have embraced 25 million people. In 1521, they were defeated by the conquistador Hernán Cortés.

baby boom Post–World War II upswing in U.S. birthrates; it reversed a century of decline.

Bactria A Hellenistic kingdom that broke away from the Seleucids around 200 BCE to establish a state in the Gandhara region of modern Pakistan, which served as a bridge between South Asia and the Mediterranean Greek world.

bactrian camel Two-humped animal domesticated in central Asia around 2500 BCE. The bactrian camel was heartier than the one-humped dromedary and became the animal of choice for the harsh and varied climates typical of Silk Road trade.

Baghdad Capital of the Islamic Empire under the Abbasid dynasty, founded in 762 CE (in modern-day Iraq). In the medieval period, it was a center of administration, scholarship, and cultural growth for what came to be known as the Golden Age of Islamic science.

Baghdad Pact (1955) Middle Eastern military alliance between countries friendly with America who were willing to align themselves with the western countries against the Soviet Union.

Balam Na Stone temple and place of pilgrimage for the Maya people of Mexico's Yucatán Peninsula.

Balfour Declaration Letter (November 2, 1917) by Lord Arthur J. Balfour, British foreign secretary, that promised a homeland for the Jews in Palestine.

Bamboo Annals Shang stories and foundation myths that were written on bamboo strips and later collected.

Bantu Language first spoken by people who lived in the southeastern area of modern Nigeria around 1000 CE.

Bantu migrations Waves of rapid population movement from West Africa into eastern and southern Africa during the first millennium CE that brought advanced agricultural practices to these regions and absorbed most of the preexisting hunting and gathering populations.

barbarian Originally a relatively neutral Greek term for non-Greek speakers, it evolved into a derogatory term used by other cultures to describe outsiders, often pastoral nomads, painting them as enemies of civilization.

barbarian invasions Violent migration of people in the late fourth and fifth centuries CE into Roman territory. These migrants had long been used as non-Roman soldiers.

basilicas Early church buildings, based on old royal audience halls.

Battle of Adwa (1896) Battle in which the Ethiopians defeated Italian colonial forces. It inspired many of Africa's later national leaders.

Battle of Wounded Knee (1890) Bloody massacre of Sioux Ghost Dancers by U.S. armed forces.

Bay of Pigs (1961) Unsuccessful invasion of Cuba by Cuban exiles supported by the U.S. government. The invaders intended to incite an insurrection in Cuba and overthrow the communist regime of Fidel Castro.

Bedouins Nomadic pastoralists in the deserts of the Middle East.

Beer Hall Putsch (1923) Failed Nazi attempt to capture Bavarian leaders in a Munich beer hall, a prelude to a planned seizure of power in Germany. Adolf Hitler was imprisoned for a year after the incident.

Beghards (1500s) Eccentric European group whose members claimed to be in a state of grace that allowed them to do as they pleased—from adultery, free love, and nudity to murder; also called Brethren of Free Speech.

bell beaker Ancient drinking vessel, an artifact from Europe, so named because its shape resembles an inverted bell.

Berenice of Egypt Egyptian "queen" who helped rule over the Kingdom of the Nile from 320 to 280 BCE.

Beringia Prehistoric thousand-mile-long land bridge that linked Siberia and North America (which had not been populated by hominins). About 18,000 years ago, *Homo sapiens* edged into this landmass.

Berlin Airlift (1948) Supply of vital necessities to West Berlin by air transport primarily under U.S. auspices. It was initiated in response to a land and water blockade of the city instituted by the Soviet Union in the hope that the Allies would be forced to abandon West Berlin.

Berlin Wall Wall built by the communists in Berlin in 1961 to prevent citizens of East Germany from fleeing to West Germany; torn down in 1989.

bhakti Religious practice that grew out of Hinduism and emphasizes personal devotion to gods.

Bhakti Hinduism Popular form of Hinduism that emerged in the seventh century. The religion stresses devotion (*bhakti*) to God and uses vernacular languages (not Sanskrit) spoken by the common people.

big men Leaders of the extended household communities that formed village settlements in African rain forests.

big whites French plantation owners in Saint Domingue (present-day Haiti) who created one of the wealthiest slave societies.

Bilad al-Sudan Arabic for "the land of the blacks"; it consisted of the land lying south of the Sahara.

bilharzia Debilitating waterborne illness. It was widespread in Egypt, where it infected peasants who worked in the irrigation canals.

Bill of Rights First ten amendments to the U.S. Constitution; ratified in 1791.

bipedalism Walking on two legs, thereby freeing hands and arms to carry objects such as weapons and tools; one of several traits that distinguish hominins.

Black Death Great epidemic of the bubonic plague that ravaged Europe, East Asia, and North Africa in the fourteenth century, killing large numbers, including perhaps as many as 65 percent of the European population.

Black Jacobins Name employed by a West Indian historian for the rebels in Saint Domingue, including Toussaint L'Ouverture, a former slave who led the slaves of this French colony in the world's largest and most successful slave insurrection.

Black Panthers Radical African American group in the 1960s and 1970s who advocated black separatism and pan-Africanism.

black shirts Fascist troops of Mussolini's regime. The squads received money from Italian landowners to attack socialist leaders.

Black Tuesday (October 29, 1929) Historic day when the U.S. stock market crashed, plunging the United States and international trading systems into crisis and leading the world into the Great Depression.

blitzkrieg "Lightning war"; type of warfare in which the Germans, during World War II, used coordinated aerial bombing campaigns along with tanks and infantrymen in motorized vehicles.

bodhisattvas In Mahayana Buddhism, enlightened demigods who were ready to reach *nirvana* but delayed so that they might help others attain it.

Bolívar, Simón (1783–1830) Venezuelan leader who urged his followers to become "American," to overcome their local identities. He wanted the liberated countries to form a Latin American confederation, urging Peru and Bolivia to join Venezuela, Ecuador, and Colombia in the "Gran Colombia."

Bolsheviks Former members of the Russian Social Democratic Party who advocated the destruction of capitalist political and economic institutions and overthrew the Provisional Government in the second phase of the Russian Revolution of 1917. In 1918, the Bolsheviks changed their name to the Russian Communist Party.

Bonaparte, Napoleon (1769–1821) French military leader who rose to power in a postrevolutionary coup d'état, eventually proclaiming himself emperor of France. He placed security and order ahead of social reform and created a civil legal code. Napoleon expanded his empire through military action, but after his disastrous Russian campaign, the united European powers defeated him and forced him into exile. Napoleon escaped and reassumed command of his army but was later defeated at the Battle of Waterloo.

Book of the Dead Ancient Egyptian funerary text that contains drawings and paintings as well as spells describing how to prepare the jewelry and amulets that were buried with a person in preparation for the afterlife.

bourgeoisie The middle class, defined not by birth or title, but by capital and property.

Boxer Protocol Written agreement between the victors of the Boxer Uprising and the Qing Empire in 1901 that placed western troops in Beijing and required the regime to pay exorbitant damages for foreign life and property.

Boxer Uprising (1899–1900) Chinese peasant movement that opposed foreign influence, especially that of Christian missionaries; it was put down after the Boxers were defeated by an army composed mostly of the Japanese, Russians, British, French, and Americans.

Brahma One of three major deities that form a trinity in Vedic religion. Brahma signifies birth. *See also* Vishnu *and* Siva.

Brahmans Vedic priests who performed rituals and communicated with the gods. Brahmans provided guidance on how to live in balance with the forces of nature as represented by the various deities. The codification of Vedic principles into codes of law took place at the hands of the Brahmans. They memorized Vedic works and compiled commentaries on them. They also developed their own set of rules and rituals, which developed into a full-scale theology. Originally memorized and passed on orally, these may have been written down sometime after the beginning of the Common Era. Brahmanism was reborn as Hinduism sometime during the first half of the first millennium CE.

British Commonwealth of Nations Union formed in 1926 that conferred "dominion status" on Britain's white settler colonies in Canada, Australia, and New Zealand.

British East India Company *See* East India Company.

bronze Alloy of copper and tin brought into Europe from Anatolia; used to make hard-edged weapons.

brown shirts Informal name for the men who joined the Nazi SA (Sturmabteilung); they participated in mass rallies and street brawls, persecuting Jews, communists, and others who opposed the Nazis.

bubonic plague Acute infectious disease caused by a bacterium that is transmitted to humans by fleas from infected rats; sometimes referred to as the "Black Death." It ravaged Europe and parts of Africa and Asia in the fourteenth century.

Buddha (Siddhartha Gautama; 563–483 BCE) Indian ascetic who founded Buddhism.

Buddhism Major South Asian religion that aims to end human suffering through the renunciation of desire, derived from the teachings of Siddhartha Gautama, the Buddha (563–483 BCE). Buddhists believe that removing the illusion of a separate identity will lead to a state of contentment (nirvana). These beliefs challenged the traditional Brahmanic teachings of the time and provided the peoples of South Asia with an alternative to established traditions.

bullion Uncoined gold or silver.

Byzantium Modern term for the eastern Roman Empire (lasting from the fourth to the fifteenth century), centered at its "new Rome," Constantinople (founded by emperor Constantine in 324 CE on the site of a Greek city, Byzantium).

Cahokia Commercial center for regional and long-distance trade in North America. Its hinterlands produced staples for urban consumers. In return, its crafts were exported inland by porters and to North American markets in canoes. *See also* "Mound people."

calaveras Allegorical skeleton drawings by the Mexican printmaker and artist José Guadalupe Posada. The works drew on popular themes of betrayal, death, and festivity.

caliphate Institution that arose as the successor to Muhammad's leadership and became both the political and religious head of the Islamic community. Although the caliphs exercised political authority over the Muslim community and were the head of the religious community, the *umma,* they did not inherit Muhammad's prophetic powers and were not authorities in religious doctrine.

Calvin, Jean (1509–1564) A French theologian during the Protestant Reformation. Calvin developed a Christianity that emphasized moral regeneration through church teachings, laid out a doctrine of predestination, and established Calvinist dominance in Geneva, Switzerland.

Candomblé Yoruba-based religion in northern Brazil; it interwove African practices and beliefs with Christianity.

Canton system System officially established by imperial decree in 1759 that required European traders to have Chinese guild merchants act as guarantors for their good behavior and payment of fees.

caravan city Commercial hub of long-distance trade, where groups of merchants could assemble during their journeys. Several of these developed into full-fledged cities, especially in the deserts of Arabia.

caravans Companies of men who transported and traded goods along overland routes in North Africa and central Asia. Large caravans consisted of 600 to 1,000 camels and as many as 400 men.

caravansarais Inns along major trade routes that accommodated large numbers of traders, their animals, and their wares.

caravel Sailing vessel suited for nosing in and out of estuaries and navigating in waters with unpredictable currents and winds.

carrack Ship used on open bodies of water, such as the Mediterranean.

Carthage City in what is modern-day Tunisia; emblematic of the trading aspirations and activities of merchants in the Mediterranean. Pottery and other archaeological remains demonstrate that Carthaginian trading contacts were as far-flung as Italy, Greece, France, Iberia, and West Africa.

cartography Mapmaking.

caste system Hierarchical social system of organizing people and distributing labor.

Caste War of the Yucatán (1847–1901) Conflict between Maya Indians and the Mexican state over Indian autonomy and legal equality, which resulted in the Mexican takeover of the Yucatán Peninsula.

Castro, Fidel (1926–2016) Cuban communist leader whose forces overthrew Batista's corrupt regime in early January 1959. Castro became increasingly radical as he consolidated power, announcing a massive redistribution of land and the nationalization of foreign oil refineries. He declared himself a socialist and aligned himself with the Soviet Union in the wake of the 1961 CIA-backed Bay of Pigs invasion.

Çatal Hüyük Site in Anatolia discovered in 1958. It was a dense honeycomb of settlements filled with rooms whose walls were covered with paintings of wild bulls, hunters, and pregnant women. Çatal Hüyük symbolizes an early transition into urban dwelling and dates to the eighth millennium BCE.

Cathedra Bishop's seat, or throne, in a church.

Catholic Church Unifying institution for Christians in western Europe after the collapse of the Roman Empire. Rome became the spiritual capital of western Europe, and the bishops of Rome emerged as popes, the supreme head of the church, who possessed great moral authority.

Cato the Elder (234–149 BCE) Roman statesman, often seen as emblematic of the transition from a Greek to a Roman world. Cato the Elder wrote a manual for the new economy of slave plantation agriculture, invested in shipping and trading, learned Greek rhetoric, and added the genre of history to Latin literature.

caudillos South American local military chieftains.

cave drawings Images on cave walls. The subjects are most often large game, although a few are images of humans. Other elements are impressions made by hands dipped in paint and pressed on a wall or abstract symbols and shapes.

Celali revolts (1595–1610) Peasant and artisan uprisings against the Ottoman state.

Central Powers Defined in World War I as Germany, Austria-Hungary, and the Ottoman Empire.

Chan Chan City founded between 850 and 900 CE by the Moche people in what is now modern-day Peru. It had a core population of 30,000 inhabitants.

Chandra Gupta II King who reigned in South Asia from 320 to 335 CE. He shared his name with Chandragupta, the founder of the Mauryan Empire.

Chandravamsha One of two main lineages (the lunar one) of Vedic society, each with its own creation myth, ancestors, language, and rituals. Each lineage included many clans. *See* Suryavanha.

Chan Santa Cruz Separate Maya community formed as part of a crusade for spiritual salvation and the complete cultural separation of the Maya Indians; means "little holy cross."

chapatis Flat, unleavened Indian bread.

chariots Horse-driven carriages brought by the pastoral nomadic warriors from the steppes that became the favored mode of warfare and transportation for an urban aristocratic warrior class and for other men of power in agriculture-based societies. Control of chariot forces was the foundation of the new balance of power across Afro-Eurasia during the second millennium BCE.

charismatic Person who uses personal strengths or virtues, often laced with a divine aura, to command followers.

Charlemagne King of the Franks from 768 CE, king of the Lombards from 774 CE, and emperor of the Romans from 800 CE until his death in 814 CE.

chartered companies Firms that were awarded monopoly trading rights over vast areas by European monarchs (e.g., Virginia Company, Dutch East India Company).

Chartism (1834–1848) Mass democratic movement to pass the Peoples' Charter in Britain, granting male suffrage, secret ballot, equal electoral districts, and annual parliaments and absolving the requirement of property ownership for members of the parliament.

chattel slavery Form of slavery that sold people as property, the rise of which coincided with the expansion of city-states. Chattel slavery was eschewed by the Spartans, who also rejected the innovation of coin money.

Chavín A people who lived in what is now northern Peru from 1400 to 200 BCE. They were united more by culture and faith than by a unified political system.

Chernobyl Site in the Soviet Union (in Ukraine) of the 1986 meltdown of a nuclear reactor.

Chiang Kai-shek (1887–1975) Leader of the Guomindang following Sun Yat-sen's death. Chiang mobilized the Chinese masses through the New Life movement. In 1949, he lost to the communists and moved his regime to Taiwan.

Chimú Empire South America's first empire; it developed during the first century of the second millennium in the Moche Valley on the Pacific coast.

chinampas Floating gardens used by the Aztecs in the 1300s and 1400s to grow crops.

China's Sorrow Name given to the Yellow River, which, when it changed course or flooded, could cause mass death and waves of migration.

chinoiserie Chinese silks, teas, tableware, jewelry, and paper, popular among Europeans in the seventeenth and eighteenth centuries.

Christendom Entire portion of the world in which Christianity prevailed.

Christianity Religion that originated at the height of the Roman Empire and in direct confrontation with Roman imperial authority, founded by Yeshua ben Yosef (Joshua son of Joseph, known today by the Greek form of his name, Jesus), whom the Romans condemned for sedition and crucified. In the fourth century CE, Christianity was officially recognized as the Roman state religion.

Church of England Official form of Christianity established in England when Henry VIII broke with Rome during the Reformation. The English monarch, not the pope, is the head of this church.

city Highly populated concentration of economic, religious, and political power. The first cities appeared in river basins, which could produce a surplus of agriculture. The abundance of food freed most city inhabitants from the need to produce their own food, which allowed them to work in specialized professions.

city-state Political organization based on the authority of a single, large city that controls outlying territories.

Civil Rights Act (1964) U.S. legislation that banned segregation in public facilities, outlawed racial discrimination in employment, and marked an important step in correcting legal inequality.

civil rights movement Powerful movement for equal rights and the end of racial segregation in the United States that began in the 1950s with nonviolent boycotts and court victories against school segregation.

civil service examinations The world's first written civil service examination system, instituted by the Tang dynasty to recruit officials and bureaucrats. Open to most males, the exams tested a candidate's literary skills and knowledge of the Confucian classics. They helped to unite the Chinese state by making knowledge of a specific language and Confucian classics the only route to power.

Civil War, American (1861–1865) Conflict between the northern and southern states of America, leading to the abolition of slavery in the United States.

clan A social group comprising many households claiming descent from a common ancestor.

clandestine presses Small printing operations, especially in Switzerland and the Netherlands, that published banned texts in the early modern era.

closing of the frontier In 1893, responding to the recent U.S. Census, the historian Frederick Jackson Turner popularized the idea that the western frontier—so long crucial to the making of American identity—had closed. His announcement spurred many to worry that having lost the manliness and self-reliance nurtured by the hard life on the frontier, Americans would grow soft and weak.

Clovis people Early humans in America who used basic chipped blades and pointed spears in pursuing prey. They extended the hunting traditions they had learned in Afro-Eurasia, such as establishing campsites and moving with their herds. They were known as Clovis people because the arrowhead point that they used was first found by archaeologists at a site near Clovis, New Mexico.

Code of Manu Part of the handiwork of Brahman priests; a representative code of law that incorporated social sanctions and practices and provided guidance for living within the caste system.

codex Early form of book, with separate pages bound together; it replaced the scroll as the main medium for written texts. The codex emerged around 300 CE.

cognitive skills Skills such as thought, memory, problem solving, and—ultimately—language. Hominins were able to use these skills and their hands to create new adaptations, like tools that helped them obtain food and avoid predators.

Cohong Chinese merchant guild that traded with Europeans under the Qing dynasty.

coins Form of money that replaced goods, which previously had been bartered for services and other products. Originally used mainly to hire mercenary soldiers, coins became the commonplace method of payment linking buyers and producers throughout the Mediterranean.

Cold War (1945–1990) Ideological conflict in which the Soviet Union and eastern Europe opposed the United States and western Europe.

colonies Regions under the political control of another country.

colons French settler population in Algeria.

Colosseum Huge amphitheater, originally begun by Flavian and completed by Titus, which was dedicated in 80 CE. The structure is named after a colossal statue of Nero that formerly stood beside it.

Columbian exchange Movement between Afro-Eurasia and the Americas of previously unknown plants, animals, people, diseases, and products that followed in the wake of Columbus's voyages.

commanderies Provinces. Shi Huangdi (First August Emperor) divided China into commanderies (*jun*) to enable the Qin dynasty to rule the massive state effectively. The thirty-six commanderies were then subdivided into counties (*xian*).

Communist Manifesto Pamphlet published by Karl Marx and Friedrich Engels in 1848 at a time when political revolutions were sweeping Europe. It called on the workers of all nations to unite in overthrowing capitalism.

compass Navigation instrument invented by the Chinese and used to determine directions with a magnetized needle, which always points to the north cardinal direction on the compass rose.

Compromise of 1867 Agreement between the Habsburgs and the Austrian Empire's Hungarian population that gave the Hungarian lands more autonomy; the empire was now renamed the Austro-Hungarian Empire.

concession areas Territories, usually ports, where Chinese emperors allowed European merchants to trade and European people to settle.

Confucian ideals The ideals of honoring tradition, emphasizing the responsibility of the emperor, and respect for the lessons of history, promoted by Confucius, which the Han dynasty made the official doctrine of the empire by 50 BCE.

Confucianism Ethics, beliefs, and practices stipulated by the Chinese philosopher Kong Qiu, or Confucius, which served as a guide for Chinese society up to modern times.

Confucius (551–479 BCE) Influential teacher, thinker, and leader in China who developed a set of principles for ethical living. He believed that coercive laws and punishment would not be needed to maintain order in society if men following his ethics ruled. He taught his philosophy to anyone who was intelligent and willing to work, which allowed men to gain entry into the ruling class through education.

Congo Free State Large colonial state in Africa created by Leopold II, king of Belgium, during the 1880s, and ruled by him alone. After rumors of mass slaughter and enslavement, the Belgian parliament took the land and formed a Belgian colony.

Congress of Vienna (1814–1815) International conference to reorganize Europe after the downfall of Napoleon. European monarchies agreed to respect each other's borders and to cooperate in guarding against future revolutions and war.

cong tube Ritual object crafted by the Liangzhu. A cong tube was made of jade and was used in divination practices.

conquistadors Spanish military leaders who led the conquest of the New World in the sixteenth century.

Constantine Roman emperor who converted to Christianity in 312 CE. In 313 CE, he issued a proclamation that gave Christians new freedoms in the empire. He also founded Constantinople (at first called "New Rome").

Constantinople Capital city, formerly known as Byzantium, which was founded as the New Rome by Constantine the Great.

Constitutional Convention (1787) Meeting to formulate the Constitution of the United States of America.

Contra rebels Opponents of the Sandinistas in Nicaragua. They were armed and financed by the United States and other anti-communist countries (1980).

Conversion of Constantine Inspired by a dream to arm his soldiers with shields bearing Christ's name, the Emperor Constantine won a decisive battle for Rome in 312 CE. Afterward, he issued a proclamation giving privileges to Christian bishops, which began the process of spreading Christianity throughout the Roman Empire.

conversos Jewish and Muslim converts to Christianity in the Iberian Peninsula and the New World.

Coptic Form of Christianity practiced in Egypt. It was doctrinally different from Christianity elsewhere, and Coptic Christians had their own views of Christology, or the nature of Christ.

Corn Laws Laws that imposed tariffs on grain imported to Great Britain, intended to protect British farming interests. The Corn Laws were abolished in 1846 as part of a British movement in favor of free trade.

cosmology Branch of metaphysics devoted to understanding the order of the universe.

cosmopolitans The inhabitants of the multiethnic cities that thrived in the Hellenistic world, literally meaning "citizens belonging to the whole world" as opposed to a particular city-state.

Council of Nicaea Church council convened in 325 CE by Constantine and presided over by him as well. At this council, a Christian creed was articulated and made into a formula that expressed the philosophical and technical elements of Christian belief.

Counter-Reformation Movement initiated by the Catholic Church at the Council of Trent in 1545 with the aim of countering the spread of the Reformation. The Catholic Church enacted reforms to attack clerical corruption and placed a greater emphasis on individual spirituality. During this time, the Jesuits were founded to help revive the Catholic Church.

coup d'état Overthrow of the established state by a group of conspirators, usually from the military.

creation narratives Various accounts of the creation of the universe and humankind's place in it, conceived by virtually all peoples.

creed Formal statement of faith or expression of a belief system. A Christian creed, or "credo," was formulated by the Council of Nicaea in 325 CE.

creoles Persons of full-blooded European descent who were born in the Spanish American colonies.

Crimean War (1853–1856) War waged by Russia against Great Britain and France. Spurred by Russia's encroachment on Ottoman territories, the conflict revealed Russia's military weakness when Russian forces fell to British and French troops.

crossbow Innovative weapon used at the end of the Warring States period that allowed archers to shoot their enemies with accuracy, even from a distance.

Crusades Wave of attacks launched in the late eleventh century by western Europeans. The First Crusade began in 1095, when Pope Urban II appealed to the warrior nobility of France to free Jerusalem from Muslim rule. Four subsequent Crusades were fought over the next two centuries.

Cuban Missile Crisis (1962) Diplomatic standoff between the United States and the Soviet Union that was provoked by the Soviet Union's attempt to base nuclear missiles in Cuba; it brought the world close to a nuclear war.

cult Religious movement, often based on the worship of a particular god or goddess.

cultigen Organism that has diverged from its ancestors through domestication or cultivation.

cuneiform Wedge-shaped form of writing, used primarily by the Sumerian, Assyrian, and Persian Empires. By impressing these signs into wet clay with the cut end of a reed, scribes engaged in cuneiform.

Cyrus the Great Founder of the Persian Empire. This sixth-century ruler (559–529 BCE) conquered the Medes and unified the Iranian kingdoms.

Daimyo Ruling lords who commanded private armies in pre-Meiji Japan.

dan Fodio, Usman (1754–1817) Fulani Muslim cleric whose visions led him to challenge the Hausa ruling classes, whom he believed were insufficiently faithful to Islamic beliefs and practices. His ideas gained support among those who had suffered under the Hausa landlords. In 1804, his supporters and allies overthrew the Hausa in what is today northern Nigeria.

Daoism School of thought developed at the end of the Warring States period that focused on the importance of following the Dao, or the natural way of the cosmos. Daoism emphasized the need to accept the world as it was rather than trying to change it through politics or the government. Unlike Confucianism, Daoism scorned rigid rituals and social hierarchies.

Dar al-Islam Arabic for "the House of Islam"; it describes the territories ruled by Muslims and is contrasted with *Dar al-Harb*, the land of war, not yet under Islamic rule.

Darius I (521–486 BCE) Leader who put the emerging unified Persian Empire on solid footing after Cyrus's death.

Darwin, Charles (1809–1882) British scientist who became convinced that the species of organic life had evolved under the uniform pressure of the laws of natural selection, not by means of a special, one-time creation as described in the Bible.

D-Day (June 6, 1944) Day of the Allied invasion of Normandy under General Dwight Eisenhower to liberate western Europe from German occupation.

Dear Boy Nickname of an early human remain (an almost totally intact skull) discovered in 1931 by archaeologists Mary and Louis Leakey. Other objects discovered with Dear Boy demonstrated that by the time of Dear Boy, early humans had begun to fashion tools and to use them for butchering animals and possibly for hunting and killing smaller animals.

Decembrists Russian army officers who were influenced by events in revolutionary France and formed secret societies that espoused liberal governance. They were put down by Nicholas I in December 1825.

Declaration of Independence U.S. document stating the theory of government on which the United States was founded.

Declaration of the Rights of Man and Citizen (1789) French charter of liberties formulated by the National Assembly that marked the end of dynastic and aristocratic rule. The seventeen articles later became the preamble to the new constitution, which the assembly finished in 1791.

decolonization End of empire and emergence of new independent states in Asia and Africa as a result of anticolonial nationalism, the weakening of the European colonial powers in World War II, and the rise of the United States and the USSR as superpowers after the war, both of whom favored ending imperial rule.

degeneration In the later 19th century, many Europeans began to fear that Darwin had been wrong: urbanization, technology, racial hybridity, the emergence of the "modern" woman, and over-refinement were causing Europeans not to progress as a species, but to degenerate. This fear was often combined with anxieties about colonialism, homosexuality, emigration, and/or the advancement of women.

Delhi Sultanate (1206–1526) Muslim Turkish regime of northern India. The regime strengthened the cultural diversity and tolerance that were a hallmark of the Indian social order, which allowed it to bring about political integration without enforcing cultural homogeneity.

democracy The idea that people, through membership in a nation, should choose their own representatives and be governed by them.

Democritus Thinker in ancient Greece who lived from 470 to 360 BCE. He deduced the existence of the atom, postulating that there was such a thing as an indivisible particle.

demotic writing The second of two basic forms of ancient Egyptian writing. Demotic was a cursive script written with ink on papyrus, on pottery, or on other absorbent objects. It was the most common and practical form of writing in Egypt and was used for administrative record keeping and in private or pseudo-private forms like letters and works of literature. *See also* hieroglyphs.

developing world Term applied to countries collectively called the Third World during the Cold War; countries seeking to develop viable nation-states and prosperous economies.

devshirme System of taking non-Muslim children in place of taxes in order to educate them in Ottoman Muslim ways and prepare them for service in the sultan's bureaucracy.

dhamma Moral code espoused by Aśoka in the Kalinga edict, which was meant to apply to all—Buddhists, Brahmans, and Greeks alike.

dhimma system Muslim law and practice that permitted followers of religions other than Islam, such as Christians, Jews, and Zoroastrians, and later Buddhists and Hindus, to choose their own religious leaders and to settle internal disputes within their religious communities as long as they accepted Islam's political dominion.

dhows Ships used by Arab seafarers. The dhow's large sails were rigged to maximize the capture of wind.

Dien Bien Phu (1954) Defining battle in the war between French colonialists and the Viet Minh that secured North Vietnam for Ho Chi Minh and his army and left the south to form its own government to be supported by France and the United States.

Din-I-llahi "House of worship" in which the Mughal emperor Akbar engaged in religious debate with Hindu, Muslim, Jain, Parsi, and Christian theologians.

Diogenes Greek philosopher who lived from 412 to 323 BCE and who espoused a doctrine of self-sufficiency and freedom from social laws and customs. He rejected cultural norms as out of tune with nature and therefore false.

Directory Temporary military committee that took over the affairs of the state of France in 1795 from the radicals and held control until the coup of Napoleon Bonaparte.

divination The interpretation of rituals used to communicate the wishes of gods or royal ancestors to foretell future events. Divination was used to legitimize royal authority and demand tribute.

Djoser Ancient Egyptian king who reigned from 2630 to 2611 BCE. He was the second king of the Third Dynasty and celebrated the Sed festival in his tomb complex at Saqqara.

domestication Bringing wild plants and animals under human control.

Dominion in the British Commonwealth Canadian promise to keep up the country's fealty to the British crown, even after its independence in 1867. It later applied to Australia and New Zealand.

Dong Zhongshu Emperor Wu's chief minister, who advocated a more powerful view of Confucius by promoting texts that focused on Confucius as a man who possessed aspects of divinity.

double-outrigger canoes Vessels used by early Austronesians to cross the Taiwan Straits and colonize islands in the Pacific. These sturdy canoes could cover over 120 miles per day.

Duma Russian parliament, first convened in 1906.

Dutch learning Broad term for European teachings that were strictly regulated by the shoguns inside Japan.

dynastic cycle Political narrative in which influential families vied for supremacy. Upon gaining power, they legitimated their authority by claiming to be the heirs of previous grand dynasts and by preserving or revitalizing the ancestors' virtuous governing ways. This continuity conferred divine support.

dynasty Hereditary ruling family that passed control from one generation to the next.

Earth Summit (1992) Meeting in Rio de Janeiro between many of the world's governments in an effort to address international environmental problems.

Eastern Front Battlefront between Berlin and Moscow during World War I and World War II.

East India Company (1600–1858) British charter company created to outperform Portuguese and Spanish traders in the Far East; in the eighteenth century, the company became, in effect, the ruler of a large part of India.

Edict of Nantes (1598) Edict issued by Henry IV to end the French Wars of Religion. The edict declared France a Catholic country but tolerated some Protestant worship. It was revoked by Louis XIV in 1685.

Egyptian Middle Kingdom Period of Egyptian history lasting from about 2040 to 1640 BCE, characterized by a consolidation of power and building activity in Upper Egypt.

Eiffel Tower Steel monument completed in 1889 for the Paris Exposition. It was twice the height of any other building at the time.

eight-legged essay Highly structured essay form with eight parts, required on Chinese civil service examinations.

Ekklesia Church or early gathering committed to leaders chosen by God and fellow believers.

Ekpe Powerful slave trade institution that organized the supply and purchase of slaves inland from the Gulf of Guinea in West Africa.

Elamites A people with their capital in the upland valley of modern Fars who became a cohesive polity that incorporated transhumant people of the Zagros Mountains. A group of Elamites who migrated south and west into Mesopotamia helped conquer the Third Dynasty of Ur in 2400 BCE.

empire Group of states or different ethnic groups under a single sovereign power.

Enabling Act (1933) Emergency legislation, enacted just after Hitler became German chancellor (prime minister), that undermined parliamentary democracy in Germany by giving the chancellor the right to dictate legislation without the approval of the Reichstag (German parliament). This legislation paved the way for Hitler's dictatorship.

enclosure A movement in which landowners took control of lands that traditionally had been common property serving local needs.

encomenderos Commanders of the labor services of the colonized peoples in Spanish America.

encomiendas Grants from European Spanish governors to *encomenderos* control the labor services of colonized people.

Endeavor Ship of Captain James Cook, whose celebrated voyages to the South Pacific in the late eighteenth century supplied Europe with information about the plants, birds, landscapes, and people of this uncharted territory.

Engels, Friedrich (1820–1895) German social and political philosopher who collaborated with Karl Marx on many publications, including *The Communist Manifesto*.

English Navigation Act of 1651 Act stipulating that only English ships could carry goods between the mother country and its colonies.

English Peasants' Revolt (1381) Uprising of serfs and free farmworkers that began as a protest against a tax levied to raise money for a war on France. The revolt was suppressed but led to the gradual emergence of a free peasantry as labor shortages made it impossible to keep peasants bound to the soil.

enlightened absolutists Seventeenth- and eighteenth-century monarchs who claimed to rule rationally and in the best interests of their subjects and who hired loyal bureaucrats to enact enlightened policies.

Enlightenment Intellectual movement in late seventeenth- and eighteenth-century Europe stressing natural laws and reason as the basis of authority.

entrepôts Trading stations at the borders between communities, which made exchange possible among many different partners. Long-distance traders could also replenish their supplies at these stations.

Epicurus (341–279 BCE) Greek philosopher who espoused emphasis on the self. He founded a school in Athens called The Garden and stressed the importance of sensation, teaching that pleasurable sensations were good and painful sensations bad. Members of his school sought to find peace and relaxation by avoiding unpleasantness or suffering.

Estates-General French quasi-parliamentary body called in 1789 to deal with the financial problems that afflicted France. It had not met since 1614.

Etruscans A dominant people on the Italian Peninsula until the fourth century BCE. The Etruscan states were part of the foundation of the Roman Empire.

eunuchs Loyal and well-paid men who were surgically castrated as youths and remained in service to the caliph or emperor. Both Abbasid and Tang rulers relied for protection on a cadre of eunuchs.

Eurasia The combined area of Europe and Asia.

European Union (EU) Western European organization that evolved out of post-1945 efforts to prevent warfare in Europe, initially by forging closer economic cooperation.

evolution Process by which the different species of the world—its plants and animals—make changes in response to their environment that enable them to survive and increase in numbers.

Exclusion Act of 1882 U.S. congressional act prohibiting nearly all immigration from China to the United States; fueled by animosity toward Chinese workers in the American West.

Ezo Present-day Hokkaido, Japan's fourth main island.

fascism Mass political movement founded by Benito Mussolini that emphasized nationalism, militarism, and the omnipotence of the state.

fascists Radical right-wing groups of disaffected citizens, often veterans of World War I, that were opposed to democracy and favored rule by a single leader. Fascist movements triumphed in Italy, Germany, Spain, Japan, and several central European countries after World War I.

Fatehpur Sikri Mughal emperor Akbar's temporary capital near Agra.

Fatimids Shiite dynasty that ruled parts of the Islamic Empire beginning in the tenth century CE. The Fatimids arose in North Africa, where they conquered Egypt and founded the city of Cairo.

February Revolution (1917) The first of two uprisings of the Russian Revolution, which led to the end of the Romanov dynasty. It ended with the forming of a Provisional Government under Alexander Kerensky.

Federal Deposit Insurance Corporation (FDIC) Organization created in 1933 to guarantee all bank deposits up to $5,000 as part of the New Deal in the United States.

Federalists Supporters of the ratification of the U.S. Constitution, which was written to replace the Articles of Confederation.

Federal Republic of Germany (1949–1990) Country formed of the areas occupied by the Allies after World War II. Also known as West Germany, this country experienced rapid demilitarization, democratization, and integration into the world economy.

Federal Reserve Act (1913) U.S. legislation that created a series of boards to monitor the supply and demand of the nation's money.

feminist movements Movements that call for equal treatment for men and women—equal pay and equal opportunities for obtaining jobs and advancement. Feminism arose mainly in Europe and in North America in the 1960s and then became global in the 1970s.

Ferangi Word taken from the Arabic word for "Franks," but referring to Europeans in general and widely used to describe the European Crusaders.

Fertile Crescent Site of the world's first agricultural revolution; an area in Southwest Asia, bounded by the Mediterranean Sea in the west and the Zagros Mountains in the east.

feudalism System instituted in medieval Europe after the collapse of the Carolingian Empire (888 CE) whereby each peasant was under the authority of a lord and typically owed him fees and/or service in exchange for protection and the right to live and work on his lands.

fiefdoms Medieval economic and political units.

First World Term invented during the Cold War to refer to western Europe and North America (also known as the "free world" or the west); Japan later joined this group. Following the principles of liberal modernism, First World states sought to organize the world on the basis of capitalism and democracy.

five pillars of Islam The five tenets, or main aspects, of Islamic practice: testification, or bearing witness, that there is no God other than God (Allah, in Arabic) and that Muhammad is the messenger of God; praying five times a day; fasting from sunup to sundown every day during Ramadan (a month on the Islamic calendar); giving alms; and making a pilgrimage to Mecca.

Five-Year Plan Soviet effort launched under Stalin in 1928 to replace the market with a state-owned and state-managed economy, to promote rapid economic development over a five-year period of time and thereby "catch and overtake" the leading capitalist countries. The First Five-Year Plan was followed by the Second Five-Year Plan (1933–1937), and so on, until the collapse of the Soviet Union in 1991. Because of the seeming Soviet economic successes, five-year plans became popular in many developing countries as a way to promote economic growth.

Flagellants European social group that came into existence during the bubonic plague in the fourteenth century. They believed that the plague was the wrath of God.

floating population Poor migrant workers in China who supplied labor under Emperor Wu.

Fluitschips Dutch shipping vessels that could carry heavy bulky cargo with relatively small crews.

flying cash Letters of exchange—early predecessors of paper cash instead of coins—first developed by guilds in the northwestern Shanxi. By the thirteenth century, paper money had eclipsed coins.

fondûqs Complexes in caravan cities that included hostels, storage houses, offices, and temples.

Forbidden City of Beijing Palace city of the Ming and Qing dynasties.

Force Publique Colonial army used to maintain order in the Belgian Congo.

During the early stages of King Leopold's rule, it was responsible for bullying local communities.

Fourierism Form of utopian socialism based on the ideas of Charles Fourier (1772–1837). Fourier envisioned communes where work was made enjoyable and systems of production and distribution were run without merchants. His ideas appealed to middle-class readers, especially women, as a higher form of Christian communalism.

free labor Wage-paying rather than slave labor.

free markets Unregulated markets.

Free Officers Movement Secret organization of Egyptian junior military officers led by Gamal Abdel Nasser that came to power in a coup d'état in 1952, forced King Faruq to abdicate, and consolidated control through dissolving the parliament, banning opposing parties, and rewriting the constitution.

free trade Domestic and international trade unencumbered by tariff barriers, quotas, and fees.

Front de Libération Nationale **(FLN)** Algerian anticolonial, nationalist party that waged an eight-year war against French troops, beginning in 1854, that forced nearly all of the 1 million colonists to leave.

Fulani A widespread ethnic group in West Africa, some of whose members embraced Islam and carried out religious revolts at the end of the eighteenth and the beginning of the nineteenth centuries in an effort to return to the pure Islam of the past.

fur trade Trading of animal pelts (especially beaver skins) by Indians for European goods in North America.

Gandharan art Buddhist sculptures, particularly from the northern Kushan territory, that show a high degree of Greek and Roman influences.

Gandhi, Mohandas Karamchand (Mahatma) (1869–1948) Indian leader who led a nonviolent struggle for India's independence from Britain.

garrisons Military bases, often built inside cities and often used for political purposes, such as protecting rulers, putting down domestic revolts, or enforcing colonial rule.

garrison towns Stations for soldiers originally established in strategic locations to protect territorial acquisition. Eventually, they became towns. Alexander the Great's garrison towns evolved into cities that served as centers from which Hellenistic culture was spread to his easternmost territories.

gauchos Argentine, Brazilian, and Uruguayan cowboys who wanted a decentralized federation, with autonomy for their provinces and respect for their way of life.

Gdansk shipyard Site of mass strikes in Poland that led in 1980 to the formation of the first independent trade union, Solidarity, in the communist bloc.

gendered relations A relatively recent hypothesis that gender roles emerged only with the appearance of modern humans and perhaps Neanderthals. When humans began to think imaginatively and in complex symbolic ways and give voice to their insights, perhaps around 150,000 years ago, gender categories began to crystallize.

genealogy History of the descent of a person or family from a distant ancestor.

Geneva Peace Conference (1954) International conference to restore peace in Korea and Indochina. The chief participants were the United States, the Soviet Union, Great Britain, France, the People's Republic of China, North Korea, South Korea, Vietnam, the Viet Minh party, Laos, and Cambodia. The conference resulted in the division of North and South Vietnam.

Genoa One of two Italian cities (the other was Venice) that linked Europe, Africa, and Asia as nodes of commerce in 1300 CE. Genoese ships linked the Mediterranean to the coast of Flanders through consistent routes along the Atlantic coasts of Spain, Portugal, and France.

German Democratic Republic Nation founded from the Soviet zone of occupation of Germany after World War II; also known as East Germany.

German Social Democratic Party Founded in 1875, the most powerful socialist party in Europe before 1917.

Ghana The most celebrated medieval political kingdom in West Africa and later the name of the first independent black African state.

Ghost Dance American Indian ritual performed in the nineteenth century in the hope of restoring the world to precolonial conditions.

Gilgamesh Heroic narrative written in the Babylonian dialect of Semitic Akkadian. This story and others like it were meant to circulate and unify the kingdom.

Girondins Liberal revolutionary group that supported the creation of a constitutional monarchy during the early stages of the French Revolution.

globalization Development of integrated worldwide cultural and economic structures.

globalizing empires Empires, such as the Han and the Roman, that covered immense amounts of territory, included huge, diverse populations; exerted influence beyond their own borders; and worked to integrate conquered peoples.

global warming Worldwide rising temperatures caused in large part by the release into the air of human-made carbons.

Gold Coast Name that European mariners and merchants gave to that part of West Africa from which gold was exported. This area was conquered by the British in the nineteenth century and became a British colony; upon independence, it became Ghana.

Goths One of the groups of "barbarian" migrants into Roman territory in the fourth century CE.

government schools Schools founded by the Han dynasty to provide an adequate number of officials to fill positions in the administrative bureaucracy. The Imperial University had 30,000 members by the second century BCE.

Gracchus brothers Two tribunes, the brothers Tiberius and Gaius Gracchus, who in 133 and 123–121 BCE attempted to institute land reforms that would guarantee all of Rome's poor citizens a basic amount of land that would qualify them for army service. Both men were assassinated.

Grand Canal Created in 486 BCE, a thousand-mile-long connector between the Yellow and Yangzi Rivers, linking the north and south, respectively.

grand unity Guiding political idea embraced by Qin rulers and ministers, with an eye toward joining the states of the Central Plain into one empire and centralizing administration.

"greased cartridge" controversy Controversy spawned by the rumor that cow and pig fat had been used to grease the ammunition to be used by sepoy gunners in the British army in India. Believing that this was a British attempt to defile their religion and speed their conversion to Christianity, the sepoys mutinied against their British officers and led a widespread revolt against British rule in 1857.

Great Depression Worldwide depression following the U.S. stock market crash on October 29, 1929.

great divide The division between economically developed nations and less developed nations.

Great East Asia Co-Prosperity Sphere Term used by the Japanese during the 1930s and 1940s to refer to Hong Kong, Singapore, Malaya, Burma, and other states that they seized during their run for expansion.

Great Flood One of many traditional Mesopotamian stories that were transmitted orally from one generation to another before being recorded. The Sumerian King List refers to this crucial event in Sumerian memory and identity. The Great Flood was thought to have led to Uruk's demise as punishment by the gods.

Great Game Competition for economic or political control of areas such as Turkistan, Persia (present-day Iran), and Afghanistan. The British (in India) and the Russians believed that controlling these areas was crucial to preventing their enemies' expansion.

Great League of Peace and Power Iroquois Indian alliance that united previously warring communities.

Great Leap Forward (1958–1961) Plan devised by Mao Zedong to achieve rapid agricultural and industrial growth in China. The plan failed miserably, and more than 20 million people died.

great plaza at Isfahan The center of Safavid power in the seventeenth century created by Shah Abbas (r. 1587–1629) to represent the unification of trade, government, and religion under one supreme political authority.

Great Proletarian Cultural Revolution (1966–1976) Mass mobilization of urban Chinese youth inaugurated by Mao Zedong in an attempt to reinvigorate the Chinese Revolution and to prevent the development of a bureaucratized Soviet style of communism. With this movement, Mao turned against his longtime associates in the Communist Party.

Great Trek Afrikaner migration to the interiors of Africa after the British abolished slavery in the empire in 1833.

Great War (August 1914–November 1918) Also known as World War I. A total war involving the armies of Britain, France, and Russia (the Allies) against those of Germany, Austria-Hungary, and the Ottoman Empire (the Central Powers). Italy joined the Allies in 1915, and the United States joined them in 1917, helping tip the balance in favor of the Allies, who also drew on the populations and material of their colonial possessions.

Greek Orthodoxy Enduring form of Christianity that arose in the "Roman" state inherited from Constantine and Justinian and eventually split off from the Roman Catholic Church. The Greek Orthodox capital was Constantinople, and its spiritual empire included the Russian peoples, Baltic Slavs, and peoples living in southwest Asia.

Greek philosophers "Wisdom lovers" of the ancient Greek city-states, including Socrates, Plato, Aristotle, and others, who pondered such issues as self-knowledge, political engagement and withdrawal, and the order of the world.

Greenbacks Members of the American political party of the late nineteenth century that worked to advance the interest of farmers by promoting cheap money.

griots Counselors and other officials serving royal families in African kingdoms and also in small-scale states. They were also responsible for the preservation and transmission of oral histories and repositories of knowledge.

Group Areas Act (1950) Act that divided South Africa into separate racial and tribal areas and required Africans to live in their own separate communities, including the "homelands."

guerrillas Small groups engaged in irregular fighting against larger regular forces; after the French word *guerre*.

guest workers Migrants looking for temporary employment abroad.

gulag Administrative name for the forced labor and "reeducation" camps established first by the Soviet Union and then by other Soviet-style socialist countries. Penal labor was required of both ordinary criminals (rapists, murderers, thieves) and those accused of political crimes (counterrevolution, anti-Soviet agitation).

Gulf War (1991) Armed conflict between Iraq and a coalition of thirty-two nations, including the United States, Britain, Egypt, France, and Saudi Arabia. It was started by Iraq's invasion of Kuwait, which it had long claimed, on August 2, 1990.

gunpowder Explosive powder. By 1040, the first gunpowder recipes were being written down. Over the next 200 years, Song entrepreneurs invented several incendiary devices and techniques for controlling explosions.

gunpowder empires Muslim empires of the Ottomans, Safavids, and Mughals that used cannonry and gunpowder to advance their military causes.

Guomindang Nationalist party of China, founded just before World War I by Sun Yat-sen and later led by Chiang Kai-shek.

Habsburg dynasty Powerful medieval monarchs whose hereditary lands lay along the Danube River, but whose domains also included, for a time, Spain and the Low Countries. Habsburg princes were regularly elected Holy Roman Emperors. In 1556, Charles V abdicated and divided the empire, and the Habsburgs, into a Spanish branch and an Austrian branch. In 1867, the Austrian Empire was reorganized into the Austro-Hungarian Dual Monarchy, and in 1918 it collapsed.

Hadith Sayings attributed to the Prophet Muhammad and his early converts, used to guide the behavior of Muslim peoples.

Hagia Sophia Enormous and impressive church sponsored by Justinian and built starting in 532 CE. At the time, it was the largest church in the world.

hajj Pilgrimage to Mecca; an obligation for Muslims.

Hammurapi's Code Legal code created by Hammurapi, the most famous of the Mesopotamian rulers, who reigned from 1792 to 1750 BCE. Hammurapi sought to create social order by centralizing state authority and creating a grand legal structure that embodied paternal justice. The code was quite stratified, dividing society into three classes: free men, dependent men, and slaves, each with distinct rights and responsibilities.

Han agrarian ideal Guiding principle for the free peasantry that made up the base of Han society. In this system, peasants were honored for their labors, while merchants were subjected to a range of controls, including regulations on luxury consumption, and were belittled for not engaging in physical labor.

Han Chinese Inhabitants of China proper who considered others to be outsiders. They felt that they were the only authentic Chinese.

Han Fei Chinese state minister who lived from 280 to 233 BCE; he was a proponent and follower of Xunzi.

Hangzhou City and former provincial seaport that became the political center of the Chinese people in their ongoing struggles with northern steppe nomads. It was also one of China's gateways to the rest of the world by way of the South China Sea.

Han military Like its Roman counterpart, a ruthless military machine that expanded the empire and created stable conditions that permitted the safe transit of goods by caravan. Emperor Wu heavily influenced the transformation of the military forces and reinstituted a policy that made military service compulsory.

Hannibal Great Roman general from Carthage whose campaigns in the third century BCE swept from Spain toward the Italian Peninsula. He crossed the Pyrenees and the Alps mountain ranges with war elephants. He was unable, however, to defeat the Romans in 217 BCE.

Harappa One of two cities (the other was Mohenjo Daro) that, by 2500 BCE, began to take the place of villages throughout the Indus River valley. Each city covered an area of about 250 acres and probably housed 35,000 residents.

harem Secluded women's quarters in Muslim households.

Harlem Renaissance Cultural movement in the 1920s that was based in Harlem, a part of New York City with a large African American population; also referred to as the "New Negro Movement." The movement gave voice to black novelists, poets, painters, and musicians, many of whom used their art to protest racism.

harnesses Tools made from wood, bone, bronze, and iron for steering and controlling horses. Harnesses discovered by archaeologists reveal the evolution of headgear from simple mouth bits to full bridles with headpiece, mouthpiece, and reins.

Hatshepsut Ancient Egypt's most powerful woman ruler. Hatshepsut served as regent and pharaoh for her young son, Thutmosis III, whose reign began in 1479 BCE. She remained co-regent until her death.

Haussmannization Redevelopment and beautification of urban centers; named after the city planner who modernized mid-nineteenth-century Paris.

Heian period Period from 794 to 1185 CE, during which began the pattern of regents ruling Japan in the name of the sacred emperor.

Hellenism Process by which the individuality of the cultures of the earlier Greek city-states gave way to a uniform culture that stressed the common identity of all who embraced Greek ways. This culture emphasized the common denominators of language, style, and politics to which anyone anywhere in the Afro-Eurasian world could have access.

hieroglyphs One of two basic forms of Egyptian writing that were used in conjunction throughout antiquity. Hieroglyphs are pictorial symbols; the term derives from a Greek word meaning "sacred carving"—they were employed exclusively in temple, royal, and divine contexts. *See also* demotic writing.

Hijra Tradition of Islam whereby one withdraws from one's community to create another, more holy one. The practice is based on the Prophet Muhammad's withdrawal from the city of Mecca to Medina in 622 CE.

Hinayana (Lesser Vehicle) Buddhism Form of Buddhism that accepted the divinity of Buddha himself but not of demigods, or bodhisattvas.

Hinduism A refashioning of the ancient Brahmanic Vedic religion, bringing it in accord with rural life and agrarian values. It emerged as the dominant faith in Indian society in the third century CE. Believers became vegetarians and adopted rituals of self-sacrifice. Three major deities—Brahma, Vishnu, and Siva—formed a trinity representing the three phases of the universe (birth, existence, and destruction, respectively) and the three expressions of the eternal self, or *atma*.

Hindu revivalism Movement to reconfigure traditional Hinduism to be less diverse and more amenable to producing a narrowed version of Indian tradition.

Hiroshima Japanese port devastated by an atomic bomb on August 6, 1945.

Hitler, Adolf (1889–1945) German dictator and leader of the Nazi Party who seized power in Germany after its economic collapse in the Great Depression. Hitler and his Nazi regime started World War II in Europe and systematically murdered Jews and other non-Aryan groups in the name of racial purity.

Hittites One of the five great territorial states. The Hittites campaigned throughout Anatolia, then went east to northern Syria, though they eventually faced weaknesses in their own homeland. Their heyday was marked by the reign of the king Supiliulimua (1380 to 1345 BCE), who preserved the Hittites' influence on the balance of power in the region between Mesopotamia and the Nile.

Holocaust Deliberate racial extermination of the Jews by the Nazis that claimed the lives of approximately 6 million European Jews.

Holy Roman Empire Enormous confederation of polities that encompassed much of central Europe and aspired to be the Christian successor state to the Roman Empire. It was headed by a Holy Roman Emperor, usually a Habsburg prince, selected by elite lower-level sovereigns. Despite its size, the empire never effectively centralized power.

Holy Russia Name applied to Muscovy and then to the Russian Empire by Slavic Eastern Orthodox clerics who were appalled by the Muslim conquest in 1453 of Constantinople (the capital of Byzantium and of Eastern Christianity) and who were hopeful that Russia would become the new protector of the faith.

home charges Fees India was forced to pay to Britain as its colonial master. These fees included interest on railroad loans, salaries to colonial officers, and the maintenance of imperial troops outside India.

hominins Humanlike beings who walked erect and are represented today only by modern humans.

Homo Genus that includes modern ("true") humans and species of premodern hominins.

Homo caudatus "Tailed man," believed by some European Enlightenment thinkers to be an early species of humankind.

Homo erectus Species that emerged about 1.5 million years ago and had a large brain and walked truly upright. *Homo erectus* means "standing man."

Homo habilis Species name meaning "skillful man." Toolmaking ability made *Homo habilis* the forerunners, though very distant, of modern humans.

Homo sapiens The first humans; they emerged in a small region of Africa about 200,000 years ago and migrated out of Africa about 100,000 years ago. They had bigger brains and greater dexterity than previous hominin species, whom they eventually eclipsed. *Homo sapiens* means "wise man."

horses Animals used by full-scale nomadic communities to dominate the steppe lands in western Afro-Eurasia by the second millennium BCE. Horse-riding nomads moved their large herds across immense tracts of land within zones defined by rivers, mountains, and other natural geographical features. In the arid zones of central Eurasia, the nomadic economies made horses a crucial component of survival.

Huguenots French Protestants who endured severe persecution in the sixteenth and seventeenth centuries.

humanism The Renaissance aspiration to know more about the human experience beyond what the Christian scriptures offered by reaching back into ancient Greek and Roman texts.

Hundred Days' Reform (1898) Abortive modernizing reform program of the Qing government of China.

hunting and gathering Lifestyle in which food is acquired through hunting animals, fishing, and foraging for wild berries, nuts, fruit, and grains, rather than planting crops, vines, or trees. As late as 1500, as much as 15 percent of the world's population still obtained food by this method.

Hyksos A western Semitic-speaking people whose name means "Rulers of Foreign Lands"; they overthrew the unstable Thirteenth Dynasty in Egypt around 1640 BCE. The Hyksos had mastered the art of horse chariots, and with those chariots and their superior bronze axes and composite bows (made of wood, horn, and sinew), they were able to defeat the pharaoh's foot soldiers.

Ibn Sina Persian philosopher and physician who lived from 980 to 1037 CE. He was also schooled in the Quran, geometry, literature, and Indian and Euclidian mathematics. He was known in Europe as Avicenna.

ideology Dominant set of ideas of a widespread culture or movement.

Il Duce Term designating the fascist Italian leader Benito Mussolini.

Iliad Epic Greek poem about the Trojan War attributed to Homer and completed several centuries after the events it describes. It was based on oral tales passed down for generations.

Il-khanate Mongol-founded dynasty in the thirteenth century and based in Persia.

imam Muslim religious leader among Sunni Muslims. Shiites believe that imams are the rightful successors to the Prophet Muhammad through Ali, the son-in-law of Muhammad, and accord them much greater political and religious legitimacy than the Sunnis do.

imperialism Acquisition of new territories by a state and the incorporation of those territories into a political system as subordinate colonies.

Imperial University University founded in 136 BCE by Emperor Wu. Important discoveries and advances were made here, including rational diagnoses of the body's functions, the magnetic compass, and high-quality paper. The university was a mechanism by which the Han state inculcated Confucian thought into the elite.

imperium Latin word used to express Romans' power and command over their subjects. It is the basis of the English words *empire* and *imperialism*.

Inca Empire Empire of Quecha-speaking rulers in the Andean valley of Cuzco that encompassed a population of 4 to 6 million. The Incas lacked a clear inheritance system, causing an internal split that Pizarro's forces exploited in 1533.

Indian Institutes of Technology (IIT) Institutions originally designed as engineering schools to expand knowledge and to modernize India, which produced a whole generation of pioneering computer engineers, many of whom moved to the United States.

Indian National Congress Formed in 1885, an anticolonial party deeply committed to constitutional methods, nonviolent protest, and cultural nationalism.

Indian National Muslim League Founded in 1906, an organization dedicated to advancing the political interests of Muslims in India.

Indo-Greek Fusion of Indian and Greek culture in the area under the control of the Bactrians, in the northwestern region of India, around 200 BCE.

Indu What we would today call India. It was called "Indu" by Xuanzang, a Chinese Buddhist pilgrim who visited the area in the 630s and 640s CE.

indulgences Church-sponsored fund-raising mechanism that gave certification that one's sins had been forgiven in return for money.

industrial revolution Gradual accumulation and diffusion of old and new technical knowledge that led to major economic changes in Britain at the end of the eighteenth century and spread to northwestern Europe and North America in the nineteenth century. The industrial revolution catapulted these countries ahead of the rest of the world in manufacturing and agricultural output and standard of living.

industrious revolution Interpretation of seventeenth- and eighteenth-century economic change, developed by Jan de Vries, that attributes the origins of the industrial revolution to northern European householders' decisions to work harder and longer hours to produce more for the market, enabling them to increase their income and standard of living.

innovation Creation of a new method that allows humans to make better adaptations to their environment. Toolmaking was an important innovation.

Inquisition Tribunal of the Roman Catholic Church that enforced religious orthodoxy during the Protestant Reformation.

internal and external alchemy In Daoist ritual, use of trance and meditation (internal) or chemicals and drugs (external) to cause transformations in the self.

International Monetary Fund (IMF) Agency founded in 1944 to help restore financial order in Europe and the rest of the world, to revive international trade, and to support the financial concerns of Third World governments.

invisible hand As described in Adam Smith's *The Wealth of Nations*, the idea that the operations of a free market produce economic efficiency and economic benefits for all.

iron Malleable metal found in combined forms almost everywhere in the world. It became the most important and widely used metal in world history after the Bronze Age.

Iron Curtain Term popularized by Winston Churchill after World War II to refer to the political, economic, and ideological division within Europe between western Europe, under American influence, and eastern Europe, under the domination of the Soviet Union.

irrigation The supply of water, other than through rainfall, to land and crops, often by means of water sluices and channels in river floodplains, to increase agricultural production.

Islam A religion that dates to 610 CE, when Muhammad believed God came to him in a vision. Islam ("submission"—in this case, to the will of God) requires its followers to act righteously, to submit themselves to the one and only true God, and to care for the less fortunate. Muhammad's most insistent message was the oneness of God, a belief that has remained central to the Islamic faith ever since.

Jacobins Radical French political group that came into existence during the French Revolution and executed the French king and sought to remake French culture.

Jacquerie A general term for peasant revolts, taken from the 1358 French peasant revolt against nobles and their restrictions.

jade The most important precious substance in East Asia. Jade was associated with goodness, purity, luck, and virtue and was carved into such items as ceremonial knives, blade handles, religious objects, and elaborate jewelry.

Jagat Seths Enormous trading and banking empire in eastern India.

Jainism Along with Buddhism, one of the two systems of thought developed in the seventh century BCE that set themselves up against Brahmanism. Its founder, Vardhamana Mahavira, taught that the universe obeys its own everlasting rules that no god or other supernatural being could affect. The purpose of life was to purify one's soul in order to attain a state of permanent bliss, which could be accomplished through self-denial and the avoidance of harming other creatures.

Janissaries Corps of infantry soldiers recruited as children from the Christian provinces of the Ottoman Empire and brought up with intense loyalty to Islam, the Ottoman state, and its sultan. The Ottoman sultan used these forces to clip local autonomy and to serve as his personal bodyguards.

Jati Social groups as defined by Hinduism's caste system.

Jesuits Religious order founded by Ignatius Loyola in Spain in the middle of the sixteenth century to counter the inroads of the Protestant Reformation. The Jesuits, or the Society of Jesus, were active in politics, education, and missionary work.

jihad Literally, "striving" or "struggle." This word also connotes military efforts or "striving in the way of God." It also came to mean spiritual struggles against temptation or inner demons, especially in Sufi, or mystical, usage.

Jih-pen Chinese for "Japan."

Jim Crow laws Laws that codified racial segregation and inequality in the southern part of the United States after the Civil War.

jizya Special tax that non-Muslims were forced to pay to their Islamic rulers in return for which they were given security and property and granted cultural autonomy.

jong Large oceangoing vessels, built by Southeast Asians, which plied the regional trade routes from the fifteenth century to the early sixteenth century.

Judah The southern kingdom of David, which had been an Assyrian vassal until 612 BCE, when it became a vassal of Assyria's successor, Babylon, against whom the people of Judah rebelled, resulting in the destruction of Jerusalem in the sixth century BCE.

Julius Caesar (100–44 BCE) Formidable Roman general who was also a man of letters and a great orator. He incited a civil war in 49 BCE; victorious, he seized power and began a series of populist reforms. He was assassinated by Senators who feared he was becoming a dictator in 44 BCE.

junks Trusty seafaring vessels used in the South China Seas after 1000 CE. These vessels helped make shipping by sea less dangerous.

Justinian Roman (Byzantine) emperor who ascended to the throne in 527 CE. In addition to his many building projects and military expeditions, he issued a new law code.

Kabuki Theater performance that combines song, dance, and skillful staging to dramatize conflicts between duty and passion; originated in Tokogawa, Japan.

kamikaze Japanese for "divine winds" or typhoons, such as the storm that saved Japan from a Mongol attack. The term also was used for Japanese suicide bombers during World War II.

kanun Highly detailed system of Ottoman administrative law that jurists developed to deal with matters not treated in the religious law of Islam.

Karim Loose confederation of shippers banding together to protect convoys.

karma Literally, "fate" or "action" in Confucian thought; this is a universal principle of cause and effect.

Kassites Nomads who entered Mesopotamia from the eastern Zagros Mountains and the Iranian plateau as early as 2000 BCE. They gradually integrated into Babylonian society by officiating at temples. By 1745 BCE, they had asserted order over the region, and they controlled southern Mesopotamia for the next 350 years, creating one of the territorial states.

Keynesian Revolution Economic ideas developed by British economist John Maynard Keynes during the Great Depression, wherein the state took a greater role in managing the economy, stimulating it by increasing the money supply and creating jobs. These ideas were only adopted by state policymakers after World War II.

KGB Soviet political police and spy agency, formed as the Cheka soon after the Bolshevik coup in October 1917 and known during the Stalinist period as the NKVD. The KGB grew to more than 750,000 operatives with military rank by the 1980s.

khan Ruler who was acclaimed at an assembly of elites and supposedly descended from Chinggis Khan on the male line; those not descended from Chinggis continually faced challenges to their legitimacy.

Khanate Major political unit of the vast Mongol Empire. There were four Khanates, including the Yuan Empire in China, forged by Chinggis Khan's grandson Kubilai.

Kharijites Radical sect from the early days of Islam. The Kharijites seceded from the "party of Ali" (who themselves came to be known as the Shiites) because of disagreements over succession to the role of caliph. The Kharjites were known for their strict militant piety.

Khmers A people who created the most powerful empire in Southwest Asia between the tenth and thirteenth centuries in what is modern-day Cambodia.

Khomeini, Ayatollah Ruhollah (1902–1989) Iranian religious leader who used his traditional Islamic education and his training in Muslim ethics to accuse the shah's government of gross violations of Islamic norms. He also identified the shah's ally, America, as the Great Satan. The shah fled the country in 1979; in his wake, Khomeini established a theocratic state ruled by a council of Islamic clerics.

Khufu The second pharaoh of the Fourth Dynasty in ancient Egypt (2575–2465 BCE), who constructed the Great Pyramid, the largest stone structure in the world. The pyramid is located in an area called Giza, just outside modern-day Cairo.

Khusro I Anoshirwan Sasanian emperor who reigned from 530 to 579 CE. He was a model ruler and was seen as the personification of justice.

Kiev City that became one of the greatest cities of Europe after the eleventh century. It was built to be a small-scale Constantinople on the Dnieper River.

Kikuyu Kenya's largest ethnic group; organizers of a revolt against the British in the 1950s.

King, Martin Luther, Jr. (1929–1968) Civil rights leader who borrowed his most effective weapon—the commitment to nonviolent protest and the appeal to conscience—from Gandhi.

Kingdom of Awadh One of the most prized lands for annexation and the fertile, opulent, and traditional vestige of Mughal rule in India.

Kingdom of Jerusalem A Crusader state established in Palestine in 1099 CE after the First Crusade. The kingdom lasted until 1187, when it was destroyed by Saladin.

Kizilbash Mystical, Turkish-speaking tribesmen who facilitated the Safavid rise to power.

Knossos Area in Crete where, during the second millennium BCE, a primary palace town existed.

Koine **Greek** Common form of Greek that became the international spoken and written language in the Hellenistic world. This was a simpler everyday form of the ancient Greek language.

Köprülü reforms Reforms named after two grand viziers who revitalized the Ottoman Empire in the seventeenth century through administrative and budget trimming as well as by rebuilding the military.

Korean War (1950–1953) Cold War conflict between Soviet-backed North Korea and U.S.- and UN-backed South Korea. The two sides seesawed back and forth over the same boundaries until 1953, when an armistice divided the country at roughly the same spot as at the start of the war. Nothing had been gained. Losses, however, included 33,000 Americans, at least 250,000 Chinese, and up to 3 million Koreans.

Koryo dynasty Leading dynasty of the northern-based Koryo kingdom in Korea. It is from this dynasty that the name Korea derives.

Kremlin Once synonymous with the Soviet government; refers to Moscow's walled city center.

Kshatriyas The military caste, one of the four Hindu castes, which was supposed to protect society by fighting in times of warfare and governing in times of peace.

Kubilai Khan (1215–1294) Mongol leader who seized southern China after 1260 and founded the Yuan dynasty.

Ku Klux Klan Racist organization that first emerged in the U.S. South after the Civil War and then gained national strength as a radically traditionalist movement during the 1920s.

kulak Originally a pejorative word used to designate better-off peasants, the term used in the late 1920s and early 1930s to refer to any peasant, rich or poor, perceived as an opponent of the Soviet regime; Russian for "fist."

Kumarajiva Renowned Buddhist scholar and missionary who lived from 344 to 413 CE. He was brought to China by Chinese regional forces from Kucha, modern-day Xinjiang.

Kushans Northern nomadic group that migrated into South Asia in 50 CE. They unified the tribes of the region and set up the Kushan dynasty. The Kushans' empire embraced a large and diverse territory and played a critical role in the formation of the Silk Road.

Labour Party Founded in Britain in 1900, a party that has drawn its support from workers and has espoused moderately socialist principles.

laissez-faire The concept that the economy works best when it is left alone— that is, when the state does not regulate or interfere with the workings of the market.

"Land under the Yoke of Ashur" Lands not in Assyria proper, but under its authority. The inhabitants had to make exorbitant tribute payments to the Assyrian Empire.

language families Related tongues with a common ancestral origin. Language families contain languages that diverged from one another but share grammatical features and a root vocabulary. More than a hundred language families exist.

Laozi Also known as Master Lao; perhaps a contemporary of Confucius and the person after whom Daoism is named. His thought was elaborated upon by generations of thinkers.

latifundia Broad estates that produced goods for large urban markets, including wheat, grapes, olives, cattle, and sheep.

Laws of Manu Part of the handiwork of Brahman priests; a representative code of law that incorporated social sanctions and practices and provided guidance for living within the caste system.

League of Nations Organization founded after World War I to solve international disputes through arbitration; it was dissolved in 1946, and its assets were transferred to the United Nations.

Legalism Also called Statism, a system of thought about how to live an ordered life. It was developed by Master Xun, or Xunzi (310–237 BCE). It is based on the principle that people, being inherently inclined toward evil, require authoritarian control to regulate their behavior.

Lenin, Vladimir (1870–1924) Leader of the Bolshevik Revolution in Russia and the first leader of the Soviet Union.

Liangzhu Culture spanning centuries from the fourth to the third millennium BCE that represented the last New Stone Age culture in the Yangzi River delta. One of the Ten Thousand States, it was highly stratified and is known for its jade objects.

liberalism Political and social theory that advocates representative government, individual rights, free trade, and freedom of speech and religion.

limited-liability joint-stock company Company that mobilizes capital from a large number of investors, called shareholders, who were not to be held personally liable for financial losses incurred by the company.

Linear A and B Two linear scripts first discovered on Crete in 1900. On the island of Crete and on the mainland areas of Greece, documents of the palace-centered societies were written on clay tablets in these two scripts. Linear A script, apparently written in Minoan, has not yet been deciphered. Linear B was first deciphered in the early 1950s.

"Little Europes" Urban landscapes between 1100 and 1200 CE composed of castles, churches, and towns in what are today Poland, the Czech Republic, Hungary, and the Baltic states.

Little Ice Age Period of global cooling beginning at the close of the Medieval Warm Period and lasting for centuries. The most extreme drop in temperature was in the 1600s.

Liu Bang Chinese emperor from 206 to 195 BCE. After declaring himself the prince of his home area of Han, in 202 BCE, Liu declared himself the first Han emperor.

llamas Animals similar in utility and function to camels in Afro-Eurasia. Llamas can carry heavy loads for long distances.

Long March (1934–1935) Trek of over 10,000 kilometers by Mao Zedong and his communist followers to establish a new base of operations in northwestern China.

Longshan peoples Peoples who lived in small agricultural and river-basin villages in East Asia at the end of the third millennium BCE. They set the stage for the Shang in terms of a centralized state, urban life, and a cohesive culture.

lord Privileged landowner who exercised authority over the people who lived on his land.

lost generation The 17 million former members of the Red Guard and other Chinese youth who were denied education from the late 1960s to the mid-1970s as part of the Chinese government's attempt to prevent political disruptions.

Louisiana Purchase (1803) American purchase of French territory from Napoleon, including much of the present-day United States between the Mississippi River and the Rocky Mountains.

Lucy Relatively intact skeleton of a young adult female australopithecine unearthed in the valley of the Awash River in 1974 and nicknamed Lucy. Lucy walked upright at least some of the time, and her jaw and teeth were humanlike. Until recently, Lucy was the oldest hominin skeleton ever discovered.

Luftwaffe German air force.

Luther, Martin (1483–1546) A German monk and theologian who sought to reform the Catholic Church. He believed in salvation through faith alone, the importance of reading Scripture, and the priesthood of all believers. His Ninety-Five Theses, written in 1517, enumerated the abuses by the Catholic Church and catalyzed a movement that became the Protestant Reformation.

Maastricht Treaty (1992) Treaty that formed the European Union, an integrated trading and financial bloc with its own bureaucracy and elected representatives.

Ma'at Term used in ancient Egypt to refer to stability or order, the achievement of which was the primary task of Egypt's ruling kings, the pharaohs.

Maccabees Leaders of a riot in Jerusalem in 166 BCE. The riot was a response to a Roman edict outlawing the practice of Judaism.

Madhyamika (Middle Way) Buddhism Chinese branch of Mahayana Buddhism established by Kumarajiva (344–413 CE) that used irony and paradox to show that reason is limited.

madrassas Higher schools of Muslim education that taught law, the Quran, religious sciences, and the foreign sciences.

Mahayana Buddhism School of Buddhist theology that believed that the Buddha was a deity, unlike previous groups that had considered him a wise human being.

Mahdi The "chosen one" in Islam whose appearance was supposed to foretell the end of the world and the final day of reckoning for all people.

maize A grain crop, also known as corn, that the settled agrarian communities across the Americas cultivated, along with legumes (beans) and tubers (potatoes).

Maji-Maji Revolt (early 1900s) Swahili insurrection against German colonialists, inspired by the belief that those who were anointed with specially blessed water (*maji*) would be immune to bullets. It resulted in 200,000 to 300,000 African deaths.

Mali Empire West African empire, founded by the legendary king Sundiata in the early thirteenth century and lasting until the beginning of the seventeenth century. It facilitated thriving commerce, with routes linking the Atlantic Ocean, the Sahara, and beyond.

Mamluks Military men who ruled Egypt as an independent regime from 1250 until the Ottoman conquest in 1517.

Manaus Opera House Opera house built in the interior of Brazil in a lucrative rubber-growing area at the turn of the twentieth century.

Manchukuo Japanese puppet state in Manchuria in the 1930s.

Manchus Descendants of the Jurchens, who helped the Ming army recapture Beijing in 1644 after its seizure by the outlaw Li Zicheng. The Manchus numbered around 1 million but controlled a domain that included perhaps 250 million people. Their rule lasted more than 250 years and became known as the Qing dynasty.

mandate of heaven Ideology established by Zhou dynasts to communicate the moral transfer of power. Originally a pact between the Zhou people and their supreme god, it evolved in the first century BCE into Chinese political doctrine.

Mande A people who lived in the area between the bend in the Senegal River and the bend in the Niger River east to west and from the Senegal River and Bandama River north to south. Also known as the Mandinka, their civilization emerged around 1100 CE, and their merchants were deeply involved in long-distances trade throughout the region.

Mandela, Nelson (1918–2013) Leader of the African National Congress (ANC) who was imprisoned for more than two decades by the apartheid regime in South Africa for his political beliefs. Worldwide protests led to his release in 1990. In 1994, Mandela won the presidency in South Africa's first free mass elections.

Manifest Destiny Belief that it was God's will for the American people to expand their economic and political dominion across the North American continent.

manorialism System in which the manor (a lord's home, its associated industry, and surrounding fields) served as the basic unit of economic power; an alternative to feudalism (a term primarily used to describe political and hierarchical relationships of king, lords, and peasantry) for thinking about the nature of power in western Europe, 1000–1300.

Mao Zedong (1893–1976) Chinese communist leader who rose to power during the Long March (1934). In 1949, he defeated the Nationalists and established a communist regime in China. Mao's efforts to transform China, such as the industrialization program of 1958 (known as the Great Leap Forward) and the Cultural Revolution of 1966, failed and brought great suffering to the people, but he has been credited with instilling China with a sense of purpose after decades of political and economic weakness.

maroon community Sanctuary for runaway slaves in the Americas.

Marshall Plan Economic aid package given by the United States to certain European nations after World War II in hopes of a rapid period of reconstruction and economic gain, thereby securing those countries from a communist takeover.

martyrs People executed by the Roman authorities for persisting in their Christian beliefs and refusing to submit to pagan ritual or belief.

Marx, Karl (1818–1883) German philosopher and economist who, together with Friedrich Engels, founded the first International Working Mens' Association and developed the economic and political theories we now call Marxism.

Marxism Form of scientific socialism created by Karl Marx and Friedrich Engels that was rooted in a materialist theory of history: what mattered in history was what ordinary people ate and how they lived and worked, not political events or philosophies. Marx believed that capitalism enslaved workers, and he predicted that eventually a revolution of the working classes would overthrow the capitalist order and create a classless society.

mass consumption Increased purchasing power in the early twentieth-century prosperous and mainly middle-class societies, stemming from mass production.

mass culture Distinctive form of popular culture that arose in the wake of World War I. It reflected the tastes of the working and the middle classes, who now had more time and money to spend on entertainment, and relied on new technologies, especially film and radio, which could reach an entire nation's population and consolidate their sense of being a single state.

mass production System in which factories were set up to produce huge quantities of identical products, reflecting the early twentieth-century world's demands for greater volume, faster speed, reduced cost, and standardized output.

mastaba Word meaning "bench" in Arabic; it refers to a huge flat structure identical to earlier royal tombs of ancient Egypt.

Mau Mau Revolt (1952–1957) Kenyan uprising orchestrated by a guerrilla movement of the Kikuyu peoples. This conflict forced the British to grant independence to the black majority in Kenya.

Mauryan Empire Dynasty extended by the Mauryans from 321 to 184 BCE, from the Indus Valley to the northwest areas of South Asia, in a region previously controlled by Persia. It was the first large-scale empire in South Asia and was to become the model for future Indian empires.

Mawali Non-Arab "clients" attached to Arab patrons in the early Islamic Empire. Because patronage was so much a part of the Arabian cultural system, non-Arabs who converted to Islam affiliated themselves with extended Muslim families and became clients of those groups.

Maxim gun European weapon capable of firing many bullets per second; it was used against Africans in the conquest of the continent.

Maya Civilization that ruled over large stretches of Mesoamerica, composed of a series of kingdoms, each built around ritual centers rather than cities. The Maya were not defined by a great ruler or one capital city, but by their shared religious beliefs.

McCarthyism Campaign by Republican senator Joseph McCarthy in the late 1940s and early 1950s to uncover closet communists, particularly in the State Department and in Hollywood.

Meat Inspection Act (1906) Legislation that provided for government supervision of meat-packing operations. It was part of the broader Progressive Movement dedicated to correcting the negative consequences of urbanization and industrialization in the United States.

Mecca Arabian city in which Muhammad was born. Mecca was a trading center and pilgrimage destination in the pre-Islamic and Islamic periods. Exiled in 622 CE because of resistance to his message, Muhammad returned to Mecca in 630 CE and claimed the city for Islam.

Medes Rivals of the Assyrians and the Persians. The Medes inhabited the area from the Zagros Mountains to the modern city of Tehran. Although expert horsemen and archers, they were eventually defeated by the Persians.

megaliths Literally, "great stones." The word *megalith* is used when describing a structure such as Stonehenge, a massive structure that is the result of cooperative planning and work.

megarons Large buildings found in Troy (level II) that are the predecessors of the classic Greek temple.

Meiji Empire Empire created under the leadership of Mutsuhito, emperor of Japan from 1868 until 1912. During the Meiji period, Japan became a world industrial and naval power.

Meiji Restoration Reign of the Meiji emperor, which was characterized by a new nationalist identity, economic advances, and political transformation.

Mencius Disciple of Confucius who lived from 372 to 289 BCE.

mercantilism Economic theory developed in Europe in the seventeenth century based on the idea that the world had a fixed amount of wealth, which meant that one country's wealth came at the expense of another's. Mercantilism encouraged the placing of tariffs on imports and the founding of colonies to enrich the mother countries and in this way drove European empire building.

Mercosur Free trade pact between the governments of Argentina, Brazil, Paraguay, and Uruguay.

meritocracy Rule by persons of talent.

Meroe Ancient kingdom in what is today Sudan. It flourished for nearly a thousand years, from the fifth century BCE to the fifth century CE.

mestizos Mixed-blood offspring of Spanish settlers and native Indians.

métis Mixed-blood offspring of French settlers and native Indians.

Mexican Revolution (1910) Conflict fueled by the unequal distribution of land and by disgruntled workers; it erupted when political elites split over the succession of General Porfirio Díaz after decades of his rule. The fight lasted over ten years and cost 1 million lives, but it resulted in widespread reform and a new constitution.

Mfecane **movement** African political revolts in the first half of the nineteenth century that were caused by the expansionist methods of King Shaka of the Zulu people.

microsocieties Small-scale communities that had little interaction with others. These communities were the norm for peoples living in the Americas and islanders in the Pacific and Aegean from 2000 to 1200 BCE.

migration Long-distance travel for the purpose of resettlement. In the case of early humans, the need to move was usually a response to an environmental shift, such as climate change during the Ice Age.

millenarian Convinced of the imminent coming of a just and ideal society.

millenarian movement Broad, popular upheaval calling for the restoration of a bygone moral age, often led by charismatic spiritual prophets.

millets Minority religious communities of the Ottoman Empire.

minaret Slender tower within a mosque from which Muslims are called to prayer.

minbar Pulpit inside a mosque from which Muslim religious speakers broadcast their message to the faithful.

Minoans A people who built a large number of elaborate, independent palace centers on Crete, at Knossos, and elsewhere around 2000 BCE. Named after the legendary King Minos, said to have ruled Crete at the time, they sailed throughout the Mediterranean and by 1600 BCE had planted colonies on many Aegean islands, which in turn became trading and mining centers.

mission civilisatrice Term French colonizers used to refer to France's form of "rationalized" colonial rule, which attempted to bring "civilization" to the "uncivilized."

mitochondrial DNA Form of DNA found outside the nucleus of cells, where it serves as cells' microscopic power packs. Examining mitochondrial DNA enables researchers to measure the genetic variation among living objects, including human beings.

Moche A people who extended their power and increased their wealth at the height of the Chimu Empire over several valleys in what is now modern-day Peru.

Model T First automobile, manufactured by the Ford Motor Company, to be priced reasonably enough to be sold to the masses.

modernism Term used to describe artistic, literary, and scientific movements of the late nineteenth and early twentieth centuries that self-consciously broke with traditional rules, practices, and forms of thought.

modernists A generation of exuberant young artists, writers, and scientists in the late nineteenth century who broke with older conventions and sought new ways of seeing and describing the world.

Mohism School of thought in ancient China, named after Mo Di, or Mozi, who lived from 479 to 438 BCE. It emphasized one's obligation to society as a whole, not just to one's immediate family or social circle.

monarchy Political system in which one individual holds supreme power and passes that power on to his or her next of kin.

monasticism Christian way of life that originated in Egypt and was practiced as early as 300 CE in the Mediterranean. The word comes from the Greek *monos*, referring to a person "living alone" without marriage or family.

monetization An economic shift from a barter-based economy to one dependent on coin.

Mongols Combination of nomadic forest and prairie peoples who lived by hunting and livestock herding and were expert horsemen. Beginning in 1206, the Mongols launched a series of conquests that brought far-flung parts of the world together under their rule. By incorporating conquered peoples and adapting some of their customs, the Mongols created an empire of four khanate states that stretched from the Pacific Ocean to the shores of the eastern Mediterranean and the southern steppes of Eurasia.

monotheism The belief in only one god.

Moors Term employed by Europeans in the medieval period to refer to Muslim occupants of North Africa, the western Sahara, and the Iberian Peninsula.

mosque Place of worship for the people of Islam.

"Mound people" Name for the people of Cahokia, since the landscape was dominated by earthen monuments in the shapes of mounds. The mounds were carefully maintained and were the loci from which Cahokians paid respect to spiritual forces. *See also* Cahokia.

Mu Chinese ruler (956–918 BCE) who put forth a formal bureaucratic system of governance, appointing officials, supervisors, and military captains to whom he was not related. He also instituted a formal legal code.

muckrakers Journalists who aimed to expose political and commercial corruption in late nineteenth- and early twentieth-century America.

muftis Experts on Muslim religious law.

Mughal Empire One of Islam's greatest regimes. Established in 1526, it was a vigorous, centralized state whose political authority encompassed most of modern-day India. During the sixteenth century, it had a population of between 100 and 150 million.

Muhammad (c. 570–632 CE) Prophet and founder of the Islamic faith. Born in Mecca in the Arabian Peninsula and orphaned when young, Muhammad lived under the protection of his uncle. His career as a prophet began around 610 CE, with his first experience of spiritual revelation.

Muhammad Ali Ruler of Egypt between 1805 and 1848. He initiated a set of modernizing reforms that sought to make Egypt competitive with the great powers.

mullahs Religious leaders in Iran who in the 1970s led a movement opposing Shah Reza Pahlavi and denounced American materialism and secularism.

multinational corporations Corporations based in many different countries that have global investment, trading, and distribution goals.

Muscovy The principality of Moscow. Originally a mixture of Slavs, Finnish tribes, Turkic speakers, and many others, Muscovy used territorial expansion and commercial networks to consolidate a powerful state and expanded to become the Russian Empire, a huge realm that spanned parts of Europe, much of northern Asia, numerous North Pacific islands, and even—for a time—a corner of North America (Alaska).

Muslim Brotherhood Egyptian organization founded in 1928 by Hassan al-Banna. It attacked liberal democracy as a cover for middle-class, business, and landowning interests and fought for a return to a purified Islam.

Muslim League National Muslim party of India.

Mussolini, Benito (1883–1945) Italian dictator and founder of the fascist movement in Italy. During World War II, he allied Italy with Germany and Japan.

Muwahhidin Term meaning "unitarians," or believers in one God, these were followers of the Wahhabi movement that emerged in the Arabian Peninsula in the eighteenth century.

Mycenaeans Mainland competitors of the Minoans; they took over Crete around 1400 BCE. Migrating to Greece from central Europe, they brought their Indo-European language, horse chariots, and metalworking skills, which they used to dominate until 1200 BCE.

Nagasaki Second Japanese city to be hit by an atomic bomb near the end of World War II.

Napoleonic Code Legal code drafted by Napoleon in 1804; it distilled different legal traditions to create one uniform law. The code confirmed the abolition of feudal privileges of all kinds and set the conditions for exercising property rights.

National Assembly of France Governing body of France that succeeded the Estates-General in 1789 during the French Revolution. It was composed of, and defined by, the delegates of the Third Estate.

National Association for the Advancement of Colored People (NAACP) Founded in 1910, the U.S. civil rights organization dedicated to ending inequality and segregation for black Americans.

nationalism The idea that members of a shared community called a "nation" should have sovereignty within the borders of their state.

National Recovery Administration (NRA) New Deal agency created in 1933 to prepare codes of fair administration and to plan for public works. It was later declared unconstitutional.

nation-state Form of political organization that derived legitimacy from its inhabitants, often referred to as citizens, who in theory, if not always in practice, shared a common language, culture, and history.

native learning Japanese movement to promote nativist intellectual traditions and the celebration of Japanese texts.

native paramountcy British form of "rationalized" colonial rule, which attempted to bring "civilization" to the "uncivilized" by proclaiming that when the interests of European settlers in Africa clashed with those of the African population, the latter should take precedence.

natural rights Belief that emerged in eighteenth-century western Europe and North America that rights fundamental to human nature are discernible to reason and should be affirmed in human-made law.

natural selection Charles Darwin's theory that populations grow faster than the food supply, creating a "struggle for existence" among species in which nature selects which individuals are "fittest" to survive and reproduce.

Nazis National Socialist German Workers Party; German organization founded after World War I and dedicated to winning workers over from socialism to nationalism. The first Nazi Party platform combined nationalism with anti-capitalism and anti-Semitism.

Neanderthals Members of an early wave of hominins from Africa who settled in western Afro-Eurasia, in an area reaching from present-day Uzbekistan and Iraq to Spain, approximately 150,000 years ago.

needle compass Chinese invention made available to navigators after 1000 CE that helped guide sailors on the high seas.

Negritos Hunter-gatherer inhabitants of the East Asian coastal islands who migrated there around 28,000 BCE but by 2000 BCE had been replaced by new migrants.

Negritude Statement of the virtues of the black identity and the validation of African culture and the African past, even in a westernizing world. This idea was shaped by African and African American intellectuals like Senegal's first president, Léopold Sédar Senghor.

Nehemiah Jewish eunuch of the Persian court who was given permission to rebuild the fortification walls around the city of Jerusalem from 440 to 437 BCE.

Neo-Assyrian Empire Afro-Eurasian empire that dominated around 950 BCE. The Neo-Assyrians extended their control over resources and people beyond their own borders, and their empire lasted for three centuries.

neocolonialism Contemporary geopolitical policy or practice in which a politically, economically, and often militarily superior nation asserts control over a country that remains nominally sovereign.

Nestorian Christians Denomination of Christians whose beliefs about Christ differed from those of the official Byzantine church. Named after Nestorius, former bishop of Constantinople, they emphasized the human aspects of Jesus.

New Deal President Franklin Delano Roosevelt's set of government reforms enacted during the 1930s to provide jobs for the unemployed, social welfare programs for the poor, and security to the financial markets.

New Economic Policy (NEP) Enacted decrees of the Bolsheviks between 1921 and 1927 that grudgingly sanctioned private trade and private property.

New Negro Movement *See* Harlem Renaissance.

New World Term applied to the Americas that reflected the Europeans' view that anything previously unknown to them was "new," even if it had existed and supported societies long before European explorers arrived on its shores.

nirvana Literally, nonexistence; the state of complete liberation from the concerns of worldly life, as in Buddhist thought.

Noble Eightfold Path Buddhist concept of a way of life by which people may rid themselves of individual desire to achieve nirvana. The path consists of wisdom, ethical behavior, and mental discipline.

Noh drama Masked theater favored by Japanese bureaucrats and regional lords during the Tokugawa period.

Nok culture Spectacular culture that arose in the sixth century BCE in what is today Nigeria. Iron smelting occurred there around 600 BCE. Thus, the Nok people made the transition from stone to iron materials.

nomads People who move across vast distances without settling permanently in a particular place. Pastoralists, nomads, and transhumant herders introduced new forms of chariot-based warfare that transformed the Afro-Eurasian world.

nongovernmental organizations (NGOs) Term used to refer to private organizations like the Red Cross that play a large role in international affairs.

nonviolent resistance *Satyagraha*; moral and political philosophy developed by Indian National Congress leader Mohandas Gandhi and taken up by other reformers, such as Martin Luther King Jr. Gandhi believed that if Indians pursued self-reliance and self-control in a nonviolent way, the British would eventually have to leave.

North American Free Trade Agreement (NAFTA) Treaty negotiated in the early 1990s to promote free trade between Canada, the United States, and Mexico.

North Atlantic Treaty Organization (NATO) International organization set up in 1949 to provide for the defense of western European countries and the United States from the perceived Soviet threat.

Northern Wei dynasty Regime founded in 386 CE by the Tuoba, a people originally from Inner Mongolia, that lasted one and a half centuries. The rulers of this dynasty adopted many practices of the earlier Chinese Han regime. At the same time, they struggled to consolidate authority over their own nomadic people. Ultimately, several decades of intense internal conflict led to the dynasty's downfall.

Northwest Passage Long-sought marine passageway between the Atlantic and Pacific Oceans.

Oceania Collective name for the lands of Australia and New Zealand and the islands of the southwestern Pacific Ocean.

Odyssey Composed in the eighth century BCE and attributed to Homer, an epic tale of the journey of Odysseus, who traveled the Mediterranean back to his home in Ithaca after the siege of Troy.

oikos The word for "small family unit" in ancient Greece, similar to *familia* in Rome. Its structure, with men as heads of household over women and children, embodied the fundamental power structure in Greek city-states.

oligarchy Clique of privileged rulers.

Olmecs A people who emerged around 1500 BCE and lived in Mesoamerica. The name means those who "lived in the land of the rubber." Olmec society was composed of decentralized villages. Its members spoke the same language and worshipped the same gods.

Open Door Policy Policy proposed by American Secretary of State John Hay in the late nineteenth century to make sure that the United States, along with other foreign nations, would have equal access to trade with China.

Opium War (1839–1842) War fought between the British and Qing China over British trade in opium. China's loss resulted in the granting to the British the right to trade in five different ports and the ceding of Hong Kong to the British.

oracle bones Animal bones used by Shang diviners. Diviners applied intense heat to the shoulder bones of cattle or to turtle shells, which caused them to crack. The diviners would then interpret the cracks as signs from the ancestors regarding royal plans and actions.

Organization of Petroleum Exporting Countries (OPEC) International association established in 1960 to coordinate price and supply policies of oil-producing states.

Orientalism Genre of literature and painting that portrayed the nonwestern peoples of North Africa and Asia as exotic, sensuous, and economically and culturally backward with respect to Europeans.

Orientalists Western scholars who specialized in the study of the East.

Orrorin tugenensis Predecessor to hominins that first appeared 6 million years ago.

Ottoman Empire Domain that encompassed Anatolia, the Arab world, and much of southern and eastern Europe in the early sixteenth century. Ottoman leaders transformed themselves from nomadic warriors who roamed the borderlands between Islamic and Christian worlds in Anatolia into sovereigns of a vast, bureaucratic empire. The Ottomans embraced a Sunni view of Islam. They adapted traditional Byzantine governmental practices but tried new ways of integrating the diverse peoples of their empire.

Pacific War (1879–1883) War between Chile and the alliance of Bolivia and Peru.

palace Official residence of the ruler, his family, and his entourage, first appearing around 2500 BCE. Eventually, palaces became defining landmarks of city life and sources of power rivaling temples.

Palace of Versailles The palace complex, 11 miles away from the French capital of Paris, built by Louis XIV in the 1670s and 1680s to house and entertain his leading clergymen and nobles, with the hopes of diverting them from plotting against him.

Palmyra Roman trading depot in what is modern-day Syria; part of a network of trading cities that connected various regions of Afro-Eurasia.

pan movements Movements that sought to link people across state boundaries in new communities based on ethnicity or, in some cases, religion (e.g., pan-Germanism, pan-Islamism, pan-Slavism).

papacy The institution of the pope; the Catholic spiritual leader in Rome.

papal Of, relating to, or issued by a pope.

Parthians Horse-riding people who pushed southward around the middle of the second century BCE and wiped out the Greek kingdoms in Iran. They then extended their power all the way to the Mediterranean, where they ran up against the Roman Empire in Anatolia and Mesopotamia.

pastoralism Herding and breeding of sheep and goats or other animals as a primary means of subsistence.

pastoral nomads Groups of people who moved their domesticated animals from place to place to meet the animals' demanding grazing requirements. Around 3500 BCE, western Afro-Eurasia witnessed the growth and spread of pastoral nomadic communities.

paterfamilias From the Latin for "father of the family," the foundation of the Roman social order.

patria Latin, meaning "fatherland."

patrons In the Roman system of patronage, men and women of wealth and high social status who protected dependents or "clients" of a lower class.

Pax Mongolica Term that refers to the political and especially the commercial stability that the vast Mongol Empire provided for the travelers and merchants of Eurasia during the thirteenth and fourteenth centuries.

Pax Romana Latin for "Roman Peace"; refers to the period between 25 BCE and 235 CE, during which conditions in the Roman Empire were settled and peaceful.

Pax Sinica Period of peace (149–87 BCE) during which agriculture, commerce, and industry flourished in East Asia under the rule of the Han.

Peace Preservation Act (1925) Act instituted in Japan that specified up to ten years' hard labor for any member of an organization advocating a basic change in the political system or the abolition of private property.

Pearl Harbor American naval base in Hawaii on which the Japanese launched a surprise attack on December 7, 1941, bringing the United States into World War II.

Peloponnesian War War fought between 431 and 404 BCE between two of Greece's most powerful city-states, Athens and Sparta.

peninsulars Spaniards who, although born in Spain, resided in the Spanish colonial territories. They regarded themselves as superior to Spaniards born in the colonies (creoles).

Peninsular War (1808–1814) Conflict in which the Portuguese and Spanish populations, supported by the British, resisted the French invasion of the Iberian Peninsula by Napoleon.

Peoples' Charter Document calling for universal suffrage for adult males, the secret ballot, electoral districts, and annual parliamentary elections. It was signed by over 3 million British between 1839 and 1842.

periplus Book that reflected sailing knowledge; in such books captains would record landing spots and ports. The word *periplus* literally means "sailing around."

Persepolis Darius I's capital city in the highlands of Fars; a ceremonial center and expression of imperial identity as well as an important administrative hub.

Peterloo Massacre (1819) The killing of 11 and wounding of 460 following a peaceful demonstration for political reform by workers in Manchester, England.

Petra City in modern-day Jordan that was the Nabataean capital. It profited greatly by supplying provisions and water to travelers and traders. Many of its houses and shrines were cut into the rocky mountains. *Petra* means "rock."

phalanx Military formation used by Philip II of Macedonia, whereby heavily armored infantry were closely arrayed in battle formation. Term also used by Charles Fourier to describe a well-ordered utopian community.

Philip II of Macedonia Father of Alexander the Great, under whose rule Macedonia developed into a large ethnic and territorial state. After unifying Macedonia, Philip went on to conquer neighboring states but was assassinated in 336 BCE at the age of 46.

philosophes Enlightenment thinkers who applied scientific reasoning to human interaction and society.

philosophia Literally, "love of wisdom." This system of thought originally included speculation by Greek thinkers on the nature of the cosmos, the environment, and human existence. It eventually came to include thought about the nature of humans and life in society.

Phoenicians Known as the Canaanites in the Bible, an ethnic group in the Levant under Assyrian rule in the seventh century BCE; they provided ships and sailors for battles in the Mediterranean. The name *Phoenician* means "purple people," referring to the purple dye they manufactured and widely traded,

along with other commercial goods and services, throughout the Mediterranean. Their major contribution was the alphabet, first introduced in the second millennium BCE, which made far-reaching communication possible.

phonemes Primary and distinctive sounds that are characteristic of human language.

piety Strong sense of religious duty and devoutness, often inspiring extraordinary actions.

plant domestication Process of growing plants, harvesting their seeds, and saving some of the seeds for planting in subsequent growing cycles, resulting in a steady food supply. This process occurred as far back as 5000 BCE, when plants began to naturally retain their seeds. Plant domestication was practiced first in the southern Levant and spread from there into the rest of Southwest Asia.

Plato (427–347 BCE) Disciple of the great philosopher Socrates; his works are the only record we have of Socrates' teaching. He was also the author of formative philosophical works on ethics and politics.

plebs In ancient Rome, term that referred to the "common people." Their interests were protected by officials called tribunes.

pochteca Archaic term for merchants of the Mexicos.

polyglot communities Societies composed of diverse linguistic and ethnic groups.

popular culture Affordable and accessible forms of art and entertainment available to people at all levels of society.

popular sovereignty The idea that the power of the state resides in the people.

Populists Members of a political movement that supported U.S. farmers in late nineteenth-century America. The term is often used generically to refer to political groups who appeal to the majority of the population.

potassium-argon dating Major dating technique based on the changing chemical structure of nonliving objects over time. It is carried out by measuring the ratio of potassium to argon, since over time potassium decays into argon. This method makes possible the dating of objects up to a million years old.

potato famine (1840s) Severe famine in Ireland that led to the rise of radical political movements and the migration of large numbers of Irish to the United States.

potter's wheel Fast wheel that enabled people to mass-produce vessels in many different shapes. This advance, invented at the city of Uruk, enabled potters to make significant technical breakthroughs.

pottery Vessels made of mud and later clay that were used for storing and transporting food. The development of pottery was a major breakthrough.

Prague Spring (1968) Popular movement that strove to create a democratic and pluralist socialism in Czechoslovakia; suppressed by Russian intervention in early 1969.

predestination Belief of many sixteenth- and seventeenth-century Protestant groups that God had foreordained the lives of individuals, including their bad and good deeds.

primitivism Western art movement of the late nineteenth and early twentieth centuries that drew upon the so-called primitive art forms of Africa, Oceania, and pre-Columbian America.

progressive reformers Members of the U.S. reform movement in the early twentieth century that aimed to eliminate political corruption, improve working conditions, and regulate the power of large industrial and financial enterprises.

proletarians Industrial wage workers.

prophets Charismatic freelance religious men of power who found themselves in opposition to the formal power of the kings, bureaucrats, and priests.

Prophet's Town Indian village in Indiana that was burned down by American forces in the early nineteenth century.

Protestantism Division of Christianity that emerged in western Europe from the Protestant Reformation.

Protestant Reformation Religious movement initiated by Martin Luther, who openly criticized the corruption in the Catholic Church and voiced his belief that Christians could speak directly to God. His doctrines gained wide support, and those who followed this new view of Christianity rejected the authority of the papacy and the Catholic clergy, broke away from the Catholic Church, and called themselves "Protestants."

Proto-Indo-European The parent of all the languages in the Indo-European family, which includes, among many others, English, German, Norwegian, Portuguese, French, Russian, Persian, Hindi, and Bengali.

Pullman Strike (1894) American Railway Union strike in response to wage cuts and firings.

Punic Wars Three wars waged between the Romans and Carthage in the third and second centuries BCE that resulted in the defeat of the Carthaginian hegemony in the western Mediterranean and demonstrated the might of the Roman military (army and navy) and the beginnings of Rome's aggressive foreign imperialism.

puppet states Governments with little power in the international arena that follow the dictates of their more powerful neighbors or patrons.

Puritans Seventeenth-century reform group of the Church of England; also known as dissenters or nonconformists.

Qadiriyya Sufi order that facilitated the spread of Islam into West Africa.

qadis Judges in the Muslim societies.

qanats Underground water channels, vital for irrigation, that were used in Persia. Little evaporation occurred when water was being moved through qanats.

Qing dynasty (1644–1911) Minority Manchu rule over China that incorporated new territories, experienced substantial population growth, and sustained significant economic growth.

Questions of King Milinda (Milindapunha) Name of a second-century BCE text espousing the teachings of Buddhism as set forth by Menander, a Yavana king. It featured a discussion between the king and a sophisticated Buddhist sage named Nagasena.

Quetzalcoatl Ancient deity and legendary ruler of Native American peoples living in Mexico.

Quran The scripture of the Islamic faith. Originally a verbal recitation, the Quran was compiled into a book soon after the death of Muhammad in the order in which we have it today. According to traditional Islamic interpretation, the Quran was revealed to Muhammad by the angel Gabriel over a period of twenty-three years.

radicalism The conviction that real change is possible only by going to the root (in Latin, *radix*) of the problem and promoting complete political and social reform. Tendencies toward radicalism can be found in every culture that develops a complex set of institutions and hierarchies, but have been found most frequently in the west since 1789.

radicals Widely used term in nineteenth-century Europe that referred to those individuals and political organizations that favored the total reconfiguration of Europe's political and/or economic systems.

radiocarbon isotope C^{14} Isotope contained by all living things. When organisms die, the C^{14} isotope they contain begins to decay into a stable nonradioactive element, C^{12}. The rate of decay is regular and measurable, making it possible to ascertain the date of fossils that leave organic remains for ages of up to 40,000 years.

Raj British crown's administration of India following the end of the East India Company's rule after the Great Rebellion of 1857.

raja The Sanskrit word for "king," used in South and Southeast Asia. It could also refer to the head of a family, but in South Asian city-states indicated the person who had control of land and resources.

Ramadan Ninth month of the Muslim year, during which all Muslims must fast during daylight hours.

Rape of Nanjing Attack against the Chinese in which the Japanese slaughtered at least 100,000 civilians and raped thousands of women between December 1937 and February 1938.

Rashtriya Swayamsevak Sangh (RSS) (1925) Campaign to organize Hindus as a militant, modern community in India; translated in English as "National Volunteer Organization."

Rebellion of 1857 (Great Rebellion) Indian uprising against the East India Company to bring religious purification, an egalitarian society, local and communal solidarity, and a return of a Mughal to the throne without the interference of British rule.

rebus Probably originating in Uruk, a representation that transfers meaning from the name of a thing to the sound of that name. For example, a picture of a bee can represent the sound "b." Such pictures opened the door to writing, a technology of symbols that uses marks to represent specific discrete sounds.

Reconquista Spanish reconquest of territories lost to the Islamic Empire, beginning with Toledo in 1061.

Red Guards Chinese students who were the shock troops in the early phases of Mao's Cultural Revolution in 1966–1968.

Red Lanterns Female supporters of the Chinese Boxers who rebelled against foreign intrusions in China at the turn of the twentieth century. Most were teenage girls and unmarried women, and they dressed in red garments.

Reds Bolsheviks.

Red Turban Movement Diverse religious movement in China during the fourteenth century that spread the belief that the world was drawing to an end as Mongol rule was collapsing.

Reich German word for "realm." Hitler claimed to be creating the Third German Reich (after the Holy Roman Empire and the German Empire that had lasted from 1871 to 1919).

Reichstag The German parliament.

Reign of Terror Campaign at the height of the French Revolution in the early 1790s that used violence, including systematic execution of opponents of the revolution, to purge France of its enemies and to extend the revolution beyond its borders. Radicals executed as many as 40,000 persons who were judged enemies of the state.

Renaissance Term meaning "rebirth" that historians use to characterize the expanded cultural production of European nations between 1430 and 1550. The Renaissance emphasized a break from the church-centered medieval world and a new concept of humankind as the center of the world.

republican government Government in which power and rulership rest with representatives of the people—not a king.

res publica Literally, "public thing"; this referred to the Roman republic, in which policy and rules of behavior were determined by the Senate and by popular assemblies of the citizens.

Restoration period (1815–1848) European movement after the defeat of Napoleon to restore Europe to its pre–French Revolutionary status and to quash radical movements.

Rift Valley Area of northeastern Africa where some of the most important early discoveries of human fossils were found, especially one of an intact skull that is 1.8 million years old.

river basins Areas drained by a river, including all its tributaries. River basins were rich in fertile soil, water for irrigation, and plant and animal life, which made them attractive for human habitation. Cultivators were able to produce surplus agriculture to support the first cities.

Roman army Military force of the Roman Empire. The Romans devised a military draft that could draw from a huge population. In their encounter with Hannibal, they lost up to 80,000 men in three separate encounters and still won the war.

Roman Catholicism Branch of Christianity established by 1000 CE in western Europe and led by the Roman papacy. In contrast to ancient Greek Orthodoxy, Western Catholics believed that their church was destined to expand everywhere, and they set about converting the tribes of northern Europe. Western Catholics contemptuously called the East Romans "Greeks" and condemned them for their "Byzantine" cunning.

Roman law Roman legal system, under which disputes were brought to the public courts and decisions were made by judges and sometimes by large juries. Rome's legal system featured written law and institutions for settling legal disputes.

roving bandits Large bands of dispossessed and marginalized Chinese peasants who vented their anger at tax collectors in the waning years of the Ming dynasty.

Royal Road A 1,600-mile road of the ancient Persian Empire that went from Sardis in Anatolia to Susa in Iran. It was used by messengers, traders, the army, and those taking tribute to the king.

Russification Programs to assimilate people of over 146 dialects into the Russian Empire.

S.S. (*Schutzstaffel*) Hitler's security police force.

Sack of Constantinople Rampage in 1204 by the Frankish armies on the capital city of Constantinople.

Sahel region The Arabic word for "coast," used to describe the area that borders the southern region of the Sahara Desert. This vast expanse of land, stretching from the Atlantic Ocean to the Red Sea, was significantly wetter and more temperate than the desert, especially in the upland massifs and their foothills, where villages and towns were able to emerge.

Salt March (1930) A 240-mile trek to the sea in India, led by Mohandas Gandhi, to gather salt for free, thus breaking the British colonial monopoly on salt.

Samurai Japanese warriors who made up the private armies of Japanese daimyos.

Sandinista coalition Left-leaning Nicaraguan coalition of the 1970s and 1980s.

Sanskrit cosmopolis A cultural synthesis based on Hindu spiritual beliefs and articulated in the Sanskrit language that served to culturally unify South Asia in place of a centralized empire.

Santería African-based religion, blended with Christian influences, that was first practiced by slaves in Cuba.

Sargon the Great King of Akkad, a city-state near modern Baghdad. Reigning from 2334 to 2279 BCE, Sargon helped bring the competitive era of city-states to an end and sponsored monumental works of architecture, art, and literature.

Sasanian Empire Empire that succeeded the Parthians in the mid-220s CE in Inner Eurasia. The Sasanian Empire controlled the trade crossroads of Afro-Eurasia and possessed a strong armored cavalry, which made them a powerful rival to Rome. The Sasanians were also tolerant of Judaism and Christianity, which allowed Christians to flourish.

Sati Hindu practice whereby a woman was burned to death on the pyre of her dead husband.

satrapies Provinces in the Persian Empire governed by a satrap. Each satrap was a relative or intimate associate of the king.

Satyagraha *See* nonviolent resistance.

scientific method Method of inquiry based on experimentation rather than on the acceptance of older authorities. Many of its principles were first laid out by the philosopher Sir Francis Bacon (1561–1626), who claimed that real science entailed the formulation of hypotheses that could be tested in carefully controlled experiments.

Scramble for Africa European rush to colonize parts of Africa at the end of the nineteenth century.

scribes Those who wield writing tools. From the very beginning, they were at the top of the social ladder, under the major power brokers.

Scythian ethos Warrior ethos that embodied the extremes of aggressive mounted-horse culture, c. 1000 BCE. In part the Scythian ethos was the result of the constant struggle between settlers, hunter-gatherers, and nomads on the northern frontier of Europe.

Sea Peoples Migrants from north of the Mediterranean who invaded the cities of Egypt and the Levant in the second millennium BCE. Once settled along the coast of the Levant, they became known as the Philistines and considerably disrupted the settlements of the Canaanites.

SEATO (Southeast Asia Treaty Organization) Military alliance of pro-American, anticommunist states in Southeast Asia in 1954.

second-generation societies Societies that expanded old ideas and methods by incorporating new aspects of culture and grafting them onto, or using them in combination with, established norms.

Second World Term invented during the Cold War to refer to the communist countries, as opposed to the west (or First World) and the former colonies (or Third World).

Seleucus Nikator Successor of Alexander the Great who lived from 358 to 281 BCE. He controlled Mesopotamia, Syria, Persia, and parts of the Punjab.

Self-Strengthening movement In the latter half of the nineteenth century, a movement of reformist Chinese bureaucrats that attempted to adopt western

elements of learning and technological skill while retaining their core Chinese culture.

Semu Term meaning "outsiders" or non-Chinese people—Mongols, Tanguts, Khitan, Jurchen, Muslims, Tibetans, Persians, Turks, Nestorians, Jews, and Armenians—who became a new ruling elite over a Han majority population in the late thirteenth century.

sepoys Hindu and Muslim recruits of the East India Company's military force.

serfs Peasants who farmed the land and paid fees to be protected by lords under a system of rule called feudalism.

settled agriculture Application of human labor and tools to a fixed plot of land for more than one growing cycle. It entails the changeover from a hunting and gathering lifestyle to one based on agriculture, which requires staying in one place until the soil has been exhausted.

Seven Years' War (1756–1763) Worldwide war that ended when Prussia defeated Austria, establishing itself as a European power, and when Britain gained control of India and many of France's colonies through the Treaty of Paris; known in North America as the French and Indians Wars.

sexual revolution Increased freedom in sexual behavior, resulting in part from advances in contraception, notably the introduction of oral contraception in 1960, which allowed men and women to limit childbearing and to have sex with less fear of pregnancy.

shah Traditional title of Persian rulers.

shamans Certain humans whose powers supposedly enabled them to commune with the supernatural and to transform themselves wholly or partly into animals.

shamisen Three-stringed instrument, often played by Japanese geisha.

Shandingdong Man A *Homo sapiens* whose fossil remains and relics can be dated to about 18,000 years ago. His physical characteristics were close to those of modern humans, and he had a similar brain size.

Shanghai School Late nineteenth-century style of Chinese painting characterized by an emphasis on spontaneous brushwork, feeling, and the

incorporation of western influences into classical Chinese pieces.

Shang state Dynasty in northeastern China that ruled from 1600 to 1045 BCE. Though not as well defined by borders as the territorial states in the southwest of Asia, it did have a ruling lineage. Four fundamental elements of the Shang state were a metal industry based on copper, pottery making, standardized architectural forms and walled towns, and divination using animal bones.

sharecropping System of farming in which tenant farmers rented land and gave over a share of their crops to the land's owners. Sometimes seen as a cheap way for the state to conduct agricultural affairs, sharecropping often resulted in the impoverishment and marginalization of the underclass.

sharia Literally, "the way"; now used to indicate the philosophy and rulings of Islamic law.

Sharpeville Massacre (1960) Massacre of sixty-nine black Africans when police fired on a rally against the recently passed laws requiring nonwhite South Africans to carry identity papers.

Shawnees Native American tribe that inhabited the Ohio Valley during the eighteenth century.

Shays's Rebellion (1786) Uprising of armed farmers that broke out when the Massachusetts state government refused to offer them economic relief.

Shi Huangdi King during the Qin era who defeated what was left of the Warring States between 230 and 221 BCE. He assumed the mandate of heaven from the Zhou and declared himself First August Emperor, to distinguish himself from other kings.

Shiism One of the two main branches of Islam, practiced in the Fatimid and Safavid Empires. Always a minority sect in the Islamic world, the interpretations of theology and politics in Shiism differ from those in Sunni Islam.

Shiites Group of supporters of Ali, Muhammad's cousin and son-in-law, who wanted him to be the first caliph and believed that members of the Prophet's family deserved to rule. The leaders of the Shiite community are known as "imams," which means "leaders."

Shinto Japan's official religion; it promoted the state and the emperor's divinity. The term means "the way of the gods."

shoguns Japanese military commanders. From 1192 to 1333, the Kamakura shoguns served as military "protectors" of the ruler in the city of Heian.

Shotoku Prince in the early Japanese Yamoto state (574–622 CE) who is credited with having introduced Buddhism to Japan.

shudras Literally, "small ones"; workers and slaves from outside the Vedic lineage.

Siddhartha Gautama Another name for the Buddha, the most prominent opponent of the Brahman way of life. He lived from 563 to 483 BCE and developed methods for overcoming life's suffering and achieving a state of grace, or nirvana.

Sikhism Islamic-inspired religion that calls on its followers to renounce the caste system and to treat all believers as equal before God.

Silicon Valley Valley between the California cities of San Francisco and San Jose, known for its innovative computer and high-technology industries.

silk Luxury textile that became a vastly popular export from China (via the Silk Road) to the cities of the Roman world.

Silk Road A series of trade routes linking China with central Asia and the Mediterranean; it extended over 5,000 miles, land and sea included, and was so named because of the quantities of silk that were traded along it. The Silk Road was a major factor in the development of cultures in China, Egypt, Persia, India, and even Europe.

Silla One of three independent Korean states that may have emerged as early as the third century BCE. These states lasted until 668 CE, when Silla took control over the entire peninsula.

Silver Islands Term used by European merchants in the sixteenth century to refer to Japan because of its substantial trade in silver with China.

Sino-Japanese War (1894–1895) Conflict over the control of Korea in which China was forced to cede the province of Taiwan to Japan.

Sipahi The Persian word for "cavalryman." *Sipahis* were expected to provide military service to the Ottoman Empire.

Siva The third of three Vedic deities, signifying destruction. *See also* Brahma *and* Vishnu.

slave plantations System whereby enslaved labor was used for the cultivation of crops to be sold for profit. Slave plantations were a crucial part of the growth of the Mediterranean economy.

small seal script Unified script that was used to the exclusion of other scripts under the Qin, with the aim of centralizing administration. Its use led to a less complicated style of clerical writing than had been in use under the Han.

social contract The idea, drawn from the works of the English writer John Locke, that all governments come into existence through agreements made between rulers and peoples; if a ruler violates those agreements, Locke argued, the people have the right to rebel.

Social Darwinism Belief that Charles Darwin's theory of evolution is applicable to humans and justifies the right of the ruling classes or countries to dominate the weak.

social hierarchies Distinctions between the privileged and the less privileged.

socialism Political ideology that calls for a classless society with collective ownership of all property.

Social Security Act (1935) New Deal act that instituted old-age pensions and insurance for the unemployed.

Socrates (469–399 BCE) Philosopher in Athens who encouraged people to reflect on ethics and morality. He stressed the importance of honor and integrity as opposed to wealth and power. Plato was his student.

Sogdians A people who lived in central Asia's commercial centers and maintained the stability and accessibility of the Silk Road. They were crucial to the interconnectedness of the Afro-Eurasian landmass.

Solidarity The communist bloc's first independent trade union, established in Poland at the Gdansk shipyard in 1980.

Song dynasty Chinese dynasty that took over the mandate of heaven for three centuries starting in 976 CE. It ruled an era of many economic and political successes but eventually lost northern China to nomadic tribes.

Song porcelain Type of ceramics perfected during the Song period that was translucent and delicate but also durable.

South African War (1899–1902) Conflict between the British and Afrikaner colonists of South Africa that resulted in bringing two Afrikaner republics under the control of the British; often called the Boer War.

Soviet bloc International alliance that included the east European countries of the Warsaw Pact as well as the Soviet Union but also came to include Cuba.

Spanish-American War (1898) War between the United States and Spain in Cuba, Puerto Rico, and the Philippines. It ended with a treaty in which the United States took over the Philippines, Guam, and Puerto Rico; Cuba won partial independence.

speciation The formation of different species.

specie Money in coin.

species Group of animals or plants possessing one or more distinctive characteristics and able to exchange genes and interbreed.

Spring and Autumn period Period between the eighth and fifth centuries BCE, during which China was ruled by the feudal system. Considered an anarchic and turbulent time, there were 148 different tributary states in this period.

Stalin, Joseph (1878–1953) Leader of the Communist Party and the Soviet Union. Stalin sought to create "socialism in one country."

St. Bartholomew's Day Massacre (1572) Roman Catholic massacre of French Protestants in Paris.

steel A metal more malleable and stronger than iron that became essential for industries like shipbuilding and railways.

stoicism Widespread philosophical movement initiated by Zeno (334–262 BCE). Zeno and his followers sought to understand the role of people in relation to the cosmos. For the Stoics, everything was grounded in nature. Being in love with nature and living a good life required being in control of one's passions and thus indifferent to pleasure or pain.

St. Patrick Former slave brought to Ireland from Briton who later became a missionary. Known as the "Apostle of Ireland," he died in 470 CE.

Strait of Malacca Seagoing gateway to Southeast and East Asia.

Strategic Defense Initiative ("Star Wars") Master plan, championed by U.S. president Ronald Reagan in the 1980s, that envisions the deployment of satellites and space missiles to protect the United States from incoming nuclear bombs.

stupa Dome monument marking the burial site of relics of the Buddha.

Suez Canal Channel completed in 1869 across the Isthmus of Suez to connect the Mediterranean Sea with the Red Sea and to lower the costs of international trade.

Sufi brotherhoods Mystics within Islam who were responsible for the expansion of Islam into many regions of the world.

Sufism Emotional and mystical form of Islam that appealed to the common people.

sultan Islamic political leader. In the Ottoman Empire, the sultan combined a warrior ethos with an unwavering devotion to Islam.

Sumerian King List Text that recounts the making of Sumerian political dynasties. Recorded around 2000 BCE, it organizes the reigns of kings by dynasty, one city at a time.

Sumerian pantheon The Sumerian gods, each of whom had a home in a particular floodplain city. In the Sumerian belief system, both gods and the natural forces they controlled had to be revered.

Sumerian temples Homes of the gods and symbols of Sumerian imperial identity. Sumerian temples also represented the gods' ability to hoard wealth at sites where people exchanged goods and services. In addition, temples distinguished the urban from the rural world.

Sunnis The majority sect of Islam, Sunnis originally supported the succession of Abu Bakr over Ali and supported the rule of consensus rather than family lineage for the succession to the Islamic caliphate. *See also* Shiites.

Sun Yat-sen (1866–1925) Chinese revolutionary and founder of the Nationalist Party in China.

superior man In the Confucian view, a person of perfected moral character, fit to be a leader.

superpowers Label applied to the United States and the Soviet Union after World War II because of their size, their possession of the atomic bomb, and the fact that each embodied a model of civilization (capitalism or communism) applicable to the whole world.

supranational organizations International organizations such as nongovernmental organizations (NGOs), the World Bank, and the International Monetary Fund (IMF).

survival of the fittest Charles Darwin's belief that as species grow and resources become scarce, a struggle for existence arises, the outcome of which is that only the "fittest" survive.

Suryavanha The second lineage of two (the solar one) in Vedic society. *See* Chandravamsha.

Swadeshi movement Voluntary organizations in India that championed the creation of indigenous manufacturing enterprises and schools of nationalist thought in order to gain autonomy from Britain.

syndicalism A political and economic system, elaborated by the French social philosopher Georges Sorel (1847–1922), that sought to replace capitalism with a workplace organization that included unskilled laborers.

tabula rasa Term used by John Locke to describe the human mind before it begins to acquire ideas from experience; Latin for "clean slate."

Taiping Heavenly Kingdom (Heavenly Kingdom of Great Peace) Religious sect established by the Chinese prophet Hong Xiuquan in the mid-nineteenth century. Hong Xiuquan believed that he was Jesus's younger brother. The group struggled to rid the world of evil and "restore" the heavenly kingdom, imagined as a just and egalitarian order.

Taiping Rebellion Rebellion by followers of Hong Xiuquan and the Taiping Heavenly Kingdom against the Qing government over the economic and social turmoil caused by the Opium War. Despite an army of 100,000 rebels, the rebellion was crushed.

Taj Mahal Royal palace of the Mughal Empire, built by Shah Jahan in the seventeenth century in homage to his wife, Mumtaz Mahal.

Tale of Genji Japanese work written by Lady Murasaki that gives vivid accounts of Heian court life; Japan's first novel (early eleventh century).

talking cures Psychological practice developed by Sigmund Freud whereby the symptoms of neurotic and traumatized patients would decrease after regular periods of thoughtful discussion.

Talmud Huge volumes of oral commentary on Jewish law eventually compiled in two versions, the Palestinian and the Babylonian, in the fifth and sixth centuries BCE.

Talmud of Jerusalem Codified written volumes of the traditions of Judaism, produced by the rabbis of Galilee around 400 CE.

Tang dynasty (608–907 CE) Regime that promoted a cosmopolitan culture, turning China into the hub of East Asian cultural integration, while expanding the borders of their empire. To govern such a diverse empire, the Tang established a political culture and civil service based on Confucian teachings. Candidates for the civil service were required to take examinations, the first of their kind in the world.

Tanzimat Reorganization period of the Ottoman Empire in the mid-nineteenth century. Modernizing reforms affected the military, trade, foreign relations, and civilian life.

tappers Rubber workers in Brazil, mostly either Indian or mixed-blood people.

Tarascans Mesoamerican society of the 1400s, rivals to and sometimes subjects of the Aztecs.

Tecumseh (1768–1813) Shawnee who circulated Tenskwatawa's message of Indian renaissance among Indian villages from the Great Lakes to the Gulf Coast. He preached the need for Indian unity, insisting that Indians resist any American attempts to get them to sell more land. In response, thousands of followers renounced their ties to colonial ways and prepared to combat the expansion of the United States.

tekkes Schools that taught devotional strategies and the religious knowledge that students needed to enter Sufi orders and become masters of the brotherhood.

temple Building where believers worshipped their gods and goddesses and where some peoples believed the deities had earthly residence.

Tenskwatawa (1775–1836) Shawnee prophet who urged disciples to abstain from alcohol and return to traditional customs, reducing dependence on European trade goods and severing connections to Christian missionaries. His message spread to other tribes, raising the specter of a pan-Indian confederacy.

Teotihuacán City-state in a large, mountainous valley in what is modern-day Mexico; the first major community to emerge after the Olmecs.

territorial state Political form that emerged in the river-basin cities of Mesopotamia, which was overwhelmed by the displacement of nomadic peoples. These states were kingdoms organized around charismatic rulers who headed large households; each had a defined physical border.

Third Estate The French people minus the clergy and the aristocracy; this term was popularized after 1789 and used to claim power for nonelite people during the French Revolution.

Third Reich The German state from 1933 to 1945 under Adolf Hitler.

Third World Nations of the world, mostly in Asia, Latin America, and Africa, that were not highly industrialized like First World nations or tied to the Soviet bloc (the Second World).

Thirty Years' War (1618–1648) Conflict between Protestants and Catholics in the Holy Roman Empire that escalated into a general European war.

Tiananmen Square Largest public square in the world and site of the pro-democracy movement in 1989 that resulted in the killing of as many as a thousand protesters by the Chinese army.

tiers-monde Term meaning "Third World," coined by French intellectuals to describe countries seeking a "third way" between Soviet communism and western capitalism.

Tiglath Pileser III Assyrian ruler from 745 to 728 BCE who introduced a standing army and instituted reforms that changed the administrative and social structure of the empire to make it more efficient.

Tiwanaku Another name for Tihuanaco, the first great Andean polity, on the shores of Lake Titicaca.

Tlaxcalans Mesoamerican society of the 1400s; these people were enemies of the powerful Aztec Empire.

Tokugawa shogunate Hereditary military administration founded in 1603 that ruled Japan while keeping the emperor as a figurehead; it was toppled in 1868 by reformers who felt that Japan should adopt, not reject, Western influences.

Toltecs A Mesoamerican people who, by 1000 CE, had filled the political vacuum created by the decline of the city of Teotihuacán.

tomb culture Warlike group from northeast Asia who arrived by sea in the middle of the third century CE and imposed their military and social power on southern Japan. These conquerors are known today as the "tomb culture" because of their elevated necropolises near present-day Osaka.

Topkapi Palace Political headquarters of the Ottoman Empire, located in Istanbul.

total war All-out war involving civilian populations as well as military forces, often used in reference to World War II.

transhumant herders Nomads who entered settled territories in the second millennium BCE and moved their herds seasonally when resources became scarce.

Trans-Siberian Railroad Railroad built over very difficult terrain between 1891 and 1903 and subsequently expanded. It created an overland bridge for troops, peasant settlers, and commodities to move between Europe and the Pacific.

Treaty of Brest-Litovsk (1918) Separate peace treaty between imperial Germany and the new Bolshevik regime in Russia. The treaty acknowledged the German victory on the Eastern Front and took Russia out of the war.

Treaty of Nanjing (1842) Treaty between China and Britain following the First Opium War; it called for indemnities, the opening of new ports, and the cession of Hong Kong to the British.

Treaty of Tordesillas (1494) Treaty in which the pope decreed that the non-European world would be divided into spheres of trade and missionary responsibility between Spain and Portugal.

trickle trade Also called "down the line trade," a method by which a good is passed from one village to another, as in the case of obsidian among early farming villages. The practice began around 7000 BCE.

Tripartite Pact (1940) Pact that stated that Germany, Italy, and Japan would act together in all future military ventures.

Triple Entente Alliance developed before World War I that eventually included Britain, France, and Russia.

Troy Important site founded around 3000 BCE in Anatolia, to the far west. Troy is legendary as the site of the war that was launched by the Greeks (the Achaeans) and that was recounted by Homer in the *Iliad*.

Truman Doctrine (1947) Declaration promising U.S. economic and military intervention, whenever and wherever needed, for the sake of preventing communist expansion.

Truth and Reconciliation Commission Quasi-judicial body established after the overthrow of the apartheid system in South Africa and the election of Nelson Mandela as the country's first black president in 1994. The commission was to gather evidence about crimes committed during the apartheid years. Those who showed remorse for their actions could appeal for clemency. The South African leaders believed that an airing of the grievances from this period would promote racial harmony and reconciliation. Other countries suffering from traumatic political, ethnic, and cultural events have adopted the South African experiment and established their own truth and reconciliation commissions.

truth commissions Elected officials' inquiries into human rights abuses by previous regimes. In Argentina, El Salvador, Guatemala, and South Africa, these commissions were vital for creating a new aura of legitimacy for democracies and for promising to uphold the rights of individuals.

tsar/czar Russian word derived from the Latin *Caesar* to refer to the Russian ruler of Kiev and eventually to all rulers in Russia.

Tula Toltec capital city, a commercial hub and political and ceremonial center.

Uitlanders British populations living in Afrikaner republics; they were denied voting rights and subject to other forms of discrimination in the late nineteenth century. The term means "outsiders."

ulama Arabic word that means "learned ones" or "scholars"; used for those who devoted themselves to knowledge of Islamic sciences.

Umayyads Family who founded the first dynasty in Islam. They established family rule and dynastic succession to the role of caliph. The first Umayyad caliph established Damascus as his capital and was named Mu'awiya ibn Abi Sufyan.

umma Arabic word for "community"; used to refer to the "Islamic people" or "Islamic community."

Universal Declaration of Human Rights (1948) UN declaration that laid out the rights to which all human beings are entitled.

universalizing religions Universal religions that are proselytized by energetic and charismatic missionaries, that foster a deep sense of community felt by their converts, and that are supported by powerful empires.

universal religions Religions that appeal to diverse populations, that are easily adaptable across various cultural and geographical areas, and that promote universal rules and principles to guide behavior that transcend place, time, and specific cultural practices.

universitas Term used from the end of the twelfth century to denote scholars who came together, first in Paris. The term is borrowed from the merchant communities, where it denoted the equivalent of the modern "union."

Untouchables Caste in the Indian system whose jobs, usually in the more unsanitary aspects of urban life, rendered them "ritually and spiritually" impure.

Upanishads Vedic wisdom literature collected in the first half of the first millennium BCE. It took the form of dialogues between disciples and a sage.

urban-rural divide Division between those living in cities and those living in rural areas. One of history's most durable worldwide distinctions, the urban-rural divide eventually encompassed the globe. Where cities arose, communities adopted lifestyles based on the large-scale production of goods and on specialized labor. Those living in the countryside remained close to nature, cultivating the land or tending livestock. They diversified their labor and exchanged their grains and animal products for necessities available in urban centers.

utopian socialism The most visionary of all Restoration-era movements. Utopian socialists like Charles Fourier dreamed of transforming states, workplaces, and human relations, not through bloody revolution but through the wholesale reorganization of society.

Vaishyas Householders or lesser clan members in Vedic society who worked the land and tended livestock.

Vardhamana Mahavira Advocate of Jainism who lived from 540 to 468 BCE; he emphasized interpretation of the Upanishads to govern and guide daily life.

varna Caste system established by the Vedas in 600 BCE.

vassal states Subordinate states that had to pay tribute in luxury goods, raw materials, and labor as part of a broad confederation of polities under the kings' protection.

Vedas Rhymes, hymns, and explanatory texts composed by Aryan priests; the Vedas became their most holy scripture and part of their religious rituals. The Vedas were initially passed down orally, in Sanskrit. Brahmans, priests of Vedic culture, incorporated the texts into ritual and society. The Vedas are considered the final authority of Hinduism.

Vedic people People who came from the steppes of Inner Asia around 1500 BCE and entered the fertile lowlands of the Indus River basin, gradually moving as far south as the Deccan plateau. They called themselves Aryan, which means

"respected ones," and spoke Sanskrit, an Indo-European language.

veiling Practice of modest dress, including covering the hair and much of the face, required of respectable women in the Assyrian Empire, introduced by Assyrian authorities in the thirteenth century BCE.

Venus figures Representations of the goddess of fertility drawn on the Chauvet Cave in southeastern France. Discovered in 1994, they are probably about 35,000 years old.

Versailles Conference (1919) International peace conference at the end of World War I intended to shape the future of the world after the war. Delegates decided on the principles that would shape the resultant five peace treaties, one for each of the Central Powers (the most well-known of these is the Treaty of Versailles, which forced Germany to pay reparations, admit responsibility for the war, and give up its colonies). The Soviet Union, which had already made peace with the Central Powers, was not invited to this conference.

Viet Cong Vietnamese communist group committed to overthrowing the government of South Vietnam and reunifying North and South Vietnam.

Viet Minh Group founded in 1941 by Ho Chi Minh to oppose the Japanese occupation of Indochina; it later fought the French colonial forces for independence. Also known as the Vietnamese Independent League.

Vietnam War (1955–1975) Conflict that resulted from concern over the spread of communism in Southeast Asia. The United States intervened on the side of South Vietnam in its struggle against peasant-supported Viet Cong guerrilla forces, who wanted to reunite Vietnam under a communist regime. Faced with antiwar opposition at home and ferocious resistance from the Vietnamese, American troops withdrew in 1973; the puppet South Vietnamese government collapsed two years later.

Vikings A people from Scandinavia who replaced the Franks as the dominant warrior class in northern Europe in the ninth century CE. They used their superior ships to loot other seagoing peoples and sailed up the rivers of central Russia to establish a trade route that connected

Scandinavia and the Baltic with Constantinople and Baghdad. The Vikings established settlements in Iceland and Greenland and, briefly, North America.

Vishnu The second of three Vedic deities, signifying existence. *See also* Brahma *and* Siva.

viziers Bureaucrats of the Ottoman Empire.

vodun Mixed religion of African and Christian customs practiced by slaves and free blacks in the colony of Saint Domingue.

Voting Rights Act (1965) Law that granted universal suffrage in the United States.

Wafd Nationalist party that came into existence during a rebellion in Egypt in 1919 and held power sporadically after Egypt was granted limited independence from Britain in 1922.

Wahhabism Eighteenth-century reform movement organized by Muhammad Ibn abd al-Wahhab, who preached the absolute oneness of Allah and a return to the pure Islam of Muhammad.

Wang Mang Han minister who usurped the throne in 9 CE because he believed that the Han had lost the mandate of heaven. He ruled until 23 CE.

war ethos Strong social commitment to a continuous state of war. The Roman army constantly drafted men and engaged in annual spring military campaigns. Soldiers were taught to embrace a sense of honor that did not allow them to accept defeat and, their leaders commended those who repeatedly threw themselves into battle.

War of 1812 Conflict between Britain and the United States arising from U.S. grievances over oppressive British maritime practices in the Napoleonic Wars.

War on Poverty President Lyndon Johnson's push for an increased range of social programs and increased spending on Social Security, health, education, and assistance for the disabled.

Warring States period Period extending from the fifth century BCE to 221 BCE, when the regional warring states were unified by the Qin dynasty.

Warsaw Pact (1955–1991) Military alliance between the Soviet Union and other communist states that was established in response to the creation of the NATO alliance.

Weimar Republic (1919–1933) Constitutional republic of Germany that was subverted by Hitler soon after he became chancellor.

Western Front Military front that stretched from the English Channel through Belgium and France to the Alps during World War I.

White and Blue Niles The two main branches of the Nile, rising out of central Africa and Ethiopia. They come together at the present-day capital city of Sudan, Khartoum.

White Lotus Rebellion Series of uprisings in northern China (1790–1800s) inspired by mystical beliefs in folk Buddhism and, at times, the idea of restoring the Ming dynasty.

Whites "Counterrevolutionaries" of the Bolshevik Revolution (1918–1921) who fought the Bolsheviks (the "Reds"); included former supporters of the tsar, Social Democrats, and large independent peasant armies.

White Wolf Mysterious militia leader, depicted in popular myth as a Chinese Robin Hood whose mission was to rid the country of the injustices of Yuan Shikai's government in the early years of the Chinese Republic (1910s).

wokou Supposedly Japanese pirates, many of whom were actually Chinese subjects of the Ming dynasty.

Works Progress Administration (WPA) New Deal program instituted in 1935 that put nearly 3 million people to work building roads, bridges, airports, and post offices.

World Bank International agency established in 1944 to provide economic assistance to war-torn and poor countries. Its formal title is the International Bank for Reconstruction and Development.

World War II (1939–1945) Worldwide war that began in September 1939 in Europe and pitted Britain, the United States, and the Soviet Union (the Allies) against Nazi Germany, Japan, and Italy (the Axis).

Wu or Wudi Chinese leader known as the "Martial Emperor" because of his many military campaigns during the Han dynasty. He reigned from 141 to 87 BCE.

Wu Zhao Chinese empress who lived from 626 to 706 CE. She began as a concubine in the court of Li Shimin and became the mother of his son's child. She eventually gained power equal to that of the emperor, and she named herself regent when she finagled a place for one of her own sons after their father's death.

Xiongnu The most powerful and intrusive of the nomadic peoples, originally pastoralists from the eastern part of the Asian steppe in what is modern-day Mongolia. They appeared along the frontier with China in the late Zhou dynasty and by the third century BCE had become the most powerful of all the pastoral communities in that area.

Xunzi Confucian moralist whose ideas were influential to Qin rulers. He lived from 310 to 237 BCE and believed that rational statecraft was more reliable than fickle human nature and that strict laws and severe punishments could create stability in society.

Yalta Accords Results of the meeting in February 1945 in the Crimean city of Yalta between President Roosevelt, Prime Minister Churchill, and Premier Stalin; the meeting was held to plan for the postwar order.

Yavana kings Sanskrit name for Greek rulers, derived from the Greek name for the area of western Asia Minor called Ionia, a term that then extended to anyone who spoke Greek or came from the Mediterranean.

yellow press Newspapers that seek a mass circulation by featuring sensationalist reporting.

Yellow Turbans One of several local Chinese religious movements that emerged across the empire, especially under Wang Mang's officials, who considered him a usurper. The Yellow Turbans, so called because of the yellow scarves they wore around their heads, were Daoist millenarians.

Yin City that became the capital of the Shang in 1350 BCE, ushering in a golden age.

Young Egypt Antiliberal, fascist group that gained a large following in Egypt during the 1930s.

Young Italy Nineteenth-century nationalist organization made up of young students and intellectuals, devoted to the unification and renewal of the Italian state.

Yuan dynasty Dynasty established by the Mongols after the defeat of the Song. The Yuan dynasty was strong from 1280 to 1368; its capital was at Dadu, or modern-day Beijing.

Yuan Mongols Mongol rulers of China who were overthrown by the Ming dynasty in 1368.

Yuezhi A Turkic nomadic people who roamed on pastoral lands to the west of the Xiongnu territory of central Mongolia. They had friendly relationships with the farming societies in China, but the Yuezhi detested the Xiongnu and had frequent armed clashes with them.

zaibatsu Large-scale, family-owned corporations in Japan consisting of factories, import-export businesses, and banks that dominated the Japanese economy until 1945.

zamindars Archaic tax system of the Mughal Empire, where decentralized lords collected tribute for the emperor from peasants working on their estates.

Zapatistas Group of indigenous rebels that rose up against the Mexican government in 1994 and drew inspiration from an earlier Mexican rebel, Emiliano Zapata.

Zheng King during the Qin era who defeated what was left of the Warring States between 230 and 221 BCE. He assumed the mandate of heaven from the Zhou and declared himself First August Emperor, to distinguish himself from other kings.

Zheng He (1371–1433) Ming naval leader who established tributary relations with Southeast Asia, Indian Ocean ports, the Persian Gulf, and the east coast of Africa.

Zhongguo Term originating in the ancient period and subsequently used to emphasize the central cultural and geographical location of China in the world; means "Middle Kingdom."

Zhong Shang Administrative central complex of the Shang.

ziggurat The stepped platform base of a Sumerian temple. By the end of the third millennium BCE, the elevated platform base had transformed into the stepped platform.

Zionism Movement advocating the reestablishment of a Jewish homeland in Palestine.

Zoroaster Greek name for the Persian religious reformer known as Zarathustra, thought to have been a teacher around 1000 BCE in eastern Iran and credited with having solidified the region's religious beliefs into a unified system that moved away from animistic nomadic beliefs. The main source for his teachings is a compilation called the Avesta.

Zoroastrianism Dominant religion of the Persian Empire, based on the teachings of Zoroaster.

Zulus African tribe that, under Shaka, created a ruthless warrior state in southern Africa in the early 1800s.

Text Credits Page 410: Ahmet T. Karamustafa, from *God's Unruly Friends: Dervish Groups in the Islamic Later Middle Period*, pp. 6–7, © Ahmet T. Karamustafa 1994. Reprinted with the permission of University of Utah Press; p. 418: "Nanak and His Teaching," from *Sources of Indian Tradition Vol. 2*, compiled by Wm. Theodore de Bary, Stephen Hay, Royal Weiler, Andrew Yarrow, pp. 536–538. Copyright © 1958 Columbia University Press. Reprinted with permission of the publisher; p. 425: "To Bibolo Semproni" from *Laura Cereta: Collected Letters of a Renaissance Feminist*, transcribed, translated and edited by Diana Robin (Chicago: University of Chicago Press, 1997), pp. 74–79. © 1977 by The University of Chicago. Reprinted by permission of the University of Chicago Press; p. 429: "Proclamations of the Hongwu Emperor," from *Chinese Civilization: A Sourcebook, 2nd Edition* by Patricia Buckley Ebrey. Copyright © 1981 by The Free Press, a Division of Simon & Schuster, Inc. Copyright © 1993 by Patricia Buckley Ebrey. Reprinted by permission of Simon & Schuster, Inc. All rights reserved.

CHAPTER 12

Photo Credits Page 438: Minnesota Geological Survey, University of Minnesota; p. 441 (top): The Lee and Juliet Folger Fund Accession No. 2013.1.1/National Gallery of Art; p. 441 (bottom): Scala/Art Resource, NY; p. 443: Granger, NYC—All rights reserved; p. 444: Rigged model of a Portuguese caravela from c. 1535 (wood) English School/Science Museum, London, UK/Bridgeman Images; p. 449: bpk Bildagentur/Bildarchiv Preussischer Kulturbesitz/Art Resource, NY; p. 450: Sarin Images/Granger, NYC—All rights reserved; p. 451 (left): Granger, NYC—All rights reserved; p. 451 (right): Pictures from History/Granger, NYC—All rights

Text Credits Page 455: Bartolomé Arzáns de Orsúa y Vela. *Tales of Potosí*. Edited by Robert C. Padden and translated from the Spanish by Frances M. López-Morillas. Providence, RI: Brown University Press, 1975. © 1975 Brown University. Reprinted with permission of University of New England; p. 463: "Zhang Han's Essay on Merchants," from *Chinese Civilization: A Sourcebook, 2nd Edition* by Patricia Buckley Ebrey. Copyright © 1981 by The Free Press, a Division of Simon & Schuster, Inc. Copyright © 1993 by Patricia Buckley Ebrey. Reprinted by permission of Simon & Schuster, Inc. All rights reserved.

CHAPTER 13

Photo Credits Page 476: © RMN-Grand Palais/Art Resource, NY; p. 478: Ms 439 f.9r Banquet scene with men drinking coffee, guests of honour sitting in a recess, entertained by three musicians, while an old man is taken ill, from an album of painting and calligraphy (vellum), Ottoman School/The Trustees of the Chester Beatty Library, Dublin/Bridgeman Images; p. 483: Winter Landscape with Skaters. c. 1608 (oil on panel), Avercamp, Hendrik (1585–1634)/Rijksmuseum, Amsterdam, The Netherlands/Bridgeman Images; p. 484: Granger, NYC—All rights reserved; p. 486: MPI/Getty Images; p. 487: MPI/Getty

Text Credits Page 491: From *Interesting Narrative of the Life of Olaudiah Equiano, or Gustavus Vassa, the African, Written by Himself: Norton Critical Edition*, edited by Werner Sollors. Copyright © 2001 by W.W. Norton & Company, Inc. Used by permission of W.W. Norton & Company, Inc; p. 500: Huang Liu-Hung, "Elimination of Authorized Silversmiths" from *A Complete Book Concerning Happiness and Benevolence: A Manual for Local Magistrates in Seventeenth Century China*, translated and edited by Djang Chu, pp. 190–191. © 1984 The Arizona Board of Regents. Reprinted by permission of the University of Arizona Press.

CHAPTER 14

Photo Credits Page 518: Scala/Art Resource, NY; p. 521: Art Resource, NY; p. 522: © RMN-Grand Palais/Art Resource, NY; p. 523 (left): Portrait of Sultan Mehmet II (1432–81) (w/c on paper), Turkish School (15th century)/Topkapi Palace Museum, Istanbul, Turkey/Bridgeman Images; p. 523 (right): V&A Images, London/Art Resource, NY; p. 524 (left): akg-images/Pictures From History; p. 524 (right): Private Collection, courtesy of the owner and D.A. King; photo by Christie's of London; p. 525: © The Trustees of the Chester Beatty Library, Dublin; p. 527: Forman Archive/REX/Shutterstock; p. 528 (left): Scala/Art Resource, NY; p. 528 (right): Granger, NYC—All rights reserved; p. 529: Wikimedia Commons; p. 530 (left): George Rinhart/Corbis/Getty Images; p. 530 (right): Underwood & Underwood/Library of Congress/Corbis/VCG/Getty Images; p. 531 (left): The Needham Research Institute; p. 531 (right): A Korean World Map/British Library, London, UK/© British Library Board. All Rights Reserved/Bridgeman Images; p. 532: P. 359–1945 Scene 12, Comparison of celebrated beauties and the loyal league, c. 1797 (colour woodblock print), Utamaro, Kitagawa (1753–1806)/Fitzwilliam Museum, University of Cambridge, UK/Bridgeman Images; p. 533 (top): © RMN-Grand Palais/Art Resource, NY; p. 533 (bottom): Map of the World, 1671 (woodblock print), Japanese School, (17th century)/Private Collection/Bridgeman Images; p. 534: Alan Tobey/Getty Images; p. 535 (top): © The Trustees of the British Museum/Art Resource, NY; p. 535 (bottom): The Michael C. Rockefeller Memorial Collection, Bequest of Nelson A. Rockefeller, 1979 © The Metropolitan Museum of Art; p. 536 (top): Minnesota Geological Survey, University of Minnesota; p. 536 (bottom): Euriskodata CDrom/Wikimedia Commons; p. 537: Trial of Galileo, 1633 (oil on canvas) (detail of 2344), Italian School, (17th century)/Private Collection/Bridgeman Images; p. 538: © RMN-Grand Palais/Art Resource, NY; p. 539: National Maritime Museum, London; p. 540: Peter Willi/Superstock; p. 542 (top): Title page of 'Encyclopedia' by Denis Diderot (1713–84), published in Paris in 1751 (engraving) (see also 157777), French School, (18th century)/Bibliotheque Municipale, Amiens, France/Archives Charmet/Bridgeman Images; p. 542 (bottom): The Pin Factory, plate 2 from Volume IV of the Encyclopedia of Denis Diderot (1713–84) and Jean le Rond d'Alembert (1717–83), 1751–52 (engraving), French School, (18th century)/Private Collection/Bridgeman Images; p. 544: Illustration of the Linnean Plant Sexual System (coloured engraving), Linnaeus, Carl (1707–78)/Natural History Museum, London, UK/Bridgeman Images; p. 545: Scala/White Images/Art Resource, NY; p. 546: Ms Palat. 218–220 Book IX Young children entering a house, from the 'Florentine Codex' by Bernardino de Sahagun, c. 1540–85, Spanish School, (16th century)/Biblioteca Medicea-Laurenziana, Florence, Italy/Bridgeman Images; p. 547 (left): Spaniard and Indian Produce a Mestizo, c. 1715 (oil on canvas), Juarez, Juan Rodriguez (1675–1728)/Breamore House, Hampshire, UK/Bridgeman Images; p. 547 (right): From a Spaniard and a Negress you a get a Half-Caste, from a Series on Mixed Marriages, Spanish School, (18th century)/Museo de America, Madrid, Spain/Bridgeman Images; p. 548: Cinchona (colour litho)/© Purix Verlag Volker Christen/Bridgeman Images; p. 549 (left): HIP/Art Resource, NY; p. 549 (right): Sarin Images/Granger, NYC—All rights reserved.

CHAPTER 15

Photo Credits Page 554: The Battle of the Pyramids, 21st July 1798 (oil on canvas), Gros, Baron Antoine Jean (1771–1835)/Chateau de Versailles, France/Bridgeman Images; p. 557: Library of Congress; p. 560: Granger, NYC—All rights reserved; p. 563 (top): Hulton Archive/Getty Images; p. 563 (bottom): Dagli Orti/REX/Shutterstock; p. 565: © BnF, Dist. RMN-Grand Palais/Art Resource, NY; p. 566 (top): The Battle of the Pyramids, 21st July 1798 (oil on canvas), Gros, Baron Antoine Jean (1771–1835)/Chateau de Versailles, France/Bridgeman Images; p. 566 (bottom): Sarin Images/Granger, NYC—All rights reserved; p. 568: © North Wind Picture Archives; p. 571 (left): Dagli Orti/REX/Shutterstock; p. 571 (right): Granger, NYC—All rights reserved; p. 572: Chasing a Slaving Dhow near Zanzibar, 1876–77 (w/c on paper), Ross-Lewin, Rev. Robert (fl.1877)/Private Collection/© Michael Graham-Stewart/Bridgeman Images; p. 575: Granger, NYC—All rights reserved; p. 577: Sarin Images/Granger, NYC—All rights reserved; p. 581: Sarin Images/Granger, NYC—All rights reserved; p. 582: The Insurrection of the Decembrists at Senate Square, St. Petersburg on 14th December, 1825 (w/c on paper), Russian School, (19th century)/Private Collection/Archives Charmet/Bridgeman Images; p. 584: Culture Club/Getty Images; p. 585: The reception of the Mysorean Hostage Princes by Lieutenant General Lord Cornwallis (1738–1805) c. 1793 (oil on canvas), Home, Robert (1752–1834)/National Army Museum, London/Bridgeman Images; p. 586: Great Eastern Hotel & Old Court House Street, Calcutta, India, 1865 (gelatin silver print), Bourne, Samuel (1834–1912)/British Library, London, UK/Bridgeman Images; p. 587 (top): Granger, NYC—All rights reserved; p. 587 (bottom): The Art Archive/REX/Shutterstock; p. 589 (left): Smokers in an opium den, from 'The Evils of Opium Smoking', (bound in an album, colour on paper)/British Library, London, UK/© British Library Board. All Rights Reserved/Bridgeman Images; p. 589 (right): © North Wind Picture Archives; p. 591: A View of the Hongs, Chinnery, George (1774–1852) (circle of)/Private Collection/Roy Miles Fine Paintings/Bridgeman Images.

Text Credits Page 583: Abd al-Rahman al-Jabarti, *Al-Jabarti's Chronicle of the first seven months of the French occupation of Egypt* (Leiden, E.J. Brill, 1975), translated by S. Moreh. © 1975 E.J. Brill, Leiden, Netherlands. Reprinted by permission of the publisher.

Italic page references indicate maps, illustrations, or chronology entries.